AF496528

INDIAN ART AT DELHI 1903

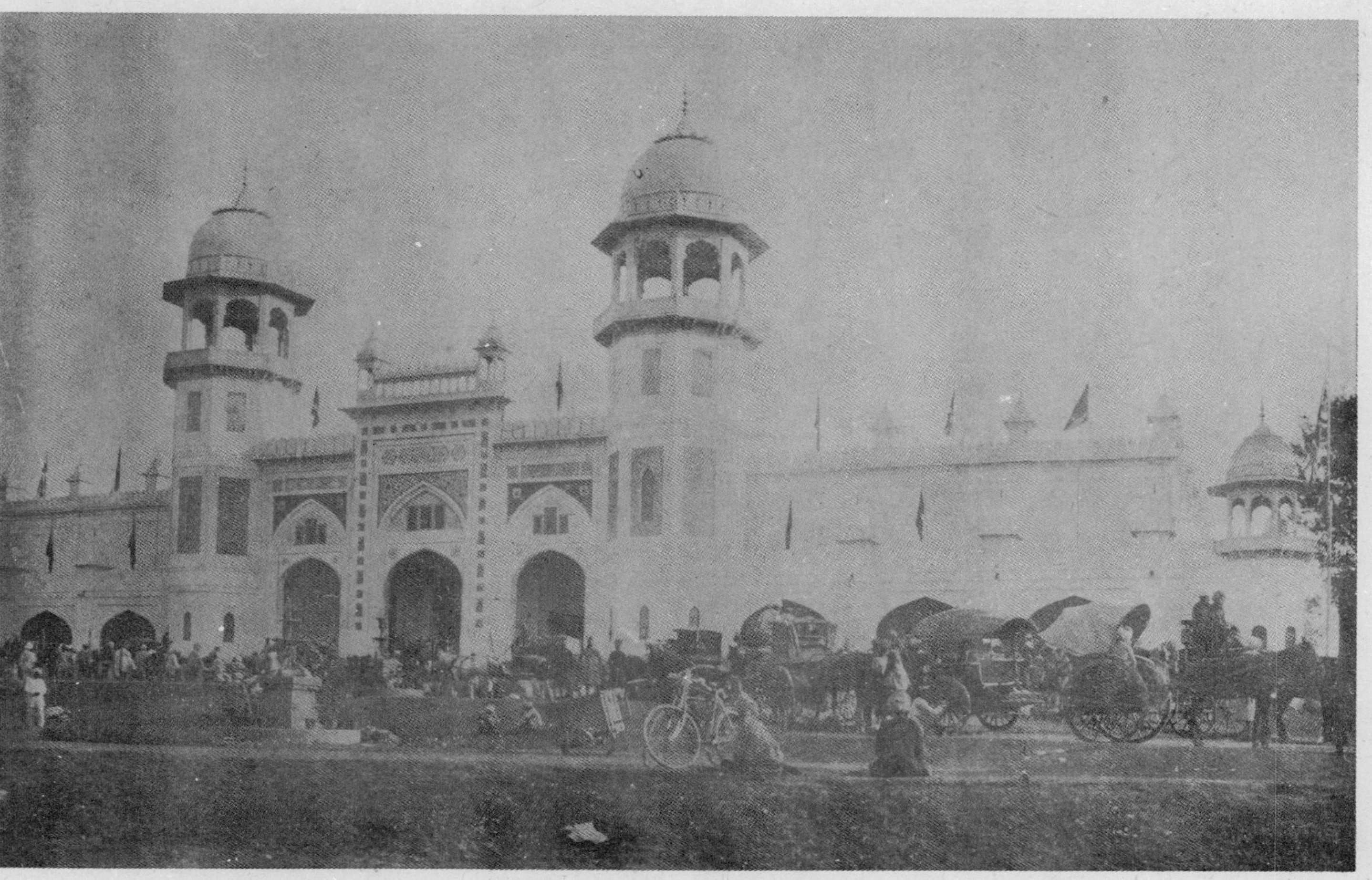

The Exhibition Buildings

INDIAN ART AT DELHI 1903

Being the Official Catalogue of the Delhi Exhibition 1902-1903

GEORGE WATT

THE ILLUSTRATIVE PART BY
PERCY BROWN

INTRODUCTION BY
NARAYANI GUPTA

MOTILAL BANARSIDASS
Delhi Varanasi Patna Madras

First Published 1903; Reprinted 1987

MOTILAL BANARSIDASS
Bungalow Road, Jawahar Nagar, Delhi 110 007
Branches
Chowk, Varanasi 221 001
Ashok Rajpath, Patna 800 004
120 Royapettah High Road, Mylapore, Madras 600 004

ISBN: 81-208-0278-0

PRINTED IN INDIA
BY JAINENDRA PRAKASH JAIN AT SHRI JAINENDRA PRESS, A-45 NARAINA INDUSTRIAL AREA, PHASE I, NEW DELHI 110 028 AND PUBLISHED BY NARENDRA PRAKASH JAIN FOR MOTILAL BANARSIDASS, DELHI 110 007.

PREFACE

THIS work has been written primarily as a Catalogue and Guide to the Indian Art Exhibition, but a secondary purpose has been kept clearly in view, namely, its possible future use as a simple and practical account of the more noteworthy art industries of India. The writer has personally experienced, during many years' association with the crafts of India, the greatest inconvenience from not being possessed of a brief descriptive catalogue that afforded a sufficiently comprehensive account to admit of identification of each style of Indian work in association with the names of the centres of production and of the chief producers. In pursuance of this necessity, the endeavour has been made to propose a classification which, while directly suited to the collections now on view and to the configuration of the Exhibition buildings, might still be capable of adoption in our Indian Museums.

The attempt to associate Indian art-wares in a systematic sequence, under certain classes, divisions, and sections, it is hoped may greatly simplify inspection and facilitate future research. But the aim has been to afford descriptions by which the articles might be severally identified, rather than to furnish traditions and historic details regarding them. In adopting this bald treatment, the writer has been fully conscious that he was of necessity depriving the subject of much of the beauty and poetry that appertains to the art crafts of this country. But he believes that in Sir George Birdwood's *Industrial Arts of India* the student already possesses a work that so completely meets that feature as to render it undesirable that the ground should be traversed a second time, in the hope of here and there amplifying what has already been so skilfully accomplished by the pioneer and chief advocate of the art crafts of India.

It seems desirable that some explanation should be afforded regarding the awards recorded by the Judging Committee. At most Exhibitions hitherto held, awards have been given to the manufacturers who placed the most imposing and effective display within the building. In fact, at many Exhibitions no attempt was made at comparative verdicts because of the knowledge of their frequent misleading character. At the Colonial and Indian Exhibition, for example, every important exhibitor received a certificate and medal. In the present Exhibition the Judging Committee had set before them a high ideal, namely, to award certificates and medals that might be accepted as denoting art merit. Moreover, the classified system deprived exhibitors of personal effort within the Exhibition. Instead of stalls being assigned to each manufacturer or trader, where they could expend money either in the preparation of special exhibits or in the display of their goods, the exhibits were personally selected by the Director or Assistant Director while on tour, and were deposited throughout the building under the various Divisions previously determined on. Each manufacturer's goods of a particular kind were, therefore, placed side by side with the corresponding goods from all parts of India, and the awards made after critical and careful comparative study. It accordingly follows that even when a certificate of being "Commended" has been given, the goods so distinguished should be viewed as possessing distinct artistic merit over many others. So also "Second Prize" by no means denotes second class goods but a high distinction, namely, the second award for that particular kind of goods in open competition with all India. When two or more identical awards have been recorded it is intended that the goods so designated should be accepted as of equal merit.

On a separate page will be found all the gold medals that have been awarded, but owing to the very extensive series of silver and bronze medals and still more so of the certificates of commendation that have been given, these have not been separately published but will be found in the text of this Catalogue under each Division and Section.

It may here be mentioned that the Jewellery Court was treated as if perfectly distinct from the rest of the Exhibition. A selected number of jewellers were assigned space and allowed to exhibit their own jewels, gold and silver plate, etc., without having to conform to the conditions that prevailed in the Main Gallery where no stalls were allowed but all exhibits classified. It was accordingly felt by the Judging Committee that it would be both invidious and possibly misleading were the attempt made to compare the one set of jewels with the other and to confer awards. Accordingly no awards were given to the goods shown in the Jewellery Court.

The writer takes this opportunity to record the invaluable assistance rendered by Mr. Percy Brown, the Assistant Director of the Exhibition and Principal of the Mayo School of Art, Lahore. Mr. Brown not only made most of the sketches of the artificers shown at work, but he carefully selected all the subjects supplied for photographic reproduction. He also went on tour for eight months and worked up the art resources of Bengal, the

United Provinces, the Central Provinces, and Central India, and part of Burma, while the writer was engaged in Madras, Mysore, Bombay, Hyderabad, Rajputana, Baluchistan, and the Panjab, as also part of Burma. To Mr. Brown, therefore, are mainly due the beautiful exhibits collected from the provinces which he visited; further, the intimate knowledge he acquired while on tour has most generously been placed at the writer's disposal, while preparing this catalogue.

In this connection it is also desirable to mention that while selecting and preparing the collections the liberal co-operation of all the art experts of India was secured. Mr. H. Tilly, Chief Collector of Customs in Rangoon, undertook to supervise the organisation of collections from that province. Mr. A. Chatterton, Superintendent of the School of Arts and Industries, Madras, took charge of the collections from the Madras Presidency. Mr. C. L. Burns, Principal of the School of Art, Bombay, acted in a similar capacity in the Western Presidency, while Mr. G. E. Brand, Officiating Principal of the School of Art, Lahore, had charge of the collections from the Panjab.

Similarly, the Superintendents and Curators of the various Museums of India most generously contributed not only loan collections from their respective Museums, but rendered every assistance within their power in forwarding the interests of the Exhibition. Under this heading has to be mentioned Sir Purdon Clarke, K.C.I.E., the Director of the South Kensington Museum, London. Permission having been obtained, through His Majesty's Secretary of State for India, a loan collection of great value and interest was forwarded to the Exhibition from the treasures of the Indian section by the South Kensington Museum.

In this way examples of Indian art manufactures were shown to the people of India of a kind hardly, if ever, met with in India at the present day.

But by far the most interesting feature of the Exhibition was doubtless the beautiful series of the finer art manufactures brought together through the public spirited munificence of the Princes and Nobles of India, who allowed the Director and Assistant Director free access to their palaces in search of the loan collections which have filled the large gallery in the Exhibition devoted to that purpose.

Lastly, it would be ungrateful were a public acknowledgment not rendered by me to the large body of District Officers throughout India, who laboured to make the Exhibition a success. While the primary responsibility of selecting and ordering the collections was thrown on the shoulders of the Director and Assistant Director, they could pay but one or at most two visits to each town. The task of encouraging the craftsmen to undertake the work required of them, of supervising and checking the special preparations, and of fixing the prices, devolved primarily on the District Officers, and through them on the Magistrates or Tahsildars of the towns of India. Without, therefore, the supervision thus exercised, the organisation of an Exhibition within the limited time available would have been next to impossible.

GEORGE WATT
Director

DELHI
January 1903

INTRODUCTION

By NARAYANI GUPTA

IF THE quality of an exhibition is to be judged by its catalogue, the Exhibition of Indian Art held at Delhi to coincide with the Durbar of 1902-03 must have been an exciting one. Its catalogue is a work of scholarship with a timeless quality which makes it a valuable book of reference for us. Its authors anticipated this when they visualized 'its possible future use as a simple...account of the more noteworthy art industries of India'. Because it has the quality of a gazetteer and an ethnographical dictionary, it is appropriate that it should be reprinted, at a time when so much of the past is disappearing and is sought to be revived.

This catalogue is the joint work of George Watt, and his young assistant Percy Brown. Watt was a botanist, and author of the formidable *Dictionary of the Economic Products of India*. Percy Brown, who had been in India only three years, was at that time the Principal of the Mayo School of Art and Curator of the Lahore Museum. He was given the task of travelling all over the country and selecting the items for display in the exhibition. He also wrote the section on 'Fine Arts' for the catalogue, and illustrated the text with sketches of the craftsmen. The major part of the writing was done by Watt.

The Delhi Exhibition was the last manifestation of interest by the British—as imperial rulers—in Indian arts and crafts. Their concern was both to learn more about them and to make them sell. This concern had not been apparent all through the decades of their rule. In the eighteenth century a considerable amount of Indian crafts and textiles had been regularly bought by the East India Company and sold in Europe. From the early nineteenth century, however, Indian goods began to lose their markets. They were effectively blocked from Britain by tariffs and by British middle-class taste, which was coming to the full flower of its vulgarity. In India, as more and more independent states were conquered, the rulers and upper classes could no longer afford to patronize artists and craftsmen. Bereft of patrons, they turned to other vocations. Some of them found employment in the Public Works Department, where their skills got eroded by the mechanical nature of the work. Fortunately, the traditions which wilted in British India were kept alive in some semi-autonomous states—Saurashtra, Rajasthan, Kashmir and Hyderabad. Small wonder, then, that in the eighteen-nineties Romesh Chunder Dutt was to accuse the British of destroying India's industries without modernizing its economy.

At a different level, one of the best-loved of British Indian administrators, Thomas Munro, said in 1812 that the quality of Indian goods was so high that Indians did not need to import anything from Europe. He also stated before a surprised House of Commons that if there were to be commerce in civilizations between India and Britain, the latter would undoubtedly be the gainer. In the seventeen-eighties Warren Hastings and William Jones had begun to systematize the British comprehension of Indian history and culture by research channelled through the Asiatic Society. Over the next fifty years, this interest was sustained by a few individuals, despite Macaulay's eloquent denigration of all Indian learning.

In the mid-nineteenth century, things looked pretty bleak. What saved Indian craftsmanship was the British passion for museums and periodic exhibitions which afforded opportunities to admire the marvels of their Industrial Revolution and of their far-flung Empire (the evocative adjective was coined by Kipling). In 1799 Charles Wilkes had carefully worked out plans for an Indian Museum, but this did not rouse much enthusiasm. Meanwhile, in the East India Company's office in London, a motley collection of items had been accumulating since the early days of empire. These were displayed in a few cluttered rooms. The biggest attraction was Tipu Sultan's mechanical tiger.

The Great Exhibition of London in 1851 was a celebration of Britain's pre-eminence as the 'Workshop of the World'. But, ironically, it was not the marvels of British industry but the Indian section which was the biggest draw. Admittedly, the crowds came more to goggle at the Kohinoor Diamond than to admire Indian craftsmanship. When Napoleon III organized an Exhibition in Paris four years later, this had an Indian section, more elaborate than that of 1851 had been—and more popular. Empress Eugenie's collection of 150 Kashmir shawls must have been the best advertisement the Kashmir weavers had had! The British understood that there was a market for Indian crafts and textiles, without risk of competition to their own products. In Britain, Indian craftsmanship became fashionable as it came to be romanticized by John Ruskin's Arts and Crafts group. Already overfurnished Victorian drawing-rooms acquired a generous sprinkling of Indian knick-knacks.

In the eighteen-fifties museums had been opened in India—the Indian Museum at Calcutta and the Prince of Wales Museum at Bombay. In London, in the eighteen-seventies, the collection from the Company's office was shifted to the South Kensington Museum (more generally known as the Victoria and Albert Museum). George Birdwood drew up a comprehensive catalogue (published as *The Industrial Arts of India*, with a long section on the Hindu Pantheon, followed by detailed descriptions of the various items on display). This sense of the need to understand Indian handicraft traditions was reflected in the officially sponsored 'handbooks of manufactures and arts' commissioned from the different provinces, and the detailed monographs on individual arts and crafts ('Art in Industry') prepared in the eighteen-nineties.

Birdwood had lamented that people had forgotten the meaning of the word 'manufacture', connoting as it had done a product crafted by hand. Now Indian manufactures were to be revived. Schools of art were opened in Lahore and Jaipur to train young men in the 'industrial arts'. In this revival, there was a danger that quality would fall victim to the needs of the mass market. The modifications made to produce salt-cellars and tie-boxes (which Birdwood fastidiously dismissed as 'mongrel articles') could, if unchecked, drive out the classic elements of Indian craftsmanship. In a determined effort to keep up the excellence, Lockwood Kipling, E.B. Havell and others began publishing, from 1886, the copiously illustrated *Journal of Indian Industrial Art*, the distinguished forerunner of *Marg*.

Indians are indebted to Lord Curzon for helping them to realize the wonder that was India. In his imperious manner, he declared that the best in the Indian heritage—fine art, crafts, architecture—be recognized and preserved. He invigorated the Archaeological Survey, planned the Victoria Memorial Museum, and used the Coronation Durbar of Delhi as the occasion for an Exhibition of Indian Art on a far bigger scale than anything held in India before. This Durbar, like that of 1877, and the subsequent one of 1911-12, meant that a large number of officials and princes gathered at Delhi. Curzon saw this as an opportunity to give publicity and open a market for the goods displayed at the Exhibition. The Durbar celebrations lasted twelve days (December 1902 to January 1903) and the Exhibition continued for six weeks afterwards, till the end of February.

The Durbar was held in north Delhi, beyond the city and the Civil Lines. The exhibition was housed in a temporary building in the beautiful Qudsia Gardens, which divided the Civil Lines from the city. Curzon's hopes were fulfilled. Forty-eight thousand people visited the 'Ajaibghar' ('The House of Wonders', the popular name for the exhibition). Goods worth Rs. 350,000/- were sold. This was enough to silence the critics who had accused Curzon of wasting money on the Durbar. The Exhibition building was planned with an eye to convenience rather than effect, and in a manner designed to facilitate its being dismantled and the building material sold. The structure (254′ × 194′ was designed in the Indo-Saracenic style with ornamentation in tile-work by Punjabi potters, and fresco painting by pupils of the Mayo School of Art at Lahore. The construction began in May 1902 and was completed in six months. The exhibition was lit by gas and open all day (it had been discussed whether it would not be a good idea to keep it open at night as well, but it was agreed that there were too many other entertainments in the evenings to make this worthwhile). At the end of the three months, the exhibition building, like all the other Durbar buildings, was dismantled and its material sold.

Curzon set a lot of store by the Exhibition. He saw its objectives as manifold. It would attract visitors and buyers from India and abroad. It would enable an accurate survey of the condition of artistic industries in India, and the extent to which these had been affected by foreign competition. It would also give new ideas to the artisans. In March 1902 he had sent letters to the various provincial governments stating that the 'main test to be applied will be that of artistic merit'. 'Our object has been to encourage and revive good work, not to satisfy the requirements of the thinly-lined purse.' It was to be an exhibition of the arts only. There was no section on industrial and economic products, as there had been in previous exhibitions. Nothing with any European influence was to be allowed. 'It is possible', Curzon was to say ruefully, 'that a few articles that do not answer to my definition may have crept in because the number of teapots, cream jugs, napkin-rings, salt-cellars and cigarette-cases that the Indian artisan is called upon to turn out is appalling.'

Watt and Brown travelled all over India, interviewing artisans, selecting specimens, sometimes supplying models and advancing money where needed. In addition to these items, which were for sale, there were many which were lent by Indian princes and by the Victoria and Albert Museum. The classification was not by provenance, as in earlier exhibitions, but according to categories. This was done in order to make this exhibition a prototype for later museums. At the same time, regional variations and even local specializations in many crafts were obvious. This came through particularly vividly in the rooms decorated in the style of different regions or towns. The richness and variety in wood-work was particularly striking. The Section of Fine Arts included paintings by Abanindranath Tagore, and some unusually powerful sculptures of famine victims by a Lucknow artist. These were not the product of any art school, and struck an incongruous note by its realism in an exhibition where everything was bright and beautiful. The verandahs were allotted to craftsmen who pursued their work during the exhibition. In sum, this was the precursor of the Festivals of India and the Dastkari Movement, and the first of its kind to be held in India and not in Britain.

Curzon has been stereotyped for generations of school children as an 'imperialist'. and has been mindlessly criticized for the first partition of Bengal. By association, one thinks of the Swadeshi Movement which was intensified as a protest against this. In this context, it is worth quoting from the speech he gave at the opening of the Delhi Exhibition on 30 December 1902:

> If Indian arts and handicrafts are to be kept alive, it can never be by outside patronage alone...I should like to see a movement spring up among the Indian chiefs and nobility for the expurgation or, at any rate, the purification of modern tastes, and for a reversion to the old-fashioned but exquisite styles and patterns of their own country. The aim of the Exhibition is to show that for the beautification of an Indian house or the furniture of an

> Indian home there is no need to rush to the European shops at Calcutta or Bombay. but that in almost every Indian State and Province...there still survives the art and there still exist the artificers who can satisfy the artistic, as well as the utilitarian, tastes of their countrymen. I hope that [the Exhibition] may in some measure fulfil the strictly patriotic purpose for which it has been designed.

Is it possible to see something in common between Curzon inaugurating the Delhi Exhibition and Bipin Chandra Pal setting a match to a pile of Manchester cloth?

This catalogue is a labour of love and of erudition. To a world of 'instant scholarship' it teaches the values of meticulous scholarship. This had been evident in Watt's earlier work. It was to be seen in Percy Brown's works on Mughal art and on Indian architecture. Watt retired from government service in 1906 and returned to England, where he continued to devote himself to the study of botany. Brown was to become Principal of the Government Art College in Calcutta, and, after his retirement in 1927, Secretary and Curator of the Victoria and Albert Museum. They are two of the many British scholars to whom we are beholden.

JUDGING COMMITTEE

President

COLONEL SIR SWINTON JACOB, K.C.I.E., I.A.

Members

COLONEL STUART BEATSON, C.B., I.A.
C. L. BURNS, ESQ.
CHEVALIER O. GHILARDI
COLONEL T. H. HENDLEY, I.M.S., C.I.E.
R. D. MACKENZIE, ESQ.
MUNSHI MADHO LAL
BHAI RAM SINGH.
E. THURSTON, ESQ.

Secretary

R. E. V. ARBUTHNOT, ESQ., I.C.S.

OFFICERS OF THE EXHIBITION

SIR GEORGE WATT, KT., C.I.E.,—*Director*
PERCY BROWN, ESQ., A.R.C.A.,—*Assistant Director*
G. E. MILNE, ESQ.,—*Secretary*
S. K. MURPHY, ESQ.,—*Assistant Secretary*

Official Agents and Bankers

MESSRS. THOS. COOK & SON, BOMBAY

LIST OF FIRST-CLASS AWARDS

Nineteen Gold Medals have been placed at the disposal of the Committee. The names of the donors are as follows:—

The Government of India . . .	5
H. H. the Maharaja of Cooch Behar .	4
H. H. the Raja of Kapurthala . .	2
H. H. the Raja of Poonch . . .	2
Raja Sir Amar Singh	2
Munshi Madho Lal	3
Raja Bahadur Ranajit Sinha of Nashipur (1 Silver and 1 Gold) . . .	1

These have been awarded as follows:—

Class I.—Metal Wares.

1. Metal ware (Copper and Brass) from Jaipur School of Art.
2. Saya Po of Toungoo—Niello work, bowl and dish.
3. Maung Yin Maung of Rangoon—Silver work.

Class II.—Stone Ware.

4. Bharatpur House.

Class III.—Glass and Earthen Wares.

None.

Class IV.—Wood Work.

5. Bhavnagar House.
6. Mayo School of Art, Lahore, for wood-carving.
7. Maung Than Yegyan of Rangoon for a carved figure in wood of a Burmese Princess.
8. Bombay School of Art—Bombay Art Furnished Room.
9. Mysore—Carved sandal-wood casket.

Class V.—Ivory, Horn, Leather, etc.

10. Fakir Chand Raghu Nath Dass of Delhi for a collection of carved ivory.
11. School of Art, Trevandrum—Ivory casket.

Class VI.—Lac, Lacquer, etc.

None.

Class VII.—Textiles.

12. Bhagwan Das Gopi Nath of Benares—Gold kinkhabs.

Class VIII.—Embroidery.

13. Trailokya Nath Dass of Dacca and Murshidabad for a pair of shawls.
14. Collection of chikan work by Kedar Nath Ram Nath & Co. of Lucknow.
15. Collection of Kashmir shawls (woven and embroidered) from H. H. the Maharaja of Kashmir.

Class IX.—Carpets.

16. Cashmir Manufacturing Co., Srinagar.
17. The Agra Central Jail.

Class X.—Fine Arts.

18. Mr. G. K. Mhatre of Bombay for the figure of a girl.
19. Bhagwant Singh of the Lucknow Industrial School for clay modelling.

Money Awards.

It was felt that a certificate, given to the exhibitor of an article, might not reach the actual maker. To meet this difficulty a fund was started to be used in rewarding actual artificers. The following are the contributions received towards that fund :—

	Rs.
The Government of India . . .	1,000
H. H. the Raja of Tipperah . .	1,000
H. H. the Raja of Nabha . . .	1,000
Hon'ble Sir E. Law, K.C.M.G. . .	1,000
Babu Manmatha Nath Ray Chowdhury of Calcutta . . .	500
Raja Bahadur Ranajit Sinha of Nashipur	500
Babu Dhanpat Sing of Azimganj .	500
Babu Dooly Chund of Calcutta .	200
Lalubhai Samaldass, Esq., of Bhavnagar	100
Indian Industrial Association, for two medals and money prizes .	100
Total .	5,900

It has been arranged that for each certificate of commendation an award of Rs. 10, for each bronze medal Rs. 20, and for each silver medal Rs. 30, should be made. Further that the letters by which certificates are forwarded may desire the owners of each article to give these money awards to the actual artificer or artificers who made the exhibits. In this way it is hoped the wishes and intentions of the donors of money may be assured, namely, to recognise individual work and merit.

The following are the total number of the awards given :—

Gold Medals	19
Silver Medals	83
Bronze Medals	115
Commendations	110
Total	327

LIST OF PLATES

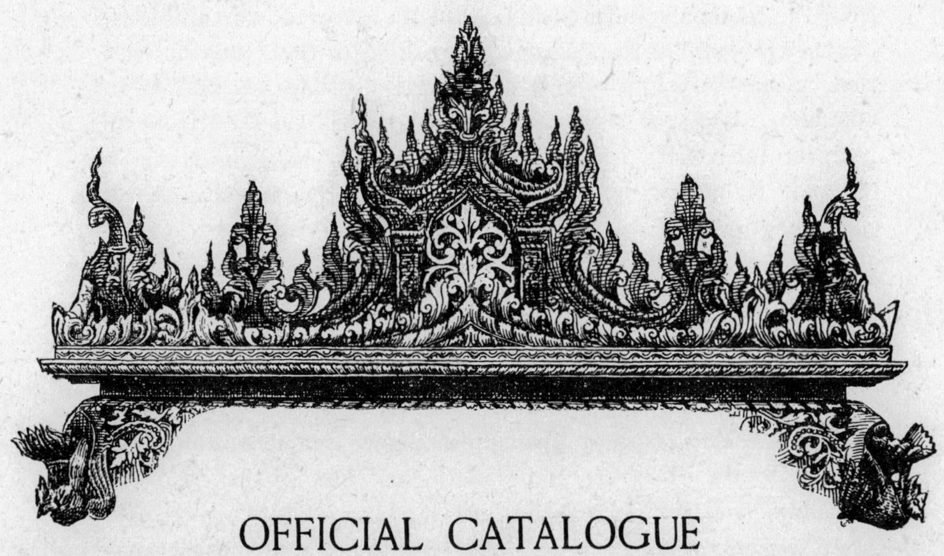

OFFICIAL CATALOGUE

OF THE

INDIAN ART EXHIBITION, DELHI.

THE Exhibition Buildings shown on the frontispiece have been erected in the Kudsia Gardens close to the Kashmir gate into the city of Delhi. They have been designed for their present function; convenience rather than effect having been aimed at. The northern or main elevation is, however, in Saracenic style, and the ornamentation in tile-work by the potters of Lahore, Mooltan, Halla and Jaipur, and in fresco-painting by pupils of the Mayo School of Art, Lahore, is worthy of special notice.

The Collections.—There are two distinguishing features of the present Exhibition which deserve particular attention. Of these the *first* is that the exhibits have been collected as the result of personal choice and selection—special efforts having been directed to the exclusion of all trace of the modern foreign influences which have tended to debase the ancient indigenous arts of India.

CLASSIFICATION. And in the *second* place an important divergence has been made from the methods of classification usually followed at exhibitions, in that the exhibits are arranged according to their kind and not their places of origin. It is thus made possible for visitors to compare, almost at a glance, productions of one kind from all parts of India both near and remote, and to make purchases in the Sale Gallery without being harassed by the importunities of competing traders.

The buildings comprise four great sections:—

(*a*) The Main or Sale Gallery.
(*b*) The Loan Collection Gallery.
(*c*) The Jewellery Gallery.
(*d*) The Artificers' Gallery of Workshops.

Plan.—The transept that crosses the entire building terminates in the Main or Sale Gallery, and has on the right the Jewellery Gallery and on the left the Loan Collection Gallery. The Artificers' Gallery is a broad enclosed verandah that runs round the entire building, sub-divided into numerous workshops, with a passage for the public in front.

Classification.—Within each of these galleries, the same main classification has been observed, namely, into:—

I.—Metal wares.
II.—Stone wares.
III.—Glass and Earthen wares.
IV.—Wood work.
V.—Ivory, Horn, Shell and Leather wares.
VI.—Lac (Lakh) and Lacquer wares.
VII.—Textiles—
(*a*) treatment after leaving the loom, such as dyeing, printing, etc.
(*b*) woven patterns.
VIII.—Embroidery, Braiding, Lace, etc., Needle work.
IX.—Carpets, Rugs, Baskets, etc.
X.—Fine Arts.

So in the same way the Classes have been referred to certain Divisions in order to still further facilitate the grouping together of goods of a particular kind. It has been found desirable to

CLASSIFICATION.

establish 50 of these divisions with several sections under each, and they are, therefore, too numerous to be detailed in this place, but a sufficient idea of their character may be obtained from the following which relates to the Metal Wares only. The goods of this class are sub-divided into:—

1. Iron, Lead and Tin wares.
2. Tinned, Painted and Lacquered wares (imitation, enamelled, damascened and encrusted wares, etc).
3. Enamelled and Niello wares.
4. Gold and Silver wares.
5. Damascened and Encrusted wares.
6. Copper and brass wares.

Location.—Exhibits in Class I—Metal Wares extend from right to left, along the entire length of the Main Gallery, but Division 1 has been placed on the extreme right and Division 6 on the extreme left, in order to admit of the Gold and Silver Wares being located in the centre of the space devoted to the class, and hence on the right and left of the great transept. It is in this great transept that exhibits in Class X—Fine Arts (such as sculpture, painting, book illumination, etc.) are set out. It will thus be observed that the system on which the divisions in Class I have been assorted, and which has been followed in locating the divisions in the other classes as well, brings the most highly artistic goods of the Metal Wares, as also of each of the other classes, into the centre of the gallery and thus into juxtaposition with the Fine Arts.

This method of grouping, while it doubtless disturbs numerical sequence, produces as it were an expansion of the Class devoted to Fine Arts, which is in accordance with the intentions and with the theories of the organisers of the Exhibition. A Fine Arts class, which is to be strictly Indian, cannot itself be a very large one. Perspective, shadow and atmosphere have never been mastered by Indian artists, and oil-painting and sculpture are arts which owe their existence almost exclusively to the Government Schools of Art. Indian indigenous art being strongest in conventionalism and decoration, it was thought wisest to treat the Fine Arts as the highest utilisation of industrial materials, and

ART ROOMS. hence the indirect expansion of that class is both logical and convenient.

Chief features of the Main or Sale Gallery.

Dispersed throughout the building will be found certain small rooms, balconies, etc. These have been set apart for the purpose of exemplifying the adaptability of the various better known styles of Indian Art, to modern household furnishing and architectural decoration. On passing through the turnstiles the visitor will discover on either side of the entrance two small rooms. These are :—

1st, Madras Room.—(*Plate No. 1.*)—That on the right assigned to the Madras School of Arts is intended to exemplify the accumulative and realistic Dravidian style of South India, often spoken of as *Swámi*. This may be said to have attained its highest development with the production of Madura and other temples built about the sixteenth century. The door by which the room is entered is an exceedingly fine example of the *Swámi* style. The coloured cornices are intended to demonstrate the possible future extended application of the art of *gesso* painting as practised in Nossam in the Karnul District. The fittings and furniture of this room have been designed by Mr. A. Chatterton, Superintendent of the School of Art, and have been purchased by His Highness the Nizam of Hyderabad.

2nd, Bombay Room.—(*Plate No. 2.*)—This stands on the left : its fittings and furniture have been the special charge of the Bombay School of Art, under the direction of the Principal, Mr. C. L. Burns. It has been designed to exemplify the elaborate and intricate Jaina style of architecture and ornamentation that still survives in the Jain temples of the province, but which was adapted to the requirements of the Muhammadans by Ahmad Shah, in the fifteenth century, when he founded the city of Ahmedabad. This style, therefore, attained its highest perfection in the production among other monuments of the Rani Sipri's tomb and the mosque of Sidi Said. The famous windows of the last mentioned have been reproduced in wood and placed in the room. These represent the phenomenon not unfamiliar to Indian travellers of a banyan tree growing out of and around a palm, until, in its snake-like entanglements of root and branch, the banyan strangles its

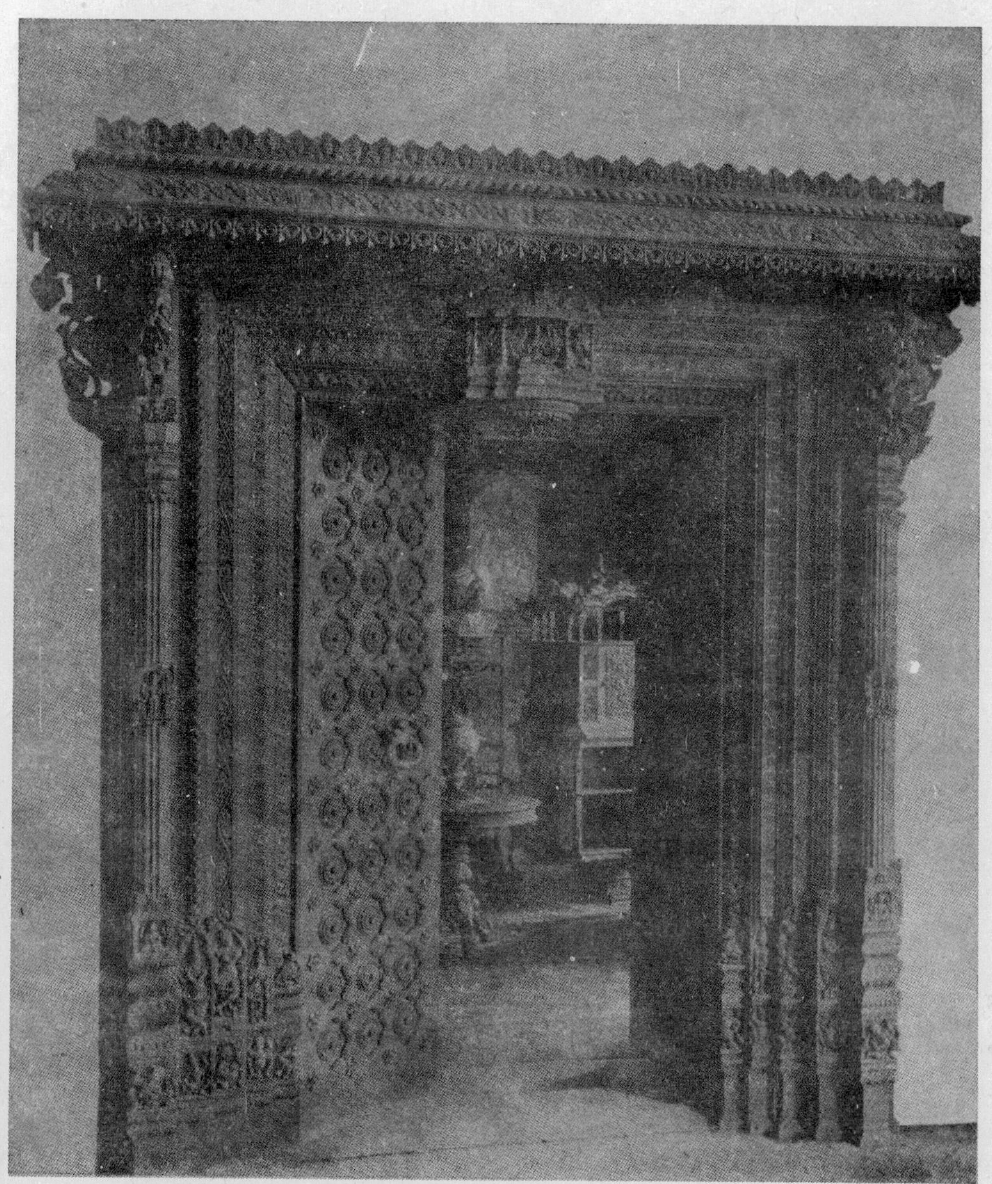

Plate No. 1 Madras Room

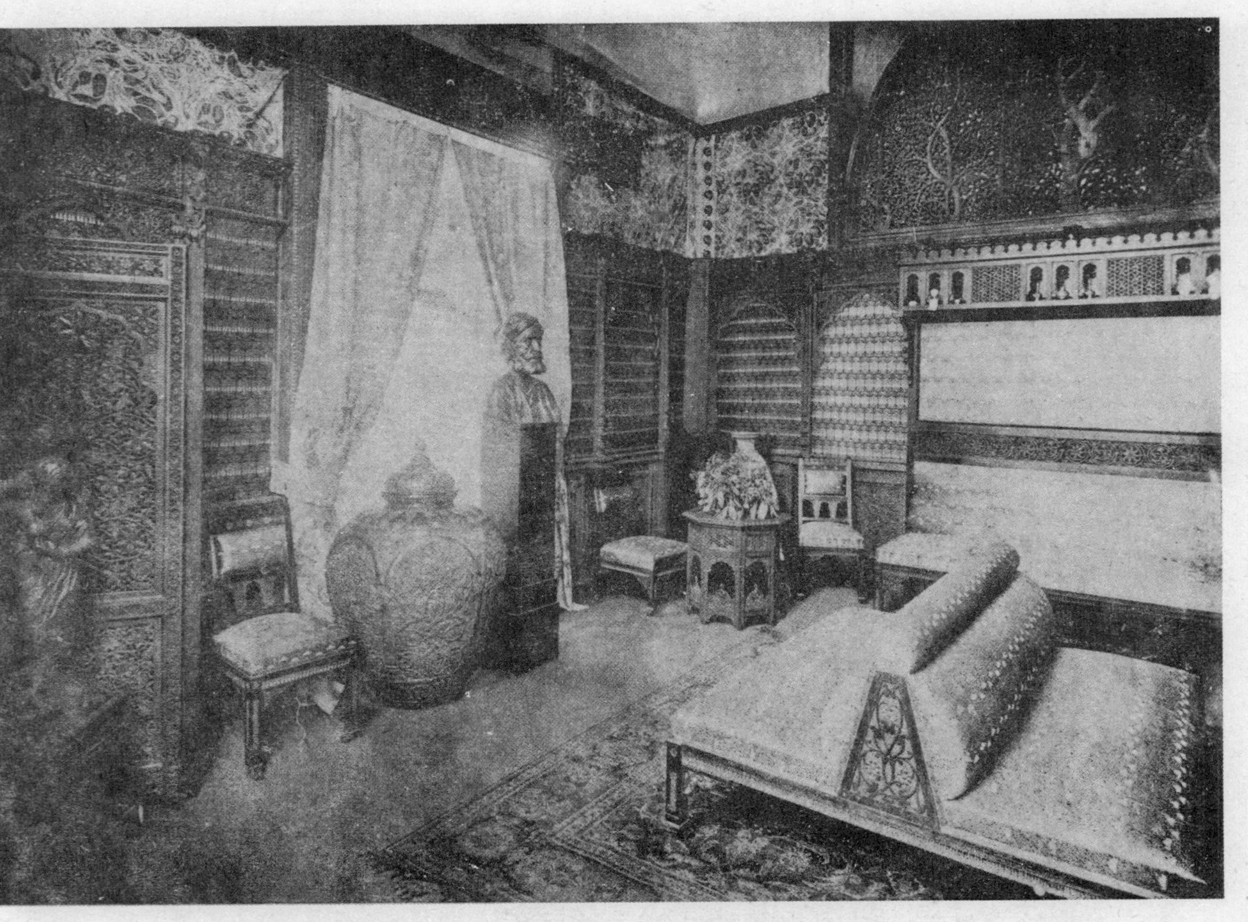

Plate No. 2 Bombay Room-Gujerat Art-furnishing

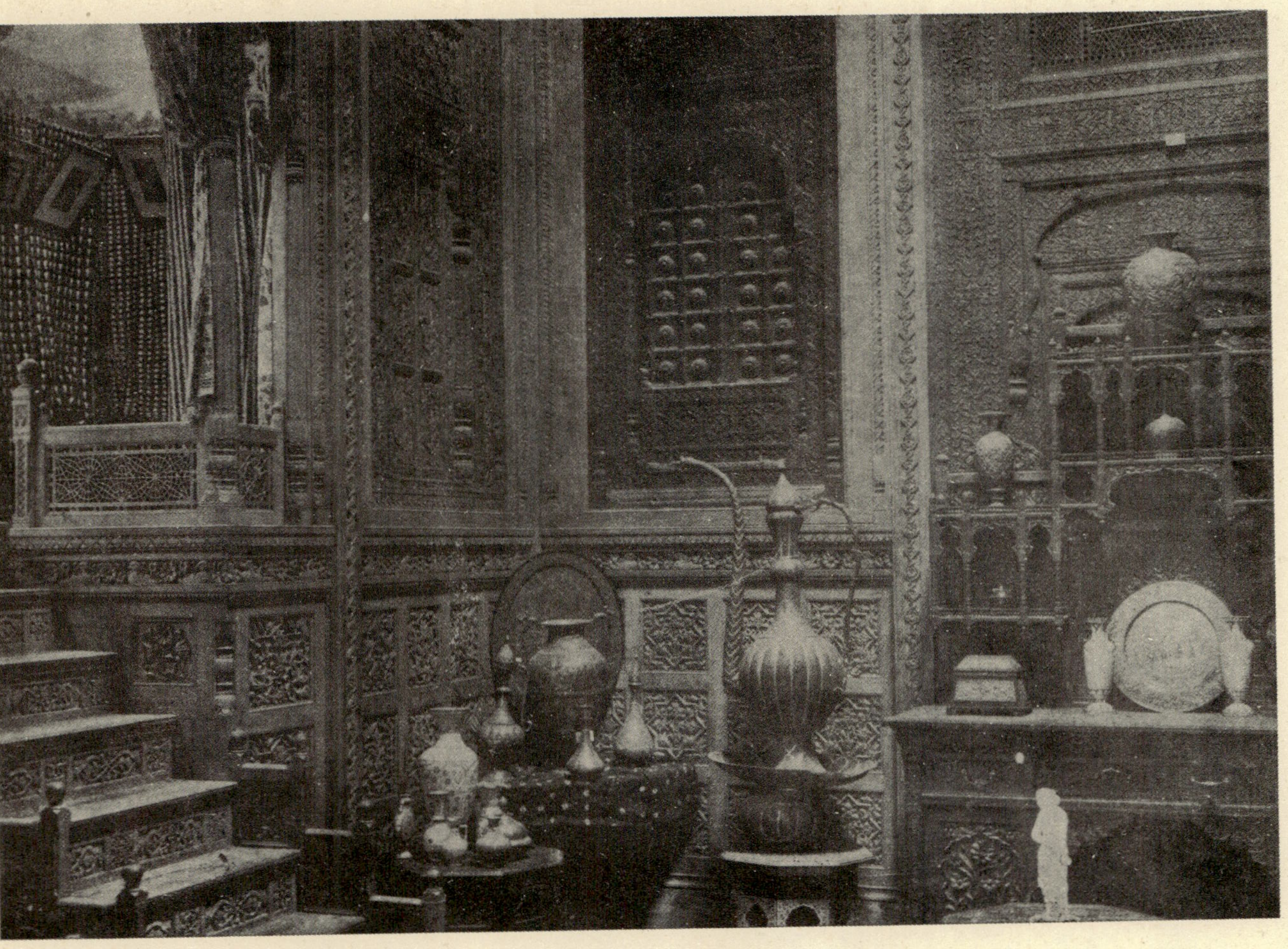

Plate No. 3 Punjab Room, Punjab Art Furnishing

ART ROOMS.

foster-parent. While this central idea has been fully conveyed, the distribution and treatment of branch and foliage has been so admirable as to produce an exquisite conventional ornamentation that has accompanied the arts of Ahmedabad in all their developments for the past 400 years without having deteriorated to any material extent.

The Bombay Room obtained the gold medal as the best example of Indian art furnishing. It has been purchased by His Highness the Nizam of Hyderabad.

A further example of Ahmedabad ornamentation has been provided in the drawing-room of the Circuit House at Delhi. Every detail in the fittings of that room has also been carefully developed on the lines of the master-pieces in Ahmedabad. Mr. C. L. Burns has had special charge of this room, and the sketch of Ahmedabad hung on the overmantel was made by him.

3rd, Panjab Room.—(*Plate No 3.*)—Further along and on the right hand side of the transept will be found the room assigned to the Panjab School of Art. This may be described as accomplished on the lines of the past 20 years' work of the School but carried out by Mr. G. E. Brand, the Officiating Principal. The walls have been panelled in the characteristic forms of wood-carving met with in Bhera, Lahore, Amritsar, Udaki and Chiniot. These, although each possessing features of its own, are commonly (excluding the more directly Muhammadan form of Chiniot) grouped under the designation of the Sikh style. They certainly attained their highest development during the period of Sikh power in the Panjab.

The balcony thrown into the Main Gallery, and which opens from the Panjab Room, is probably the finest example of the modern development of Panjab wood-carving ever shown (Plate No. 21). It is supported on foliated arches with fluted scaly pillars. The chief panels have been prepared under the personal supervision of Bhai Ram Singh, whose name is so prominently associated with the Lahore School of Art. The room itself manifests one of the most fascinating features of Panjab wood-work, namely, the *bukhár-cha* (or bow window) which commonly rests on an upturned lotus flower. It is largely to the presence of the *bukhárcha* that Lahore owes its striking individuality among the cities of Northern India.

ART ROOMS.

The interior fittings of the Panjab Room as well as its external ornamentations have been specially selected and executed, to demonstrate all that is beautiful and distinctive in Panjab decoration. It obtained a gold medal for superiority in wood-carving, and has been purchased by His Highness the Nizam of Hyderabad.

4th, Burma Room.—Opposite the Panjab Room will be found that devoted to Burma. The fittings originally intended for this room were found too large and too numerous for the space available; in consequence a large overflow had to be carried to the Refreshment Room on the opposite side of the Main Gallery. It may be said that there are two widely different styles of Burmese wood-carving—one bold and effective, the other deeply cut and elaborate. The former is devoted to the uses of every-day life, the latter to pagodas and monasteries. The walls of the Refreshment Room have been arcaded with a series of steering chairs, from ordinary river boats, the carved and elevated portions being made to arch overhead (Plate No. 19). Across the transept in the middle of the Main Gallery have been thrown three arches in rich wood-carving. The central arch was made by the wood-carvers of Mandalay (Plate No. 31) and the two side ones by those of Rangoon. The writer selected from the pagodas and monasteries the main features that were desired to be followed in the construction of these arches, so that they may be said to represent the finest masterpieces that exist. Mr H. L. Tilly, Chief Collector of Customs, a well-known expert on Burmese art, very kindly supervised the preparation of these arches and also of most of the other Burmese exhibits from Rangoon and Moulmein.

In the Burmese Room itself will be found some of the most charming examples of the elaborate and deeply cut carving, characteristic of the monasteries. The glass mosaic shrine in the Refreshment Room is a careful reproduction, in section, of one of the finest shrines in the great pagoda of Rangoon. It has been made in wood instead of stone and cement, so that it may be taken to pieces and removed. It is shown in the middle of the arches given on Plate No. 31. The numerous articles of furniture and fittings are all specially selected to exemplify the best features

STONE BALCONY.

of Burmese art, many of which have been contributed by Messrs. Beato & Co. of Rangoon and Mandalay. The gong stand, made by Maung Po Nyun of Rangoon, is one of the most wonderful and beautiful examples of this art ever produced (Plate No. 31-A). The tympanums shown on the walls are exact copies of those in the Salim Chang (monastery), Mandalay. The door, half natural size, is a reproduction from the same monastery. There will also be seen in the Burmese Room three small steering chairs, two exactly like those in the Refreshment Room and one much more elaborate and delicate. Near the window have been placed two spandrils, copied at the writer's request from one of the monasteries of Prome. Lastly, the full size doors shown in the room as also in the Refreshment Room are four selected by the Burmese Government from the series submitted to the recent competition for superiority in style and workmanship.

5th, Jodhpur Balcony.—(*Plate No. 14.*)—This beautiful structure (known locally as a *jhároka*) will be found attached to the left hand end wall of the Main Gallery. It is an exact reproduction in red, yellow and white sandstone of the carving usually met with in the towns of Rajputana. Its most striking features are its richly carved brackets, its lace-like fringes and pendants and its elegant floral ornamentation in which a deep sharp groove, to mark the midribs of the leaves, gives a finishing touch in shadow that suggests the survival of a style that possibly attained perfection in wood before being applied to stone. This most exquisite example of a highly characteristic style of stone work was prepared by the master mason of the Jodhpur State and has been purchased by His Highness the Nizam of Hyderabad (see p. 69).

6th, Mysore Stone Carving.—On the walls close to the Jodhpur Balcony and the Travancore House will be discovered a series of carved stones. These, like the numerous other loan exhibits in the Loan Collection Gallery, have been secured through the extreme liberality of His Highness the Maharaja of Mysore, who has permitted the rich mine of art materials, presently available from the works connected with the construction of the new palace, to be drawn upon. The slabs shown exemplify the main

TYPICAL HOUSES.

features of the stone carvings being adopted for the new palace. They are made in blue pot-stone, and for depth of carving and relief are unsurpassed by any other stone work in India.

7th, Travancore House.—Alongside of the Jodhpur *jhároka* will be seen a section of a house, for which the Exhibition is indebted to the generosity of His Highness the Maharaja of Travancore. Although not full size, it is identical, in every detail of shape, furnishing and wood-carving, with the houses used by the better class people of the State. At the far end of the gallery will also be seen a stand which has been specially designed to exemplify the chief decorative features of a Travancore temple. The juxtaposition of the Travancore House with the Jodhpur *jhá-roka* manifests in a striking manner the great diversity and immense possibilities of development in Indian decorative art.

8th, Bhavnagar House.—(*Plate No. 28.*)—This will be found on the left hand of the Refreshment Room. It has been specially contributed by His Highness the Maharaja of Bhavnagar, and is intended to demonstrate all the best features of a Rajput Chief's house in Kathiawar. Mr. Proctor Sims, the State Engineer, has given this reproduction his most careful attention, and it may safely be accepted that it is true in every detail to the architecture and household furnishing that prevailed a century ago and which to a large extent still survives in Kathiawar. The head carpenter of Bhavnagar, when told that he was to follow carefully the time-honoured rules in designing and constructing the model-house required for the Exhibition, expressed the greatest pleasure at this order, as he regarded the modern departures as degenerations. As the building progressed, he observed that the finger of God was pointing the way, and that mistakes were accordingly impossible. In support of this belief he quoted the ancient rules of his craft, such as that, if the nine planets, the twelve signs of the zodiac and the fifteen dates of the lunar month were kept in line together, Vishwakarma had told that they would subtend a right angle. Further, that the breadth of the façade should be divided into 24 equal parts, of which 14 in the middle and 2 at each end should be left blank, while the remaining two portions should each form windows or *jálís*. The space between the plinth and

BHAVNAGAR HOUSE.

the upper floor should be divided into nine parts, of which one should be taken up by the base of the pillar, six parts by the column, one by the capital and one by the beam over it. He then added that, should any departures be made from these rules, the ruin of the architect and death of the owner were sure to follow.

The Kathiawar House is, in fact, constructed in conformity with conditions and rules that have taken hundreds of years to evolve to their present perfection of beauty and dignity. The wood-carving will be at once admitted as graceful and artistic, especially the peacock-like (*morli*) elaboration of the protruding joist ends, the pendants and veils of the brackets and capitals, and the curtain-like assortment of the component parts of the scrolls and other ornamentations. The Bhavnagar House has been purchased by the Indian Museum, Calcutta, for Rs. 10,000. It secured a gold medal, being viewed as equal with the Panjab Room as the finest examples of wood-carving in the Exhibition.

The style adopted in the Bhavnagar House is one of the most prevalent and striking met with in Gujerat, and very possibly originated in ancient Cambay and from a Hindu rather than a Jaina conception. In Broach and Surat a modern development is met with, in which fluted or even twisted pillars have garlands encircling the columns, and festoons and tassels of flowers carved on the architraves.

9th, Baroda Balcony.—Over the door into one of the offices of the Exhibition, and thus against the south wall of the Main Gallery, has been thrown a Baroda Balcony. This will be seen to closely resemble the Bhavnagar House but to manifest many developments mostly of a local character. The balcony was selected by the writer in consultation with Mr. G. R. Lynn, the State Chief Engineer, who kindly undertook to supervise its construction. It cost in all Rs. 1,264. The original is an old house seen in the main street of the city of Baroda.

10th, Ahmedabad House.—Across the west end of the Refreshment Room, and thus facing the Bhavnagar House, has been reconstructed an old house from Ahmedabad which, through a happy accident, was secured for the Exhibition. The house had to be pulled down, in consequence of certain improvements being

STONE BALCONIES

accomplished by the Municipality. It illustrates the more distinctly Hindu style of wood-work as contrasted with that of the Jaina.

11th, Agra House.—This will be found on the right hand of the Refreshment Room and forming a portion of the south wall of the Main Gallery. The façade is in white sandstone and is a reproduction of a portion of a Hindu temple in Agra city, and cost Rs. 3,000. This may be spoken of as in the recent Hindu style (seventeenth or eighteenth century for the most part), which was strongly influenced by the great Muhammadan architects of Northern India and reached its highest development in the palaces of Dig, Bharatpur and some portions of Fatehpur Sikri.

12th, Fatehpur Archway.—Between the Kathiawar and Agra Houses will be seen a triple archway, in plaster-of-paris, which constitutes the central feature of the south wall of the Main Gallery, facing the grand transept. This is a copy of an archway in the Mayo School of Art, Lahore, which was designed originally by Mr. J. L. Kipling, mainly from Fatehpur Sikri.

13th, Bijapur Door.—This is a paper impression made by Mr. C. L. Burns and the pupils of the School of Art, Bombay, of one of the doorways into the famous tomb of Ibrahim Rozah. The style shown is the second in importance, after Delhi and Agra, of the great schools of Saracenic Art in India, and was selected for the ornamentation and furnishing of the boudoir in the Circuit House. The graceful arch and beautiful brackets (adapted from the Chalukyans) are its most striking characteristics.

14th, Bharatpur House.—(*Plate No. 15.*)—Passing round the gallery to the extreme right (the west end), the central portion of the end wall will be found encased in a richly carved sandstone façade. This was intended as the residence of the Court barber some 80 years ago, but owing to the death of the then Maharaja was never actually finished. With the permission of His Highness the Maharaja of Bharatpur, the portions of this most interesting house, shown in the Exhibition, have been conveyed to Delhi and erected by the State Engineer. Mr. J. A. Devenish, who, while Engineer of the State, commenced the work, has been permitted to supervise the reconstruction, although he is no longer

MODEL HOUSE.

connected with the State. Unfortunately the entire building brought to Delhi could not be constructed, but the portion shown is true to the peculiar style of Dig and Bharatpur and will be admitted as one of the most perfect specimens of carving shown in the Exhibition. Having been carved so many years ago, this marvellously beautiful structure may be accepted as uncontaminated by European influence. Its most striking architectural features are its double cornices and projecting eaves. Fergusson, the historian of Indian architecture, alluding to these features, observes that "for extent of shadow and richness of detail" these "surpass any similar ornaments in India, either in ancient or modern buildings." It is not to be wondered at, therefore, that the Judging Committee have awarded this charming house the gold medal as the best example of stone-work shown in the Exhibition (see p. 70).

15th, The Mysore Carved Wooden Door. — (*Plate No. 30.*) — This beautiful door has been carved on the model of a door in a portion of the old palace of Mysore that escaped the destruction of the great fire. The replica was constructed under the orders of the Executive Engineer in charge of the new palace works. It is a faithful reproduction and one of great interest. The frame is exceedingly simple and massive, though richly carved. The scrolls are mostly in pinnate foliage, a conception that seems to have originated with the Chalukyan architects and became diffused throughout the central tract of India and along the western coast of Gujerat. This beautiful door has been secured by the Madras Central Museum.

Above the Mysore Door have been placed two reproductions in wood of the stone architraves of two doors in the great Chalukyan temple of Hullabid—the prototype very possibly of most of the art conceptions of west Central India. The huge animal with floriated tail and wreathed in garlands recurs again and again in numerous forms, and might be regarded as the ultimate key-note of the decorative arts of the region mentioned. The two examples have been purchased by the Calcutta and Panjab Museums.

16th, Nepal Model House.—This will be found against the western wall of the main hall. It is a faithful copy of one of the

BIKANIR WINDOW.

palaces in Nepal. This style is very Chinese in its feeling and is uncontaminated with the Muhammadan art denomination of India, though influenced by the recent conversion of the people to a modified form of Hinduism. The style is accumulative, appliqué and executed in several different coloured woods. By passing within the square formed, a vivid conception is given of the court-yard. On the way near to the Nepal Model House will be found a selection of Nepalese wood-carving (Plate No. 25) that may be accepted as illustrative of the style.

17th, Bikanir Window.—This beautiful structure is a reproduction in sandstone of one of the windows within the old palace of Bikanir. It was used in former times by the Maharaja, who sat within and conversed with his people seated in the outer hall. On the termination of the audience the wooden doors were closed. The stone work is typical of the style introduced some 200 years ago, while the door is a beautiful example of *gesso* painting of the same period. The door has been most obligingly lent by His Highness the Maharaja.

Having now briefly indicated some of the more striking features of the Main Gallery it becomes necessary to take up *seriatim* the classes and divisions of goods shown there.

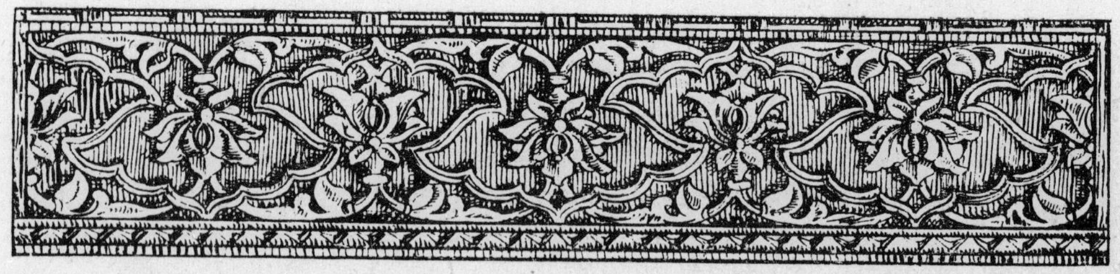

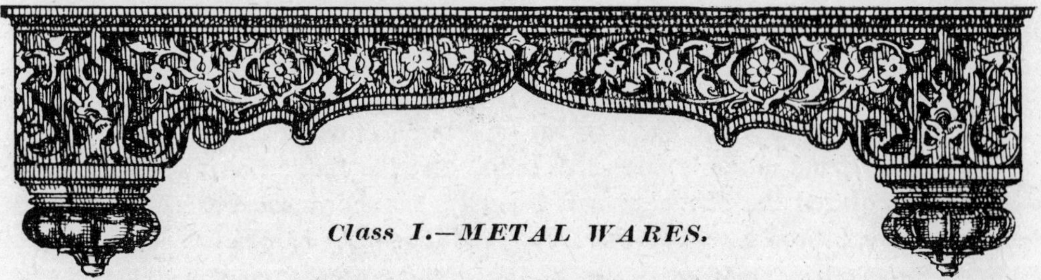

Class I.—METAL WARES.

DIVISION 1. IRON.

AFTER wood-work the metal manufactures are perhaps the most important of all the art wares of India. Most of the Indian household utensils are made of metal, hence metal takes the place of the porcelain and glass of Europe. The shapes most in use were possibly derived from the fruits, shells, horns or leaves utilised by primitive man, and even to the present day ascetics use the shell of the gourd and of other fruits in place of metallic vessels. According to popular opinion copper is regarded as the purest of metals; brass is most frequently employed by the Hindus and copper by the Muhammadans.

Classification into Divisions.

As assorted within the Exhibition, the Divisions into which the metal wares have been relegated run as follows:—

Division 1. Iron, Lead and Tin wares.
Division 2. Tinned, Painted and Lac-coloured wares.
Division 3. Enamelled and Niello wares.
Division 4. Gold and Silver plate.
Division 5. Damascened and Encrusted wares.
Division 6. Copper and Brass wares.

Location in Exhibition.

It will thus be seen that gold and silver are placed in the middle of the gallery and adjacent to the transept. On the right, methods of surface colouring are exemplified, such as enamelling, lac-colouring and tinning. On the left, methods of ornamentation by combining metals together, such as damascening, encrusting, etc.

The divisions may now be taken up categorically.

Division 1.—Iron, Lead and Tin Wares. (*Plate No. 4.*)

DIVISION 1. IRON.

The collections shown under this division are not very comprehensive, although the materials iron, lead and tin recur again and again in the other divisions. The antiquity and excellence of the Indian knowledge in iron may be judged of from the famous iron pillar at the Kutub near Delhi, from the numerous examples of wrought iron, also hammered and perforated brass gates, at the forts and tombs of India, and from the superb collections of ancient arms to be found in the armouries of India. At the Exhibition it will be discovered the School of Art, Bombay, has shown some excellent wrought-iron gates, windows, etc , and that from Baroda has been procured a complete series of the designs usually employed in Gujerat in the production of wrought-iron balustrades. Burma has for many years been known to have attained high proficiency in wrought iron. Near the Arakan pagoda of Mandalay numerous workshops exist for the production of the iron *Thees* or the umbrellas placed as weather-cocks on the pagodas of Burma. At the pagodas also balustrades in iron are so frequently used that this demand has given birth to a fairly large import trade in very inferior cast-iron imitations of the beautiful Burmese designs in wrought iron. Of *Thees* there are two widely different forms, the Burmese and the Shan; one of each of these will be found in the Exhibition, utilized as hanging lamps (see Plate No. 12 to the right).

Bombay School of Art.

Engraved Steel.

The engraving and carving of iron and steel was some years ago an important industry in India, and Kanara, Madura, Malabar, Vizagapatam and Mysore were famous for this work. Some of the arms procured from the Tanjore Palace and from the Madras Museum manifest a perfectly marvellous skill in the art of steel-carving (see Plate No. 4). Throughout India the dealers in art curiosities offer for sale swords, daggers, shields, helmets, in carved steel, and in a few localities the art is still practised, such as in Udaipur, Jaipur and Jodhpur. The collection of arms shown in the Sale Gallery may be said to consist of three or four sets of engraved steel, the more important being a series from Jaipur, a large assortment from Hyderabad Deccan, and a set from Kach. A complete chain armour has been obtained from Jaipur valued at

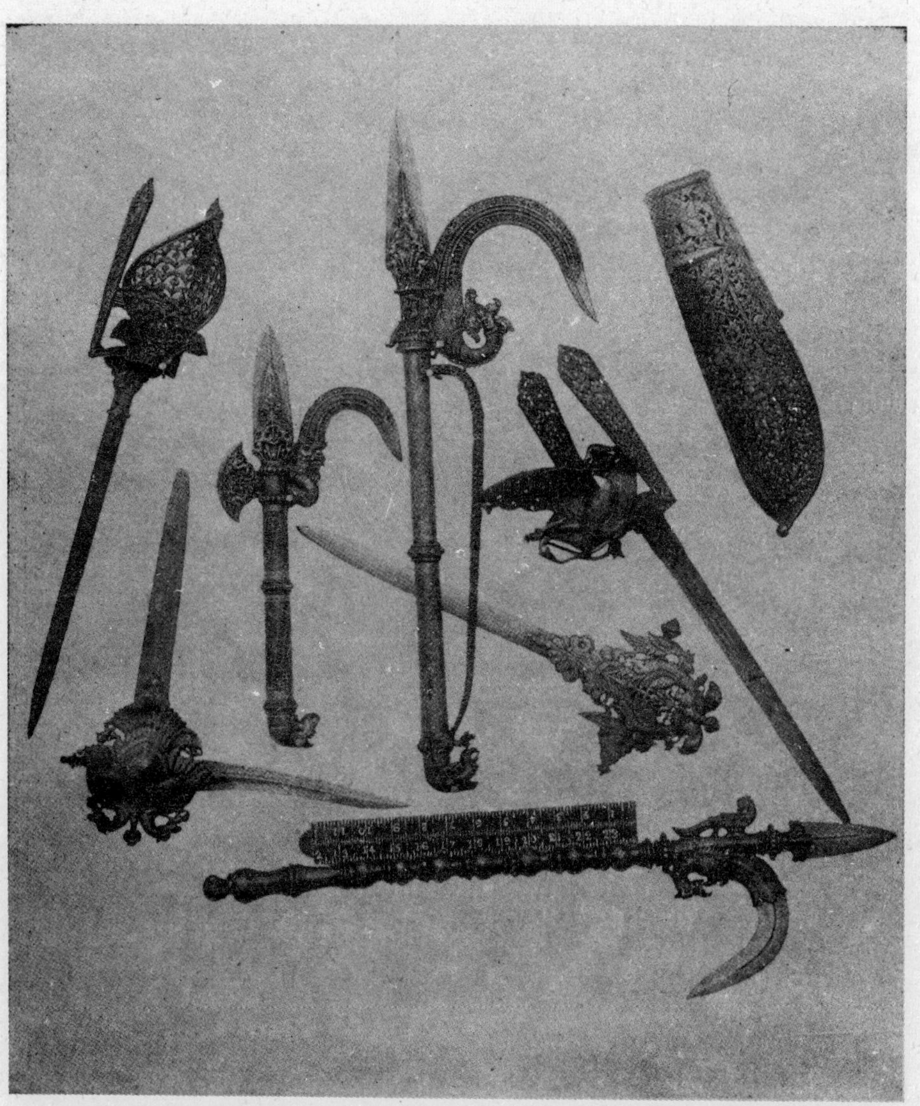

Plate No. 4 Carved Steel Tanjore Arms-

Rs. 300 and a lamp-stand from Sialkot Rs. 50; these may be quoted under this division as examples of Indian wrought iron. For further particulars regarding carved steel see the remarks and illustrations in connection with the Loan Collection Gallery.

DIVISION 2. TINNED METAL.

Chain Armour.

AWARDS AND CHIEF EXHIBITS.

AWARDS.

First Prize with silver medal to the Bombay School of Art for wrought-iron grills (No. 1648, etc.).

Second Prize with bronze medal for iron grills from Baroda procured through the Chief Engineer.

Commended for chain armour for a lady (No. 1753), made in Jaipur, exhibited by Messrs. Panna Muhammad Alla Baksh & Co. of Ajmir Bazar, Jaipur.

Commended for steel armour, head piece (damascened) and gauntlet (No. 1094); also large shield engraved steel and gold damascened (No. 1089), exhibited by Messrs. Nur Buksh Khuda Buksh & Co. of Jaipur.

Commended for large shield engraved steel damascened with gold (No. 1990), exhibited by Messrs. Amir Buksh & Sons, Ajmir Gate, Jaipur.

Division 2. Tinned, Painted and Lac-coloured Wares.—(*Plate No. 5.*)

Centres of Production.

Manipulation.

In this division have been placed all the goods that may be spoken of as imitating enamelled wares. The art is an old one and assumes considerable importance in several centres. Of these the most noted are Moradabad, Jaipur, Peshawar and Kashmir. The process of manipulation is the same in all, namely, the design is chased on the metal, the excavations thus made are then loaded with black or variously coloured lac (*lakh*) applied by a hot bolt, which fuses and distributes the lac over the surface. The excess smeared beyond the design is removed by sand or brick-dust and water, by sand-paper or by means of a file. The surface is next polished, and the pattern thus appears in colours within the metallic surface. Should the vessel have been gilded, silvered or tinned, the coloured ornamentations are shown on a gold or silver or a tinned background. Sometimes (as in Peshawar) the tinned-

DIVISION 2. TINNED METAL.

copper vessels are simply chased, when a red or copper pattern shows through the white metal surface.

The following are the *Chief Styles and Examples* of this division :—

1st :—Tinned Metal.—(*Plate No. 5.*)

(1) Tinned Metal.

This is largely turned out in Kashmir and various towns of the Northern Panjab; the art seems to have come from Persia. The Muhammadans use copper cooking and eating vessels, and hence these have to be tinned before they can be employed with safety. The ornamentation of tinned ware is thus essentially Muhammadan in origin. But there are various fairly distinctive styles and patterns in use, of which the following may be enumerated and examples of each cited :—

Various Styles. (A) Kashmir.

(A) In KASHMIR there are several designs such as (*a*) the *Floral Rosette* on a black background. This is probably Turkoman in origin. It consists of numerous small rosettes assorted on a spirally twisted line which passes all round the object and forms an intricate pattern in bunches of rosettes. The best examples are an *aftábá* with *tasht* (No. 4908), Rs. 75, by Kashmir State; a shield (No. 2938), Rs. 31, by Lassoo of Srinagar; a *suráhi* (Plate No. 5-A), by Kashmir State ; and a lamp-stand (No. 4901), Rs. 55, also by the Kashmir State, etc. (*b*) The *Arabesque style*, one of great beauty and much suited to this class of ware. The design consists of elongated flamboyan figures that convey the first impression of being composed of Arabic inscriptions arranged geometrically. When more closely examined the pattern is seen to be a complex design of quaintly bifurcated and minutely interlaced floral scrolls. This style of ornamentation, as also the rosette pattern, is met with in all forms of Kashmir metal ware, as also in the older and better examples of papier-maché. The most commendable samples of Arabesque tinned wares are an octagonal tray (No. 2956), Rs. 22, by Lassoo of Srinagar; a *samavár* (No. 4905), Rs. 37, by Kashmir State; and a Persian tea-pot (Plate No. 5-A), Rs. 22, by Lassoo of Srinagar. Formerly Kashmir used to turn out copper, not tinned but with Arabesque designs showing on the gold (sometimes even gilt) surface. There is only one example of this kind in

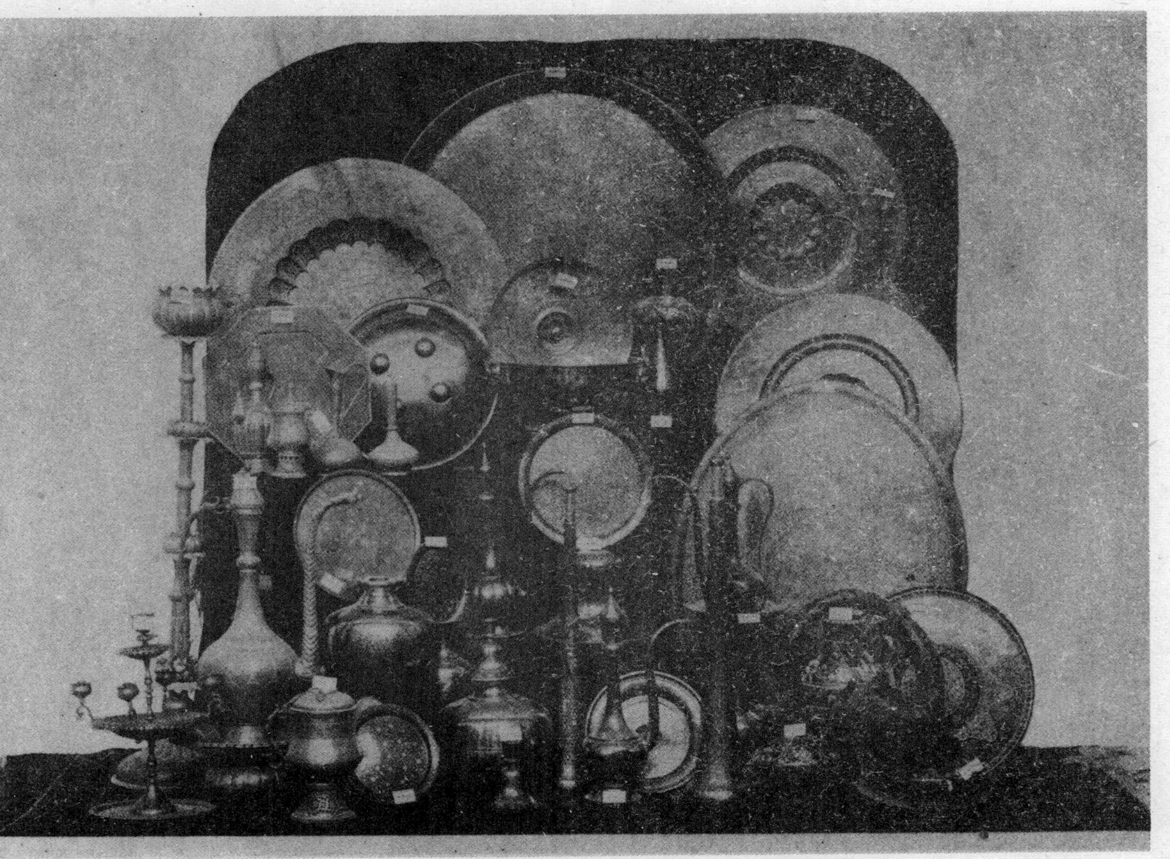

Plate No. 5 Tinned, Painted and Lacquered Metal Wares

the Sale Gallery, namely, an octagonal plate (Plate No. 5). Many examples will, however, be found in the Loan Collection Gallery, especially those procured from the South Kensington Museum. This work was, as a rule, extremely beautiful because of the ornamentation not being over-burdened, and liberally and gracefully spaced. (*c*) The *Modern Kashmir pattern* such as the excellent Samarkand coffee-pot (No. 2727), Rs. 37; the copper flower bowl with Persian inscription (No. 2650), Rs. 56; an *aftábá* and *tasht* by Lassoo, silver and copper-smith of Kashmir.

DIVISION 2. TINNED METAL.

(B) Peshawar.

(B) In PESHAWAR and the NORTHERN PANJAB the style of ornamentation differs but slightly from that of Kashmir, except perhaps in the circumstance that a very large trade is done in copper-chased goods not loaded with lac or other pigment. These are for the most part in the Arabesque design, and when colour is employed it is often a preparation of lamp-black not of coloured lac. Of this class of goods Messrs. Mull Chand & Sons of Peshawar have sent the following amongst others:—Six large trays (*sínís*) (Plate No. 5-A), each Rs. 75, these have been commended by the Exhibition judges; copper *aftábás* (6 in number) (Plate No. 5-A), Rs. 10 each, which have also been commended; large *aftábá* and *tasht* (No. 4360); beggars' bowls (*kashkols*), Rs. 15 each (No. 4353); water bottles (*kúzas*), Rs. 7. In a good many of these articles, as also in numerous examples of the collection generally, the copper is simply incised through the tinned surface, thus showing the pattern in bright colour. The largest *aftábá* and *tasht* is an admirable example of modern tinned, engraved and black coloured ware. It is priced at Rs. 125, and was made by Messrs. Mull Chand & Sons, and has been purchased by the Bombay School of Art.

Incised but not coloured.

(C) Moradabad repoussé Tin.

(C) From MORADABAD have come several examples of a craft practised here and there, at widely remote localities, all over India. Wood is first carved, then over the surface are placed thin plates of tinned copper (*nakáshi*). These are hammered on to the wood and are then securely fixed by pins and retained over the surface of the wood, thus producing a sort of *repoussé*. The

DIVISION 2. LAC-COLOURED METAL.

large settee (No. 146) made by Niaz Ullah of Moradabad is perhaps the best example; it is priced at Rs. 44.

AWARDS FOR TINNED METAL.

Kashmir Ware.

AWARDS.

Second Prize with bronze medal for lamp-stand (No. 4901); the *aftábá* and *tasht* (No. 4908); and an embossed jar (No. 4906) —all exhibited by Kashmir State.

Peshawar Ware.

Second Prize with bronze medal for large trays (*sínís*) and an *aftábá* and *tasht* by Messrs. Mull Chand & Sons of Peshawar.

2nd :—Painted Wares.—(*To extreme right and lower corner of Plate No. 5.*)

(2) Painted Wares.

Painted metals have been received from BELGAUM, the colours employed being mostly red and gold and the designs mythological. These are made by Fakerapa of that town and consist of vases, plates and *lotás*, at prices from Rs. 2 to Rs. 10 (No. 788). The art is unimportant though curious and interesting. From BAREILLY and TILHAR in the United Provinces painted metal trays (No. 3701) have been received. These are made by Nathoo Khan, painter of Bareilly. The colours mostly used are Aspinal, though the designs are ancient and distinctly Oriental.

3rd :—Lac-coloured Metal.—(*Centre of Plate No. 5 and right hand side of Plate No. 5-A.*)

(3) Lac-coloured Wares. (A) Moradabad.

(A) MORADABAD.—The original and to this day the chief centre of this craft may be said to be Moradabad. The system of ornamentation appears to have been designed to imitate the class of encrusted ware known as *bidrí*. The lac was accordingly coloured black, the copper vessels were tinned and an extensive background chased or punched away, thus leaving the floral ornamentation in relief. The depressions were then loaded with black lac, fused by a hot bolt, and the excess rubbed off with sand-paper or powdered brick. In consequence a liberal background in black was produced with, on the surface, a floral design in white metal. This form was known locally as *bidrí*. Some 50 or 60 years ago the pattern was bold, but through successive

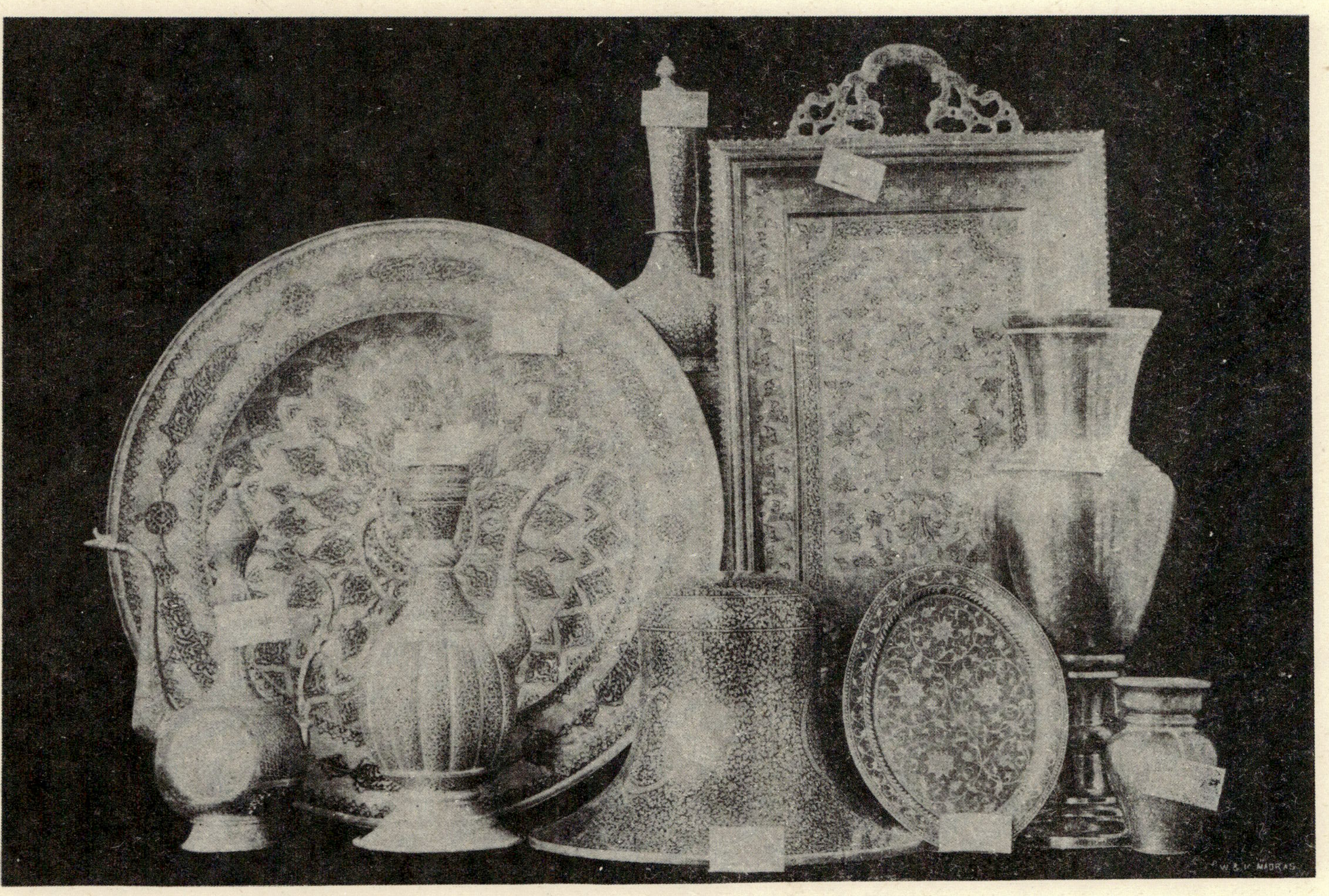

Plate No. 5-A Selected Patterns in Tinned and Lac-coloured Metal Ware

changes this gradually gave place to a more minute style known as *marori* and later still to a form—*the charakwan*—in which the pattern is in black or other coloured lac and the background in brass. **DIVISION 2. LAC-COLOURED METAL.**

(*a*) Of the *bidrí* style the best examples are a large *hukka* bowl (Plate No. 5-A) made from an old sample selected by the writer; a *garhá* (No. 127); a series of oval plates or trays (Plate No. 5-A) copied from old samples in the Calcutta and Lahore Museums (Nos. 136, 139, 141); a pair of Indian clubs (in diamond pattern) (No. 135), Rs. 62-8; and a large tray (No. 136), Rs. 200—all made by Sheik Hafiz Azizuddin of Moradabad; these are specially worthy of attention. (*b*) Of the *marori* work, perhaps the best examples are a ewer made by Mahomed Yarkhan (No. 122), Rs. 87; two spitoons shown on right of Plate No. 5-A in minute *marori*; and a large *hukka* bowl (No. 131), Rs. 94, made by Sheik Hafiz Azizuddin. (*c*) Of the *charakwan* work, perhaps the best illustration is a *garhá*, Rs. 40, made by Sheik Hafiz Azizuddin, a ewer and basin made by Mahomed Yarkhan (No. 126), Rs. 100, and a rectangular tray shown on Plate No. 5-A. **Various Styles of Work.**

AWARDS FOR LAC-COLOURED METAL.

(*a*) *Bidrí form.*

First Prize with silver medal for collection (chiefly Nos. 127 and 139) by Sheik Hafiz Azizuddin of Moradabad. **AWARDS.**

Second Prize with bronze medal for ewer and basin (No. 122) and spitoon (No. 116) by Mahomed Yarkhan of Moradabad.

(*b*) *Marori form.*

Commended for a ewer (No. 124) and casket (No. 107) by Mahomed Yarkhan of Moradabad.

(*c*) *Charakwan form.*

Second Prize with bronze medal for an *aftábá* and *tasht* (No. 126) by Mahomed Yarkhan of Moradabad.

Recently a further development has taken place in Moradabad ware in which coloured flowers and even mythological subjects are inserted within the elaborate *marori* pattern. In such instances the colour portions are spoken of (though incorrectly) as

DIVISION 2. LAC-COLOURED METAL

enamel. A good example of this is the pair of small vases, Rs. 43, made by Mahomed Yarkhan.

(B) Kashmir.

(B) KASHMIR.—Lac has for long been used in Kashmir for the purpose of colouring brass and copper wares, but the practice has almost entirely died out in recent times, and in the Exhibition will be found only one or two specimens, such as the candlesticks (No. 2547) by Lassoo of Srinagar.

(C) Jaipur.

(C) JAIPUR.—Within the past few years Jaipur has taken to imitating Moradabad in the production of *marori* and *charakwan* work, but with an abundance of colours added in questionable taste. The best example of this ware is a tray (No. 1026) at Rs. 50 and a ewer (No. 1039) made by Nur Bux and Khudda Buksh of Jaipur. Lastly, a large shield showing scenes in the Ramiana on a field of white lac with red roses and green leaves (No. 1001), Rs. 500. A further development has taken place in Jaipur, in which engraved designs mostly mythological (large oval tray, Plate No. 4) are produced in elaborate colours on a metallic background.

AWARDS.

AWARDS.

No awards were given for the lac-coloured metal of Kashmir or of Jaipur, a verdict that it is hoped may check the further development of these highly-coloured wares.

Concluding Note.—It will thus be observed that both in Moradabad and Jaipur, the modern tendency has been to discontinue the elaborate process of producing a coloured background and to substitute a coloured design on a metallic surface. Obviously the latter can be much more cheaply and quickly done, and when accomplished skilfully is often more pleasing than the overelaboration of the older method. The danger lies in the cheapening process and in the substitution of European for Oriental designs. The chief pattern employed in *charakwan* work is admittedly European, the source of the design having been shown to the writer as a piece of English calico-print. An even more serious danger lies in the fact that Muhammadan craftsmen, in response to a popular

Degeneration.

demand (and following the lead of the Hindu workers of Jaipur), are taking to the production of Hindu (often mythological) designs, with which they are not only quite unfamiliar but in personal (religious) antipathy. Further, in order to meet a depraved taste they are taking to the use of glaring, mostly aniline, colours that are bound to fade within a few weeks. The art of ornamentation of copper and brass by means of lac is essentially Muhammadan, and its adaptation by the Hindu workers of Jaipur could hardly escape the degeneration that is rapidly becoming more evident.

DIVISION 3. ENAMELLING.

Division 3.—Enamelled and Niello Wares.—(*Plate No. 6.*)

1st, Enamelling.—Enamelling may be described as the art of colouring and ornamenting the surface of metal by fusing over it various mineral substances. Success depends on the skill and resources of the operator and the materials employed. The range of colours attainable on gold is much greater than on silver and still more so than on copper or brass. This peculiarity is to a certain extent overcome by silvering or gilding the surfaces intended to be enamelled. There are known to exist three or four forms of enamelling, such as the *cloisonné* of Japan and China, in which wires are fastened by a gum or simply impinged or in others welded to the surface of the metal, in elaboration of the design, much as in some forms of filigri. The various spaces thus outlined are next loaded with the colouring materials, and the article placed in the furnace until the glasses fuse, when the purpose of the wires becomes apparent, namely, to save the various colours from being intermixed and the design thereby hopelessly destroyed.

Various Forms.

The second form is known as *champlevé* in which the metal is engraved or chased, repousséd or blocked out in such a way as to provide depressions within which the colours can be imbedded. In Jaipur, Kach, Bhawalpur, Delhi, Lucknow, Benares and Rampur and other towns of India the pattern is chased, in Kashmir repousséd, and in Multan it is blocked out by means of dies.

Chief Centres.

But in India the resources of the jeweller are limited, though his results are often extremely beautiful. His furnace is very small and his methods of heating defective, hence comparatively small articles only can be enamelled, the colours being applied time after time, those that can stand the greatest amount of heat being first used and the others in order of their fusibility.

A third mode and that which prevails for the most part in Kashmir is to paint the surface with a sort of silicated or readily

DIVISION 3. ENAMELLING.

fusible paint and then to subject the article to a moderate heat, sufficient to melt the paint but not to cause the colours to fuse together.

Materials used.

The flux used is invariably borax, tin oxide being added to lower the required temperature but with the further result of making the glass or enamel opaque. The colours are silicates and borates of the metals, the chief being a yellow produced through the use of chromate of potash; violets through carbonate of manganese; blues through cobalt oxide; greens through copper oxide; browns through red iron oxide, blacks through cobalt—copper, manganese and red iron oxides being used along with a glass composed of 100 parts of quartz, 50 borax and 200 red lead. The brillinat reds attained by the Jaipur, Delhi and Benares workers on gold are the most difficult of all colours to produce, and their secret is therefore more or less rigorously preserved. White or ivory colour is also difficult, but is obtained from antimoniate of potash, hydrated iron oxide and carbonate of zinc, added to the ordinary glass.

Manipulation.

Colonel T. H. Hendley, C.I.E., has published a most admirable account of the art of enamelling. He tells us that "the engraving is done with steel styles and the polishing is completed with similar tools and agates. The surface of the pits in the gold is ornamented with hatchings, which serve not only to make the enamel adhere firmly, but to increase the play of light and shade through the transparent colours. The enameller or *minakar* now applies the colours in the order of their hardness, or power of resisting fire, beginning with the hardest. Before the enamel is applied, the surface of the ornament is carefully burnished and cleansed. The colours are obtained in opaque vitreous masses from Lahore, where they are prepared by Muhammadan *manikars* or bracelet makers. The Jaipur workmen state they cannot make the colours themselves."

Jaipur Style.

JAIPUR.—(*Plate No. 67 in Loan Collection.*)—The various styles of enamelling met with in India are so different that they can be readily recognised. Jaipur stands pre-eminent—the oldest and best school of work, though within recent years the most skilled artificers have removed to Delhi. It is somewhat difficult to write a description by which this kind of work may be recognised. It is

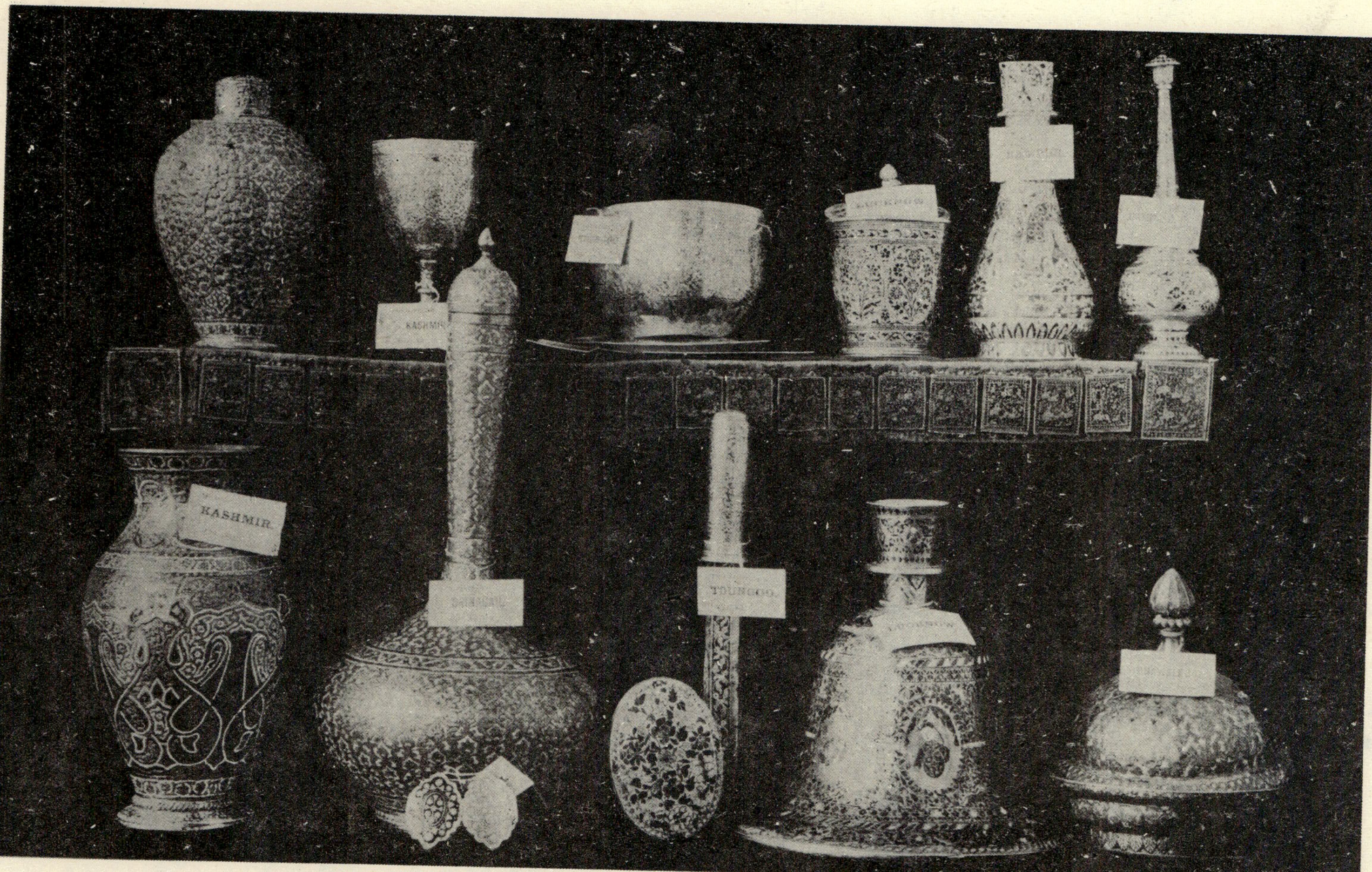

Plate No. 6 Enamelled and Niello Wares

invariably done on the purest gold (22 carat), and the plate is so engraved that all but the faintest lines of the metal disappear and the entire surface becomes as it were a sheet of translucent enamel. Formerly every attention was given to effect, and a background or field colour was regularly employed, most frequently a rich creamy white. Within the past few decades this has been discontinued, and complex and intricate designs substituted, in which it can hardly be said there is a field colour at all. The result is distinctly inferior and may be described as garish rather than artistic. The utilitarian spirit of the times is also marked by the production of a large assortment of sleeve links, lockets, bracelets, brooches and the like, and the decoration of the backs of pieces of jewellery, in place of enamelling being the chief ornamentation of charms, sword hilts, plates, etc., as in former times. The smallness of the articles turned out may have dictated the change in style, but the result is anything but complimentary to "the master art craft" of India, as enamelling has been called by Sir George Birdwood. This change seems also to have accompanied the subordination of the artificers to the money lenders and traders. The best known trader is the famous Jaipur Jeweller, Sughan Chand, Sobhag Chand, who has a splendid display of modern work in his show cases within the Jewellery Court of the Exhibition. The contrast between that work and the fine series of old enamels, doubtless made in Jaipur, that may be seen in the Loan Collection Gallery will abundantly confirm the opinion that a distinct decline in artistic merit has to be accepted as characteristic of the modern trade in these beautiful wares.

DIVISION 3. ENAMELLING.

Degeneration.

Subordination of Artificers.

BHAWALPUR—(*Plate No. 6*)—has long enjoyed the reputation of being an important centre for gold enamelling. Objects of a large size are produced, such as finger bowls, cups, vases, etc., the enamel being mostly in a rich deep blue intermixed with green. In the Loan Collection will be found a superb series of this work, the vase in bold blue diaper being specially commendable. In this school of work the pattern is large, the enamelled surfaces considerable, and the spacing in gold graceful. Occasionally the enamellers raise the pattern by a thick deposit of opaque white enamel (or "slip") subsequently coloured on the surface. This work

Bhawalpur Style.

DIVISION 3. ENAMELLING.

thus comes to very closely resemble Chinese copper enamelled vases, plates, cups, etc. In the Loan Collection will be found a superb example of this work in the form of the enamelled scabbard shown on Plate No. 68-A, fig. 1.

KACH.—The enamellers of Bhuj have recently attained high proficiency in the art of enamelling. A sample of their work in the Loan Collection (Plate No. 68-A, fig. 2.) will be seen to equal, if not excel, the finest enamelling of Europe. The whole surface is uniformly coloured, only the faintest lines of gold being left by the engravers of the plate, so that the enamelling looks like the most delicate French *cloisonné*, but in design closely resembles the embroidery of Kach.

KASHMIR.—In the Loan Collection (Plate No. 69) will be found an enamelled plate from the Kashmir Museum. This closely resembles Persian work, and, but for the subject (*Devi* being attended by *Parbatti*), might be mistaken for Persian enamelling. The whole surface is covered and appears to have been painted in a rich silicate or enamelling paint. This work is of a very different character from that presently to be described under copper and brass enamels (fig. 1).

Multan Style.

MULTAN is famed for its small ornaments, such as buckles, bracelets, studs, etc., done in two or three shades of blue. The articles are in silver, struck off from a die so as to leave small rims of silver to demark the patches of colour. The enamelling is quite opaque and the yellows and reds (occasionally employed) very inferior. A specimen will be seen on Plate No. 6 resting against a *suráhi* from Srinagar.

Benares Style.

In BENARES the art of enamelling seems confined to the production of large patches of colour in imitation of jewels, or as a setting to jewels, rather than in the elaboration of a floral or other design that could be regarded as a distinct style of enamelling. In the Exhibition, both in the Main Gallery and in the Jewellery Court, numerous examples of this work may be seen. Usually the enamel is employed to give the ground colour required in the production of gold and jewelled ornaments such as *pachísí* markers, and the design is produced with diamonds or other stones set within the coloured field.

LUCKNOW and RAMPUR.—(*Plate No. 6.*)—These towns are known for their enamels. The prevailing feature is an etched pattern on silver in which green and blue with a small patch of yellow and brown enamel is given. The etching is so minute and at the same time so abundant as to give the ornamented article, when viewed at a distance, the appearance of being corroded in verdigris. The absence of a background or any well-marked scheme of composition or colour, renders this style of work distinctly inferior in artistic merit to any of the other Indian schools of enamelling. It is, moreover, burdened with animal forms to an extent perfectly astonishing, seeing that it is for the most part made by Muhammadans and sold to Muhammadans. It is, at the same time, by no means cheap. In the Exhibition a glass case will be found full of this work. The more noteworthy samples are a large *hukka* bowl with *chilam*, etc., complete; a beautiful little oval box with rich floral design, quite unlike most of the examples of Lucknow work, shown on Plate No. 6 resting against a dagger. Sir George Birdwood, in his *Industrial Arts of India,* gives on Plate 38 a superb example of Lucknow or Rampur work. The design is clearly engraved in the way characteristic of these towns, but the spacing and designing is charming, and so far superior to anything of the present day as to leave some doubt of the identification here made being correct. Occasionally, however, old samples of Lucknow and Rampur work are found that show that this style of work attained a far higher degree of merit than is reached by the present craftsmen.

DIVISION 3. ENAMELLING.

Lucknow Style.

Samples on View.

Old Specimens.

LAHORE.—In many towns of the Panjab a style of enamelling prevailed some half a century ago that seems to have practically disappeared. The articles were deeply repousséd and the depressions loaded with a rich blue enamel that gave great effect to the ornamentation. In the Lahore Museum there are some splendid examples of this work.

Panjab Style.

KANGRA and HAZARA turn out crude enamellings in blue and yellow that much resemble that of Multan.

In PARTABGARH, in Rajputana, a peculiar style of work is practised that has been spoken of as a form of enamellings. The article is made of a piece of green or red coloured glass, or thick layer of enamel, the crude material for which is imported from

Quasi-Enamelling.

DIVISION 3. ENAMELLING.

Manipulation.

Kashmir. A frame or silver wire, of the exact size and shape of the glass, is next made, and across this is attached a sheet of fairly thick gold leaf. This is then embedded on lac and the pattern punched out and chased on the gold. The glass is then semi-fused, and while still hot the rim of silver and film of gold are slipped over the edge and pressed on to the surface of the glass. The article is again heated, until a sort of fusion takes place and the gold and glass become securely united. Before mounting the article, a piece of silver tin-foil is placed underneath the glass to give it brilliancy. Mr. Brown shows in Plate No. 7 two Partabgarh enamellers at work. The man on the right is punching out the gold pattern on a bed of lac; on the left the other operator is fusing the gold on to the glass. On the little table alongside will be seen various pieces of the prepared glass or bed of enamel cut into the required shapes. On the floor a series of belts, brooches, plates, made in this ware will be seen, while hung as it were on the wall has been placed a sample, natural size, showing the gold design on the surface of the dark coloured glass. Stretched across the middle of Plate No. 6 will be seen a belt made in this style of enamelling.

In RATLAM a similar form of imitation enamelling is practised, a shade of blue being produced.

CHIEF EXHIBITS ON VIEW.

Chief Exhibits on View.

Having now indicated the chief centres of production, the materials used and the characteristic features of each Indian school of enamelling, it may be useful to discuss the collections on view. The following very brief abstract may accordingly be given of the more commendable examples of Enamelled and Niello wares in the Exhibition:—

Kashmir Copper and Brass Enamels.

KASHMIR.—The painted enamelling of this State on copper or brass is good of its kind, but much coarser than that on silver. The copper and brass enamels are never translucent, and while they do not readily crack off, they seem to become of a duller colour with the ageing of the metal. The pattern is punched (repousséd), and the hollows thus produced charged with a readily fusible glass paint. The goods produced may be described as intermediate between the fine enamellings of Jaipur, Delhi and Benares and the lac-coloured wares of Moradabad.

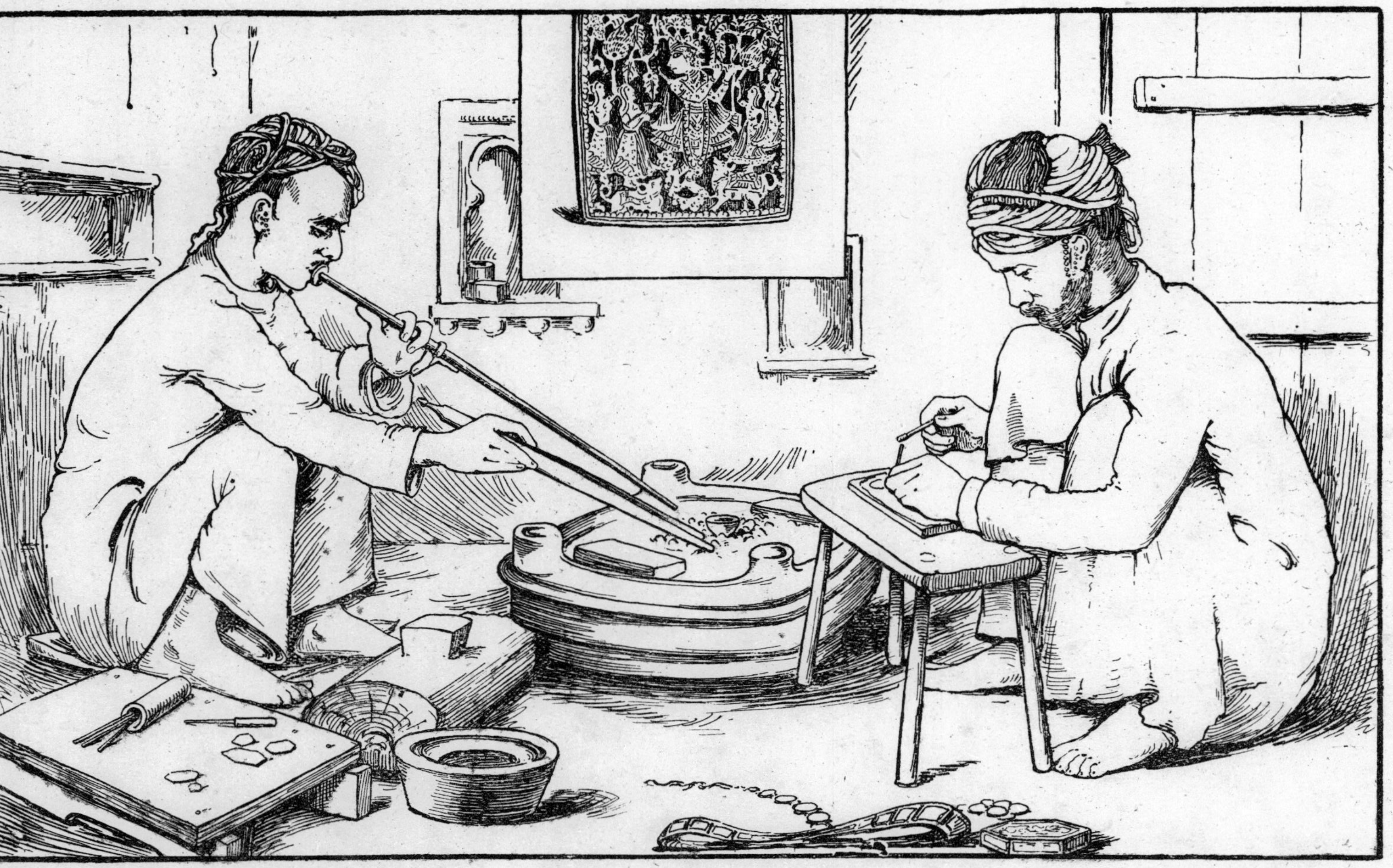

Plate No. 7 Enamellers-Pertabgarh, Rajputana

DIVISION 3. ENAMELLING.

As with tinned wares so with enamels there may be said to be two or three widely different styles and qualities turned out in Kashmir, of which the following are worthy of note:—

(*a*) *The Shawl Pattern* (*Plate No. 6,* jar and cup).—The best examples of this in the Exhibition are: — a large copper and gold vase (*Martabán*) (No. 2202), Rs. 246; a beggar's bowl (*Kashgar*) (No. 2203), Rs. 111; a gourd-shaped bowl (No. 2222), Rs. 21; a small vase, in the so-called almond work (No. 2206), Rs. 44—all by Habib Joo, silversmith of Srinagar, Kashmir; an *aftábá* by Lussoo, copper and silversmith of Srinagar, Rs. 30; a gourd-shaped vase (constricted in the middle) (*tumba*) in brass (No. 2540) by the same, Rs. 19, and many others.

(*b*) *The Arabesque Style* (*Plate No. 6, suráhi*).—Good specimens are: the copper and gold enamelled *suráhi* (No. 2791) by Habib Joo, silversmith of Srinagar, Rs. 59; a jar (No. 3773) copper and gold enamel by Subhana, copper and silversmith of Srinagar, Rs. 73.

(*c*) *The Rosette Pattern* (*Plate No. 6*, Bokhara jar).—This is similar to the corresponding class of goods in the tinned and papier-maché wares. The chief examples are a copper and gold jar (No. 3793) by Subhana of Srinagar, Rs. 24; a small circular tray by the same, Rs. 14; a copper and gold enamelled *suráhi* (No. 2219) by Habib Joo, Rs. 41.

(*d*) *The Embossed Form.*—*Aftábá* and *tasht* in copper and gold (No. 2213), Rs. 281 for the two pieces, by Habib Joo of Srinagar; a copper and gold lotus bowl (No. 2611), Rs. 87; a copper and gold Bokhara jar (No. 3778), Rs. 40, and a copper and gold Bokhara jar (No. 3791) small size, Rs. 25, by Subhana of Srinagar; a *suráhi* by Habib Joo, Rs. 56.

Kashmir Copper and Brass Enamels.

(*e*) *The Mosaic Style.*—A coarse form of enamelling, bold and effective, composed of large patches of colour but with little of the feeling of Kashmir art about it. The examples are a large vase (No. 2354) by Habib Joo of Srinagar, Rs. 258; a small *lotá* (No. 2750), Rs. 25.

Occasionally, instead of gilding the copper prior to enamelling it, the silversmiths either silver or tin it. A good example of this class of goods will be found in the Exhibition in the form of an *aftábá* and *tasht* (No. 2936) by Lassoo, silversmith of Srinagar, Kashmir.

DIVISION 3. ENAMELLING.

Kashmir Silver Enamels.

Before leaving this State it may be added that a small assortment of silver enamels will be found on the lowest shelf of the stand employed for copper and brass. The best specimens of these are the small *suráhis*, in two shades of blue, and the finger bowls and dessert plates by Habib Joo and by Subhana: prices for a *suráhi*, Rs. 24, for a finger bowl and plate, Rs. 55, and for a goblet, Rs. 40. In the silver enamels the blues are particularly rich and translucent.

Multan Enamels.

MULTAN.—In this town the silversmiths have for many years enjoyed the reputation of producing very pleasing small silver enamels, in various shades of opaque blue, yellow or scarlet. The silver is stamped on a die so arranged as to leave thin lines to separate and demark the glass as if in imitation of *cloisonné*. The best examples are—*surma dánis* made by Wasna Ram, goldsmith, Rs. 13; bangles, 18 in number, Rs. 37; buckles, Rs. 7, larger size, Rs. 11; and a numerous assortment of such small goods.

BENARES.—A set of gold *pachísí* markers and dice, richly enamelled, have been contributed by B. Moti Chand of this city. These are most admirable examples of the best style of translucent enamelling in rich, warm, life-like colours, price Rs. 2,500 for the set.

Lucknow Enamels.

LUCKNOW.—The enamel of this town, like that of Benares and Jaipur, has the silver chased or engraved to receive the glass. The colours are mostly greens and blues with indifferent browns, yellows and oranges. The design is realistic but usually deficient in composition, hence at a distance the articles look as if corroded. On closer inspection animals, birds and men are seen to be dispersed over a floriated surface. The chief defect of the style is the absence of main decorative lines to fix and guide observation. The best examples are the large *hukka* (Plate No. 6), with two *chilams* and their covers (*sarposhes*), and one mouthpiece (*mohnal*), price Rs. 2,860; one *thali* with *pán-dán*, Rs. 625; one pair (*churi*) bangles, Rs. 156; and one *changhara*, Rs. 825; one drinking-glass with cover, Rs. 666; lastly, a *chilam* and *chamal*, Rs. 888—the best piece—exhibited by Gopi Nath Lachmi Narain.

DIVISION 3. ENAMELLING.

Rampur Enamels.

RAMPUR STATE.—A bold and effective style of enamelling in greens and blues with fairly well marked sub-division of spaces is practised in this State. The example shown is a *hukka* made by Ram Prasad and Pershadi Lal, Rs. 101 (Plate No. 6).

Jaipur Enamels.

JAIPUR holds, and justly, the highest reputation of all the towns of India for enamelling. Sughan Chand and Sobhag Chand, Jewellers of that City, employ all the best workmen and, as that firm has secured a space for their wares in the Jewellery Court, their stock of beautiful articles on view should be examined in connection with the above brief observations on Indian enamelling.

LOAN COLLECTION.—In the Loan Collection Gallery a superb display of old enamels will be found, mostly in the form of sword and dagger handles, scabbards, *hukkas*, bowls, etc., those from Jaipur, Jodhpur, Kach, Bhawalpur, Chamba, etc., being specially worthy of study.

Niello Ware.

Niello Ware.—(*Plate No. 6*, bowl and dagger.)—This old art still survives in one or two localities of Burma. Only the purest silver can be used. The desired pattern is punched, then chased, in order to lower the background of the design, and the hollows thus produced are loaded with an amalgam of lead 2 parts, silver 1 part and copper 1 part. The article is next placed in the charcoal furnace on which fragments of cocoanut shell have been placed to give dense black smoke. It is there retained until the materials fuse and unite with the silver. The flux employed is a mixture of borax, crude sulphate of ammonia and sulphur. The excess colouring matter is then rubbed off and the silver polished, when the design, in bright silver, appears on a black background. Niello may thus be regarded as a form of enamelling; it is most effective and quite permanent but difficult to make, and hence the art is not popular owing to the great temperature required and the sulphurous fumes produced. It is practised by but one or two persons in Burma, and appears to be quite unknown to the craftsmen of India, though pieces of the ware may be picked up all over the country, thus very possibly indicating a former widespread knowledge in the art.

Materials and Manipulation.

DIVISION 3. ENAMELLING

Examples on View.

The following are the examples made by Saya Po of Toungoo:— a silver bowl and plate, gilt inside (No. 405), Rs. 375; four Shan daggers with Niello handles, damascened blades and silver repoussé scabbards (No. 406), Rs. 57 each; Shan swords (*da*), (Nos. 407—9) with Niello handle and silver repoussé scabbard, Rs. 188 to Rs. 250. From Kashmir has been obtained a small specimen of this ware in the form of a scent bottle, price Rs. 10. The design is quite unlike anything used in Kashmir at the present day, and the owner claims that the bottle in question is very old, though, in his opinion, made in Kashmir. If this be correct, the art of Niello ornamentation is no longer practised in that State.

AWARDS FOR ENAMELLED AND NIELLO WARES.

(*a*) *Niello Ware.*

AWARDS.

First Prize with Gold medal to Saya Po of Toungoo for Niello ware in form of bowl and plate (No. 405), also swords and daggers (Nos. 406—9).

(*b*) *Gold Enamels.*

Second Prize with silver medal for gold enamelled markers (No. 1652) to B. Moti Chand of Benares.

Third Prize with bronze medal to Bombay School of Art for both gold and silver enamels.

Third Prize with bronze medal to Partabgarh State for the quasi-gold enamel characteristic of that State.

(*c*) *Silver Enamels.*

Third Prize with bronze medal for a set of finger bowls and plates (Nos. 2964 and 2966) by Subhana, silversmith of Srinagar, Kashmir.

Commended two *suráhis* in old shawl pattern in two shades of blue (Nos. 2343 and 2344) by Habib Joo, silversmith of Srinagar, Kashmir.

Commended for large series of blue enamels to Wasna Ram of Multan.

(*d*) *Copper and Brass Enamels.*

First Prize with silver medal for an *aftábá* and *tasht* (No. 2213) Rs. 280; a *tumba* jar (No. 2222), Rs. 24, made by Habib Joo, silversmith of Srinagar, Kashmir.

Second Prize with bronze medal for an *aftábá* and *tasht* (No. 3784), Rs. 80; a jar (No. 3773), Rs. 73, by Subhana, silversmith of Srinagar, Kashmir. DIVISION 4. GOLD AND SILVER PLATE.

Commended for an *aftábá* and *tasht* in silvered enamel (No. 2956), Rs. 81, by Lassoo, silversmith of Srinagar, Kashmir.

Commended for a Bokhara jar (No. 3791), Rs. 29, by Subhana, silversmith of Srinagar, Kashmir.

Division 4.—Gold and Silver Plate.

Styles of Indian Plate.

The Gold and Silver Plate of India, until very recently, could be readily referred to four or five well-marked types or styles of ornamentation. Within the past few years, however, the silversmiths of India and even of Burma have taken to producing any or all the styles, the result being that it has become difficult, if not impossible, to affirm where a piece of plate may have been made.

In the Jewellery Court and also in the Loan Collection Gallery a fair assortment of gold plate will be found. In art conception this is identical with the silver work. Accordingly the gold may be treated conjointly with the silver plate. Bhawalpur is perhaps most famed, in recent times, for its gold plate of purely native design, though any of the goldsmiths of India can and do produce gold plate such as tea and coffee sets, though nearly all the modern work is in purpose, design and ornamentation essentially European.

CHIEF EXHIBITS ON VIEW.

Location of Collections.

The Gold and Silver Plate shown in the Sale Gallery of the Exhibition is placed in the transept and within the bay immediately adjacent. It may assist the visitor, therefore, if the collection be dealt with categorically and in the sequence in which arranged.

On the right hand side of the transept will be found the silver plate of the Madras Presidency, including Bangalore and Hyderabad; on the left that of the Bombay Presidency, including Kathiawar, Kach and Sind. Within the bay to the left of the transept will be discovered the silver plate of the Panjab, the United Provinces, Rajputana and Central India, the Central Provinces, Bengal and Burma, in the sequence mentioned.

DIVISION 4. GOLD AND SILVER PLATE.

Madras Presidency Silver Plate.

Madras Presidency.—BANGALORE.—The characteristic feature of the silver plate of this area may at once be described by saying that it is (or rather was) *swámi*—that is to say, composed of mythological medallions and canopied niches, in imitation of the encrusted and agglutinated style of work characteristic of all South India art. (Plate No. 8, fig. 8) Some of the best examples may be stated to be: a large silver cup with handles, Rs. 1,062; and silver punch bowl, Rs. 541; a silver flower vase, Rs. 599; a silver bowl Rs. 156; a silver bowl, smaller size, Rs. 78; a silver cup, Rs. 80—all by C. Krishniah Chetty, Jeweller of Bangalore. The same silversmith also sends a number of pieces in Calcutta (Bhowanipore) style, such as a flower vase, Rs. 554; a silver punch bowl with spoon, Rs. 680.

Swami Ware.

Messrs. Barton & Sons of Bangalore have contributed four specimens in *swámi* style, the most interesting being a fruit stand, representing the *nandí* (or sacred bull) of Vellore temple, the dish being thus placed above the canopy.

Mysore Silver Ware.

From MYSORE have been received six silver miniature idols and a water bottle or *surâhi* made by Subbiah and Channa Nanjiah, of excellent workmanship, the idols being priced at from Rs. 70 to Rs. 80; also a silver *pán* leaf box, Rs. 98. A panel showing the Mysore diety *Chámundi* by Anekal Krishna Chari is specially worthy of mention.

MADRAS.—A second and equally fine series is contributed by Daday Khan, of Mount Road, Madras, of which the following may be mentioned:—a large silver punch bowl in *swámi* with wooden plinth, in rich bold floral design, Rs. 937; a similar but smaller bowl, Rs. 293; another bowl in Bengal (Bhowanipore) rural style, Rs. 306; a silver claret jug in *swámi*, Rs. 123; a silver tea service in *swámi*, Rs. 293; and a second tea service also in *swámi*, Rs. 261.

Trichinopoly Style.

From TRICHINOPOLY—(*Plate No. 8, figs. 3 and 4*)—have been procured a rose-water sprinkler and heart-shaped *pán-dán* box and a coffee-pot by A. Visvanada Asavi & Co. Of these the rose-water sprinkler is exceptionally fine, having the characteristically twisted and alternate bands of polished and frosted silver. The *pán-dán* is a reproduction of an old specimen seen by the writer

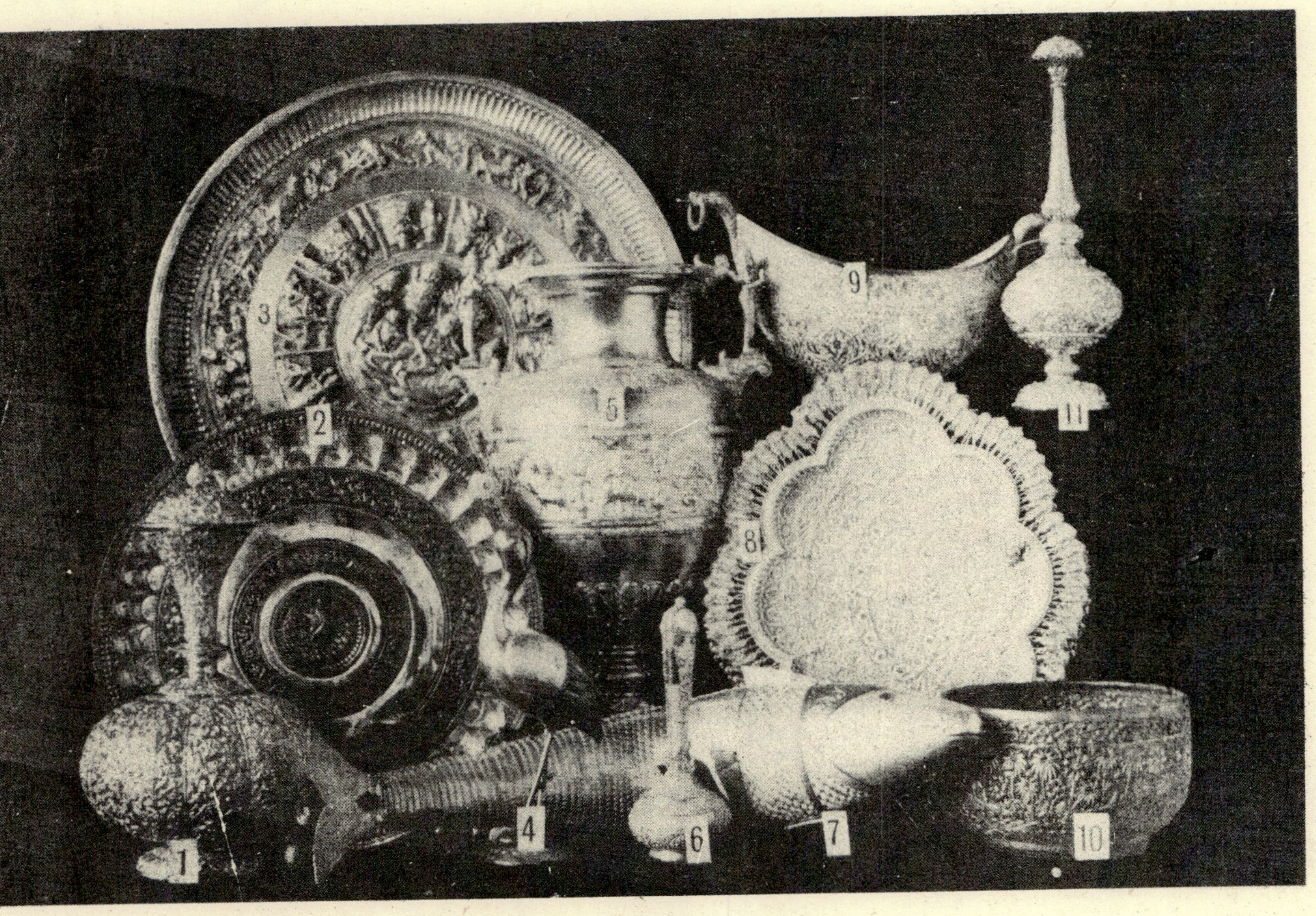

Plate No. 8 Selected Silver Plate of India

DIVISION 4. GOLD AND SILVER PLATE.

Filigri.

while in Trichinopoly, but the replica, while good, has lost the charm of the original, in consequence of not being so sharply and clearly repousséd. In Trichinopoly a form of filigrain jewellery is produced that is quite as good artistically and far superior in suitability and wearing power to that of Cuttack and Dacca. A few specially selected samples of this will be found in the collection, such as the necklace made by Muthusami Naidu, price Rs. 62.

From COCONADA has come a rose-water sprinkler, a reproduction of a good old specimen shown to the writer while on tour, but in which sufficient prominence has not been given to the chain of dancing *gopís* with crossed sticks above and below their heads. It was made by Kommojee Papayya of Coconada, price Rs. 65. This style of work may be said to be characteristic of Godaveri and of the East Coast of India generally.

Godaveri Style.

From AURANGABAD has been sent a rose-water sprinkler which is unlike any others shown in the Exhibition, and is priced at Rs. 35.

Travancore Silver.

From TRAVANCORE STATE has been contributed a small but curiously interesting collection of silver, constructed from the silver coins (*chukrams*) of that State. Of these may be indicated an oval tray, price Rs. 125; a circular tray with Krishna in the centre, price Rs. 81; and a picture frame, Rs. 62.

Bombay Presidency Silver Plate.

Bombay Presidency.—In Bombay Presidency there may be said to be two very well marked styles of silver plate with several subsidiary schools; these are the Poona and the Kach. In the former a very bold and deep form of repoussé prevails, the chief subjects being in half relief and the silver usually oxidised; in the latter school a graceful and intricate floral design in shallow repoussé (of probable Dutch origin) is practised. This consists of polished encircling lines or branches on a frosted background, the floral scroll, like that of the windows of Ahmedabad, having no beginning or ending, but in which a composite flower recurs at repeated intervals (Plate No. 8, fig. 6).

POONA.—(*Plate No. 8, fig. 10.*)—Amongst the best examples of this style may be mentioned a large silver vase (*burni*) with lid, the work showing the ten incarnations of Vishnu, made by M. K. Godbole of Poona, Rs. 625; a silver tray (*tabák*) with hunting figures, made by Hitapa Buchana, goldsmith of Poona, Rs. 528; a silver bowl (*kunda*) by the same maker, Rs. 446.

Of KACH, perhaps the finest examples are a silver flower vase or table centre, richly chased in floral design, Rs. 1,515; a silver card tray, Rs. 200; a silver bowl, Rs. 359—all made by Soni Oomersí Mawji & Sons of Bhuj, under the special supervision of His Highness the Maharao of Kach. Mr. Percy Brown's sketch (Plate No. 9) shows the Bhuj silversmith engaged at his work, while around him has been assorted a selection of his characteristic wares.

Ancient Style. From BIJAPUR have been secured two silver salvers in the old style characteristic of that country, Rs. 117 and Rs. 149. The design is deeply and richly chased, the scroll flowing forward and never reversed or inverted, as with the scrolls in most other forms of silver plate.

SHOLAPUR has contributed two circular trays in silver gilt; the design in some respects closely resembles that on the Bijapur trays and is accomplished in fairly bold repoussé, subsequently chased. Small engraved medallions are placed at intervals within the scrolls, thus giving a pleasing variety. These plates were prepared by Sheshappa Besappa, Sonar, of Sholapur, under the supervision of Ratsaheb Malappa Basappa Warad, and were thought so highly of by the Judging Committee that they were awarded a first prize (Plate No. 8, fig. 5).

In BARODA a curiously interesting style of both silver and copper repoussé may be said to be characteristic of this State. The article is first made in wood richly carved, then silver or copper plates are held over the surface and hammered until they assume the pattern given to the wood. Of this kind of work will be found a silver repoussé stool on *shisham* wood by Mistry Raghunath Tribhuvan & Sons, Visnagar, price Rs. 302. Baroda also turns out a remarkable form of moulded and chased work, in both silver and copper, in the form of immense massive anklets, price Rs. 93.

Peculiar Repoussé.

AHMEDABAD.—From this town has come an address casket made by Harilal Morarji of Gheekanta, price Rs. 400. This is a beautiful piece of work, with realistic medallions and jungle

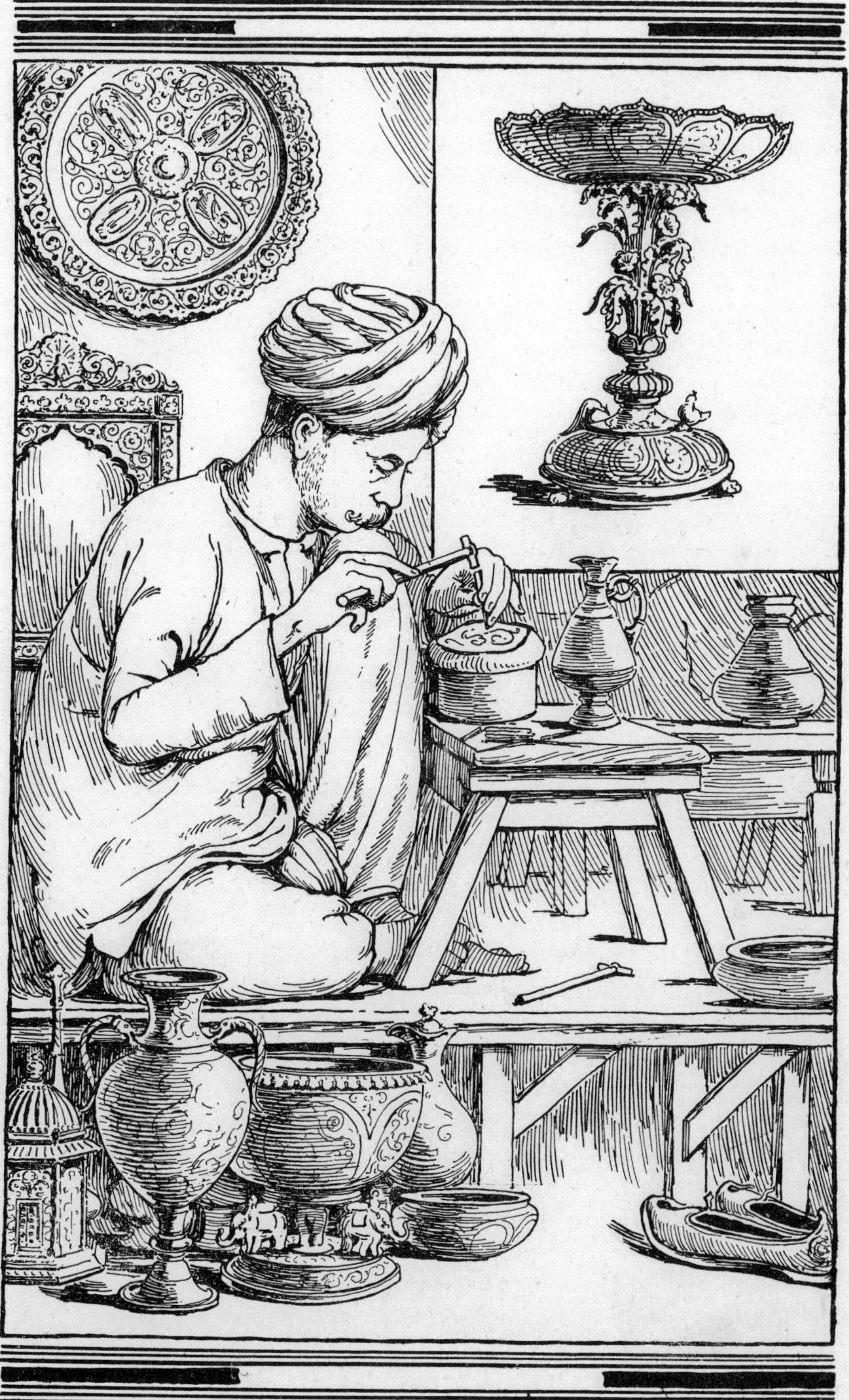

Plate No. 9 Bhuj (Cutch) Silversmith at work

scenes, the scroll work being of the Ahmedabad window type.

DIVISION 4. GOLD AND SILVER PLATE.

Kashmir Silver.

Panjab.—The most important locality in the production of silver plate in this Province is unquestionably KASHMIR. Some few years ago that State had practically only three of four styles of silver ornamentation, all being forms of exceptionally intricate and flat repoussé which closely resembled the patterns employed both in the copper and papier-maché wares of the State. These may be indicated as follows:— (*a*) *The Shawl Pattern*—perhaps the most beautiful and characteristic of all forms of silver ornamentation in India but which has got into disfavour with the silversmiths of Kashmir owing to the trouble and expense in producing it. They have, in fact, discovered that for the ordinary purchaser a few bold designs, which can be done in half the time required for the shawl pattern, will fetch the same or nearly the same money. The best examples of shawl pattern silver in the collection are a beggar's bowl, Rs. 210; a smaller specimen of the same, Rs. 124; a silver Yarkand jug, Rs. 121; a silver kettle on stand, Rs. 230; two beautiful oval shaped trays, Rs. 73 and Rs. 94; finger bowls and plates, Rs. 61; a tea-pot, Rs. 147. (*b*) *The Arabesque Style* (Plate No. 8, fig. 12.) usually parcel-gilt; the best examples of this are a large beggar's bowl, Rs. 344, by Habib Joo of Srinagar; a smaller size (*kashroul*), Rs. 128; a finger bowl and plate by Habib Joo, Rs. 61; a finger bowl by Subhana, Rs. 71, etc. (*c*) *The Rosette Style*—of which the most striking examples are a silver jug, Rs. 26; a rose sprinkler (*goláb pash*), Rs. 53. (*d*) *Wire work*—the *kángri* or fire basket is often reproduced in silver wire, a specimen is priced at Rs. 52. (*e*) *Modern Chunár* (or plane tree) *pattern*—of this class of goods there may be said to be two or three stages in development, the *first* in which the foliage is almost entirely suppressed, the ornamentation being confined to the flowers of the plane tree, interspersed with a richly convoluted line pattern. Of this, good specimens will be seen in the Exhibition, such as the silver tray and tea-pot to match, at Rs. 96 and Rs. 163; a silver coffee-pot, Rs. 93; a round bowl, Rs. 68. The *second* stage in which diminutive leaves are freely interspersed with the flowers, as, for example, a cup, Rs. 394; a claret jug, Rs. 114. The *third* stage,

Cheap Work.

DIVISION 4. GOLD AND SILVER PLATE.

those in which the leaves become almost natural size and the work correspondingly coarse, as in the claret jug priced Rs. 150; the Kashgar bowl with *chunár* leaves of natural size, Rs. 164.

Lastly, the *Lhassa Style*—in which the handles and spouts are in massive dragon form. This may be either plain, as in the silver tea-pot at Rs. 160, or chased or repousséd in any of the styles already mentioned, as, for example, the tea-set priced at Rs. 227, which may be described as being ornamented in a mixture of Kach and *chunár* patterns.

HOSHIARPUR.—From this town three very quaint rose-water sprinklers have been received, perhaps more curious than beautiful or artistic, price Rs. 60 to Rs. 70.

Lucknow. Palm Pattern.

United Provinces.—LUCKNOW.—(*Plate No. 8, figs. 1 and 2.*)—Some few years ago there was only one style of silver work in Lucknow, namely, a jungle scene, which consisted of closely compacted palms. This may be almost said to have entirely disappeared, and Lucknow now imitates the styles of all other parts of India, without having anything characteristic of its own. The best specimens are: a punch bowl by Durga Parshad and Manohar Dass, Rs. 871; a silver tea-set by the same, Rs. 313, and a silver-gilt *hukka* by Ajodhia Pershad Jaganath. A good example of the palm form of repoussé will be seen under the Division devoted to Copper and Brass (shown in Plate No. 8, fig. 2).

BENARES.—B. Moti Chand, Rais of Benares, exhibits a few specimens of *Ganga-Jamná* silver (part silver, part gilt), such as a rose-water sprinkler at Rs. 63. So also a pair of elephant and tiger-headed maces (*sota*) are sent by Bhagwan Dass Gopi Nath, Rs. 563, a pair of stick maces (*asa*) by the same contributor also priced at Rs. 563. Lastly, a salver by Kalyan Das Brothers, Benares, silver-gilt, Rs. 32.

Engraved Designs.

RAMPUR STATE has contributed a few specimens of silverware, such as the *abkorá* and *thálí sirpash*, Rs. 59. A gold tumbler and plate shown to the writer while in Rampur was most beautifully engraved with English birds, flowers, etc., in imitation of the patterns found on certain guns in the possession of the owner.

Central Provinces.—SAUGAR has furnished one or two silver trays, in a style strongly suggestive of Chalukyan influence and

DIVISION 4. GOLD AND SILVER PLATE.

closely allied to the silver and gold plates of Mysore and Bijapur. The best sample is priced at Rs. 103.

Central India and Rajputana.—ALWAR STATE has supplied a few specimens of silver and silver-gilt plate, the ornamentation being entirely engraved on a smooth polished surface. The designs appear to have been suggested from a study of European tea-sets, though Indian subjects have been substituted in most cases.

Filigri Work.

JHANSI produces a fair amount of filigrain work, much after the style turned out at Cuttack and Dacca; of these the *pán* box, Rs. 320, is the best example. The design is usually spirally assorted.

GWALIOR exhibits a number of specimens of silver-gilt wares, such as the *attar-dán*, consisting of six pieces, from UJJAIN, Rs. 325; a *goláb-pash* or rose-water sprinkler from INDORE, Rs. 130; and a large plate, Rs. 272; a *goláb-pash* in stork pattern from Gwalior, price Rs. 82, and a similar but smaller sample, delicately engraved, Rs. 40 (Plate No. 8, fig. 4).

DHAR exhibits two beautiful stork-pattern *goláb-pashes* (rose-water sprinklers), Rs. 112.

DHOLPUR supplies a beautifully formed little *chatri*, Rs. 625.

Bengal Presidency.—In the Lower Provinces there may be said to be four great centres for silver-ware, *viz.*, Calcutta, Cuttack, Dacca and Monghyr. CALCUTTA (Bhowanipore) produces a form of ornamentation in which rural (as distinct from hunting and jungle) scenery is depicted on a frosted surface. It is a style now imitated in nearly every silver-manufacturing centre of India, the characteristic Bengal hut being nearly everywhere shown, though probably quite unfamiliar to the majority of repoussé workers who are engaged in this traffic. Samples have been contributed to the Exhibition from Lucknow, Bangalore, Madras and Bombay.

Frosted Jungle Style.

CUTTACK.—(*Plate No. 8, fig. 7.*)—has for many years been famous for its silver filigrain work, of which a large assortment may be seen in the Exhibition.

Filigri Work.

The production of filigri is perhaps the most interesting branch of the silver and goldsmiths' craft. There is, however, something about this art that suggests a foreign origin. Sir George Birdwood

DIVISION 4. GOLD AND SILVER PLATE.

observes: "The silver filigrain work, in which the people of Cuttack in Orissa have attained such surprising skill and delicacy, is identical in character with that of Arabia, Malta, Genoa, Norway, Sweden and Denmark, and with the filigrain work of ancient Greece, Byzantium and Etruria, and was probably carried into the West by the Phœnicians and Arabs, and into Scandinavia by the Normans, and in the course also of the mediæval trade between Turkistan and Russia." In India there are certain well marked centres of the craft, of which apparently Cuttack may have been one of the earliest, as it is to this day the most important. It was carried south along the east coast and attained a footing at various places, more especially TRICHINOPOLY and north and east to DACCA and RANGOON. In Dacca a superior form, known as *mandila*, was produced during the seventeenth century, but for some few years this has been discontinued. The art seems also to have moved north into Central India and Rajputana, and attained considerable importance in JHANSI, where a peculiarly flat form, spirally assorted, is met with. At KOTA STATE a certain amount of filigri work is also produced very similar to that of Jhansi.

Centres of Production.

Employment of Children.

Perhaps no art is more interesting to the student than filigri. A large portion of the work is accomplished by children, often not more than eight or ten years of age,—the sons or pupils of the silversmith. Their nimble fingers and quick eye-sight are indispensable to the success of the work. The master craftsmen prepare the materials and form the frames of the designs. Only the purest silver can be employed, but this is alloyed with a small amount of lead before being used. It is drawn into flat wire, and subsequently twisted on itself to give it the appearance of minute ropes or strings. The frame of a leaf or petal having been made in silver, this is given to one of the boys who cuts the wire into certain required lengths. Each of these he seizes between the forefinger and the thumb and turns one end round in the form of a half roll. He then impinges the wire within the frame and adds one after another, until the interior is packed as full as it will hold of rolled up wire. It is then passed on to the master silversmith, who sprinkles it with a soldering salt, places it on a piece of mica, and then holds it in the furnace until the packing of wire becomes

Manipulation.

soldered together and to the frame. The skill lies in not causing the solder to fuse over more than the desired points of attachment. Leaf by leaf and petal by petal being thus prepared, they are then wielded together in the desired form. The process of cleaning and whitening the silver is one of great interest but more or less a secret of the craft.

DIVISION 4. GOLD AND SILVER PLATE.

Samples on View.

The samples of filigri most worthy of mention are a pair of oval plates (No. 143) made by Chintamoni Jethi of Cuttack, Rs. 286 each; a *hukka* made by Nanda Jethi of Cuttack (No. 128), Rs. 805; an *attar-dán*, floral stand, (No. 126) also by Nanda Jethi, Rs. 563.

DACCA.—Filigri work, exactly similar to that of Cuttack, is produced in Dacca; one sample only need be mentioned, *viz.*, an elephant-formed *attar-dán* (No. 92), Rs. 500, made by Krishna Charan Kamnakar.

Lastly MONGHYR.—(*Plate No. 8, fig. 9.*)—At Kharakpur in Monghyr (as also in one or two other localities in Bengal), silver fish *attar-dáns* are manufactured with great skill; the largest one on view is priced Rs. 218, and measures 18 inches in length.

Silver Fish.

Burma.—(*Plate No. 9-A.*)—From RANGOON, MOULMEIN, TOUNGOO, PROME and THAYETMYO have been procured an extensive series of silver plate in the form of bowls, jars, plates, etc. The best samples were, however, forwarded by the Burma Government on loan. Had the specimens of the loan set been for sale, they could have been disposed of several times over. These were made by Maung Yin Maung and others. Of the sale collection there may be said to be two widely different styles, one characteristic more or less of Rangoon, the other of Moulmein. In the former the surface is frosted, in the latter polished or burnished. In a Rangoon bowl the main surface of the silver is usually left a dull white, with small portions of the design here and there burnished. In both styles of work the silver is strongly repousséd and mainly in human forms or with *belus* in hunting or sporting scenes.

Burmese Bowls.

Rangoon and Moulmein Styles.

Manipulation.

The principal articles made by the Burman silversmiths are the well known bowls. These are beaten up from discs of silver rather larger and very much thicker than a rupee; one of these

DIVISION 4. GOLD AND SILVER PLATE. discs is taken and beaten into a small shallow saucer, another is put on the bottom and hammered until it unites with the former and the saucer begins in consequence to gradually assume the shape of a cup. This process is continued until the desired size and shape is obtained. The thickness of the metal in a good bowl, before being decorated, is over one-eighth of an inch. The bowl is then filled with lac and the pattern traced, then respoussêd and finally chased. The great relief desired often leads to perforations, even in the best workmanship, but these are filled up afterwards by patches of silver soldered on the inside and hammered into the metal, the face of the bowl for that purpose being imbedded in lac.

Chief Specimens on view. A representative collection has been sent from MOULMEIN. It comprises, amongst others, several good specimens of "double work" as in the bowl to the right in Plate No. 9-A. In this style the design is embossed as usual but the ground perforated. The article is, in consequence, lined, a space being left between the outer perforated portion and the lining. A rich effect is thus obtained through the shadows of the outer perforated surface being thrown on the inner lining. The best examples of this work are a bowl and stand (No. 5), price Rs. 563, and a betel box with stand (No. 14), price Rs. 563, both examples being the work of Maung Kyi Maung of Moulmein

From RANGOON an extensive series of bowls, trays, powder boxes, etc., has been secured. Of these special mention may be made of No. 177, Rs. 398, and No. 200, Rs. 436, made by Maung Po Kin, and a splendid sample (No. 5) exhibited by F. Beato & Co., Ld., price Rs. 937.

From PROME was procured a remarkably good old bowl (No. 255) for Rs. 375, and from Thayetmyo another old specimen of high merit, price Rs. 350.

AWARDS FOR SILVER AND GOLD PLATE.

AWARDS. First Prize with gold medal to Maung Yin Maung of Rangoon for silver table centre, Rs. 1,000.

First Prize with silver medal for silver parcel-gilt tray by Sheshappa Bas Appa of Sholapur (No. 3944), Rs. 263.

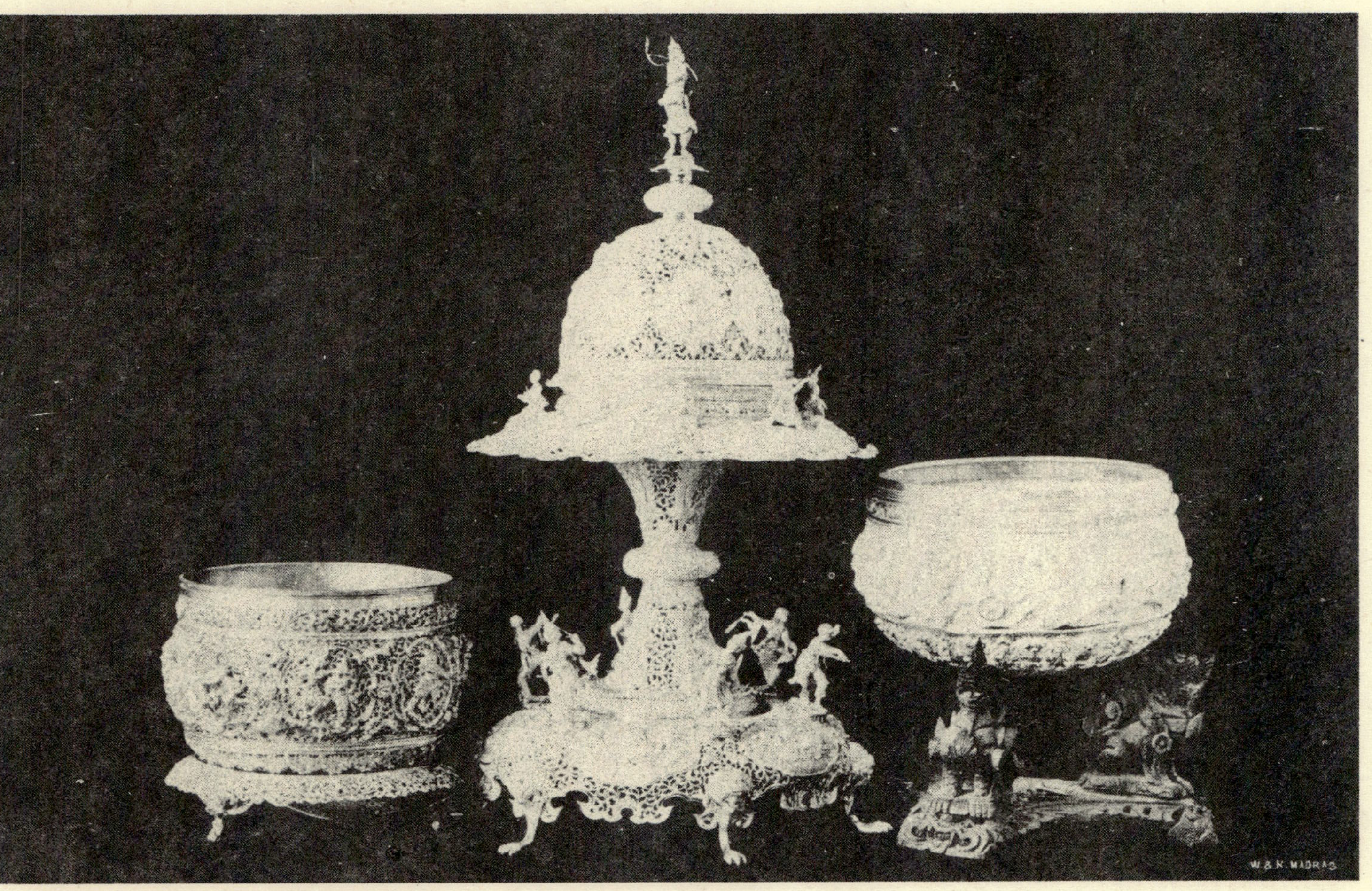

Plate No. 9-A Silver Plate of Burmah

Metal Wares.

DIVISION 4. GOLD AND SILVER PLATE.

First Prize with silver medal for filigri *hukka* (No. 128), *attar-dán* (No. 126) and silver filigri box (No. 130), by Nanda Jethi of Cuttack.

First Prize with silver medal for bowl (No. 177), Rs. 399, by Maung Po Kin of Rangoon.

Second Prize with silver medal for Kach silver plate (Nos. 1200, 1201, 1215, 1227, 1228, 1229, 1233) to Soni Oomersí Mawji of Bhuj.

Second Prize with silver medal for bowl and stand (No. 14), Rs. 563; silver *dah* (No. 20), Rs. 100; pongye bowl (No. 11), Rs. 700; betel box (No. 14), Rs. 563—by Maung Kyi Maung of Moulmein.

Third Prize with bronze medal for tray made by Vishnu Ganesh Purandhare of Poona (No. 775), Rs. 513.

Third Prize with bronze medal for casket (No. 3208), Rs. 906, also silver bowl (No. 3206), Rs. 343, made by Framji Pestonji Bhumgara, made in Madras.

Third Prize with bronze medal for *sota* or mace (No. 1577), Rs. 563, with elephant head, made by Bhagwan Das Gopi Nath of Benares.

Third Prize with bronze medal for gold and silver caskets (Nos. 3957 and 3958), Rs. 500, and a large assortment of silver plate, made by C. Krishna Chetty of Bangalore.

Third Prize with bronze medal for three pairs of candlesticks (Nos. 256, 652, 3695) for Rs. 360 to Rs. 656 the pair, made at the Madras School of Arts.

Third Prize with bronze medal for collection of silver plate by Daday Khan of Madras.

Third Prize with bronze medal for collection of silver-gilt ware (Nos. 2351, 2686, etc.) by Habib Joo, silversmith, Srinagar, Kashmir.

Third Prize with bronze medal for collection of silver plate (Nos. 2665, 2688, etc.) to Subhana, silversmith, Srinagar, Kashmir.

Third Prize with bronze medal for candlestick (No. 1253), Rs. 135, made by Soni Mawji Raghavji of Bhuj, Kach.

Commended—water vessel made by Subbhiah and Channi Nanyiah of Bangalore.

DIVISION 4. GOLD AND SILVER PLATE.

Commended for silver bowl in fish pattern (No. 3230), Rs. 32, by Durga Pershad and Manohar Das of Lucknow.

Commended silver tea-set of three pieces (No. 3284), Rs. 313; also tray (No. 3283), Rs. 250, made by Gauri Shankar Har Narain of Lucknow.

Commended for silver-gilt *hukka* (No. 3238), Rs. 250, made by Ajodhia Pershad Jaganath of Lucknow.

Commended for *chukram* tray (No. 900), Rs. 105, made at Quilon in Travancore.

Commended for *chámandi* panel (No. 3915), Rs. 125, made by Anekal Krishna Chari of Bangalore.

Commended—silver anklet (maize pattern), made at Dabhoi in Baroda (No. 1501), Rs. 85.

Commended for *attar-dán* (rose-water sprinkler) (No. 4035), Rs. 72, made by Parbh Dial and Milcawa Mull of Hoshiarpur.

Commended for silver tea-pot with engraved hunting scenes on polished silver (No. 3555), Rs. 149, made by Panna Lal of Alwar.

Commended for silver fish (18 inches long) (No. 234), Rs. 218, by Babu Shivanandan Prasad Singh of Monghyr.

Commended for *attar-dán* in form of silver elephant (No. 92), Rs. 500, made by Krishna Charan Kamnakar of Dacca in Bengal.

Division 5.—Damascened and Encrusted Wares.—
(*Plate No. 10.*)

Wire Damascening.

These names indicate degrees of the same art rather than distinct arts. They both denote the surface ornamentation of one metal through the application of one or more metals. In damascening (*koftgari*) proper, it is usual for iron or steel to be ornamented with gold or silver wire. In the various forms of encrusted work the ground metal is rarely steel and the applied metals are rarely in the form of wire. In true damascening the design is chased on the steel surface with a hard and sharp style, and the wire, held by one hand within the grooves, is hammered by the other, until it is made to literally unite with the steel. Of encrusted wares there may be said to be two chief forms, the one with the applied metal raised above the surface, the other with it below the surface.

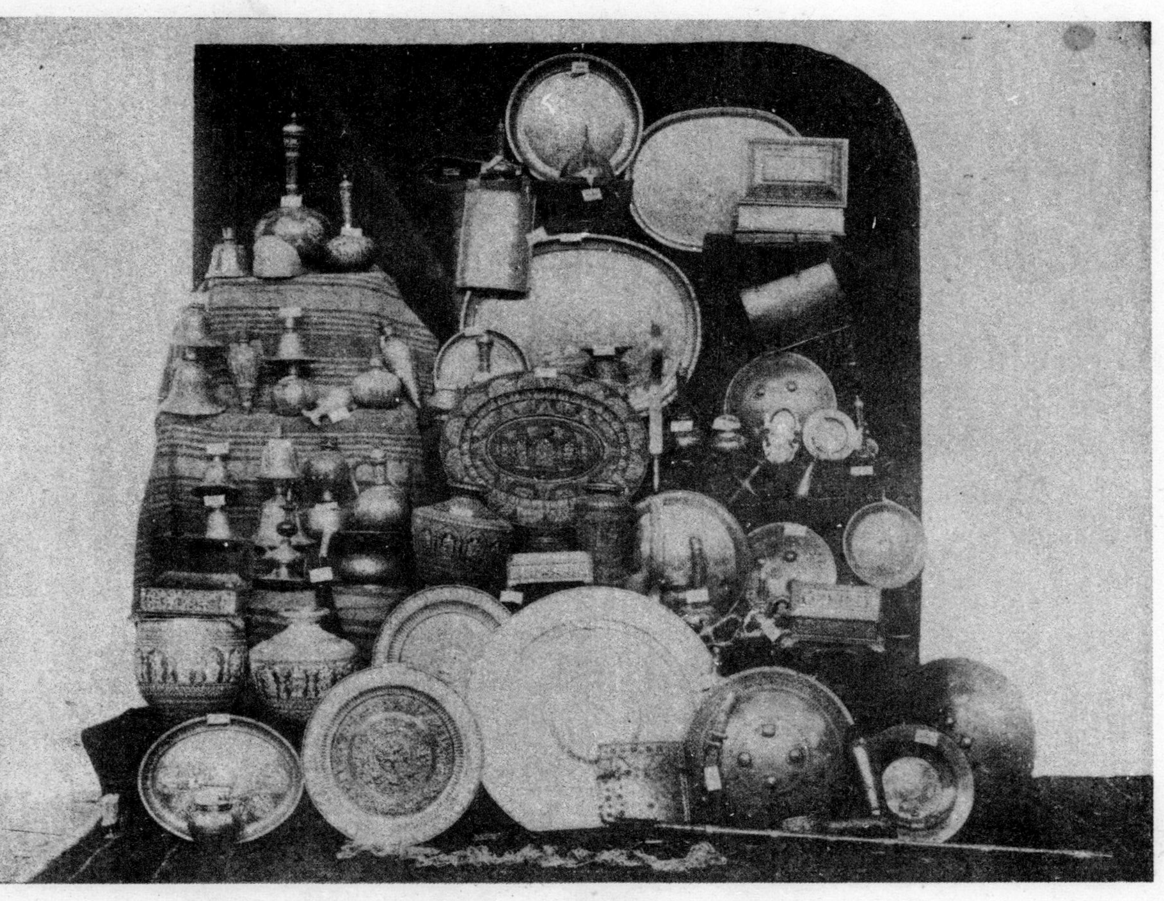

Plate No. 10 Damascened and Encrusted Wares

DIVISION 5. DAMASCENED AND ENCRUSTED WARES.

Forms of Encrusted Ware.

(A) Tanjore ware is representative of the first style of encrusted work. A piece of silver or brass is taken and repousséd on a bed of lac. When finished this is held over the surface of the metal upon which it is to be attached, its outline is scratched, then chased until the groove produced is able to receive the edge of the applied piece. This is finally secured by having the rim of the ground metal hammered over it.

(B) The flat form (represented by *bidrí* ware) differs in that the pattern of the desired appliqué ornamentation is completely excavated and the metal placed within and secured by hammering. But there are two modifications of this, one in which the exact form and ornamentation of the applied metal is practically finished before being attached, and the other, and very often the most beautiful, in which the design is only crudely cut out on the ground metal, the applied metal being fixed and at the same time hammered and chased into form. In this condition, therefore, the applied metal is mainly above the surface, much as in Tanjore ware.

With these introductory remarks it may now be desirable to deal with each manifestation of the arts of Damascening and Encrusting Metals:—

1st, Koftgari.—ARMS.—The art of damascening appears to have taken its origin with the ornamentation of swords and other weapons. On the decline of the Sikh power, the *koftgari* workers of Sialkot and Gujerat diverted their skill to the ornamentation of articles for domestic use. To this day, however, they still prepare damascened sword and dagger handles, scabbards, shields, helmets, etc. The best examples of this work to be seen in the Exhibition are sword handles (Nos. 4143 and 4145), by Shabab Din, son of Imam Din, prices Rs. 50 and Rs. 100. In Jaipur, Alwar, Datia, Jodhpur and in Serhoi, the art of damascening sword handles attained high proficiency. A shield, has been arranged to display the damascening of Jaipur, which is mostly silver or gold on steel in elaborate and intricate patterns. In Datia and Jodhpur the work is very similar, as, for example, sword handle (No. 10), price Rs. 31. In Serhoi (Plate No. 11-A, figs. 10 and 11), a

DIVISION 5. DAMASCENED AND ENCRUSTED WARES.

background of frosted silver is given round the gold, producing thereby a characteristic style which, although not confined to Serhoi, is more or less peculiar to that State. The same system is occasionally practised in Sialkot, as for example the gauntlets (No. 4161), Rs. 50. A shield has been designed to exhibit a full display of SERHOI arms as also a further shield to display a special series of JAIPUR arms, mostly those that manifest engraved and damascened steel. One of the chief centres of damascened arms in India is doubtless HYDERABAD in the Deccan (Plate No. 11-A, fig. 15). A large shield has been arranged to show a selection of the silver and a second the gold damascening of that State.

The above brief reference may suffice to denote the older manifestations of the art of damascening. Mr. Brown's sketch (Plate No. 11) of the damascene worker in Datia, shows the artist with his appliances engaged damascening a sword hilt. His reels of gold and silver thread are in front of him, and an enlarged hilt on the wall shows the pattern turned out.

PANJAB.—Of modern work it may be said that Gujerat and Sialkot in the Panjab, and more recently Jaipur, Alwar, Serhoi and Lahore, turn out large quantities. The materials employed are steel plates engraved in minute arabesque designs, into which silver and gold wire are hammered. But there are various forms or qualities of this work, the most valuable being that known as

Forms of Koftgari.

(A) Teh Nashán.

(A) *Teh Nashán* or deep *Koftgari* (Plate No. 11-A, figs. 1, 2 and 3).—In this the steel is deeply engraved and thick gold or silver wire hammered into the grooves. It is then filed down, cleaned and blued, until it forms a perfectly smooth and polished surface. At times when both gold and silver are used (*Ganga-Jamná*), certain parts of the gold are mixed with copper in order to obtain a pinkish tint. The surface is blued through the action of fire only. A good example of this style is the small boat-shaped tray from Jaipur (No. 2141), Rs. 100, and the circular tray from Sialkot, Rs. 50.

(B) Ordinary.

(B) Ordinary or shallow *Koftgari* (Plate No 11-A, figs. 6 and 7).—In this case the design is engraved in shallow grooves or scratchings, and a very fine wire is hammered into these. The amount of silver and gold employed is accordingly very small, and in consequence the surface cannot be polished and smoothened

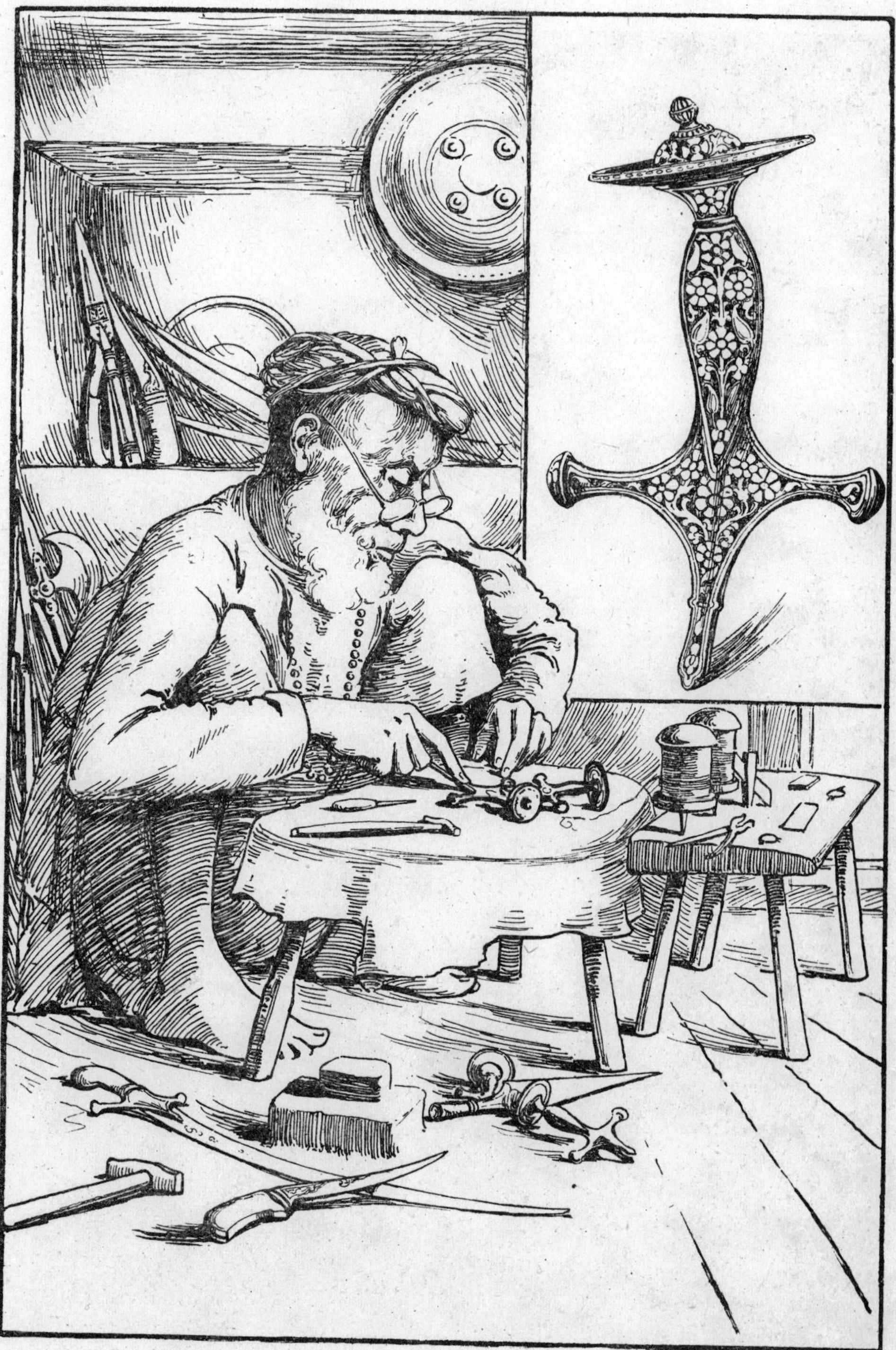

Plate No. 11 Damascene Worker, Datia. Central India

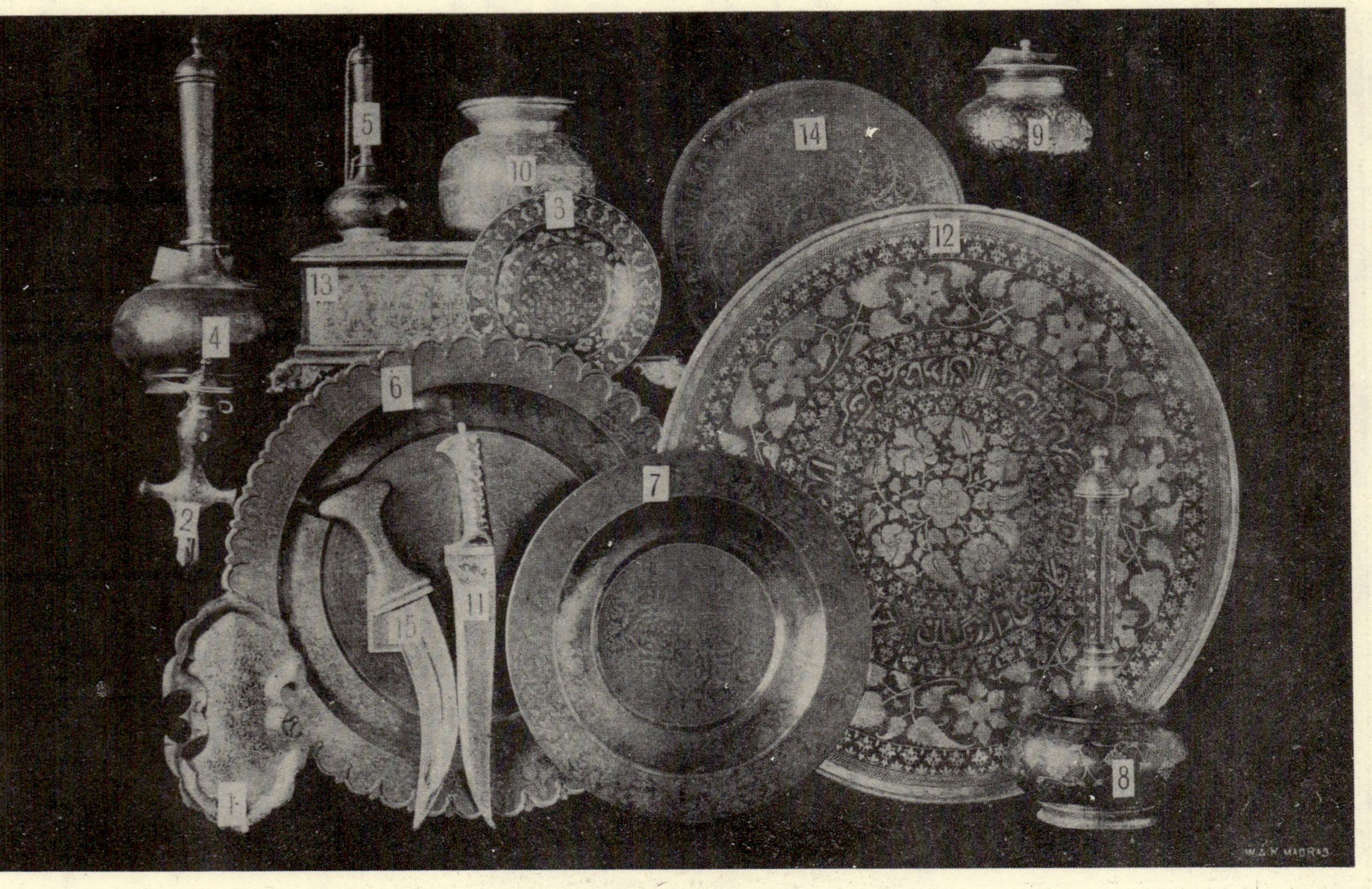

Plate No. 11-A Wire Damascening or Koftgari

as in the *teh nashán* without removing the gold and silver wire. Accordingly, with the cheaper forms of *koftgari*, the wire can be readily felt on the surface. (C) Lastly, the cheapest form of all is a sort of imitation *koftgari*. This is called *Dewálí* (Plate No. 11-A, fig. 12). The surface is smoothened with a file and afterwards with pumice stone. The pattern is then scratched with the style and lime juice sprinkled over it to thoroughly cleanse the surface. It is next heated and gold leaf (lifted with a pair of pincers) is applied and lightly hammered, then rubbed with the *mori* stone, which causes the gold to adhere to the portions of the surface scratched for its reception. The best example of *dewálí* work in the Exhibition is the plate (No. 3906), Rs. 75, made by Sultan Mahamad of Sialkot.

DIVISION 5. DAMASCENED AND ENCRUSTED WARES.

(C) Dewali.

RAJPUTANA.—The degree of hammering applied to *koftgari* causes the gold or silver to spread out in all three forms of work. In Rajputana it would appear that a fourth system prevails, namely, *dewálí* work subsequently scratched to remove portions of the gold and produce a closer similarity to wire inlaying.

Scratched Koftgari.

SIALKOT and GUJERAT.—(*Plate No. 11-A, figs. 4—9 and 12.*) —The most desirable examples are:—from GUJERAT a tray by Fazal Ahmad, Rs. 131; a *tháli* (tray) by Abdul Aziz, Rs. 150; another by Maula Bux, Rs. 93; a *suráhi* by Mahomed Azum, Rs. 25; a *golábdani* by the same maker, Rs. 81; and a *surâhi* by Abdul Aziz, Rs. 37. From SIALKOT a *surâhi*, silver and gold on iron, by Koftgan Nazar Mahamad, son of Kutubdin, Rs. 50; a *surâhi*, silver and gold on iron, by Nurdin, Rs. 15; a *lota*, silver and gold on steel, by Budha, Rs. 62; a shield, gold and silver on steel, by Golab Din, Rs. 125; a *tháli*, gold on steel, by Budha, Rs. 62; a *cháraina* (set of armour) by Musa, son of Khush Mahamad, Rs. 150; a *thali*, silver and gold on steel, by Haji Mahamad Yar, son of Sultan Mahamad, Rs. 125.

Samples on View.

From LAHORE a shield in gold damascening by Aim Din, Rs. 156; a *cháraina* (set of armour) by the same maker, Rs. 1,871. From JAIPUR, a tray, gold on steel, by the School of Art, Rs. 100; a *dhál* (shield) by Khuda Buksh, Rs. 125; a *koft surâhi* (goblet) also by Khuda Buksh, Rs. 25; a *surâhi*, gold on steel, by the School of Art, Jaipur, Rs. 56. It may be added, of the two last

DIVISION 5. DAMASCENED AND ENCRUSTED WARES.

named specimens, that they are perhaps the most highly finished and best examples of *koftgari* in the Exhibition.

Travancore.

TRAVANCORE may be said to have a style of *koftgari* of its own, which consists of roughened steel with gold wire beaten into it in the form of floral designs of a strongly Dravidian type; this may be seen in the tray, gold on iron, by the School of Art, Trevandrum, Rs. 62 (Plate No. 11-A, fig. 14), and the casket (fig. 13).

2nd, Bidri Ware.—(*Plate No. 11-B*, the series with labels Hyderabad Deccan.)—In the Nizam's territory an industry exists which bears the name of the town in which it originated, *viz.*, Bidar.

Early Account of Bidri ware.

One of the earliest accounts of this craft may be said to be Dr. Benjamin Heyne's paper published in the *Asiatic Journal* for March 1817. He opens that paper by the statement that "the Hindus have since time immemorial not only excelled their neighbours in the management of metals for useful and curious purposes but are even acquainted with alloys unknown to our practical chemists." "Biddery (*vidri*) ware is used particularly for *hukka* bottoms, and dishes to hand betel about to visitors, where more precious metals are not attainable. It is of a black colour, which never fades and which, if tarnished, may be easily restored. To relieve the sable hue it is always more or less inlaid with silver. It is called Biddery ware from the place where it was originally, and I believe is still exclusively, made; for though the people of Bengal have utensils of this kind, I have nowhere seen any new ones for sale, which would be the case were they manufactured there." Dr. Heyne then gives a full description of each stage and process in the production of *bidri* ware. The artificers complained of the decline of the craft, which they said gave formerly employment to hundreds in place of the tens now engaged. He examined the alloy used, and found it to consist of 24 parts of tin to 1 of copper.

Composition of the Alloy.

In reply to Dr. Heyne's statement that *bidri* ware was exclusively made in Bidar, Mr. Wilkins wrote, shortly thereafter, that it was also made in Benares, but that the alloy contained zinc in place of tin along with copper. The composition of the alloy seems to vary somewhat: the difference indicated by the two above passages still seems to prevail. In Lucknow the chief

DIVISION 5. DAMASCENED AND ENCRUSTED WARES.

Manipulation.

metal is zinc, the others, lead, tin and copper, being added each in the proportion of $\frac{1}{16}$th of the zinc. In Hyderabad, zinc seems to be greatly reduced and lead much increased. In Murshidabad lead is entirely omitted. The desired vessel is first moulded then reduced to the exact shape on the turning lathe. It is next engraved or chased in varying depths according to the quality or kind of *bidri* that is desired to be produced. It is thereafter smoothed, polished and coloured to a dark green or black colour by means of a paste made by sal ammoniac and saltpetre, moistened in rape seed oil and thickened with charcoal. In Murshidabad and Lucknow blue vitriol is added. The vessel is slightly heated by placing it in the sun, then rubbed with the colouring preparation and allowed to cool for several hours. It is thereafter washed and rubbed with a little oil, when the colour is found to be permanent. *Bidrí* does not rust, and only breaks by a severe blow, but it is very heavy and clumsy.

Centres of Production.

The chief centres of production are HYDERABAD (Bidar mainly), LUCKNOW, MURSHIDABAD, PURNEA and to a small extent KASHMIR.

Chief Forms of Bidrí.

There are two main forms of *bidrí*, much as in *koftgari*, according to the depth of embedding and the quality of the metal affixed to the surface. These are known as *Teh Nashán*, or deeply cut work and *Zar Nashán*, (or *Zar buland*), raised work. In the former the pattern is deeply excavated and the silver or gold cut to the exact size and shape of the chased pattern. After being embedded, the surface is smoothed and polished, the silver or gold ornamentations being then within or below the surface.

Zar Nashán or *Zar buland* work greatly resembles Tanjore encrusted ware. The outline of the pattern is engraved, the silver leaf held over and rubbed with the finger until a tracing of the design is imparted. The leaf is then cut into the desired pieces, each a little larger than the space it is intended to cover. The margin or rim of each is bent over, and the cavity thus formed filled with a piece of soft lead. This is next inverted over the space and the margin of the structure pressed into the engraved outline. Lastly, it is hammered or punched all round so as to

DIVISION 5. DAMASCENED AND ENCRUSTED WARES.

cause the surface metal to embrace and fix the applied piece. The process is then finished by the silver leaf being punched or chased on the surface in completion of the desired pattern.

Brass Zar Nashán ware.

A form of *zar nashán* is met with in Sialkot in which the ground metal is brass and the finished article overlaid with both silver and gold. But the process pursued is different from that followed in any of the centres of *bidrí* ware production proper. The pattern is only partially engraved. The silver or gold is fixed within the grooves, then worked up on the surface by chasing and punching. This gives a far richer effect than is produced by either of the forms of simple encrustation of previously prepared ornamentations.

Patterns met with in Bidrí ware.

DESIGNS.—HYDERABAD.—One of the oldest and at the same time most beautiful patterns employed in true *bidrí* portrays the poppy plant, a design which recurs all over India. It is one of the most frequent patterns employed by the *kinkhab* weavers, the leaves being in silver and the flowers in gold. Good examples of this style will be found in the extensive series of *bidrí*, contributed by Haji Hasan, an Arab trader in Hyderabad (Plate No. 11-B), in the coffee-pot and two bell-shaped *hukka*-bowls. Sir George Birdwood's *Industrial Arts of India* (Plate 32) may be mentioned as a most admirable example of this style. It would, however, necessitate the production of a special treatise to give anything like a satisfactory conception of the many beautiful designs met with in Hyderabad *bidrí*. Perhaps after the poppy pattern, the most prevalent is that in which wire alone is used in the elaboration of a minute ornamentation in silver crosses or stars, assorted in a diagonal fashion. In Purnea and Murshidabad, wire alone is never used (at the present day), but the silver or gold, in fairly large patches, is cut in the form of flowers or animals and deeply imbedded and polished along with the rich surface polishing characteristic of the *bidrí* of Bengal. Sir George Birdwood's Plates Nos. 34 and 35 do not represent the *bidri* of Purnea and Murshidabad of the present day.

Other examples worthy of special study are a beautiful *hukka* in gold *bidrí*, in diaper pattern, made by Trailokya Nath Dass of Murshidabad seen in Plate No. 11-B.

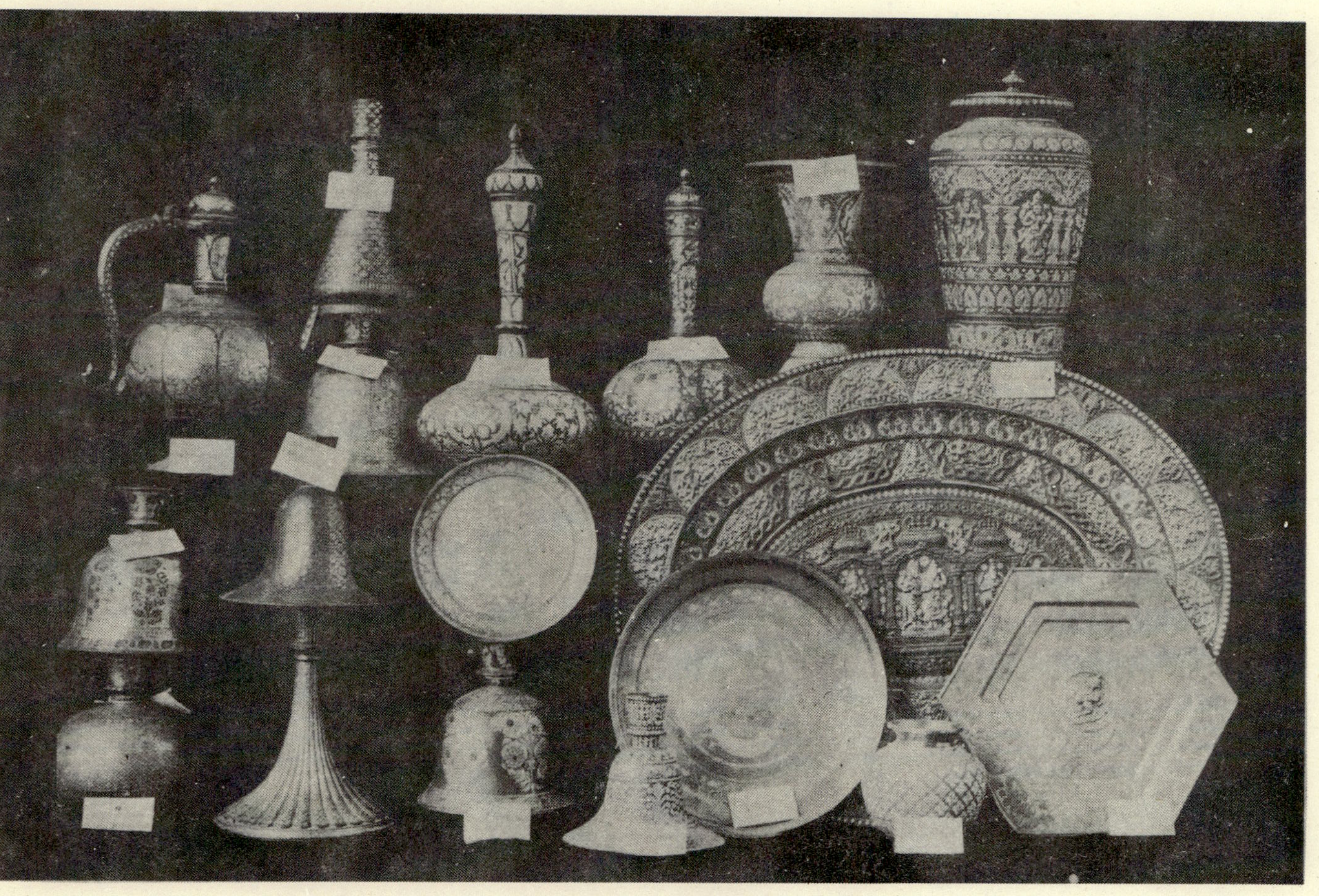

Plate No. 11-B Encrusted Ware

DIVISION 5. DAMASCENED AND ENCRUSTED WARES.

From Kashmir have been received a few examples of erect *hukka* bowls in gold and a flower vase in silver *bidrí* procured from Subhana, silversmith of Srinagar. The designs in these are worked in wire imbedded below the surface, but remarkably little wire is employed, much less than in any other form of *bidrí* ware. The design may be said to be invariably a diaper.

LUCKNOW.—The art of manufacturing *bidrí* in this town, as already indicated, seems to have been carried from Bidar during the time of the Kings of Oudh. In Lucknow, however, it early assumed a very different type—the description described above as *Zar buland.* Large patches of silver, in the form of fish, flowers and leaves, are encrusted all over the surface. The best examples of this work are a *hukka* (No. 1036) and *surâhi* (Plate No 11-B) made by Chandu Beg of Lucknow. For a time this type of work prevailed in Oudh but gradually it changed and assumed a second condition in which realistic designs were produced in a minute and complex manner much after the fashion evolved at Purnea and Murshidabad Of this modern work a large assortment will be found, the most note-worthy being the large *hukka* by Kadar Beg and Chandu Beg of Lucknow, and the *surâhi* with vine-leaf pattern (Plate No. 11-B) by Ramana of Hyderabad.

Tanjore Ware.

3rd, Tanjore Encrusted ware.—(*Plate No. 9-B.*)—The encrusted ware of South India is referable to two sections:—*first,* that of Tanjore, in which the applied portions stand in bold relief; *second,* that of Tirupati in which the applied metal is smooth and level with the surface. The best examples of these two forms may be said to be the following:—TANJORE SERIES—a large circular brass tray by M. Karupanna Pathar & Co., of Tanjore, elaborately covered with silver encrustrations in *swámi* form, Rs. 250; a circular copper plate with silver *swámi* work by Amnuga Pathar of Tanjore, Rs. 100; large copper bowls in the original *swámi* designs of Tanjore with pillars dividing the mythological subjects, much as in Plate No 14 in Sir George Birdwood's *Industrial Arts of India*; a round copper tray of Tanjore work, made in the Madras School of Arts, Rs. 50; brass address box, oblong size, with *swámi* carved work by Guvmsawmy Pathar of Tanjore Rs. 187; a circular brass plate, medium size, with silver *swámi*

DIVISION 5. DAMASCENED AND ENCRUSTED WARES.

Tirupati Ware.

work, Rs. 56; octagonal brass plate with silver *swámi* work by Ramalunga Pathar of Tanjore, Rs. 50; a small *chumbu* (*lotá*) of copper with silver *swámi* work much as in Sir George Birdwood's Plate 15), made by the School of Arts, Madras, Rs. 25. TIRUPATI SERIES—a large oval brass tray of copper and silver encrustations, which has attained the first award for encrusted ware,—also a similar tray with silver on brass (No 4530), price Rs. 150.

It would seem probable that the original of these crafts (Tanjore and Tirupati) consisted of brass and copper only and that the use of silver proceeded from a European suggestion. But by far the most serious departure has been the substitution of large patches of fine silver leaf, blocked out on a die, in place of the multitude of small pieces (hand chased) that were formerly employed, in the ornamentation of the copper or brass surface.

Trichinopoly Ware.

TRICHINOPOLY SERIES.—In Trichinopoly a still more curious process of encrustation prevails, in which brass vessels are encrusted on the surface with zinc The best examples of this are a plate, Rs. 18, a *suráhi*, Rs. 15, made by Melapulujur Asari.

Turquoise Work.

4th, Kashmir Turquoise work.—Although in no way connected with *bidrí* ware it may be convenient to mention. in this place that into Kashmir has been recently introduced a sort of mosaic in brass, in which the recesses of a pattern are compacted with fragments of false turquoise embedded in cement The best examples of this work are a picture frame, Rs. 14, and an octagonal tray, Rs. 15.

AWARDS FOR DAMASCENED AND ENCRUSTED WARES.

(*a*) *Damascened or Koftgari work.*

AWARDS.

First Prize with silver medal for boat-shaped small tray (No. 1490), Rs. 100, made in *teh nashán* style at the School of Art, Jaipur.

First Prize with silver medal for plate (No. 3977), to Golam Muhammad of Sialkot—ordinary *koftgari* work of a very high order.

First Prize with silver medal for shield (No. 621) from Hyderabad Deccan, done in rich gold *koftgari* on finest steel, made by Piraji of Hyderabad.

DIVISION 5. DAMASCENED AND ENCRUSTED WARES.

First Prize with silver medal for collection of swords, daggers, etc. (Nos. 840—926), with hilts in gold and silver damascening, exhibited by Haji Hasan, Arab trader in Hyderabad.

First Prize with silver medal for tray in ordinary *koftgari* work (No. 3983), Rs. 100, and tea tray (No. 3985), Rs. 125, made by Haji Muhamad Yar of Sialkot.

Second Prize with silver medal for set of armour (*charina*), (7 pieces), (No. 3925), Rs. 313, the larger foliar ornamentation in *dewálí* the other portions ordinary *koftgari*, made by Malaka Imam Din of Sialkot.

Second Prize with silver medal for shield (No. 3982), Rs. 125, engraved steel with pattern in *dewálí* work; sword hilt (No. 3986), Rs. 100, and tray (No. 3998) in *teh nashán* work, by Kazi Gulab Din of Sialkot.

Third Prize with bronze medal for a collection of swords, daggers, etc., with hilts in *Ganga-Jamní koftgari* (Nos. 4351-2-3), Rs. 14 to Rs. 16, made in Sirohi State.

Third Prize with bronze medal for *suráhi* in *dewálí* and *koft* (No. 4525), Rs. 75; and a shield (No. 4828), Rs. 75, made by Muhamad Azim of Gujerat.

Commended for large tray in Oriental style (central leaf work in *dewálí* and marginal scrolls in ordinary *koftgari* work), made by Abdul Aziz of Gujerat.

Commended for large tray (No. 4531), Rs. 50 (*dewálí* work but good design), made by Abdur Rahim of Gujerat.

Commended for *suráhi* (No. 3989), Rs. 28, made by Muhamad Buksh of Sialkot.

Commended for large tray in *koft* work (No. 3976), Rs. 63, made by Budha of Sialkot.

Commended—a small *suráhi* (No. 3968), Rs. 31, ordinary *koftgari*; a large plate in *Ganga-Jamní* work (No. 3945), Rs. 75, made by Fazal Karim of Sialkot.

Commended—a small tray in soft steel inlaid with gold wire with figure of Krishna in the centre (No. 893), Rs. 62, made by the School of Art, Travancore.

Commended for nut-cutter damascened in gold wire, made by Saghbatullah of Alwar (No. 3525), Rs. 44.

(*b*) *Bidrí ware* (*or quasi-encrusted ware*).

DIVISION 5 DAMASCENED AND ENCRUSTED WARES.

First Prize with silver medal for an extensive series of old ware (Nos. 779, 783, 826-7 and 833-*a* to *f*), by Haji Hasan, Arab trader of Hyderabad.

Second Prize with silver medal for *hukka* bowl in *teh nashán bidrí* with gold, made by Trailokya Nath Dass of Murshidabad.

Second Prize with silver medal for *hukka* (No. 5027), Rs. 338, *teh nashán bidrí*, and *hukka* (No. 5037), Rs. 300, *zar nashán bidrí*, made by Kadar Beg and Chandu Beg of Lucknow.

Third Prize with bronze medal for new *bidrí suráhi* (No. 791), Rs. 119; *suráhi* (No. 827-*e*), Rs. 18, by Haji Hasan of Hyderabad.

Commended—a *suráhi* (No. 760), Rs. 22, in modern *teh nashán bidrí*, in vine pattern, made by Ramanna of Hyderabad.

(*c*) *Encrusted ware proper.*

First Prize with silver medal for large oval tray (No. 3801), Rs. 150, made by Rama Chari of Tirupati, North Arcot.

Second Prize with bronze medal for pair of small *lotás* (Nos. 3698-9), Rs. 20 each, made at the Madras School of Arts.

Second Prize with bronze medal for copper bowl with silver (No. 119), Rs. 250, made by V. Kristna Pathar & Co. of Tanjore.

Commended—a copper bowl with silver (No. 115), Rs. 125, made by Kasi Ram Pandia & Co. of Tanjore.

Commended—large oval salver (No. 120), Rs. 250, made by Karuppama Pathar of Tanjore.

Commended—covered *chumbu* of lead and brass (Nos. 387-8-9), Rs. 12, made by Melapalijar Asari of Trichinopoly.

Division 6.—Copper and Brass Wares.—(*Plates Nos. 12 and 13.*)

Metals and Alloys.—The provinces of India have each two or three centres noted for their copper and brass wares, and accordingly a corresponding number of widely different art conceptions are practised in the ornamentation of these metals. Copper is called *tánbá* in Hindustani; zinc *jasta* and tin and pewter are *ránga*, though the latter is an alloy of tin and antimony; lastly lead is *sísa*. These metals two or more—are utilised in the

Metallic Alloys.

DIVISION 6. COPPER AND BRASS WARES.

manufacture of the alloys used in India. Brass or *pital* is made from copper and zinc in varying proportions, usually 2 of the former to 1 or 1½ of the latter. The alloy is very rarely made in India at the present day, the bulk being imported in the form of sheet brass. *Bharat, kaskut* or *kánsá* is an alloy of copper, zinc and tin, and is much cheaper than brass though inferior in colour. *Phúl* or *kánsi* is the most constant of the alloys of India and corresponds to the bell-metal of Europe or white brass. On account of its bright colour and the polish that it takes, this metal is in much demand for ornamental purposes. It usually consists of 7 parts of copper to 2 parts of tin. In the Hindu *Shastras* gold and copper pots are held to be the purest, next to these come silver and brass and lastly those of iron. According to the Muhammadan sacred books earthen vessels are preferable to metallic, brass being specially detestable (*makrúh*) but the prohibition against copper is evaded by its being tinned, since tin eating vessels are approved. The Hindu prohibition against *phúl* or bell-metal is unreasonable since it is by far the most sanitary metal of all those in use in India. Milk and curds cannot be kept in brass and nothing acid can be cooked in it, hence it may be said that the best cooking vessel that the Hindu possesses is under the ban of vexatious ceremonial restrictions. The impurity of *phúl* is attributed to its being an alloy containing *ránga* or pewter.

Purity of the Metals.

Industrial Aspects.

Craftsmen.—It would be beyond the scope of this work to deal with the purely industrial aspects of the copper and brass-smiths' crafts, suffice it to say therefore that a considerable range exists in the knowledge and skill manifested by the Indian craftsmen in the utilization of these metals and their alloys. In Burma, for example, idols of a perfectly stupendous size are cast in brass by a mere handful of operators (at each foundry yard) whose appliances, judged of by the standard of European necessity, would be pronounced absolutely inadequate. In many parts of India, such for example as in Rajputana, the chain bangles worn by the peasants are moulded and sold for a few annas the pair that would, by the superior knowledge and labour-saving appliances of Europe and America, be impossible of production at many times the price charged. Between these extremes in magnitude and intricacy

DIVISION 6. COPPER AND BRASS WARES.

may be said to lie the range of domestic and sacred utensils, in the production of which every village possesses its skilled coppersmiths, but so profitable apparently is the craft that it has drawn to its ranks men of nearly every caste in addition to the hereditary workers—the *Kaseras* and *Thatheras*.

Shapes of Domestic Vessels.

Ordinary domestic utensils are rarely ornamented because by ordinance they require to be scoured with mud, after being used and before being washed with water. But the shapes of these vessels are often extremely graceful and the finish and style of one locality far superior to that of another. The copper or brass vessel of most general use by the Hindus is the *lotá*, a globular melon-shaped vessel flattened from the top and having an elegantly reflexed rim by which it is carried suspended between the fingers and thumb. In shape this doubtless originated from the partially expanded flowers of the sacred lotus, its name thus coming from the same root as the Latin *lotus*, "washed," and the English lotion, "a wash." With the Muhammadans the *lotá* (or *tonti*) has been given a spout because the Quran ordains that a man shall perform his ablutions in running water, hence the water when poured out of the *tonti* is considered to be running water. It is carried by holding the rim at one side and it thus dangles instead of being (as with the Hindus) suspended from the middle of the hand. The shapes of the *lotá* and *tonti* and their respective uses have given birth to two widely different forms of both domestic and decorative metal works, characteristic of India. For example, the spout and the use of copper, more especially when tinned, has originated a whole range of forms and designs not only quite unknown to the Hindus but next to impossible with the materials permitted by their religion.

The Lota.

Ceremonial Implements.

Ceremonial Implements.—Some of the most beautiful and interesting copper and brass wares of India are those directly required for ceremonial purposes or which have been derived from the implements used at the temples. The *kosa* or *panchpatr*, the spathe-like vessel used in raising water, and the similarly shaped spoon, *kusi* or *achmani*, employed by the priests in sprinkling holy water and making drink offerings, are beautiful symbolic objects largely drawn upon in decorative art. The *dhupdání* or

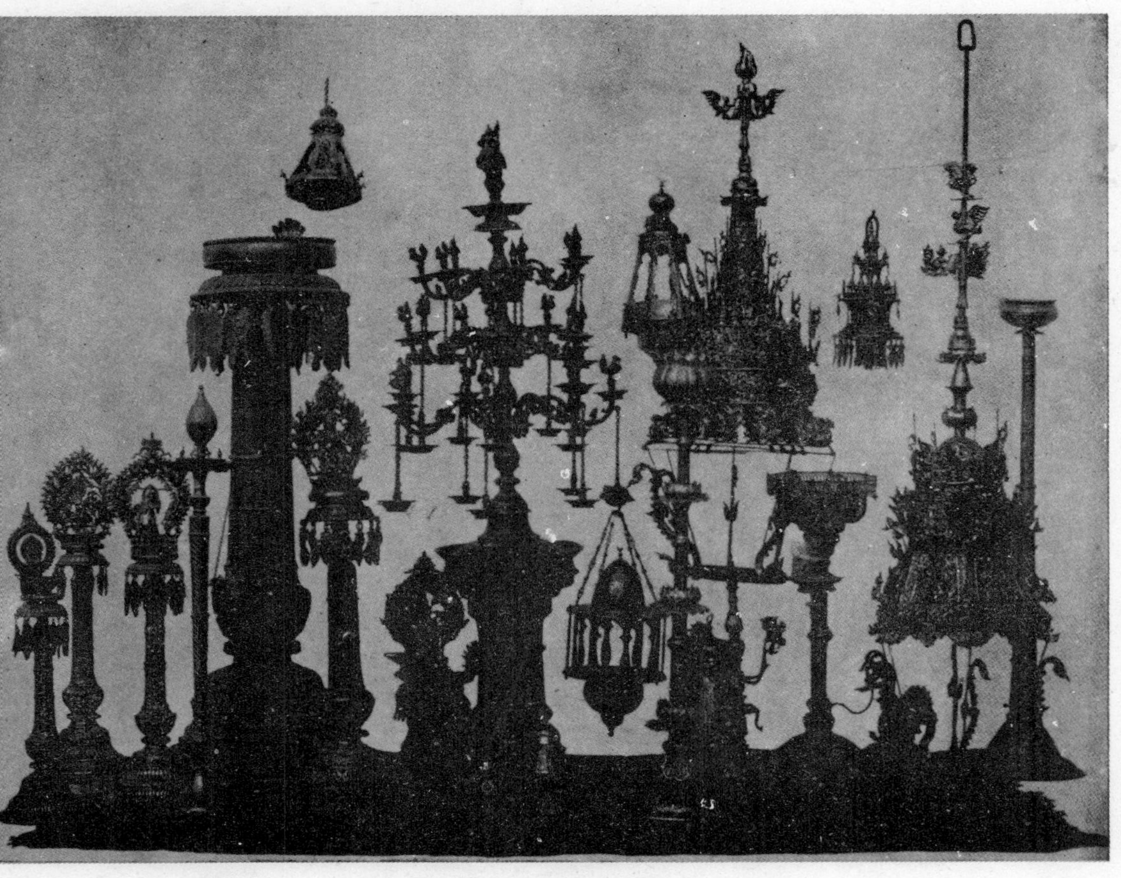

Plate No. 12 Metal Lamps

DIVISION 6. COPPER AND BRASS WARES.

Lamps and Bells.

censer is often extremely beautiful. The *sinhasan* or idol throne of lotus-leaf pattern has originated much that is admirable in India. The lamp (*arti*) (Plate No. 12), more especially the hanging lamps, as also the bells (*ghantá*) that occur in almost every temple, have stimulated art conception until it might fairly well be said that few articles of Indian production are more beautiful, especially the chains by which these are suspended. So again it might in all fairness be remarked that the restrictions imposed by religious conceptions have alone prevented the copper and brass founders of India from producing statuary of a high order. As it is, many centres turn out idols and figures that manifest not only a high skill but much artistic feeling, especially those that portray the youth and pastoral existences of Krishna.

Idols.

But to attempt an enumeration of even the more remarkable and beautiful examples of the every-day copper and brass wares of India would necessitate the production of an elaborate treatise. It may, therefore, suffice to indicate, province by province, the chief styles of ornamental treatment of the metals here dealt with more especially that may be seen at the Exhibition.

CHIEF EXHIBITS ON VIEW.

Panjab and Northern India.—AMRITSAR and LAHORE:—Following the lead of the golden temple, Amritsar has for some years past turned out a fair amount of very superior repoussé in brass and copper. The goods in question are in low relief, the pattern sharp and crisp and the designs mostly Italian. The best examples of this work are the door made by Dullu Mall, price Rs. 625, and three copper and brass plates (*thális*) at Rs. 31.

KASHMIR enjoys the reputation of producing two well marked forms of copper and brass, the one from Kashmir proper, the other from the Ladakh or Thibet territory of that State. For many years both these forms had a good reputation, but recently the attempt to cheapen production has resulted in the destruction of the art feeling of these goods and in the manufacture of articles of such a flimsy nature that they cannot be handled without falling to pieces. It is, therefore, most unfortunate that it has to be affirmed that the brass and copper wares of Kashmir from being once in great demand have become almost unsaleable. This significant fact has been abundantly demonstrated at the present Exhibition.

DIVISION 6. COPPER AND BRASS WARES.

Kashmir copper and brass wares may be described as manifesting an elaborate form of low repoussé, which is devoid of the boldness of other styles but relieved by a higher repoussé carried over the surface. Pierced ornamentation is also freely introduced, thereby strengthening the Persian character of these wares. The best examples in the Exhibition are the following:—Four large circular trays in copper, Rs. 150 each. These were made by Subhana of Srinagar and are by far the best samples shown. After these may be mentioned a circular tray, Rs. 62; a large flower vase, Rs. 62; a jar with massive handles, Rs. 18; an octagonal tray, Rs. 15.

Of the THIBETAN work the following may be inspected:—A Lhassa tea-pot, Rs. 93 (Plate No. 13); a *samavár*, Rs. 25; a Yarkand shield, Rs. 37, and a large assortment of similar wares.

United Provinces. (*Plate No. 13.*)—In these Provinces there are two specially marked centres in the production of copper and brass ware; these are LUCKNOW and BENARES. The former mainly deals in copper, the latter in brass. In Lucknow, moreover, the material is treated very much more artistically and effectively than in Benares. It is repousséd in a bold style without any surface chasing, additional effect being given by frequent perforation. In the Exhibition will be found several large trays (*sínís*) in this style made by Makhan Lal Narain Das, price Rs. 100; also a basket (*pitári*) and *pán-dán* (*mukaba*). The frequent use of the crescent shows the Muhammadan influence, but there are two widely different styles—a Hindu and a Muhammadan; the best workers belong to the former and do not, as a rule, perforate their copper or make use of the crescent ornamentation unless specially prepared for the Muhammadan market.

Lucknow.

BENARES ware is too well known to be here described, but a good example may be seen in the Loan Collection Gallery kindly contributed by His Highness the Maharaja of Mysore. It is punched brass and in a colour and design (excepting in the very finest and most expensive specimens) anything but pleasing. It is, however, cheap and is the best known style of Indian metal work met with in Europe, and has accordingly done much to lower the desire to possess examples of Indian brass and copper

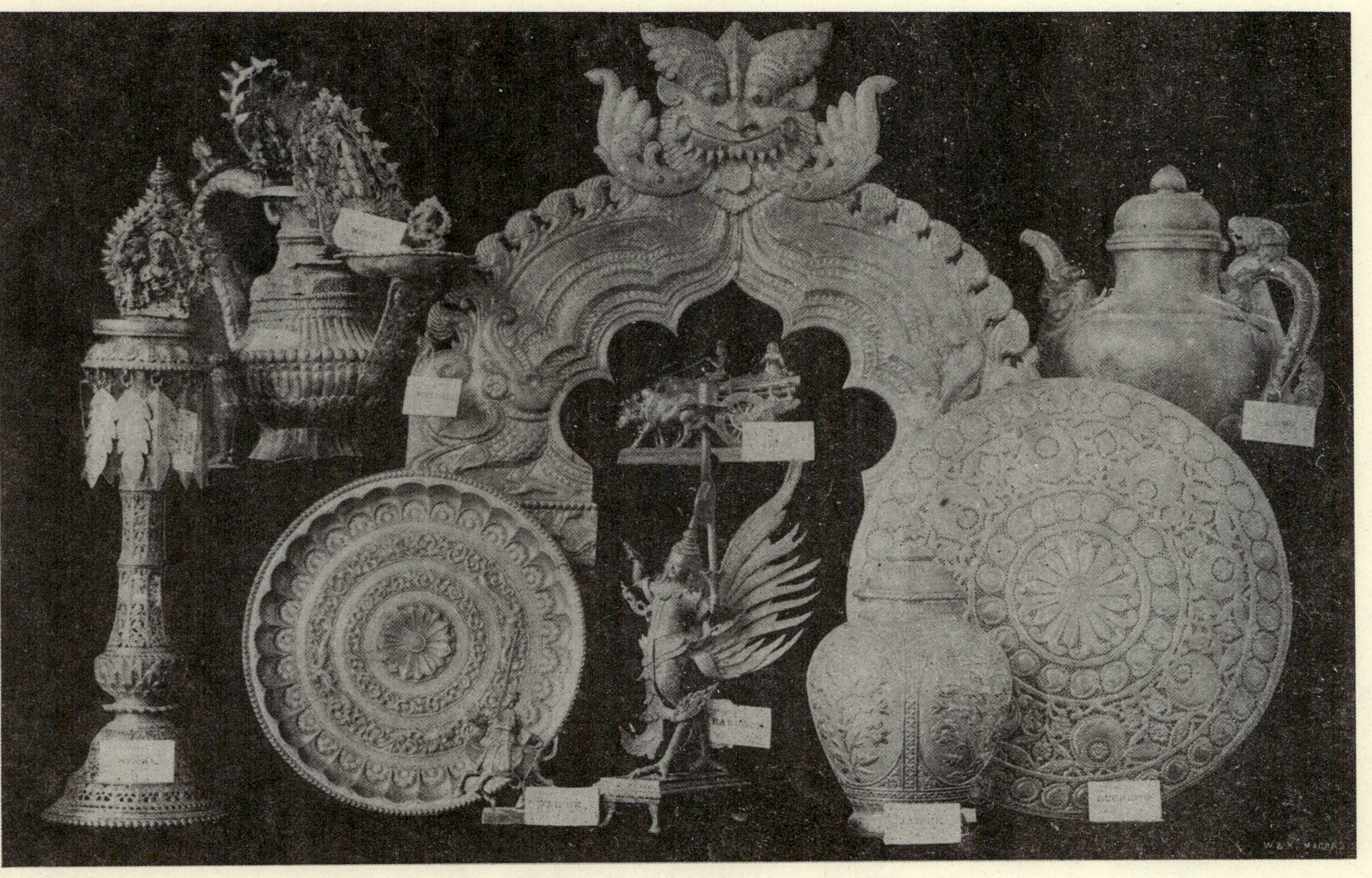

Plate No. 13 Brass and Copper Ware

DIVISION 6. COPPER AND BRASS WARES.

wares. While arranging for the collections intended for this Exhibition, the writer inspected, in the town hall of Benares, a large assortment of the brass ware of that place. All but one or two pieces were bad in design and worse in execution. They had departed from the fine old patterns that made Benares famous for its brass wares, most being poor imitations of *swámi* silver or of Poona copper ware. Many were in degraded European shapes and purposes. It was accordingly decided that unless very superior articles were specially produced, on the lines of certain old samples picked up in the city, Benares brass would have to be excluded. Only two samples were finally received at Delhi and neither of these have been sold, so that Benares ware may be said to be entirely absent from this Exhibition of Indian Art.

Jaipur.

Rajputana, Central India.—There are several centres noted for the production of copper and brass in these Provinces, the most important being JAIPUR, BIKANIR, DHOLPUR, UJJAIN and INDORE. The manufactures of Jaipur may be taken as representative and within the past few years the trade in this class of goods from that State has immensely increased and it is satisfactory to have to add in some respects improved. The articles are more conscientiously made, cheaper and better than in most other parts of India. The style followed is polished brass in rich but not overburdened repousse, the designs being often in modern Arabesque such as in the famous Jaipur tables, that within the past ten or fifteen years have assumed the condition of a distinct item of trade. Instead of being repousséd, the copper is often simply engraved. The best examples of Jaipur work shown in the Exhibition may be said to be an electro-plated and gilt brass *Ramayana* embossed shield with carved *shisham* wood stand 4½ feet by 3¼ feet, Rs. 1,500; a large beggar's bowl (*kamandal*) in brass, elaborately embossed and standing 4½ feet high, price Rs. 275; another of the same, richly engraved, standing 5½ feet high, Rs. 375; an embossed *rastila* vase, Rs. 62; a snake-handled water jug (*surâhi*), with Krishna on the top, Rs. 40; a brass table richly embossed with astronomical figures, Rs. 119, all made at the School of Art. An oval gold-plated shield in repousse work with figures of the Mughal Emperors placed in a carved *shisham* wooden stand,

DIVISION 6. COPPER AND BRASS WARES.

Rs. 438; a brass bullock cart with load of wood (Plate No. 13), made by Messrs. Panna Mahomed Alla Buksh & Co., Rs. 12. These and several other examples are exceptionally fine and remarkably cheap for the finish and style given to them. Having said so much in praise of the Jaipur brass and copper wares, it is satisfactory to have to add that these personal opinions have subsequently been abundantly confirmed by the Judging Committee in their having awarded to Jaipur, more especially its School of Art, the gold medal for the best collection of metal work shown in the Exhibition.

Bombay.—In the Presidency of Bombay there are several centres noted for copper and brass manufacture. Those of greatest repute, from an art point of view, are POONA, BOMBAY and BARODA, while NASIK has a high reputation for the manufacture of cooking utensils. In Poona, just as with silver plate, the habit prevails of producing copper and brass in bold massive repoussé. The School of Art, Bombay, has for years past pioneered a high development in repoussé ware. The following examples may be specially mentioned as good examples from that institution:—A large copper pot and a large copper and brass vase, Rs. 375 each.

Poona.

In BARODA, repoussé brass is largely produced by hammering thin plates of brass on to carved wood-work and fixing the plates permanently over the wood. So also copper anklets of a massive and striking character are largely produced at Baroda. Of the former work the best example is a brass repoussé stool on teak-wood, made by Mistry Raghunath Tribhuvan & Sons of Vishnagar; of the latter a copper *kalla* (anklet), chrysanthemum pattern, made by Hurgovind Hira of Dabhoi near Baroda.

KATHIAWAR produces very curious copper boxes used for locking up valuable articles of personal adornment. These are circular in shape, stand on three massive tapering feet and have immense hasps and padlocks. They are exceedingly curious but not very ornamental.

From BIJAPUR have been received two plates of an interesting and strictly Hindu character. In general feature they are flat, the highest portion being in the centre. The ornamentation is strictly in circles. Starting from the central medallion there are three or four zones of chased floral scrolls, one of the most striking features of which is that the pattern flows onward. The rim of the plate has the double finger-print impressions in a form met with throughout the whole Mahratta country and closely associated with Chalukyan art.

DIVISION 6. COPPER AND BRASS WARES.

Madras.—South India has several centres of artistic copper and brass manufactures, the most noteworthy being MADRAS TOWN, MADURA, MYSORE and VELLORE. A considerable trade is done in Madura in the manufacturing of idols, toys, insects, statuettes, ornaments, etc., the chief manufacturer being Malai Kan Ashary. The Madras School of Art turns out a good deal of very massive repoussé, of which good examples will be seen in the general collection and in the Madras room. Vellore has a style of work all its own, namely a form of perforated brass, the mythological figures having portions plain and polished, others engraved.

Mysore.

In MYSORE are manufactured brass plates with floral concentric scrolls closely resembling those of Bijapur, already described. In Sir George Birdwood's *Industrial Arts of India* (Plates 9, 10 and 11), examples of one phase of this style will be seen. But from Mysore have been received and shown in the Exhibition a large assortment of such trays, not in gold as in Sir George Birdwood's examples, but in brass. These are round, oval and octagonal in shape—very possibly in the shapes and manifesting the ornamentation turned out in that State for centuries. They are in strict accord with the ornamentation of the temples now spoken of as Chalukyan and display great dignity in proportion and quality in ornamentation. In fact this style is capable of greater development than almost any other form of metallic treatment met with in India. At present it may be said to be utterly neglected. The Madras School of Arts furnished to the Exhibition, however (in brass), a charming reproduction of an old silver tray believed to have come from TRAVANCORE. This manifests all the peculiarities of the Chalukyan decoration in massive repoussé richly chased on the surface. It is shown on Plate No. 13 without a label. A charming example of a brass canopy for a Hindu god (*prabhavala*) has been made and exhibited by Venkata Krishnappa, Rs. 25, showing in the centre and background of Plate No. 13.

DIVISION 6. COPPER AND BRASS WARES.

There are also several finer examples of this work in the Loan Collection Gallery. They are identical with the silver example figured in Sir George Birdwood's *Industrial Arts of India* (Plate 8-*bis*) as coming from Madura. The *yálí* (or demon) spouting forth life, which occurs all over these canopies, is a remarkable feature of all Chalukyan art and almost of necessity fixes the place of their production in Mysore. A large assortment of richly chased trays by the Art Department of the Mysore Government will be found well worthy of careful study. The designs are peculiarly Chalukyan.

Bengal Presidency.—Bengal has no special art manufacture in copper and brass, but NEPAL and SIKKIM, the frontier States of that Province, have each highly characteristic manufactures of this kind. From Nepal has been received a fine display of hanging, standard and hand lamps, perhaps the best series ever shown at any Exhibition. (See Plate No. 12 on left hand side.) Of these may be mentioned a brass lamp 6½ feet high, Rs. 1,314, a brass standard lamp with figures of *Ganesh* and *Bharon*, Rs. 80, and a brass standard lamp without figures, Rs. 180. Two of the Nepal lamps are shown on Plate No. 13

Burma—has contributed two most admirable candlesticks in the form of birds with human heads, made by Maung Po Kyew of Prome, Rs. 65 each (one shown in the centre of Plate No. 13); also a set of gongs from Mandalay. The gongs of Burma are famous all over the world and are of two kinds, round and triangular. To show the Burmese brass and copper crafts it would have been necessary to display a large assortment of idols from ½ foot to 10 or 15 feet in height. This was found impossible and from an art point of view hardly necessary.

AWARDS FOR COPPER AND BRASS.

(a) Copper and Bronze.

AWARDS.

First Prize with gold medal to Jaipur School of Art for a collection of copper and brass wares.

First Prize with silver medal to the Mayo School of Art, Lahore, for a pair of copper vases, Rs. 136 the pair.

First Prize with silver medal to the Madras School of Arts for pair of copper bowls, Rs 24, and one large *ghará* in bold and deep repoussé, Rs. 77; also salver in brass (No. 528).

First Prize with silver medal to the Bombay School of Art for collection of copper repoussé.

Second Prize with bronze medal for insects in bronze(No. 472), Rs 32, made by Pounaswami Arary of Madura.

Second Prize with bronze medal for collection of large and boldly repousséd trays (*sínís*), (No. 4982), Rs. 100 ; large *hukka* (No. 5,000) ; and circular box of perforated copper (No. 5003), made by Makhan Lal Narain Dass, of Abyagunj, Lucknow.

Third Prize with bronze medal for lamp-stand in form of statue of *kanahaya* (birdman), made in bronze (Nos. 4 and 5), Rs. 65 each, made by Maung Po Kyew of Prome.

Third Prize with bronze medal for large copper tray in old shawl pattern (No. 2574), Rs. 150 ; also No. 3577, a jug, Rs. 10 ; No. 3590, Bokhara jar, Rs. 7, made by Subhana of Srinagar.

Commended for collection of copper ware in modern though good design, more especially Nos. 2575 and 3741, small claret jug made by Lassoo of Srinagar.

Commended for copper anklets (No. 1078), Rs. 10, made by Huragovind Hira, of Dabhoi, Baroda.

(*b*) *Brass.*

First Prize to the Jaipur School of Art, the gold medal mentioned above. The best examples in brass are, however, a goblet (No. 1611), Rs. 18 ; a vase (No. 1681), Rs. 23 ; pierced betel box (No. 1642) ; a Ramayana shield (No. 1684), Rs. 1,500 ; models of carts, etc. (No. 1631), etc.

First Prize with silver medal to Panna Muhammad Alla Buksh of Jaipur, for hanging lamps (Nos. 1756, etc.,) and models of carts (No. 1771, etc.).

First Prize with silver medal for a copper and brass door (No. 1604), Rs. 500, made by Dulu, silversmith of Amritsar.

Second Prize with bronze medal for trays richly chased (Nos. 3517, 3516, 3524, etc.), procured from the Artware Department, Mysore Government.

Third Prize with bronze medal for deeply chased trays (No. 5819, etc.) from Bijapur.

Third Prize with bronze medal to Nur Baksh and Khuda Buksh of Jaipur, for models of animals (No. 1100) and hanging lamps (Nos. 1043, 1044).

DIVISION 6. COPPER AND BRASS WARES.

Commended for brass repousséd trays (Nos. 1607-8) made by Ghulam Jiláni of Amritsar.

Commended for large embossed circular salver (No. 772), also bowl (No. 769), exhibited by Mr. M. K. Godbole, Poona.

Commended for series of circular trays in perforated brass (No. 701), made by Oeriya Munisami Achari of Saidapet, Vellore.

Commended for stool in wood, coated with brass repousséd on the wood (No. 1589), Rs. 50, made by Mistry Raghu Nath Tribhuvan and Sons, Baroda.

(*c*) *Nepal and Kashmir brass* (*Old work*).

First Prize with silver medal for large series of old Nepal brasses, *i.e.*, hand-lamps, hanging lamps and stand lamps, exhibited by His Excellency the Prime Minister of Nepal.

Second Prize with bronze medal for collection of old Thibetan (and imitation old Thibetan) brasses (Nos. 2901 and 2922), exhibited by Lassoo, silversmith, of Srinagar, Kashmir.

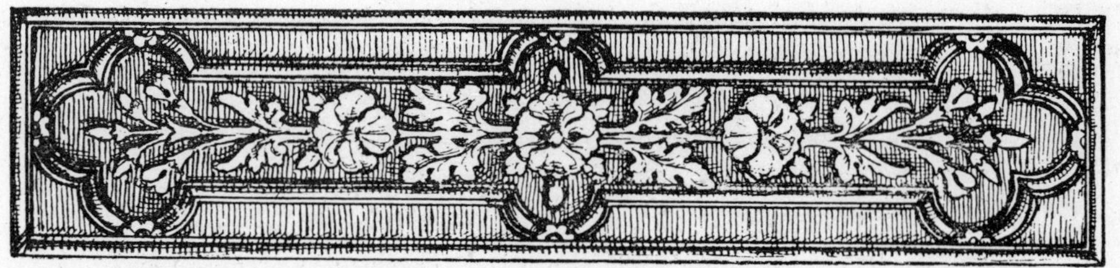

Class II.—STONE AND GLASS WARES, INCLUDING INLAID STONE.

THE articles placed under this Class have been referred to the following groups:— **DIVISION 7. STONE-CARVING.**

Division 7. Stone-carving of all kinds (Architectural, Domestic and Religious, etc.)

Division 8. Lapidary work and Seal engraving, Precious Stone cutting, etc.

Division 9. Glass ware.

Division 10. Inlaid Stone-work.

The articles indicated by these Divisions might be dealt with under numerous headings: for example, the materials used (sandstone, marble, etc.); the purposes served (architectural, domestic, religious); or the nature of the designs pursued. These and such like considerations might be each seized upon for the classification of the stone wares of India. Wood-carving being the more widely known and doubtless the earlier craft, it may be the preferable course to attempt greater detail in discussing the art conceptions manifested in wood rather than those in stone work. This view of the case may be accepted as likely to prove satisfactory, when it is recollected that the persons who engage in both wood and stone-carving when Hindus belong to the same caste and have thus the same conceptions and traditions. The observations that will be found below, under Class IV—Wood-work, may therefore be read conjointly with the briefer statement, here given, of the Stone-work (more specially Stone-carving) of India, as represented in the Exhibition.

DIVISION 7. STONE-CARVING.

Stages in Development.

It may, for convenience, be said that in Indian stone-work there are three great stages or types—(*a*) corresponding with the excavation of cave temples and the construction of topes, (*b*) the building of Hindu, Chalukyan and Jain temples, and (*c*) of Pathan and Mughal mosques, tombs and palaces. In other words, stone-work first assumed importance in India with the Buddhist topes and cave temples. For convenience these may be accepted as having been constructed and excavated between the years 250 B.C. and 400 A.D. They may accordingly be taken as affording the only certain knowledge available regarding the constructive features and decorative designs that prevailed in India during the period named. But, since the older cave temples and the rails and gateways of the topes depict wooden structures, it may be safely assumed that their constructive and decorative designs had come down from an even greater antiquity than the dates mentioned. The majority of the early Buddhistic monuments that bear actual or relative dates, follow a sequence in change that portrays the gradual absorption of the concrete or personal doctrines of Hinduism with the loss of the abstract impersonal conceptions of Buddhism. Emblematic and natural ornamentation is in consequence seen to give place to sacerdotal and idolatrous forms, until the avowed contest for popular favour of the co-equal faiths of Hinduism, Jainism and Buddhism are depicted at Ellora.

Temple-building Period.

Passing over the gap of several centuries, spoken of as the dark ages, down to the period that gave birth to the majority of the older constructive temples of India, the curtain rises to disclose the complete disappearance of Buddhism, the insignificance of Jainism, and the ascendency of Hinduism such that it no longer seeks the seclusion of caves nor regards the contest for popular favour as necessary. Thus it may be accepted that from aboriginal thoughts and arts to Hindu, Jaina and Buddhistic, and back again to the modern Hindu or Brahmanical forms, the Indian arts were gradually evolved and nurtured, until from a foreign source there came by far the most important disturbing element of all, namely, the invasion and conquest of India by various races of Muhammadans.

Mosque-building Period.

Then came the period of mosques, tombs and palaces Pathan and Persian arts were gradually established in India, more especially in the northern tracts, and from about 1200 to 1600 A.D. began to be adopted by even the conquered races. But the Emperor Akbar, having seen the political danger of exclusive reliance on foreign modes of thought, when dealing with a conquered country, pioneered a new departure, namely, the liberal adoption of all that was beautiful and commendable in the indigenous arts of India. He introduced the system of encrusting marble with other coloured stones, in place of the coloured tiles of his Pathan and Persian predecessors. He authorised a liberal use of life portraiture in both animal and vegetable forms. In other words, Hindu treatment of Muhammadan subjects became the rule, not the exception. The fort of Agra and portions of the palace were built, the palaces of Fatehpur Sikri were designed and constructed, and the tombs of Sikandra and Itmad-ud-Daula and many of those in Lahore were built. The absence of timber and the sparing use of the true arch may be spoken of as some of the most significant features of this style of stone-work.

Indo-Saracenic Style.

In 1627 Shah Jahan ascended the throne, and very shortly after turned his attention to architectural and decorative arts. In consequence he originated the style of stone-work that has more specially received the name of Indo-Saracenic. The political precepts of his father and grandfather were blended, so to speak, into a style of art that might almost be viewed as having lost eclecticism and become a dazzling picture in photographic detail, precipitated on the very borderland of dignity and propriety. Its faults are the loss of the restraining influences that centre around the principles of construction, proportion, and composition. In consequence, when the hands of the great Emperor architect were withheld by his usurping son, it tumbled over almost instantly into the tawdriness and eccentricity of the palaces of Oudh and the tombs of Junagad.

Among the long list of beautiful buildings that owe their existence to the Emperor Shah Jahan, the following may be specially mentioned :—the Khas Mahal of Agra (completed in 1637), the Jumma Masjid of Agra (in 1644), the Táj Mahal of

DIVISION 7. STONE-CARVING.

Agra (in 1648), the Mote Masjid of Agra (in 1653) and the Jumma Masjid of Delhi (in 1658).

Blending of Hindu and Muhammadan Styles.

It may thus be said that from Akbar's time forward Hindu artificers were much more freely utilised by the Muhammadans, and were given a comparatively free hand to follow their own conceptions in the ornamentation of the buildings required of them. In time they became not only experts in adapting their own arts to the wants of their conquerors, but soon imbibed all that was good in the architecture of their masters. In consequence, there has hardly been a Hindu temple constructed in Northern India from the date named to the present day, that is not strongly Saracenic in style and feeling. Below will be found particulars of the façade of a temple, made in Agra of white sandstone, as also portions of a rich man's house from Bharatpur and of a window from Bikanir, reproduced from the palace—all these edifices were built originally for Hindus. A comparison between them and the Jodhpur *jhároka* will at once show how strongly the Saracenic influence has been exercised. The Jodhpur *jhároka* has very little in it that can be traced to the Muhammadan architects save its flattened arch and pointed and suspended eaves. But even these features belong to the period of decadence of Saracenic art, and shortly after their adoption became more Hindu than Muhammadan. In every other respect the Jodhpur *jhároka* exemplifies the stone-carving of the Rajputs, with the prevailing character of all Hindu work strongly marked, namely, its want of breadth redeemed by exuberance in ornamentation. Hindu stone-carving is essentially wooden, and it might be said that it has to be rendered on a foreign model before its beauties can be fully appreciated. It was this circumstance that gave the unity and beauty of Shah Jahan's Saracenic architecture, namely, Hindu conceptions adapted by Hindus to forms and structures supplied to them. (See page 116.)

Characteristic features.

Modern Change.

But all this has been changed in a perfectly surprising manner. In travelling from one end of India to the other in the study of crafts and industries, one circumstance is brought home to the observer more forcibly than almost any other, namely, that while a very large percentage of the skilled labour is Muhammadan, the industries are financed and controlled by Hindus. The division of labour is often carried to remarkable extents. For instance, the designers in the *kinkhab* craft are exclusively Muhammadans, the weavers largely Hindus, while the owners of factories and the traders in *kinkhabs* are almost exclusively Hindus. This state of affairs prevails all over India, and even in Rajputana the majority of the stone masons are Muhammadans.

Thus, during the lapse of the past three or four centuries, the Indo-Saracenic art and architecture have not only dwindled to insignificance, while that of the Hindus has been maintained and strengthened, but the Muhammadans, from being the employers of skilled labour, have become themselves the skilled artificers working under Hindu masters.

Division 7.—Stone-Carving. – (*Plates Nos. 14, 15 and 16.*)

Chief Centres.

The chief centres of stone-work in India (both ancient and modern) are :—(*a*) In Rajputana – Chittor and Mount Abu for ancient monuments, and Udaipur, Bikanir, Jodhpur (Makrana), Jaipur, Alwar, Ajmir, Jaisalmir for modern work, in both marble and sandstone. (*b*) In Central India—Sanchi, Díg, Fatehpur Sikri and the Sas Bahu temples and Jaina sculptures of Gwalior for ancient monuments, with Bharatpur, Dholpur, Gwalior (fort) for modern work in sandstone. (*c*) In the Panjab—the Græco-Buddhist Gandhara remains in the Peshawar district, the ancient temples of Kashmir (Marttand) and the Kutab Minár for ancient work, with the fort, palace, and city of Delhi for modern and recent work. (*d*) In the United Provinces, the best known localities for stone-work are Agra, Muttra (Brindabun), Mirzapore and Jabalpur, the last mentioned for marble. (*e*) In the Central Provinces two districts have attained a fairly high reputation for their stone-work, namely, Chanda and Bhandara. (*f*) In Bengal there is very little stone of any kind, and the art of stone-carving is therefore practically unknown to the people of the Lower Provinces, except in the tracts traversed by hills, such as Chutia Nagpur and Orissa. In these sub-provinces of Bengal, stone-carving is met with in the districts of Manbhum, Shahabad (Sasseram), Gaya, Monghyr, Bhuvaneswar and Puri. (*g*) In

Bombay Presidency good sandstone and rough marble, or rather various forms of lime-stone, are met with, the best known carvers and masons being in Rewa Kanta, Ahmedabad and Kathiawar. The ancient monuments of greatest repute in Bombay Presidency are the cave temples of Elephanta, Kanerhi, Nasik, Karli, Ajunta and Ellora, and the mosques, temples and palaces of Bijapur, Kanara (Mudbidri), Ahmedabad, Girnar and Palitana. (*h*) Of Madras Presidency there may be said to be several centres of modern stone-carving which compare most unfavourably with even the work of three or four centuries ago. The best known of the ancient monuments in stone are Amravarti, Mahavallipuram, Hampee, and the temples of Madura, Congeveram, Tanjore, Ramisseram, Pirur (near Coimbatore), Vellore, Seringam and many others. (*i*) In Mysore and Hyderabad there are many localities with ancient and also modern buildings of great beauty and interest, in stone, such as Somnathpur, Baillur, Hullabid in the former, and Hammoncondah, Warangal, Golconda in the latter. The best modern work may be said to be the pot-stone carvings for the new palace of Mysore.

With these few introductory observations it may now be desirable to draw attention to :—

1st, Examples of Architectural Stone-work. - In the Exhibition will be found six examples of architectural stone-work. These are as follows, commencing from the transept and passing to the left in the Main Gallery:—*1st*, *The Bikanir Window* :—This is a reproduction in red sandstone of a window in the old palace of Bikanir. It manifests a style which was introduced into Rajputana over 250 years ago and which prevails to the present day. Its most striking feature is the flattened arch of the roof with pointed eaves, seen opposite in the Jodhpur *jhároka*. This very possibly was derived from the bamboo huts of Bengal, and was adopted in the first place by the great architects of the later Mughal times to a limited extent, but carried by the Sikhs of the Panjab and the Hindus of Rajputana into every detail of their architecture. The doors shown within this structure illustrate a style of *gesso* wood-painting which came to India about the same period and for a century or so was widely patronised in all the centres of

Bikanir Window.

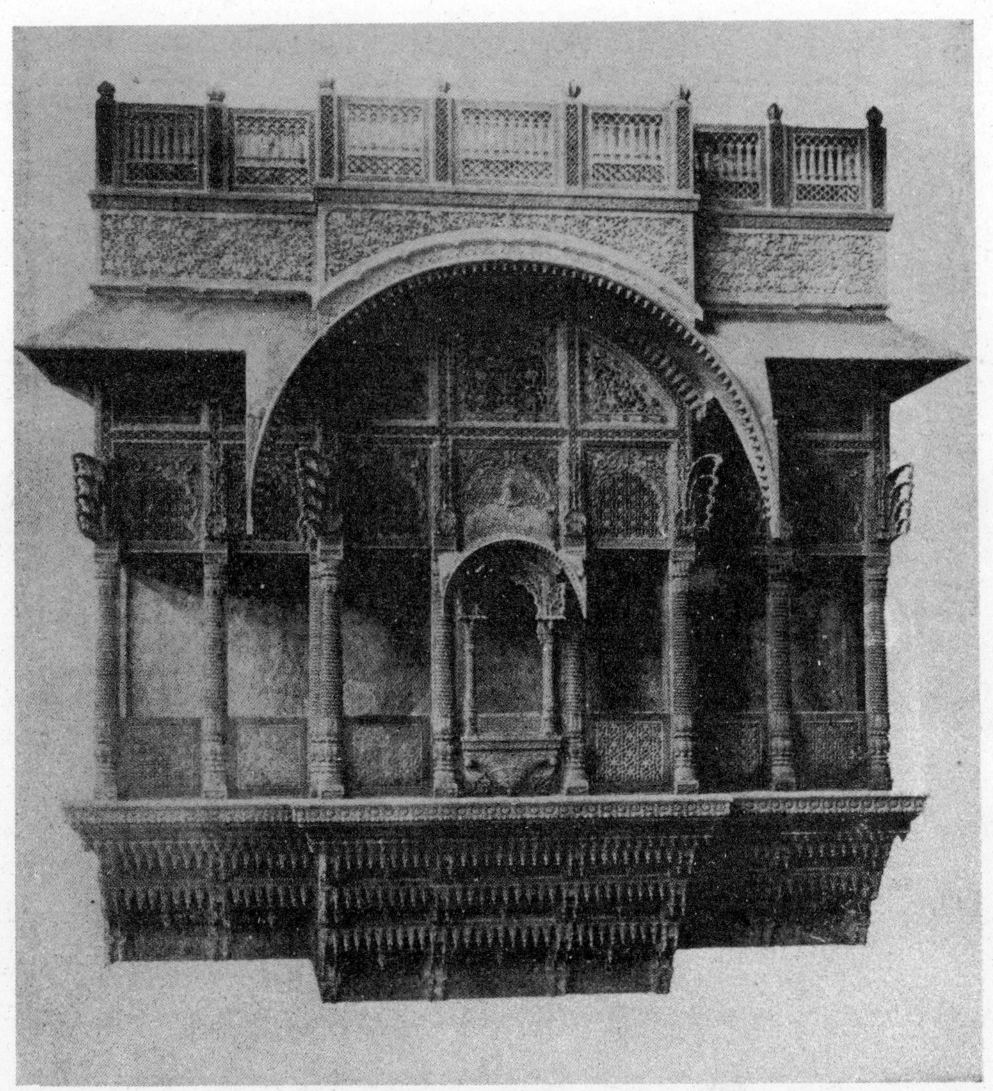

Plate No. 14 Jodhpur Jarokha in red and white Sandstone

DIVISION 7. STONE-CARVING.

Indian enlightenment. Through the kindness of His Highness the Maharaja of Bikanir the original doors from the palace are shown within the stone-work reproduction.

Mirzapore Work.

2nd, Mirzapore Fire place and Overmantel. – This has been prepared in order to illustrate the Hindu style of stone-work of the Lower Provinces of India. It is fairly characteristic of the style which may be said to be one infinitely better suited to temple ornamentation than to European requirements.

Mysore Work.

3rd, Mysore Pot-stone Work. – The specimens shown have been most generously lent by His Highness the Maharaja of Mysore and are portions of the stone-work of the new palace. The style originated with the Chalukyan temple builders (see wood-carving). The great floriated *yálí* and the art conceptions that centre around that antediluvian monster are everywhere present. What is likely to impress the observer most, however, with these Mysore carvings will doubtless be the deep under-cutting, by which the stems, leaves and flowers are in complete relief and appear as if placed in front of the stones from which they have been carved. The middle of a set of three panels shows the patron saint of Mysore (*Chámundi*); it is an admirable piece of sculpture work produced in more than half relief.

Jodhpur Work.

4th, The Jodhpur Jharoka. – (*Plate No. 14.*)—This charming sandstone building is a reproduction of an old house in the city of Jodhpur, prepared at the writer's suggestion, by the chief mason of the State. The Exhibition is greatly indebted to His Highness the Maharaja for having permitted the skill of his State to be so extensively drawn upon as was necessary for the accomplishment of this beautiful piece of work in the limited time available. It is not only a faithful copy, but is fully abreast of any of the old master-pieces of Rajputana. It has, however, been already briefly described in the foregoing remarks as also in the Introductory Chapter, to which the reader is referred for further particulars (p. 7).

Agra Work.

5th, The Agra House. – This is a faithful copy of one of the walls of a Hindu temple in Agra, showing more especially the gateway. It is in white sandstone and in a style that may be said to give tokens of being the outcome of a transition from one

DIVISION 7. STONE-CARVING.

condition of stone-carving to a widely different one. It is Díg in ornamentation and Saracenic in structure.

Bharatpur Work.

6th, Bharatpur House.—(*Plate No. 15.*)—The Introductory Chapter (p. 10) furnishes the particulars regarding this house, and further details seem unnecessary. It illustrates the stone-work of Díg and Fatehpur Sikri, and was made about 80 years ago. It is therefore a pure example of a style that holds an important position in the various schools of Indian stone-work. Unfortunately, as constructed in the Exhibition, it is incomplete It was found that the walls of the Exhibition would not support the complete structure, and one portion of it had therefore to be very nearly entirely omitted. In its full condition there would have been an inner richly carved wall and an outer trellis, with pillars supporting the projecting double eaves.

II.—Chief Examples Illustrative of the Minor Industries.—(*Plate No. 16.*)—Turning now to the special bay devoted to stone and glass ware, the assortment of small articles there shown may be regarded as representative of the stone-carving, lapidary work and stone-inlaying of India. The materials used are sandstone, marble, alabaster, soap-stone, false jade, pebbles, etc. The chief centres in these minor industries are as follows:—*for sandstone*—Mirzapore, Agra, Gwalior, Bharatpur, Jodhpur, Karauli Bikanir, etc.; *for marble*—Jaipur, Jodhpur, Jabalpur, Jaisalmir (Nummulitic lime-stone), etc.; *for lapidary work, including precious stone cutting*—Bhera, Delhi, Jodhpur, Jaipur, Cambay, Jabalpur, Banda, Rangoon, etc.; *for inlaying*—Agra, Bharatpur and Mysore; *for glass mosaic*—Udaipur, Alwar, Rangoon.

Chief Centres.

The following are the principal exhibits under each of the above mentioned sections:—

Sandstone.—The most interesting specimens have come from Gwalior such as a pair of wall brackets, Rs. 237; a pair of round vases on stands, Rs. 211 (Plate No. 16, fig. 3); a pair of square flower vases, Rs. 237; two pairs of candlesticks, in French style. In the grounds in front of the building, near the fountains, will be seen a red sandstone parapet as also two quaint and beautiful sandstone chairs (Plate No. 16, fig. 5). These have been specially supplied by His Highness the Maharaja of Jodhpur.

Sandstone flower-pots.

Balustrades.

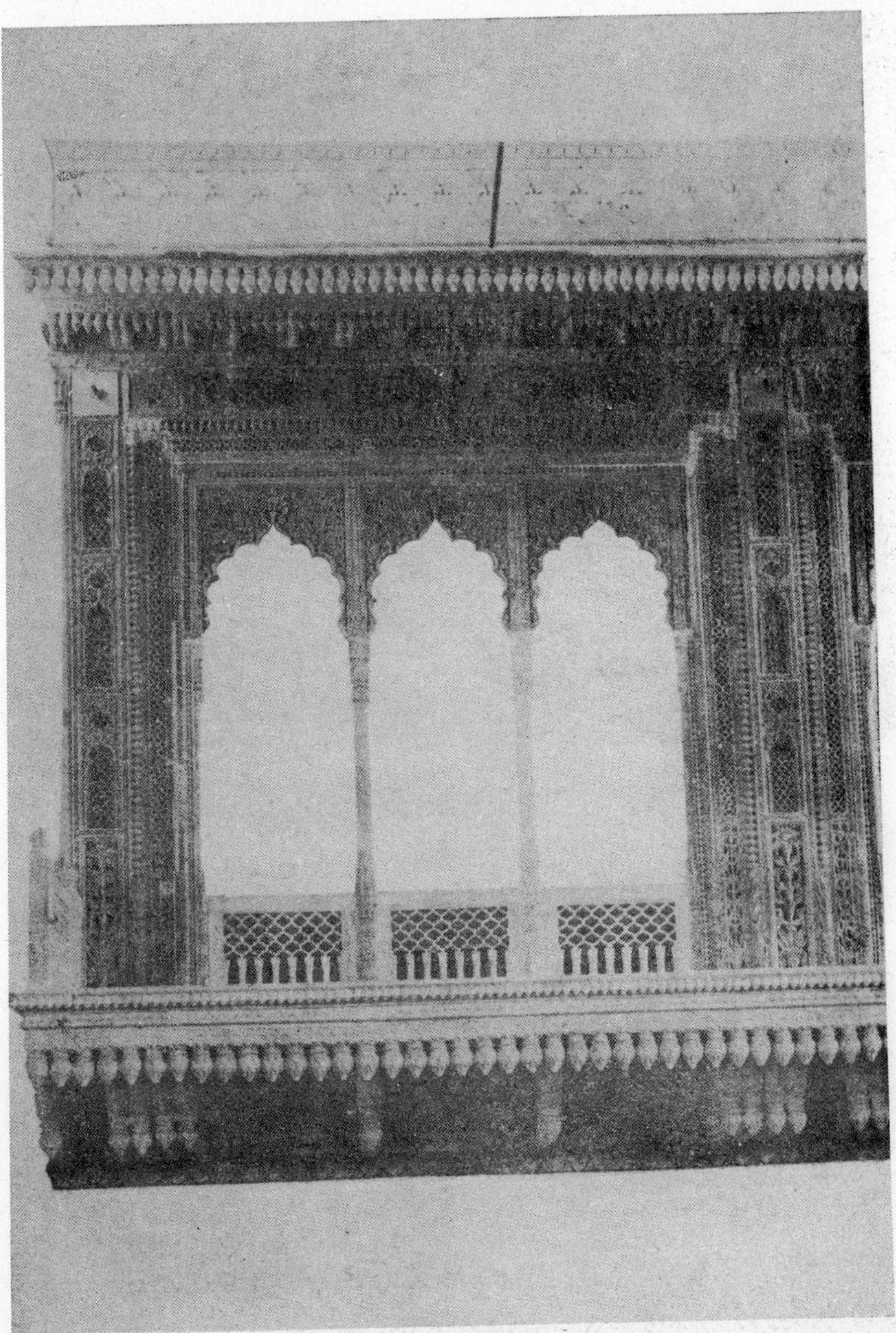

Plate No. 15 Bharatpur Facade in White Sandstone

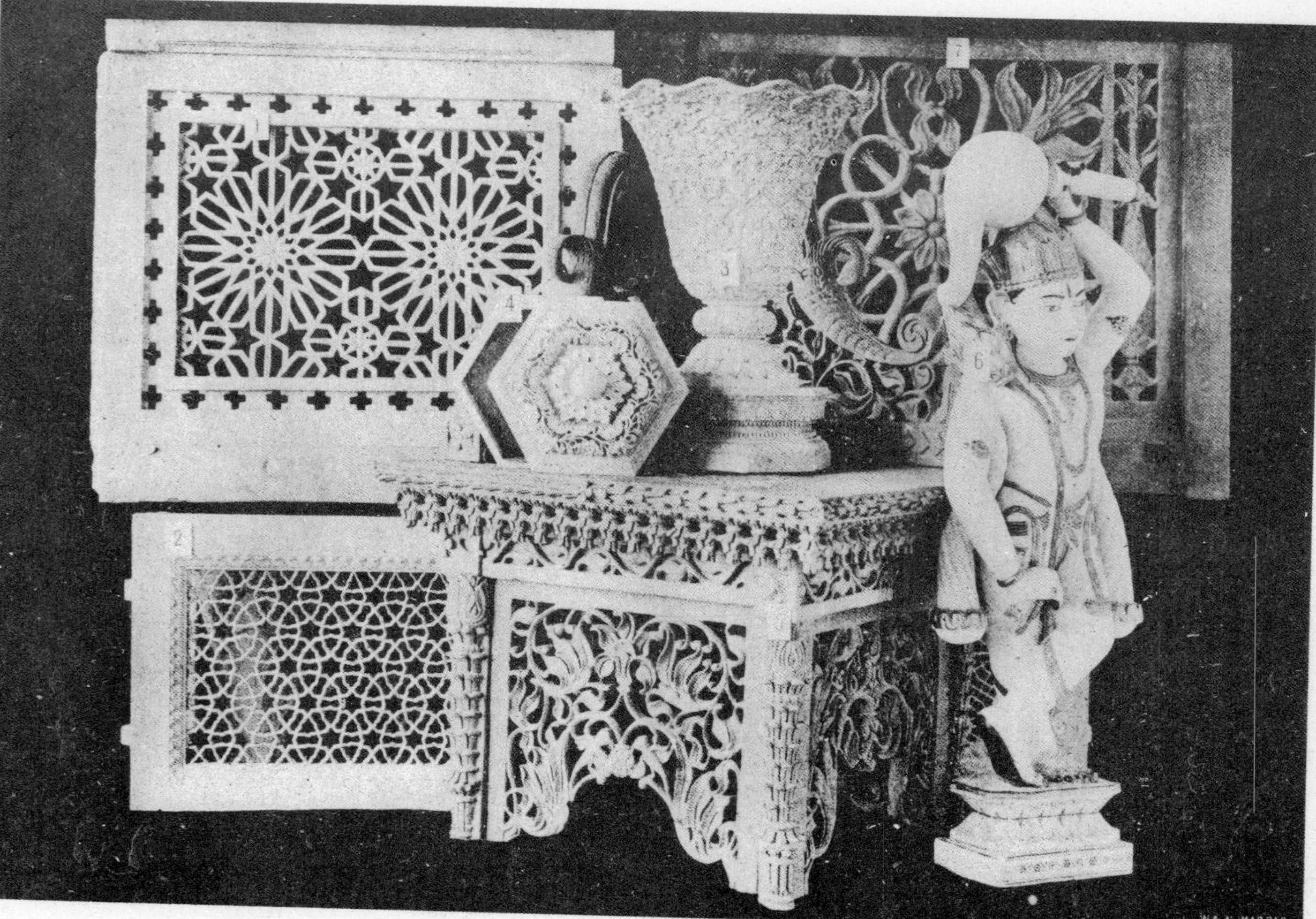

Plate No. 16 Selection of Minor Stone Work

DIVISION 7. STONE-CARVING.

Jalis.

The panels of the parapet are remarkably well designed and executed examples of sandstone *jálís*. On the *chabútras* placed on the steps of the main entrance will be found balustrades in white sandstone (Plate No. 16, fig. 1). These have been furnished by His Highness the Maharaja of Bharatpur and will be readily admitted to give a graceful finish to the façade. Seth Mul Chand, of Ajmir, has most obligingly contributed reproductions of the *jálí* panels of his own house (Plate No. 16, fig. 7), as also two red sandstone lamp-posts in order to illustrate the more characteristic styles of modern Jain stone-work. Several *jálí* panels, brackets, etc., from Karauli, Gwalior, etc. (Plate No. 16, fig. 2), have also been sent to the Exhibition that are worthy of careful study.

Jaipur Marble Figures.

Marble Statuettes, etc.—Perhaps the best example of marble statuary in the Exhibition is the familiar subject of a cow and calf, made in Jaipur, Rs. 425 (doubtless after a European model), but it may be mentioned that there are shown several complete sets of Hindu idols, in assorted sizes (Plate No. 16, fig. 6), as also a large number of animals and other articles in black, white and red marble, all more or less in conventional forms and positions. Jodhpur has contributed a *chatrí*, price Rs. 1,500 (Plate No. 17), six chairs and several garden benches in white marble, also a graceful table with thin white marble top, red marble pedestal and black marble stand (Plate No. 17 to right). A marble bench, probably very old, has been sent from Moradabad, price Rs. 1,500. Nepal has furnished a model of a Buddhist pagoda in red marble, Rs. 15, and another, Rs. 20; also several black and white marble panels carved in low relief in rich forest scenes which portray Krishna in various phases. Madura is represented by copies of pillars in the great temple; these appear to be in black marble, Rs. 125. Carved black marble lions have come from Mysore, Rs. 25. A black marble seated Buddha from Jaipur, Rs. 437, etc., as also several white marble Buddhas from Rangoon.

Jaisalmir Cups.

Pudding-stone and Yellow Lime-stone—Is made into cups, bowls, paper-weights, small tables etc., at Jaisalmir. A large series of these are shown by Imam Bux and Mubanik, masons; these range in price from Rs. 2 to Rs. 10.

Alabaster and Soap-stone.—(*Plate No. 16, fig. 4.*)—A fair

DIVISION 7. STONE-CARVING.

assortment of this class of goods will be found in the Exhibition, of which the Táj, made by Nathoo Ram and Sons, Rs. 625, is doubtless the best example. The model of Salim Chisti's tomb at Fatehpur Sikri by Permanand Brothers of Agra, is another admirable example. Of soap-stone proper, a small hexagonal box from Agra, price Rs. 37, (fig. 4) is an excellent specimen of this kind of work; it is by Nathu Ram and Sons.

Division 8.—Lapidary Work. — (*Plate No. 17, mostly on the left.*)

Jade work.

False Jade and Purbeck Marble (Suleimani) Bhera Stone-work.—The green jade stone, worked up at Bhera in the Panjab and a few other localities in India, has been classed as false jade or rather a very pure form of serpentine called Bowenite; it is known in the vernacular as *sang-i-yeshm*. It is softer and more easily worked than the jade which forms so important an article of import trade with Burma. Indian jade comes down the Indus from some part of Afghanistan, possibly mainly from Gandamak, and is sold at Attock. Recently the stone has greatly risen in value, owing to the supply having been almost cut off through the Amir of Afghanistan having placed the traffic under restraint and imposed a heavy export duty. The stone known to the natives as *suleimani* (a form of Purbeck marble) has similarly and for the same reason assumed an almost prohibitive price, though a large proportion of the stone comes from the Salt Range in the Panjab.

A very attractive series of stone-work of both jade and Purbeck marble has been received from Bhera, of which the best specimens are a square chess table of Purbeck marble inlaid with mother-of-pearl and dark green jade, Rs. 2,500; two tables in green jade, inlaid with Purbeck marble, with accompanying *suráhis* and tumblers in the same materials (Plate No. 17); two sets of afternoon-tea services cut in green jade, with tray for the same, in Sialkot gold damascened ware, all by Muhamad Amin; as also numerous small jade caskets from Rs. 30 to Rs. 600. The specimen that attracted most attention was a book-rest in pale green jade bound in gold damascened steel. This was purchased by His Excellency the Viceroy. (See Plate No. 74, fig. 7.)

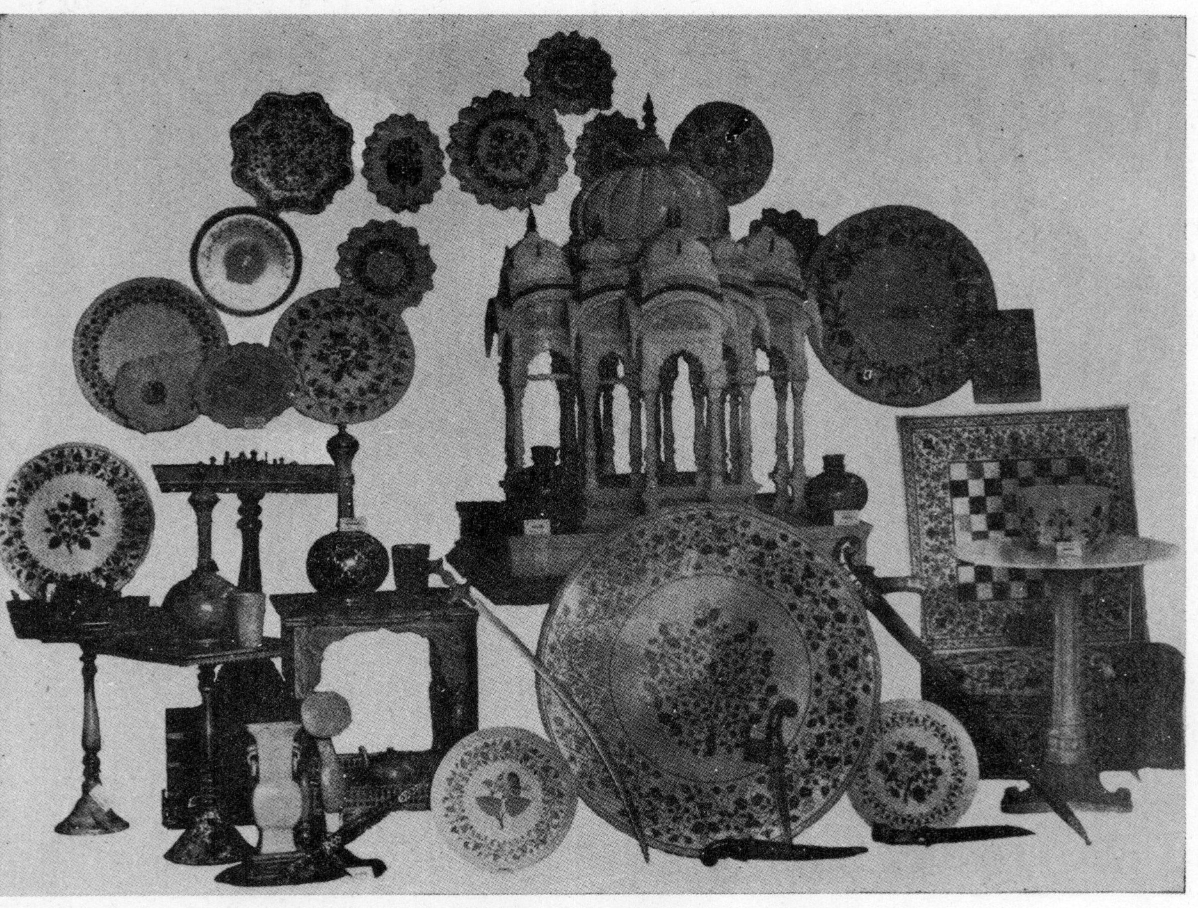

Plate No. 17 Collection of Lapidary Work including Stone-inlaying

Jewelled Jade.—Cups, *hukka*-bowls, caskets, sword and dagger handles and such like articles, made of Indian false jade or foreign true jade, are often richly jewelled. A large collection of these beautiful objects will be seen both in the Loan Collection and Jewellery Galleries. Plate No. 75 shows a few of these, the two *hukka*-bowls (figs. 7 and 8) being procured from His Highness the Maharana of Udaipur, the central vase (fig. 2) from His Highness the Maharaja of Kashmir—a trophy of the subjection of Leh—and the dagger (fig. 1), a weapon of great interest, exhibited by Babu Madho Das of Benares. The exhibitor says of it that it was "presented with other valuables by Lord Cornwallis, after the death of Tippu Sultan, to the ancestors of Babu Madho Das (*alias* Madhoji), the present owner, who had lent the Government of the day three crores of rupees to prosecute the war." It is for sale, and has been priced at Rs. 1,00,000; but it may be added that the rubies, emeralds and diamonds are beautifully carved: the weapon in addition to its historic interest is one of great intrinsic and artistic merit.

From Banda has been received an old jade casket with gold ornamentation, price Rs. 750.

Historic facts.

Agates and other Minor Gems.—The lapidary workers of India have been known from the remotest antiquity. "The agate vases of Broach and Cambay have been famous under the name of Murrhine vases from the time of Pliny."—(*Birdwood.*) "It is probable that the polished and cut pebbles of India have been spread over the world to an extent of which few people are conscious. It is said that the pebbles which the tourist or visitor is induced to buy at many well-known sea-side and other resorts in Europe, as mementos of the place, have not only been originally produced but have been cut and polished in India. If it be so, the trade is a more creditable one than that which sends sham jewels to Ceylon, because the stones are really what they pretend to be, true pebbles, and they are often extremely beautiful objects."

Cut Pebbles.

CAMBAY AND BANDA STONE WARES.—A feature of the pebble trade of India that is not very generally known may be here mentioned, namely, that the stones can be and are largely coloured

DIVISION 8. LAPIDARY WORK.

artificially. The following particulars may be given from a long and interesting report written by Mr. J. M. Campbell :—The stones are collected near the village of Ratanpur near Cambay, and classified into two sorts, *viz.*, those that should be and those that should not be baked. The stones that are not baked are a form of onyx called *mora* or *bawa-ghori*, the cat's eye or *chashamdar* or *dola*, and a yellow half clear pebble called *rori* or *lasania*. All others are baked to bring out their colours. After exposure to the sun or by being baked in a fire of cowdung, light browns become white and dark browns deepen into chestnut. Of yellows, straw colours become rosy, and orange is intensified into red; other shades of yellow become pink. Pebbles with cloudy shades become converted into brightly veined stones in red and white. Red cornelians range in colour from flesh colour to blood red. The deeper and the more uniform the colour the greater the value. So again, the larger and thicker the stone, the more is it valued.

Baked Carbuncles.

Agate Cups.

From Cambay has come to the Exhibition an extensive series of agates, carbuncles, etc., in the form of cups, sword-handles, caskets, beads, brooches and the like. The prices of these range according to size and quality. Boxes 3 to 4 inches in size are from Rs. 30 to Rs. 40; sword-handles, about Rs. 70; and a set of large chess-men, Rs. 375. Large red carbuncles suitable for brooches vary from Rs. 3 to Rs. 10. A similar collection of moss agates, etc., has been received from Banda and from the pebble-works of Jabalpur, some of the finest being valued at Rs. 100, while others are only Rs. 2 and Rs. 3. Similarly, Banda has contributed a large assortment of knife-handles in bluish green pebble at Rs. 3-8 each, and an extensive series of buttons, studs, and other small ornaments. (*Conf.* with Plate No. 74.)

Moss Agates.

Banda Stones.

Garnets.—Cut garnets in the form of necklaces and other small articles of personal adornment constitute an important section of the lapidary craft of India. The chief centre in the production of these goods is doubtless Jaipur. The best stones are procured from the Rajmahal mines of Jaipur, from Udaipur, and from Kishangarh. The qualities known are the so-called amathystine or Oriental garnets, which are usually cut in the form of pendants for jewellery, and the more valuable noble or alamandine garnets.

A large assortment will be found both in this division as also in the Jewellery Gallery, and perhaps no very good purpose would be served by enumerating the separate articles. The chief merchants are Sugun Chund, Sobhag Chund, of Jaipur.

Rock Crystals—Are largely cut in various places in India and made into sword and dagger handles, into beads and other ornaments, or into buckles, necklaces and the like. These are turned out fairly extensively in Jaipur. The Kashmir so-called rock-crystal buckles are made of "paste diamonds" specially imported for the purpose. Throughout the Exhibition true rock crystal will be found utilised in various ways, but by far the most interesting series are doubtless the sword and dagger handles and the cups and *hukka* bowls in the Loan Collection. (See Plate No. 74.)

Crystal Cups.

Turquoise.—A large trade is done in India in the manufacture and sale of jewellery of various sorts made in turquoise. Perhaps with no other stone has the art of fabrication been carried to a higher perfection than with turquoise. Glass coloured on the surface is produced with all the defects natural to the true stone, so that, unless scratched to ascertain if the colour is only on the surface, it is next to impossible to detect the true from the false. To give a deeper shade, a surface dressing in colour is sometimes imparted to the true as well as the false stone. This may be instantly detected by rubbing the stone between the fingers with a little oil or butter. If the stone becomes lighter coloured on the side rubbed with the fat, it is of necessity either a false stone or a poorly coloured turquoise that has had its tint artificially deepened.

Imitation Stones.

The chief traffic in turquoise is from Kashmir, and within the past few years a new industry has arisen in that State in the production of picture frames and other small objects in copper, with a surface layer of fragments of false turquoise compacted by a cement. This has already been alluded to under Metals, but it is probable that the correct place for this modern monstrosity is in the present class along with true and false turquoises.

Turquoise Frames.

Rubies, Diamonds, etc.—It does not fall within the scope of this catalogue to deal with the traffic in mining, cutting, and setting

DIVISION 9. GLASS WARE.

the precious stones. The Jewellery Gallery has been specially set apart for this purpose.

Division 9.—Glass Ware.

From Patna, in Bengal, a consignment of glass has been obtained. A certain percentage of the forms are artistic and in good taste, but a still larger series has to be characterised as a miserable imitation of English ware, in bad taste and worse execution. In the Loan Collection Gallery will be seen some excellent *hukka* bowls in cut glass. Those from the Victoria and Albert Museum, London, are beautifully cut. If correctly identified, as Indian work, they display a knowledge in glass in the 17th and 18th Centuries that was infinitely superior to that possessed at the present day.

Division 10.—Inlaid Stone Work.

It seems desirable to separate as carefully as possible the inlaying of a stone from the piecing together of numerous small coloured stones, glass or pottery imbedded in cement, but not let into special excavations prepared for their reception. The words "Inlaid" and "Mosaic" sufficiently indicate these two kinds of work, and yet they are hopelessly confused by most writers. With a view to enforce their distinction, they have been referred below to independent Divisions, and from the circumstance that in India mosaic is mostly done in earthenware or glass and invariably set in cement, the mosaics have been placed under Class III, and treated as examples of cement work (see page 96).

History of Indian Inlaying.

From the nature of the designs employed, Sir George Birdwood has ably upheld that the Inlaid work of the Táj of Agra and the other great Indo-Saracenic monuments of India is in all probability an indigenous art. It has for many years been contended by other writers that it was purely and simply Florentine *pietra dura* introduced into India by Austin de Bordeaux. This latter opinion rests upon two circumstances: (*a*) certain examples, such as the tablet representing Orpheus charming the animals (Plate No. 17-A, fig. 5), a portrait that has been presumed to depict Austin himself, and (*b*) the fact that Father Da Castro, who lived in Lahore at the time the Táj was under construction, is said to have told Father Manrique (who arrived in India in 1640.) that the Táj was designed by a Venetian architect named Geronimo Verroneo and the inlaying done by the Frenchman, Austin de Bordeaux. But the use of marble inlaid on red sandstone was well-known in India long before the Táj Mahal was conceived. This will, for example, be seen at the tombs of Toghlak Humayún, near Delhi. By Akbar the art of encrusting coloured stones on a marble or sandstone surface was freely substituted for colour tiles and tile mosaics. Itmad-ud-Daula's tomb is to this day one of the most beautiful examples of inlaying, and this was completed in 1620, while the Táj Mahal was not finished until 1648. On the other hand, many of the flowers vividly depicted in the inlaid marble of the Indo-Saracenic tombs and palaces could hardly have been familiar to the stone-workers of Agra and Delhi, such as the tulip, the iris and the Imperial lily, though as ornamental designs they became so completely engrafted to the art that at the present day they are carved and inlaid with a life-like accuracy that is singularly remarkable. What is even still more curious, as designs they are known to the stone and wood-carvers of Northern India by names utterly unconnected with the vernaculars for these plants in the alpine tracts where they are to be found.

Floral Designs used.

The glory of the higher art manufactures of Indian stonework may be said to be this inlaying on marble. The great centre for the craft is doubtless Agra, though in other parts of India it is not unknown. The inlaid marble work of Bharatpur is in some respects superior to that of Agra. The usual style is marble inlaid with the inferior gems, such as agate, cornelian, lapis lazuli, etc. The following may be mentioned as the best example on view in the Sale Gallery:—a circular table made by Nathu Ram & Sons, of Agra, Rs. 437, the prevailing feature in the ornamentation being pale yellow roses with pink buds. Next comes a chess board, price Rs. 1,625, the border panels being broad and rich with numerous pink flowers; a round plate with undulated rim and elaborate red and green floral designs, made by Nathu Ram & Sons, sculptors of Agra, Rs. 312; a similar plate with a wreath of ivy and spray of jasmine, made by Behari Lal & Sons, of Agra, Rs. 62; a circular plate inlaid with mother-

Inlaid work on View.

DIVISION 10. INLAID STONE WORK.

of-pearl, by Nathu Ram & Sons. From Bharatpur have been received three marble slabs, the most important being an iris pattern panel. Lastly, from Mysore has come a large slab of bluish marble richly inlaid and the design derived from the flowers of the gourd, a modern conception that re-appears in Mysore carved ivory.

On Plate No. 17-A, fig. 4, will be seen a bowl made at the suggestion of Mr. Percy Brown from designs in the Táj. This obtained the silver medal of the Exhibition. None of the present-day examples approach in beauty of design and richness of colour the admirable series of Agra inlaid work sent to the Loan Collection Gallery by C. W. McMinn, Esq., I.C.S., of Hill Tipperah. On Plate No. 17-A will be found three of these most admirable examples, *viz.*, figs. 1, 2 and 3. The first is a charming vine scroll, in which the bloom of the grape is attempted by the separate pieces of which each fruit is constructed. The second is a chess board with a perfectly life-like tracery of the passion flower; while the third is a circular table in bold encircling scroll of conventional flowers.

Awards for Stone Ware including Inlaid, Marble and Stone Mosaics.

(*a*) *Architectural work.*

First Prize with gold medal for the Bharatpur house in white sandstone, done in the style of the palaces of Díg.

Second Prize with silver medal to the Jodhpur *Jhároka*, in three colours of sandstone and carved in the characteristic style of stone-carving met with in Rajputana.

Second Prize with silver medal to Agra white sandstone doorway.

Third Prize with bronze medal to the Mirzapore fireplace and overmantel.

Commended for stone-carving, Suba Bhika of Gwalior.

(*b*) *Lapidary work.*

Second Prize with silver medal for green jade book-rest (*rehl*) (No. 21); jade *suráhi* and tumbler (No. 44); also Purbeck marble *suráhi* and tumbler with table inlaid with mother-of-pearl, made by Mahomed Amin of Bhera.

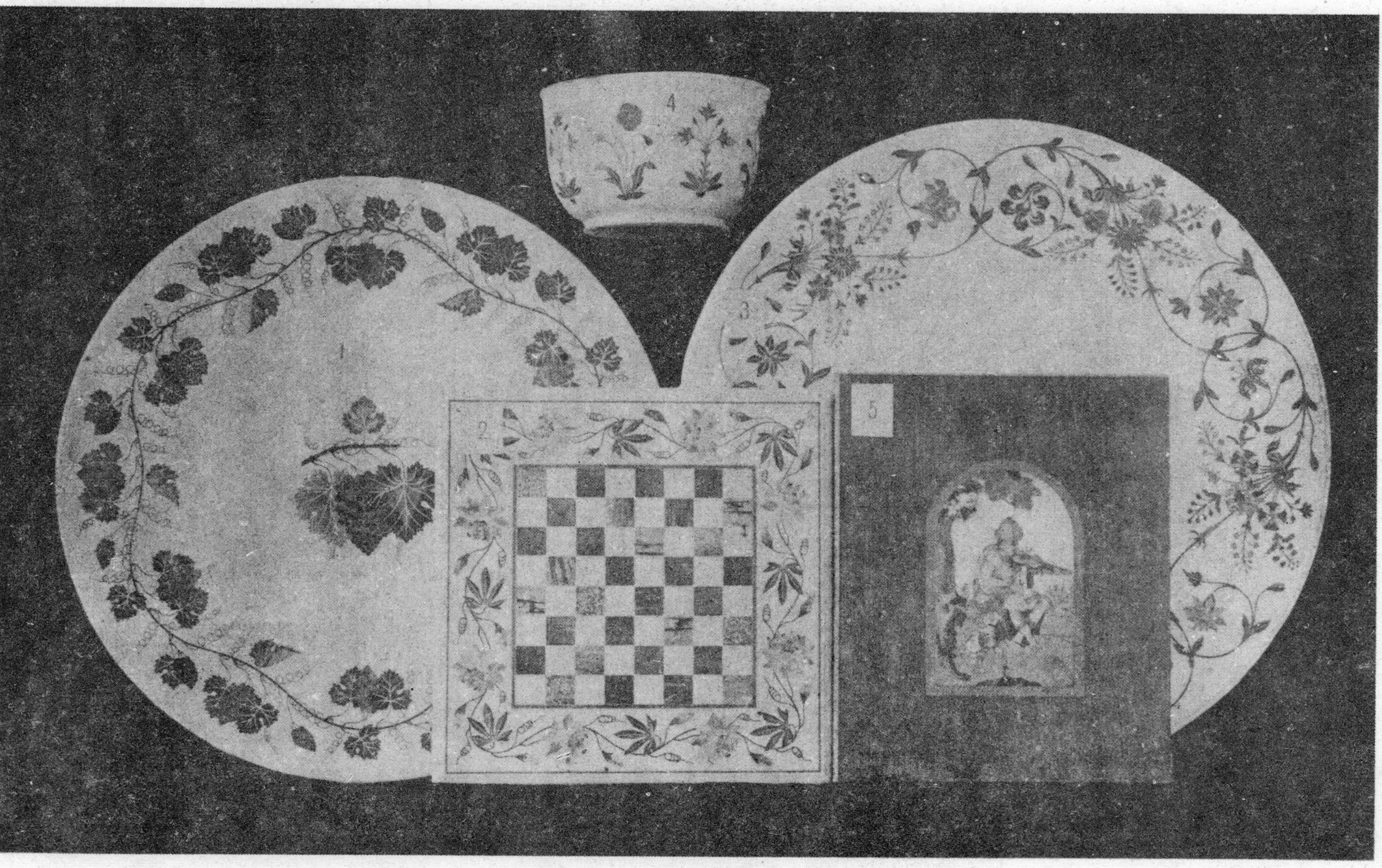

Plate No. 17-A Selected Inlaid Stone Work

Third Prize with bronze medal for collection of lapidary work (knife-handles, moss agates, etc.) by Lal Khan of Sudder Kotwali, Banda.

Commended for collection of lapidary work, mostly in agate and cornelian, exhibited by the Cambay Darbar

(*c*) *Glass Ware.*

Commended—a collection of Patna Glass in native shapes and forms made by Ahmad Hasain.

(*d*) *Inlaid Marble.*

First Prize with silver medal for bowl (No. 940) made by Behari Lall and Son of Agra.

Second Prize with bronze medal for three reproductions of inlaid marble panels at the palace of Díg (especially one with erect spray of Hibiscus in flower) awarded to the Bharatpur State.

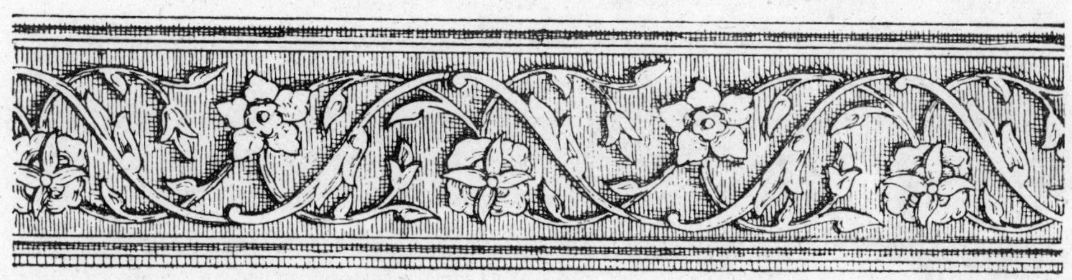

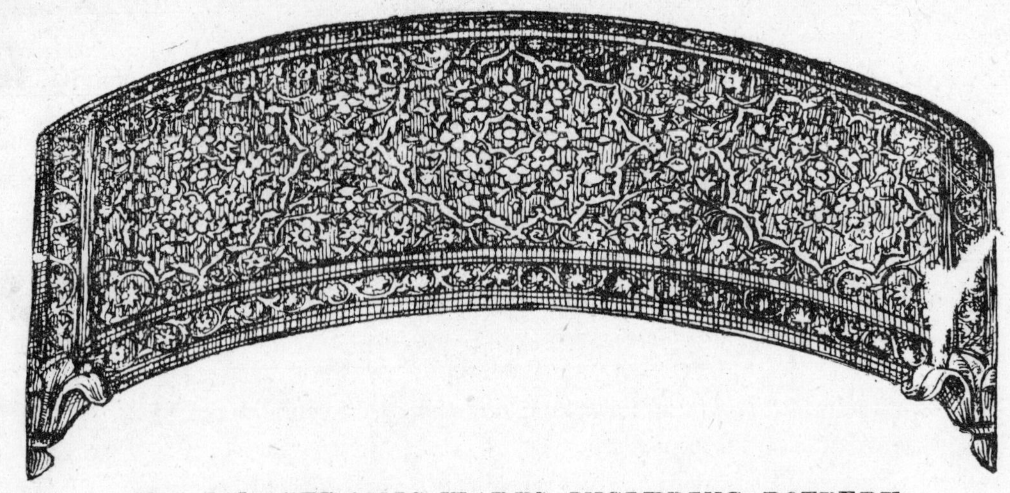

Class III.—CERAMIC WARES, INCLUDING POTTERY, CLAY MODELS, PLASTER AND CEMENT WORK, MOSAICS, Etc.

DIVISION 11. POTTERY.

THE articles under this Class have been referred to the following:—

Division 11. Pottery.

Division 12. Plaster-of-Paris and Cement work—Mosaics.

The absence from India of a good and abundant Kaolin has doubtless greatly retarded the higher developments of the potter's craft, but perhaps less severely than the social and religious customs of the people. There are three widely different classes of pottery—(*a*) that produced by aboriginal tribes, (*b*) by Hindus and (*c*) by Muhammadans. According to Hindu observance, pottery is easily defiled and has to be broken whenever polluted, since it cannot be cleansed in the same way as brass. So again pottery has to be thrown away on certain prescribed occasions, whether polluted or not. Thus has come into existence an immense traffic with the Hindus in cheap rubbish, but no demand whatever for higher class pottery. The artistic skill of the Hindu potter or *kumhár* has in consequence been developed in the manufacture of jars in which to store grain, spices, pickles, rather than in the production of eating or drinking vessels. Where not intended for use with water, glazing would be almost unnecessary, and very possibly the prevalence of painted or lacquered, in place of glazed pottery, in the hands of the Hindus, is due to this circumstance. With the Muhammadans it may safely be inferred the glazing of

Glazing unnecessary.

DIVISION 11. POTTERY.

pottery originated with the production of the tiles used in the ornamentation of their tombs and mosques, even although with them no religious objection existed against the employment of earthen vessels for eating and drinking purposes. It may accordingly be inferred that in India the introduction of glazed earthen vessels was subsequent to the establishment of even the earliest Muhammadan dynasty. There are possibly two exceptions to this view, namely, (*a*) the appearance of glazed pottery among the Dravidians of South India, and (*b*) the fragments of glazed pottery found in the Charsada excavations in the Peshawar district.

Ancient Pottery.

In VELLORE, in North Arcot, there has survived an art in glazed pottery that seems to have been more widely known in South India than at the present day and to be of indigenous origin. Sir George Birdwood figures and describes identical pottery to that of Vellore as being produced at Madura, during the time when he wrote his *Idustrial Arts of India*. The writer made careful inquiry recently, on two separate occasions, while in Madura, but could find no trace of such pottery. Terra-cotta assumes a greater importance, however, with the Hindus of South India than in the more Northern tracts, and pottery of high quality and in a style quite unlike that of Northern India is produced at numerous centres. One of the best accounts of South Indian pottery was that written by Surgeon-General G. Bidie, while in charge of the Madras Central Museum. He specially mentions that of Sivaganga, Madura, Udiyagiri, Salem, Vizagapatam, Kistna, Godaveri and others. The habit of constructing large earthenware animals, to be placed in sacred groves near human dwellings, may have had much to say to the accumulative style of architecture peculiar to the Dravidians. From about the fourteenth and fifteenth centuries terra-cotta gods and animals, etc., have at all events been extensively used in the ornamentation of both temples and dwelling houses, and the art of glazing pottery, as already remarked, seems to have been there spontaneous, not acquired.

South Indian Pottery.

But the potters, whether Hindu or Muhammadan, are referred to two septs—the *kumhár* or village potter who as a rule

Two Septs of Potters.

DIVISION 11. POTTERY.

produces non-glazed pottery and confines himself to the ordinary articles of household and agricultural use; the artistic potter or *kuzagár* (*kashigárs*) who makes artistic wares (*kágazi*), often glazed. In the latter case he is usually a Muhammadan, though there are notable exceptions, such as the Hindu *kuzagárs* of Delhi. It also frequently happens (as in Multan) that the chief art workers (*kuzagárs*) do not make their own pottery, but purchase sun-dried vessels from the potter (*kumhár*). There are thus many powerful arguments in favour of the opinion that the glazed pottery of India, as generally accepted by art collectors in Europe, originated with the Muhammadan traffic in coloured tiles, used in mosques and tombs. When the demand for these goods declined, the art of the *kuzagár* was diverted to the production of jars (*martabáns*), *surāhis* and such like ornamental wares. It would also appear fairly certain that every 10 to 20 years, for some time past, has witnessed radical changes in this modern demand for glazed art pottery. For example, the series of samples selected from the Calcutta International Exhibition of 1884, and deposited in the Indian Museum, Calcutta, when contrasted with the collections at present on view at the Indian Art Exhibition of Delhi, shows that not only have the designs and schemes of colour, formerly characteristic of each school of work, changed, but they have deteriorated in character, finish and purity of colour. The cheapening process and larger demand, like the makers' names (but in even more glaring characters), have been stamped on every sample. They have each and all lost the little individuality they possessed and mainly through the attempt at copying each other. What a few years ago would have been called Jaipur has gone back again to its original home, Delhi; Jaipur has become Persian; Khurja and Rampur have become inferior Multan; Multan has become Halla; and Halla, Bombay. It can hardly be a matter of surprise, therefore, that the older collections of Indian pottery, such as that of South Kensington Museum, London, bear little or no relation to the Indian pottery of the present day, and hence it may almost be said that Sir George Birdwood's Plates (Nos. 71, 72, 73 and 74) do not portray the Sind pottery as now understood.

Change.

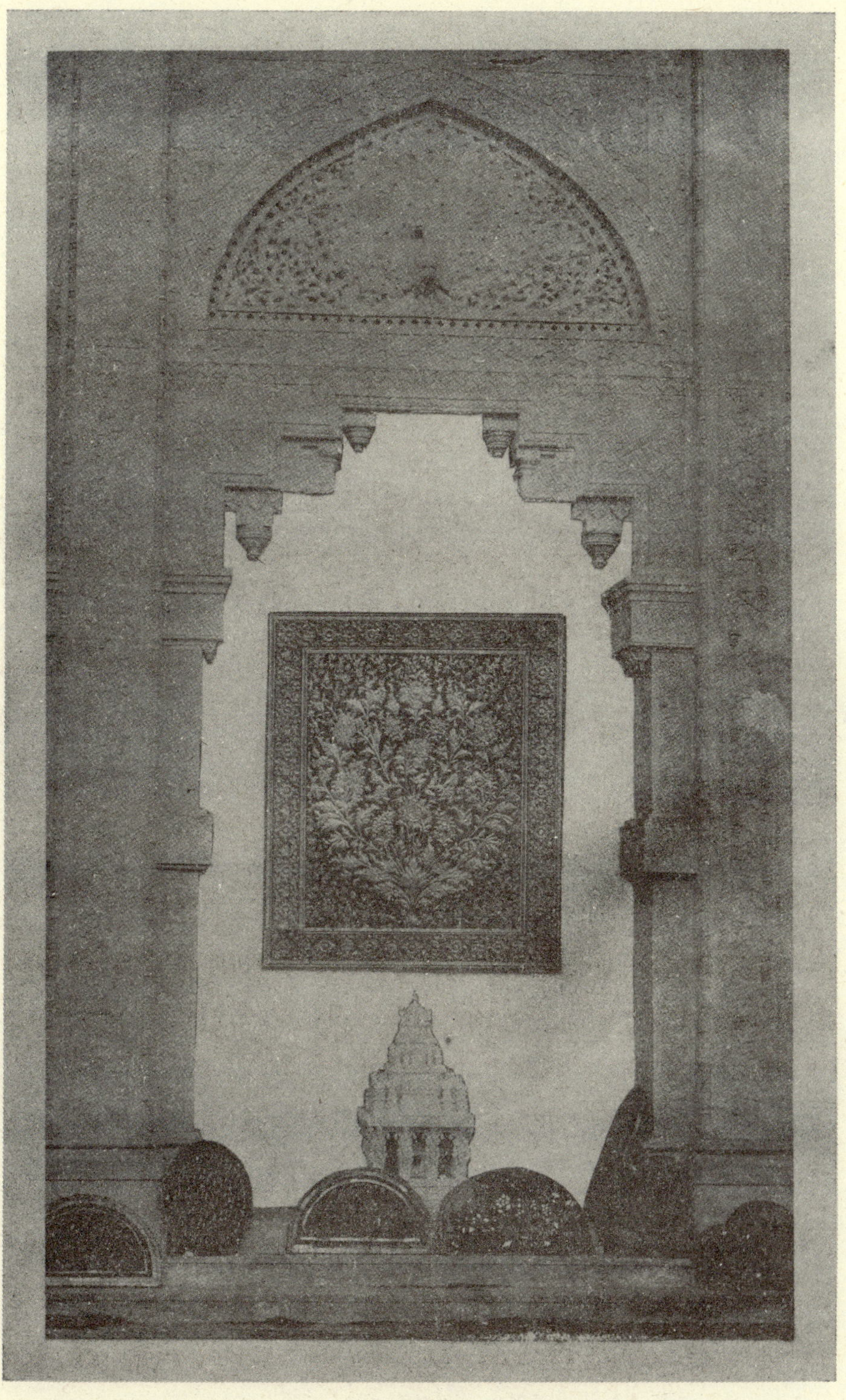

Plate No. 18 Plaster of Paris and Cement including Transparencies and Bikanir red and gold panels

Every-day Pottery.

All have changed, and changed for the worse. But when one turns from the so-called ornamental or glazed pottery to study the unglazed and painted wares, the story that has to be told is distinctly more interesting and less disappointing. The shapes of the *kalasas* or water jars, of the *kapálas* or cooking pots, of the *pátras* or platters, of the *sarakás* or goglets, of the *lotás*, and other such vessels, are not only graceful but highly instructive. The hand of change has less severely affected these articles. It accordingly seems possible that, were a complete series of all the pots used in carrying water, or in boiling rice, or in holding milk, etc., to be collected from each and every race of people and from all parts of the Empire, much of great interest would be learned, not only from the standpoint of the arts and industries of the country but as object lessons in historic and anthropological sciences. The shapes vary with every few hundred miles, and are severely isolated according to the races of people and the traditions of the country. The primitive methods of ornamentation shown on them might also afford suggestions of great value in the study of Indian decorative art. All this has been very nearly neglected and the scholars of Europe and America may be said to have been groping in the dark, with fragments of prehistoric pottery, while the prototypes of many of the most instructive forms and designs they are dealing with, are still produced by the village potters of India and might be studied with great advantage.

A valuable study.

In the Indian Museum, Calcutta, the writer attempted some few years ago a classification of the ceramic collections of that institution into:—

Classification.

(*a*) Unglazed or terra-cotta pottery:

(*b*) Painted or stained and varnished but not glazed pottery:

(*c*) Glazed pottery.

This serves a useful purpose, since over large tracts of India the art of glazing is quite unknown, though highly ornamental pottery is nevertheless produced. Of painted pottery there may be said to be two kinds—painted or stained *before firing*, and painted, lacquered or stained *after firing*. While the art of glazing may thus be quite unknown, a high proficiency is often attained in colouring pottery. The materials and methods employed for this purpose are extremely local and such as to remove any doubt as to their being indigenous. In fact they are frequently exceedingly ancient crafts, much more so than that of glazing, which in Northern India at all events does not very possibly date further back than the fifteenth century. Unglazed pottery has been abundantly proved to be closely associated with the earliest Buddhist remains and the tumuli of South India (Salem). According to some writers Chingiz Khan, after his conquest in China in 1212 A.D., brought back with him a Chinese wife, and through her the Chinese art of glazing pottery is believed to have been carried to Persia and subsequently to India, more especially Sind. Be that as it may, the oldest building in India with glazed tiles still on it, is the Killa Koná mosque of Delhi, which dates from the middle of the sixteenth century or toward the close of the Pathan dynasty. With the solitary exception of the glazed pottery of Vellore, already mentioned, all the present-day glazed pottery of India is essentially of Muhammadan origin It is Indo-Saracenic in design, is made mainly by Muhammadans, and until quite recently was sold exclusively to Muhammadans. From being designs originally intended for the ornamentation of mosques and tombs, it has by the modern demand been diverted to the construction of ornamental jars (*martabáns*), *surάhis* and the like, so that it is not after all to be wondered at that it should show a tendency to drift from one condition and style to another, according to the caprice of demand.

Muhammadan Glazed Pottery.

Division 11.– Pottery and Clay Modelling.

With these introductory remarks it may now be desirable to discuss the various forms of Indian pottery separately. Since, however, few, if any, of the examples of unglazed and painted pottery have been received at Delhi, it may suffice to deal with the unglazed and painted forms very briefly and to devote greater detail to the glazed ware

(A) Unglazed or Terra-cotta Ware (Bhande).—This is met with all over India, but certain localities are more especially famed for the superior quality of their crude pottery. Commencing from the north, the following may be given as those of greatest merit:—Hazara, Bannu, Jallandhar, Gujranwala, Bhawalpur, Jaipur (Bassi), Jodhpur (Gudha), Alwar, Seoni, Ahmedabad, Pattan in Baroda, Kholapur, Broach, Ratnagiri, Kanara, Aligarh, Azamgarh, Chunar, Jabalpur, Ranigunj, Sewan, Dacca, Khulna, Assam, Pegu and other parts of Burma, Vizianagram, Rajamundry, Madura, Salem, Coorg, Malabar, Travancore, etc.

Designs.—In some cases it is made so thin that it has been called *kágazi* (paper pottery). Of this nature may be mentioned the terra-cotta of Gujranwala, Bhawalpur, Alwar, etc. In other instances a design is moulded on the surface by the fingers prior to its being fired. The best example of this may be said to be the classic-like designs of the Aligarh pottery. But by far the most instructive patterns are those adopted by the village potters. They consist for the most part of fancy lines, cut as the plastic material is revolving on the wheel, or are imprinted from blocks kept for that purpose. Occasionally a higher art is manifested when the designs are incised or carved on the half-dry surface.

Black Pottery.

Black Pottery.—Much has been written on the subject of the colour and polish or varnish given to these forms of pottery. From a vast antiquity black pottery has been made and extolled, such as the black antique ware of the Greeks. There are many places in India that have a high reputation for this kind of pottery, such as Sewan and Khulna in Bengal; Azamgarh and Aligarh in the United Provinces; Ratnagiri in Bombay; Madura in Madras; and Tavoy in Burma. The black colour seems almost invariably to be produced by the same process, *viz.*, the confinement of the smoke during firing and the supply of some material within the kiln that will generate much smoke. In the finer work of Sewan and Azamgarh, the articles are fired within a closed jar so as to prevent contact with the flame, the jar being placed within the kiln. Alongside of the articles that are to be blackened is usually placed some damp straw and cow-dung or oil cake. But before being fired the pottery is polished and painted or washed with a special preparation called the *kabis*. This is comprised of yellow earth (a form of fuller's earth) known as *piari mitti*, of powdered mango bark and of *sajji mitti*, or crude carbonate of soda. It is used with all the finer qualities of unglazed pottery, the confined smoke of cow-dung being the additional ingredient that imparts the black colour.

Varnish.—The range of vegetable substances used in the same way as the mango bark in the above preparation is very remarkable, and in each case it is claimed that these vegetable ingredients give the *kabis* its polishing property over the clay. One that may be here mentioned is the polishing material employed at Seoni in the Central Provinces, *viz.*, the bark of the *tensa* tree. So again the leaves of the bamboo and of the *vasaka* (*Adhatoda Vasica*) are employed in certain forms of *kabis.* Oil is also largely used and seems to effect some change on the consistence or grain of the pottery even although the firing must be supposed to destroy the oil itself. In Hoshiarpur the glaze consists of *biroza* resin (*Pinus longifolia*) dissolved in turpentine and mustard oil, burned into the clay much as in the tar used during the time of Herodotus.

Colours.—To impart colour to the whole surface or portions of the surface, the vessels are coated with special clays or coloured earths, such as ochre (*geru*), chalk or talc (*abrak*). These take the place of the *engobe* or *slip* in glazed pottery, the material given beneath the *fritt* or glaze. The wash with special earths is thus an initial stage in the higher forms of the ceramic art. In fact, all that is missing from painted and stained pottery is the use of a flux such as borax, common salt or oxide of lead, with the paint. The heat employed in stained non-glazed pottery is also not sufficient to fuse the materials. Colour is thus imparted before the firing, and is fixed by the firing without the formation of a glaze. The most skilled craftsmen in this more or less specially Indian form of pottery, are nearly invariably Hindus. The *kumhárs* (the makers of water pots,—*kumhá*— as their name implies) are poorly paid but hold an honourable position in the village community, and are as a rule much respected.

Lac-coated Pottery.—After being fired, unglazed pottery is often smeared with lac and other substances to make it impervious to fluids. The black and red pottery of Madura, for

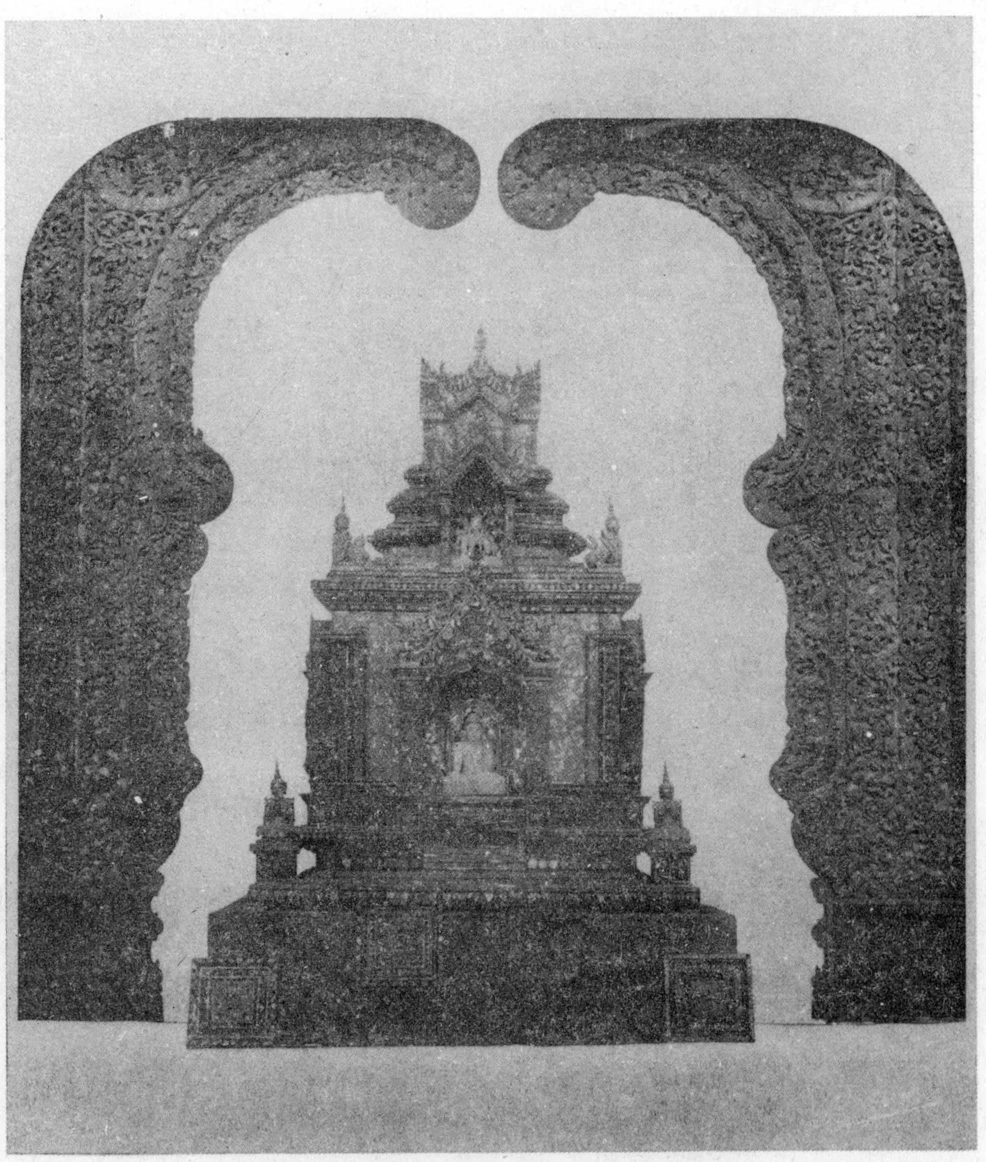

Plate No. 19 Mosaic Work and Glass Wares (showing in back-ground Burmese Carved wood as a wall decoration)

example, according to Dr. Hunter, is smeared with a mucilaginous material obtained from a species of *Abutilon,* over the stained surface. Much has been written on the antiquity of smearing pottery with a black or red inner layer and of polishing the surfaces of vessels in place of glazing them. This is practised in many parts of India, such as in the preparation of the toddy pots of Gujerat, lac being the substance in most general use. So also in Panipet pottery is extensively used that has been coated with a thin layer of lac. Dr. Bidie observes, of the ancient pottery of South India, "In some cases the external surface has a varnished appearance which was produced by rubbing it with the seeds of a *Gyrocarpus* and burnishing. Some of the cup-like vessels of the cairns are covered in the interior with a black lacquer-like varnish." It was the smearing of the surface of pottery with coloured bees-wax that led to the name encaustic pottery and in India lac, a far superior material, is simply substituted for the wax.

Lac smeared.

Encaustic Pottery.

In RAJPUTANA, pottery is sometimes coated with many layers of differently coloured lac, one layer over the top of the other; a pattern is then elaborated by scratching through so as to reveal the various colours.

(B) Painted Pottery and Models.—The centres that have attained the greatest repute for their painted pottery are:—Peshawar, Jallandhar, Hushiarpur, Jhajjar (in Rhotak), Pind Dadan Khan, Gujranwala, Rawalpindi, Bhawalpur, Lahore, Kota, Amroha, Lucknow, Atraula (in Gonda), Sitapur, Sasseram (in Shahabad), Salem, Madura, etc.

A volume might be written on the art conceptions manifested by this craft. The colour is given after the pottery has been fired. It is in fact the school from which much of the modelling and painting of India has been evolved; it is intimately connected with the production of idols and other sacred objects and with the frescoing of the walls of temples and houses: hence is utterly unconnected with the kindred Muhammadan art of glazing pottery. The black pottery of Pind Dadan Khan, painted in red, is as different from the gilt painted pottery of Peshawar and the yellow and red painted ware of Lahore as it is possible to imagine. The less pretentious colourings of the rural pottery of India, like

DIVISION II. POTTERY.

those of the Nicobar Islands are, however, far more ancient and very much more interesting than the designs shown on the Indian pottery usually found in collections. While the majority of the designs are undoubtedly Hindu in origin, others are closely associated with one or other of the great Muhammadan dynasties.

Sasseram Pottery.

There could hardly, for example, be anything more surprising, to the student of Indian art, than a visit to Sasseram in the Shahabad district, in order to study the wonderful tomb of Sher Shah, a splendid building in the later Pathan style which dates from 1545 A.D. Suddenly, while passing through the hamlet that now marks what must at one time have been an important town, the visitor has his attention directed to the remarkable industry that there survives in painted pottery. This would seem to be the sole remnant of a school of art that most probably was focused around the first great Muhammadan administrator of India—Sher Shah. It is Pathan (Turkish) in feeling and would seem to have lived through all the past ages without having either assumed importance or migrated a hundred miles from its present location. This curiously interesting pottery is of no intrinsic value but nevertheless deserves recognition. It has been too long neglected, in fact, by collectors of Indian art, for it has much to teach. And yet it has not been so much as mentioned in any of the Manuals, Art Journals or special Monographs that have appeared on the Art Manufactures of India.

In art design it stands as distinct from the painted (non-glazed) pottery of Gonda, Peshawar, Lahore and other places as it is possible to imagine. It is floral, and consists of rosettes assorted on a distinctly geometric plan. The colours chiefly used are white, yellow and blue (the last being varnished into green), on a dull ground colour. In Gonda the field is usually green and the flowers red and yellow. In Sasseram there is a Hindu-like exuberance and profusion of colour out of all keeping with the solemnity and dignity of Sher Shah's tomb, which is possibly alone to be accounted for by its greater antiquity.

Models.—The modelling, painting and dressing of clay figures, proceeds primarily from the preparation of idols. It is in consequence essentially a Hindu art. The centres of this work are Poona, Lucknow and Krishnagar, though every village has its potter who turns out idols and toys in clay.

DIVISION II. POTTERY.

For some years Poona models have practically ceased to be made and the Krishnagar modellers, while they have failed to advance above the preparation of toys dressed in actual cloths, have steadily raised their prices to a prohibitive extent. In Lucknow, on the other hand, a high standard has recently been attained in the production of artistic terra-cotta models. Indeed, the series of these sent to Delhi was of such merit that it was decided to place them in the class devoted to Fine Art instead of under this division. It is satisfactory to have to add that they were subsequently awarded a gold medal by the Judging Committee.

Lucknow models.

(*C*) ***Glazed Pottery.***—The glazed pottery of India may be said to be mainly produced at the following places, commencing from the north while moving east and west to south:—Peshawar, Lahore, Jallandhar, Sialkot, Delhi, Jaipur, Ajmir, Bikanir, Multan, Tatta, Hallá, Kach, Bombay, Bharampur, Bulandshahr (Khurja), Rampur, Lucknow, Jabalpur, Allahabad, Mirzapore, Ranigunj, Vellore, Coorg, Malabar (Feroke) and Burma. The collection shown at the Indian Art Exhibition is fully representative of these various centres.

PESHAWAR.—(*Plate No. 20, fig. 1.*)—The pottery of this northern town has been spoken of as resembling majolica. It is a rough "*faience*." The reddish earth body or "paste" is coated with a dressing in white earth—the "slip" or "*engobe*" which consists of a preparation of *karia mitti* or chalk, obtained from the Khaibar. It is then dipped into the glaze of which the basis is lead oxide. For the ordinary greenish white pottery, nothing else is needed. But when it is desired to ornament the plate or jar, the design is outlined on the unburnt glaze, with a paint made of manganese, and the details are filled in with a preparation of copper. When burned, green leaves, outlined in brown, are produced on a dirty white. Sometimes the glaze is more thoroughly fused and the colours then run and the brown takes a purplish tint. Further colours are red, obtained from a red earth, and black, from a stone of dark colour—both procured from the Khaibar. Blue is produced from *lajaward* or cobalt. The prevalent form is green

Indian Majolica.

DIVISION II. POTTERY.

Peshawar.

and pink on a milky white, but in the earlier work the patches of colour were assorted so as to give, at a distance, the effect of bunches of flowers. Recently shades of blue and green alone have been produced with hardly any attempt at artistic effect. The glazing seems, however, to have improved and the pottery has come much more largely into competition with the imported Russian, Chinese, Dutch and English pottery for which there is a large local demand. Pottery is so extensively used in Peshawar that it would seem desirable every effort should be made to educate the local potters in the higher flights of their craft with a view to checking the imports. It has been pointed out that one of the chief difficulties in this direction is the restriction imposed on the sale of lead by the local authorities.

DELHI and JAIPUR.—(*Plate No. 20, fig. 4.*)—The pottery of these towns has a peculiarity of great interest. It is not made of clay but of ground felspar (*burbura*) mixed with gum or starch. It cannot, in consequence, be formed on the potter's wheel but has to be moulded or wielded by the hand. It is known locally as *kám-chíní.* The art appears to have originated in Delhi, the chief artist, some 30 years ago, being a Hindu *kumhár* called Bhola. It seems probable that the suggestion for its production arose from a desire to compete with the imported jars, known as *martabáns,* and which came to Delhi all the way from the fort of that name on the coast of Burma. These jars were in demand for the purpose of storing pickles and were at first made in shape and colour to exactly resemble the imported article. Later on they were ornamented, but only in response to the European desire did they become ornate. One of the pupils of Bhola was induced to join the School of Art, Jaipur, and thus gave birth to the fairly large modern demand in Jaipur pottery. In the Indian Museum, Calcutta, some of the examples of Delhi pottery, produced by Bhola, are placed almost side by side with Pegu (*Martabán*) jars, obtained direct from Burma. Their similarity in shape and material is very striking. At first the designs and colouring adopted by the Delhi potter were strongly Hindu in feeling and coloration, but later on they became (perhaps in imitation of Multan) much more Muhammadan and then consisted of rich shades of pale blue

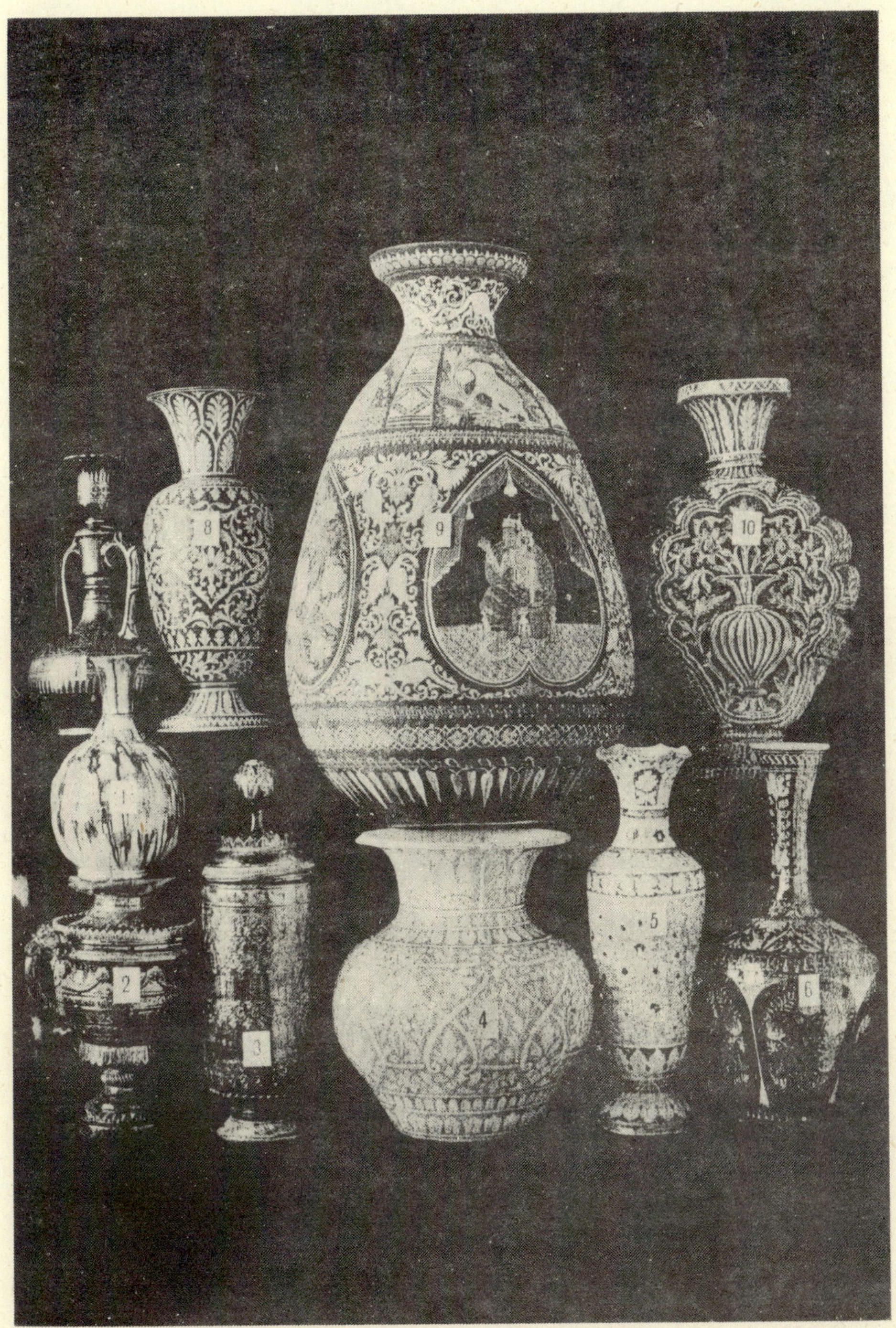

Plate No. 20 Certain Forms of Indian Pottery

(occasionally also green) on a granular but pure white surface.

Jaipur formerly differed from Delhi and attained its reputation and traffic through the use of two shades of blue—cobalt and turquoise—on a very pure opaque white. Recently Jaipur has turned its attention to modern Persian models and has produced pottery with an admixture of green leaves and brown and yellow flowers that to most persons is distinctly inferior to the older work.

MULTAN.—(*Plate No. 20, fig. 5.*)—Long anterior to its production of vases, plaques and other such ornamental wares, Multan, like Halla and other towns within or bordering on Sind, had a large trade in the production of glazed tiles. The close proximity, geographically, of Sind and Beluchistan to Persia and the intimate relation that for long existed between these two countries, doubtless accounts for many of the specially Persian characteristics of the arts of this north-western section of India. The ancient buildings of Sind and Beluchistan are mostly in brick, the ornamentation accomplished being chiefly by tiles. The oldest tomb in Tatta dates from 1572 A. D. (the year in which Akbar annexed Sind) and others up to the date of the tomb of Nawab Amir Khan, 1640 A.D., are all richly adorned with tiles in cobalt and turquoise blues on a white ground. These were the prototypes of the pottery of Halla, Tatta and Multan, until the demand for novelty dictated the series of changes that have marked the downward course in the traffic. That the artistic pottery of Multan like that of Sind originated with the production of tiles and for centuries lived through the demand for such goods, may be viewed as confirmed by the circumstance already mentioned, namely, that the *kashigárs* of Multan do not make the clay pots, vases, *surāhis*, etc., that they paint and glaze, but purchase them from the ordinary village potter or *kumhár*.

Some few years ago the spirit of the times, dictated doubtless by the vicissitudes of trade, led the *kashigárs* of Multan to imitate the greens, yellows and browns, as well as the blues on a blue (not white) background, produced fairly successfully in Sind. The result may be described as most disastrous. The depth of the blues and whites of Multan, which was the glory of

DIVISION 11. POTTERY. the evolution of centuries of patient study and discovery, has been completely effaced. The work of to-day is slovenly, the design weak and the colours dull and unfeeling. The modern work, with its abortive efforts at new colours, manifests so serious a decline from that of even 20 years ago that the death blow may be said to have been given to the industry.

Munshi Sher Mohamed, Painting Master of the Lahore School of Art, has kindly furnished the sketch, Plate No. 20-A, as also that of the Multan *kashigár* at work with characteristic wares around him. This has been given as the title-page of this publication. On the bottom of that illustration (and at the writer's suggestion) has been shown a border design taken very faithfully from a panel of lotus pattern found on a stone slab derived from the Buddhistic remains of Gandhara. The original is in the possession of the Lahore Museum and may be taken as dating from some time before the birth of Christ. It portrays life from youth to manhood, old age and death, the water (*bhavsagar*) being the eternity of existence. This beautiful conception is crystallised into the arts of India and appears again and again both in Hindu and Muhammadan decoration, but hardly, if ever, in such vivid portraiture as that of the early Buddhistic stone-carvers.

SIND and BOMBAY.—(*Plate No. 20, figs. 6 and 9, respectively.*)—The pottery of these two centres may be taken conjointly since it is well known that the Bombay School of Art, on its organising a class of pottery, imported from Halla its foremen potters. On this account doubtless arose the close similarity of much of the pottery of Bombay, as understood at the present day, with that of Sind. A little later, however, Mr. Griffith (then Principal of the

Ajunta Pottery. School of Art) gave the pupils of the pottery class a new conception when he caused them to follow the ancient Buddhist designs and schemes of colour depicted by the frescos on the walls of the cave temples of Ajunta. These two styles have passed down and given to Bombay the reputation it has attained of possessing art pottery. The town of Bombay (in fact the Presidency of Bombay if Sind be excluded) had no glazed pottery prior to the establishment of the ceramic class and pottery works in connection with the School of Art.

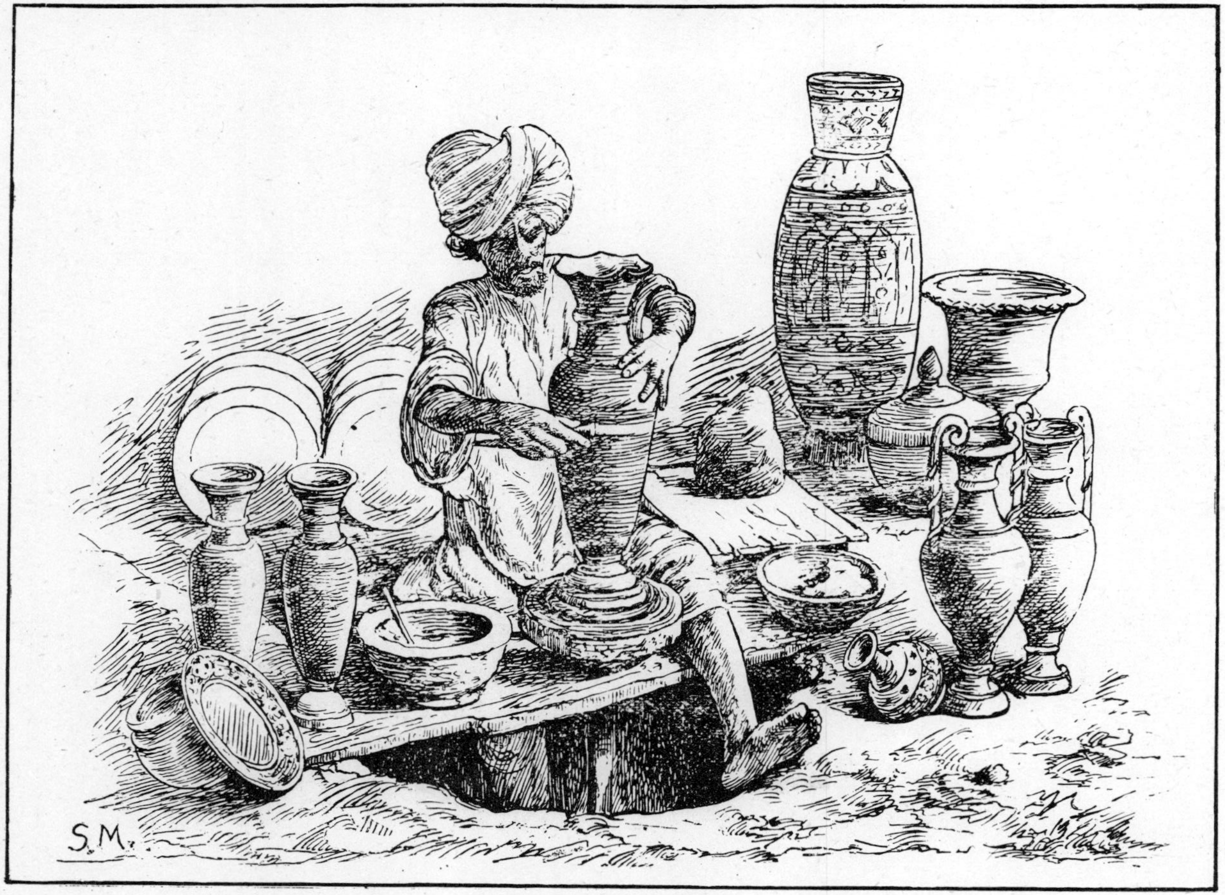

Plate No. 20-A Indian Potter

Sind pottery admirably represented by Sir George Birdwood's Plates Nos. 70 and 75 (*Industrial Arts of India*), may be said to have consisted until quite recently of two forms—(*a*) vases, etc., for domestic use and ornament, and (*b*) tiles for the decoration of tombs and mosques. The former were curiously enough usually made in two or at most three shades of the same colour. If blue, the ground was in pale blue and the pattern in one or two shades slightly darker. If yellow, the ground was the palest shade and portions of the design were almost brown in colour. So with the greens. But usually the floral ornamentation was assorted within panels or medallions, the flowers being in a lighter shade than the local panel field. But a peculiarity of Sind pottery that at once separates it from Multan may be here mentioned, *viz.*, the pattern is first painted with a white slip then by the colour. This raises it slightly above the level of the field. The tiles were nearly always like those of Multan, white field with blue design.

Within the past few years the Halla potters have taken to imitating the floral designs introduced by the Bombay School of Art, with anything but a happy result.

BULANDSHAHR (KHURJA) and RAMPUR.—(*Plate No. 20, figs. 8 and 10, respectively.*)—The style of work turned out in these two localities is so very similar, at the present day at all events, that there would be little advantage in keeping them distinct. Originally Khurja produced a peculiar style of pottery of its own, the pattern being raised by the use of slips into slight relief. It consisted of a warm orange brown or pale claret coloured field with slightly darker floral designs picked out in white and blue. A little later it took to producing the same style of work in a rich green-blue. Rampur was originally famed for its deep green-blue *surâhis*, in one uniform colour and without any pattern worked on them. A little later it took to ornate work in one or sometimes two shades of green-blue with a pattern distinctly moulded above the surface. Now-a-days both Rampur and Khurja manufacture articles in quaint shapes such as the undulated forms of the pumpkin, the constricted melon (beggar's

DIVISION 11. POTTERY.

bowl) and the flat water bottle, etc. Very recently Khurja has taken to imitating Multan, with ridiculous results. Its blues are dull and faded and the design devoid of soul.

Green Pottery.

VELLORE in NORTH ARCOT.—(*Plate No. 20, figs. 2 and 3.*)—Mention has already been made of this pottery. It is manufactured from a fine pure white clay that on the potter's wheel yields readily to the most delicate treatment. It burns into a beautiful light coloured and firm terra-cotta that lends itself readily to glazing and painting. When not glazed it is very porous and clean and in the form of *surâhis* or water bottles, with a double or outer perforated protecting shell, is largely used and much appreciated for the cool water that may be drawn from such bottles after being stored for an hour or so. When glazed it is either in a clear emerald green or deep dull brown. In the former a beautiful effect is produced through the colours having run during firing, thus giving a marbled or shaded effect. The ornamentation is chiefly by dog-tooth-notching of the edges and by the stamping of patterns on the plastic material.

Martabán Jars.

BURMA.—The pottery of Burma, more especially of Pegu, has been famed from ancient times. Sir Henry Yule gives several references to the *martabán* jars, dating back to 1508. In the provincial Gazetteer the remark occurs that "Pegu Jars are still made and are still popular, but they are no longer exported even to India, where indeed they have learned to make them." On the other hand Mr. Lockwood Kipling while discussing the question of the jars made in Delhi and which bear the vernacular name of *martabán* observes: "In 1869 the writer, while passing through Delhi, purchased a number of jars and took them to the London Exhibition of 1870 where their fine texture of glaze, a rough duck-egg like coating, was admired by connoisseurs, notably by the late Mr. Fortuny, a celebrated Spanish painter, then visiting England. One of these articles, by the way, happened to be marked *martabán*, the native name for a jar, and was afterwards described on a museum label as coming from Martaban, a port on the Burmese coast." This curious story has a double interest in that it proves the comparative antiquity of the Burmese ceramic art

DIVISION 11. POTTERY.

and the very modern character of the application of the Indian potter's skill to domestic purposes. There would seem little doubt that the *martabáns* sold in India, a century ago, were entirely imported from Burma and were distributed as regular articles of trade even to such remote inland towns as Delhi.

The most curious forms of Burmese pottery are the quaint urns used for storing the ashes of the *Hpungis*. But the *Martabán* jars and water vessels are by far the most interesting. In shape and method of treatment of the clay and of the colouring materials, these might be placed alongside of the classic pottery of ancient Greece and Rome without attracting more than a passing observation of being a slightly different kind, in a remarkably good state of preservation.

It has been upheld that Burma acquired its knowledge of pottery, more especially its glazed wares, from China. There seems some truth in this surmise since the best work is turned out in proximity to the Shan States or by people who have been largely influenced by the Shans.

Division 12.—Plaster-of-Paris and Cement work.

Many parts of India may be said to be famed for their marble-like cement-work, stucco or *chunám*. This is made with lime, mixed with sand and either plaster-of-paris or powdered marble and very often sugar, or some glutinous substance such as the gum from the *bel* fruit. When patiently beaten and smoothed almost until quite set, it assumes a remarkably hard consistence and an exceedingly fine polish. In Bikanir the walls of houses so coated are beautifully carved, just as the stucco is about to set. The head-piece to this chapter (page 80) shows a portion of a carved ceiling in a ruined summer house in the Kudsia gardens, Delhi. This may be described as a form of *sgraffito* and when quite dry is usually most elaborately painted and gilded (see middle of Plate No. 18). Throughout Rajputana a curious art exists in which *jálís* or perforated panels, made in plaster-of-paris, are sawn through their thickness into two sheets or are separately made and subsequently united by liquid plaster after fragments of coloured glasses have been placed within the perforations. Panels with coloured glasses so made are used as

DIVISION 12. PLASTER-OF-PARIS AND CEMENT WORK.

transparencies. A few of these panels have been laid on the ground on Plate No. 18.

Although Gypsum exists abundantly in India, plaster-of-paris, except as an ingredient in certain cements, does not seem to have been ever used by the natives as a moulding material. The numerous figures that have been found in the prehistoric remains of India, made of plaster, were clearly carved, not moulded.

Mosaics.—In the Exhibition numerous examples of mosaic work will be found, in most of which cement or simply plaster-of-paris has been used as the impacting and imbedding material. In Udaipur the pattern is drawn on paper. Glass is then cut into the desired shapes and gummed over the portions of the design as required for each colour. When finished, the paper with its adhering design in glass is inverted over a carefully prepared bed of partially dry *chunám.* The glass is pressed home into the *chunám* and left in that position until the bed has dried and set completely. The paper is then washed off when the glass mosaic is seen on a polished *chunám* or marble-like surface. In some of the more recent of the ndo-Saracenic palaces the ceilings are done in rich geometric design made of fragments of mirror glass set in cement. This is known as *shísh* work. Mr Kipling has carefully described the mirror mosaic work in the Shish mahal or glass palace of Lahore "The building," he says, "is the work of both Shah Jahan and Aurangzib; and the more gaudy portions are due to the later times of the Sikhs. The effect of this *shísh* or mirror mosaic, though brilliant, narrowly escapes the charge of vulgarity. The principle on which the work is constructed, particularly in its application to ceilings, is identical with that of many examples at Cairo, and in other places all over the East."

In Burma the material used to fix the glass in the mosaics is the sap of a tree known as *thítsí.* In the Exhibition there will be found numerous examples of Burmese glass mosaics, from the shrine placed within the refreshment room to the numerous panels that will be found in the stall devoted to mosaics generally.

Of pure plaster-of-paris work some admirable examples will be found, such as the statues by the Bombay sculptor, Mr. G. K.

Mhatre: the figures made by the various schools of art: the model of a Dravidian temple by the School of Arts, Madras, and lastly the great triple arch that forms the facade of the refreshment room already described in the Introductory Chapter. **DIVISION 12. PLASTER-OF-PARIS AND CEMENT WORK.**

AWARDS FOR POTTERY AND GLASS WARES INCLUDING CEMENT AND PLASTER-OF-PARIS WORK.

(*a*) *Pottery.*

First Prize with gold medal for series of clay models that will be found recorded under Class X, Fine Arts. **AWARDS.**

First Prize with silver medal to the Bombay School of Art for collection, unglazed pottery.

First Prize with silver medal for Nos. 1 a plate—*rikabi*—and for a blue glazed jar from Multan made by Golam Hosain.

First Prize with silver medal for collection of pottery, more especially vases Nos. 1106, 1137, 1609, also tiles on facade of building made by the Jaipur School of Art.

Second Prize with bronze medal for vases and *rikabis* (Nos. 412, 417, 328, 356 and 377) made by Muhamad Husain of Multan.

Second Prize with bronze medal for vases (Nos. 2710, 2723 and 2993) to Abdul Hafiz, Potter, of Khurja in Bulandshahr.

Commended for plate—*rikabi*—(No. 275) made by Ahmad Buksh of Khurja in Bulandshahr.

Commended for dark blue *guldan kalan* (No. 3666) also *changail suráhi* (No. 3690) made by Nabi Buksh, Rampur City.

Commended for collection of green pottery, more especially (No. 725) the tall tubular jar and cover made by Arunachella Udayan of Karigeri, Vellore.

(*b*) *Glass and Earthenware Mosaics.*

Commended for earthenware mosaic panels shown on main façade of building made at Lahore School of Arts.

Commended for glass mosaics exhibited by the Udaipur Darbar.

Commended for glass mosaic shrine set in *thítsí* made in Rangoon.

(*c*) *Plaster-of-paris and Cement Work.*

Second Prize with bronze medal for triple archway made by pupils of the Mayo School of Art, Lahore.

DIVISION 12. PLASTER-OF-PARIS AND CEMENT WORK.

Commended coloured and gilded *sgraffito* panels (Nos. 2110, 2111 and 2114), reproductions from Bikanir Palace made by Bhura Usta and Sita Ram.

Commended for model of Dravidian temple (No. 3687) made at the School of Arts, Madras.

Commended for panel of plaster-of-paris mosaic (No. 2777) exhibited by the Udaipur Darbar.

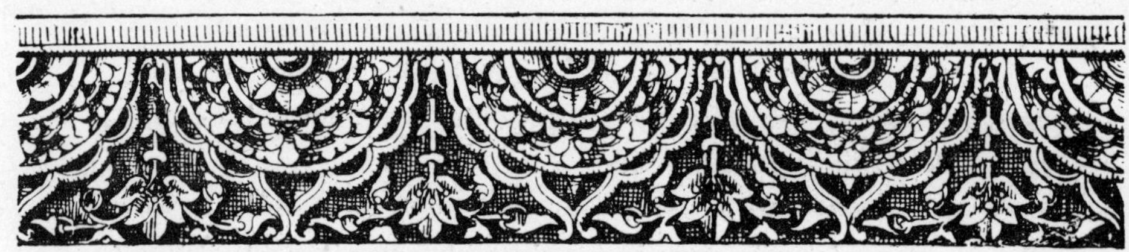

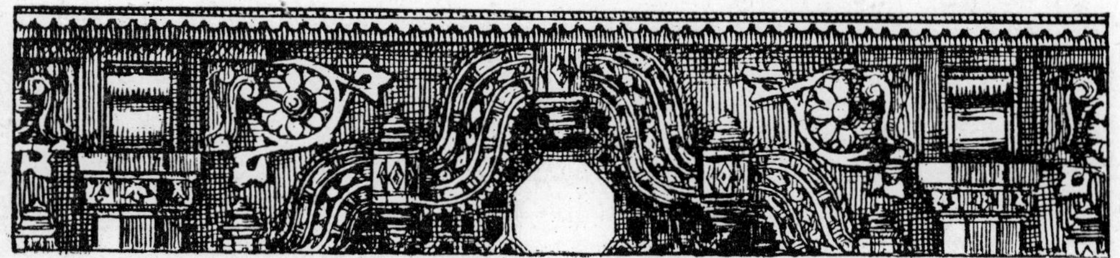

Class IV.—WOOD-WORK.

DIVISION 13. WOOD-CARVING.

THERE is perhaps no feature of Indian Art that manifests so great a diversity nor so many points of interest as that of wood-work. Fergusson has pointed out that none of the constructive buildings of India have an antiquity anything like so great as that of the excavated temples. He explains this statement by the opinion that, as in Burma to the present day, temple and house construction was, in ancient India, entirely in perishable wood and hence the antiquity of the cave temples may be relatively determined by their degree of departure from a purely wooden to a lithic conception. The earliest constructive buildings, moreover, show their undoubted wooden origin by the presence of unnecessarily large stones, by the survival of essentially wooden constructive features, by the dove-tailing and bolting together of the parts, by the production on the turning lathe of the pillars and by the absence of any knowledge in the use of cement. It will thus be seen that no aspect of Indian Art can have so much to teach the student as that of wood-work. It has a vast antiquity but in addition has been influenced and diversified in each important section of the Empire by the texture of the most abundant and most suitable timber, and by the religious sentiments and racial peculiarities of the people. With no very great effort the migration of forms and designs and the social evolutions and eruptions of succeeding races, can be

Wooden to Lithic Forms.

Modifying Influences.

DIVISION 13. WOOD-CARVING.

followed in the wood-carving. A grammar of decorative art might, in fact, be written from the study of wood-carving alone, and the circumstance that the wood and stone-carvers belong to one and the same caste, may be accepted as an additional evidence in favour of the gradual production of the one from the other and that at no very ancient date. Both in Peshawar in the extreme north of India and Rangoon in further India, the tradition exists that wood-carving originated in connection with boat-building—a by no means improbable circumstance.

In a brief work, such as the present, it would be undesirable to expand this line of reasoning further. The object has been served by the few remarks already made, *viz.*, to advise the reader of the historic importance of the carpenter's craft and the rich assortment of constructive and decorative designs that may be looked for in the splendid display of wood-work on view within the Exhibition. As met with in architecture, furniture and cabinet work,

Methods of Ornamentation.

wood is ornamented in various ways such as by carving, inlaying, veneering, painting, lacquering, etc. The chief woods employed

Timbers Employed.

for ornamental work in India are teak, *shisham*, *deodár*, sandal-wood, ebony, walnut, *tun*, *ním*, Madras red-wood (sometimes called black-wood), *dudhi* or white-wood, red-cedar, *sal*, *rohira*, *babul*, jack-wood, etc., the order enumerated being approximately that of their importance. The art conceptions seen in wood-work have been greatly influenced by the grain of the timber employed, such as the deep under-cutting and sculpture that is possible with teak, red-wood and walnut, the low relief of *shisham* and *deodár*, the incised designs of ebony, the intricate and minute details of sandal and the barbaric boldness of *rohira*, *sal*, and *babul* (*kikar*) and other coarse grained and hard woods.

Divisions Formed.

The following are the divisions that have been established, and the arrangement of the collections, in the order in which assorted within the Exhibition, commencing from the eastern extremity and passing to the western end of the Main Gallery:—

Division 13. Carving for architecture, furniture and cabinet work.
Division 14. Inlaying with other woods, with ivory, etc.
Division 15. Sandal-wood, Engraved, Inlaid, Veneered.

DIVISION 13. WOOD-CARVING.

Division 16. Veneering, Appliqué, Marquetry, Lattice-work (*pinjra*), in woods, metals, porcupine quills, tortoise shell, etc.

Division 17. Painted, Stained, Imitation Inlaying (with matallic amalgams), etc.

Division 18. Papier maché and Imitation Papier maché.

Division 19. Ornaments, Toys, Models, etc.

Division 20. Minor wood-work, *e.g.*, engraved fruits, pith work, etc., etc.

It may be desirable to discuss these divisions in detail and to allude to the more noteworthy examples of each that may be seen in the Exhibition. The importance of this subject may be judged of by the circumstance that household furnishing and ornamentation, in the European acceptation, might almost be said to be unknown to the simple primitive life of the Native of India. All must have a *chárpai* (a bedstead) and with the peasant this is made of variously ornamented feet and bamboo shafts, with the prince, of ivory, silver or gold—they are identical otherwise. Caskets for jewels, *pán-dáns* and *attar-dáns*, a few quaint oil lamps, and occasionally a trunk for the storage of State-robes, also cushions and pillows, mats and rugs, floor and ceiling cloths, door curtains and wall drapings, hand punkhas and a few eating and drinking vessels, which, with the very poor, are in unglazed pottery or brass, with the middle classes in copper or brass ornamented, with the rich in silver or with the very rich in gold. Such may be accepted as a fairly comprehensive enumeration of the essentials of indigenous household furnishing. In some parts of the country low settees (*chaukis*) and reed stools (*moráhs*) are in demand but chairs and sofas are of modern introduction. Tables, knives and forks, crockery, glass-ware, table and wall ornaments and the like, are quite foreign to the Native mind and superfluous. Thrones and State-chairs have, however, been made from the most ancient times and are usually named after the animal or chief object portrayed, such as the "lion throne," "the lotus-lion throne," "the peacock throne," "the conch-shell throne," "the goose throne," "the pitcher throne," etc. Thrones are also named after the material used in their construction, such as "the golden throne."

Dwelling House.

Thrones.

DIVISION 13. WOOD-CARVING.

The reed or grass stool, made in hour-glass form and known as the *moráh*, is identical in shape with the lotus-throne on which the gods are represented in Indian sculpture and painting. Throughout the Exhibition *moráhs*, draped in Jodhpur printed cotton cloth, have been furnished in place of chairs.

Guest House.

In the houses of the rich, however, special apartments, furnished in European style (as a rule in the most tawdry and discordant fashion possible) are set apart for formal receptions or the accommodation of European guests. Some 30 years ago the late Mr. B. H. Baden Powell wrote that in India wealth was displayed by extravagant indulgence in foreign luxuries rather than in the barbaric pageants of former times. This is not only doubly true of to-day but it may be added that European ideas of comfort are steadily creeping into the every-day life of the people and accordingly a demand for household furnishing has set in, which, by careful guidance may assume vast importance to the carpenters and cabinet-makers as also to the other art craftsmen of India.

Division 13.—Wood-carving in Architecture, Furniture, etc.

Wood-carving.

There is hardly any necessity to separate wood-carving, as seen in Architecture, from that usually met with in Cabinet-work, since the peculiarities of the latter are in India of comparatively modern growth. The preferable course may be to deal with wood-carving in a provincial sequence.

1st:—Panjab wood-carving.—(*Plates Nos. 3, 21, 22.*)

Chief Types.

There are in the province four great types, with numerous local manifestations under each. These may be spoken of as the wood-work of the plains, produced by Muhammadans, Sikhs or Hindus, and that of the hills, turned out by aboriginal tribes controlled for the most part by what has been spoken of as "Tree and Serpent Worship" or still further to the north by the Buddhism of Thibet and China. In the wide range of work met with, the most powerful influence has undoubtedly been that of the Muhammadan. The Sikh art is but a recent adaptation from the Muhammadan, constructed on more or less Hindu lines, while the pure Hindu wood-carving (the most ancient of the three) may be described as a reintroduction into the Panjab and is seen in its highest condition, in the Eastern and Southern Panjab, such as in Ludhiana and Hissar. Most towns in the province, however, possess fine old doors of Hindu origin which carry down to us decorative designs that existed long anterior to the introduction of the Muhammadan style.

DIVISION 13. WOOD-CARVING.

Centres of Production.

The important centres for ornamental wood-work and furniture, in the Panjab, may be given as follows (in alphabetical order):—Amritsar, Batala, Bhera, Chiniot, Gujerat, Hariana, Hissar, Hoshiarpur, Jallandhar, Kashmir, Lahore, Ludhiana, Peshawar and Udaki. The essential features of the Muhammadan and Sikh work may be said to be their direct adaptation to *deodar* and subsequently very possibly to *shisham* wood. They are in consequence flat or in low relief, with little undercutting (except in the very recent walnut wood-carving of Kashmir). They are largely constructed on a geometric basis with the foliage elaborately veined and twisted and dispersed in diapers. Lastly in the modern Sikh and Hindu adaptations grotesque animal forms or mythological subjects are introduced freely. It is generally contended that the Sikh style of wood-carving took its birth in the towns of Amritsar, Batala, Hariana and Udaki, in other words in the districts of Amritsar and Gurdaspur.

Leading Characteristics.

In illustration of the varying styles met with, it may be said that in Bhera the imposed architectural forms, such as the pilasters, are in less than half relief, the panels are mostly floral and the carving in sharp, V-shaped section. The wood used is mainly *deodar*. In Chiniot, on the other hand, the pilasters stand out boldly, the panels are geometric, for the most part in *pinjra* (or lattice) work, and the carving is in rounded outline, dispersed within a rich diaper tracery. The strongly Arabic character of the framed or carved geometric (*pinjra*) panels is one of the most remarkable features of this work. A striking peculiarity also is the art of inlaying with brass. The wood used is *shisham*, known locally as *tahli*. In Amritsar there prevails a distinct renascent feeling, doubtless derived from the Golden Temple, and in Udaki occurs a remarkably flat style of work in arabesque design, a beautiful example of which will be found in the Panjab Room.

DIVISION 13. WOOD-CARVING.

In Peshawar the main feature is the very elaborate and minute *mauj* or *pinjra*-work done in walnut-wood (Plate No. 38). The pieces are dowelled together, not glued, but do not fall to pieces even when the frame is removed. As the result of a suggestion given in connection with this Exhibition olive-wood has been tried for the framework of *pinjra* panels. In Kashmir, of former times, the characteristic feature was the bold and effective (sometimes notched or carved) *pinjra*-work, in *deodár* wood, and the graceful geometric panellings (*khatamband*) applied to ceilings—a speciality of Kashmir so far as India is concerned. These are in pine wood and are cheap and most effective. Recently in Kashmir a most unfortunate departure has taken place into realistic carving in walnut, in which bunches of water lilies or sprays of *chunar* (plane) leaves are carved over the surface of tables or other articles, the one object apparently being to display a marvellous degree of undercutting but with a corresponding loss of art feeling. Throughout the Panjab, popular fancy has turned to under-cutting, fret-saw perforations and minute (in place of bold) *pinjra*-work. The change will, by most persons of taste, be admitted as of doubtful merit.

Recent Developments.

In Hoshiarpur inlaying with ivory or copper has been a peculiarity for many years past but perverted and distorted in adaptation to the demand for European house-furnishing (Plate No. 32). Simla, the chief centre of this trade so far as Northern India is concerned, has drawn on the craftsmen of Hoshiarpur and Jallandhar and given birth to every possible process of scamping and cheapening work. The chief demand for inferior work has, however, been in Europe and America, where small tables, picture frames, and brackets, in a most inartistic red-wood, have, for some years past, been exported by ship loads, with the starvation of the superior wood-carving industry of the province. In all low class work the fret-saw invariably displaces the *pinjra*-maker, cheap and more easily worked woods drive *deodár*, *shisham* and walnut from the market, while bone takes the place of ivory in inlaying. In these abominations, it is thought sufficient proof of an Indian character to introduce some portion of a mosque or temple, and that being done all attention to such details as suitability of design or nature of ornamentation can be disregarded

Cheap work.

DIVISION 13. WOOD-CARVING.

In Gujerat a large trade has been organised in modern furniture and materials and appliances for games, which, while not falling within the scope of an Art Exhibition, may in passing be mentioned as having attained high proficiency. Kartarpur in Jallandhar has similarly a great reputation for the manufacture of chairs on a wholesale scale. **Furniture.**

It may perhaps suffice to conclude this cursory sketch of Panjab wood-carving by drawing attention to the leading peculiarities of a door and a window. Beautiful examples of these will be found both in the division devoted to Architecture and in the Panjab Art-furnishing Room (Plate No. 3).

The Door or Chaukat.—Persons with any pretensions to social position, consider it essential to have a carved door. This in the Panjab is in fact a sign of position and wealth. No branch of wood-carving could be more instructive than a study of the doors met with in the various provinces of India. In the Muhammadan style of the Panjab the parts are severely conventional and isolated, being often purchased separately. The outer frame might be spoken of as many times larger than is actually essential. It embraces a series of panels both over the primary lintel and alongside of the jambs—the combined structure perhaps covering one-third of the total elevation of the house. It usually embraces two *mihráb* arches (one cusped, the other flat) supported on superimposed pilasters which are more or less imbedded. The contained panels are mostly in *pinjra*-work (or carved imitation *pinjra*) and thus elaborately geometric. The floral scrolls and tracery consist for the most part of rosettes assorted on a diaper. In the older and finer examples the over-door assumes the form of a sort of balcony, carried forward on cantilever brackets, the extremities of which are developed into a most fascinating series of pendants and tassels, a system spoken of as *Akbari*. **Muhammadan Style.**

Turning now to what has been called the Sikh and Hindu styles. The chief peculiarities of these are the great reduction in size of the frame; the absence of the projecting over-door; the fact that *pinjra* panels when present assume the condition of windows above the door rather than being integral parts of the **Sikh and Hindu Styles.**

DIVISION 13. WOOD-CARVING.

door itself; the frequent absence of the cusped *mihráb*; the door panels much more numerous and conspicuously carved: their assortment being often traceable to the *swástika* symbol; lastly, and by far the most strongly marked peculiarity of all, the substitution of life subjects, carved on the scrolls or in bold relief in the panels, in place of conventional designs and *pinjra*-work. In the scrolls it is customary to find that the same flower or fruit is rarely repeated while the effect desired is in no way marred through the profusion of vivid portraiture.

Vivid Portraiture.

Pinjra panelling is much more frequent in Sikh than in Hindu work, but more massive and less complex in design than in the Muhammadan, while the individual parts are at the same time carved or notched in elaboration of the pattern. It in fact more closely resembles the lattice-work of the Deccan and the perforated jamb panels (and fan-lights) of the Chalukyan architecture of the Southern Mahratta country, than the minute and intricate *pinjra* of the purely Muhammadan style, such as presently produced at Chiniot and Peshawar.

In the older and purer examples of Hindu door architecture and carving, such as those to be seen in the gullies of Lahore and in the splendid example on view in the Loan Collection Gallery (Plate No. 26, page 117) (which came from Chittor originally some 400 years ago), the entire structure is flat, devoid of superimposed or projecting portions and remarkable for its intricacy of design, its sharp crisp carving and its bold elaboration in detail. The higher portions of the carving look in fact as if originally prepared as blocks for the calico-printer, the edges of the minute incised pattern being brought to a smooth surface. There is little or no undercutting and, except in the over-door panels, no trace of the fantasy and grotesque which so often disfigure recent Hindu and to some extent modern Sikh work. In fact even the over-door, but for the insertion of a representation of *Ganesha*, is usually carved in a most curiously intertwined design as if portraying festoons of cloth and garlands of flowers, braced together into long interwoven lines.

Hindu Fantasy.

With all three forms (Muhammadan, Sikh and Hindu) the doors are as a rule studded with metal bosses or are overlaid with brass ornamentations, mostly in diaper form. The actual door

DIVISION 13. WOOD-CARVING.

which consists of two leaves, is hung on pivots, not hinges, and the overlapping portion (the parting bead called the *bindí* in the Panjab) is lavishly ornamented. In fact with the poor this is often the only part of the door that manifests any trace of wood-carving. In some of the older examples (such as the Chittor Door above alluded to) the *bindí* is however absent.

The modern Hindu and Sikh doors of the Panjab are so governed by Muhammadan influence that but for their vivid representation of living forms they can with difficulty be separated as distinct styles of architecture and carving.

***The Window and the Balcony* (*Bari and Bokharcha*).**—The former is usually flat and consists of a simple frame with a *mihráb* arch and spandrel (*mergol*) supported on pilasters, with, on the level of the floor of the room, a balustrade of one to three carved panels, closing in the lower third of the window frame. The shutters are often highly artistic and frequently glide upwards in one, two or three boards, instead of swinging on hinges sideways. The latter—the balcony or *bokhárcha*—is one of the most striking and beautiful features of Panjab architecture which in some towns is so popular as to be almost ruined through its very superfluity. It rests on an upturned lotus-flower masonry platform (*pendi*) which is often realistically painted, while the dome (*gumbaz*) is in the fluted lotus form. It is most frequently half hexagonal in plan, with three openings or windows. The windows (*bari*) are canopied by cusped arches, supported on the ordinary fluted pilasters (*tham*) and, as panels (*tili*), above the arch and as a balustrade, on the floor level, are placed *pinjra* frames. Excellent examples of miniature *bokhárchas* will be seen within the Panjab Room (Plate No. 3 and in Plate No. 22, fig. 3).

The Bokharcha.

CHIEF EXHIBITS ON VIEW.

Panjab Room and Balcony.—(*Plates Nos. 3 and 21.*)—By far the most instructive exhibit of this division may be said to be the small room specially furnished by the Mayo School of Art, Lahore, to exemplify the adaptability of the Panjab style to modern house-furnishing. The walls have been provided with a lofty dado, in illustration of the peculiarities of Bhera, Chiniot and Udaki wood-carving, while the balcony (Plate No. 21) which

Panjab Room.

DIVISION 13. WOOD-CARVING. opens into the Main Gallery, may be said to be one of the finest examples of the modern developments of Panjab (Sikh) wood-carving ever shown.

LAHORE WORK.—The School of Art has for many years past guided not only the workers in Lahore city, but throughout the province has striven to conserve and develop all that is beautiful in the various styles met with, the result being that Lahore itself practically combines the styles of the province. Plate No. 22-A shows a Panjab wood-carver at work on one of the brackets of the Panjab Balcony (Plate No. 21). Behind him has been placed a characteristic overmantel and on the floor a panel from the Panjab Room (Plate No. 3). The sketch has been supplied by Munshi Sher Muhamed. The following are the more noteworthy examples on view:—*Bokhárchas* from Rs. 20 to Rs. 50, tables, Rs. 40 to Rs. 45, by Lala Sant Ram (Plate No. 22, fig. 3).

AMRITSAR WORK.—(*Plate No. 22, fig. 2.*)—The carvers of Amritsar have perhaps the highest reputation of all the many skilled wood-workers of the provinces. Particular attention may be directed to the Cabinet, Rs. 500, the window (*bari*), Rs. 312, the tables, Rs. 100, shown by the well-known firm of Messrs. Devi Sahai Chamba Mal. A beautiful screen by Thaker Singh has been classed under *pinjra*-work though of course it might equally well appear under this division. It is offered for sale at Rs. 625.

CHINIOT WORK.—Although this town has a style of wood-carving of its own (already briefly described) it is best known for its brass inlaying on *shisham* wood. The most noteworthy cabinet maker is Mahommed Hussain.

JALLANDHAR.—The wood-carvers of this town have developed a style of their own that resembles that of the United Provinces. In Plate No. 22, fig. 1, is shown a rectangular table made by Barkat Ali of Jallandhar which has been purchased by His Excellency the Viceroy.

KASHMIR WORK.—The wood-carving of Kashmir State is so very similar to that of the Panjab that there would be no advantage in assigning it an independent position. The population of the State doubtless came mainly from India and brought with them their arts, somewhere in the 14th Century. In this respect

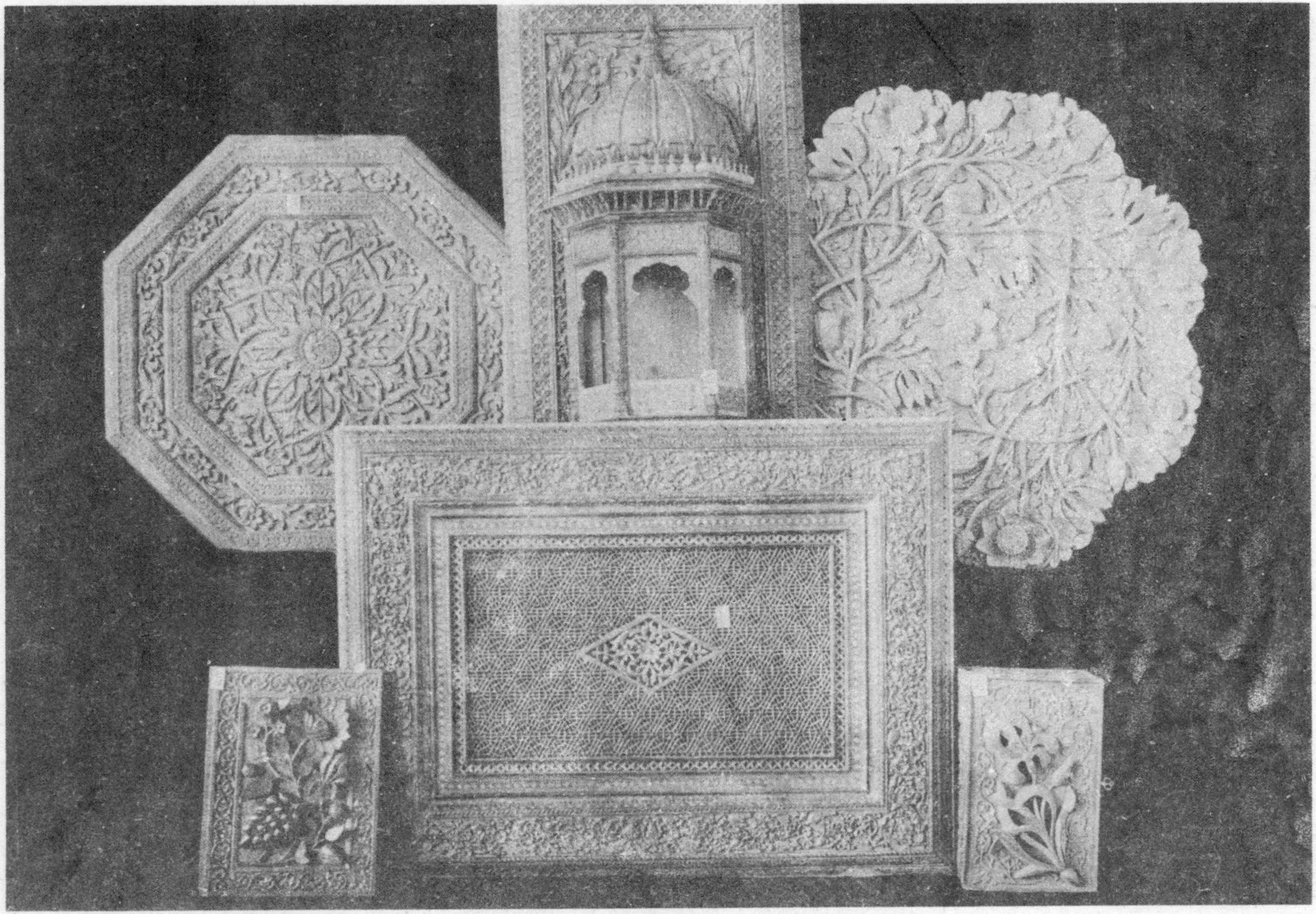

Plate No. 22 Punjab and Kashmir Carving

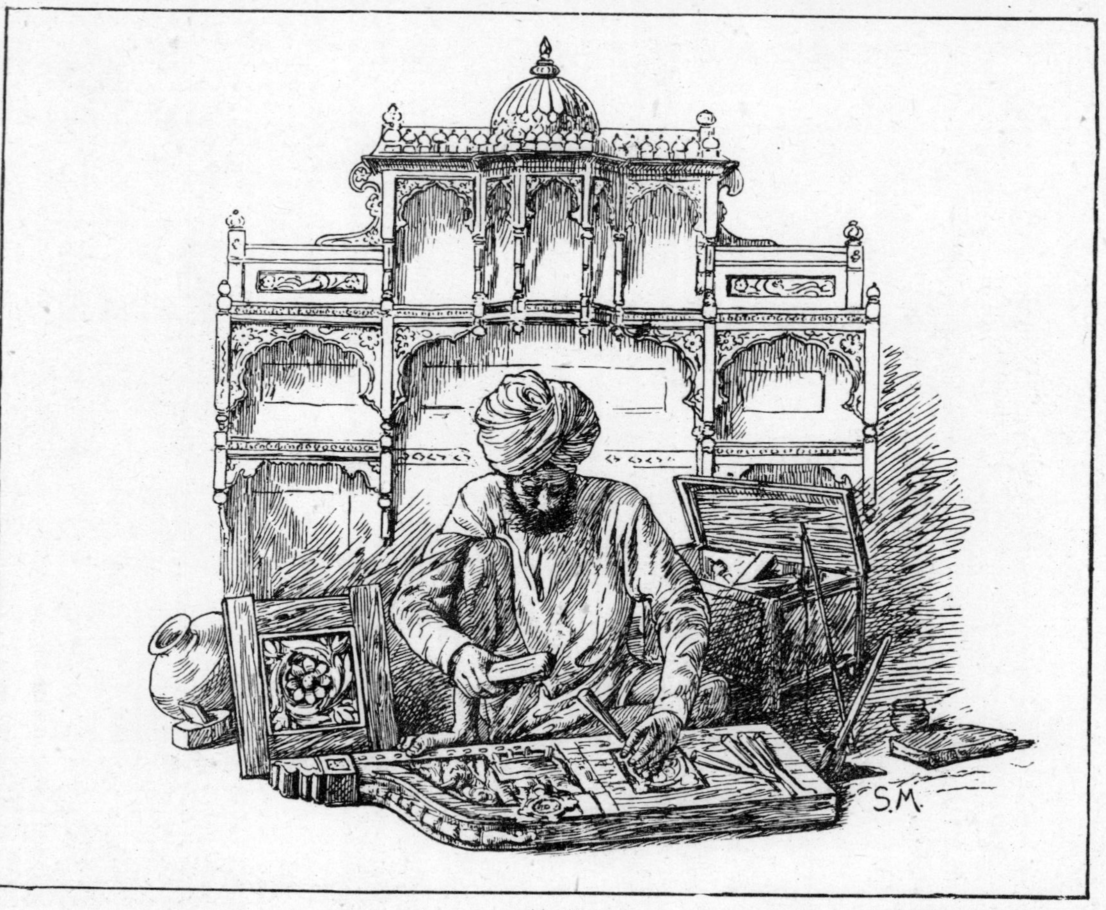

Plate No. 22-A Punab Wood Carver

DIVISION 13. WOOD-CARVING.

Kashmir is very different from the other great Himalayan State, Nepal, which drew its people and their arts mainly from the North. The present-day arts of Kashmir bear little or no trace of the Grecian Doric of its Martand, Avantipore and Bhaniyar temples (700 to 1260 A. D.), still less of its more ancient Buddhism. The artificers are Muhammadans and their crafts are of Indian or Persian origin. But none of the bold *pinjra*-work and simple but effective wood-carving, that characterised the wood-work of the State some 15 to 20 years ago and possibly for centuries previously, will be found in the Exhibition. That style took its birth with the conception that raised some of the famous mosques such as Chakoti—a wooden building which, till a few years ago, was the admiration of all visitors but which by the earthquake of 1885 was levelled to the ground, much as its still more ancient masterpiece, the temple of Martand, had been demolished. The wood-work of Kashmir to-day seems to have originated by a European suggestion, given some 8 or 10 years ago. The series shown in the Exhibition (Plate No. 22, figs. 4, 5, 6) are all good of their kind. By some persons this style is admired, by others regarded as superfluous and burdensome through the under-cutting rendering the walnut-wood dull and unfeeling which no realism or skill can overcome.

Doric Art. Buddhist Art. Muhammadan Art. Modern Realistic Art.

The screens, tables, picture frames, etc., shown have been produced by Jubbar Khan, Habib Joo, Lussoo, Subhana, Khizra and other wood-carvers and art dealers in Srinagar. Small drawing-room tables of the very best style and workmanship, average from Rs. 20 to Rs. 100 according to size. Perhaps one of the most surprising features of the Exhibition may be said to have been the avidity with which every bit of this modern Kashmir work was purchased.

2nd : United Provinces of Agra and Oudh—Wood-Carving.

Wood-work constitutes a by no means unimportant aspect of the architecture of these provinces. It is carved, painted or inlaid and the timbers mostly employed are *shisham* and *sal*. For furniture and other ornamental purposes, the woods are *shisham*, ebony, *nim*, and white-wood (*dudhi*). The chief centres (in alphabetical

Timbers Used.

DIVISION 13. WOOD-CARVING.

Centres of Production.

sequence) are Aligarh, Azamgarh, Bareilly, Bijnor (Nagina) Budaun, Bulandshahr, Farukhabad, Ghazipur, Lucknow, Mainpuri, Muttra, Saharanpur, etc.

Leading Characteristics.

Following the course adopted above, the wood-work of these provinces may be studied from the example of a door (Plate No. 23). Perhaps its most remarkable features might be said to be the strongly Hindu or Sikh tendency. The lower or cusped *mihráb*, described in connection with the Panjab Door, is absent, but the upper flat arch is present and embraces a large over-door panel (below the second lintel) which carries in the centre of a diaper pattern the figure of *Ganesha*. There are no superimposed and half imbedded pilasters, though the door frames are carved into numerous beads that manifest either spirally arranged garlands or portray dwarfed pilasters that carry the flattened arch and spandrel of the over-door. *Pinjra* panellings (as described under the Panjab) are unknown, but the door leaves are panelled in boards that are richly carved, in geometric designs, with floral rosettes within the meshes.

Door and Window.

The door and window frames are massive (square on section) and flat on the surfaces—peculiarities preserved in the ultimate elaboration. They are cut up and carved (as already indicated), on the upper half or two-thirds of their length at least, into numerous parallel imitation beads and frames, but on the lower third are preserved in their massive form and developed into rich and most effective basement panels.

Nature of Carving.

The carving is below the surface of the structure but nevertheless fairly deeply under-cut. Excepting in the door leaves it is rarely placed under geometric restraint but is free, bold and graceful. It is cut in rounded, not sharp V-shaped section. The tips of the leaves and of the floral petals are thickened and compressed and turned over in a curious manner, suggestive of a plastic material, a feature by which this style of work may be instantly recognised.

Structural Features Imitated.

It may thus be said that, through carving and surface ornamentation, structural features are imitated that do not exist in the scheme of door construction. Though the general effect is undoubtedly admirable, a careful study of such doors and a comparison with those from other parts of India, leaves the impression

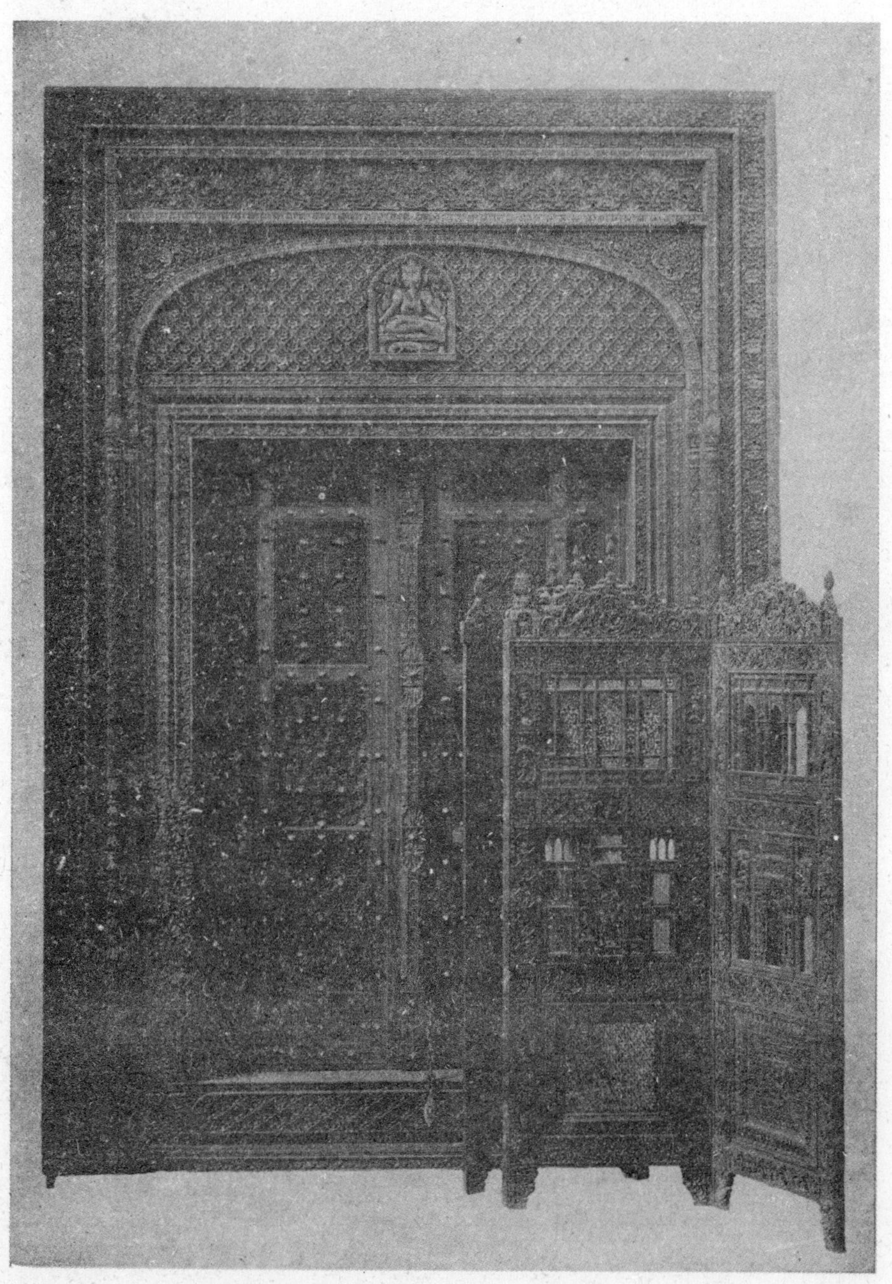

Plate No. 23 Selection of the Wood Carving of the United Provinces

that an effort has been put forth to recover by the carver's art the dignity disregarded by the joiner.

DIVISION 13. WOOD-CARVING.

Chief Exhibits on View.

SAHARANPUR.—Against the eastern wall of the Main Gallery of the Exhibition there will be found a good example of a door (Plate No. 23) made in this style at Saharanpur by Surja Mistri. It was prepared for the Lucknow Museum but has been sent on loan by that institution to Dehli. In the Calcutta Museum there is an even finer example which was procured from Saharanpur some 20 years ago.

Saharanpur White-wood Work.

Saharanpur used to enjoy a great reputation in the manufacture, in vine pattern, of carved caskets, bread plates, trays, salad knives and forks, picture frames and the like, done in the soft white-wood known as *dudhi*, but though this still survives it has given place to the modern wholesale traffic in the production of vulgar and common-place brackets, folding octagonal tables, etc., in red *tun* and mulberry woods, cut by the machine fret-saw and exported to Europe and America by the thousand, and there accepted apparently as typical examples of Indian wood-carving. This new traffic has very nearly killed the beautiful *shisham* wood-carving of Saharanpur and of one or two other neighbouring towns. As illustrative of the modern trade, however, one or two of the best examples of fret-saw work in "cigar-box wood" (as it is popularly described) will be found against the south wall of the Main Gallery. These are exhibited by Aziz Din, price for the over-mantel Rs. 100, for the screen Rs. 75.

Saharanpur Modern Red-wood Work.

Should replicas of the Saharanpur Door be desired these could be obtained to order for about Rs. 1,000 but could not be turned out in less than a year for each door.

Farukhabad Work.

FARUKHABAD has enjoyed the reputation of producing some of the finest wood-carving of these provinces. The art seems to be confined to at most one or two families and the finer specimens to one man. In the Loan Collection Gallery will be seen a screen (Plate No. 23) produced by Nek Ram, Mistri, the most expert carver of Farukhabad. This may be taken as representative of the best work of that place though, in conformity with modern craving, fret-work panels have unfortunately been introduced. It will be seen

DIVISION 13. WOOD-CARVING.

Special Features.

by comparison with the Saharanpur Door that the floral carvings of this screen are in close conformity with the style already briefly described. One of the special features of this work is the method of carving the pinnacles, struts and other adventitious ornaments. These are completely excavated into cage-like traceries, often with idols left within, such as are seen in Burmese ivories. In the Main Gallery a few additional examples of Farukhabad work (picture frames, brackets, etc.) will be found and offered for sale at moderate prices.

NAGINA, in BIJNOR DISTRICT, is the centre of a graceful style of ebony carving. This has attained a high proficiency, in the cabinet-maker's trade, but does not seem to have had a prototype in architectural wood-work. It most closely resembles the intricate incised carving on the very oldest of Hindu doors already mentioned. Tables, chairs, caskets, picture frames, walking sticks and other such articles are turned out (Plate No. 24) richly chased by a delicate and crisp surface ornamentation that is purely floral and which can hardly be described as restrained by geometric tracery.

Nature of Carving.

It is cut in imitation of panels and frames, to suit the surfaces treated, and the borders are often in simple dog-tooth (*kingrí*) pattern. The chief floral conception may have been suggested by the scorpoid twisting and thickening of the flowering tips of the wild heliotrope. The effect of the carving is enhanced by the clever way the background is punched in minute circles. This not only gives a finish to the work but relieves and heightens the carving. For picture frames and caskets this style of work is well suited and has been taken advantage of by the miniature painters of Delhi to set off their choicest productions. (See Fine Arts in the transept.)

Isolation of Art Industries.

There is perhaps no more surprising peculiarity of the Indian Arts, than their sudden and unexpected appearance in isolated localities, often remote from the sources of the materials required. Nagina is a remarkable example of this. It is a small and unimportant village, many miles from the nearest forests of ebony and distant from either a large city or a possible wealthy patron. The craftsmen are Muhammadans who, until comparatively recently, were in a state of abject poverty. There are only four

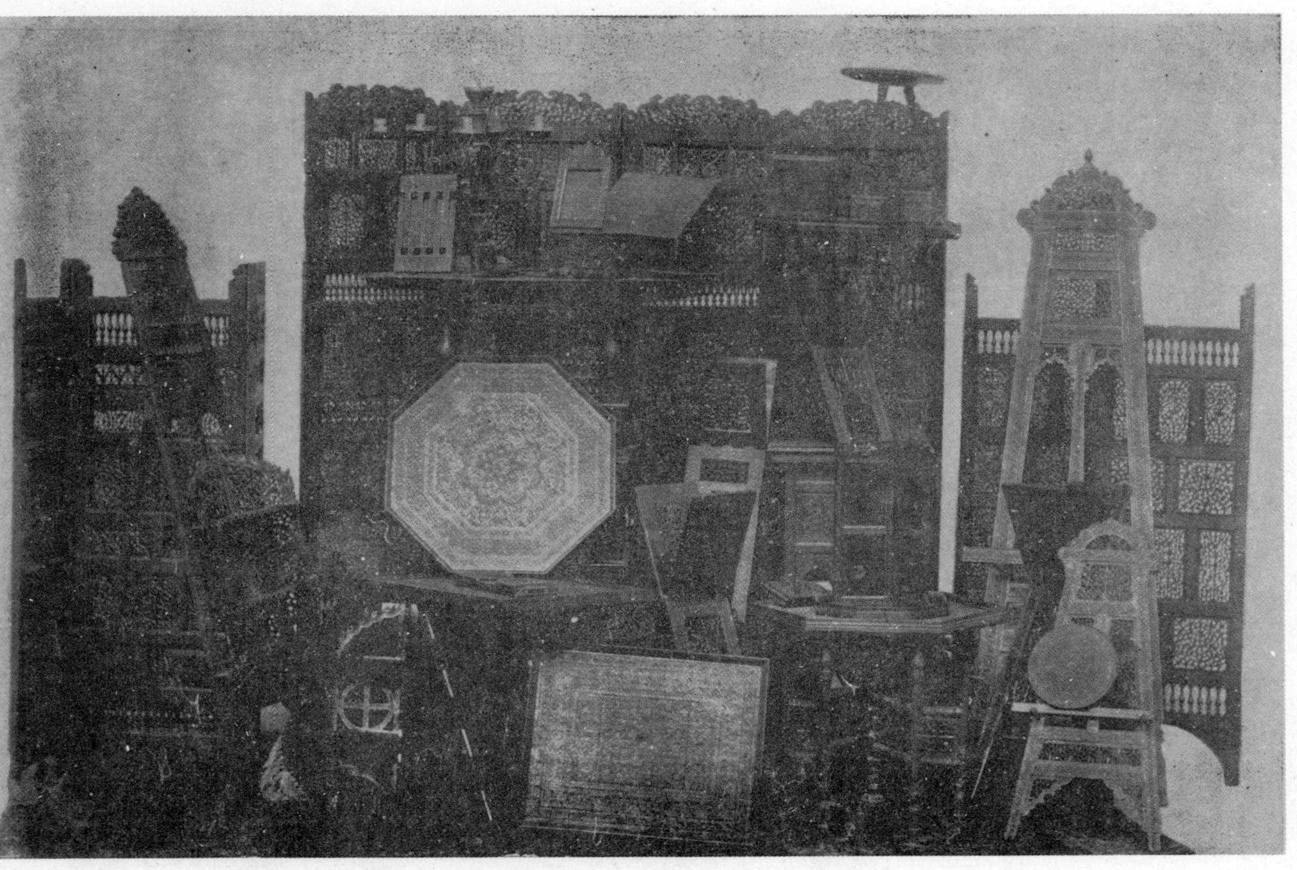

Plate No. 24 Nagina Wood Carving in Ebony

shops each giving employment to perhaps half a dozen workmen and for many hundred miles in every direction around this little art oasis, there are no other workers in ebony and hardly any wood-carvers of any description. From one end of India to the other this particular style of incised wood-carving occurs nowhere else except in the village of Nagina.

The following are some of the more remarkable examples of this work and the names of the better craftsmen:—A screen No. 3801, price Rs. 1,250, by Abdulla. An overmantel No. 3911, price Rs. 650, by Moula Buksh, and a table No. 3875, price Rs. 156, by Murad Buksh.

3rd:- Central Provinces Wood-carving.

NAGPUR and several other large towns have had a considerable reputation for wood-carving and the door that will be found attached to the south wall of the Main Gallery of the Exhibition may be accepted as fully representative of the style of work that is characteristic of these provinces. It will be seen to bear a strong similarity to the Mahratta (or Deccan) style and thus to blend almost imperceptibly into the Chalukyan art which, like a belt, severs the Indo-Aryan from the Dravidian styles, as it stretches from shore to shore across the peninsula from about Mysore on the west to the mouths of the Kistna and Godaveri on the east.

The doorway (No. 38, price Rs. 575) was executed by Ramji. The leaves of the door are divided into ten square panels, each of which contains one of the incarnations of Vishnu as described in Hindu mythology. The jambs are flanked by square tapering pilasters in the middle of which are carved two figures representing *Jay* and *Vijay* (luck and ill-luck) and at the top amongst foliage are *Gurud* and *Maroti*. In the centre of the lintel is the usual representation of *Ganpati* and at the bottom of the steps are two demons (*shankhardev*). Above the whole is a cornice richly decorated with elaborately carved pendants, the whole of which is supported by corbels in the shape of animal heads. A striking feature is the corner pendantives which are very elaborately carved. They represent lotus flowers and support figures riding on peacocks.

4th :—Bengal Wood-carving.

DIVISION 13. WOOD-CARVING.

Wood-carving is by no means a characteristic feature of the Lower Provinces. In Gaya and Maldah there are some good examples to be seen in connection with old houses and the wood-carvers have a local reputation. (See page 143.) As illustrative of the insignificance of the art in Bengal, it may be mentioned that in the Native town of Calcutta scarcely a door or window can be discovered that displays any trace of wood-carving or in fact any architectural features of interest or beauty. In furniture making, a certain skill has been attained by the carpenters but exclusively in European designs and mostly through the training imparted in the workshops of European firms.

5th :—Nepal Wood-carving.—(*Plate No. 25.*)

It seems desirable to treat the Arts of this State quite independently of those of the provinces to which it is adjacent, owing to the fact that in art conceptions it is more nearly rated to Thibet and China than to India. The comparatively recent engrafting of Hinduism to its earlier Buddhism has given the only Indian feeling that can be traced in the work of its skilled artificers. The valley was never conquered by the Muhammadans and in consequence its arts are uncontaminated by Indo-Saracenic influences. But freed from the restraint usually imposed by Muhammadanism, the exuberance and fantasy of both Hinduism and Buddhism have in Nepal been allowed to run riot. Fergusson says "the style may be called barbarous, and the buildings have the defect of being principally in wood; but their height, their variety of outline, their wealth of carving and richness of colour are such as are not to be found in Benares or any other city of the plains. The real point of interest in the Architecture of Nepal lies in the fact that it presents us with a complete microcosm of India as it was in the 7th Century, when Hiouen Thsang visited it—when the Buddhist and Brahmanical religions flourished side by side, and when the distinctive features of the various races were far more marked than they have since become under the powerful solvent of the Muhammadan domination." Passing over a gap of many centuries and coming down to about 150 years ago, Nepal was conquered by the Gurkhas and its various petty States absorbed

Absence of Muhammadan Influence.

A Microcosm of Ancient India.

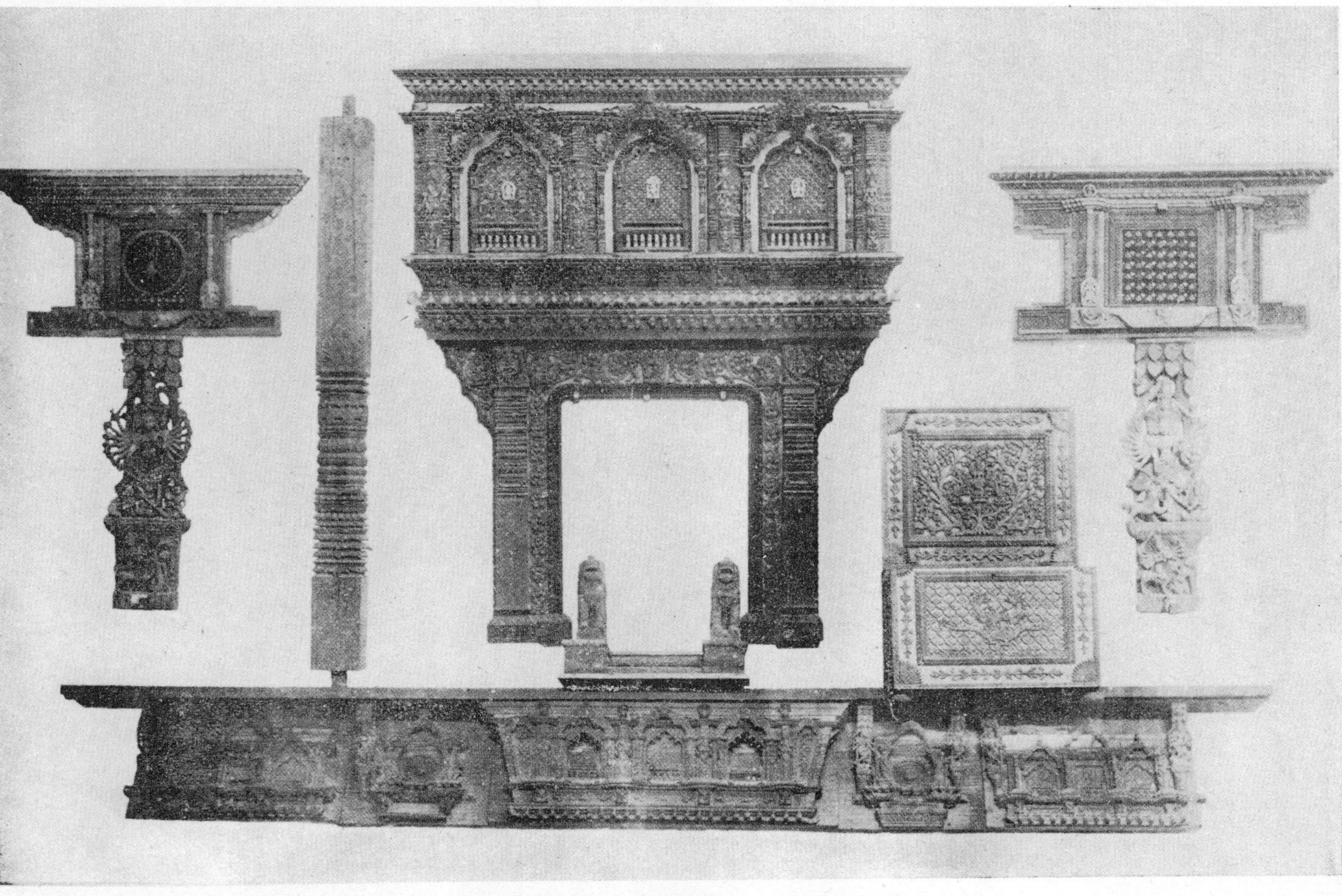

Plate No. 25 Wood Carving of Nepal

DIVISION 13. WOOD-CARVING.

and merged into a central administration that gave more attention to military than to domestic affairs. The Newar craftsmen—the artists of the State—the chief workers in metal and wood—found accordingly little or no market for their skill, hence for many years past the art industries have been declining both in merit and importance. The older houses and temples of Katmandu and other towns show the proficiency that once existed.

Chief Features of the Style.

The examination of Nepal wood-work first suggests the observation of its strongly Chinese feeling; then its curious practice of superimposing structural features—a sort of appliqué in wood-work—arrests attention; lastly the superfluity of animal forms engrosses the observer's thoughts. The strutted roof-supports are seen to be carved into a multiplicity of gods perfectly bewildering; below this is a frieze of lion heads, still lower a border or wavy line of serpents, next a profusion of carved pillars with hardly any two alike and lastly imitation brackets, spandrels, over-doors and other such superimposed structures that portray a medley of gods, demons, dragons (*bijlis*), serpents and other fantastic animals—for which there is no parallel in the wood-work of India. Projecting windows, perforated panels and massive lattice-work enclosures, are prominent features of the style, but the doors are, as a rule, unimportant and hardly if ever carved.

Imitation Structures.

Chief Exhibits on View.

On the western end of the Main Gallery will be seen the court-yard of a house in section and much reduced in size though sufficiently large to show every detail. Also on the walls a few articles (fire-place, brackets, etc., Plate No. 25) prepared by the Newar wood-carvers in adaptation of their art to modern house furnishing. There will also be seen a remarkably beautiful trunk ornamented entirely in appliqué, two shades of pale coloured wood only being employed. These admirable examples have beeen furnished by the Nepal Government. Not only are they built up, as it were, of numerous pieces of wood, one over the other, but the colours of the wood employed are carefully chosen to give the effect in light and shade that is specially desired. The *titiboshi* wood is pale coloured, easily worked and cheap. It is

Applique in Wood-work.

Woods used.

DIVISION 13. WOOD-CARVING.

accordingly used for the larger parts. The *sattisal* is of dark reddish colour, heavy, hard and close grained, hence largely sought after for carving and is placed over the *titiboshi* wood. The *sakua* is of a still darker red colour, while the *champá* is pale yellow. These are the woods mostly in demand and their assortment is carefully considered so as to give the quaint barbaric effect desired.

The art of Nepal may thus be spoken of as quite unlike anything met with in India proper though it recalls some of the features of the Burmese crafts.

6th :—Rajputana, Central India, Sind and Beluchistan Wood-carving.—(*Plate No. 26.*)

Throughout the whole of the wide range of country indicated under this section, the chief if not the only timber sufficiently abundant and at the same time suitable for wood-work, is the *babul* (*kikar*) or other species of the gum-arabic kind. The *rohira* might be mentioned as the next most abundant and suitable wood. But the deserts and rainless tracts embraced, afford numerous rich supplies of variously coloured and admirable marbles and sandstones, suitable for house construction, hence the ornamental carving met with is, for the most part, in stone, not in wood. In fact the wood-carving that does occur in any abundance might be described as of a very elementary (almost aboriginal) character while the stone-work is of a far higher order than that met with in any other part of India One feels inclined accordingly to guess that the wood-work most characteristic may be the survival of an art practised by the aboriginal races, while the stone-work may be the craft of a highly cultured and invading race who attained their proficiency in wood before they were compelled to apply their skill to stone. The reader may recollect that (under Class II—Stone-work, p. 66) the endeavour has been made to show that the lace-like fringes and moveable pendants and the lattice-like perforated screens with minute and elaborate stone-carving, seen in the region above indicated, are features better suited to wood than to stone. The contention has in consequence been put forth that, were the effort desirable, it might be shown fairly satisfactorily that the

Early Style.

Fully Elaborated Style.

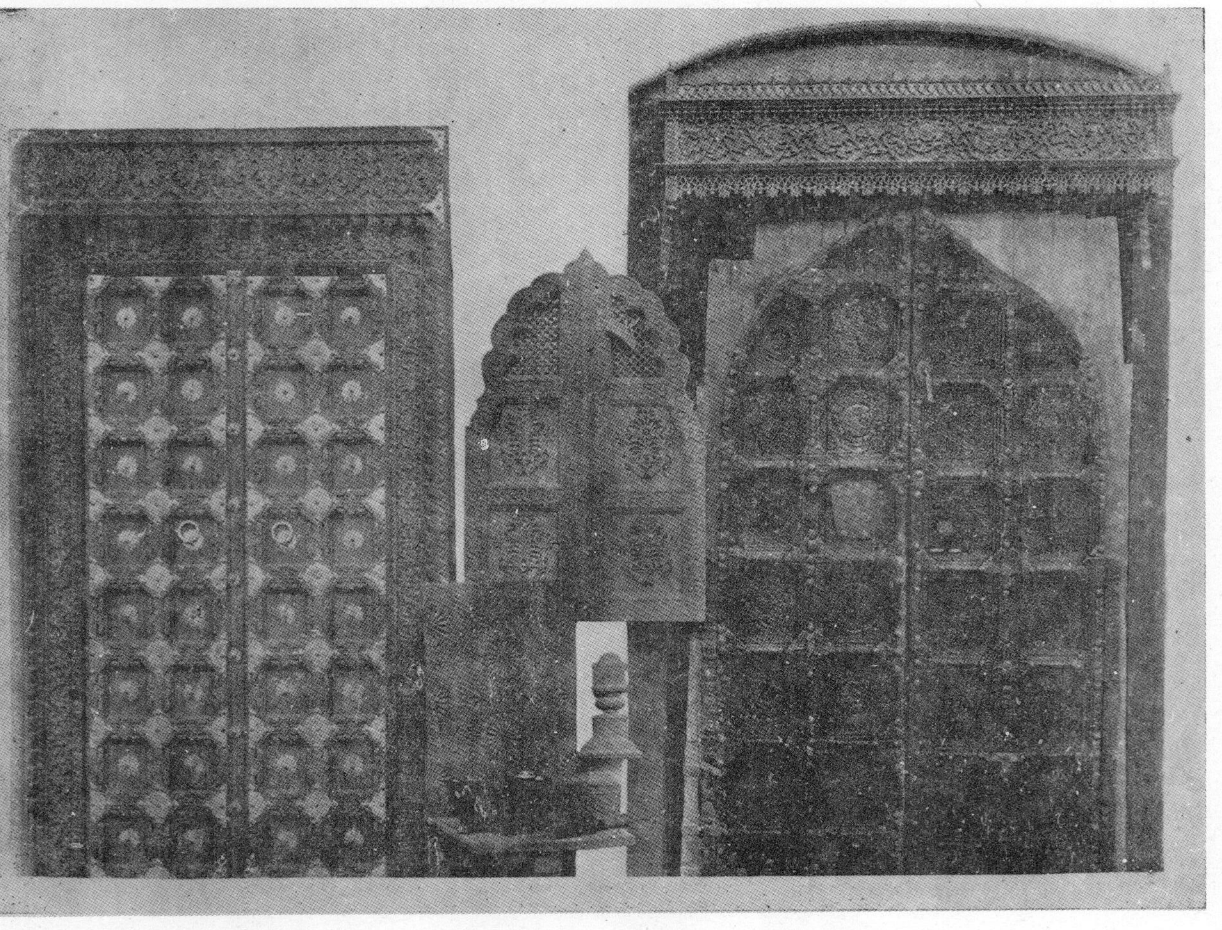

Plate No. 26 Wood-carving of Rajputana, Central India, Sind, and Baluchistan

skilled wood-carving of India (that existed prior to the Muhammadan domination), might be traced in the stone-work of Rajputana and Central India, rather than in the bulk of the wood-work of the present day. It is significant that in none of the palaces of the princes and nobles of Rajputana and Central India, are there examples of fine old wood-carving. Wood-work in these rich repositories of art might in fact be regarded as conspicuous by its absence while, as if in compensation, sandal-wood and ivory-carving hold fairly prominent positions. Indeed the arts of carving in these materials have attained some importance locally, though the centres of these crafts are remote from the regions of supply. (For further particulars the reader should consult Class V, below.) **DIVISION 13. WOOD-CARVING.**

It would seem almost certain that the early wood-carving of the country here indicated was, a few centuries ago, exclusively incised, that is to say, scratched or cut below the surface and notched or dog-toothed on the margins. While hunting up the collections shown in the Exhibition, the writer discovered, in a store-room of the Dargah of Ajmir—the tomb and mosques of the revered Khwaja Sahib—two pairs of doors. These were lying on the floor and utterly neglected. On inquiry the information was elicited that they had been brought by the Emperor Akbar, from the third destruction of Chittor in 1580. Assuming this report to be correct (which there seems every likelihood to be the case), these doors are amongst the oldest examples of Hindu wood-carving in existence. Plate No. 26 (to the right) gives a fairly good impression of the constructive and decorative peculiarities of one of these. It will be seen that there are two leaves; that there is no *binai* or overlapping bead (such as described above under the Panjab Door, p. 107); that the ornamentation has been made to fit into a simple pointed arch, a flat portion of the door surface being left both on top and bottom to rest against the top of the door frame and the door-step, just as in the old Bikanir Door shown on Plate 32; lastly that the carving is flat, incised and in primitive designs such as would alone have been possible to crude workers on an exceptionally difficult timber. There is no trace of the Hindu exuberance in animal forms, characteristic of recent ornamentation and (it thus seems possible) that just as in the older doors, to be seen in Lahore **Chittor Door.**

DIVISION 13. WOOD-CARVING.

and other towns, so in the Chittor Door, the only sculpture work present was the idol placed within the spandrel.

CHIEF EXHIBITS ON VIEW.

Marwar Work.

MARWAR.—Alongside of the Chittor Door and to the left have been shown on Plate No. 26, a characteristic modern door and window from Marwar. These are in *rohira* wood (*Tecoma undulata*) and, for the most part, display the skill that may be obtained in simple notching or dog-toothed ornamentation. The clever perforation of the window-panel gives the effect of the transparencies and mosaics of Rajputana in a most surprising manner, the flowers and peacocks showing up as if in coloured glass, through the study of light and shade that has been accomplished. These have been furnished by the Mehkura Raj, Marwar, Jodhpur, the price of the door being Rs. 219 and of the window Rs. 62. In the same plate has been shown an over-door placed above the Chittor Door. This may be accepted as illustrative of the modern style of work that has crept into the country from the Panjab. The scrolls manifest flowers and birds, carved in fairly high relief. This has been contributed by the Jodhpur State and is for sale, the price being Rs. 81.

Kach Window-shutters.

In KACH STATE window-shutters are often highly artistic objects. They consist of a perforated tracery of wood placed over looking glasses. The carving is bold, twisted and profusely flowering.

Jaipur Style.

In Jaipur a modern school of wood-carvers exist who work in *shisham* wood. They turn out a striking style of work, *viz.*, intricate, deeply cut, compact and heavy, as if portraying fruits rather than flowers.

Bikanir.

Bikanir is famous for its carved red sandstone but its wood-carvers are also experts. In Plate No. 26 will be seen an opium pestle and mortar and glove box from Bikanir. The painted and gilded marble, cement and wooden panels of the older palaces of Bikanir, manifest in a remarkable degree the high skill attained. One of these will be seen on Plate No. 18; and three have been placed below the Bikanir sandstone window on the north wall of the Main Gallery and against the outside of the Burmese Room.

Indore.

In Indore, wood-carving is liberally used in house decoration.

DIVISION 13. WOOD-CARVING.

Waziri Charpai. Head-pieces.

Though remote and isolated both in style and location from the other articles, a crude chair has been shown in Plate No. 26; this was procured from the Waziri country. While exploiting the resources of the town of Bannu, the writer's attention was drawn to a curious feature in the *chárpais* used by the Waziris. At the head and at the right-hand corner, these possessed an erect and curiously carved board. It was explained that this was intended as a back-rest, so that the *chárpai* might be used during the day as a sort of chair or couch. The chairs have been constructed to show the peculiar and primitive wood-carving characteristic of these bed-heads; it might almost be spoken of as the prototype of the style of work seen on all the oldest examples of wood-carving met with in India.

7th :--Bombay Wood-carving.– (*Plate No. 27.*)

Various Styles.

This has to be severely isolated into at least two if not three widely different styles of indigenous work as well as one or two foreign crafts that have become securely engrafted to the province. The Jaina and Saracenic wood-carving of Ahmedabad and Gujerat generally (including the Hindu form of Kathiawar), are collectively as distinct from the Chalukyan and Saracenic arts of Khandesh, the Deccan and the Mahratta country, as it is possible to imagine. It is extremely difficult, however, to convey, in a few brief sentences, a satisfactory conception of these characteristic and widely different styles of architectural and ornamental wood-work. The following may be given as a few of the more prominent features:—

Historic Facts.

(A) GUJERAT may be spoken of as comprising two great forms (*a*) the Jaina or Hindu style and (*b*) its Muhammadan adaptation and development. So in the same way it would not be very far from correct to regard the Saracenic Art and Architecture of India as referable to three great schools with numerous minor offshoots, *viz.*, the glorious Mughal conception that attained its highest state in the tombs, mosques and palaces of Agra and Delhi (1494–1750 A.D.); the dwarfed style of the kings of Gujerat (with their capital at Ahmedabad, 1396—1572 A. D.), where loss of breadth may be spoken of as redeemed by elaboration in detail;

Saracenic Forms and Influence.

DIVISION 13. WOOD-CARVING.

and lastly the graceful dignity and boldness of the Bijapur work (1489—1660 A.D.). The more remarkable features of these three schools of Muhammadan Art and Architecture have governed the industries of India for many centuries and carried down to the present day much that was beautiful in the Hindu and Jaina ornamentation of times and dynasties almost lost and forgotten otherwise.

Jaina Architecture.

It would necessitate the production of an elaborate treatise, to portray with any degree of accuracy a conception of Jaina architecture—the undisputed model upon which the chief peculiarities of the Ahmedabad Saracenic have been evolved. With the disappearance of Buddhism (in the 7th Century), India may be viewed as having had three great religious faiths—Jainism in the West, Vishnuism in the East and Shivism in the South. Jainism reached the zenith of its course about the 11th Century, when some of the finest of its temples were constructed, such as those of Abu and Girnar. As the Jain religion gradually lost its hold of the people and became contaminated or amalgamated with the two great factions of Hinduism, the arts and architecture of the Jains lost their individuality.

Influence of Religious Thought.

Dominant Characteristics.

The dominant characteristics of the Jaina art may be said to proceed from the conception of an arch. This was horizontal, never formed by radiating voussoirs. Each succeeding layer was made to project beyond the preceding, until the centre was reached. The degree of projection was governed by the size of stones available and hence, with large stones, the layers were reduced in number and became continuous brackets, thus originating a flat not a pointed arch. To the south this developed into interrupted brackets, hence the bracketed capitals and flat-roofed halls of a thousand pillars, that are perhaps the most significant peculiarities of Hindu architecture. In other words the bracket became a formative feature that governed both the character of the building and the nature of the ornamentation. To the north the horizontal arch similarly gave birth to the horizontal dome, a conception that allowed of its construction on pillars. To reduce the square form to the circular, 12 pillars were necessary, the corners being bridged across by architraves. With larger

The Arch.

The Bracket.

The Dome.

buildings an aggregation of pillars and bridging architraves, upon the principle indicated, up to 56 or more became possible. Obviously, however, this system was governed by the length and strength of the stone available and a maximum of say 12 to 15 feet was almost necessarily the limit. To overcome this defect two contrivances were resorted to (*a*) the production of bracketed capitals that might expand the distance between the pillars; (*b*) a support or strut, carried to the middle of the architrave, starting from an additional bracket placed about one-third from the top of the shaft. Both the brackets and struts became highly ornate features and are carved and sculptured into fantastic forms, while essentially assorted on horizontal and concentric rings. Lastly, there being no lateral thrust the necessity for a keystone did not exist and in consequence the stone that completes the dome was developed, within the structure, into a superb pendant which "hangs from the centre of the dome more like a lustre of crystal drops than a solid mass of marble or of stone."

DIVISION 13. WOOD-CARVING.

Bracketed Capitals.

Struts.

The Pendant.

The varied outline, the light, grace and delicacy of Jain temples, have to be seen to be appreciated. They practically justify the intricacy of the ornamentation that universally prevails. With a larger structure and one where reliance was placed very nearly exclusively on proportion and shade, elaboration soon becomes not only useless but in bad taste. With the Jaina arts and architecture it might almost be said that no elaboration could be in excess of the propriety and necessity of the style.

Jain Ornamentation.

(B) DECCAN.—Similarly the second great group of Bombay Presidency wood-carvings, *viz.*, that of Khandesh and the Deccan, may be viewed as possessing both a Hindu and a Muhammadan type. The latter attained perfection with the tombs, mosques and palaces of Bijapur and the former—a survival of a still more ancient art—evolved into splendour with the establishment of the Kalyan dynasty, somewhere in the 6th Century. This may be spoken of as the Chalukyan style and stated as severing India into Northern and Southern sections. It has also been speculated that the Chalukyans were by religion Jains originally, though for many centuries their descendants have been Hindus. Their arts in consequence manifest a co-equal tendency to Jaina and Hindu feeling.

Bijapur Saracenic.

Chalukyan Architecture.

DIVISION 13. WOOD-CARVING. The Muhammadan art of this region (as already remarked) may be regarded as having taken its birth with the architecture of Bijapur. This will be seen in the paper impression furnished by Mr. C. L. Burns, Principal of the School of Art, Bombay, and placed near to the Agra House. The fittings of the boudoir in the Circuit House have also been designed to exemplify other features of this style and special attention may be drawn to the fire-place, adapted by Mr. Percy Brown, from Ibrahim Razah's mosque, and made by the stone-carvers of Jodhpur.

It may serve the immediate purpose of this work, namely, the exemplification of the more striking styles of wood-carving met with in Western India, if a few of the better known developments be now discussed and reference made to the examples in the Exhibition.

CHIEF EXHIBITS ON VIEW.

Ahmedabad Style. AHMEDABAD.—The elaborate and intricate Jaina and Hindu styles of architecture and ornamentation (Plate No. 27) that still survive in the Jain and Hindu temples of the Western Presidency and which were adapted to the requirements of the Muhammadans in the 15th Century, may be said to have attained their greatest perfection in the tombs and mosques erected during the Ahmedabad dynasty. These are more Indian in feeling than are the Saracenic buildings of any other part of India. In fact the minarets are simply elongated temples with the niches containing vegetable scrolls in place of idols. This special development in panelling, rapidly assumed the form of screen and window tracery, in many respects unsurpassed for beauty and elegance in any part of the world. In the Rani Sipri's tomb and mosque and in the Sidi Said's mosque, of the Bhudder palace, the finest examples of this art may be seen. The famous windows of the last mentioned have been reproduced for the Exhibition in wood. They represent the phenomenon, not unfamiliar to the Indian traveller, of a *banyan* tree growing out of and around a palm until, in its snake-like entanglements of root and branch, the *banyan* strangles its foster parent. The equal spacing, the assortment and distribution of the parts, carries

Window Tracery.

The Banyan Tree.

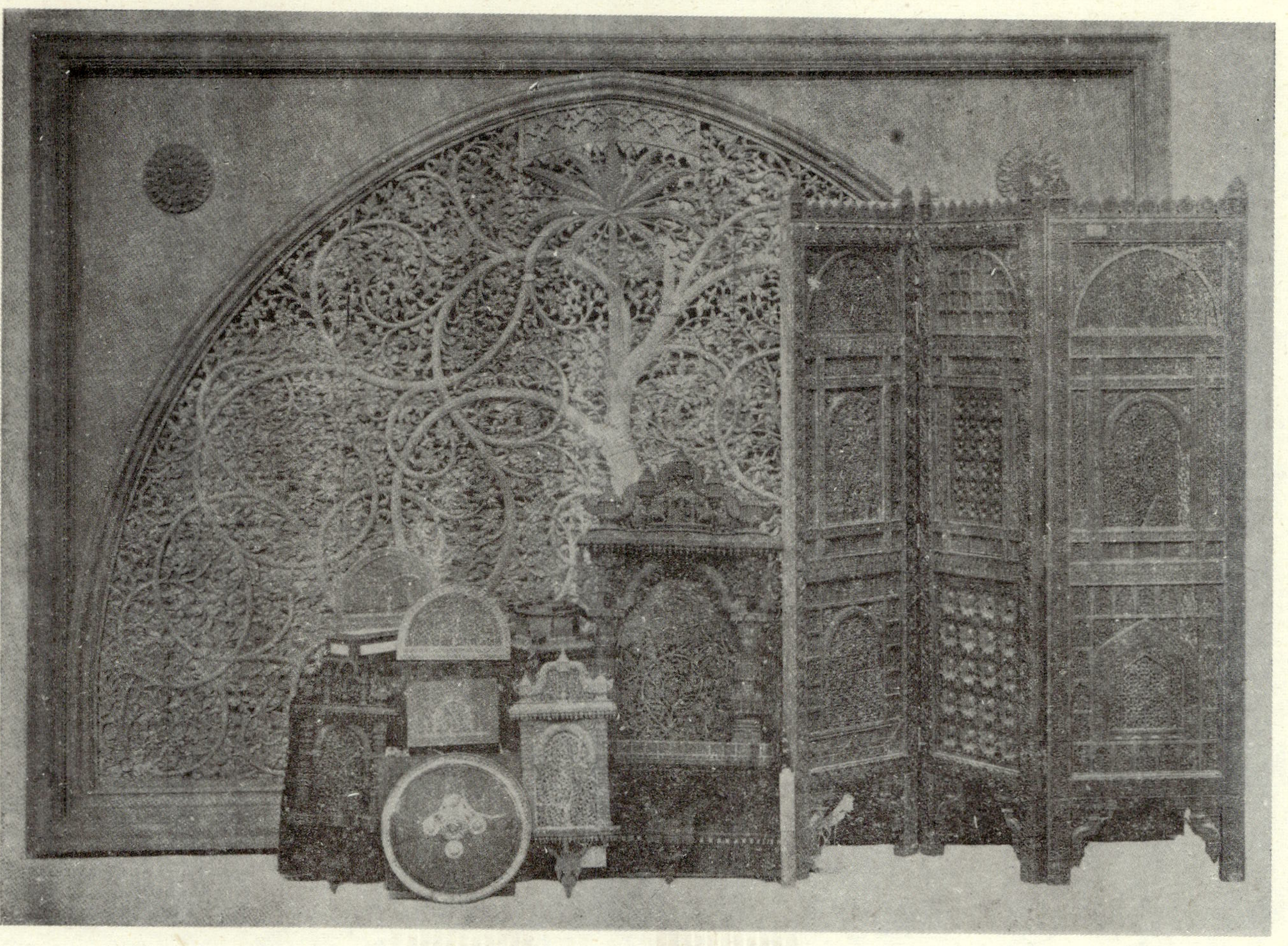

Plate No. 27 Wood Carving of Ahmedabad

DIVISION 13. WOOD-CARVING.

this conception into the highest domain of conventional decorative art, while the atmosphere of nature is uncontaminated. Its inception may be traced to the Jamma Musjid and its perfection seen in the Sidi Said mosque, but for 400 years it has pursued the arts of Ahmedabad without deterioration to any material extent. It is repeated time after time, in the carved stone, wood, sandal and ivory, in the carved hide-shields, in the *kinkhabs* and other textiles, and in the gold and silver plate and jewellery, until it has become the most characteristic feature of Ahmedabad art. Plate No. 27 shows a group of carved wooden articles, hide-shields, etc., from Ahmedabad, with in the background a faithful reproduction (in full size) of one of the Sidi Said windows. It will be noted that everywhere the minarets of the mosques are drawn upon for the uprights in the screens, brackets, etc., while the tracery is invariably after the encircling contortions of the *banyan* tree.

Intricate Style.

In addition to these peculiarities the arts of Ahmedabad, from the temples and mosques to the cabinet makers' productions, show an intricacy and elaborateness that recalls the ebony wood-carvers' work of Nagina, rather than the architectural wood and stone carvings of any other part of India. It is this rigorous attention to detail that makes the work so much more expensive than that from all other art centres.

Ahmedabad House.

The more strictly Hindu style, of recent date in Ahmedabad, may be studied in the carved house from that city which has been placed across the west end of the Refreshment Room and thus facing the side door into Bhavnagar House. This was secured by the writer, through the kind assistance of Mr. W. O. Alcock, Assistant Collector of Ahmedabad. The house had to be pulled down, by orders of the Municipality, and thus, through a happy accident, became available for the Exhibition. The wood-carving it displays is in the style that prevailed about 150 years ago. The scaly pilasters will doubtless be much admired and admitted as recalling those of the sandstone *jhároka* of Jodhpur. In constructive details this Ahmedabad House closely resembles that of Bhavnagar.

Numerous brackets and other such articles will be found on the

DIVISION 13. WOOD-CARVING.

tables of the Exhibition executed in the best Ahmedabad style. Of these the following may be mentioned :—

A teak wood carved bracket (No. 4652) priced at Rs. 205; a smaller one of similar wood (No. 902) and a large bracket in black-wood (No. 906) carved at Kalupar and priced at Rs. 280.

In Mangrol (Kathiawar) good wood-carvers are to be found who produce black-wood exactly as in Ahmedabad. A few examples will be found in the Exhibition by Kachra Doolabhram.

Bhavnagar House.—(*Plate No. 28.*)—Turning now to the more Hindu style of wood-carving, seen in Gujerat, the charming reproduction of a portion of a palace, contributed by His Highness the Maharaja of Bhavnagar, may be accepted as fully characteristic of the purest and best work of former times. This will be found on the left-hand side of the Refreshment Room. Mr. Proctor Sims, the State Engineer of Bhavnagar, has given this reproduction his most careful attention and it may accordingly be accepted that, in constructive details, in ornamentation and in furnishing, it is an accurate and faithful reproduction of a portion of a Rajput Chief's palace in Kathiawar. Plate No. 28 shows the front elevation of the building which it will be noted consists of a ground floor and an upper storey. The lower windows are in a rich form of lattice, consisting of rounded balls beautifully carved and fixed together in geometric form. This style of *pinjra* recalls at once the turned lattice-work of Egypt and the perforated stone panels of the Chalukyan temples. The painted ceiling of the lower room represents the moon-light dance of *Krishna* and the *Gopis* (or milk-maids), while flowers are being showered upon them from the clouds.

Characteristic Features.

Mr. Proctor Sims informs the writer that, when the head carpenter of the State was told His Highness had given orders that, in constructing this model house, he was to follow most carefully the time-honoured rules and traditions of his craft, he expressed the greatest pleasure since he regarded the modern departures (all too common) as degenerations. As the work progressed he observed that the finger of God was pointing the way and that accordingly mistakes were impossible. In support of this belief he quoted the ancient rules of his craft such as that if the nine planets,

Modern Degeneration

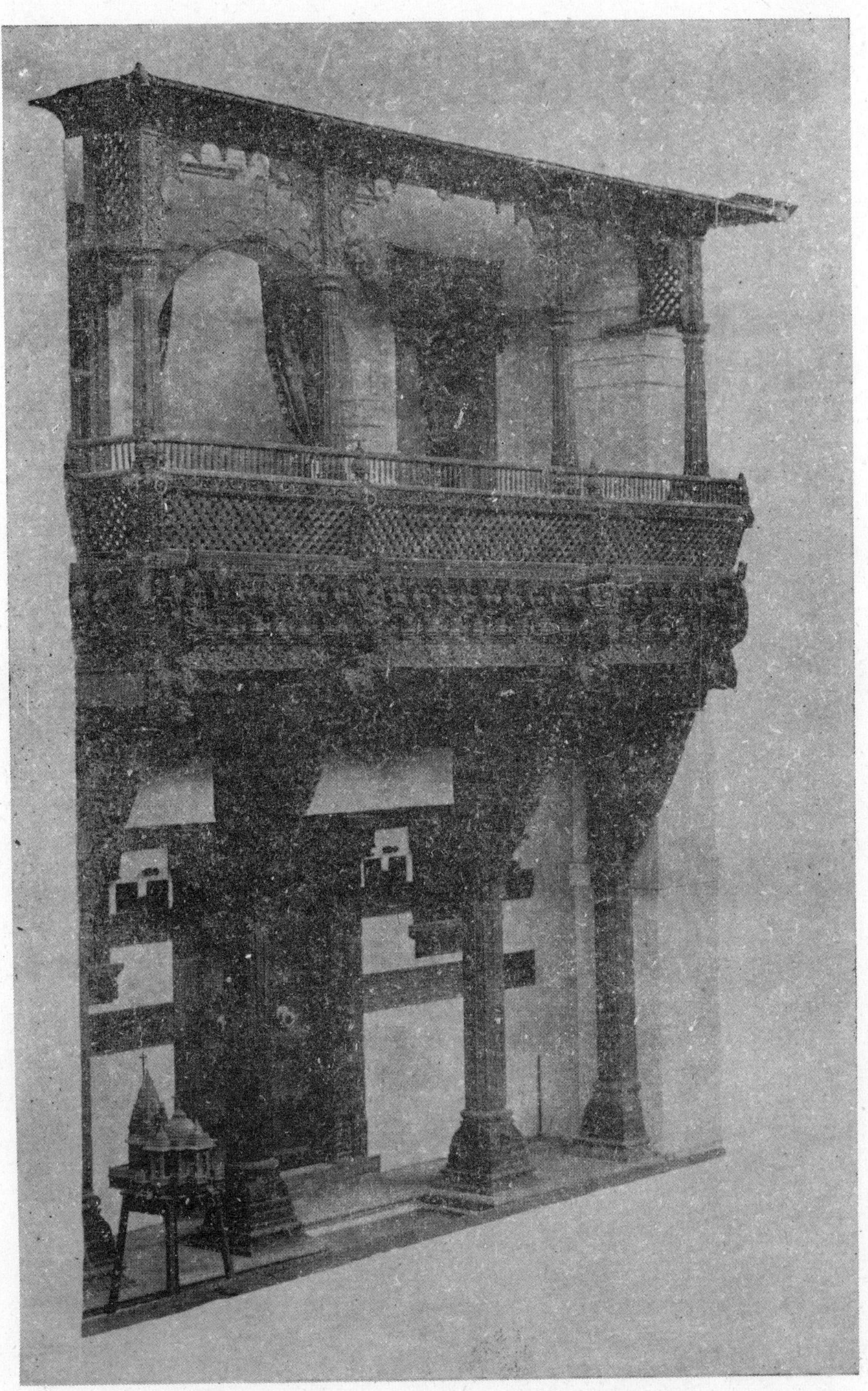

Plate No. 28 Bhavnagar Room (Wood-carving in Hindu Style of Kathiawar)

the twelve signs of the zodiac and the fifteen dates of the lunar month, were kept in line together, Vishwakarma had told that they would subtend a right angle. Further that the breadth of the room should be divided into 24 equal parts, of which 14 in the middle and 2 at each end should be left blank, while the remaining two portions should each form windows or *jális*. The space between the plinth and the upper floor should be divided into nine parts, of which one should be taken up by the base of the pillar, six parts by the column, one by the capital and one by the beam over it. He then added that should any departures be made from these rules, the ruin of the architect and death of the owner were sure to follow. **DIVISION 13. WOOD-CARVING.**

Is it to be wondered at that the Kathiawar House should be beautiful and dignified when constructed under conditions and rules that have taken hundreds of years to evolve to their present perfection? The wood-carving will be at once admitted as graceful and artistic, especially the peacock-like (*morli*) elaboration of the protruding joist ends, the pendants and veils of the brackets and capitals, and the curtain-like festoonings of the component parts of the scrolls and other ornamentations. The struts supporting the upper balcony are deeply under-cut, the design being richly interwoven with animal subjects and foliar elaborations. In these it is not infrequent to find the motto "Live and let live" portrayed. A man is represented shooting, with the bow and arrow, a falcon which is about to strike a pigeon, while a snake has that instant bitten the man. The Bhavnagar style is one of the most prevalent and characteristic met with in Gujerat, and very possibly originated in ancient Cambay and from a Hindu rather than a Jaina conception. **A Purpose in Ornamentation.**

Bhavnagar House has been purchased for the Indian Museum, Calcutta, where it will be reconstructed.

The Baroda Balcony, thrown over the door into the Exhibition office, will be seen to bear a close resemblance, in most of its details, to the Bhavnagar House but to manifest numerous modern or local developments. This singularly graceful structure was made under the supervision of Mr. G. R. Lynn, State Chief Engineer of Baroda, and by the carpenter who **Baroda Style.**

IVISION 13. WOOD-CARVING. constructed the pigeon-house shown at the Colonial and Indian Exhibition of London. The tail-piece shown on page 98 shows a portion of the festooning scroll work not only seen in the Baroda Balcony but throughout the wood-work of Gujerat and Kathiawar.

Bombay Black-wood Furniture.—This art was introduced into Bombay many years ago and to this day is mainly produced by the Portuguese inhabitants. At one time no house in Bombay was considered well furnished that had not many pieces of this work. For some years past, however, popular fancy has changed and good black-wood can hardly be procured. Some three or four samples will be found in the Exhibition and offered for sale at moderate prices.

8th :—Mysore and Coorg.—(*Plate No. 29.*)

It has already been observed that a powerful art influence, generally spoken of as the Chalukyan, took its birth with the establishment, in the 6th Century, of the Kalyan dynasty. This survived, in its integrity and purity, till the dark ages, say from about 750 to 900 A.D., when the craftsmen were gradually converted to Hinduism and thus diverted their skill to the production of a mixed form of Hindu and Chalukyan art. This has, however, preserved, to the present day, sufficient of its original conception to now constitute a perfectly distinct style from that of other parts of India and one which has exercised a very considerable influence on the art crafts of the southern peninsula. From the town of Kalyan, in the Nizam's territory, the Chalukyan inspiration spread east and west until it extended from the Southern Mahratta country and Mysore to the Bay of Bengal (between the mouths of the Kistna and Godaveri) and north until it embraced the whole of the Deccan, Khandesh and Berar. It thus severed the Dravidian arts and architecture of the southern extremity from those of the Indo-Aryan and Saracenic of the northern sections of India.

It has been surmised, from the many points of similarity of the older temples of this class (met with in the central tracts of India) to the modern Jaina structures of the western and north-western

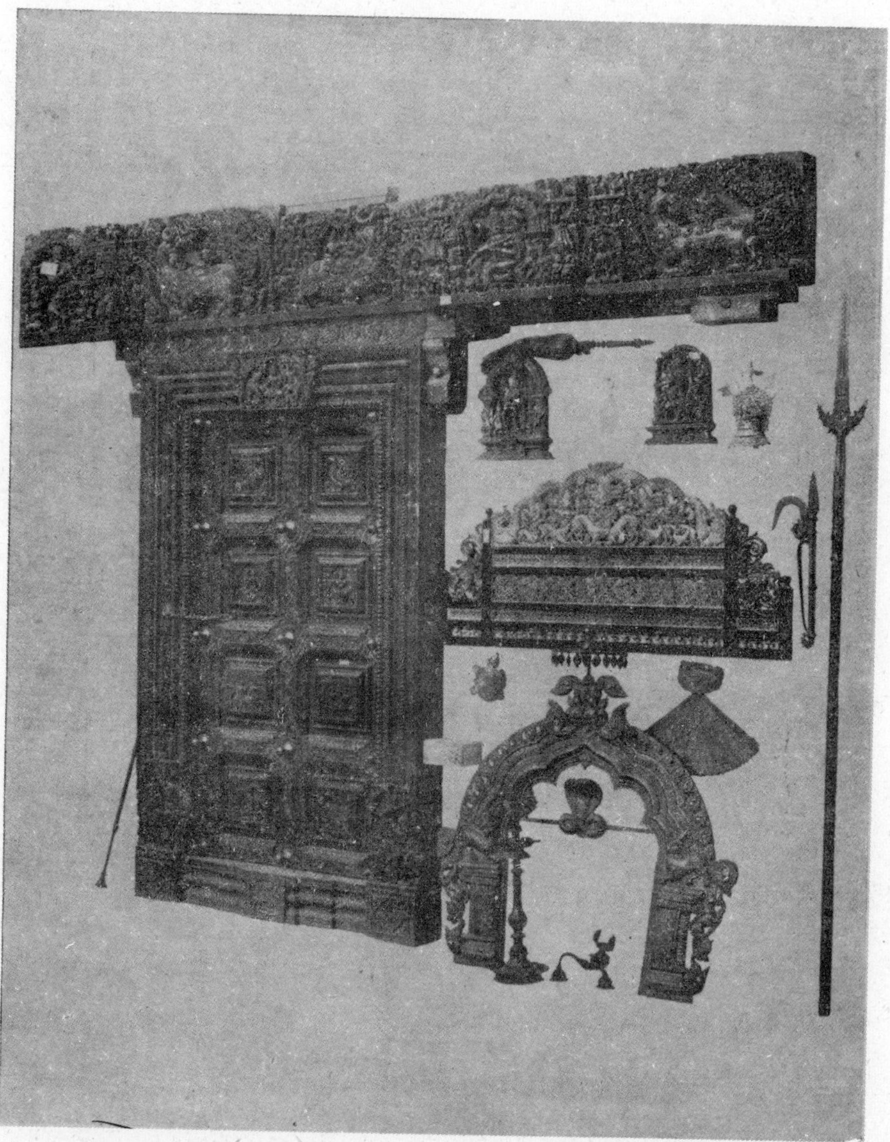

Plate No. 29 Mysore door and other articles in Chalukyan style

portions of the Bombay Presidency, that the builders of these monuments were originally Jains or perhaps followed a faith that possessed many tenets in common with both Buddhism and Jainism. The later monuments gradually show, however, a stronger and still stronger taint of Hinduism, until in Hallabid, the last and in some respects the grandest of all, they are purely Hindu temples. The building of Hallabid was suddenly left off through the conquests of the Muhammdans in 1310 A.D., and at the same time the art instincts of the people, in this tract of country, were so completely annihilated that nothing new has since been produced by them. **DIVISION 13. WOOD-CARVING.**

The continuity of great works and the preservation of a style of art from generation to generation is only possible through the guiding and controlling power of religion. A decadence of the Chalukyan art was accordingly instantly started, when Hindu influence was brought to bear upon it. Sculpture changed from a decorative and high art, to the production of conventional statuary, intended to portray celestial forms.

Personal Adornment.

Turning now from the temple to the homestead, it may be remarked that house and personal ornamentation usually follow the types established in the sanctuary. The great prototypes of the secular ornamentation, of the region here dealt with, may accordingly be said to have been the temples of Hammoncondah (near Warangal), in Hyderabad, and of Somnathpur, Baillur and Hallabid, in Mysore. The sandal-wood carvers of to-day copy the statues and idols of the niches and the panellings of the walls of these temples. The bracketed pillars and massive over-door frames and architraves, with their niches and idols, are regularly copied and have become features in secular construction. The perforated stone windows and fan-lights, doubtless originated the massive form of lattice (*pinjra*) work, peculiar to the Deccan and Gujerat. Lastly, the celestial animals of the later developments of this style may be presumed to have taken their birth from the Chalukyan five-fold friezes of first the elephant, then the lion, next the horse and above that the ox and last of all the bird. The bird depicted, however, often resembles the swan or goose,—the vehicle of the creator, Brahma,—at other times it is a *garuda* in monster form, such as a two-headed bird, an elephant-headed

Five-fold Animal Friezes.

DIVISION 13. WOOD-CARVING. bird, a heavy-bodied elephant upon hippopotamus-like, short legs, a winged bull, or a monster tortoise. From each and every one of these semi-aquatic mythical animals are seen to emerge, from the tail or the mouth, a profusion of living things as if borne from the waters of Narā to people the dry land. So also the bodies of these strange animals are garlanded with plants and flowers, upon which rest terrestrial animals and birds, while from their tails are produced a profusion of floral and foliar ornamentations that involve the whole structure upon which they are portrayed. The peculiar twistings and feather and fan-like expansions of these foliar tails, it will presently be shown, become dominant features in the ivory, sandal and other wood-carvings, as also in the jewellery, fabrics and carpets of the country indicated.

Chief Exhibits on View.

Against the south wall of the Main Gallery, and toward its western extremity, will be found three carved wooden doors. These have been specially selected to exemplify three stages or degrees in Chalukyan art. They are as follows: the Bellary Door (Chalukyan and Dravidian), the Mysore Door (pure Chalukyan), and the Bangalore Door (a modern development).

The Mysore Door.—(*Plate No. 29.*)—The original of this is in the portion of the old palace of Mysore that was not destroyed by the great fire that effaced so much of value and beauty. The replica was specially carried out under the orders of the Executive Engineer in charge of the new palace works, supervised personally by Mr. B. K. Venkatavaradiyengar, the President of the Committee appointed by the Mysore Government to procure the articles required for the Delhi Exhibition. It is a faithful reproduction and one of great interest. It will be observed that the frame is exceedingly simple and massive, though richly carved. Above the door-frame is placed a narrow lintel which must serve a purely ornamental purpose. A frieze of goose pattern runs along its length. The door itself consists of but one leaf, it swings on pivots, not hinges, and has deep wings intended to embrace both the door-step and lintel. It is richly and elaborately panelled, the 8 panel boards having bold animal forms carved

DIVISION 13. WOOD-CARVING.

on them in strong relief. The massive panel frames have rosette-like expansions at the joints and around the brass bosses, that give a finish and dignity to the whole structure, most unusual in Indian wood-work. It may be observed that the goose, carrying a wreath of flowers and possessing a floriated tail, constitutes a prominent feature in the ornamentation which, except for the statue of Lakshmi on the lintel, has little or no trace of Hindu ornamentation, as understood in Northern India.

Distinctive Feature.

The Hallabid door-lintel.—Placed over the Mysore Door (Plate No. 29) but unconnected with it, will be seen two reproductions in teak wood, of the stone lintels in the famous Chalukyan temple of Hallabid. These were prepared at the writer's request from the originals in the Bangalore Museum. The mythical monster animal, discussed above, will be seen clearly portrayed. Its foliated tail and floral ornamentations of the body are the features of most interest, from the stand-point of decorative art. The peculiar forms these assume may be traced in practically every art of Mysore and a large portion of that of South India generally, where found uncontaminated with modern and specially European influence. The foliage will be seen to represent a pinnate leaf with numerous scorpoid flowering branches dispersed within the scrolls. In exemplification of the importance of this observation and with a view to illustrate other forms of the mythical animal so commonly portrayed and its domination of the arts of South India, a selection of articles has been hung on the walls around the Mysore Door. Of these may be noted (*a*) two sandal-wood carvings, the one showing an elephant-headed hippopotamus, the other an elephant-headed goose, depicted on the name-plates below the statues; (*b*) an ivory tortoise, wreathed in flowers; (*c*) a settee head-piece in ivory (rescued from the old palace of Mysore and possibly 16th Century work), ornamented in dragon forms; (*d*) a small casket in silver, showing the double-headed goose; (*e*) lastly, two carved steel weapons, a halberd and elephant *ankus*, which manifest numerous animal forms of ornamentation of the kind here indicated. The green and white carpet hung on the walls above the Bellary Door is a reproduction from an old Hindu design which came very

Foliated tail.

Nature of Ornamentation.

DIVISION 13. WOOD-CARVING. possibly from Warangal and which doubtless was intended to depict the double-headed goose.

The Bangalore Door.—This has been specially constructed under the supervision of Mr. J. Cameron, Superintendent of the Bangalore Museum. It is in *karachu* (*Hardwickia binnata*) wood —a wood that can only be carved when green. The style of ornamentation of this door may be spoken of as an evident degeneration from the other type and one in which the pinnate leaf has become larger and coarser (almost Acanthus-like) than in the Mysore sample. The door consists of two leaves and has an inner lintel, within the frame, which supports a miniature niche for the idol.

Pinnate Foliage.

9th :—South India (Dravidian) Wood-carving.

So much stress has already been laid on the importance of the influence of architectural conceptions on the arts and crafts of India, that it seems desirable to extend to South India a similar method of treatment.

The Chief Dravidian temples of South India date from about the 10th to 18th Centuries ; the more important ones having been constructed about the 15th and 16th Centuries. They consist of a fane placed more or less in the centre of a series of enclosures with gateways (or *gopurams*) passing through these and leading up to the temple itself. The outermost gateway is the largest and most conspicuous structure while the sanctuary may be the smallest or even the least important. The bathos of this arrangement is, however, sometimes redeemed through the sculptures of the temple being superior to those of the *gopurams*, thus very possibly indicating greater antiquity for the sanctuary. A study of the Dravidian temples in the sequence of their ascertained dates, reveals a most remarkable decline in artistic merit as having taken place with the approach to present times.

Perhaps the most significant feature of these monuments may be said to be the effort expended by their designers to force admiration through the display of inordinate human labour, in place of scientific and artistic skill. They are not constructed on any preconceived plan. The effects of proportion and of light and shade are utterly disregarded. For example, in the mouth of a *yáli* (or

Characteristic Features.

lion-shaped demon) the tongue may be so cut from the solid rock that it can be moved while it cannot be extracted from between the teeth. A chain of many free links may be formed out of a stone, five or six feet in length, and then uselessly suspended from the ceiling. A *rath*, or carriage for the god, may be hewn out of a huge boulder so that its wheels may be turned round by the hand although the carriage cannot be moved upon them. Such are the triumphs of past labour, that the visitor is invited to inspect, or he may be asked to examine and purchase, the equally absurd results of the present-day effort at marvellous production, consisting of a carving that can hardly be seen by the naked eye (a statue of Krishna cut from a tamarind seed), "The Lord's Prayer" inscribed on a grain of rice, or a table mat constructed of grains of rice; superfluity of labour thus made to take the place of intelligent and rational skill. This feature permeates the Dravidian arts and accounts for the agglutinations and endless repetitions that everywhere prevail, in the ornamentation of the temple or of the *swámi* encrustation in the metal wares and jewellery.

DIVISION 13. WOOD-CARVING.

Superfluity.

The next most striking feature of this style of work may be said to be the ingenuity displayed to utilize to the full the bracketed pillar. In place of struts thrown out to support the middle of the architrave (as in the Jaina form of flat roofing), supplementary or bracket shafts are introduced with transverse purlins supporting the rafters; by this means the middle space is widened. In the older examples these supplementary pillars are free from the pier, or at most are attached to it by open-work panels, much as in the Hallabid perforated windows. So again they are at times exceedingly beautifully formed and are clustered around the pier in a highly artistic manner. Lastly their purpose may be utterly disregarded and the pillars made so slender that they serve the purpose of sounding boards rather than of supports for the roof. The more recent temples have the bracket shafts attached to the pier, and very often carved into *yáli* or lion-headed monsters. As works of art these *yáli* pillars are usually as barbarous as they are architecturally superfluous. They constitute, however, a highly characteristic feature of Dravidian form and thought,

Bracketed Pillar.

Supplementary Pillars.

Yali Pillars.

DIVISION 13. WOOD-CARVING.

but have exercised comparatively little influence on the art crafts of South India, when contrasted with the value of the figures met with in the Chalukyan style. It has been surmised that the conception of these *válís*, or animal supplementary pillars, as also of the idols, etc., that are piled one on the top of the other, from the base to the apex of the *gopurams*, may have originated from the ancient practice of placing large terra-cotta figures within groves near the homesteads—a practice that prevails to this day over a large tract of Southern India. The *yálí* pillars are distinctly lithic not wooden conceptions and their progression into wood-carving may, therefore, be regarded as due exclusively to European suggestion.

Double Curve of the Cornice.

One other feature of Dravidian architecture and the last that need be here mentioned, may be stated to be the double flexure of the cornice and the ogee-like ornamentation that runs along its crest,—perhaps the most beautiful and valuable contribution made by this style, to the decorative arts of India. The ogee arch of the Buddhist rock-cut temples became with the early fathers of Indian art almost a sacred emblem and thus passed down to the monolithic temples of Mahavelipuram and from these into the Hindu architecture of the Dravidians.

EXAMPLES ON VIEW.

The Madras Room (*Plate No. 1*) should be studied—more especially the door—with a view to learning the chief features of the wood-carving of South India traceable to the Dravidian style of architecture. The fittings of that room have been prepared by the pupils of the Madras School of Arts under the personal guidance of Mr. A. Chatterton, B. Sc., the Superintendent. These will be seen to manifest numerous reproductions of the *yálí* pillars and of the agglutinated style of ideas and forms so prevalent in South India. The two superb Dravidian side-boards (Rs. 4,000), the writing table (Rs. 275), the lamp stands (from Rs. 106 to Rs. 165), the easel (Rs. 165) and many other articles exhibited both in the Madras Room and in other parts of the building have been made at the School of Arts and are all for sale.

MADURA.—This town was long famous for a simple and elegant

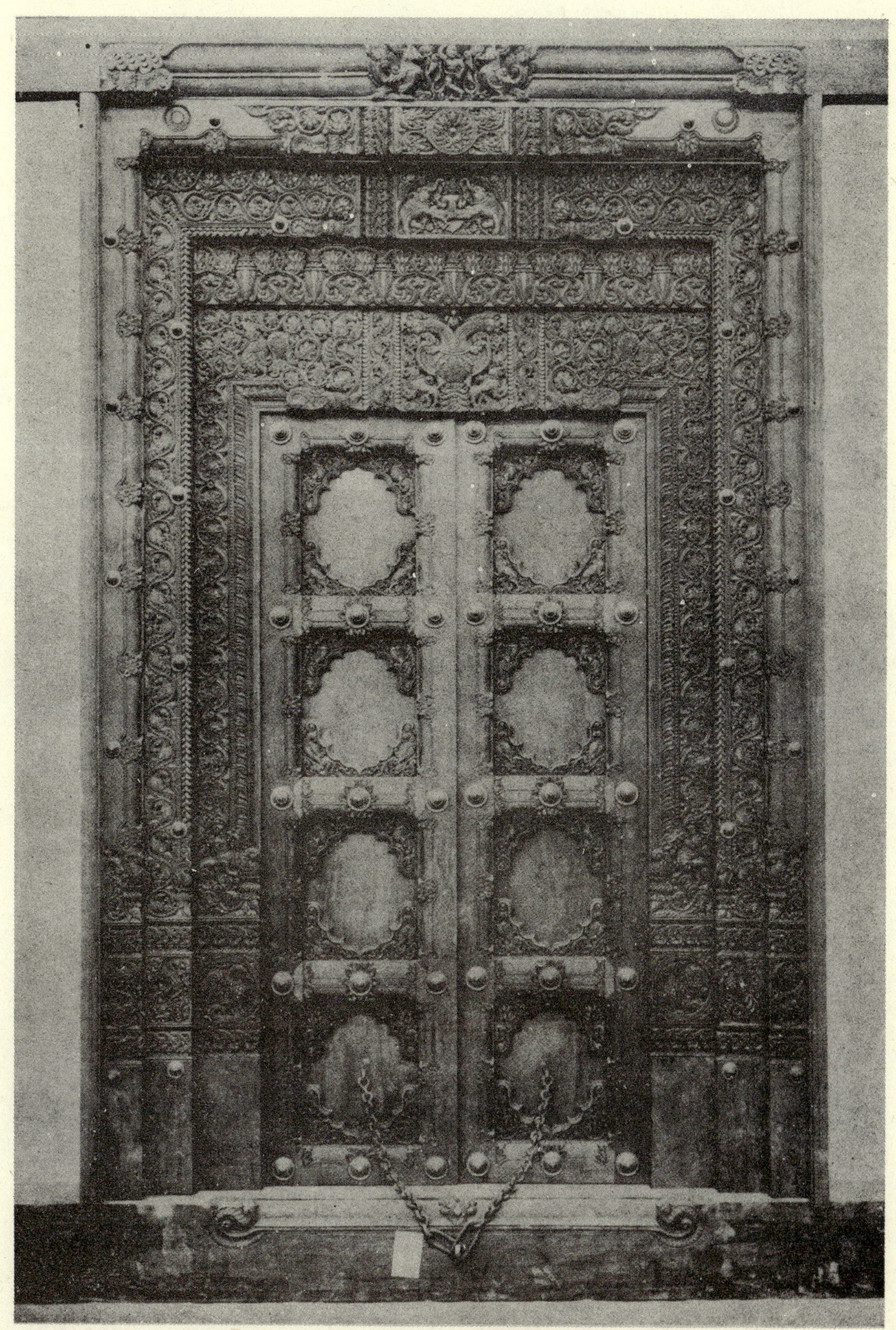

Plate No. 30 Bellary Door—Dravidian Style

style of incised black-wood tables – ebony or more frequently *shisham* made black through treatment with cocoa-nut oil. These tables used to be sold from Rs. 5 to Rs. 100 according to size and workmanship, but they are hardly if ever now produced although two have been specially made for the Exhibition. The design was plotted out by means of a pair of compasses, while the feet were in the form of elephant-heads with extended trunks passing to the floor. Recently the Technical School of Madura has pioneered into new flights in which Burmese and other styles have been copied while a further development of Dravidian style has also been matured where the *yáli* figures of the great temple are copied as the feet of the tables, etc. At the suggestion of the writer two of the most suitable figures in the great temple have been reproduced in wood as lamp stands at a half the original size. (Plate No. 63.) These are on view (Rs. 600 each) and will doubtless be much appreciated since they have been admirably prepared, and the Quixotic expression of the dancing archer cleverly rendered from the granite of the original. These have been purchased by the Indian Museum.

The Bellary Door (Chalukyan and Dravidian, Plate No. 30) is one of the most dignified structures in the Exhibition. It was made at the writer's request by a carpenter whose ancestors had made nearly all the beautiful doors of Bellary city. He was found at work on parts of the door and was simply required to devote a little more care and attention to it than he had originally intended. It will be seen to consist of three frames—one within the other—the innermost bearing the double-headed goose whose tail has given birth to the elaborately interwoven scroll of the frame. The charm of the door lies in the refinement given through the portions left without any carving and in the ogee-like pattern running round the double curved smooth frames of the door panels. It will thus be seen that this door manifests both Dravidian and Chalukyan feeling in its construction and ornamentation. It is thus hardly correct (as has been done inadvertently on the plate) to describe the Bellary Door as Dravidian. The tail-piece of page 169 shows one of the border patterns and another will be discovered as largely used by

DIVISION 13. WOOD-CARVING.

the copper and brass smiths of Calicut in their embossed and pierced caskets.

Malabar.—The Cannanore Central Jail has for many years enjoyed the reputation of turning out some good wood-work as also charmingly engraved cocoa-nuts. It would appear from the character of the carving that the inspiration must have come from Burmese prisoners since the style might be spoken of as a greatly modified form of Burmese carving. The design is first deeply incised then the edges of the floral scrolls and figures, thus brought into low relief, are rounded off and their surfaces scratched in imitation of veins, shadows, etc. This somewhat resembles the old fashioned "Bombay black-wood furniture" but is much flatter and never under-cut, so that in reality it more nearly resembles the wood-carvings of the aboriginal tribes of Fiji or New Zealand. It is distinctly quaint. A writing table is for sale (Rs. 250), and also a stationery holder (Rs. 31).

The Travancore House.—This beautiful and instructive addition to the Exhibition has been furnished by His Highness the Maharaja of Travancore. It has been constructed against the eastern wall of the Main Gallery alongside of the Jodhpur *jhároka* or projecting stone window. Travancore House is intended to depict one of the most striking features in the houses of the well-to-do inhabitants of that State. The gable verandah (if it may be so described), is true in every detail to those commonly seen in Travancore. It is richly carved, the rafters and purlins being developed into a special type of ornamentation quite unknown in any other part of India. This may be said to be first met with in the porches or outer corridors of the Dravidian temples, to the extreme south, such as at the great temple of Tinnevelly. It recalls forcibly the similar corridors and carved passages around the pagodas as also the verandahs and open gable rooms of the monasteries of Burma.

His Highness the Maharaja has also contributed a model in carved wood of a temple. This is intended to exemplify the leading decorative features of Travancore wood-carving.

10th :—Burma Wood-carving.—(*Plates Nos. 31 and 31-A.*)

DIVISION 13. WOOD-CARVING.

Except in the construction of religious buildings, such as the pagodas, masonry edifices have from time immemorial been practically prohibited to the Burmans. This circumstance has led to a great development of all the arts available for the ornamentation of wood-work. From the palace of the king or the priest, to the hut of the peasant, the Burmese people live, and have done so through all past ages, in wooden houses. Like Solomon's house made of the cedars of Lebanon and the palaces of Nineveh and Persepolis, they are perishable edifices, which by a few hours' conflagration or a few years' neglect, may be reduced to dust and ashes.

Wooden Houses.

It has already been observed that, from the wooden character of most of the early stone excavations and buildings of India, it may be inferred that they are repeating structures that had attained popularity and almost inseparable association with certain religious aspirations in wood, long anterior to their being constructed in stone. In this view, therefore, Burma can be accepted as carrying down to us some conception of the conditions that very possibly prevailed in India prior to the dark ages. We can imagine, for example, the fringe of palaces and monasteries that may have surrounded the topes and rails of Bharhut, Sanchi and Amravati, as we are forced to believe that the ruined pagodas that skirt (for 8 miles) the tongue of land within the great bend of the Irrawaddy river at Pagan (in Burma itself) must at one time have been dispersed through a populous city, of wooden palaces and houses, long since completely effaced.

Sumptuary Desires.

The admirable nature of the very abundant teak wood of Burma naturally aided the aspirations of the people for artistic houses, while the wealth of the soil admitted of a large percentage of the population being released from agricultural labour and thus free to satisfy the sumptuary desires of the wealthy. In consequence it is hardly a matter for surprise that wood-carving should have advanced beyond both suitability and necessity. It has in Burma become an art in which superfluity of wealth has dictated exuberance in treatment. The deep under-cutting of

DIVISION 13. WOOD-CARVING.

wood-work that can depict faithfully a triumphal arch covered with a profusion of vines and other flowers, with birds and squirrels resting on the twigs within its tracery, and which can be looked at not only on both sides but along the edge and through and through and still every detail remain vivid and life-like, can alone be compared with that profligacy of human labour already mentioned in connection with the Dravidian arts. Immense sums have, and are still expended on wood-carving in Burma, with, in consequence, exceptionally high wages paid to the most skilled carvers. It is not, however, alone in the extravagance in detail that a parallel may be drawn between the work of the Burman and that of the Tamil and Telugu people of Madras. There are so many striking similarities in the form of their sacred edifices, that one is disposed to think these can hardly be coincidences. They in fact challenge comparison not only with South Indian to Burman art, but with these collectively to Assyrian and Babylonian. The prevalence of radiating and pointed arches in certain of the brick buildings of Pagan, long anterior to the introduction of a true arch in India, is most significant. So again the great human-headed and winged lions of Burma might be looked upon as the lineal descendants of those that adorned the portals of Nineveh. But underneath all Burmese art and Burmese Buddhism there is a strong vein of the ancient demon worship, now a deep-rooted superstition. The distortions and twistings of the floral carvings in wood and ivory, of the chasings of metal ware, of the draperies of the sculptures, of the painted cloud effects, of the attitudes and expressions of the human figures, each and all are tainted with the *bilu* or demon. So all-important is this feature that without a knowledge of its existence, most of the designs are inexplicable.

Characteristic Features.

Three Styles.

In Burma there may be said to be three very distinct styles of wood-carving—the bold massive form seen on rudder chairs of boats, etc., the deep and elaborate under-cutting of the screens at the pagodas and monasteries and the simple incised carving of the house-doors and window-shutters. The writer desired to have these three forcibly demonstrated at the Exhibition and accordingly secured the rudder chairs of three ordinary river

Rudder Chairs as Panellings.

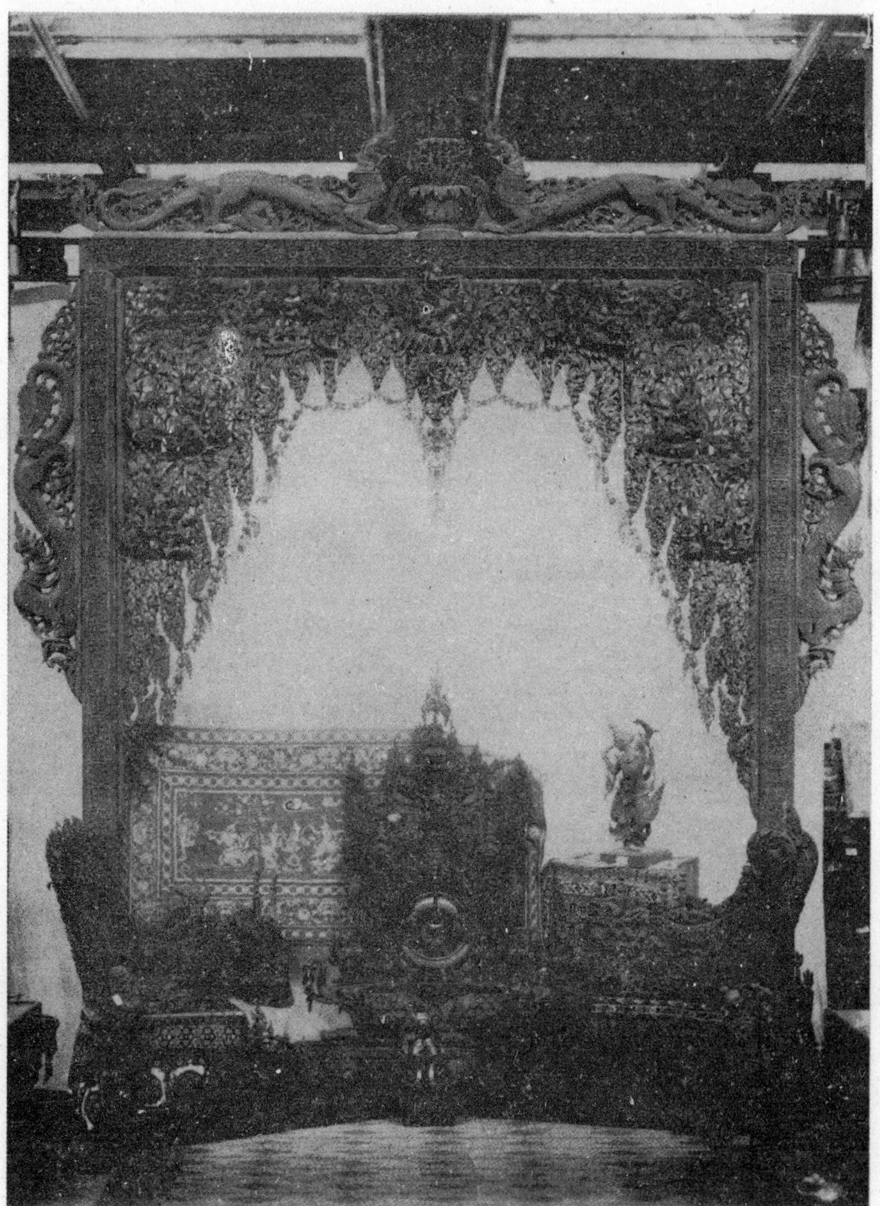

Plate No. 31(1) Wood Carving of Burma

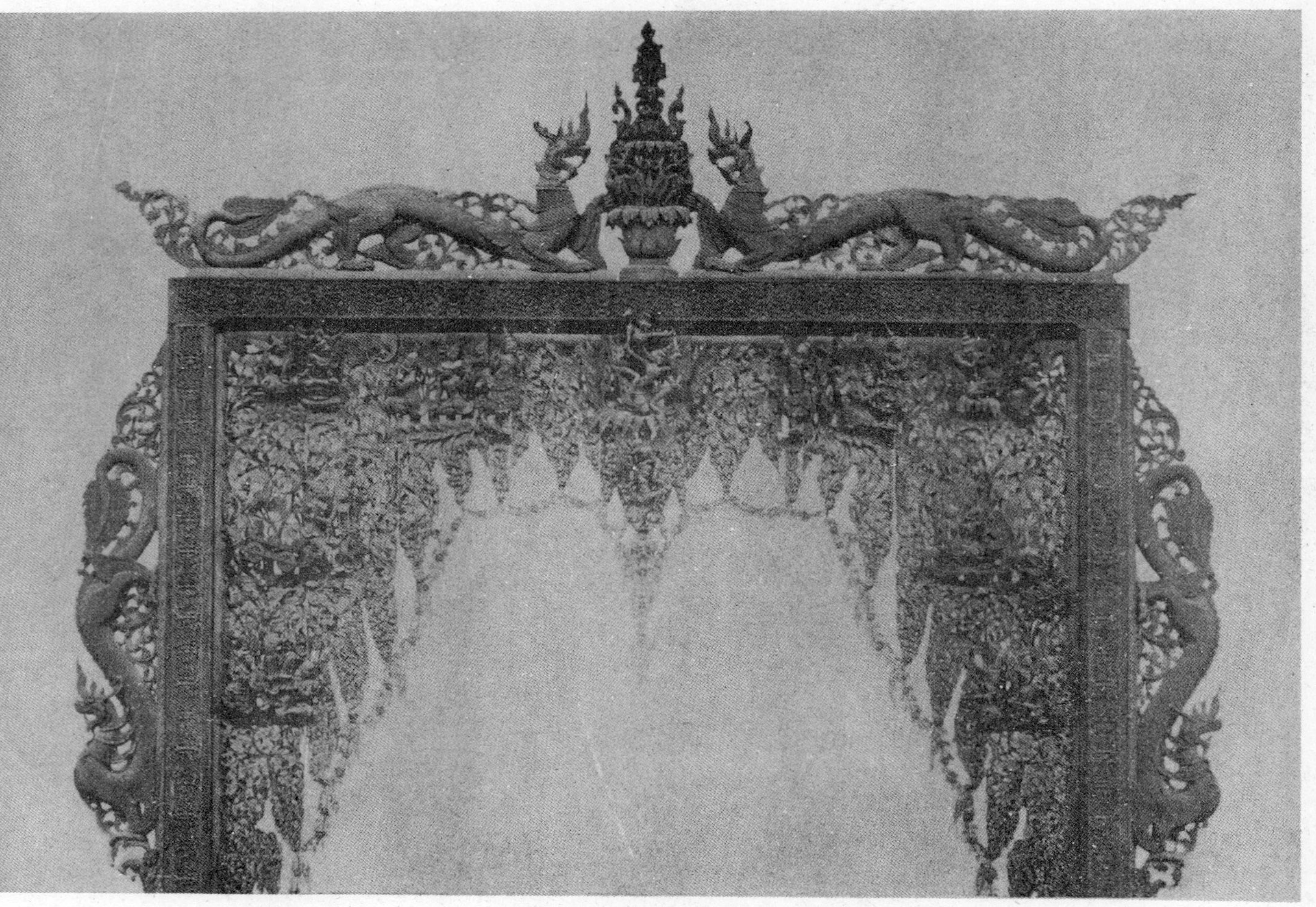

Plate No. 31(2) Wood Carving of Burma

boats. These have been turned on end and fixed against the south wall of the Refreshment Room (Plate No. 19) thus forming a simple and effective ornamentation. Near the floor and constituting a sort of basement panel, where the extremities of the rudder chairs converge and unite, have been placed two pairs of window-shutters. The originals from which these were copied were found on a house at Toungoo, the replicas being secured through the kind offices of Mr. C. R. Wilkinson, the Deputy Commissioner, Toungoo. Mr. H. L. Tilly, Chief Collector of Customs, Rangoon, having been instructed to supervise the preparation and despatch of goods for the Delhi Exhibition, from that town, was good enough to accompany the writer on a visit to the workshops of the chief carvers, *viz.*, Maung Po Thit, Maung Kaung Biu, Maung Po Nyun, and Maung Than.

DIVISION 13. WOOD-CARVING.

Screens at the Exhibition.

Arrangements were thereafter made for these craftsmen to copy two of the screens in the Shweydagon pagoda and to prepare certain gong-stands, wooden statues, rudder chairs, etc., for the Exhibition. The head-pieces to Chapters V and VI show certain features of this kind of Burmese wood-carving.

MANDALAY.—Subsequently, while on a visit to Mandalay, arrangements were entered into by which certain screens, doors, tympanums, etc., after the pattern of those in the Salin Kyaung, should be copied by Saya Khin, the most famous carver of Amarapura.

The series of Burmese wood-carving was thus organised with the object of presenting examples in its original form, rather than in the frequently putrid adaptations of it that are prepared for the European market. It was believed the finer and more elaborate work might be directly used for wall decoration, in the interior of houses, and the bolder and stronger work for out-door ornamentation, such as garden houses, band-stands, etc.

CHIEF EXHIBITS ON VIEW.

The splendid series of Burmese wood-carvings thus secured will be found in the Refreshment Room, in the Burmese Room, (on the left of the transept), and in the Main Gallery—the portion devoted to wood-carving. They also form a screen across the

DIVISION 13. WOOD-CARVING. main transept of the building of which the central arch came from Mandalay and the two side ones from Rangoon. The central arch was specially prepared from a selection of designs from the great pagoda in Rangoon and also the beautiful but little known Salin Kyaung of Mandalay. It has been purchased by His Highness the Maharaja of Nepal.

In the Refreshment Room will be found the large rudder chairs, Rs. 100 the pair; certain carved doors, supplied by the Local Government from their annual competition for good workmanship, these cost Rs. 431 each; and the four window shutters, Rs. 50.

In the Main Gallery have been placed six half life-sized statues admirably carved and sold for Rs. 73 each. Also two small figure gong-stands, Rs. 25. These were specially made to order, the idea being taken from two figures in the appliqué-work of one of the pagoda screens. Across the transept have been carried the three arches already mentioned; the left-hand screen by Maung Po Thit, has been sold for Rs. 1,500; the middle screen by Sayo Khin, for Rs. 2,000, and the right-hand screen by Maung Po Thit, for Rs. 1,500. They are good examples of their kind of work.

In the Burmese Room will be discovered an exquisite gong-stand by Maung Po Nyun, Rs. 1,500, a charming rudder chair by Saya Taung, Rs. 513, and two more rudder chairs boldly cut by the same maker, Rs. 50 each. A pair of tympanums, reproduced from those in the Salin Kyaung; two doors by Maung Than, Rs. 431 each; a door one quarter natural size from the Salin Kyaung, Rs. 250; and lastly a frieze copied from parts of the monastery near the great pagoda of Prome, Rs. 125.

A good collection of miscellaneous wood-work is contributed by Messrs. Beato & Co., of Rangoon, and may be said to constitute the furniture in the Burmese Room. This comprises amongst other things a carved screen (No. 37), price Rs. 250, a gong stand, Rs. 250, and an overmantel (No. 38), Rs. 187.

AWARDS FOR WOOD-CARVING UNDER DIVISION 13 (ARCHITECTURE AND FURNITURE).

AWARDS. First Prize with gold medal awarded to His Highness the Maharaja of Bhavnagar for Architectural wood-carving as seen in Bhavnagar House. (Plate No. 28.)

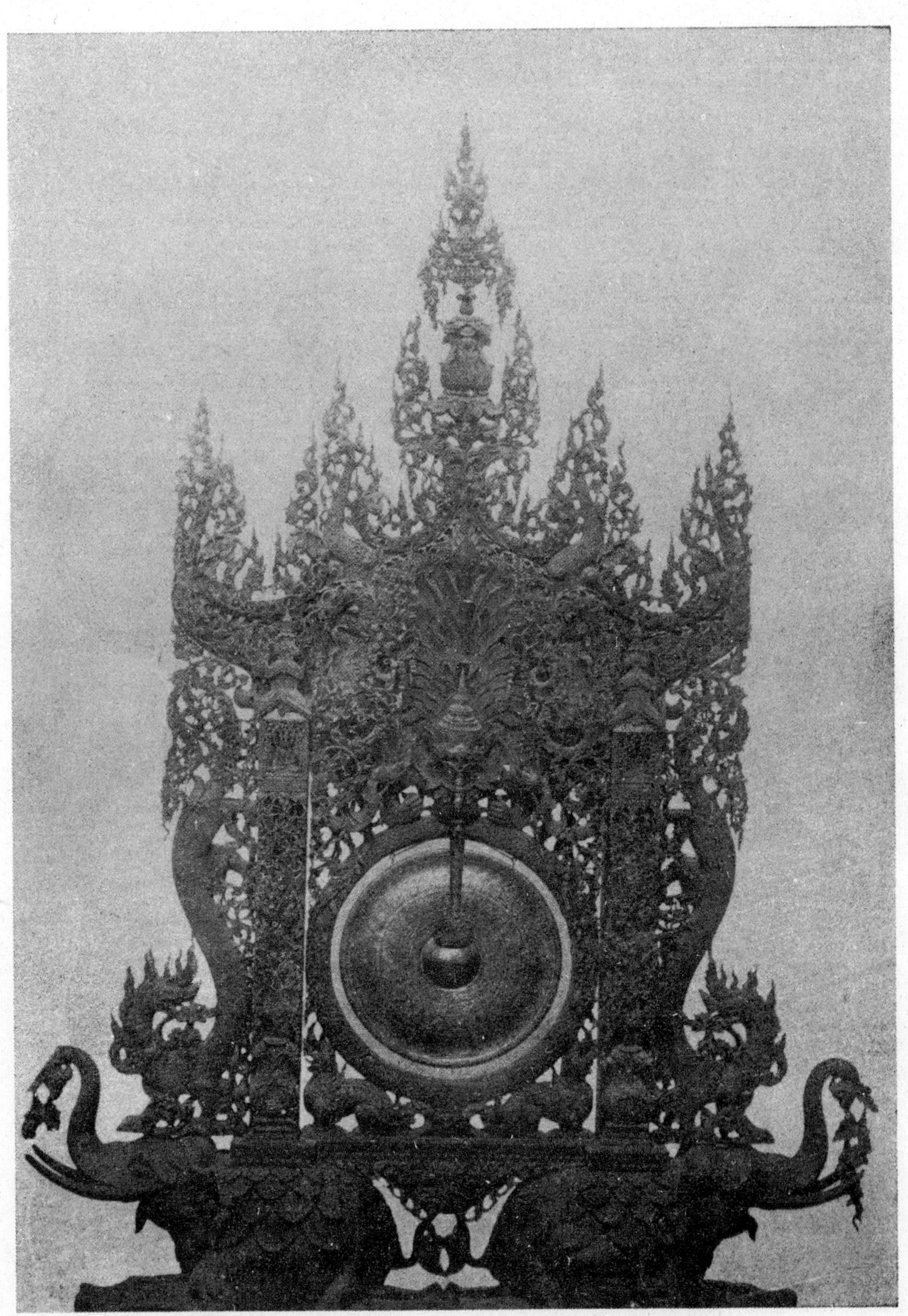

Plate No. 31-A Burmese Carved Wood Gong Stand

DIVISION 13. WOOD-CARVING.

First Prize with gold medal awarded to the Mayo School of Art, Lahore, for wood-carving shown on the balcony of the Panjab Room. (Plate No. 21.)

First Prize with gold medal to the School of Art, Bombay, for its room furnished and decorated in Gujerat style. (Plate No. 2.)

First Prize with gold medal for Burmese Princess in carved wood made by Maung Than Yegyan of Rangoon. (Plate No. 64.)

First Prize with silver medal to the Madras School of Arts for the carved doorway at the entrance to its Dravidian Room. (Plate No. 1.)

Second Prize with silver medal to the Madras School of Arts for a sideboard in Dravidian style (No. 644).

Second Prize with silver medal to the Bombay School of Art for a sideboard.

Second Prize with silver medal for sideboard made by the Mayo School of Art, Lahore.

Second Prize with silver medal for Burmese gong-stand made by Maung Po Nyun of Rangoon. (Plate No. 31-A.)

Second Prize with silver medal for Burmese archway made by Saya Khin of Mandalay. (Plate No. 31.)

Second Prize with silver medal for bracket in black-wood (No. 906) made by Panachand Bhagwan of Ahmedabad. (Shown in middle of Plate No. 27.)

Third Prize with bronze medal to Messrs. Beato & Co., of Rangoon and Mandalay for furniture in Burmese Room.

Third Prize with bronze medal for balcony made under the supervision of the State Chief Engineer of Baroda.

Third Prize with bronze medal for a doorway made by Surjan Singh of Saharanpur. (Plate No. 23.)

Third Prize with bronze medal for replica of a door in the old palace of Mysore made by the Executive Engineer of the new palace. (Plate No. 29.)

Third Prize with bronze medal for a carved door made by Hussain Perasaib and Peeransahib, carpenters, Bellary. (Plate No. 30.)

Third Prize with bronze medal for replica of a pillar (No. 503)

DIVISION 13. WOOD-CARVING. (in the form of a huntsman) from the great temple of Madura, made under the supervision of the Principal of the Technical School of Madura. (Plate No. 63.)

Third Prize with bronze medal for carved table (No. 3804) and another table (No. 3867) in black ebony made by Abdulla, Mistri, of Nagina in Bijnor (shown in Plate No. 24).

Third Prize with bronze medal for a bracket (No. 4652) made by Somnath Bhadar Das of Panchpati, Ahmedabad.

Third Prize with bronze medal for two reproductions in wood of certain architraves in Hallabid temple, also carved doorway in *Hardwickia binnata* wood (No. 3348); made under the instructions of Mr. J. Cameron, Superintendent of the Bangalore Museum. (For former, see Plate No. 29.)

Third Prize with bronze medal to Barkat Ali, of Jallandhar, Panjab, for overmantel (No. 836), panel (No. 830), table (No. 835), and table (No. 838). (See Plate No. 22, fig. 1.)

Commended for old carved doorway purchased through the Collector, made by carpenters in Mainpuri in the United Provinces.

Commended for carved overmantel exhibited by Messrs. Davee Sahai Chamba Mull of Amritsar.

Commended for carved walnut tray (No. 2766) made by Habib Joo of Srinagar, Kashmir.

Commended for carved walnut screen (No. 2870) made by Jabbar Khan of Srinagar, Kashmir.

Division 14.—Inlaying.

The subject of wood-carving having been dealt with more or less in detail, there seems hardly any occasion to devote to the other Divisions of wood-work so much consideration. Inlaying, for example, is an art rarely practised by itself. There is no special craft devoted to it, and the designs adopted differ in no essential from those of carving. It may accordingly be regarded as an aid to wood-carving and one resorted to mainly for special effects. At the same time there are a few centres that have for long years past enjoyed the reputation of having expert inlayers, hence certain styles of wood-work may be instantly recognised by the

DIVISION 14. INLAYING.

Materials Used.

peculiar form of this art which they adopt. Inlaying may be accomplished by other woods, by ivory, by bone, by mother-of-pearl or by metals. It may be in large pieces or in fine wire, the former becomes a kind of encrusting and the latter a form of damascening. At times marquetry and veneering come to resemble inlaying, owing to a ribbon or veneer, composed of many parts and materials, being first separately prepared then inlaid *en masse* as may be desired. When simply fastened to the surface this becomes appliqué or veneering proper. (See Plate No. 37.)

Centres of Production.

The following are the chief Indian centres of inlaying :—

Hoshiarpur and Jallandhar (with Simla as a summer resort), where ivory or bone and also brass are inlaid on *shisham*; Chiniot, where brass alone is used—both towns of the Panjab. Mainpuri, in the United Provinces, where copper or brass wire are employed. Recently (and in questionable taste), Nagina, in Oudh, has made a bid for inlaying its ebony work with ivory or bone. Mysore, where ivory on *shisham*, rosewood or ebony, is the form of the art adopted. Monghyr, in Bengal, where ivory or ebony is practised. Some beautiful inlaying is also turned out both at Ratnagiri and Aurangabad, but apparently at the Industrial Schools of these places only. Lastly, in Nepal, ivory is inlaid on black-wood.

Plate No. 32 shows a group of inlaid wood-work, those from Mysore being to the right, those from Northern India to the left. The art has for long been followed in Mysore. His Highness the Maharaja has recently given great encouragement to its extension by having many of the doors and articles of furniture, required for the new palace, done by the inlayers of the State. The chief firms that turn out this class of goods, may be said to be Messrs. Ahamed Ali and Mahomed Mukhdum, Ganesiam & Co., and Yusuf Ali & Sons The last mentioned have sent only a few samples, but these perhaps the best finished of all. One of the most beautiful and perhaps also ancient examples of Indian inlaid work may be said to be the door from the Palace of Bikanir shown to the extreme right of Plate No. 32.

Process of Inlaying.

The method of inlaying is practically the same in all parts of the world. The ivory or bone is first formed into long strips of a

DIVISION 14. INLAYING.

required shape, then cut transversely into a number of thin slips. These are laid on their places and the outlines of the spaces required, scratched on the wood. These are then cut out and the ivory imbedded with glue or other cement as required. A peculi-

Chief Characteristics.

arity of Mysore work and the one that gives it its great charm, is the fact that the surface of the ivory is ornamented with black designs. This is accomplished by scratching a pattern on the surface of the ivory, then smearing over with black lakh (lac), fused by means of a hot bolt. The excess of lakh above the surface is next removed by scraping with the edge of a flat knife. The black ornamentations thus shown below the surface are, in the case of large pieces of ivory, done before being inlaid, but with the small pieces may subsequently be accomplished. An even more important feature of the superiority of Mysore work over that of Hoshiarpur, Jallandhar, etc., may, however, be said to be the more artistic designs adopted, the better workmanship displayed and the more durable wood employed. The surfaces are not overloaded with ivory and the articles have a finish and style about them that is most pleasing and exceptional with Indian work, while the price is not materially greater than that of Hoshiarpur and other localities. These introductory observations should be compared with the remarks below on Ivory.

CHIEF EXHIBITS ON VIEW.

Ivory and Bone Inlaying.—It may perhaps serve a useful purpose to discuss each of the centres of inlaying a little more fully and to indicate the collections now on view, under two sections, *viz.*, inlaying with (*a*) ivory, bone and other woods, and (*b*) with metals.

1. HOSHIARPUR and JALLANDHAR (Plate No. 32).—The art of inlaying has been long practised in these towns, to meet certain native requirements. To Mr. Coldstream must be attributed the honour of having inspired the present trade in European furniture. For many years low settees (*chaukis*), used by the natives, also pen-cases, walking-sticks and the like have been regularly produced but recently the shops of the Indian art-dealers have been flooded with tables, cabinets, etc., elaborately spotted all over with ivory or bone. The absence of any definite scheme of orna-

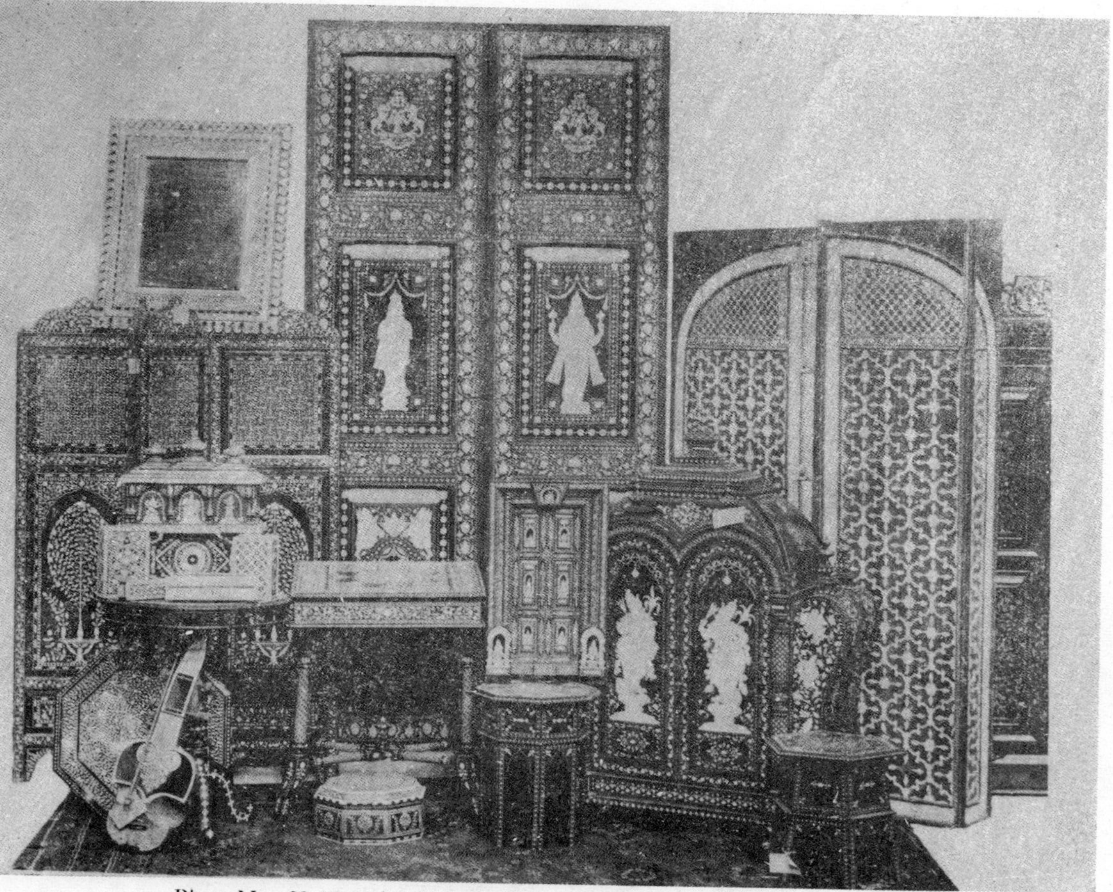

Plate No. 32 Wood inlaying with Ivory Bone or Mother-of-Pearl

mentation and the overelaboration usually pursued, are the chief faults of this style of work, together with an inherent tendency to the cheap but nasty.

The best examples in the collection may be said to be the almirah from Lahore; the looking-glass from Hoshiarpur made by Jeyram Das and Karam Chand, price Rs. 115; some three or four small tables from Lahore and Hoshiarpur, Rs. 30 to Rs. 50; a work-box from Hoshiarpur by Atma Ram and Ganga Ram, Rs. 75; and a looking-glass from Amritsar, Rs. 110. It seems needless to specialize further the numerous excellent examples displayed on the tables of the Exhibition. All or nearly all are made at or near Hoshiarpur, those from Lahore and Amritsar being sent by dealers are in all probability Hoshairpur or Jallandhar work.

2. NAGINA, in Oudh, has for some time past taken to produce inlaid work. It is doubtful if ebony inlaid with ivory can be made attractive. In the case of the Nagina work it is overloaded with minute specks of white. Only a few pieces have been shown—a screen valued at Rs. 2,000 and a bracket at Rs. 988 are those best deserving of mention.

3. MONGHYR.—For many years this town has been famed all over Bengal for turning out black ebony work-boxes, inlaid with ivory. These are known to the trade as "Monghyr boxes." The pattern of ornamentation was formerly a minute spray of flowers in stiff conventionalism. Recently the inlayers seem to have got a new conception. They turn out cabinets, card-tables and other such articles in response to the universal modern demand for articles of quasi-European household furnishing. The style of ornamentation has also changed and perhaps improved though it is difficult to form an opinion as to the origin of the design or its possible future developments. Three circular pieces of ivory, one larger than the other two, are inlaid at fixed intervals, while the interspaces of ebony are incised and punched, thus giving an effective back-ground to the diaper of ivory. Of this kind of goods may be mentioned a cabinet, Rs. 125, a card-table, Rs. 62-8, a tea-table, Rs. 31, and a work-box, Rs. 25. As compared with other ebony work this is remarkably cheap and

DIVISION 14. INLAYING.

serviceable, though monotonous when more than one sample is seen. All these articles have been made by Kali Charan of Monghyr.

4. NEPAL.—The inlaying of ivory on black ebony seems to be practised to some extent in this State. The picture frames supplied will be doubtless much admired. They display a neatness in execution and elegance in scroll ornamentation that will be a surprise to most persons who are accustomed to associate quaint appliqué rather than finished inlaying with Nepal.

5. RATNAGIRI—Has contributed two writing tables produced by the pupils of the local Industrial School. Although these are European in feeling both in construction and ornamentation they are good examples of inlaying in which two or three shades of wood have been carefully selected so as to produce a desired effect; price Rs. 375 and Rs. 335 each.

6. AURANGABAD.—A somewhat similar style of coloured wood inlaying to that of Ratnagiri is practised at this town, one example of which, a small glove-box, price Rs. 50, may be discovered in the Exhibition: it has been purchased by His Excellency the Viceroy. This is ornamented with three shades of wood interspaced with brass.

7. MYSORE.—The best specimen of inlaid work shown in the Exhibition, will doubtless be admitted to be the door from the palace of Mysore which has been placed in the Loan Collection Gallery. (See Plate No. 32.) In the Main Gallery will be found numerous fine examples, all for sale. Among these may be specially mentioned the splendid drawing-room cabinets (Rs. 950 to Rs. 1,150) made by Ganesiah and Co.; the lady's writing table, Rs. 458, from the Mysore Museum; the large assortment of small tables, mostly in quaint octagonal forms, Rs. 25 to Rs. 60; the miniature doors, Rs. 250, made by Messrs. Ahamad Ali and Muhamad Mukhdum; the stationery racks, Rs. 65 to Rs. 150; lastly a charming casket (spoken of as an address box), by Messrs. Ahamad Ali and Muhamad Mukhdum, ebony inlaid with ivory and silver, price Rs. 625. One or two rosewood writing tables, with roll tops, inlaid with white woods, have also been contributed by Ganesiah and Co., of Mysore, at a cost of Rs. 340

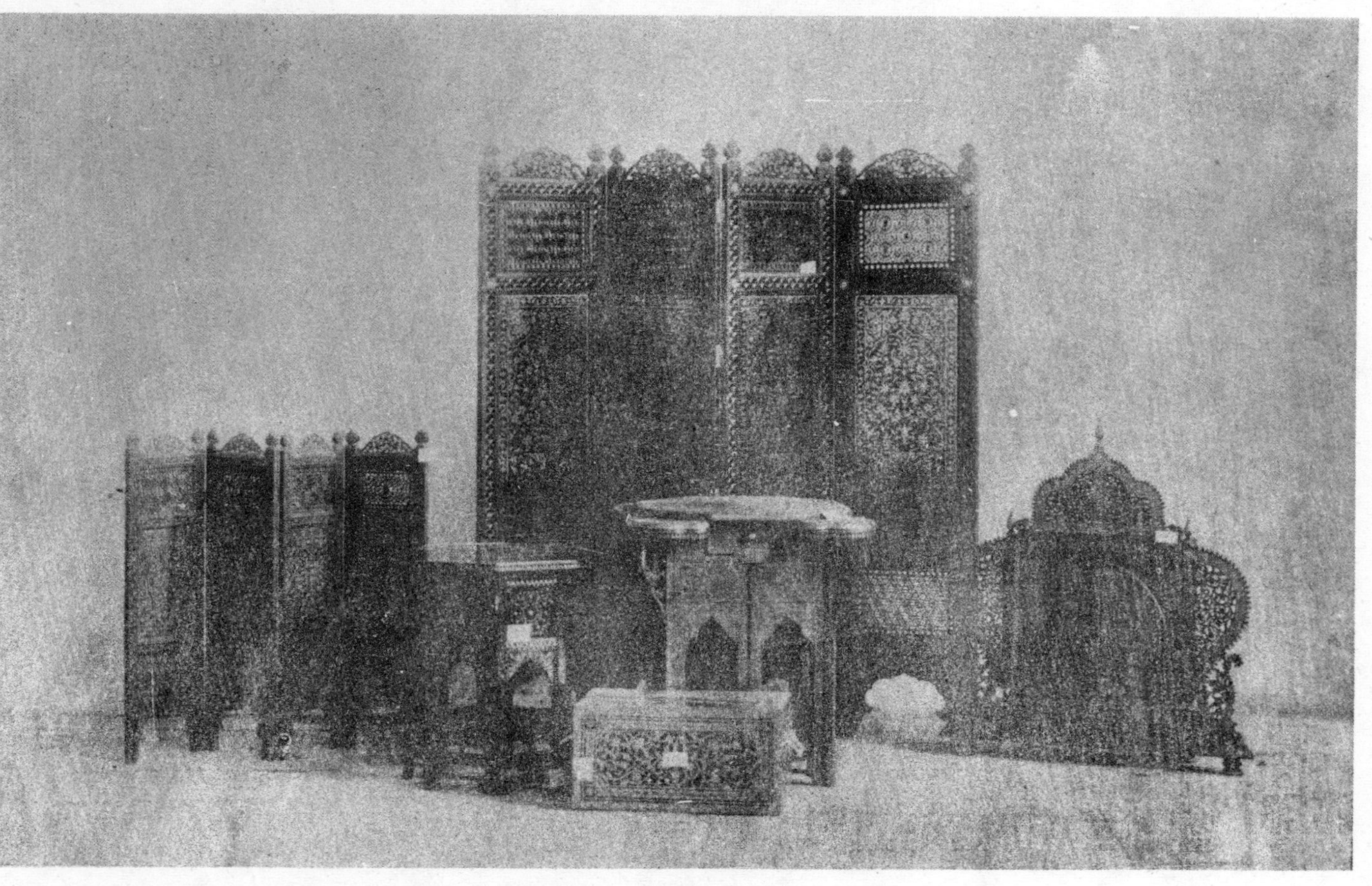

Plate No. 33 Inlaying with Metal (Mainpuri, Chiniot, etc.)

each. Messrs. M. Yusuf Ali & Sons, Artware makers of Mysore, have sent a few admirably finished articles such as a vase, Rs. 75, a small work-box, Rs. 55, and a walking-stick, Rs. 100. (*Conf.* with Class V.)

Metal Inlaying.—Turning now to Metal Inlaying, there are two or three centres where this is practised, the chief being Chiniot and Lahore in the Panjab and Mainpuri in the United Provinces. Of course in many other places metal may be and is used to a limited extent. For example, both in Hoshiarpur and Jallandhar the art is an old one, but these towns can hardly be regarded as having evolved features in metal inlaying that are in any way distinctive.

CHINIOT.—The art of inlaying with brass, as practised in this locality, would seem to have originated with the preparation of camel-panniers (*kajawas*). It has recently, in the hands of Muhammad Hussain, risen to a higher order. Some of the screens turned out by that carpenter are exceedingly beautiful and remarkably cheap. His usual charge for a four-leaved screen is about Rs. 150, but if finished on both sides, Rs. 200 or Rs. 250. With one or two exceptions the examples shown in the Exhibition are not up to his best standard. Chiniot work is bolder, freer and better in design than the inlaying of Hoshiarpur or Jallandhar and the contrast of the metal with the darker wood used in Chiniot is distinctly superior to that with the wood employed in Hoshiarpur. The best example is the screen shown in the background of Plate No. 33.

LAHORE and AMRITSAR.—Sant Ram of Lahore has contributed a few small screens, prices Rs. 43 to Rs. 88, and there will also be found various drawing-room tables more or less inlaid with brass, at prices from Rs. 30 to Rs. 50. (To left of Plate No. 33.)

MAINPURI in the UNITED PROVINCES.—This District has for many years been noted for its beautiful wood-work inlaid with brass-wire. Mr. Percy Brown's sketch (Plate No. 34) shows the Mainpuri operator at work and Plate No. 33 gives a selection of the metallic inlaid wood-work of India, Mainpuri being represented by the wall-cabinet and card table. In an issue of the *Indian Art*

Journal (1887), Mr. F. S. Growse, C.I.E., told the story of the *tar-kashi* (wire-work) of Mainpuri. It can alone be done on the best seasoned black *shisham* wood, the copper being beaten into very thin sheets, then cut into fine wire. The pattern is first drawn on paper, then stencilled on to the wood. It usually follows a more or less geometric conception, but is finally evolved into an endless profusion of winding and encircling golden lines. The pattern is scratched or incised on the wood and the wire hammered within the hollowed lines. The dots that diversify the design run up to many thousands, in a space of a few inches. These are minute coils of wire twisted up on the point of a needle. They are made by little boys. The card table shown on Plate No. 33 is a beautiful example of this style of work and has been purchased by His Excellency the Viceroy.

Until comparatively recently the *tar-kashi* produced consisted of sandals (*kharauns*) used while bathing, pen-cases, work-boxes, etc.; these and such like small articles are apparently made at other centres besides Mainpuri (and Pilibhit may possibly be one) since there is hardly a local fair in the United Provinces, Behar and even Bengal that they are not offered for sale. To Mr. Growse more especially and to one or two other officers stationed in Mainpuri, has to be attributed the expansion of the craft to its present more important position. The art is best exemplified by plates or trays. A plate 12 inches in diameter will occupy one workman for 20 days. This circumstance conveys a fairly accurate idea of the cost of the work. Speaking of doors, Mr. Growse observes that the application of wire inlaying to architectural purposes was his own conception, no doors of the kind having ever yet been set up in any Native house. The door sent to the Indian Art Exhibition from Mainpuri while a fine old bit of work displays no *tar-kashi* as was hoped it might when ordered.

TRAVANCORE.—In the Exhibition a most admirably finished piece of inlaying work will be found in the form of a work-box. This was made at Travancore and is for sale, price Rs. 310. It is beautifully inlaid with copper, the design being quite unlike anything shown from other parts of India.

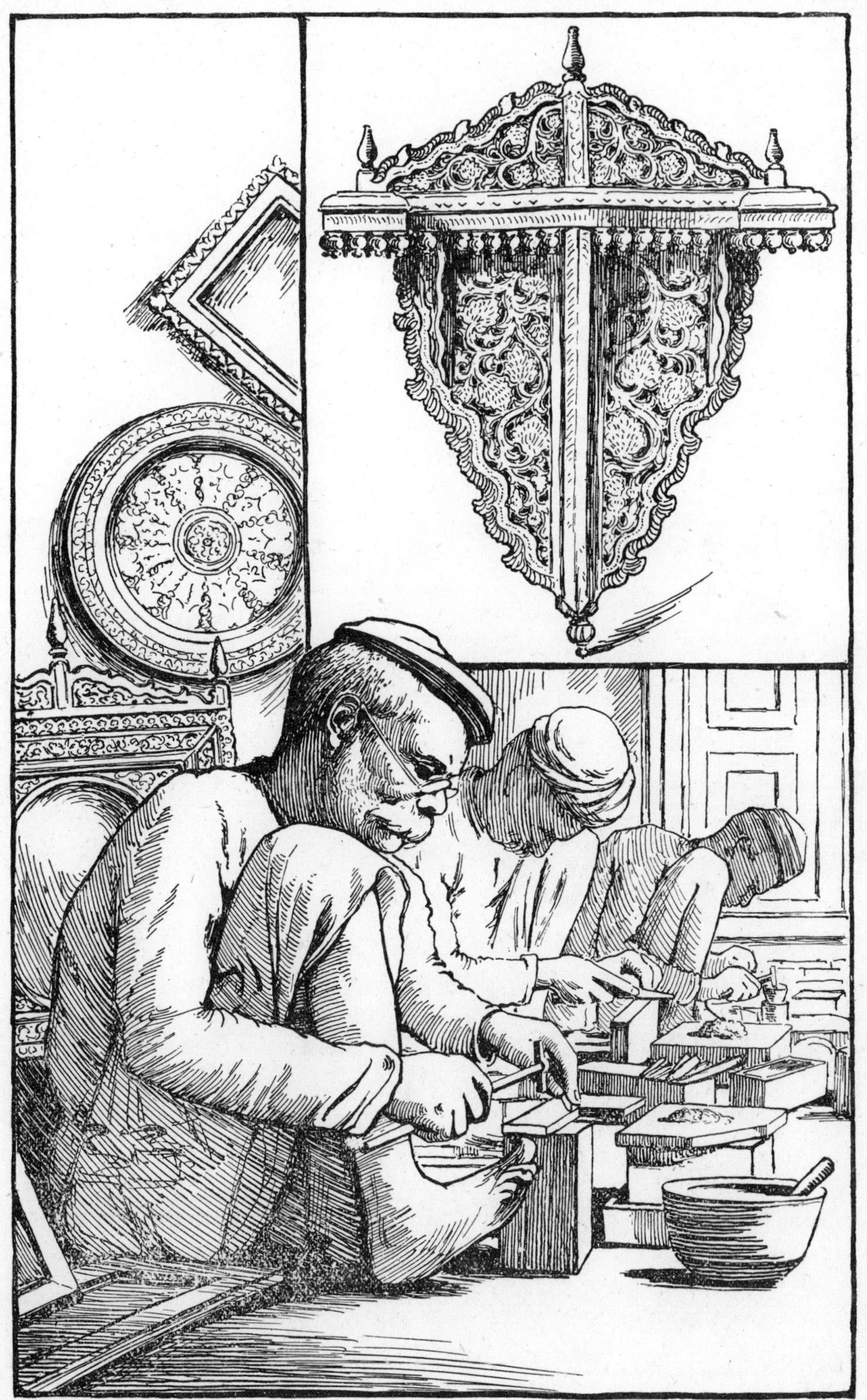

Plate No. 34 Wire Inlayers, Mainpuri U.P

AWARDS FOR WOOD-WORK UNDER DIVISION 14 (INLAYING).

DIVISION 14. INLAYING. AWARDS.

First Prize with silver medal to Ganeshiah of Mysore for a cabinet inlaid in ivory.

First Prize with silver medal to Kanhaiya Lal Madan Mohan of Mainpuri for a table inlaid with metal.

Second Prize with silver medal to Ahmed Ali and Mahomed Makhdum of Mysore for a cabinet inlaid with ivory.

Second Prize with silver medal to Atma Ram and Ganga Ram of Hoshiarpur for two boxes inlaid with ivory.

Third Prize with bronze medal to Maula Baksh and Dost Mahomed of Chiniot for a screen inlaid with metal.

Third Prize with bronze medal to Alleppy of Travancore for a box inlaid with metal.

Third Prize with bronze medal to the Industrial School of Aurangabad for box inlaid with wood and metal.

Third Prize with bronze medal to Kali Charan of Monghyr for a cabinet of ebony inlaid with ivory.

Commended for cup inlaid with ivory, Yusuf Ali & Sons.

Commended for table inlaid with metal, Bhagwan Singh of Jallandhar.

Commended for screen inlaid with metal, Muhammad Hussain of Chiniot.

Commended for almirah inlaid with ivory, exhibited by Mr. G. B. Bleazby, of Lahore.

Commended for screen inlaid with ivory and ebony by Jeyram Dass and Karam Chand of Hoshiarpur.

Division 15.—Sandal-wood.

Sandal-wood is the most popular and most expensive of all woods. It is with the Natives of India engraved, inlaid or veneered and made into a variety of most beautiful and artistic articles. Of *chandan* (sandal-wood) it might in fact be said that after ivory it is the material best suited for ornamental treatment. It is utilized at many localities, remote from the regions of production, such as Cuttack in Bengal; Delhi in the Panjab; Indore and Alwar in Rajputana; and Ahmedabad and Surat in Bombay. The chief centres of sandal-wood carving are, however, Sorab and Sugar in Mysore; Travancore, Trichinopoly,

Centres of Manufacture.

DIVISION 15. SANDAL-WOOD.

Tirupati, Madura and Coimbatore in Madras; and Kanara, Surat, Ahmedabad and Bombay in the Western Presidency. There are said to be three qualities of the wood dependant on the age of the tree, the locality of production, and the position in the stem from which derived. As a rule the darker the colour the better the quality.

The art of sandal-wood carring is usually confined to one or two families. In Mysore, in the Shimoga District, the most important centre of the craft, there are, for example, not more than eight families with 35 artizans in all. These are known as *gudigars*. They claim to have come from Goa and to owe their name to the circumstance that they were originally the hereditary carvers and painters of the temple (or *gudi*). The resemblance of the name *gudigar* to *kondikar* (the ivory carvers of Bengal) suggests a possible caste identity. The instruments

Tools used and Mode of Operation.

employed by the sandal-wood carvers are extremely simple, *viz.*, a saw, a plane, a mallet, a hone or fine-grained hard stone, and an assortment of various kinds and sizes of chisels and a few engraver's tools—some extremely minute and delicate. The operation is started by either drawing the pattern that is intended to be produced on the smooth and white-washed sandal-wood, or on a piece of paper pasted over its surface. This is then engraved or outlined in every detail; the interspaces between the lines are next cut away, thus leaving the pattern in low relief; and lastly the design itself is carved in the minutest detail by chisels fine and still finer, as the work progresses. In this way every effect of light and shade, every curve and expression, and every texture that may be desired is fully portrayed.

Characteristic Features.

The minuteness and intricacy in elaboration aimed at are alone equalled by the results attained by the ivory carver. The chief and only flaw in this most charming craft is the fact that the joinery is unsatisfactory and the fittings worthless. With truly artistic indifference to minor details the sandal-wood carver will devote days and weeks to the carving of panels or figures on a block composed of several small pieces stuck together by glue while he is fully conscious this will give way and thus ruin his work in a few months' time. This defect can alone be

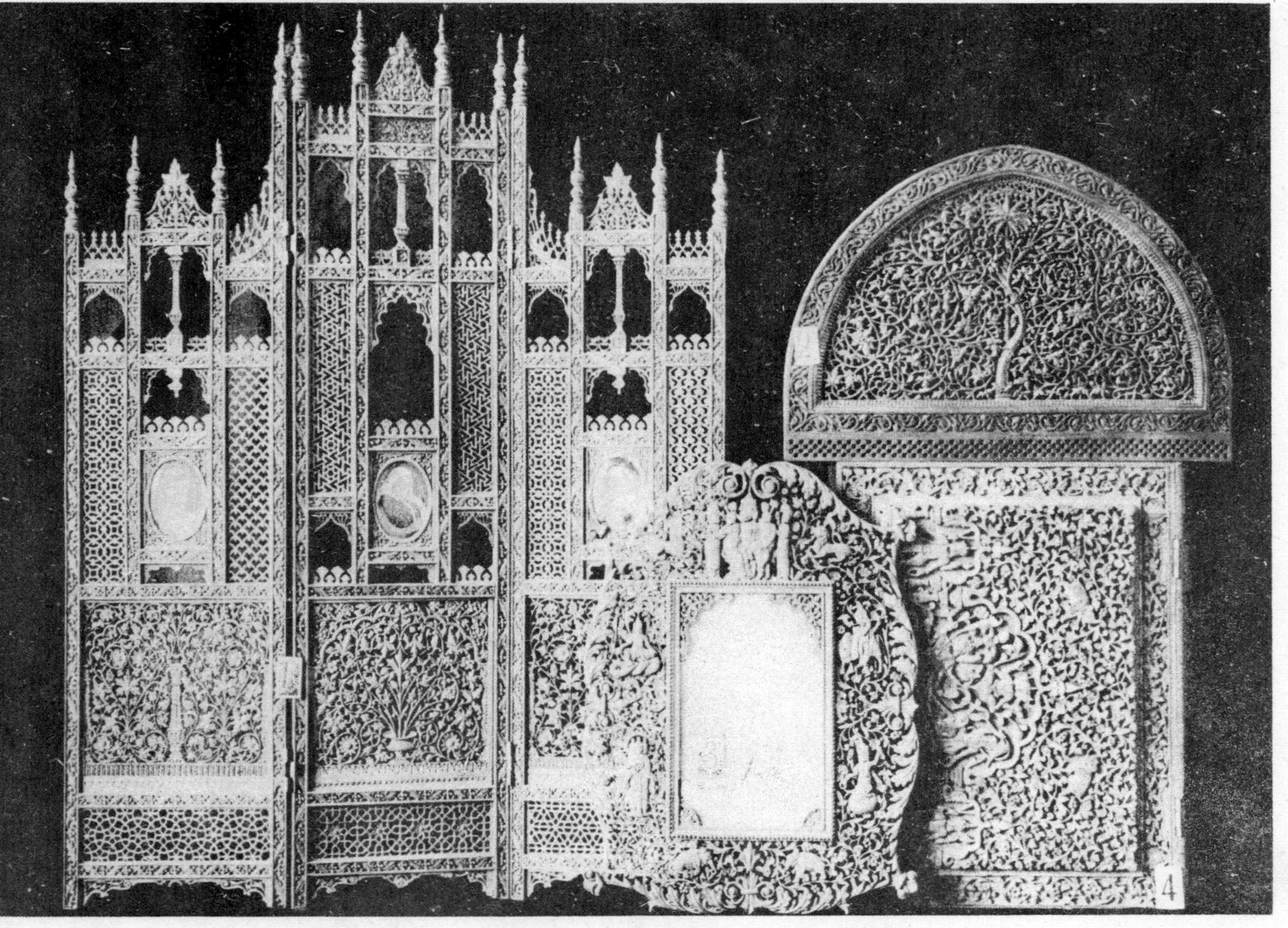

Plate No. 34-A Bombay, Ahmedabad and Surat Sandalwood

DIVISION 15. SANDAL-WOOD.

remedied by the sandal-wood work, when produced, being taken to pieces and reset by a professional cabinet-maker. No persuasion and no inducement has ever succeeded in remedying these defects. The artizans are profligate, apathetic, indigent and of intemperate habits. If their work be not desired they are ready to starve; but to change their social position, their modes of life or their craft customs, they will not. The number of good artists is extremely limited and a rule is carefully observed, *viz.*, that, if a youth does not show natural aptitude, no attempt is made to train him to the higher flights of the carver's art. Accordingly a large percentage of the sons of carvers become carpenters or even agriculturists and do not learn their ancestral trade. These considerations thus naturally narrow the possibility of any great expansion, the more so since no person outside the caste is ever admitted to the fraternity. The cheap, ordinary goods, that can be produced by indifferent skill, are those that pay. It accordingly amounts to a favour to undertake the more expensive and more troublesome work. Under these circumstances it is useless to explain the possible new markets and high prices that might be secured for good and conscientious work.

Habits of the Craftsmen.

Paying Goods.

Chief Styles.

SURAT, AHMEDABAD and BOMBAY.—(*Plate No. 35-A.*)—Sandal-wood carving has one constant characteristic, *viz.*, its application to small objects. It is accordingly elaborate and minute but while that is so there are several well marked types. In the Bombay, Surat and Ahmedabad work, for example, there may be traced a strongly Jaina tendency. The branches of the trees constantly assume the encircling feature of the Ahmedabad window panellings. The foliage is large, bold, deeply and freely cut, with the individual leaves having upturned tips and coarsely serrate margins. Interspersed with the foliage, a profusion of temples, also human and mythological subjects occur, but these display remarkably little conventionalism and artistic grouping and no trace of perspective. Reliance is apparently placed upon massiveness. As a rule the houses and figures are jumbled together without any study of effect. In fact the sandal-wood work of Gujarat, as a whole, bears evidence of having been adapted from a previous art, most probably ebony-carving, there very

DIVISION 15. SANDAL-WOOD. largely practised to this day, rather than of being an original conception in direct adaptation to the possibilities of the material.

KANARA sandal-wood work on the other hand is much nearer in art feeling to that of Mysore than to Bombay. Hindu mythological subjects occur in profusion but in artistic assemblages, the surfaces ornamented being as a rule panelled or recessed for the idols and the foliage much more minute and more sharply cut than in Bombay and Surat work.

MYSORE sandal-wood carving follows closely the type of stone carvings of Hallabid and Belgavi and the floral ornamentation is of the nature already fully detailed in connection with

Chalukyan Style. Chalukyan wood-carving. The foliage, for example, is pinnate but thrown out in fan-like sprays with the tips of the individual portions rolled up. The mythological figures are invariably placed within canopied panels, assorted between floral scrolls, which follow some fixed and highly artistic plan. The elephant-headed animal, with foliated tail, or the goose carrying in its bill a spray of flowers are ever present and recurrent features (see Plates Nos. 29 and 30). The style has in fact been fully and beautifully adapted to sandal-wood and there is no trace of the make-shift treatment of the Surat and Ahmedabad work.

CHIEF EXHIBITS ON VIEW.

MYSORE.—In the Loan Collection Gallery there will be found what is perhaps one of the most perfect samples of sandal-wood ever produced. This is intended as a spandril for a door-way in the Darbar Hall of the new palace at Mysore. Plate No. 36 gives a fair impression of this wonderful piece of wood-carving. It depicts the incident in the life of the youthful *Krishna* when he stole the garments of the *gopis* or milk-maids while they were bathing. Nature seems to rejoice with the advent of the god on earth; every bough of the tree, every bird and animal as also the fish in the waters, sing his praise, while the contentment of the trooping homeward of the cattle is simply admirable.

In the Sale Gallery will be found a unique series of mythological sandal-wood sculptures, a few of which have been given in Plate No. 35. There are representations of the three families

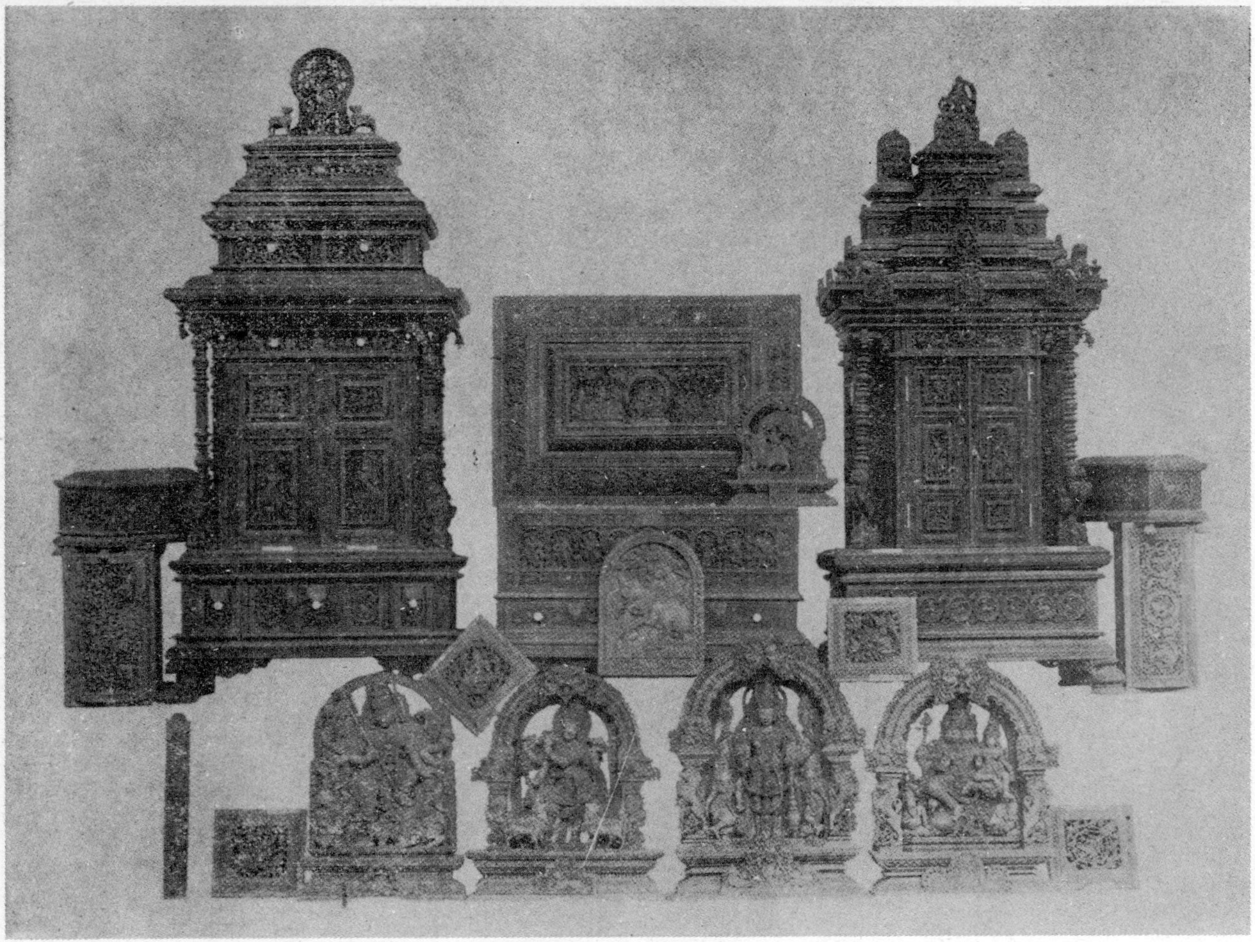

Plate No. 35 Carved Sandal-Wood

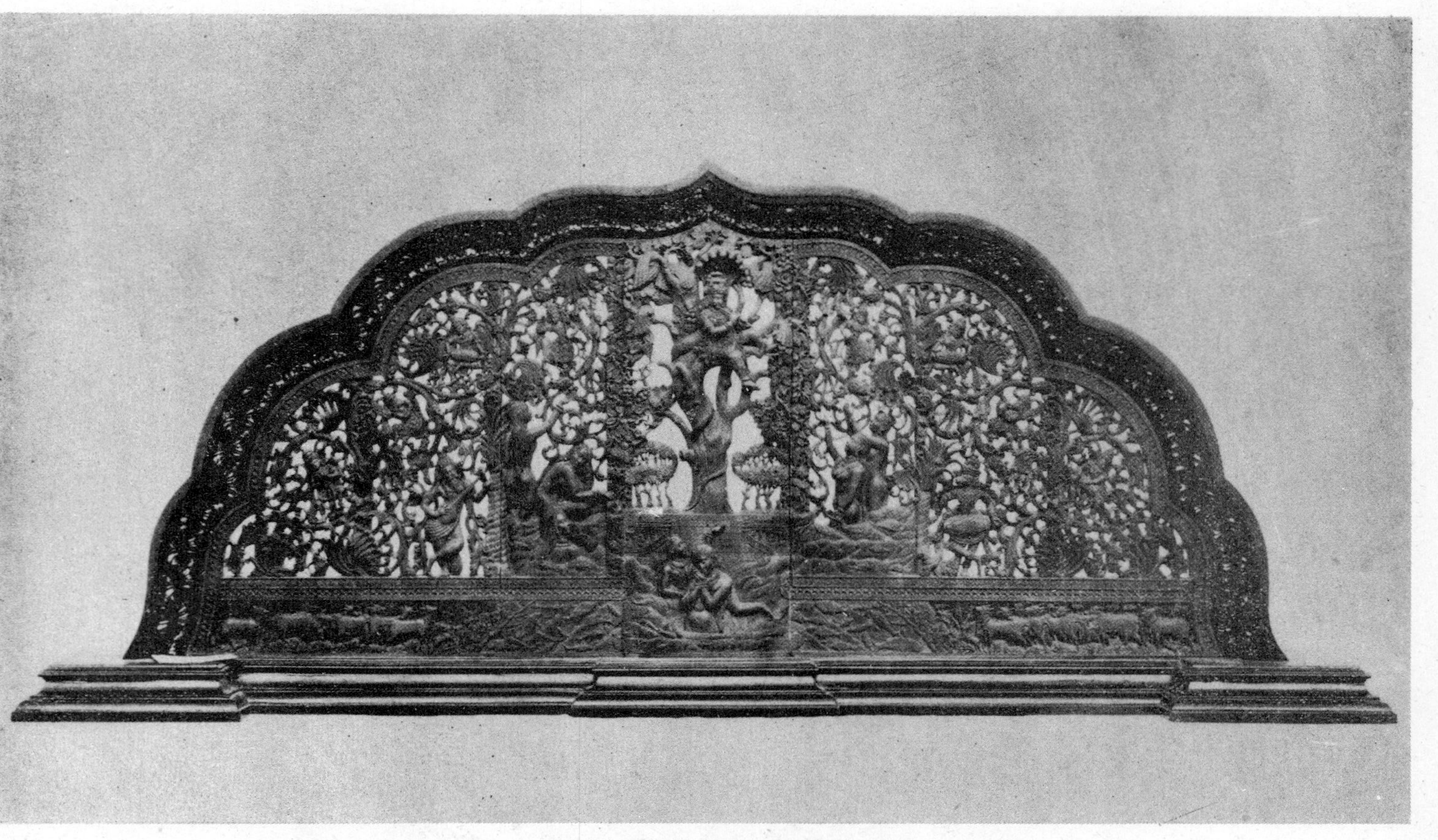

Plate No. 36 Sandal-Wood (Spandril from Mysore Palace.)

DIVISION 15. SANDAL-WOOD.

of gods, 4 being Shivite, 13 Vishnavite and 1 Brahma. They were made under the supervision of the Executive Engineer in charge of the new palace works at Mysore. The following are a few of the more commendable pieces :—

(*a*) ***Chamundi***— (*Plate No. 35*).—An emanation of the goddess *Durga* who was sent to destroy the demons *Chánda* and *Munda* and who subsequently bore their conjoint names. The carving is simply wonderful, every detail being faithfully brought out; price Rs. 255.

(*b*) ***Brahma***—(*Plate No. 35*).—The first member of the Hindu triad and the supreme creator of the universe; Rs. 184.

(*c*) ***Krishna***—(*Plate No. 35*) as the cow-keeper playing on his lute and charming the cattle; Rs. 266.

(*d*) ***Iswara***—within the mantle formed of a skin which he stripped from *Asura*, a demon disguised as an elephant; Rs. 186.

(*e*) ***Lakshmi***—the goddess of wealth with two attendant elephants throwing water; Rs. 239.

(*f*) ***Saraswati***—the goddess of learning playing on the *vina*; Rs. 184.

Amongst the very large series of admirable caskets, cabinets and other articles procured from Mysore, the following may be specially mentioned :—

(*g*) ***A cabinet*** (*see Plate No. 35*) made by Mudgod Herannappa of Surat, price Rs. 1,500. This is one of the most carefully prepared specimens of this work ever exhibited.

(*h*) ***Work-box*** by Shapur Subbrayappa, Sugar Dudda Puttappa, Ganapati Kesarappa, M. Puttappa Thimmappa and Veerappa. This was specially prepared at the writer's request, and by the most expert carvers of the State. The cabinet work was done with extra care and the carvers were instructed to produce the very best article that it was possible to accomplish, no particulars as to the ornamentation having been given. The panels on the four sides will be seen to depict hunting and forest scenes with much feeling, in a style that recalls the ivory carving of Japan and China, while the border patterns are charmingly beautiful examples of Chalukyan ornamentation; price Rs. 1,438. Plate No. 36-A shows a portion of the top of this box.

DIVISION 15. SANDAL-WOOD.

(*i*) ***Kheda Elephant-catching***—(*Plate No. 35*).—This represents a sylvan scene in the Mysore elephant-catching operations; Rs. 115.

(*k*) ***Sandal-wood temple*** sent by the Bangalore Museum, price Rs. 408.

(*l*) ***Work-box*** made by Banarsi Subhana of Sorab; Rs. 1,000.

(*m*) ***Album boards*** by Jade Gopalappa of Sorab; Rs. 138.

BOMBAY (*Plate No. 35-A, fig. 1*).—A miniature three-folding screen of exquisite workmanship done by Doolab Rai Gullab Rai, price Rs. 625, purchased by His Highness the Nizam of Hyderabad.

SURAT (*Plate No. 35-A, figs. 3 and 4*).—A large selection of this class of goods will be found of which the following may be mentioned as representative:—Combination jewel-case and glove-box by Jamsetji Nasarwanji Petigara, Rs. 156; a shawl-box Rs. 156; a glove-box Rs. 81, and a charming picture-frame by Harkison Parshotam, price Rs. 150. (Fig. 3.)

BARODA has sent a few unimportant examples of sandal-wood, such as glove-boxes and the like, by Hurgovind Hira Dabhoi.

AHMEDABAD (*Plate No. 35-A, fig. 2*) contributes a large and selected assortment of this class of goods such as cabinets, glove-boxes, book-covers, book-holders, panels (fig. 2), etc., by Parbhudas Rughnath Petigara.

It would take many pages to enumerate even the most noteworthy of the admirable collection of sandal-wood carving on view. The above by no means mentions even the names of all the commendable articles to be seen, though it may serve the purpose of this publication, namely, to direct attention to the display under the heading of carved sandal-wood, the chief types of that work that may be studied, and the better known carvers.

AWARDS FOR WOOD-CARVING UNDER DIVISION 15 (SANDAL-WOOD).

AWARDS.

First Prize with gold medal for the work-box (*h*) to Mistris Shapur Subbrayappa and Sagar Dodda Puttappa and to Carvers Ganapati Kesavappa, M. Puttappa Thimmappa and Veerappa of Mysore. (Plate No. 36-A.)

First Prize with silver medal for a figure of *Iswara* exhibited by the Executive Engineer of the Mysore Palace.

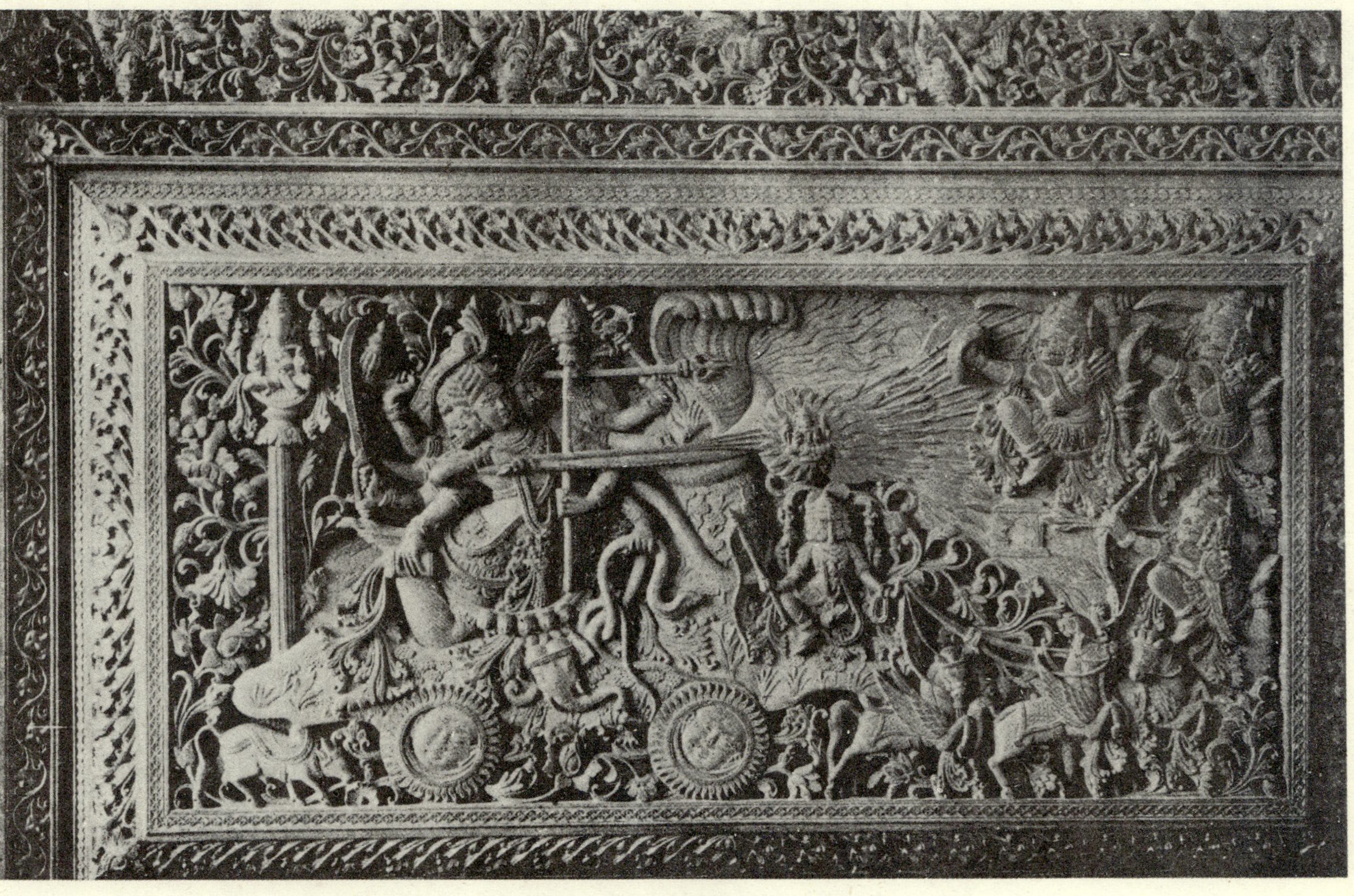

Plate No. 36–A Portion of Lid of Mysore Sandalwood Work Box

Second Prize with silver medal to Banarasi Subhana of Sorab for a Mysore cabinet. (Plate No. 35.)

DIVISION 16. VENEERING, APPLIQUÉ, MARQUETRY.

Second Prize with silver medal to Doolabhdas Ghellabhai of Bombay for a photograph frame in the form of a table screen. (Plate No. 35-A, fig. 1.)

Third Prize with bronze medal to Harkison Parshotam of Surat for a photograph frame. (Plate No. 35-A, fig. 3.)

Third Prize with bronze medal to Mudgod-Herannappa of Surat for a cabinet.

Third Prize with bronze medal to Jamsetji Nasarwanji Petigara of Surat for a writing box.

Commended for photograph frames, Parsotam Narbharam of Surat.

Commended for a carved panel, Parbhudas Rughnath of Ahmedabad. (Plate No. 35-A, fig. 2.)

Division 16.—Veneering, Appliqué, Marquetry, Lattice (Pinjra) work, etc.

1. ***Veneering,*** as applied to the furniture and the cabinet-makers' trades in Europe and America, is fortunately at present hardly if ever practised in India.* The economy secured by gluing to the surface of articles made in cheap wood, a veneer (or paper-like sheet) of a more expensive timber, would, if applied to every-day articles, be quite unsuited to the transitions of temperature and humidity to which most parts of India are subject. But the art of veneering is by no means unknown to the Indian craftsmen. Sandal-wood, tortoise-shell, horn, porcupine-quills and ivory are regularly veneered and fixed by glue, or pegged down by nails, to the surface of articles made of a cheaper material. This art has attained high proficiency in Vizagapatam where chess-tables and men, dressing cases, work-boxes, tea-caddies, jewel-cases, glove-boxes, picture-frames, etc., have for many years past been extensively manufactured in sandal and other woods, veneered with tortoise-shell or bison and buffalo-horn and these again overlaid by delicate fret-work and carved ivory.

Characteristic Features.

During a recent visit to VIZAGAPATAM, the writer inquired carefully into the origin of the floral designs employed. These

* *Conf.* with remarks below on Mysore Ivories and mother-of-pearl inlaying.

DIVISION 16. VENEERING, APPLIQUÉ, MARQUETRY. came into existence apparently with the fathers and grandfathers of the present craftsmen. The flowers usually depicted are the European eyebright, the convolvulus, the rose and other flowers with which of course the operators are quite unfamiliar and simply copy blindfoldly, the one from the other. But on further inquiry, older designs of an indigenous or Hindu origin were discovered, in the possession of the master craftsman. The art is thus by no means a modern one, as commonly affirmed, and this may be seen by some of the examples in the possession of the Raja of Vizianagram. It would seem possible that it **Chairs and Howdahs.** originated with the desire for State chairs, howdahs and the like, and was diverted into its present form at the suggestion of Europeans who very possibly furnished the rustic and foliar decoration that has characterised the goods produced for the past fifty or sixty years. The older samples (such as certain chairs in Government House, Calcutta, and in the palace of Vizianagram) are mostly ornamented by pale green or blue and pink lakh, not by black alone, as in the more recent goods.

The restriction of the craft to three or four workshops in one town, that give employment to perhaps 60 persons in all, once more illustrates the extremely local character of many of the crafts of India. A large percentage of the display of Vizagapatam work, on view at the Exhibition, has been specially prepared and the designs selected by the writer. It is believed that some of the older patterns may be recognised as superior, both in artistic merit and finish, to the goods usually procurable. The surfaces of the ivory veneers have, as just stated, patterns etched or engraved upon them. By a process of what might be called *sgraffito*, lakh variously coloured is fused over the surface of the **Lakh Ornamentation.** engraved ivory. The etched portions are thus loaded or charged with colour. The superfluous lakh is then scraped off and the ivory surface polished. The coloured ornamentation is thus shown on a white ivory background. This exceedingly simple and beautiful art is capable of considerable development and expansion, into many other branches of wooden and metallic decoration since, where pure lakh and metallic pigments (not aniline dyes) are used, it is more permanent than paint or even some forms of enamelling (*minákarí*). At the present day it is practised by the inlayers of Mysore State and the Vizagapatam and Kota State veneer box-makers and by the metal workers of Moradabad, Jaipur, Peshawar and Kashmir.

DIVISION 16. VENEERING, APPLIQUÉ, MARQUETRY.

Carved ivory Veneers.

The appliqué ivory is, however, at times simply carved, not lakh-coloured, and the caskets and boxes thus ornamented come to resemble solid not veneered ivory. This is perhaps the most desirable form of Vizagapatam ware. Her Excellency Lady Curzon having admired a casket in this style of work, in the possession of the Indian Museum, Calcutta, a competition between the three chief craftsmen in Vizagapatam was instituted, the result being the six exceedingly beautiful and carefully finished caskets, now on view at the Exhibition (Plate No. 43, fig. 3). The writer is much indebted to Mr. W. B. Ayling, the Collector of the District, for the great personal interest he took in seeing that the Calcutta model was shown to the craftsmen and faithfully followed. In consequence certain improvements have been effected, a fact which shows that the skill for fine work has not died out in India; skilled labour is being starved through the modern demand for cheap goods, but it is not dead.

CHIEF EXHIBITS ON VIEW.

A large jewel-case with arched lid, made by Ganugula Ramalingram, price Rs. 875. A smaller jewel-case with massive ivory fret-work by Lala Venkata Das, price Rs. 312. A carved ivory cabinet with coronation of Rama on lid panel, by Ganugula Ramalingram, price Rs. 625. Carved ivory cabinet with elephants on top panel by Lala Venkutu Das, Rs. 625. A jewel-box on buffalo-horn and fret-work ivory by Golti Lakshmaya, Rs. 375; the same with tortoise-shell, Rs. 437. An ivory etched cabinet with Rama's coronation and *swámis* by Lala Venkata Das, Rs. 187. A sandal-wood box with etched ivory gods and goddesses by Ganugula China Veerama, Rs. 312. Handkerchief-box with solid ivory central lid panel by Ganugula China Veerama, Rs. 82.

2. ***Appliqué work*** has incidentally been mentioned in the above passages, that deal with the special craft of Vizagapatam. Variously ornamented thin sheets of ivory are fastened, by ivory or silver pins, over the surface of the boxes and other articles,

DIVISION 16. VENEERING, APPLIQUÉ, MARQUETRY.

previously veneered with sandal-wood, with tortoise-shell or with horn. At times the ivory simulates the brass bindings of trunks, at other times becomes panels and medallions in the scheme of ornamentation. But appliqué in wood-work assumes in many parts of India much greater importance, as a decorative art, than is exemplified by the Vizagapatam box trade. In Plate No. 32 has been shown to the extreme right a door which His Highness the Maharaja of Bikanir allowed the writer to remove from one of the oldest portions of his ancestral palace. It is believed the door dates from the 17th Century. The top triangular portions show inlaying with ivory, the lower portions appliqué of ivory over wood, while the frames are charming examples of ivory-carving.

Plate No. 25 gives a representative series of the wood-carving of Nepal. It has already been explained that one of the most striking features of the wood-work of that great Himalayan State is the extensive use made of the art of ornamentation by appliqué. The trunk seen in the plate is one of the most fascinating examples of this art ever shown, two colours of pale wood having alone been employed. It is strongly Chinese in its designs but nevertheless it exemplifies the degree of knowledge in this art that prevails in India. Brass and Copper are largely overlaid on wooden structures, such as on some of the finest of the ancient doors on the forts and palaces of India.

3. ***Marquetry*** (*Plate No. 37, also* ***Plate*** *No. 61, fig. 4*), erroneously spoken of as inlaid work, is largely practised in India. It has been placed, as a matter of convenience, under this Division. It is known locally as *Sadeli* work and the chief centres of the craft are Ahmedabad, Baroda, Bombay and Surat. It would appear that the art came to India from Persia (Shiraz) through Sind, perhaps 300 years or so ago. Certain of the doors in the old palace of Nurber near Jaipur are ornamented in this style. (1630 A.D.) It was first acquired by the Hindus and then subsequently taught to the Parsis. The so-called "Bombay boxes" were apparently "*Sadeli* boxes" though the expression was early made to embrace carved wood or ivory boxes as also boxes partly of sandal and partly of *sadeli*, or simply of carved-wood and *sadeli* mixed, provided they were made in Gujarat.

Centres of Production.

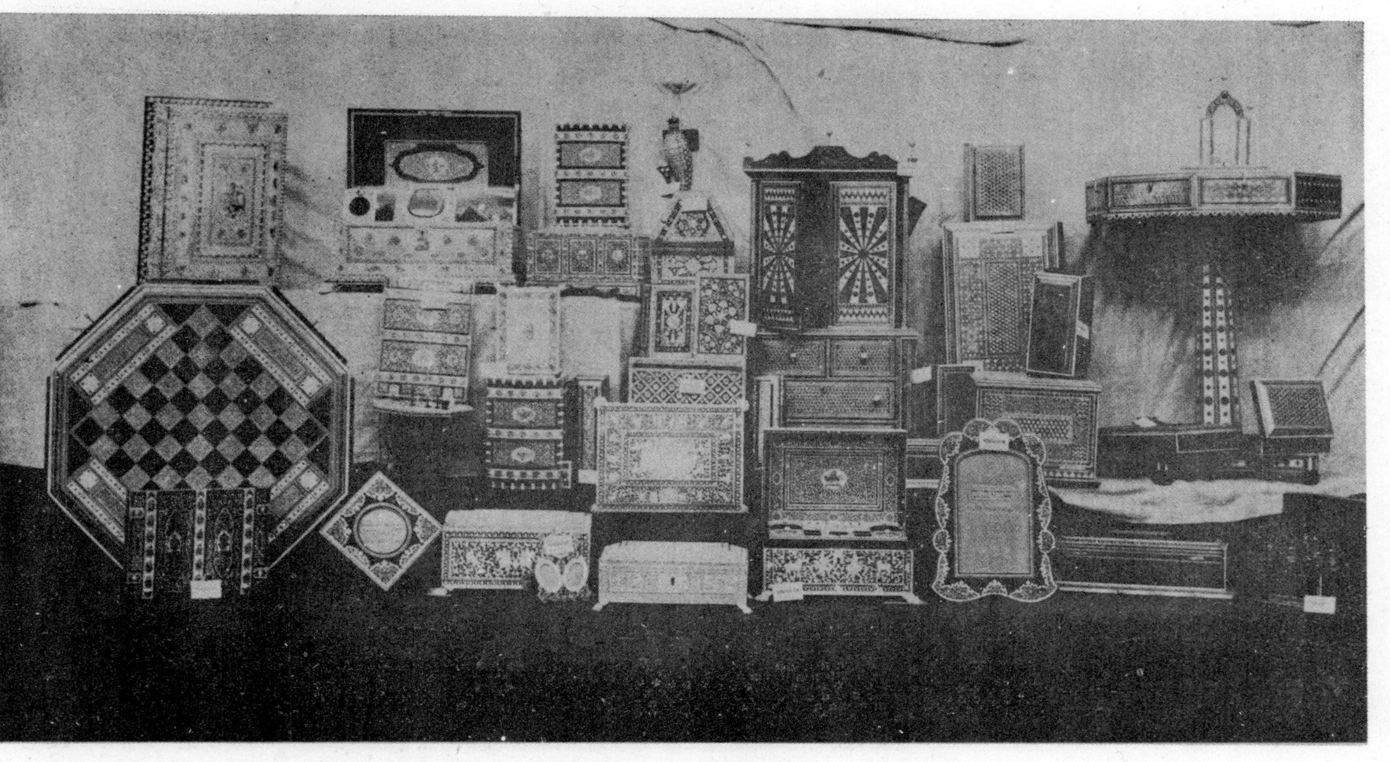

Plate No. 37 Marquetry and Veneering (Bombay, Surat, and Vizagapatam work.)

DIVISION 16. VENEERING, APPLIQUÉ, MARQUETRY.

The materials employed are ivory and horn (plain, or coloured green and blue) black ebony, red-wood and tin or silver. These are cut into long thin strips of various shapes and are glued together in such a manner as to show, on transverse section, geometric patterns of rich and varied design, believed to be traceable to an original floral conception. Thin strips or veneering ribbons are thus made by transverse section on a series of parellel strands and these ribbons are then glued to the surfaces of the boxes, cabinets, etc., as desired. Sometimes panels of richly carved sandal-wood or of black ebony, are framed in *sadeli* ware, or at other times the surfaces of the cabinet or other article are entirely covered with *sadeli*.

CHIEF EXHIBITS ON VIEW.

A fairly comprehensive series of *sadeli* work will be found in the Exhibition. Of these may be mentioned the chess-table exhibited by Framjee P. Bhumgara of Bombay, price Rs. 375. The erect cabinet shown by Muncharam Govind Ram of Bombay, price Rs. 625. The shawl box by Verji Vandas Sedasive of Bombay, price Rs. 187. The writing-desk by Kachra Doolabhram of Mangrol, Rs. 125, and the black ebony tea-caddy with borders of *sadeli* by Jamsetji Nasarwanji Petigara of Surat.

4. ***Kota Marquetry.***—[*Plates Nos. 32, 37, 42 (fig. 1) and 42-A (fig. 1).*]—At Etawa in Kota State, Rajputana, is produced a charming manifestation of an art best described as a form of marquetry. Special veneers of horn are built up by pieces of ivory and mother-of-pearl being inlaid on the horn. These veneers are then affixed to boxes of sandal or *shisham* woods, or to natural horns (used as powder flasks) and other such articles. Occasionally direct inlaying, in certain portions of the design, is practised, but usually strips of ornamented buffalo-horn are veneered to the surfaces of the boxes or other articles. Instead of veneering ribbons another method is sometimes pursued, namely, to form small diamond-shaped pieces of horn and to ornament these with ivory or mother-of-pearl and when ready, to piece them together in a quaint diaper fashion. (Plate No. 42, fig. 1.)

The ivory employed in Kota work is richly elaborated with floral designs in black lakh and the mother-of-pearl may also

DIVISION 16. VENEERING, APPLIQUÉ, MARQUETRY.

have a few colour spots or lines imparted to it, in order to bring out the flower or leaf intended to be portrayed. This, so far as the writer is aware, is the only fairly extensive use of mother-of-pearl as an ornamental material in inlaying or marquetry, practised in India on wood, though a corresponding industry exists both in Bhera and Agra in inlaying mother-of-pearl on stone (see the article "Shells" below).

Although the art as seen in Kota has not risen above that of the production of small articles, it has a charming individuality in its methods and designs. It is an illustration once more of the spontaneity and isolation of the Indian crafts which recalls the somewhat parallel case of the Dacca manufacture of bangles and other ornaments from conch shells in the heart of Bengal—and thus several hundreds of miles from the sea—the source of the materials of the craft. So in the same way it recalls the Nagina ebony-carving and the Pali ivory-turnery.

Chief Exhibits on View.

The following are some of the better examples of Kota work in the Exhibition:—A stationery-holder, Rs. 62; a jewellery-box, Rs. 50; a pen-holder, Rs. 16 and a powder flask, Rs. 17-8.

5. ***Lattice (Pinjra) Work.***—(*Plate No. 38.*)—So much has already been said regarding the various styles of lattice work in India and their possible historic sequence, that it may be regarded as hardly necessary to devote a special section of this work to the subject. But on the other hand the art gives so much character to the carpentry and cabinet work of certain localities that it may help to elucidate these, if the subject be dealt

Description. with separately, even if very briefly. By *pinjra* is meant lattice work built up of minute laths arranged in geometric forms so as to display their edges. They are held in position by the pressure they exert one against the other, by certain main lines being dowelled together and by the frame of the panel within which assorted. They are rarely if ever glued together and in good work are so accurately fitted and balanced that they do not fall to pieces even when the frame is removed.

As with inlaying, so with *pinjra* work, there is no separate craft devoted to this art. It is resorted to by the carpenters and

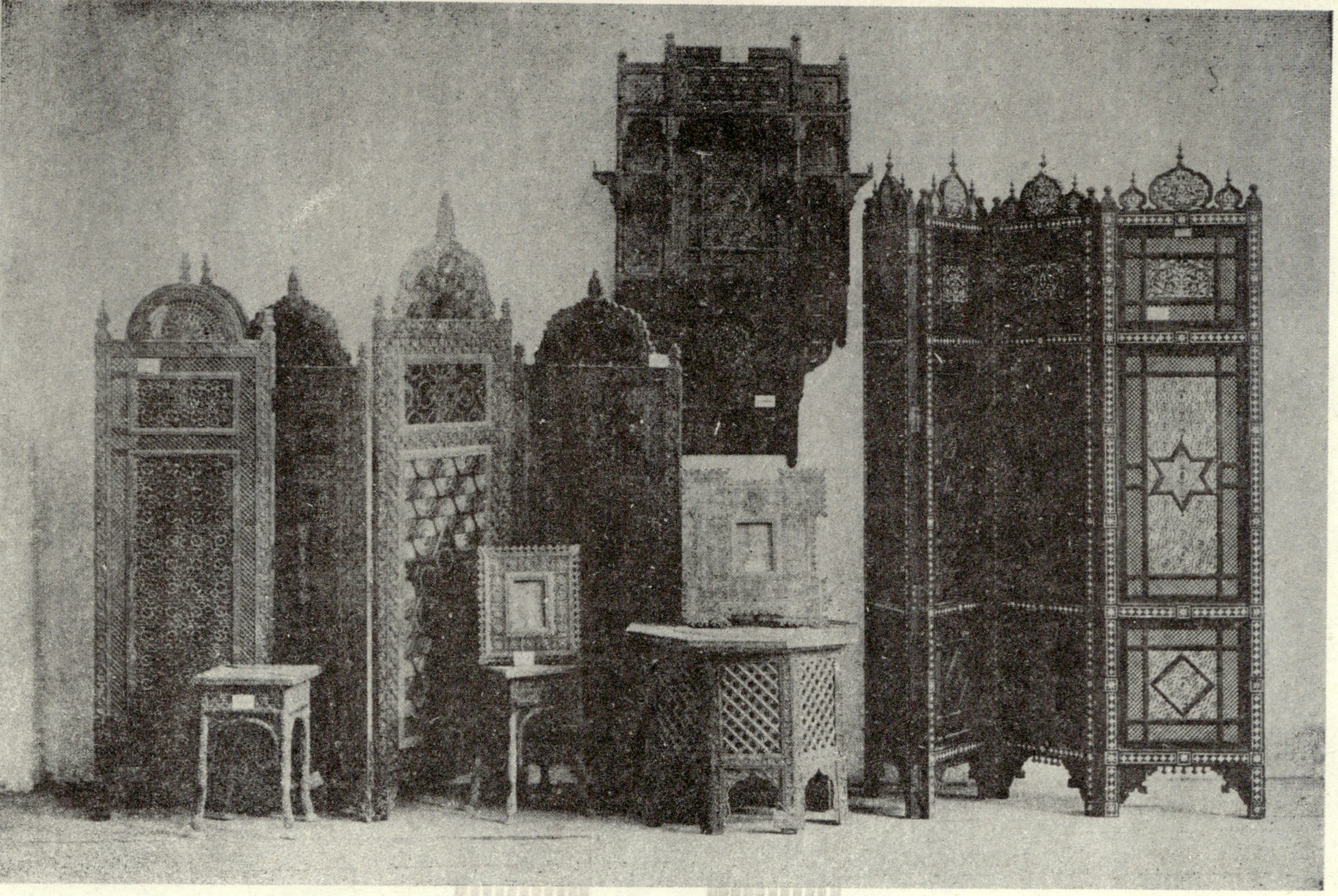

Plate No. 38 Selection of Pinjra work

cabinet-makers to secure certain effects but proficiency is not attained by every carpenter. There is in fact as much skill and artistic feeling required in designing and making a *pinjra* panel as in carving or inlaying. Certain localities have attained a great reputation for their *pinjra*. In some the massive and bold style of former times is still preserved but in others a minute kind has taken its place. Of the Panjab, Peshawar has a great reputation for delicate and intricate *pinjra* and Lahore and Chiniot for bold, massive work.

CHIEF EXHIBITS ON VIEW.

There are two sets of examples, the one from Peshawar, the other from Lahore and Amritsar. Of the former special attention may be drawn to the large three-fold screen in which walnut, sandal, ebony and olive woods have all been used to produce the charming assortment of colour in elaboration of the design. This was made by Mull Chand & Sons and is priced at Rs. 625. (See Plate No. 38 to left of wall bracket.) Another screen of a bolder and simpler though more effective kind, by the same maker, is placed to the left. Numerous tables, also in *pinjra* work, are shown, prices Rs. 50 to Rs. 80. The small square ones have the feet in carved olive wood and the *pinjra* panels backed by boards to give greater stability. They are priced at Rs. 50. Picture frames in many sizes and forms are also on view and these run from Rs. 11 to Rs. 25. On the wall near by has been hung a bracket, made of walnut, which like all the above is by Mull Chand & Sons. This, while perhaps less successful than the screens and tables, is a good example of Peshawar minute *pinjra* work.

Turning now to the second series, *viz.*, those from Lahore and Amritsar, it will be observed that the *pinjra* work of these towns is not only more massive but constructed primarily on a rectangular rather than a circular conception. The individual laths are at the same time notched on the surface, a circumstance that greatly enhances their beauty. Messrs. Daví Sahai and Chamba Mull of Amritsar have exhibited a most admirable screen of this kind, Rs. 600; and Thaker Singh, also of Amritsar, shows another admirable piece that has many charming features of special

DIVISION 16. VENEERING, APPLIQUÉ, MARQUETRY.

interest, especially the rich carving on the one side and inlaying shown on the other. This is on sale, price Rs. 625. (Plate No. 38 to right.)

AWARDS FOR WOOD-CARVING UNDER DIVISION 16.

(VENEERING, APPLIQUÉ, MARQUETRY.)

AWARDS.

First Prize with silver medal to Ganugula China Veerama of Vizagapatam for veneered ivory casket.

First Prize with silver medal to Lala Vankata Das of Vizagapatam for a casket of veneered ivory and tortoise-shell.

First Prize with silver medal to Ganugula Ramalingram of Vizagapatam for caskets veneered in ivory and tortoise-shell.

Second Prize with silver medal to Golti Lakshmaya of Vizagapatam for caskets veneered with sandal-wood, ivory and buffalo-horn.

Second Prize with silver medal for wooden appliqué box exhibited by H. E. the Prime Minister of Nepal.

Second Prize with silver medal to Mull Chand & Sons of Peshawar for *pinjra* screens.

Third Prize with bronze medal to Oukar of Etawa, Kota State, for marquetry powder flask.

Third Prize with bronze medal to Muncharam Govindram of Bombay for a cabinet.

Third Prize with bronze medal for a *pinjra* screen by Thaker Singh of Amritsar.

Third Prize with bronze medal for a *pinjra* screen by Daví Sahai Chamba Mull of Amritsar.

Commended for a marquetry chess-table by Framjee P. Bhumgara.

Commended for a *pinjra* screen by Palla Singh of Amritsar.

Commended for a *pinjra* fire-place by Dastkhat Mistri of Peshawar.

Commended for four *pinjra* overmantels by Sant Ram of Lahore.

Divisions 17 and 18.—Painted Wood-work, Papier Maché, and Imitation Papier Maché.

When the classification of Indian Arts, adopted for the Exhibition, was being framed, it was not known how far some of the

Divisions then entertained might be represented by the collections ultimately brought together. The experience since obtained has shown that the painted wood-works of Bareilly and Tilhar, for example, have either entirely disappeared or become so poor in quality that they are unworthy of a place in an Art Exhibition. So in a like manner some of the industries have been materially changed, within the past few years, and their classification become an impossible task. The so-called papier maché of Kashmir, is nowadays very largely painted wood-work, hence more than one half the goods produced in Kashmir and popularly spoken of as papier maché would have to be transferred from Division 18 to 17. Bearing these circumstances in mind it seems the preferable course to deal with painted wood, papier maché and other kindred methods of ornamentation collectively. It may, however, be convenient to refer the remarks that follow to the two sections:— **DIVISIONS 17 AND 18. PAINTED WOOD AND PAPIER MACHÉ.**

(*a*) *Painted Wood-work.*

SAVANTVADI.—(*Plate No. 39 to left.*)—Perhaps the most striking example of painted wood met with in India is the very peculiar art that has for long existed in the Native State of Savantvadi. That interesting and almost inaccessible State has, until quite recently, preserved its crafts remarkably free from Western influence. Its painted wood-work has, however, been largely degraded by wholesale adoption of European designs and colourings, the result being that the art has lost its special charm. The wood-work is painted in oil paints, with red or black as a background. It has borders of brilliant green leaves and pink flowers and in the centres of the panels mythological groups boldly painted. The supports and feet of the brackets or tables are usually done on the turning-lathe and display a most delicate and charming touch in lac line colouring. This circumstance has probably suggested the description of Savantvadi work as being a form of lac-ware. Its chief feature is the oil-painted flat surfaces, not the small turnery details. The rims of Savantvadi tables, etc., are usually fringed with the sweetly smelling *khas-khas* matting, ornamented with beetle wings and gold braid. **Description.** **Oil Painted.**

DIVISIONS 17 AND 18. PAINTED WOOD AND PAPIER MACHÉ.

This style of painting and decoration is applied to brackets, tables, caskets, shrines for the family deity in which numerous folding doors display the various incarnations of the god. Among the specimens on view, the following may be specially mentioned. A wall cabinet in black with brilliant red and green floral decorations and mythological subjects, Rs. 75; octagonal table with turned and lac-coloured feet and crimson top with mythological figures, Rs. 19. These and many other examples of this art are made by Narayan Ramchandra Kelkar.

MUZAFFARGARH in the Panjab has been famed for its painted bows and arrows (—*kaman*—a bow). These are often extremely beautiful and the art designs shown on them may be viewed as having been the originals of much of the wood-painting of the Panjab. In consequence wood-painting in this district is commonly spoken of as *kamangiri*.

Kamangiri.

JHANSI turns out boxes, trays and the like painted black and with dull green and red floral designs—the box to left bottom corner of Plate No. 39. They are not of a very artistic order and the carpentry is so poor that they cannot be handled without falling to pieces. The trays are designed, moreover, on a modern European pattern as if in imitation of common japanned metal ware.

GWALIOR has a fair amount of painted wood and basket-work, the latter being quaint and original but hardly worthy of a place in an Art Exhibition. A few examples have been furnished and will be found in this Division.

BIKANIR.—Gilded and painted wood and stone form a striking feature of the house-decoration of Bikanir. In the Loan Collection Gallery and also in the Bikanir Window on the north wall of the Main Gallery, will be seen several painted doors. As the designs in these have been built up by mud or other materials, and after being picked out with colour, have been varnished over the surface, these doors, and the art they exemplify, fall under Division 28. But there is much of what must be treated as pure wood-painting in the houses of Bikanir and of other towns of Rajputana generally. The writer asked that a portion of the wall paintings in the old palace of Bikanir should be copied. These will be

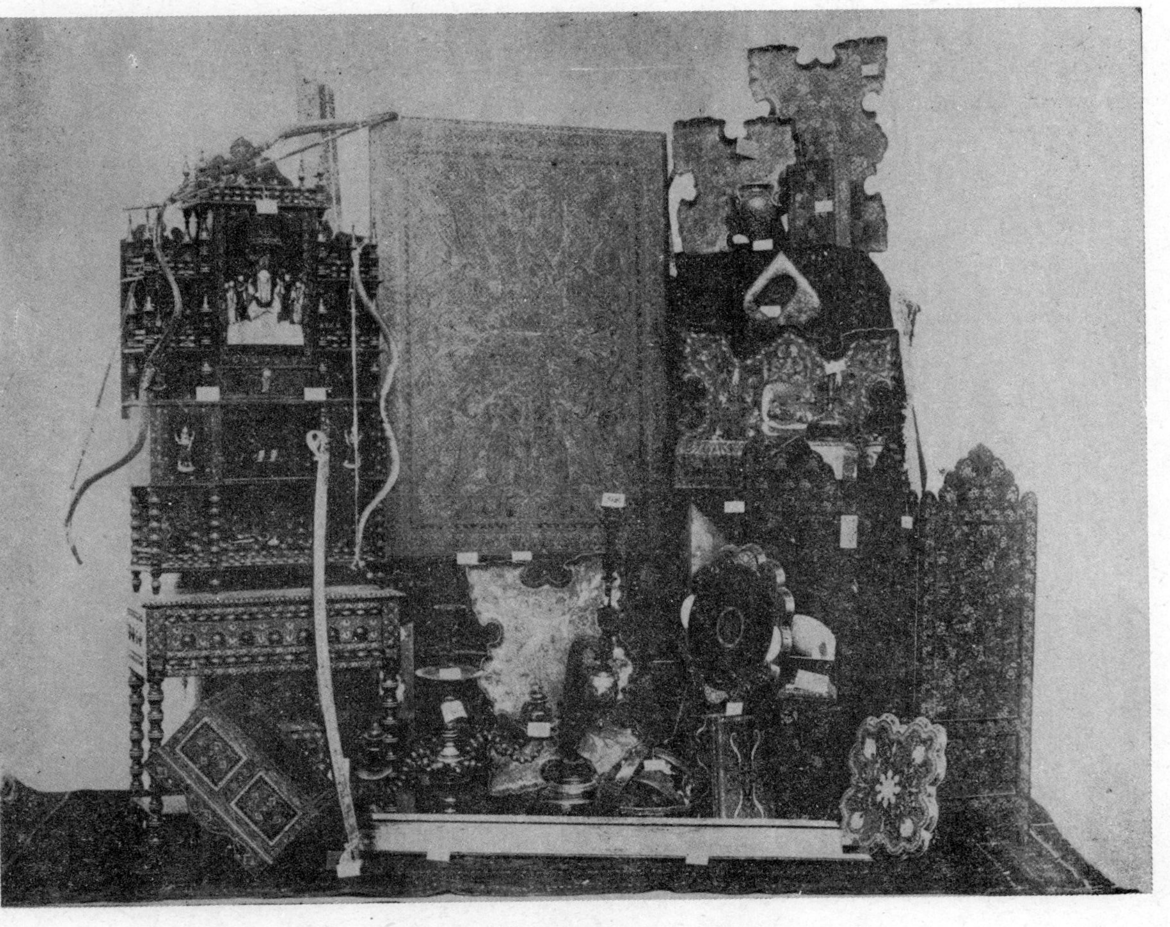

Plate No. 39 Painted Wood Papier Mache, Imitation Inlaying, etc

seen on two boards. They represent a heavy thunderstorm with lightning flashing through the clouds, while down below and nearer the earth storks may be observed. This most curious and beautiful wall decoration has a strongly Chinese feeling that it is difficult to account for. The same form of clouds will be seen on the Tonk hide-shields and observed to recur now and again all over Rajputana and Central India. In fact, the method of painting and varnishing Tonk shields is so very like Japanese work that the shields have been spoken of as illustrative of a knowledge (in India) of the Japanese art of lacquering.

DIVISIONS 17 AND 18. PAINTED WOOD AND PAPIER MACHÉ.

(*b*) *Papier Maché and Imitation Papier Maché.*

Although practised here and there all over India by Kashmiris or Persians settled in various localities, papier maché is produced on a commercial scale in Srinagar only. In Lucknow, for example, a Persian who has settled there turns out admirable work, and at Muzaffarnagar a fairly extensive papier maché industry exists but it may suffice for the purpose of this work if attention be chiefly directed to Kashmir.

Sir Walter Lawrence in his *Valley of Kashmir* makes some trenchant observations regarding the Art Industries of that State (page 373 *et seq.*). "I am afraid," he observes, "that the influence of the outside world on the art wares of Srinagar has not on the whole proved salutary. The citizens of Srinagar have a common saying to the effect that when the taxation went the prosperity of the city went also, and they explain this by the fact that the removal of taxation led to the breaking up of what were practically guilds sanctioned and protected by the State. When the taxation was removed, outsiders rushed in, and competition at once reduced prices of art wares. Copper work which sold at Rs. 7 per seer in the days of taxation now sells at Rs. 3, and this is the case with many other art wares. But in arguing that the prosperity of the city has departed, the citizens omit sometimes to explain that in the days of taxation the State exercised a vigorous supervision over the quality of the raw material and of the manufactured articles. In the good days of the shawl trade no spurious wool was brought in from Amritsar to be

DIVISIONS 17 AND 18. PAINTED WOOD AND PAPIER MACHE.

mixed with the real shawl-wool of Central Asia, and woe betide the weaver who did bad work or the silversmith who was too liberal with his alloy.

"There is no such supervision nowadays. Competition has lowered prices, and the real masters of weaving, silver, papier maché and copper-work have to bend to the times and supply their customers with cheap inferior work. Ask an old artist in papier maché to show the work that formerly went to Kabul, and he will show something very different from the miserable trash which is now sold.

"But the Pathans of Kabul paid the price of good work: the visitors to the valley want cheap work, and they get it. It is very difficult to arrest the deterioration of art work. The Kashmiris have the artistic instinct, but artists must live, and their livelihood depends on the market for art wares." "The surroundings of the Kashmir artisans" concludes Sir Walter Lawrence "are miserable and squalid, and it is sad to contrast the beauty of the art work with the ugliness of the workmen's lives. They are, however, a difficult people to deal with, for they will make no effort to help themselves."

Designs in Papier Maché.

Until quite recently there may be said to have been only two or three fairly distinctive patterns employed by the papier maché workers of the "Happy Valley." The modern stuff has multiplied with each step in its downward career. The writer was much surprised to find while in Kashmir that neither in the Palace nor in the State Museum, have there been preserved samples of the fine old forms of Kashmir papier maché, so much appreciated by collectors of Indian art. The two chief forms of the old school might be said to have been the minute rose pattern and the pale coloured shawl pattern. So completely have these disappeared that it would not be far from correct to affirm that when Kashmir thinks of reviving its former beautiful art of papier maché, it will have to go to the Museums of Europe and America for the most desirable models. Another and even more serious fact may be mentioned, namely, that by far the major portion of the papier maché of Kashmir at the present day is solely and entirely painted wood. This has cheapened the cost of production and altered

DIVISIONS 17 AND 18. PAINTED WOOD AND PAPIER MACHÉ.

the entire character of the goods. But this change had been fairly established by the time of the Panjab Exhibition in 1864 and the downward career of the industry seems to have quickened since, with each decade. Kashmir papier maché in its true form differs considerably from that of Europe. The paper is never exactly reduced to a pulp. It is simply softened and pasted together, layer upon layer, within a mould until by repeated slow drying and replacing within the mould while additions are made the article attains the correct shape and desired thickness. While moist it is wrapped round with a thin muslin rag and covered with a layer of a dressing material said to be plaster-of-paris (or *gach*). The article is next smoothed and rubbed down till it is given the required uniform surface to allow of the ground colour (*zamin*) being imparted. When this is dry the pattern is painted in water colours and when thoroughly set is glazed by the purest and most transparent varnish procurable. This is usually made from copal (*sundras*) dissolved in turpentine, not boiled in oil.

Varnish used.

But Kashmir papier maché is at present practically a name for a class of wooden goods with certain designs painted on a light coloured ground and coated with a special varnish. As just stated it has been cheapened in every possible direction, the substitution of wood for pulp being the most disastrous. This has altered the entire character of the goods. The charming coffee-sets so admirably finished that the warmest coffee might be drunk with impunity from them, are no longer procurable. The many-cornered trays, too troublesome to be made of wood, have all but disappeared. The *suráhis* and numerous other quaint vessels that might be moulded of pulp readily enough but which could not be produced without much labour and expense from wood, have been steadily displaced. Flat goods, such as picture-frames, screens and the like, are now almost the only articles produced and in these even, the precaution to coat the wood with a thin layer of pulp or to dress the surface in the manner followed with papier maché proper, has practically been abandoned so that the Kashmir papier maché has come to mean a particular kind of painted and varnished wood-work.

Painted Wood.

CHIEF EXHIBITS ON VIEW.

DIVISIONS 17 AND 18. PAINTED WOOD AND PAPIER MACHÉ.

The following may be given as indicative of the chief decorative methods at present pursued and as denoting the most commendable examples of this ware on view at the Exhibition :—

Chief Patterns.

(1) *The Shawl Pattern*—(*Plate No. 39-A, fig. 4*).—One of the most noteworthy examples of the series is doubtless the rectangular table which the writer discovered in the State Toshakkhana of Kashmir and which has been placed in the centre of the articles that are more or less in the same style of ornamentation. (Plate No. 39.) It is made of wood but has been fairly liberally coated with pulp and the surface-dressing material preparatory to being painted. The ground colour, unlike the lampblack generally employed in Europe, is pure white, and seems to consist of the specially smoothed and dressed surface material usually employed before the designs are painted in water colours.

This beautiful old table has been purchased for the Lahore Museum. Placed around it will be seen an assortment of small tables, trays, etc., all in the shawl pattern (Plate No. 39-A, fig. 4). These are priced at from Rs. 20 to Rs. 40 and are made by Jabbar Khan of Srinagar.

(2) *Rose Pattern*—(*Plate No. 39-A, figs. 2 and 5*).—Some years ago a beautiful style of work was largely turned out. This consisted of bunches of small red roses and birds clustered gracefully together, all over the surface, according to some scheme of shape and colour. This has almost entirely disappeared and in its place has come the modern rose pattern with separate sprays of flowers that look as if culled from the family herbalist or the child's scrap book and stuck down here and there without any purpose except, perhaps, a display of colour. The flowers most popular in this work are the cherry blossom, the double anemone, the tulip, the hyacinth, the rose, etc., flowers with many of which the Kashmiris are most probably quite unfamiliar. As illustrations of this modern rose pattern the following articles may be mentioned, *viz.*, the large screen (to the extreme right of Plate No. 39) that forms the centre of the set, price Rs. 100, the pair of square flower vases, price Rs. 37-8 each,

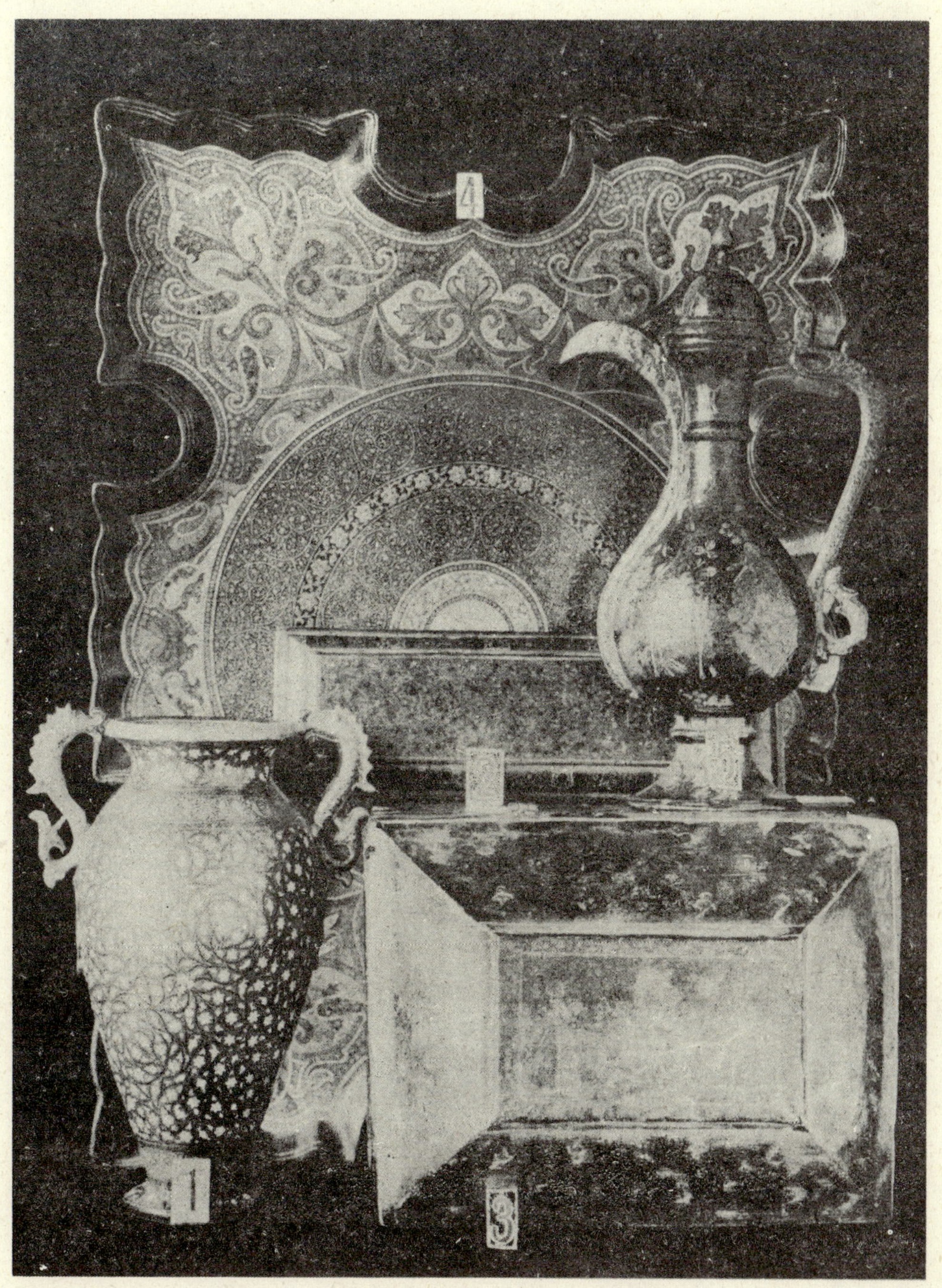

Plate No. 39-A Designs in Papier Mache

the pair of beautiful *suráhis,* Rs. 5 each, and the Persian octagonal table, Rs. 37-8, all the work of Jabbar Khan of Srinagar. Lastly a fine old example in the form of a pen-holder, Rs. 16 (Plate No. 39-A, fig. 2). This has the minute rose pattern with birds within the twigs. Though small and dull coloured, this is perhaps the best piece in the whole series.

(3) *Gold Arabesque Pattern—(Plate No. 39-A, centre of tray, fig. 4)*.—One of the old designs still occasionally produced is a gold arabesque design. This is rendered on a dull gray or brown ground colour. The best example of this is a small octagonal table with central arabesque gold design and shawl pattern border made by Jabbar Khan, price Rs. 37-8.

(4) *Yarkand Pattern—(Plate No. 39-A, fig. 1)*.—This has a dark background with gold rosettes arranged spirally, from numerous separate centres all over the surface, and white flowers drawn as it were on the tops of the golden foliage. It is a beautiful old design rarely produced at the present day. In the collection a small octagonal table of this style will, however, be found, price Rs. 37-8, as also a pair of vases one of which obtained the first prize and is shown as fig. 1.

(5) *White and Gold Pattern.*—Formerly a large percentage of the Kashmir work consisted of articles painted in a cream white and gold scroll with bright border patterns, usually in pale blue. There is but one sample in the collection namely a small paper rack (No. 2555).

(6) *Handkerchief Pattern.*—This is very rarely seen nowadays. It might be described as a reproduction in shades of red and orange of the embroidered handkerchiefs produced in Kashmir, Chamba and Kullu, in which human figures and hunting scenes are portrayed. In the more modern examples of this class a Hindu feeling has been given by the introduction of mythological subjects.

(7) *Lastly the Modern Stuff*—Mostly pale coloured and with realistic photo-transfers or coloured life-sized flowers stuck down over the surface of the white, pink, pale blue and gold ornamentations, the wood having received little or no previous dressing. There are many examples of this kind too numerous to be mentioned.

(8) *Lhassa Table.*—From Kashmir has been procured an example of the folding table characteristic of Ladakh and Thibet. The

DIVISIONS 17 AND 18. PAINTED WOOD AND PAPIER MACHÉ.

wood is carved and painted in the peculiarly Chinese style of that country, namely in gold, red and green medallions, price Rs.17-8.

(9) *Lahore Painted Wood or Papier Maché.*—Before leaving this subject it may be mentioned that a small octagonal table has been sent from Lahore by Sant Ram, price Rs. 27. This closely resembles the Kashmiri so-called papier maché but the design on the top is very peculiar and unlike anything sent from Kashmir. It consists of closely compacted circles of white and dark blue on a pale blue ground with floral elaborations across and connecting the circles together.

(10) *Papier Maché proper*—Is represented in the Exhibition by a few good examples such as the following:—A coffee set and tray in Yarkand Pattern, price Rs. 40; a large tray in handkerchief (*rumal*) pattern, price Rs. 43; a tray, Kabul shape, and in arabesque design of decoration but with shawl border pattern, price Rs.19; a shawl pattern tray of good workmanship and design, Rs. 37-8; a many-angled tray in recent rose pattern, Rs. 37-8; a pair of small boat [*kishti*]-shaped trays in arabesque designs, Rs. 6 each; and port-folio boards in modern flower pattern, Rs. 25. These are all the work of Jabbar Khan of Srinagar. Some fine old samples of papier maché have been received from Bikanir that were probably made there. These are shown on Plate No. 39, figs. 3 and 5.

AWARDS FOR PAINTED WOOD-WORK, PAPIER MACHÉ AND IMITATION PAPIER MACHÉ, UNDER DIVISIONS 17 AND 18.

AWARDS

First prize with silver medal for a papier maché table exhibited by Kashmir Darbar.

Second prize with silver medal to Jabbar Khan of Srinagar for papier maché collection.

Second prize with bronze medal for a papier maché box forwarded through the Collector of Bareilly.

Commended for a papier maché box by Masitulla of Mozaffarnagar.

Commended for a corner cabinet in painted wood by Narayan Ramchandra Kelkar of Savantvadi.

Commended for two painted wood panels by Shah Mahomed of Bikanir.

Divisions 19 and 20.—Minor Wood-works, such as Toys, Models, Engraved Fruits.

For the reasons already given these two divisions may be dealt with conjointly and very briefly since there are few articles of sufficient merit to be classed as art manufactures in this position. DIVISIONS 19 AND 20. MINOR WOOD-WORKS.

Sola Pith Models.—At one or two localities remote from each other the material employed in the manufacture of "Sola topis" is worked up more or less artistically. In Dacca in Bengal, and in Rangoon and Mandalay in Burma, it is made into artificial flowers and in Trichinopoly in Madras into models of temples. Pommusami Pillai exhibits a model of Tanjore temple, price Rs. 100.

Carved fruits.—An extensive collection of carved cocoanuts and other fruits have been obtained from Cannanore, Travancore and Mysore. The more interesting specimens may be said to be the carved double cocoanut, price Rs. 100, made by the Cannanore Central Jail; "not at home" boxes, Rs. 18-12; salt and pepper stand, silver mounted, Rs. 32.

From Travancore a cocoanut vase, Rs. 12-8; a silver mounted sugar basin and spoon, Rs. 44. From Mysore a powder box, price Rs. 7. From Savantvadi a carved cocoanut teapot decorated with amalgam of mercury, Rs. 3-12.

AWARDS FOR WOOD-WORK UNDER DIVISIONS 19 AND 20 (MINOR WOOD-WORK, MODELS, TOYS, ENGRAVED FRUITS).

Third prize with bronze medal to Narayan Ramchandra Kelkar of Savantvadi for *hukka*. AWARDS.

Third prize with bronze medal for a collection of carved cocoanuts exhibited by the Superintendent, Central Jail, Cannanore.

Third prize with bronze medal to Pommiswami Pillai of Trichinopoly for a pith model of Tanjore temple.

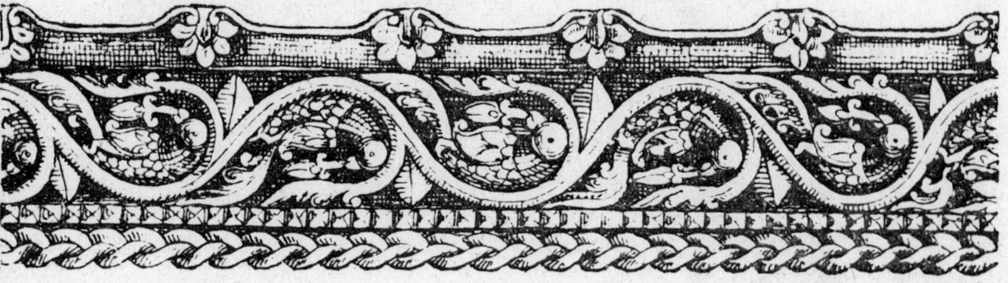

Class V.—IVORY, HORN, TORTOISE-SHELL, BONE, LEATHER AND SKINS, FEATHERS, Etc.

DIVISION 21. IVORY CARVING.

Animal Products.

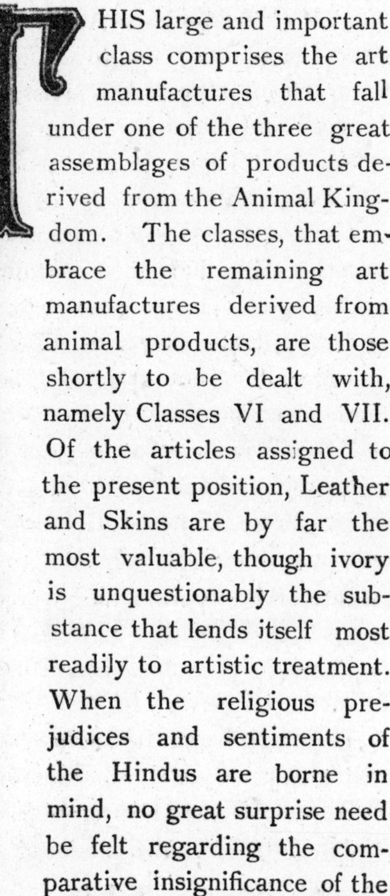

THIS large and important class comprises the art manufactures that fall under one of the three great assemblages of products derived from the Animal Kingdom. The classes, that embrace the remaining art manufactures derived from animal products, are those shortly to be dealt with, namely Classes VI and VII. Of the articles assigned to the present position, Leather and Skins are by far the most valuable, though ivory is unquestionably the substance that lends itself most readily to artistic treatment. When the religious prejudices and sentiments of the Hindus are borne in mind, no great surprise need be felt regarding the comparative insignificance of the available information (in the publications of the ancients) regarding the art industries that largely depend for their existence on the taking of animal life. This is, however, a subject that has been so fully commented on by numerous writers that it need hardly be more than alluded to in this place; the contention has been advanced that these industries are in India of recent introduction.

DIVISION 21. IVORY CARVING.

History of Ivory.

The domination of the Muhammadan faith most certainly extended their importance, as it largely removed the objection that may be assumed to have existed against undue prominence, but that the Muhammadans did not introduce these industries can be abundantly demonstrated. Siva, for example, is universally represented either dressed in or seated on a tiger's skin Deers' skins were regularly used by the Brahmans in ancient times. In the Rig Veda mention is made of leathern water buckets similar to those employed at the present day. In fact it might safely be inferred that the objection to animal products or even to animal matter as food, crept into the later Aryan times when these invaders had settled down in India and had become severed into inimical races who contested territorial possessions.

So again in the Rig Veda the king is spoken of as riding on an elephant and Indra's Vahan is the elephant Airavat. In the wars of the Ramayana and the Mahabharata elephant corps were employed, so that it is thus a fairly justifiable inference that when the elephant was thus regularly caught and tamed, during these remote periods, the uses of ivory could hardly have been unknown. In fact in the Ramayana mention is made of the ivory carvers along with the other guilds—a circumstance of considerable interest since at the present day there is no special caste devoted to the art of ivory-carving. But that the craft is not wholly of modern origin, still less a product of English influence and trade, may be conclusively inferred from the writings of the early European travellers in India. Terry in his Voyages to the East Indies (1655) makes mention of the skill of the Indian craftsmen in making "cabinets, boxes, trunks and stand dishes, curiously wrought within and without; inlaid with elephant's teeth or mother-of-pearl, ebony, tortoise-shell and wire, etc." Although there are not many examples of authentic old ivories to be found in India, sufficient exists to justify the inference that from about the time of Terry's visit, if not from a considerably earlier period, ivory-carving was as skilfully accomplished as at the present day. The more interesting examples of old ivories will be found discussed below, under the names of the provinces of India from which they have been procured.

DIVISION 21. IVORY CARVING.

Shells.

But to return to the assemblage of products placed under the present class, the conch shell (*sankha*) and the ammonite (*shalgrama*) are sacred emblems with both the Hindus (Vishnu) and the Buddhists, and in some of the most ancient topes that have been opened and their relics examined large quantities of cowries, identical with those used as coins at the present day, have been found. Bracelets made of the conch shell are frequently worn by newly married females. They are presented by the bride's father on the occasion of certain preparatory festivities to the wedding ceremony.

Division 21.—Ivory-Carving, Painting, Staining, etc.

Position of the Craft.—While touring through India, in connection with arrangements for the Indian Art Exhibition, the writer had occasion to visit nearly all the best known centres of ivory-carving as also to inspect the palaces of a large percentage of the most important princes and nobles of India. Certain circumstances were forced on his attention that may be usefully mentioned. Of these the *first*, that nowhere was ivory-carving found to occupy the prominent position that it might have been anticipated to hold in a country where ivory has been known and apparently artistically worked up for many centuries. The injunctions that are believed to prohibit the use of ivory as a material in the construction of idols for the public temple or the private sanctuary, may be held as largely accounting for this circumstance. But that ivory should not take a more honourable position in the furnishing and ornamentation of the palaces of the rich is, to say the least of it, significant. Here and there fabulous sums have been expended on special chairs, *howdahs* and thrones, made of ivory, or in weaving rugs and fans of threads cut from the tusk of the elephant, but ivory ornaments or ivory as a decorative material was found to be, comparatively speaking, rare. In the *second* place even where ivory was fairly extensively used no antique examples were discovered. Perhaps the most interesting old ivories of undoubted Indian origin were three charming pieces from Orissa which will be alluded to below in connection with the province of Bengal.

Unimportant Position.

No Antiques.

DIVISION 21. IVORY CARVING.

Materials used.—A *third* circumstance may be mentioned, namely, the very extensive use of a substance that must be characterised as an ivory substitute. In none of the extensive series of monographs on ivory (recently published by the various Governments and Administrations of India) is any mention made of this material and yet there is hardly an armoury or a centre of ivory work where it is not to be seen in fair abundance. Ivory is in Indian as in European commerce spoken of as the "elephant tooth" but a second substance is called the "fish tooth" (*machlí-ka-dant*). This is always of a dirty (oily) yellow colour with the texture looking as if crystallized into patches. The significance of being called in every language and dialect of India "fish tooth" at once suggests a common and, most probably, foreign origin for the material. Upon inquiry it was found that it was more highly valued for sword and dagger hafts and more extensively used for these purposes than is ivory. It is put through an elaborate and protracted process of curing before being worked up. The crude "fish tooth" is wrapped up in a certain mixture (*masala*) and retained in that condition for various periods, the finer samples for as long as 50 years. The advantages are its greater strength, finer and smoother surface, and greater resistance (less liability to slip in the hand) than is the case with ivory.

Ivory Substitute.

So far as the writer has been able to discover, the "fish tooth" of Indian trade is mainly, if not entirely, the so-called fossil ivory of Siberia—the ivory of the Mammoth—a substance that has lain for countless ages in the frost-bound drifts of Liakoff and New Siberia. It is also possible that a fair amount of hippopotamus or "sea-horse ivory" and even of the "walrus ivory" finds its way to India by passing like the Siberian ivory by land routes to India. And from the antiquity of some of the swords, found in the armouries of the princes of India with "fish tooth" hafts, it would seem possible that there has existed for centuries a traffic in carrying this material to India.

Mammoth Ivory.

Forms of Ivory.—There are two well marked forms of ivory—the African and the Asiatic. As a general rule the nearer the equator the larger, finer and more expensive the ivory, but there are many local manifestations that are best accounted for very

Forms of Ivory.

DIVISION 21. IVORY CARVING.

possibly by the food on which the animals have fed. For some unaccountable reason Ceylon ivory has been for years past becoming shorter and less valuable than the Indian. African ivory is closer in grain and not so liable to turn yellow as the Indian, but the ivory of the East Coast of Africa is superior to that of the West. By "dead ivory" is meant ivory that has been stored for a considerable time until it has lost the oil or gelatine that gives elasticity to "green ivory." To in part restore this lost property the ivory carvers keep the samples upon which they are engaged carefully wrapped up in damp cloth, overnight, until the carving has been completed. While this saves the ivory from chipping off in the carver's hands, it causes it to warp and split soon after and to rapidly lose colour—defects that seriously retard the Indian Ivory-carving Art.

Uses of Various Qualities.

A large percentage of the Mozambique and Zanzibar ivory finds its way to Bombay and is re-exported to Europe under what is spoken of as the East Indian trade. From this African supply the Indian carvers draw their most prized ivory. It is, therefore, perhaps only a repetition to observe that the Indian carvers recognise a vast difference between the Bombay (mostly African), the Deccan, the South Indian, the Assam and the Burman ivories, and an expert worker will point out the particular styles of work for which each quality is suitable. In Hoshiarpur, for example, the hair-like lines of inlaid work are invariably done in the bluish white African ivory procured from Bombay, but as this is more expensive than the Indian dull opaque or chalky ivory, it is most sparingly employed. The purity, opacity and stability of the Travancore ivories when compared with the flimsy brittle goods of Murshidabad, are doubtless largely due to the superiority of the green ivory invariably employed by the workers in the former, over the old brittle ivory of the latter, locality.

Centres of the craft.

Centres of Production.—There are four localities in India and one in Burma that have come to be spoken of as famous for their ivory manufactures; these are DELHI in the Panjab, MURSHIDABAD in Bengal, MYSORE and TRAVANCORE in South India and MOULMEIN in Burma.

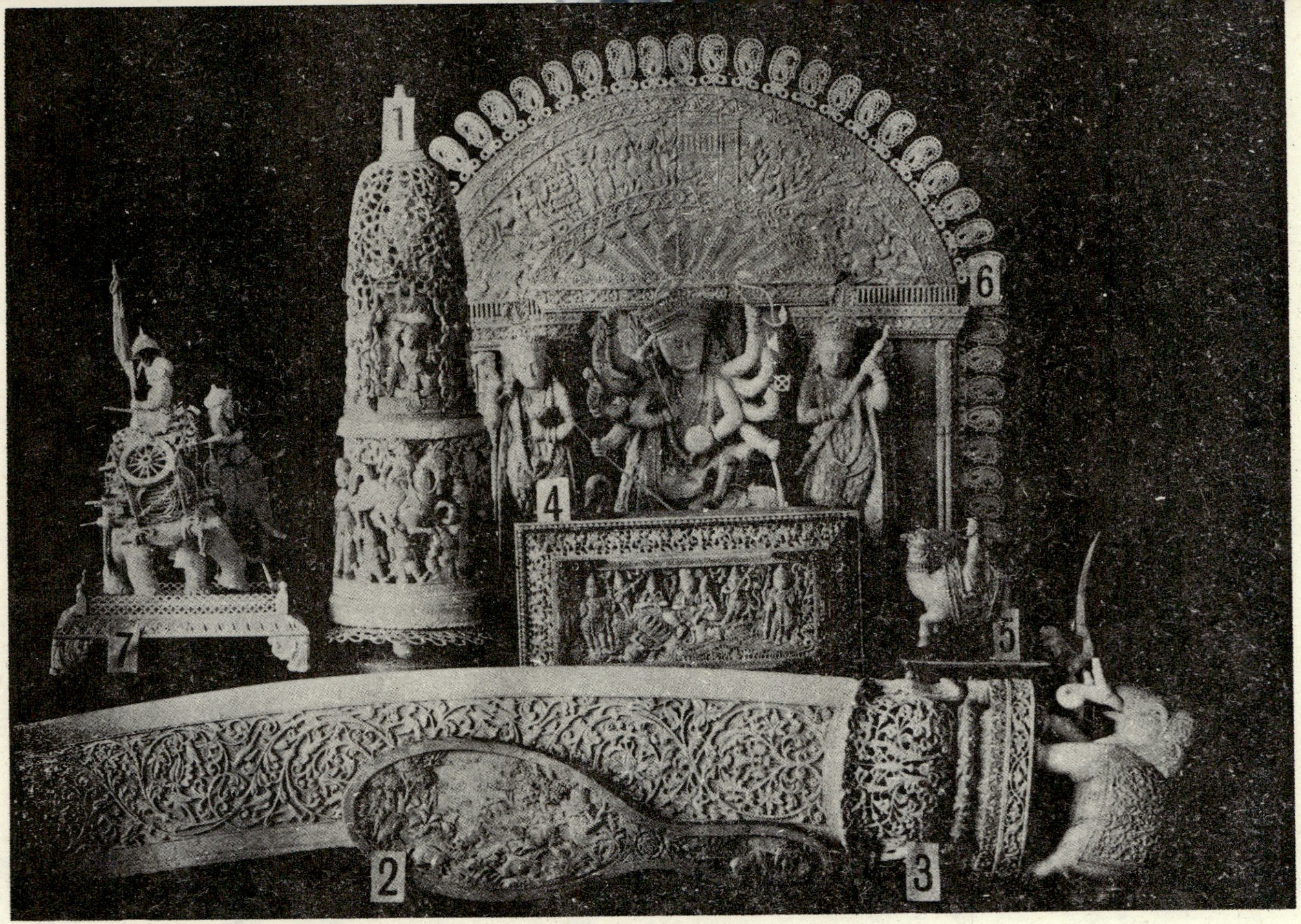

Plate No. 40 Typical Ivories

DIVISION 21. IVORY CARVING.

In the PANJAB the other centres are Delhi, Amritsar, Patiala, Ludhiana, Multan, Dera Ghazi Khan, Gujranwala, Hoshiarpur and Lahore. In LUDHIANA an extremely modern traffic has assumed some importance, *viz.*, the manufacture of billiard balls. In PATIALA a fairly old industry exists in shallow surface floral tracery—a minute and elaborate style in which, although the designs are good, the workmanship and joinery are very bad. In the palace there is a *howdah* that is perhaps one of the oldest authentic samples of Panjab ivory-carving. The Darshani Door at the Golden Temple, Amritsar, is inlaid with ivory, much of which is stained in the characteristic way, *viz.*, with green and red. These doors probably date from Ranjit Singh's restoration of the temple in 1802 A. D. Among the loan collections obtained from the Victoria and Albert Museum of South Kensington, there is a cabinet described as 19th Century Cingalese work. This is exceedingly like much of the Patiala ivory of to-day. It consists of a minute design, the branches of the floral scrolls being open, and profusely encircling, while the twigs may be described as thin, rounded and lying on the surface of the smooth field. Plate No. 40, fig. 5, shows a camel made in Patiala.

Panjab Ivories.

Patiala Style.

From Mir Muhammad Hussain Khan, miniature painter of DELHI, has been received a small casket carved in a remarkably flat style, the foliage being exceptionally large for the size of the design. The surface is broken up into distinct sections demarked by cuspid medallions and alternate straight lines formed through the stalks of rosettes of broad leaves. This is almost identical in every detail with a small box sent from the Victoria and Albert Museum of South Kensington, and which is said to be carved in "Persian style with conventional floral ornaments in foliated medallions: Mughal of the 17th Century."

Mughal Style.

In DELHI and AMRITSAR the industry would appear to have originated with the requirements of the grandees of the Muhammadan Court and subsequently with those at the Sikh Court. The Muhammadan feeling of the older Delhi work is its most striking peculiarity. The modern work has absorbed all styles and become mainly Hindu. It consists of a rich flat arabesque tracery with lace-like perforations arcading mythological or animal panels. In

DIVISION 21. IVORY CARVING.— former times the articles usually produced were bed posts, *chauris*, *surmadanis*, back-scratchers, bangles, etc. With the Sikhs, on

Sikh Style.

the other hand, the use of a comb, to be worn in the hair, became almost a matter of faith, and as the Sikhs were not restrained from life portraiture, to them very possibly may have to be attributed the introduction of relief work and statuary. It has been suggested that "the absence of any living tradition of its antiquity in the Panjab is due to the displacement of the old Hindu kingdoms by the Delhi Empire." But so little absolute proof have we of the patronage of Hindu kings in this direction and so essentially modern are the existing records of the craft, that, if speculation be permissible at all, it would seem in more accord with the facts to affirm that the modern art of Panjab ivory-carving originated, if not by, at least contemporaneous with, the Delhi Empire.

It is, however, somewhat remarkable that the chief artistic workers at the present day, are Hindus. In the now famous Lala Fakir Chand Roghu Nath Dass's shop at Delhi about 20 or 30 hands are employed and the majority are Brahmans. Ivory-carving is as a rule hereditary. The sons of carvers begin to be instructed when little more than ten years of age. For some time they are kept engaged on drawing, then from one stage to another they are progressed until they become master craftsmen. The average training for ordinary work takes about seven years but for the higher flights (assuming the possession of natural

No special Caste.

talent) the apprenticeship may be extended to 25 years. There is, however, no special caste identified with the craft like that of the *sonárs* or silversmiths. In some parts of the country the ivory carvers are carpenters by caste; in others silversmiths and in a third Muhammadans, as for example, those of Ludhiana, Dera Ghazi Khan and many other centres. The absence of a recognised caste of ivory carvers is one of the strongest points in favour of the contention that the industry, as it exists at present, is a comparatively modern one. In further support of

Modern Trade.

this view it may be said that in Delhi, some 40 years ago, there hardly existed an ivory-carving industry while to-day Delhi is one of the chief centres of the craft in India. This remarkable development is doubtless entirely the result of the great influx of sight-seers, hence the goods turned out are mainly such as meet the requirements of the European demand. Richly designed and carefully finished caskets, glove boxes, table ornaments, (in the form of elaborately caparisoned elephants, camels, horses, etc.), also model carts, carriages, etc., paper cutters (some of monster size with elephant handles, Plate No. 40, fig. 3), and a large assortment of card cases, whist markers, chessmen and the like. It has been observed that in the figure carving of the Panjab there is always a stiffness, a want of flexibility and a clumsiness that is most reprehensible. "It is often a little exasperating," writes Mr. Ellis, "after admiring the perfect symmetry of the tracery designs, to be confronted with an animal round which these designs are worked, apparently taken out of a child's "Noah's Ark," without joints, and with its left side invariably concave and its right convex." The figure work is certainly much inferior to the rich tracery and complete perforation practised. It might be spoken of as perspective sculpture that is true to nature when viewed from one position only. All the same it is clever because it is an artistic adaptation to the necessity for economy and the difficulty to obtain blocks of the required size and thickness. The economy effected by perspective work has doubtless led to the formation of panels and canopies of gods such as the Durgas turned out in Murshidabad (Plate No. 43 to the extreme right, also Plate No. 40, fig. 6) and imitated at Delhi and Patiala.

DIVISION 21. IVORY CARVING.

Perspective Sculpture.

Chief Examples on View of Delhi Work.

The splendid series of samples shown by Lala Fakir Chand Roghu Nath Dass of Delhi, secured a gold medal as the best collective display of ivory at the Exhibition. Some of the pieces are remarkably fine and most have been sold—perhaps the best proof of their high merit. Plates Nos. 40 and 61 give some of the best examples. In the former, fig. 3 shows a large paper cutter. This splendid piece of work took three years to make. The handle represents an elephant standing on a pedestal of admirable relief foliar carving; the scroll on the blade is bold Mughal work. Fig. 7 shows an elephant loaded with guns, camp equipage, etc., each article including the chains cut from solid ivory. This

Delhi work.

DIVISION 21. IVORY CARVING.

is a marvellous piece of work, more wonderful than artistic, but it shows the great skill that has been attained when the links of a chain, each not more than the size of a pin's head, can be cut from solid ivory so that they are distinct and within each other.

Ivory Mats.

This has its parallel in the equally absurd feat of weaving mats from threads of ivory. This is done at various centres and in the Exhibition some half a dozen mats are on view from Delhi, Bharatpur, Murshidabad, Tipperah, etc. Two of these have been hung up so as to form the background of the series of ivories shown on Plate No. 43.

Perforated Work.

Plate No. 61, though intended to display miniature painting on ivory—an art that has attained marvellous perfection in Delhi—represents three caskets that might be said to be each of its own kind a triumph of Lala Fakir Chand Roghu Nath Dass's skill. Fig. 1 shows a large box richly chased in foliated scrolls; fig. 2 a small casket perforated until its *jálí* work has reduced the ivory to lace; lastly, fig. 3 shows a glove box that was much admired by the Judging Committee. In this a combination of all the styles of carving in Northern and Western India may be said to be displayed. The large panels depict mythological scenes, the upright panels are in Ahmedabad style and the scroll work, in bold floriation of Mughal pattern. The painted medallions represent the more noteworthy buildings of Agra and Delhi.

In the UNITED PROVINCES there can hardly be said to be an industry in ivory. Small articles are turned out by the carpenters in most large towns, especially of Agra, Gonda, Lucknow and Benares. The Maharajas of Benares have always retained Court carvers who have made fairly creditable work, but no historic examples have been as yet discovered in these provinces. Lala Heera Lal of Lucknow has sent to the Exhibition a set of chessmen about 4 inches in height. These are realistically carved in the form of kings, knights, etc., dressed in the 14th or 15th Century costumes of England and coloured green and red.

Centres.

In RAJPUTANA and CENTRAL INDIA there are numerous centres of ivory turnery and carving. Of these special mention may be made of Jaipur, Ajmir-Merwara, Alwar, Bikanir and the

DIVISION 21. IVORY CARVING.

village of Pali in Jodhpur where there has been developed an extensive manufacture in bangles, *surma-dánís* (antimony boxes) chessmen, etc. Figures of animals are made in Rewa and paper cutters, sword hilts, combs, etc., at Ratlam, Dhar and Alipura.

Isolation of Industries.

JODHPUR.—As a curious instance of the tendency of Indian art trades to be isolated and local, the Pali (Jodhpur) craft in ivory-carving and turnery may be given. Situated on the old trade route from Bombay to Delhi *viá* Ahmedabad and Ajmir, that little town has for centuries absorbed a large proportion of the imported ivory. This is worked up into bangles of graduated sizes so as to cover the arm almost from the shoulder to the wrist. They are usually so elaborately coloured and ornamented with lac, beads and gold leaf, that a cheaper material might easily be substituted. The colours most fashionable, as with ivory staining and colouring in nearly every part of India, are red and green with black lines and circles. Such bangles are largely worn in Western Rajputana and are exported all over India. It is an old custom for the maternal uncle to present the bride with ivory bangles which are worn for the first year after the wedding. This practice prevails all over India except perhaps in the United Provinces and Oudh, in the Deccan and Madras.

Bangles.

In a set of chessmen from Jodhpur, the raja and wazier take the place of the king and queen, the elephant of the castle, the horse of the knight, and the camel of the bishop, with human heads as the *piadas* or pawns. In another set all the pieces are like salt and pepper boxes, and differ from each other only in massiveness or length. One of the most striking peculiarities of Jodhpur (Pali) ivories is the manner in which they are ornamented, namely, by circles and lines loaded with pink, green or black lac.

JAIPUR.—Certain doors in the Amber Palace which date from 1630 A. D., are inlaid with ivory and *sadeli* work similar to that described at page 156. These are in fact the oldest examples of this work in India.

Miniature Statues.

ALWAR STATE has sent to the Exhibition several miniature ivories, for example, a camel with driver, the rope being a fibre of ivory not thicker than a human hair; also a cow and calf, less than half an inch in length.

DIVISION 21. IVORY CARVING.

Bikanir old Work.

BIKANIR.—In the old palace of Bikanir the writer discovered certain doors richly inlaid and overlaid with ivory that very possibly are 18th Century style of work. One of these has been shown to the extreme right of Plate No. 32. In the same palace the walls are painted in a curiously Chinese design of clouds and thunderbolts with storks circling below (see initial illustration to this Chapter, page 170. The carved ivories, veneers and overlayings, while no doubt Mughal, have a Chinese feeling about them. In fact throughout Rajputana and Central India there is a Chinese taint in the art that brings to mind the tradition of Chinese teaching in the pottery of Sind and the Japanese or Chinese character of the Tonk shields, presently to be described (Division 28).

Ungot dans.

From UDAIPUR has been secured, for the Loan Collection Gallery, a delightful series of thumb guards (*ungot dáns*), used in shooting with the bow and arrow. Most of these are made of ivory, others rock crystal and still others of metal. They are richly coated all over with pale green, or dark claret red, or deep brown or other colour of lac. Through this and on to the white below a delicate design has been scratched which usually depicts some hunting scene, such as a fight between two elephants, or a sportsman spearing a tiger while in the act of seizing its kill. In other instances the pattern consists of oriental floral scrolls, the white flowers having a rich effect imparted to them by the margins of the petals or leaves being gilt. The designs on many of these thumb guards are so essentially Chinese that it is difficult to suppose that they could have been made in India. The feeling and touch are essentially Chinese but not more so than are the illustrations of a copy of the Shahnamah in the Loan Collection Gallery, said to have been painted in India in 1616 A. D. The doors of the Bari Mahal are overlaid with ivory that has been coloured with lac etchings. The date of these doors has been given as 1711 A. D.

BENGAL—has several centres that turn out ivory-carving and ivory inlaid work. These are Murshidabad, Rungpur, Dacca, Tipperah, Chittagong, Monghyr, Patna, Calcutta, Dumraon, Durbhanga and Orissa. Mr. G. C. Dutt has written a most excellent monograph on the ivory work of Bengal. He there narrates the tradition of the introduction of the craft into MURSHIDABAD. This, it would seem, came from Delhi, in connection with the demand for back-scratchers. A Hindu having seen the Muhammadan artist at work was induced to produce copies of his wares and so successful was he, more especially his son, that the industry soon changed hands and has been confined ever since to a small community of the *baskar* (*kondikars*) caste of Vaisnavs who in many respects recall the *gudigars* of Mysore and Kanara (page 148). Both are the hereditary idol makers, the one working mostly in ivory and the other mainly in sandal wood.

DIVISION 21. IVORY CARVING.

History of Murshidabad ivories.

While the Bengal ivory workers have produced for some years past a large assortment of table ornaments, such as elephants, models of bullock carts, processions, marriage ceremonies, and such like, for the European market mainly, they seem, at a still earlier date, to have almost exclusively turned their attention to the possibility of being able to meet a local demand for certain representations of the gods. For example, the popularity of the festival of Durga and the large demand for the characteristic groups of idols used on that occasion, doubtless suggested the flat panel of deities with an encircling canopy, borne on classic pillars. Though made in ivory, it is identical with that produced in clay or in sola pith and worshipped during the great festival season of Bengal. In the centre of the entablature is the consort of Siva in her incarnation of the warrior who slew the demon or giant Mahisha and thereafter took the name of *Durga* (*Chamundi*, page 150). She has ten hands and with one is represented as thrusting the spear into the demon and with another holding up by its tail the cobra seen stinging his face. Around her are grouped Lakshmi, Saraswati, Kartikiya and Ganesa.

Durgas.

This flat and flimsy style of ivory work was first made in Murshidabad but it is now copied in Delhi and Patiala and finds a market all over India. Without fear of contradiction it may be characterised, from the art point of view, as a modern abomination that could hardly have originated in any other province

Flat sculptures.

DIVISION 21. IVORY CARVING.

than Bengal, where a distorted conception of Doric architecture has passed current as indigenous art for at least half a century. In the background of Plate No. 40 (fig. 6) will be seen portions of an ivory panel of *Durga* and another on the extreme right of Plate No. 43.

ORISSA.—It is therefore pleasant to turn from this feature of Bengal ivory-carving to that met with in Cuttack and Puri.

Old examples.

That ivory-carving has been long known in Orissa may be inferred from one of the inscriptions on the walls of the audience hall of the temple of Jaganath in Puri—a temple that very possibly was originally Buddhist. The presentation to the temple of couches, *chauris*, bangles, all made in ivory, is there recorded. So also it is well known that the Rajahs or Chiefs of the Tributary States have for many years retained carvers and that through these a high proficiency has been attained in ivory work. Amongst the many beautiful samples of ivory-carving, sent to the Delhi Exhibition, few are more interesting than three fine old bits contributed by the Chief of the Nayagurh State. The letter that accompanied these most admirable samples states that they were made by one Gobind Ratan of Nayagurh about 50 years ago. They are as follows:—

A tortoise.

(*a*) A splendid tortoise (possibly representing *Kúrma* as *Kasyapa*). It consists of 4 pieces of ivory and is 8 inches long by 6 inches wide. Plate No. 77 shows two positions. The body of the animal is represented as wreathed and garlanded with flowers held in the mouth while entangled within these floral ornamentations are two charmingly carved and cleverly stained paraquets. The floral work is deeply cut, is liberally dispersed with large composite flowers that look like moon-stones or lotus-leaf discs and the deeply under-cut foliage recalls very forcibly the sandal wood work of Mysore. The shell of the tortoise is removable and from the photograph will be seen to be richly and deeply engraved. The zones of scroll work and the garlanding of the body of the animal are strongly suggestive of Chalukyan art. The

Forward scrolls.

outermost scroll is a beautiful example of the forward and upward flow, alternated and rarely inverted, but often with a double scroll in opposite direction, that is so commonly met with in

DIVISION 21. IVORY CARVING.

this school of early Indian decoration. In consequence of the direction of the scroll a meeting and starting point is almost indispensable. The former becomes an arbitrary line and the latter takes the form of a double-headed *yáli,* from the mouth of which the scroll is seen to flow. In the idol canopy from Mysore, shown on Plate No. 13, will be seen a good example of the grotesque animal heads, so often introduced at the meeting or starting points of decoration of this kind.

But to revert to the Nayagurh tortoise, the life-like texture and anatomy of the legs and neck of the animal, raise the artist who produced this wonderful creation to a position of equality with the ivory carvers of Europe, Japan or China.

A statue of Krishna.

(*b*) A statuette of Krishna (Plate No. 76). The drapery and ornaments of this exquisite piece of work indicate the locality of its production. Moreover the designs shown on the girdle and lotus pedestal so closely resemble the scroll work of the tortoise already described, that there would have been no difficulty in affirming that the two pieces of ivory were made by the same person, had this circumstance not been known. The method of dressing and ornamenting the hair, while it still lives to a certain extent in Orissa and along the mountainous tracts between the Mahanuddy and the Kistna, has practically disappeared from the rest of India and is only seen in fairly ancient idols of Krishna. In the more recent statues the hair is tied in a knot and is not left as a jewelled pendant hanging to the waist.

Jewelled Hair.

(*c*) The third sample from Orissa is a beautiful piece of solid ivory measuring 8½ inches in length and 3½ inches in thickness. It represents the infant Krishna kissing his toe, but there is a peculiarity not often seen in recent representations of this popular subject, namely, the hair is shown as in a profusion of short curls.

Ivory Mats.

TIPPERAH—has enjoyed the reputation (along with Sylhet) of being one of the most ancient seats in Bengal of the art of ivory carving and ivory mat-weaving. Certainly one of the most beautiful pieces of ivory work in the Indian Art Exhibition is the ivory chair furnished by His Highness the Maharaja of Tipperah. This is a splendid piece of massive and graceful work. It is said

DIVISION 21. IVORY CARVING.

of Tipperah that the art of *kinkhab* weaving is practised as an amusement by the ladies of the Court. The gold brocade with which the ivory chair has been upholstered was woven in the palace.

NEPAL.—Ivory-carving is carried on to a limited extent as also inlaying of wood with ivory. The work is very neatly finished, is strongly Chinese in feeling and usually assumes the form of figures of gods, combs, chop-sticks, etc. There are two charming picture frames among the set obtained from Nepal at the Exhibition and a large punkah with an exquisitely carved handle in quaint diaper design.

ASSAM.—Ivory-carving in the times of the Ahom kings was an important craft. Only two or three persons are now known to practise the art, the best being Fiznur, a Muhammadan of Jorhat. He makes back-scratchers, salad spoons and forks and the like.

BOMBAY and SIND.—Mr. C. L. Burns has written a monograph on the ivory work of this Presidency. He tells us that the art is little known. A certain amount of turnery and carving may, however, be seen in Poona, Kanara, Surat, Baroda, Karachi, Halla, Kathiawar and Kach. The samples sent from Bombay to the Indian Art Exhibition are in the Loan Gallery mainly. Mr. Burns observes that "it must be confessed that compared with the work produced during the middle ages in Europe and in Japan before 1860, the old Indian work is childish in its technique and poor in design. It has none of the exquisite feeling and beauty of workmanship of the former, nor the complete craftsmanship, humour and insight of the latter." This opinion may be true of the work turned out in the Western Presidency, but it would seem too sweeping a generalization when applied to India as a whole, more especially Travancore and Mysore.

Brahminabad Chessmen.

Many writers have alluded to the fact that one of the most interesting discoveries, regarding the ivories of India, was made a little more than half a century ago when a set of ivory chessmen was discovered during the excavations on the site of the city of Brahminabad in Sind. That city was destroyed by an earthquake early in the 8th Century. If it may be accepted that these ivories were made in Sind or even in India and were of the period suggested through the locality of discovery, then they would very likely have to be accepted as the oldest examples of Indian ivory at present known. They have been deposited in the Victoria and Albert Museum of South Kensington, London. Although that institution has sent to the Indian Art Exhibition some exceedingly interesting Indian and Ceylon ivories, the Sind chessmen have not been received. Perhaps the next oldest authentic example of ivory work in India is the inlaid door-ways of the Ashar Mahal of Bijapur, made in 1580 A. D.

DIVISION 21 IVORY CARVING.

MADRAS PRESIDENCY:—TRAVANCORE.—The ivory carvings of Travancore and Mysore must be given the very foremost position among the ivories of India. The sets of samples sent to the Indian Art Exhibition by His Highness the Maharaja of Travancore and His Highness the Maharaja of Mysore, while at once the most artistic and most interesting on view at Delhi, are hardly sufficient to justify the expression of definite opinions nor the production of an essay that could be accepted as giving a fair conception of the art feelings and instincts of these master carvers. To accomplish this it is essential that the methods of work and the decorative designs, not only of Mysore and Travancore, but of each and every one of the numerous minor localities of ivory-carving in the Presidency, should be critically studied and the stories they have to tell linked up with those of all other parts of India. This has not been done and is of urgent importance if the craft is to be guided into higher flights than it has as yet attained.

Defective knowledge.

During the rapid tour through South India, made in connection with the Indian Art Exhibition, arrangements were entered into for collections from Travancore, Mysore, Godaveri, Tirupati, Vizianagram and Vizagapatam, and not a few antiques were thereby brought to light that have hitherto escaped notice. But it is believed, were a protracted inquiry instituted, the missing links in the history of Indian ivory might be forthcoming. From the Victoria and Albert Museum, South Kensington, London, have been received some half a dozen South Indian ivories, presumed to date from the 17th and 18th Centuries (Plate No. 79). These abundantly confirm the impression left in the writer's mind, from the study of the beautiful collections procured direct from Travancore and Mysore, that the art conceptions of the ivory carvers, like

Loan collections from London.

DIVISION 21. IVORY CARVING.

those of the sandal wood workers, centre around the early Chalukyan and Buddhistic traditions rather than the more recent Dravidian and Indo-Aryan schools of South Indian decoration. There is something about the ivory work of the Southern Peninsula that at once brings to mind the complexity and intricacy of the pinnate and palmate floration (interspersed with grotesque animal forms) met with in the wall ornamentations of the temples of Baillur and Hullabid or even of the ancient Jaina temple of Mudbidri, rather than of the *swámi* style of the Tamil country proper. In other words the ornamentation that it is desired to urge as more immediately associated with the ivory of South India would seem to link together the people of the Eastern and Western Ghats with those of the Deccan. But, when the country indicated fell under Hindu influence, it doubtless became strongly Dravidian and hence manifested the Burmese tendency that is so striking and unexpected a peculiarity of the art of the Tamil-speaking people.

Chalukyan Style.

Examples of South Indian, (mostly Travancore and Mysore) Ivories on View.

The beautiful ivory statuette of Krishna (Plate No. 76), discussed above in connection with the ivories of Orissa, belongs to this Deccan series. It manifests in a most striking manner the fantastically twisted, pointed and rigid draperies, the massive ear ornamentations and the many-storied form of the head-piece of Burmese sculpture. This many-storied form may be recognised in the figures of the casket shown on Plate No. 79 (fig. 1); also the jewelled, tasselled and plaited hair (forming a long tail), on the casket (fig. 2) and the human figures in the central floriated portions of the comb (fig. 3) may be admitted as vividly bringing to mind the silver ware of the Godavari (Plate No. 8, fig 11). In all these examples the peculiar foliage and the nature of the grotesque animal forms that are seen to give birth to the scroll work (Plate No. 79, fig. 4) are almost precisely that seen on Hullabid and on the wonderful sandal-wood carvings of Mysore.

Godavari Style.

The casket (fig. 4), according to the label attached to it by the authorities of South Kensington, is supposed to be Cingalese

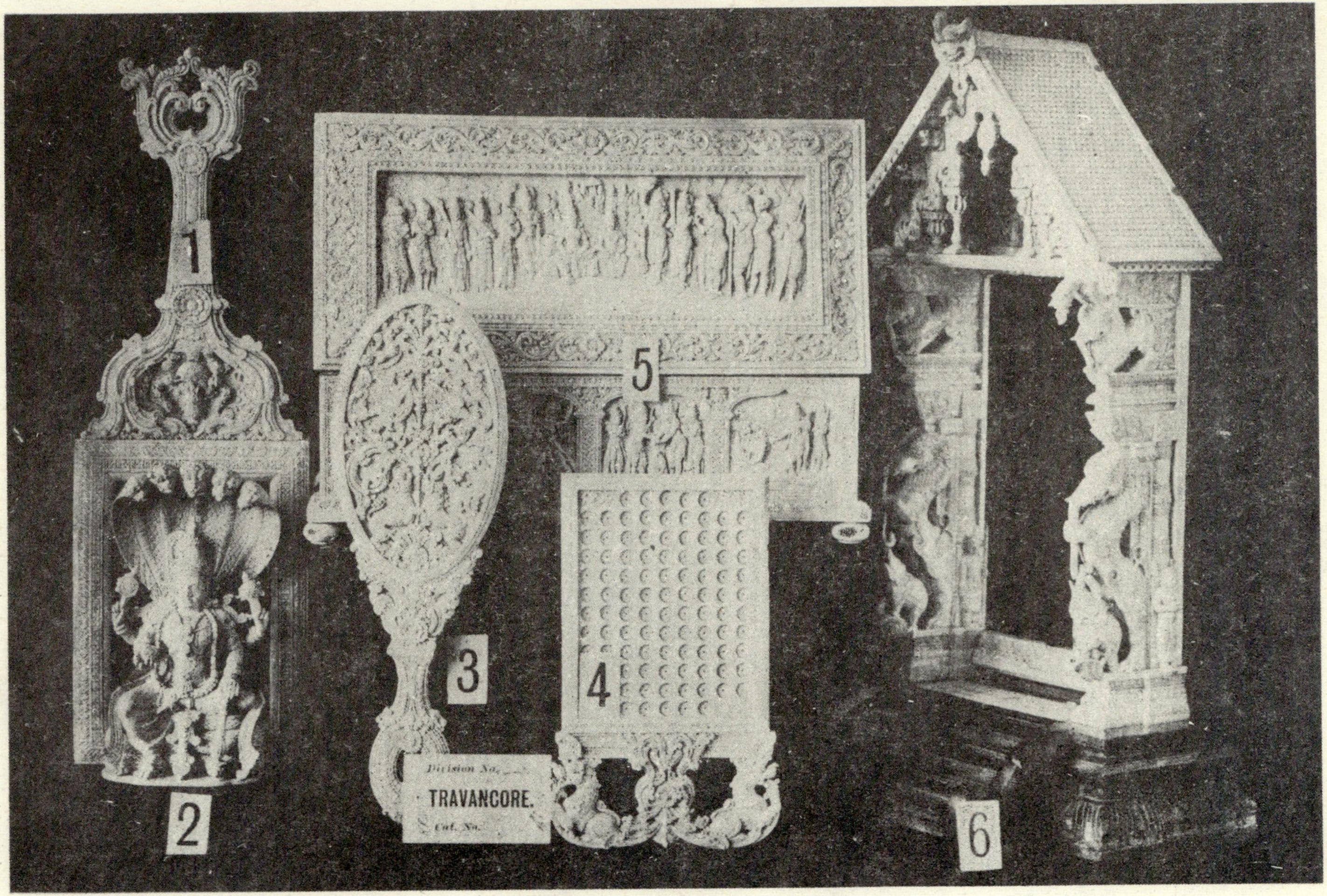

Plate No. 41 Travancore Ivories

and of the 19th Century. That may be so, for it is more difficult to separate the Ceylon from the Travancore and Mysore ivories than these from the purely Dravidian work. The Madras Museum possesses two pieces of old ivory (Plate No. 79, fig. 5) that are almost identical with several bits sent from the Victoria and Albert Museum, and said to be Cingalese of the 17th Century. But these Madras and South Kensington Museum old ivories collectively recall very forcibly the designs on the embossed and perforated brass caskets from Calicut, figured in the Album of *Madras and Burmese Art Wares* (Plate XXI), published in 1886 by the Madras Government. Through these brass wares the link is next made to the designs on the Bellary Door (Plate No. 30 and tail-piece page 169) as also to the *kinkhábs* of Tanjore (Plate No. 81). It may thus be safely inferred that designs that occur again and again in the wood, metal, ivory, textiles, etc., have more than a purely accidental or recent association with the people by whom they are produced.

DIVISION 21. IVORY CARVING.

Old samples from Madras.

Turning now from these historic examples of South Indian, possibly Travancore ivories, it may be useful to refer briefly to some of the more remarkable examples of recent work sent to Delhi by His Highness the Maharaja of Travancore. Plate No. 41 gives a selection of these. In order that the designs might be seen more clearly the selection was made, however, from the smaller pieces in the collection. One of the most beautiful examples (but unfortunately for the reason given, one that could not be reproduced) is a hexagonal shrine with idols placed within the six triangular niches thus formed. This is shown in the middle of Plate No. 43. The pillars, canopies, spandrils, roofing, etc., of this beautiful piece of work are admirable and manifest, in a forcible way, the great peculiarities of this style of ivory such as its massive form, purity in design and excellence in finish. But the shrine or *Rama mandar* here described is much more Dravidian in form than is commonly seen in the work of Travancore. This was made in the School of Art, Trevandrum. The stand is in buffalo-horn and all the structure including the idols in the purest and best ivory.

Recent Work.

The hand looking-glass (Plate No. 41, fig. 1) is a clever

DIVISION 21. IVORY CARVING.

example of the adaptation of Chalukyan foliage to a small object. The drawing is perfect, the curves graceful and the feeling, that of a style of ornamentation that has borrowed nothing from foreign influence. The massive idol (fig. 2) represents Vishnu seated on the snake with a canopy formed by a five dog-headed hood. This is illustrative of the greater attention that is paid to statuary in Travancore than in any other centre of Indian ivory-carving. Instead of being in perspective and such that it must be placed against a flat surface it is as fully developed behind as in front and can be viewed from all sides.

Brush-back.

The brush-back (fig. 3), is solid ivory with a boldly drawn floral scroll, interspersed with animal forms, seen to originate and receive the floriation. From the standpoint of design this is perhaps the most admirable and perfect of the many beautiful works received from Travancore. In order that it may be more fully appreciated it has been shown a second time (Plate No. 42, fig. 2) alongside of a loan collection brush-back obtained from the Palace of Mysore. These remarkable pieces of work admirably illustrate the two great styles of South India—Travancore, true to its ancient conventional designs, Mysore (fig. 1) modern jungle scenery, in which a high proficiency has been attained both in sandal-wood and ivory.

The money-counting board (Plate No. 41, fig. 4) is another splendid achievement of decorative art, which demonstrates the purity in design and feeling that is so remarkable a feature of these Travancore ivories. The small circular holes are intended, when filled, to count 100 *chukrams*. The handle consists of dignified floriations proceeding from lion griffins.

Casket.

The casket (fig. 5) was awarded a gold medal by the Judging Committee of the Exhibition. This is a piece of work of which Travancore may be justly proud, but it is very much more Dravidian (*swámi*) than are most of the other ivories of the State. It represents, by its twelve panels round the sides, the various incidents, in regular historic sequence, of the story of the Ramayana, while on the lid is carved the final scene—the coronation ceremony.

Doorway.

Lastly the doorway (fig. 6) is a delightful model of the approach to a temple or house in Travancore, showing a flight of

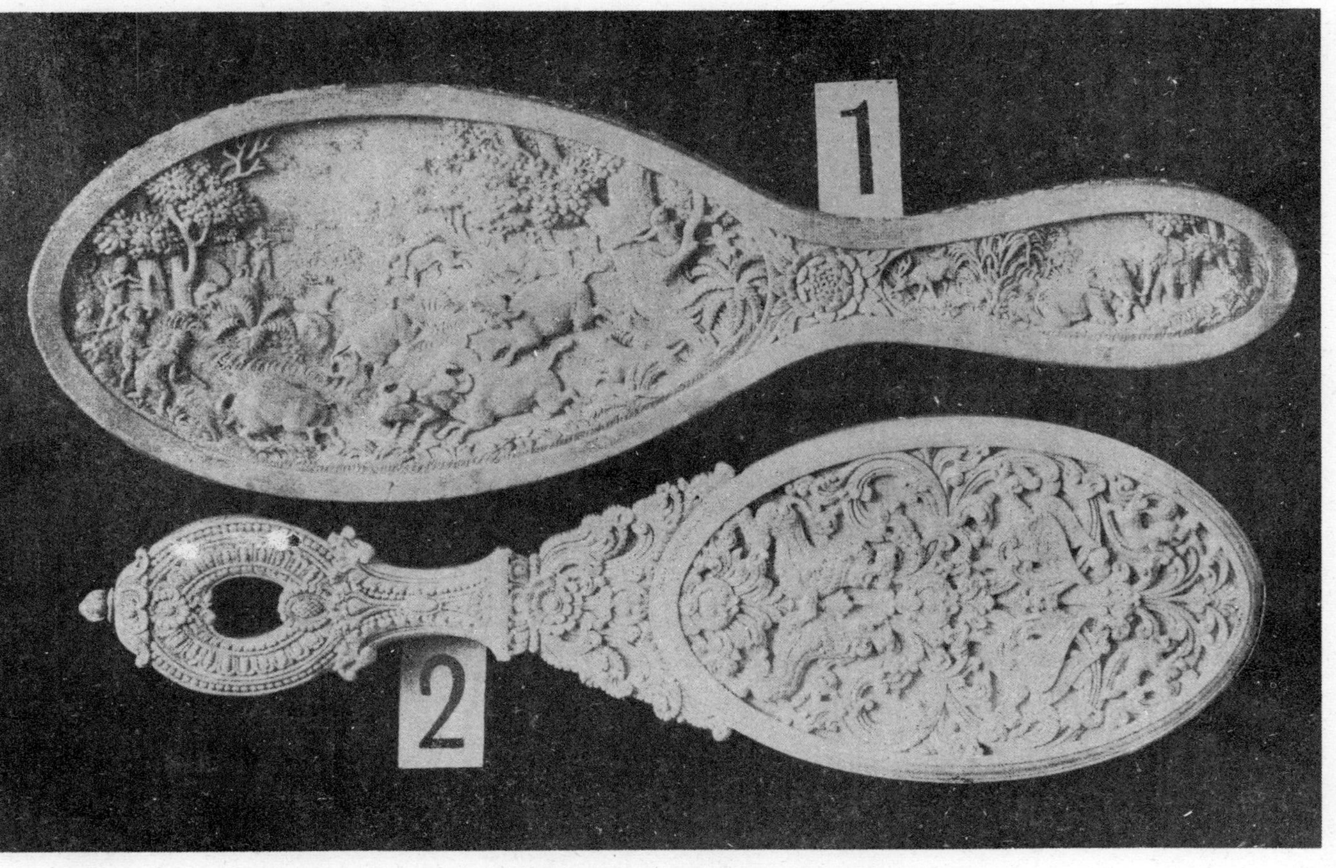

Plate No. 42 Mysore and Travancore Ivories

DIVISION 21. IVORY CARVING.

steps and moon-stone that strongly recall the similar structures in the ancient Buddhist pavilion of Anuradhapura in Ceylon. It illustrates all the peculiarities of the quaint style of wooden architecture, met with in the extreme south—its Dravidian double *yáli* pillars, its floral scrolls, suspended like draperies from straight, not curved, eaves and its great elaboration in detail of beams, joists, etc.,—peculiarities that in some respects give an aboriginal (or pre-Dravidian) turn to the art and architecture of Travancore.

Dragon Panels.

MYSORE and COORG.—From the Palace of Mysore have been received several very charming ivories. The settee back-rest (Plate No. 78) is believed to be early 17th Century work. It might be described as a tympanum-shaped and perforated panel of intertwined four-footed and feathered dragons, of all shapes and sizes, richly carved, gilded, stained and lacquered. Underneath is a band of cuspedly arched panels each filled in by perforated ivories, depicting trees with birds on the boughs and animals resting beneath. The frames of the whole structure are elaborately veneered with ivory every portion of which has been engraved and loaded with pigment (most probably lac), the colours being, as with all modern Indian work, pale green and a delicate magenta. This very remarkable piece of ivory will be seen to possess a strongly Burmo-Chinese feeling, but that it was made in Mysore there seems no occasion to doubt. It was copied some years later in a second back-rest (seen to the left of Plate No. 43), which in some respects may be regarded as an improvement on the original. It is made of more massive ivory but is spoiled by having iron rods driven through it, to bind the pieces together, in place of the gilded bands placed on the outside of the original. The ivory of the new copy has been discoloured by the iron, it has not been gilded or stained, and it has been framed in wood, in place of ivory veneers.

Antique Back-rests.

From the Palace has been received the brush-back shown on Plate No. 42, fig. 1. This has been already alluded to briefly but deserves further recognition. It is perhaps one of the most perfect pieces of realistic carving in the Exhibition. It portrays practically every feature of jungle life and sport. The foreground, middle distance, distance and clouds, are all faithfully treated and,

Jungle Scenes.

DIVISION 21. IVORY CARVING.

in a manner that is most surprising, every detail is shown and still the atmosphere of high class painting has not been materially disturbed nor the picture overburdened. On the reverse is an exceedingly clever modern design. The *karela* gourd is the subject. The composition, balance and harmony raise this little sketch to that of the highest decorative art.

Decorative Art.

The Palace of Mysore has next contributed a charming casket (Plate No. 40, fig. 4). This is bound in richly repoussé gold. It is understood it was prepared as a gift to a Royal personage, but owing to the death of the Prince was never presented. The side panels depict jungle life and sport, one of the most beautiful showing elephant catching. The panel on the lid is a mythological subject. The floral ornamentation is in the characteristic style discussed in connection with the sandal wood of Mysore.

Inlaying Work.

One of the most important trades of Mysore town may be said to be that of inlaying wood with ivory. The skill displayed by the Mysore inlayers far excels that of Hoshiarpur and other localities in Northern India. This subject has already been alluded to (pages 141-144) and Plate No. 32 shows a large assortment of the work. The two best samples are the cabinet and the door. The latter has been lent by His Highness the Maharaja and is one of those to be used in the new palace. Mysore inlaid ivory is richly loaded with black lac after the fashion practised in Vizagapatam (see page 142).

Old samples.

But a comparison of the modern with the old samples of inlaying is greatly in favour of the former. From the Victoria and Albert Museum of South Kensington has been received a panel showing old inlaying, presumed to be Indian. This will be seen on Plate No. 43-D, fig. 2. It consists of a veneer of *sisham* wood inlaid with ivory. But instead of cutting the openings to the exact size and shape of the stalks, leaves, birds, etc., to be inlaid, larger openings were made, the ivories were placed within and the remaining spaces filled up with molten lac coloured to imitate as closely as possible the surrounding wood. This method should be compared with the account of inlaying already given (pages 141-144) and with veneering (page 153)

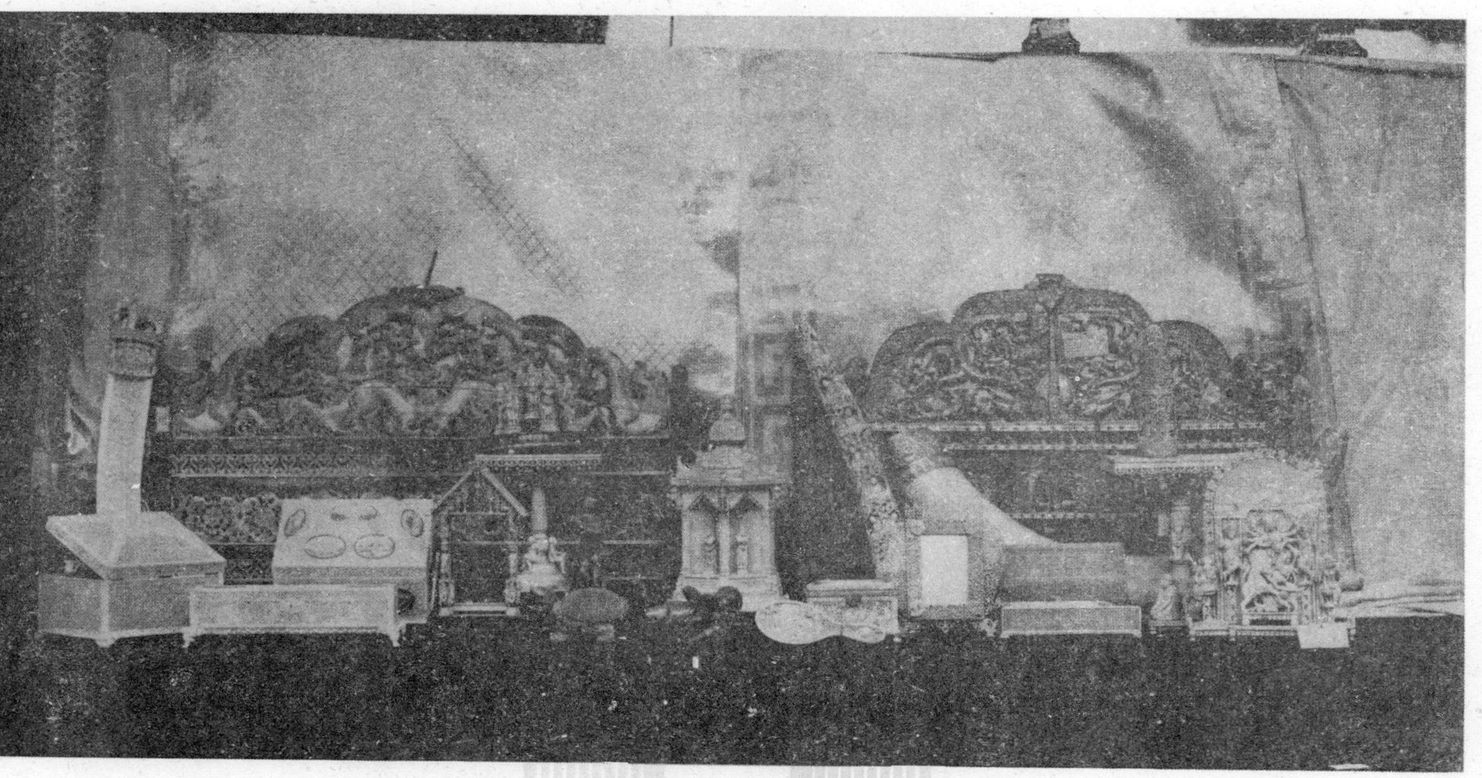

Plate No. 43 Carved Ivory (Ancient and Modern.)

DIVISION 21. IVORY CARVING.

VIZAGAPATAM.—Turning now to the Madras Presidency proper, there are several centres that have a fair trade in ivory. Vizagapatam is the centre of the veneered ivory work of India. This has already been fully discussed above (page 154) and need not be more than incidentally noticed in this place. Some of the finest examples seen by the writer are the howdahs and chairs in the possession of His Highness the Raja of Vizianagram. These are carved in a low flat style very much like the ivory-carving of Patiala and with none of the exuberance of the Travancore and Mysore styles. They are coloured with lac, mostly in shades of green and blue, and are identical with a sofa and set of chairs in Government House, Calcutta. In Vizagapatam a large amount of ivory-carving, as well as ivory-staining, is practised but mostly as veneers or appliqués over sandal wood, horn or tortoise-shell boxes. In addition to the assortment shown on Plate No. 37 one of the characteristic caskets made in Vizagapatam has been shown on Plate No. 43-A, fig. 3. It will be observed that the delicate trellis of ivory thrown over the tortoise-shell is richly carved as well as perforated, the designs being in graceful geometric scrolls, with medallions of mythological and animal subjects thrown within the floriation. It differs widely from the scroll work described and figured (Plate No. 79, fig. 3), in connection with the ivories of the Deccan and Travancore.

Lac-coloured Ivories.

Carved Veneers of Ivory.

TIRUPATI and GODAVERI—Have a fair amount of traffic in ivory but mainly in the production of miniature idols. The skill of these carvers seems to have gone forth more in the direction of the production of marvels than of art treasures. It is not uncommon to find an idol of Krishna playing on his lute, either cut from a grain of rice or a seed of the tamarind or a fragment of ivory so minute that the aid of a magnifying glass is required to discover the good or the bad points of the work. Mangu Kotilingam of Masulipatam has shown miniature statues of this kind both in tamarind seed and ivory, one of the latter representing a horse with rider, the entire size being under ½-inch in length. So also tamarind seeds in the form of elephants, camels, etc., made by Ramaswami Naidu of Tirupati have been sent to the Exhibition, some of them being remarkably clever.

Miniature Idols.

DIVISION 21. IVORY CARVING.

BURMA.—The traditions of Burmese ivory-carving would seem to point to the art having come from India. There are said to be three centres of this carving, *viz.*, Moulmein, Pyinmana and Rangoon. The articles chiefly turned out are handles to swords, (*das*), daggers and knives; picture frames; paper cutters; stands for silver bowls; chessmen; chairs; images of Gautama Buddha, etc. Whole tusks are carved with as many as 20 to 30 statues shown within a trellis-like covering of pierced ivory to which the tusk has been reduced (Plate No. 43).

Carved Tusks.

The marvellous is a distinct feature of both the wood and the ivory-carving of Burma, so much so that it may be remarked that artistic composition and adornment of structure are alike disregarded and substituted by incredible details often extremely beautiful in themselves, but superfluous and in bad taste when seen collectively. But it is somewhat significant that the design and pattern used in ivory-carving is the bold massive work seen on boats, not the more delicate lace-like fringes of the spandrils of pagodas. When done in ivory the parts are of course much reduced, but the pattern is there all the same, its large undulating foliage and rosettes of flowers taking the place of the vine leaf and tendrils of the more elaborate and less artistic work of the pagodas. This may possibly be accepted as indicating a greater antiquity and purity than is generally supposed, for there is nothing to show that the ornamental wood-work of the boats has been imported or modified by recent changes and influences.

Possible Antiquity.

From MOULMEIN has been received a good series of ivories though none of an exceptionally fine type. The best piece is a half tusk carved by Maung Po Hla in the form of an erect ornament standing on a silver pedestal. This has been shown on Plate No. 40, fig. 1. It portrays the birth, conversion, flight and life of the founder of the Buddhistic faith. As is usual with this style of work a floral trellis has been thrown over and around the chief sculptures and panels.

Other specimens worthy of special notice are the series of large tusks by Messrs. Beato and Company, RANGOON, priced at Rs. 1,000 each. In these a double layer of trellis work has been carried round the idols. Special mention may next be made of

Statuary.

the separate idols and statues of ivory made by Maung Po Hla of Moulmein. Perhaps one of the most graceful samples of Burmese ivory sent to Delhi is the picture frame, also by Maung Po Hla, (seen on Plate No. 43). In this a trellis work of foliage has been thrown over the statues that are within the texture of the frame. This beautiful piece is priced at Rs. 75.

DIVISION 21. IVORY CARVING.

AWARDS FOR DIVISION 21.—IVORY—CARVED, PAINTED, STAINED, ETC.

AWARDS.

First Prize with gold medal to Lala Fakir Chand Roghu Nath Dass of Delhi for collection of carved ivory.

First Prize with gold medal to School of Art, Trevandrum, for a carved ivory casket.

First Prize with silver medal to Maung Po Hla of Moulmein for series of Burma ivories.

Second Prize with bronze medal to Messrs. Beato & Co. of Rangoon.

Third Prize with bronze medal to Nilmani Bhasker of Murshidabad, for an ivory casket.

Third Prize with bronze medal to Girish Chandra Bhasker of Berhampur, Murshidabad, for a carved ivory procession.

Third Prize with bronze medal to Murari Mohan Bhasker of Murshidabad, for a carved ivory "Durga."

Commended for a carved ivory elephant with *howdah* by Nimai Chandra Bhasker of Murshidabad.

Commended for a carved ivory boat by Durlari Chandra Bhasker.

Divisions 22 and 23.—Horn, Antlers, Bone, Porcupine Quills, Tortoise-shell, Feathers, Feather Quills, Horse-hair, etc.

There is perhaps hardly any great advantage in keeping these various materials distinct in this work, though separate places have been assigned to them in the Exhibition. In fact it will be found that the exhibits that might be dealt with under these various divisions overlap each other as well as the manufactures of still other divisions. For example TORTOISE-SHELL is in India not as a rule manufactured by itself but is mainly employed as a veneer by the Vizagapatam fancy-box makers.

DIVISIONS 22 AND 23. HORN, ETC.

It has therefore been dealt with under Division 16. To a very small extent the Ceylon art of making combs, paper cutters, etc., from pure tortoise-shell is practised but not as a regular industry. In Bombay and some of the towns of Gujarat tortoise-shell is occasionally made into ornaments, card-cases, etc., but the trade is very unimportant except as a veneer on fancy boxes. So in the same way, though there is a fairly extensive traffic in the manufacture of combs, buttons, shoe-horns, walking sticks and the like from pure BUFFALO-HORN, the chief use of the material in the Indian Arts is as a veneer. PORCUPINE QUILLS are to a small extent employed in South India mainly in veneering fancy wares, and PEACOCK QUILLS are similarly utilized in embroidering leather. BONE is extensively used as a substitute for ivory in inferior inlaying, but in Peshawar *surma-dánís* (antimony boxes) are artistically made from camel bone and the same material is used for the white bosses shown on the lac work of Dera Ismail Khan. (Plate No. 44-A, fig. 7.)

Camel Bone.

Horse-hair.—This is woven into small baskets and boxes in Burma, but as these are coated with lacquer they have to be treated as examples of lacquered ware (see Plate No. 41, fig. 5). It thus comes about that the majority of the art manufactures derived from the animal products, mentioned above, can hardly be dealt with in this position. The following may suffice:—

Buffalo-horn.—The chief forms of horn used in the Indian Art Industries are buffalo and bison, since there are religious objections to the use of cow-horn. A cup made of rhinoceros-horn is much prized by Hindus, but that material is too scarce to be of much value. BUFFALO-HORN is by far the most largely employed but the least beautiful. It is made by the Indian workers in horn (*kangi-sáz*) into cups, tumblers, combs, musical instruments, work boxes, powder-flasks, bows and arrows, *hukka* mouth-pieces, scent bottles, snuff-boxes, pen-holders, walking stick and umbrella handles, sword, dagger and knife handles, and many other such articles. The centres of the trade are Cuttack, Monghyr, Satkhira (Khulna District), Hooghly and Serampore in BENGAL, where combs, brooches, necklaces, snake bangles and the like are made. In BHUTAN large horns, often

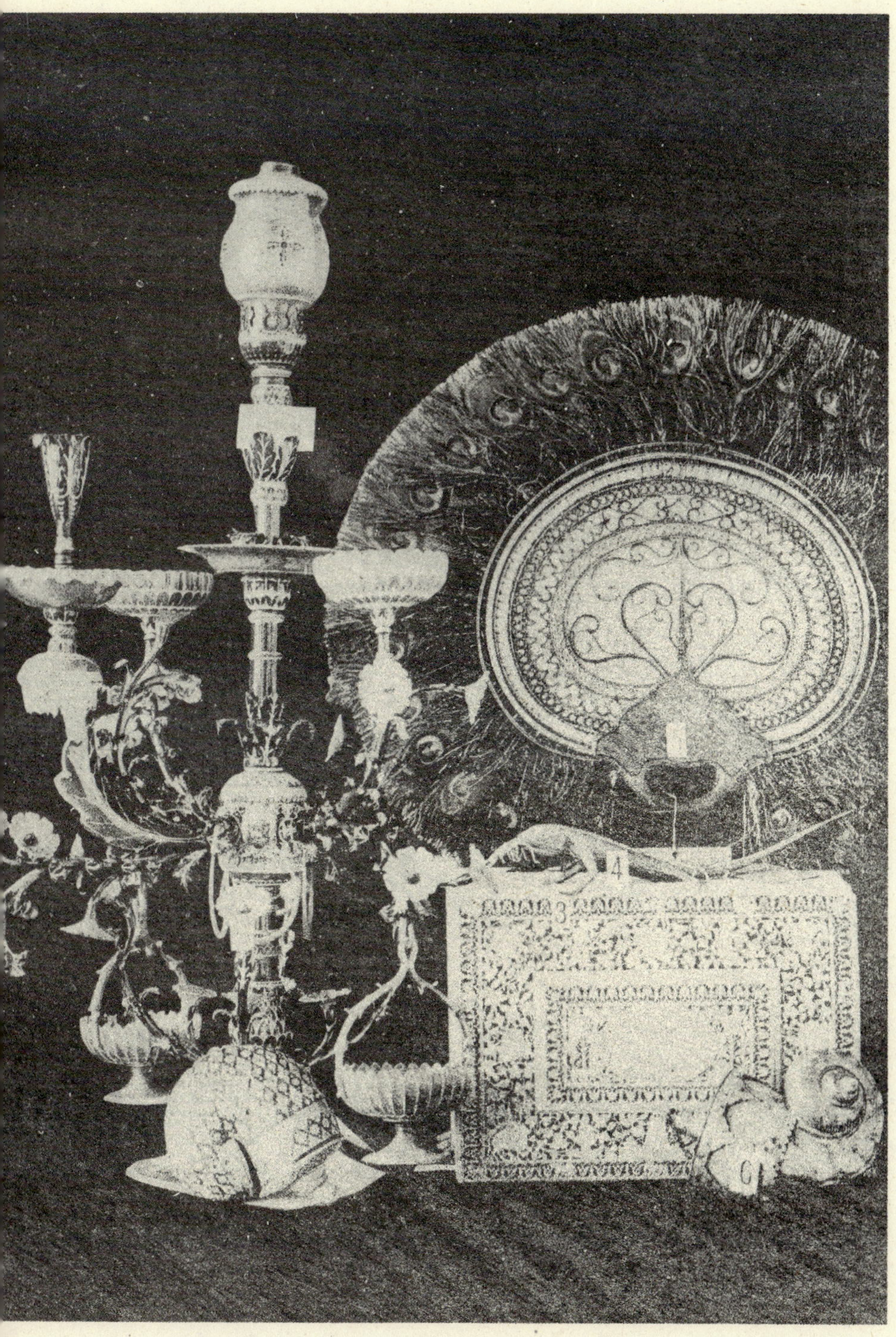

Plate No. 43-A Horn, Shell and Feather Work

richly ornamented, are used for carrying milk; and in NEPAL the rhinoceros-horn cups used in oblations to the gods are produced. In ASSAM, Sibsagar turns out salad spoons of buffalo-horn with quaint elephant handles. Of RAJPUTANA, mention may be made of the JAIPUR bows, ornamented in diaper pattern, and of the KOTA veneered work (page 157—Plate No. 37 and Plate No. 43-A, fig. 1.) The RAJKOTE combs, BARODA spoons, KATHIAWAR knife handles and the SURAT and AHMEDABAD boxes veneered with horn are all well known and are mostly of so little artistic merit that they hardly deserve a place in this work. BARODA sometimes, however, attempts articles of a higher character, such as the chameleon with scorpion in its mouth, made by Jagjivan Narbheram, carpenter of Nandod, Rajpipla, price Rs.10 (Plate No. 43-A, fig. 4). **DIVISIONS 22 AND 23. HORN, ETC.**

So much has already been said of the extensive use of buffalo-horn by the fancy-box makers of VIZAGAPATAM, under the division devoted to veneered wares (page 153) that nothing further need be said. A good example of this work, richly overlaid with carved ivory, is shown on Plate No. 43-A, fig. 3. But from MADURA has been received a large assortment of most admirably made and life-like animals in horn. Of this special mention may be given to the blood-sucker, the crab and scorpion, made by Pomusawmi Sary of Therkuvaral Street, Madura. They have not only the life-like expression of the animals but are cleverly jointed. The scorpion was so highly thought of by the Judging Committee of the Exhibition that it received a bronze medal. In this instance the horn is cleverly stained and polished so that it looks like jet. **Horn Animals.**

In MYSORE umbrella handles, powder boxes, buttons and other such articles are made of buffalo-horn and often richly inlaid with ivory and copper. Curiously interesting money boxes are constructed in this way at a cost of from Rs. 2 to Rs. 10, according to the richness and quality of the inlaid work. The best makers are Ganesiya and Yusaf Ali & Sons of Mysore. In COORG knife and *kukri* handles are made of buffalo-horn.

Bison-horn—is a more artistic material than buffalo and lends itself better to treatment. In RATNAGIRI and SAVANTVADI a fairly large trade exists in working up bison-horn into ornamental

DIVISIONS 22 AND 23. HORN, ETC.

Ratnagiri Bison-horn.

wares. In the *Agricultural Ledger* (No. 10 of 1897), Mr. E. H. Aitken published a most interesting account of the Ratnagiri work. The following passages may be extracted from that paper:—"The art of making ornamental articles in bison-horn is carried on by a very small number of men, who are also carpenters and metal workers, especially at Viziadrug. It does not appear to be an ancient art: they state that it has existed for four or five generations, and has been handed down from father to son in the few families which practise it." "The reason given for working in bison-horn is that the articles for which there is most demand are small stands for offerings, and other things which are used by Brahmans, and if they were made of cow-horn the Brahmans would have nothing to do with them. The horns are mostly procured from Malabar, and cost as much as Rs. 1-8 or Rs. 2 for a single horn."

Manipulation.

"The process of manufacture is as follows:—A portion of horn is kept moist with cocoanut-oil and heated before a fire until it becomes almost as soft as wax. This may take an hour or more. It is then worked, or pressed, into the required form, either with the hands or by means of moulds made of hard wood, and finished off with scraping tools and a small lathe. It remains to polish the whole and ornament parts of it with simple but graceful designs. The ornamentation is done in line with a fine, double-pointed, steel graving tool. The tools used in this work are indeed all extremely simple, and there are not many of them. A small, rude lathe, a fine saw, a few triangular blades, without handles, for scraping and polishing, a pair of compasses or callipers, three or four graving tools of sizes, with perhaps a file or rasp, and moulds made for the occasion, complete the necessary equipment."

Ornamentations Scratched.

Traditional Figures.

"It does not appear that the men work from any models or designs. Most of the figures are traditional. Perhaps the commonest article made is a *nandi*, or sacred bull, supporting a flat tray about seven inches in diameter, with a cobra rising out of the middle of it and rearing over it with expanded hood. The bull is in one piece, made from the solid half of the horn, which is always black. A hole is drilled in the back of the bull, in which is fixed the pedestal of the tray. This is another piece, and consists of a simple stem of solid horn, turned on the lathe. The tray is made from the base of the horn and is almost transparent. This is always made in a mould, after the horn has been thoroughly softened, and a good deal of labour is expended on it, the edges being scolloped and the border elaborately ornamented. But, alas, it is fastened to the stem with a common screw nail. The cobra is also made from the translucent section of the horn and must be moulded into shape with the hands. It is fixed so that the head rears over the middle of the tray, while the tail, passing through a hole in the bottom, twines round the stem. The eyes and mouth of the cobra and the scales on its back are most minutely worked out. It will be observed that this is all line engraving. There is scarcely anything that can be called carving in the whole work. Moulding and scratching are the only processes to which the material lends itself."

DIVISIONS 22 AND 23. HORN, ETC.

Moulded Trays.

Transparent Snake hood.

"Other articles commonly made are small ornamental cups, covers for tea-cups, buttons and beautifully translucent, round boxes or caskets for holding tooth-powder or other toilet requisites. Some of the best workmen, however, design and make much more ambitious works than these. A candelabrum, or lampstand, of most artistic design and elaborate workmanship, was lately sold in Bombay. But even original and complicated pieces of work like this appear to be carried through without any model or design. The idea is in the workman's head, and the details grow under his hand. The figures employed in ornamentation are of a kind familiar to us in brass work and embroidery, and even rustic mural decoration, consisting of circles with regular and undulating circumferences, radiating lines, loops and rings arranged in graceful, conventional patterns. As has been said, the principal purchasers of this ware are Brahmans, but the finer pieces of work are hawked about among Europeans, or wealthy natives, until a purchaser is found."

A Candelabrum of Horn.

In the Exhibition a very large assortment of bison-horn manufactures will be seen. The most beautiful sample (Plate No. 43-A, fig. 2) was made to order for a distinguished official

Examples on view.

DIVISIONS 22 AND 23. HORN, ETC.

whose death occurred immediately preceding the Delhi Darbar. It is perhaps one of the finest specimens of this ware ever seen. It was made by Vithal Gangaram Wadaya at a cost of Rs. 650. Many of the other examples shown were made by Gopat Shiveram Wadaya, and a third maker, Bhikkoo Vishram Wadaya —also of Ratnagiri—has sent excellent horn wares.

Antlers such as those of the black buck are largely made into knife and dagger handles and sometimes mounted in silver as pen-holders. They are not artistic and only a very few have been shown at the Exhibition.

Feathers.—It is perhaps hardly necessary to allude in this catalogue to any other than that of the peacock. This is largely used in ornamental work, for example, in the manufacture of fans, *morchals* or *chauris*, and braids, etc., to be used for trimming dresses and other purposes. The chief centres of manufacture are Benares, Nepal, Jhansi, Aurangabad, Savantvadi and Mysore.

Fnns.

It is customary for fans to be made of the root of the sweet smelling *khas-khas* grass and to be ornamented with gold braid, beetle wings or peacock feathers. The series of these beautiful objects at the Exhibition will be found to be most varied, but curious to say the demand for them has been very small indeed.

Chief Centres.

The centres of production have each their own little peculiarities in methods of treatment. In JHANSI the fans are perfectly circular and provided with a straight handle. The feathers are methodically arranged in perfect and symmetrical zones and both surfaces are completely compacted. Fans 3 to 4 feet in diameter of this kind may be had for Rs. 5 to Rs. 10, those smaller for Rs. 1 to 2 or 3. In MYSORE the fans are kidney shaped (see Plate No. 43-A, fig. 5) with a flat handle within the notch. The middle of the fan is built up of *khas-khas* with a fringe of peacock feathers given on the surface. In SAVANTVADI fans are kidney shaped, but with a central prolongation from the middle of the notch to give attachment to the handle. They usually are made to revolve around the handle and are elaborately ornamented with gold braid and spangles, beetle wings and tufts of dark claret coloured silk. Lastly, the fans from NEPAL are like those of Savantvadi, in shape and in the peculiarity of revolving around the handle, but they are elaborately embroidered in gold, a spray of gold spangles being shown in the middle of the eye of each feather. Medallions of idols, carved in wood or ivory, are also let into the fan and form centres around which the design in gold embroidery is developed. The whole interior of the fan is composed of feathers and the embroidery is so arranged as to show the blue eyes through the design. Lastly, and doubtless to give a delicate finish, white quills, bound together with gold wire, are employed as dividing lines or bands in the scheme of colour thus supporting the delicately carved ivory handle. Fans in this rich style cost about Rs. 300 each, but they are distinctly much more artistic than one is accustomed to think possible with an Indian fan.

DIVISIONS 22 AND 23. HORN, ETC.

Fans.

AWARDS FOR DIVISIONS 22 AND 23.—HORN, ANTLERS, FEATHERS, etc.

Third prize with bronze medal to Vithal Gangaram Wadaya for a candelabrum.

AWARDS.

Third prize with bronze medal to Malai Kan Asary of Madura for models of reptiles, etc., in horn.

Commended for horn work-boxes, etc., inlaid with metal and ivory, Ganeshia of Mysore.

Division 24.—Leather and Skins.

Leather holds an important position in the industries of India but in only a very few instances can it be regarded as rising to the position of a material that is used artistically. The following may be given as the chief artistic purposes to which leather and skins are put :—

Shoes and Sandals (*chaplis*) have been used from the most ancient times. We read, for example, of Bharata having placed the shoes of his step-brother Rama on the throne of Oudh as a symbol of the rightful heir to the throne. Coats and trousers of skins are also frequently mentioned. In fact it seems likely that from Buddhism came the injunction against taking animal life and consequently the prejudice, such as it is, against leather.

Historic Reference.

Shoes are often elaborately embroidered and even jewelled and some of them, therefore, become art manufactures. The places

DIVISION 24. LEATHER AND SKINS.

Chief Centres.

most famed for artistic shoes are Cuttack, Patna and Saran in BENGAL ; Rampur, Lucknow, Agra, Jhansi and Saharanpur in the UNITED PROVINCES ; Kohat, Rawalpur, Peshawar, Bhawalpur, Dera Ghazi Khan, Batala and Hosiharpur, also Kashmir in the PANJAB ; Chanda in the CENTRAL PROVINCES ; Jaipur and Bikanir in RAJPUTANA ; Surat, Ahmedabad, Poona, Ratnagiri and Hyderabad Sind in BOMBAY ; Raichur, Salem, Trichinopoly, Madras and Mysore in SOUTH INDIA. These are the chief centres of the native trade in artistic shoes, but of course CAWNPORE stands out pre-eminently as the commerical centre of the modern trade in boots, shoes, saddlery and trunk manufacture.

Belts, Powder-flasks, Pen-cases, etc.—Very many artistic articles are made that would fall under this section. The sword-slings and belts from PESHAWAR, Bannu, Kohat, Derajat and Quetta are often very beautiful, being richly embroidered. These are in the trade spoken of as "Frontier Belts." In QUETTA the leather used is of a dark red colour, ornamented with green, and then embroidered in minute circles, compacted between parallel lines ; this work is in golden yellow silk and in a minute form of chain stitch. The *kator-dán* is also similarly and richly embroidered, only that a fair amount of magenta silk is employed and the rosettes are larger. In DERA GHAZI KHAN (Plate No. 43-B, fig. 2) the leather used is thick soft strips of *sambar* skin ornamented with green leather and coarse chain stitch needlework, in red and yellow wool. The *postin-doz* (or fancy leather worker from Peshawar to Quetta) makes pocket-books and water bottles (*chagul*) but he never touches shoes. The powder-flasks, bullet-cases, flint and steel pouches, attached to the frontier belts (*kamr-khisa*), are often very neatly made and beautifully embroidered. The powder-flask has a curved neck and may be either moulded from one piece over a clay block, subsequently washed out, or it may be built up of pieces, each richly embossed or engraved after having been beaten into the required shape. Water bottles of some interest come from MADRAS and in LAHORE, Sirsa and Hissar leather bowls for *hukkas* are made and richly encased in brass or silver and ornamented with green

Frontier Belts.

Embroidered Leather.

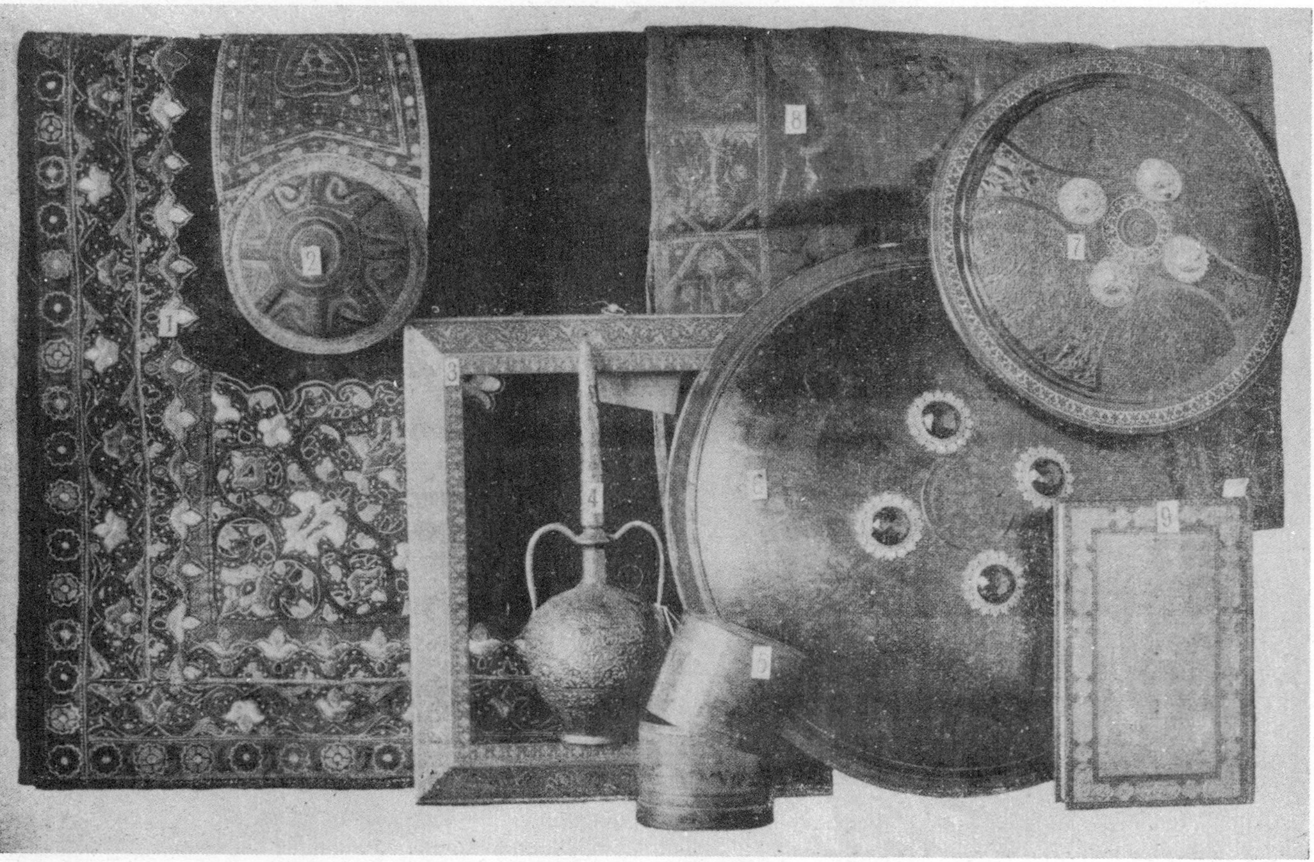

Plate No. 43-B Leather and Skin Manufactures

DIVISION 24 LEATHER AND SKINS.

leather. The leather is sometimes smoked, before being finished, with a view no doubt to colour and at the same time harden the bowl. In that condition it may be given a rich polish. Small boxes, such as pen-cases, cigar-boxes, dressing-cases, etc., are produced at BILASPUR and at ANANDPUR in Hoshiarpur District, as also in NEPAL. These are in black leather ornamented with green and other coloured portions sewn on the surface with peacock quills which are in addition made to embroider the surface.

Gloves, Socks, Trousers, Coats.—From many parts of Northern India articles of the above mentioned kind are procured. The socks (buskins), trousers and coats made at KANGRA and HOSHIARPUR (Mahalpur and Lalwan) are famed all over the Panjab and are made of deer skin leather (*sambar*) resembling dark chamois. AFGHAN *postins* or coats of skin with the wool turned inwards are richly embroidered. BANNU buskins, in soft red leather, are also well known. The hood placed over the head of the hawk is made of leather and is often very elegantly embroidered in gold. These come mainly from HOSHIARPUR.

Postins

Saddlery, Saddle Cloths, Mats, etc.—Cawnpore is famed all over the East for its saddlery, but it is not ornamented in any way. Ornamental camel trappings are made at KHERI in Jaipur State. BIKANIR also has a good reputation for its camel saddles, water bottles, etc. KUNDLA in Kathiawar produces curiously interesting horse trappings. In SARAN in Bengal saddlery is produced overlaid with velvet and richly embroidered in gold wire. One of the most striking features of the goods thrown into this position is doubtless the manufactures of INDORE. These are made of green and magenta silk or cotton velvet, fastened on the top of leather by a multitude of small brass or sometimes gold nails arranged so as to elaborate a certain design. But from the art stand-point a position of far greater importance would have to be assigned to the embroidered leather sheets of HYDERABAD, SIND (Plate No. 43-B, fig. 1). These consist of *sambar* leather and have central medallions, borders and corner pieces done in appliqué with black, red or green leather, elaborately embroidered over the surface, in chain stitch and with silver and gold wire judiciously intermixed. The designs are bold and

Embroidered Sheets.

DIVISION 24. LEATHER AND SKINS.

effective but the scheme of colour barbaric, *viz.*, yellow field, green foliage and magenta flowers—the prevailing features.

The Chiefs in some parts of UDAIPUR STATE wear broad belts that completely envelop the whole of the body. These are made of *sambar* skin with red, yellow and black cloth patch-work and satin stitch embroidery over the surface. They are exceedingly curious and must be viewed as the survival of a costume that had its origin in the troublous times through which that State passed many years ago.

Table covers. GORAKHPUR in Oudh turns out a fair amount of saddle cloths, table covers, etc., in the form of embroidered *sambar* leather, in satin stitch. CHANDA, in the Central Provinces, was at one time a town of large size that did a considerable trade in leather manufactures. It was the capital of one of the aboriginal dynasties—that of the Gonds. Its embroidered leather has been spoken of as the last relic of its past magnificence. This is done on a beautiful deep dark Indian red skin, mostly as sheets or table covers. It is embroidered in gold-wire laid in parallel lines and intermixed with green silk, the designs being largely conventional forms of fish within dog-tooth borders. (See Plate No. 43-B, fig. 8.)

Table Mats. In NOSSAM, in the Karnul District of Madras Presidency, small table mats of leather are prepared and quaintly painted. These represent women grouped in fantastic attitudes so as to collectively form the outline of a horse, an elephant, etc. In JAIPUR and elsewhere playing cards (instead of being made of fish scales as is usually the case) are often made of thin pieces of leather elaborately painted and lacquered.

Playing Cards.

Oil Bottles (Kopis).—These are generally made of sheep or camel skin. The skin is first softened, then stretched over a clay mould of the desired form and when set the clay is washed out. They are of all sizes, from the small flask used to oil the wheels of country carts to the large jars in which oil is carried. In LAHORE and elsewhere they are ornamented with bits of paper pasted on the skin before it is varnished, and in BIKANIR with a paint made of fine brick dust, subsequently coloured and varnished. (See Plate No. 43-B, fig. 4.)

DIVISION 24. LEATHER AND SKINS.

Embossed and Engraved Leather and Skins.—The position of first importance in this division must of course be assigned to the skill attained by the book-binders in embossing and engraving leather. There are several minor centres where this art is practised to-day, but for centuries it has been a special feature of the State of ALWAR in Rajputana and is still accomplished by the binders of that State in a manner that has called forth the admiration of all lovers of Indian art. There seems little doubt, however, that proficiency was attained at many localities, during the Mughal dynasty, since the beautiful books that have been handed down, with the greatest care, in the libraries of the nobles, display a skill and artistic feeling as superior to that attained by the Alwar workers of to-day as these are to the book-binders of AHMEDABAD and PESHAWAR.

Ancient Book-binding.

It would be indeed a task of no ordinary kind to compress into a few sentences a conception of the beautiful designs met with on the older books found in the libraries of India. Several papers on this subject have, however, been given in the *Journal of Indian Art*, and to that publication the reader is referred. The tail-pieces of the present and two succeeding chapters have been traced from the design on one of the book covers shown at the Exhibition, and on Plate No. 43-B (fig. 9) will be seen a book-cover—the famous Gulistan from the Alwar Library. That exceedingly beautiful volume, which has been valued at £13,000, was re-bound some few years ago in the style shown in the photograph. It has been embossed, then coloured in blue and gold. But many of the finer old examples show the leather richly engraved, the field below being usually in pale blue and the elevated floral design in gold and white. In Plate No. 43-B (fig. 3) will be seen a picture frame done in Alwar in stamped, stained and gilded leather.

Embossed Leather.

Embossed leather, in the form of powder-flasks, is produced at PESHAWAR and BIKANIR. In the former a modern development has taken place in the production of book-covers, blotters and such like articles, in response to the requirements of the European residents. In AHMEDABAD a considerable trade used to be carried on in embossing long strips of dark red and gold

DIVISION 24. LEATHER AND SKINS.

stained leather to be used as book covers for the narrow sale-books kept by the shop-keepers in Gujarat and Bombay. These were often very beautiful, but the trade in them has sunk to insignificant proportions or been entirely discontinued, since the writer failed to procure, for the present Exhibition, a set of book-covers, similar to those supplied in 1884 to the Indian Museum, Calcutta. Recently a European manufacturer (Mr. A. Leslie of Bombay) has started a business in the production of embossed book-covers, blotters, etc. Although the designs employed are Oriental, the method of treatment is essentially European.

Carved Rhinoceros-hide.

Carved Shields, Work-boxes, etc.—One of the most artistic articles made of skin may be said to be the carved rhinoceros-hide shields, boxes, etc., that are produced at AHMEDABAD, SURAT, BARODA and KACH. An example is shown on Plate No. 43-B (fig 7). The designs most generally used are panels showing intricate and elaborate carving after the windows of the Said Sibi Mosque, with dividing and elevated gilded lines between the panels, or the designs are bold floral scrolls derived most probably from the rose and run round the shield as a broad border pattern without any dividing lines.

Transparent Shields.

Instead of being carved the skin is sometimes so carefully cured as to become almost transparent. Large shields without a flaw or discoloration and pale amber coloured are very expensive and accordingly are often richly jewelled. The sample shown on Plate No. 43-B (fig. 6), lent by His Highness the Máharana of Udaipur, has emerald bosses. A large assortment of such shields will be found in the Loan Collection Gallery, many of them not only triumphs of the skin-curer's art but of the jeweller's skill.

AWARDS FOR DIVISION 24.—LEATHER AND SKINS.

AWARDS.

Second Prize with silver medal for illuminated and tooled book-binding to Qari Abdul Salam of Alwar.

Third Prize with bronze medal to Parshotam Das Narbheram of Surat for carved rhinoceros-hide casket.

Third Prize with bronze medal to Bhagwan Das Khashial of Ahmedabad for carved rhinoceros-hide shield.

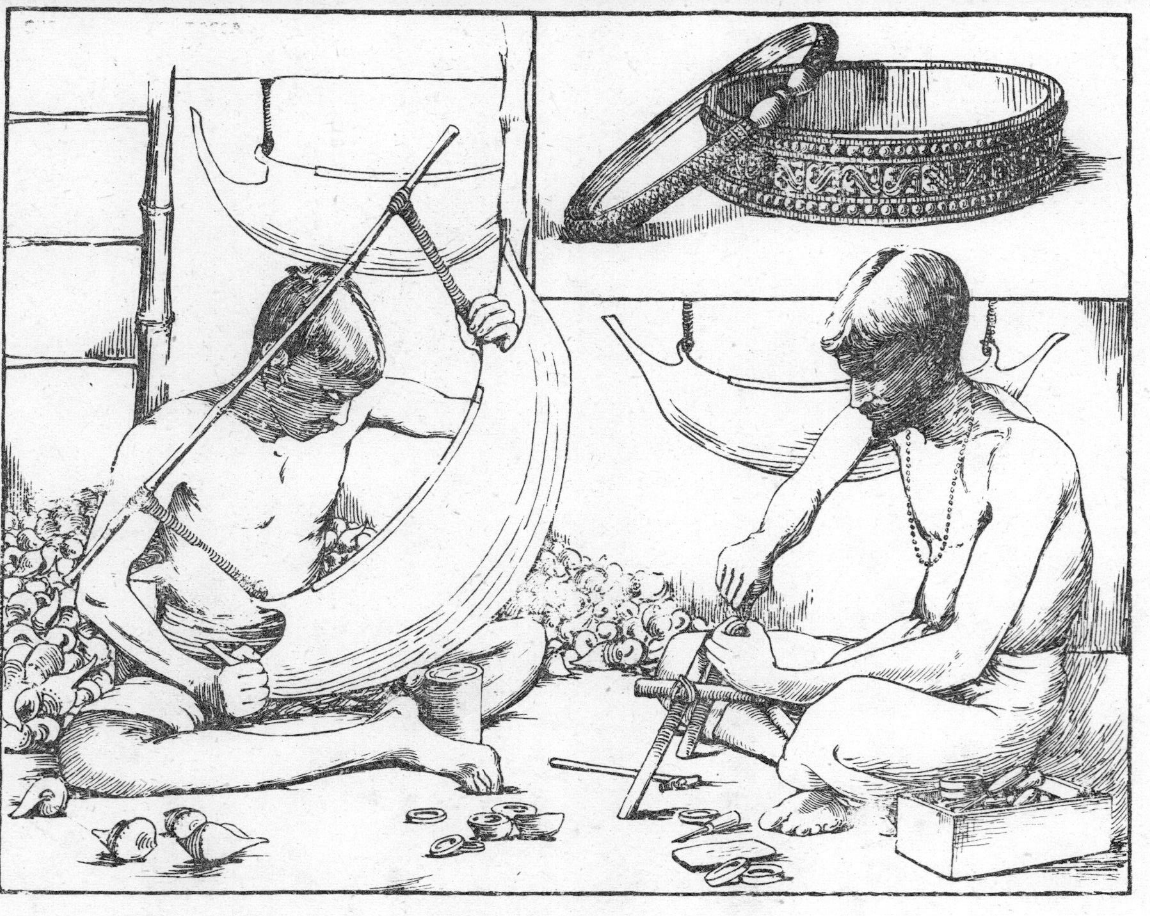

Plate No. 43-C Dacca Shell Carvers

Third Prize with bronze medal to Mukhtiorkar of Hyderabad, Sind, for embroidered leather camel saddle covers.

DIVISION 25. SHELLS AND MOTHER-OF-PEARL.

Commended for embossed leather, Mr. A. Leslie of Bombay.

Division 25.—Shells, Mother-of-Pearl, etc.

Conch Shell.—Bracelets and armlets or charms made of conch shell have been in use in India from time immemorial, and recently a further trade has originated in the manufacture of table-napkin rings, brooches and crude cameos, for the European market.

Shell Bracelets—are known as *sankhas* and the workers *sankharis.* The shells cut into amulets, are richly carved, coloured with lac or decorated with bands of gold let into specially drilled grooves. Large fully formed shells are necessary for the best bracelets and as a rule only one can be cut from each shell though two or three small bracelets or rings, suitable for children, may be made from the same shell.

Bracelets.

In Plate No. 43-C, Mr. Brown shows the Dacca *sankharis* cutting and carving the conch shells. What strikes the onlooker is the seemingly unnecessary large size and unwieldy form of the saw that is employed. The ease with which this is handled, however, shows that its weight and shape may represent a saving of power. At all events the shells held by the feet as in a vice are cleverly cut to the required shape by these expert workers.

A common design shown on these wares is a chain of fish or of doves or a conventional design evolved from these, in which the body of the animal assumes the form of a fan or wing, alternately on one side and the other of the bracelet. Another design consists of a series of conch-shells boldly carved on the surface of the bracelet and still a third of a chain, the links of which are completely perforated. Some bracelets are very broad and thick, others delicately formed and neatly ornamented with notches on the edge and diamond shapes along the centre. The colours most generally used are shades of red and green, forcibly recalling the ornamentation of ivory. The process of application is the same, namely, coloured lac fused within an engraved pattern, by means of a hot bolt, the excess being removed by the subsequent dressing and polishing of the surface.

Designs cut.

Colours used.

DIVISION 25. SHELLS AND MOTHER-OF-PEARL.

Chief Centres.

The chief centres of the trade are Dacca, Pabna, Dinajpur, Rungpur, Burdwan, Balasore, Bankura, etc., in BENGAL, and Sylhet in ASSAM, but nowhere else in India—a further illustration of the remarkably local nature of many Indian Art industries.

Other Shells.—According to Colonel Hendley (*Jour. Ind. Art*, 1886), aqua-marine shells are carved into ornaments, but although special inquiry was made in connection with arrangements for the Indian Art Exhibition, no samples of these could be procured from Jaipur. Cowrie and other shells are often made into fancy boxes, menu-holders and such like trinkets at Diamond Harbour in Bengal and at Pondicherry in South India. Cowrie Shells are largely used in the manufacture of camel *galubans* or ornamental trappings hung around the neck of the animal. They may be described as broad ribbons of coarse cloth ornamented with shells and small metal or mirror bosses with, at their extremities, large tassels of coloured wool. They have been used as curtain fastenings.

Cowrie Shells.

Mother-of-pearl is procured in connection with the Pearl and Chank fisheries of South India. The article penetrates all over the country but curiously enough is not worked up to the extent that might be anticipated, though a fairly large trade exists in exporting the shells.

Ahmedabad inlaying.

AHMEDABAD INLAYING.— Sir George Birdwood (*Industrial Arts of India*, p. 282) makes a brief reference to the art of ornamentation with mother-of-pearl. "I was not aware," he writes, "of the existence of any remains of this beautiful art in India until I read Mr. Lely's report on the wood canopies over the Shrines of Shah Alam * at Sarkhej, and on a stone in the marble tomb of one of the Sultan Ahmad's queens. 'The simpler designs,' writes Mr. Lely, 'were formed by filing pieces of mother-of-pearl to the required size, and letting them into the pattern cut in the block of wood. The more elaborate designs were with fragments of different coloured mother-of-pearl worked into cement, and laid on the surface to be ornamented. Of the coarser and commoner kinds of inlaying a little is still used for the frames of

Two kinds.

* Shah Alam's Tomb dates from 1475 A. D.

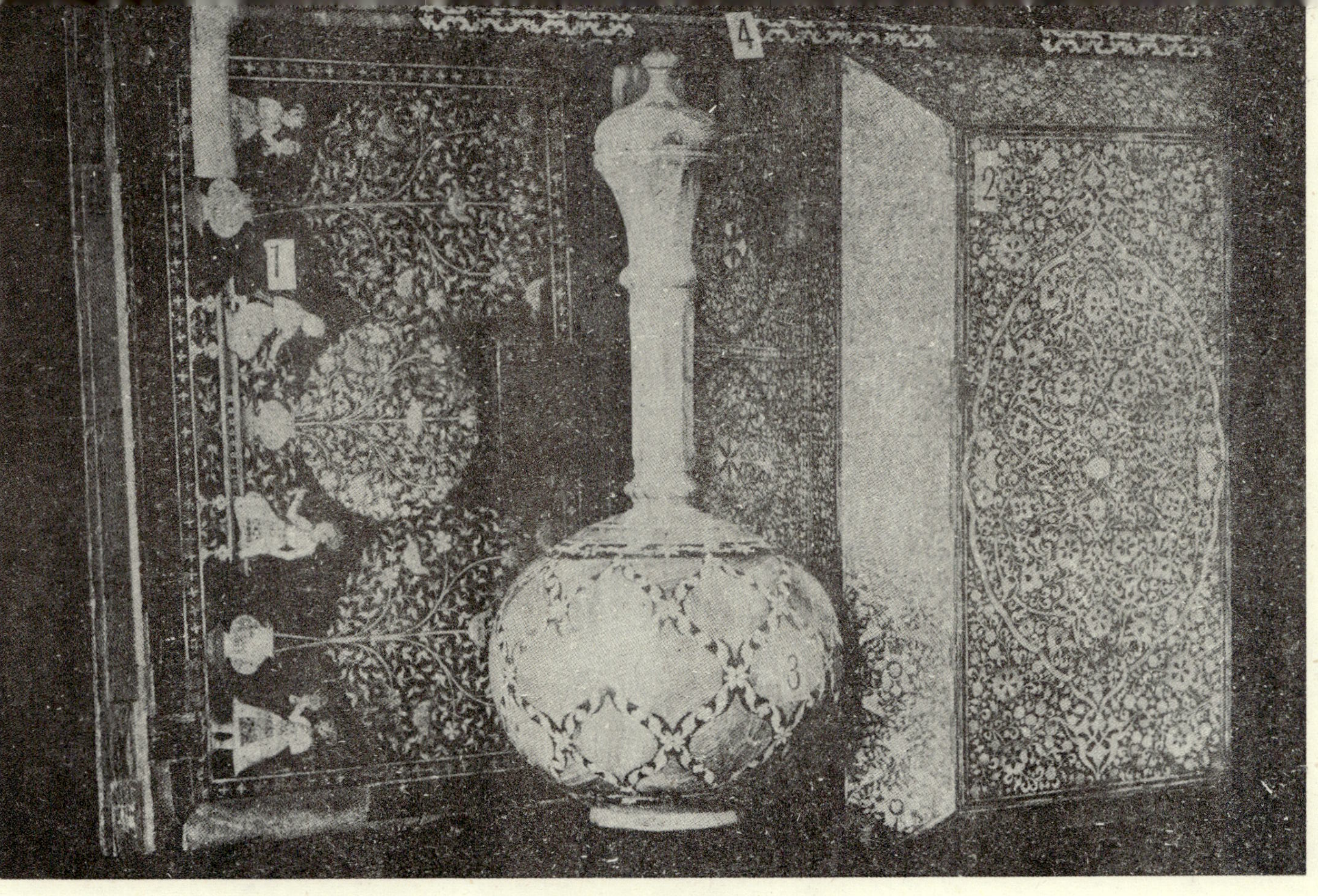

Plate No. 43-D Mother of pearl

tamburas, *rubabs*, and other guitars and violins. No one now practises the former kinds of inlaying, and only one man supports himself by inlaying musical instruments.'" But examples of old mother-of-pearl work are much more frequent than the above passage might lead one to suppose. Perhaps the best of all is the canopy over the tomb of Salim Chisti at Fatehpur Sikri (1581 A. D.).

DIVISION 25. SHELLS AND MOTHER-OF-PEARL.

Kota Inlaying.

KOTA STATE.—But at Etawa in Kota State and here and there throughout Rajputana inlaying with this material is met with. In Plate No. 43-A (figs. 1 and 6) will be seen illustrations of Kota work. This has already been briefly alluded to (p. 157) and need not be further detailed except to enforce observation on a point of some importance, namely, that in all the modern work the pieces of mother-of-pearl are imbedded in coloured and sand-hardened lac and within much larger spaces than there would appear any occasion to have to cut for their reception. Occasionally they are built up as a separate veneer, the parts of which have been consolidated by lac-cement.

Imbedded in lac.

Used in Lapidary.

BHERA and AGRA.—In these centres of lapidary work mother-of-pearl is largely used and has been so from time immemorial. In Plate No. 43-D (fig. 4), the portion of a walking stick, made at Bhera, will be seen. This is composed of Indian jade, but it may be observed that at certain intervals it is ornamented with gracefully formed black bands (made of lac-cement) with, imbedded within these, pieces of mother-of-pearl. So also on the same plate (fig. 3) there will be recognised a Purbeck marble *suráhi*, similarly ornamented with bands of black lac-cement, with mother-of-pearl sunk within them as if inlaid. It will thus be seen that instead of cutting out spaces, the exact size of the mother-of-pearl, and filling these up without showing any trace of the cement, it is customary for the cement itself to be treated as an ornamental feature and doubtless it is much easier to cut out bold lines to be loaded with lac and mother-of-pearl than to cut a multitude of small recesses for each piece of the shell. But why this habit should only prevail with mother-of-pearl and never with coloured stones it is difficult to comprehend.

Imbedded in Lac.

DIVISION 25. SHELLS AND MOTHER-OF-PEARL.

OLD WORK.—From the Victoria and Albert Museum of South Kensington there has been received a cabinet supposed to have been made in India. This is completely covered with a rich Oriental design in mother-of-pearl (Plate No. 43-D, fig. 2), but in this case instead of the shell being imbedded within specially prepared recesses, the whole surface is coated with a thick layer of lac-cement, so that the design is, as it were, veneered on the surface. If this may be accepted as having been made in India, it is an art that has entirely disappeared and is most nearly simulated by the Burmese and Siamese as also the Udaipur glass mosaics in which in the former the coloured pieces of glass are sunk within the lacquer material (*thítsí*) and in the latter within a specially prepared *chunám* (p. 96).

Imbedded in Lac.

Reference has already been made to a second fine old piece of inlaid work, sent to Delhi from the South Kensington Museum. It is shown on Plate No. 43-D (fig. 1), and may be briefly described as a veneer of *shisham* wood in which holes were crudely cut in part conformation with a scheme of inlaying and within these large openings, pieces of ivory or mother-of-pearl were placed and finally fixed by means of lac-cement.

AWARDS FOR DIVISION 25.—SHELLS AND MOTHER-OF-PEARL.

AWARDS.

Third prize with bronze medal to Dwarka Nath Nag of Dacca for carved shell bracelets.

Commended for carved shell work, Prem Chandra Sur of Dacca.

Commended for camel *galubans* decorated with cowries, Messrs. Mull Chand of Peshawar.

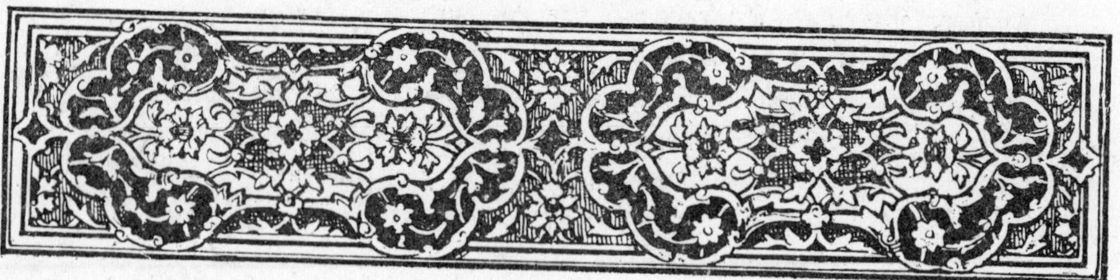

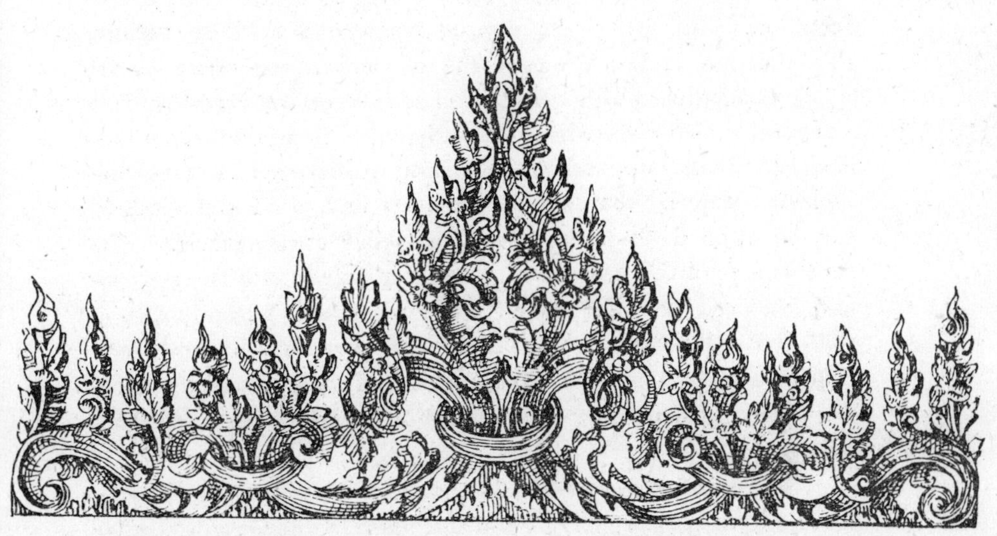

Class VI.—LAC, LACQUER, VARNISH, WAX, AFRIDI WAX-CLOTH, Etc.

DIVISION 26. LAC OF INDIA.

THE major portion of the materials used in the manufacture of the articles that have been arranged under this Class are derived from the Animal Kingdom. But though they hold an honourable position among the art crafts of India it may be said that none of them assumes specific importance. They have been assorted under the following :—

Division 26.—Lac of India.

Division 27.—Lacquer-work of Burma.

Division 28.—Varnished wares.

Division 29.—Wax and Afridi Wax-cloth.

Lac and Lacquer.—A distinction between lac-turnery and lacquer-ware, implied by the title given to this class, may probably be regarded as an innovation in nomenclature. Their separation serves, however, both an industrial and an art purpose' while helping to remove many sources of ambiguity. Lac is an animal resin applied either in the dry state, and distributed by the heat generated by friction, or in the form of a spirit varnish. **Animal Resin.**

DIVISION 26. LAC OF INDIA.

The craft of lac-turnery is essentially Indian and it might be said that the resin—lac—in some form is used in almost every art industry of india, and in the form of bracelets it holds an honourable position in the domestic life of perhaps one-third of the entire population of this country. Lacquer, on the other hand, is a vegetable oleo-resin which naturally exists in a liquid state, and is either directly applied by a brush or is thickened by ashes into a plastic material that may be moulded and, while still adhesive, can be applied to surfaces in bass-relief ornamentation. The various uses of this substance have originated with the Burmese and Siamese art that more closely resembles Japanese lacquer than Indian lac-work. One point in common may be here mentioned, namely, that with the exception of indigo, practically all the other pigments used in the lac and lacquer-wares are metallic oxides.

Vegetable Oleo-resin.

Varnished Wares.—Various varnishes are used in India (including copal) to give a gloss and finish to the painted wood and papier maché (already described in Divisions 17 and 18). In a few instances, however, varnishing rises to a separate and special art conception that simulates indifferently Japanese lacquer and Japanning.

Vegetable Oil.

Wax-cloth.—The so-called Afridi wax-cloth has little in common with the lac, lacquer or varnished wares. The chief material is a vegetable oil, boiled until it assumes, when thrown into cold water, a thick consistence which, with mineral pigments, comes to resemble lacquer. Burmese lacquer and Afridi waxwork are both of them coloured varnishes rather than paints. The distinction, therefore, between painted wood-work and varnished wares (especially when the former may to some extent be encrusted with mud, brick-dust, paper pulp, etc.) is sometimes a matter of uncertainty. It serves, however, the purpose of emphasising the existence in India of special art conceptions (as different from ordinary painted wood-work as from lac or lacquer), to assign a separate place to the varnished wares of India.

Beeswax.

Lastly, ***Beeswax,*** though by no means extensively employed in India, is used as a resist in some of the most curious and interesting forms of dyeing as also tinsel printing and, by the Burmese, is largely employed in their brass (idol) moulding and casting. DIVISION 26. LAC OF INDIA.

Division 26.—Lac-ware of India.

Materials.—It is probable that one of the very earliest utilizations of lac was the preparation of personal ornaments. At the present day one of the most important uses of the resin is the part it plays in the production of the bracelets of the peasantry. These, while often extremely pretty, and, from the industrial point of view, most interesting, were not thought worthy of a position in this Exhibition. The designs met with in lac-turnery on the other hand are frequently distinctly artistic and they have accordingly been freely admitted. The series on view, while by no means as good as might have been expected, is fairly representative of all the styles most worthy of study. But it must not be forgotten that lac is extensively employed as a decorative material in the metal and ivory crafts as well as in that of wood-turnery. In connection, therefore, with the remarks that follow, the reader should consult pages 18 to 21 and so also the various passages in the chapter on Ivory, more especially the account given of the Vizagapatam industry (page 191), which deal with the colouring of that substance. **Ornaments.**

The turner (*kharádi*) with his lathe is met with in every village of India and has an assured position in the community. He prepares toys, nests of boxes, bed-posts, *pán dáns*, *hukka* mouth-pieces, and the like. A long list of woods are mentioned as used by the turner, the selection depending upon the purpose intended. For ornamental objects light coloured and uniformly grained woods, that are not liable to warp or split, are indispensable. The pigments employed are orpiment, sulphur, white lead, red mercury, prussian blue, lamp-black and indigo. Recently, however, aniline dyes have been almost universally adopted with the result that the delicate artistic colours formerly produced have practically disappeared and the articles made at the present day fade and tarnish to such an extent as to render them no more desirable objects. Metallic effects are produced by mixing the lac with powdered mica, with powdered tinfoil and **Pigments.** **Metallic Tints.**

DIVISION 26. LAC OF INDIA.

imitation gold leaf or with an amalgam of mercury, lead and tin. These metals, if used in large particles, give a quaint mottled appearance that simulates the grain of stone and sometimes gives a rich effect. Mottled metallic wares may be said to be a peculiarity of Mysore State, while ornamented work such as the better examples of various kinds presently to be described are almost invariably Muhammadan.

Coloured Lac.

Manipulation.—Shellac is melted by being held over the fire until rendered plastic. It is then placed on a stone and a small quantity of pigment (previously dissolved in water or oil) is deposited within a hollow formed on the surface. This is closed over and the lac vigorously hammered and pulled out with the hands until the colour is uniformly mixed. The hammering continues the heat, so that as the operation proceeds the mixture gradually assumes the consistence of India rubber. The coloured lac is then formed into sticks about the length and thickness of black-lead pencils or many times thicker, as may be desired These sticks of sealing-wax are known as *battís* and are the form in which both the lac and pigment are applied to the wood-work. After the article has been prepared and smoothed, a stick of sealing-wax *battí*) is pressed against it, as it revolves on the lathe. The heat generated melts the lac and thus colours the wood irregularly. A small piece of hard wood is next pressed firmly on the revolving article when the colour is effectually diffused. Lastly, a cotton rag, dipped in sweet oil (preferably sessamum), is held against the revolving object, when the lac takes a polish that it never subsequently loses.

Polishing.

Obviously the first conception, in lac ornamentation, must be a direct adaptation to a revolving object, hence the articles are either uniformly coloured in one shade or are ornamented by rings and bands of different colours. In the higher flights of lac-turnery, however, a diversity and richness in effect is produced that it seems essential should be described briefly in this place.

Chief Art Conceptions seen in Lac-turnery.

1. ***Plain Ornamentation.***—This has already been indicated by the few sentences given above. The chief centres are Patna,

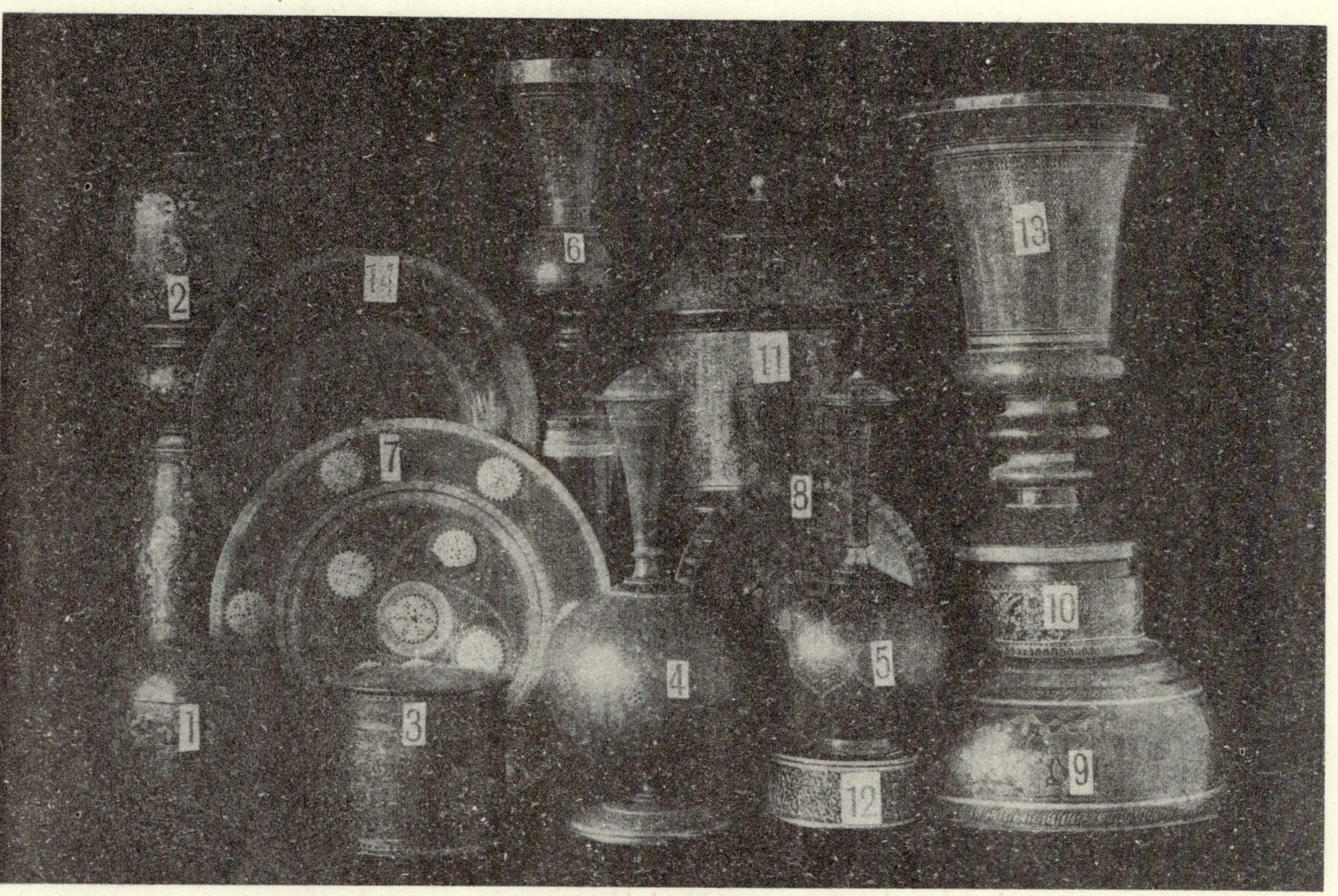

Plate No. 44 Lac Work of India

DIVISION 26. LAC OF INDIA.

Murshidabad, Birbhum in BENGAL; Sylhet in ASSAM; Saharanpur, Agra, Lucknow, Fatehpur, Benares and Mirzapur (the "Benares toys" of trade) for the UNITED PROVINCES; Shahpur, Ferozepur, Hoshiarpur in the PANJAB; Alwar, Jodhpur, Marwar, Bikanir in RAJPUTANA; Savantvadi and Bombay town in the BOMBAY PRESIDENCY; Salem, Nandyal, Podanur in MADRAS; and lastly Bangalore and Chenapatna in MYSORE. These are the centres that turn out superior work in plain lac-ware, but practically every town of any note has its lac turners.

Chief Centres.

An article intended to be ornamented with lac is first turned to the desired shape and polished with a fine powder made from broken pottery. This polishing has the effect of filling up the pores. Should cracks or joints exist, these are plugged up with wood, waste lac or other materials, and at the same time pieces of cloth are glued across such imperfections. Articles so treated are again coated repeatedly with a preparation of glue and pottery dust. They are polished after each coating with a sort of chisel made from the leaf-stalk of a palm. All the imperfections and joints are thus made to disappear completely and a smooth and uniform surface is produced. This art is practised all over India, especially in the ornamentation of wooden toys, bed-posts, *pán*-leaf-boxes, etc. It is perhaps one of the most ancient and widely known methods of wood ornamentation in India. Certain towns are famous for the rich blending of colours, the depth of tone, and the fine polish produced by the local *kharádis*. This is, for the most part, due to several layers of colour and polish having been imparted, the one on the top of the other.

Preparatory Treatment.

Purity of Colour.

2. ***Abrí or Cloud Work.***—The turnery, after being polished and glued in the ordinary way, has a coating of yellow lac applied all over. The operator then takes in his hand a specially prepared *batti* of red or orange colour. This is exceptionally hard, sharply pointed and not thicker than a lead pencil. In some cases the pigments used in colouring these hard *battis* have been dissolved in water, others in oil. By allowing the red hard oil *batti* to tremble in the hand and to thus touch the revolving object interruptedly, numerous irregularly shaped spots are

Spots are imparted.

DIVISION 26. LAC OF INDIA.

imparted. By next using a water-prepared black *battí* of large size and soft texture, black borders are communicated to the red spots. Lastly the interspaces are filled up by a white water *battí*.

By various modifications of the process thus briefly indicated are produced the pleasing cloud effects that have given origin to the name *ábrí* for this kind of lac ornamentation. It is practised all over India, but seems to be carried to the greatest perfection in Hoshiarpur (in the Panjab), and in Bombay and Sind. (See Plate No. 44, fig. 12 and the pedestal of fig. 13.)

Fiery Glow.

3. ***Átíshí or Fire Work.***—The peculiarity of this style may be said to be that, after the article has been carefully prepared and polished with pottery-dust, it receives a coating of finely divided tinfoil made into a paste with glue, the coating being either uniform or made up of a multitude of minute dots after the fashion of the *ábrí* work. Over the top of the tin, a layer of red or yellow lac is next given, with the result that the object obtains a rich fiery glow. It is then polished on the lathe by means of a stone known as the *mohrá* (a form of agate); this communicates so much heat that the lac becomes more transparent than is the case in the other methods of lac ornamentation.

Átíshí is largely practised in Hoshiarpur, Jampur and Dera Ghazi Khan, in the Panjab. Without exactly manifesting a fiery glow, the lac toys and boxes of Indargarh, in Rajputana, and of Podanur, in Madras, exhibit a depth of colour and purity of polish that approaches closely to the *átíshí* style. (In Plate No. 44 the circular box upon which vase, fig. 6, is standing, as also the middle portion of the pedestal in fig. 13, are in this style.)

4. ***Nákshí (or Pattern) Work.***—Of this style there are two well marked sections.

Etched Work.

(SECTION A)—ETCHED NAKSHI.—In this class of turnery the object is coated with first one colour, then on the top a second, a third or a fourth, uniformly all over. The *battís* employed are for the most part soft and water-prepared. The first colour is usually yellow, the next red, followed by green and last of all by black; but, of course, any assortment or number of colours may be imparted layer upon layer, the one on the top of the other. With a fine chisel or style the lac-coated surface is now scratched, the hand being made to move lightly or to press heavily as may be necessary to bring out the colour required from the numerous layers beneath the surface. In this way, upon a black background, yellow stems and leaf stalks, green leaves and red flowers with yellow or parti-coloured veins and shadings may be elaborated in a manner analogous to the *sgraffito* of the Italians.

Various Local Styles.

In PAKPATTAN, in Montgomery (Plate No. 44, fig. 6), the floral designs are usually produced in browns and reds and they manifest a softening and blending of the colours that bespeak great skill and delicacy of touch. In FEROZEPUR (figs. 4 and 5), the fern-like ornamentation of red on a brown or green surface assumes a geometric arrangement of spaces. IN DERA ISMAIL KHAN (fig. 7), ivory buttons or discs are given as centres for an elaborate and minute floral design. In JAIPUR (figs. 1 and 2), hunting scenes are cleverly etched in which the shading and colouring of the figures are attained through the varying degree of pressure given to the chisel. In HOSHIARPUR (fig. 3), the floral designs are largely in green with yellow and red flowers, but the surface is usually panelled and has animal forms freely dispersed amid the floral. In INDRAGARH, in Rajputana, the design is yellow blending into green on a deep black background (figs. 8 and 10). And lastly, in BANNU, the pattern is bold and highly artistic. It is in red flowers with yellow borders standing out on a black background (fig. 9).

Throughout India this art of lac-etching is known and practised, the designs varying with the art instincts and religious feelings of the people. Usually it is only resorted to for the ornamentation of small portions of plain lac-ware. In other localities plain lac-work seems never to be produced, and the most ordinary articles of every-day use are elaborately ornamented with etched *nákshi*. The artistic workers in lac (more especially the *nákshi* form) are invariably Muhammadans.

(SECTION B)—SCRAPED NAKSHI.—An example of *átíshi* ware polished with oil, has patterns, floral designs, or hunting

DIVISION 26. LAC OF INDIA.

Scraped Work.

scenes, etc., subsequently worked on the surface. This is accomplished by scraping off the lines, loops or patches of the oil-varnish and then applying a water-prepared *batti* as the article revolves on the lathe. The portions scraped off receive the new colour, but none of the intervening oil varnished spaces do so. The article is again oil-varnished all over and further portions scraped off when these in turn are given the further colour desired. This is repeated time after time until the floral and other designs or pictures have every outline and detail of colouring imparted to them. This art attains its highest perfection in HOSHIARPUR in the Panjab (Plate No. 44, fig. 11), as also Jodhpur in Rajputana. It often happens, however, that the advantage of the alternate oiling of the surface and the use of specially prepared *battis* is not understood. In that case the result just described is more laboriously obtained by scratching off the portions to which it is desired to impart colour, then coating the whole surface with the new colour and subsequently removing, by pumice stone, the surface coating until the new colour is alone revealed within the places that had been etched for its special reception. The box shown (fig. 11) had the mythological figures and animals shown on it elaborated while it was revolving on the turning-lathe by one or other of the methods here described.

Zig-Zag Ornamentation.

But occasionally longitudinal and parallel lines are scraped on a lac-coated surface, one after the other, and the superfluous colour removed until the article is seen to have a ground colour with a multitude of lines running along its length. If now it be desired to cause these to become variegated, an eccentric movement is communicated to the lathe while a piece of hard wood is pressed firmly against the lac coating. The result of this is that the straight lines are dragged into the zig-zag form shown on the vase (fig. 13).

Painted lac-ware.

5. ***Painted Ornamentation.***—In this class of work the articles to be ornamented are repeatedly and carefully coated with fine pottery powder. Thereafter they are elaborately smoothed and polished. When a sufficiently good surface has been obtained, certain portions (panels or medallions) upon which bunches of flowers, groups of animals or hunting scenes are to be shown,

receive a coating of white paint or chalk. The desired illuminations are then made in water colours by a brush and, when quite dry, are varnished over with lac dissolved in spirits of wine. The articles are again placed on the lathe and the designs completed by one or all of the methods of ordinary lac ornamentation.

Painted Designs.

This art attains its highest perfection in Hyderabad (Sind) and seems also to have been skilfully accomplished in Alwar. In Benares and elsewhere crudely painted designs are sometimes given to otherwise plain lac ornamentation. Unfortunately, owing to the rich glaze of the lac varnish, the delicate paintings on the HYDERABAD (SIND) dish (Plate No. 44, fig. 14) have not been brought out to advantage. The illustrations (Plate 65), given in Sir George Birdwood's *Industrial Arts of India* are, however, admirable examples of the Hyderabad (Sind) lac-work; and Plate 66 is the form of *nákshí* made at Jaipur and Plate 64 is Indargarh *nákshí*, not Sind work as produced to-day. In fact the beautiful art of lac painting has for years past been steadily disappearing from Sind. Only one or two persons now practise it and according to the traditions they came originally from Zanzibar. They could with difficulty be induced to make the articles shown at the Exhibition. One of the most striking peculiarities of this style is that no ground colour is given, so that the rich texture of the wood shows through the transparent lac varnish. The borders and certain restricted parts are colour-lac coated and scratched (*nákshí*) but only with a view to give panellings or borders and rich contrasts. The result is indeed highly commendable and the Sind lac-work deserves an honourable position among the Art Crafts of India.

6. ***Tinfoil ornamentation.***—In many parts of India, the art of preparing coloured tinfoil is fully known and largely utilized. A fragment of coloured lac is placed on a sheet of tinfoil and held over the fire until the lac completely covers the sheet. Tinfoil coloured in this manner is regularly sold and largely employed in the manufacture of imitation jewellery, in the production of tinsel decorations and as an adjunct in ornamental turnery. In many parts of India spools, shuttles and other industrial implements, more especially flat surfaces that cannot be treated on the

DIVISION 27. LACQUER-WARE OF BURMA.

turning-lathe, are ornamented by clipping up coloured or plain tin-foil into various shapes and forms and gumming these, as desired, over the surface. When the pattern has been completed, the surface is painted over with a spirit and lac varnish, or if capable of treatment on the turning-lathe, it is covered in the ordinary way. By colouring the varnish yellow, the tinfoil shows up as if in gold. Instead of lac, the varnish may be made by boiling myrrh, copal and sweet oil, for some hours, and when cool applying it with a brush. In Baroda lac-turnery is regularly ornamented with tinfoil underneath the varnish. In the Exhibition the most beautiful example of this style of work may be said to be the child's swinging cot, No. 1526, Rs. 62.

AWARDS FOR DIVISION 26.—LAC OF INDIA.

AWARDS.

Third prize with bronze medal to Shedooram Mahadeo of the Jaipur School of Art, for collection of lacquered articles.

Commended for a lacquered cradle—Itcharam Premji of Baroda.

Commended for series of painted lac-ware made by Umedali Vighamel of Hala District, Hyderabad, Sind.

Commended for a pair of gold lacquered vases—Ismail of Jampur, Dera Ghazi Khan.

Commended for a lacqured bowl—Shahband of Bannu.

Division 27.—Lacquer-ware of Burma.

The chief material in this craft is the oleo-resin *thitsí* of the tree known to botanists as *Melanorrhœa usitata.* This is employed in its liquid state as a varnish or it may be thickened by ashes or by saw-dust to a plastic condition and used as a moulding material or as a cement for mosaics. It may be coloured with lamp-black, with gold leaf, with vermillion (not red lead), with orpiment or with indigo and may be applied with a brush or by the hand direct or while revolving on the turning-lathe. It may be applied as an ordinary varnish on wood-work, or utilized to render paper or cloth water-proof (as in the manufacture of Burmese umbrellas); or employed as putty to fill up defects in wood-work or to close the meshes of basket-work, so as to convert

Condition. Pigments. Various Uses.

such articles into water-tight drinking cups, boxes, etc., or it may be the cement used in the manufacture of glass mosaics; or lastly, and by far its best known purpose, it may be employed as the chief material in the production of Burmese lacquer-ware.

There are three chief types of lacquer-work—(1) the Pagan basket-ware; (2) the Prome gold lacquered boxes and baskets and (3) the Mandalay boxes, thrones, etc., with moulded lacquer ornamentations. Up to a certain point these may be regarded as identical and may, therefore, be so far described collectively.

Manipulation and materials.—There may be said to be two main stages in Burmese lacquer-work—*1st*, loading articles with the thickened *thitsí*. Whether made of wood, of basket-work, of horse-hair, etc., all the imperfections, cracks, joints, meshes, etc., are filled up by a putty made of the commoner sort of *thitsí* mixed with saw-dust or cow-dung ashes. Layer upon layer, for some 20 to 30 times, the *thitsí* is applied, while bits of cotton rags are at the same time stretched across and around the joints or cracks and thus imbedded within the *thitsí*. After each application the article is laid aside for a few days to slowly dry in the damp, confined atmosphere of an underground pit. It is again and again removed, washed in water, rubbed down, smoothed, polished with sand-paper and various stones and again coated with fresh layers of thickened *thitsí*. If circular it is placed on the turning-lathe and gauged to the required size, the excess deposits of lacquer being removed by scouring. In the case of basket-ware, the articles are held on the lathe by special blocks, but so delicately are they treated that films of horse-hair are coated with the lacquer, gauged, polished, and again and again coated and still the finished article hardly exceeds in thickness that of ordinary shirting cotton cloth. (See Plate No. 43-B, fig. 5.) **Loading.**

2nd.—Varnishing Stage. When the required degree of loading has been attained, the articles are rubbed all over by the hand with pure *thitsí* (mostly obtained from the Shan States) as a varnish. They are set aside as usual to dry, then rubbed down and again coated with the fine quality of *thitsí* and water obtained after boiling glutinous rice and cow-dung ash (a preparation known **Varnishing.**

DIVISION 27. LACQUER-WARE OF BURMA.

as *thayo*). After drying, they are again varnished with pure Shan *thitsí*, and if it be desired to have a black article it is coloured with lamp-black or if red with vermillion (red mercury). It may now be regarded as finished, or at all events ready to receive ornamentation, if such be desired, by either of the following three processes.

Chief Art Conceptions.

Pagan Lacquer Boxes.

1. ***Pagan Ware.***—This is mainly, if not entirely, done on basket-ware or horse-hair boxes. Plate No. 44-A, fig. 3, shows the lid of a circular box of bamboo wicker work about 18 inches in diameter, and fig. 4, a horse-hair betel-nut-box about 3 inches in diameter, both richly ornamented in the Pagan fashion.

Manipulation.—This is accomplished as follows:—The article prepared as described is put on the turning-lathe and the gloss removed, thus leaving a perfectly smooth, usually black, surface.

Engraving.

It is then handed over to the designers and engravers who are often young girls. By means of a fine metallic scriber a certain portion of the pattern is engraved all over; the spacing and assortment being done unerringly by the eye and without any previous delimitations or drawings. *En passant* it was observed that a monkey that had to be drawn at a certain recurring position was made by first drilling the holes for its eyes, thus apparently fixing the position and attitude of the head. The tail was then cut out, the body followed and last of all the legs. Or, where some portion of a tree or animal had to be of a different colour from the rest, that portion only was cut at intervals all over the box or basket, so that the pattern that was in the operator's head remained a complete mystery till many stages had been passed through.

Colouring.

After being engraved the article is handed to another operator who places it on the turning-lathe and taking a small quantity of some dry metallic pigment, rubs it all over and thereafter by means of a cloth removes the surface excess. The engraved pattern is then seen loaded with colour and to fix this the article is once more varnished, placed aside to dry in the pit and after some days is removed, smoothed and again engraved for other portions of the design. These are in their turn charged

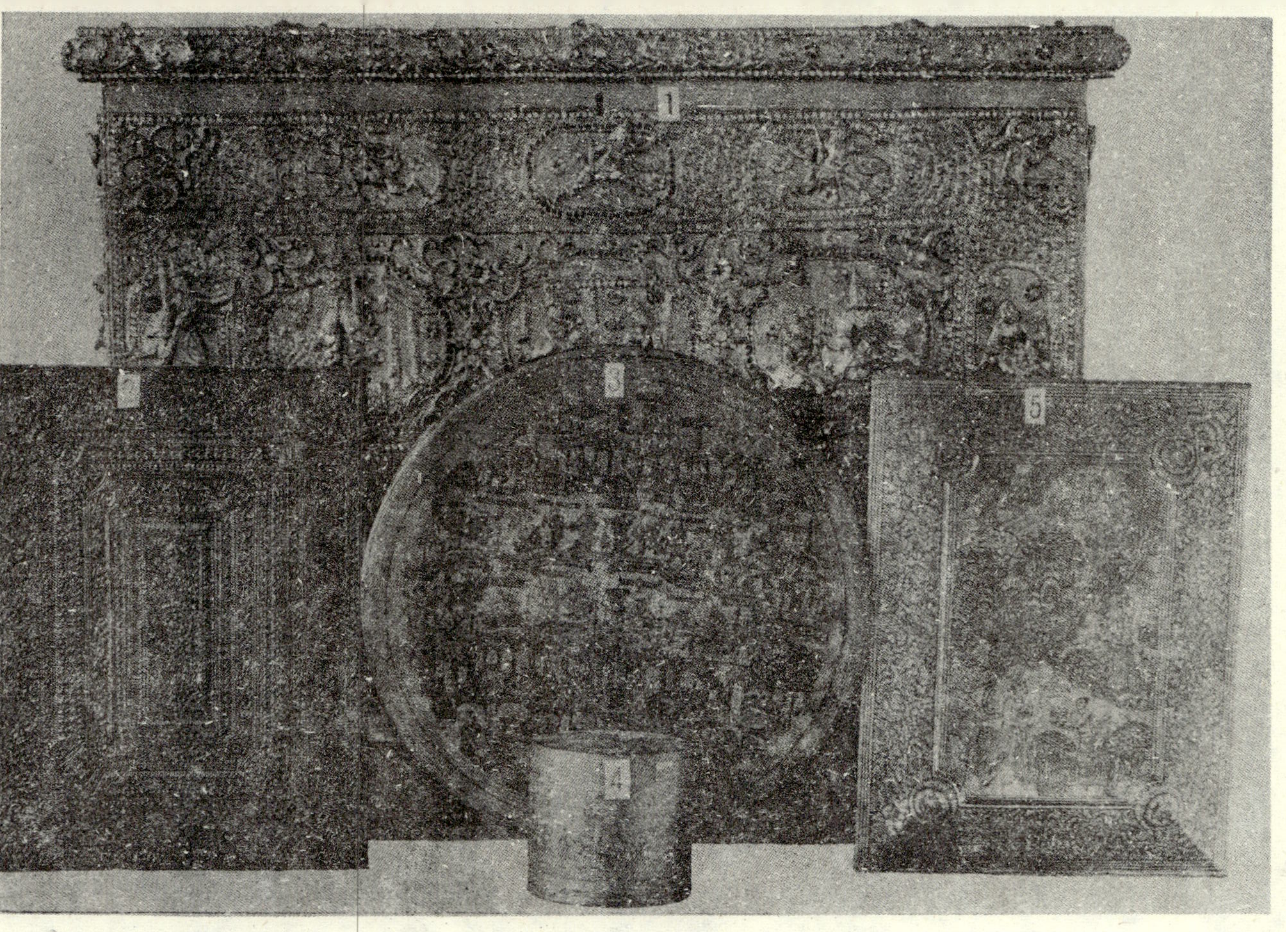

Plate No. 44-A Lacquer Work of Burma

with colour, again varnished over, set aside once more, again polished, and so on until every detail has been accomplished.

DIVISION 27. LACQUER-WARE OF BURMA.

Scheme of Colours.

Colours used.—Green is a favourite colour with the Pagan lacquer workers by which the effects of vegetation are produced. This is made of indigo mixed with finely powdered orpiment (yellow arsenic). The ground colour is usually black, but before the article is finished, the dominant colours are red and green. The patterns are outlined in red, the bodies of the figures, etc., remaining in black (within the red outlines) and a new background is imparted by finely drawn checkered lines in green.

Suggestion for Lac workers.

It will thus be seen that in principle this closely resembles the scraped *nákshí* lac-work of India, but is simpler and less troublesome, through the colours loaded into the engraved designs being used in the form of a powder. Were the Indian workers to adopt this process, giving a coating of transparent lac over each colour stage, they might produce results hitherto not dreamt of by them.

Designs.—The patterns used by the Pagan workers are overburdened. There is an entire absence of any knowledge in the value of spacing or of contrasts. They recall the Chinese willow pattern in so far that rivers, seas, boats, houses, trees are assorted in zig-zag panoramic effects within winding panels (see Plate No. 44-A, fig. 3). The trees shown are mainly the cocoanut and the plantain, while the scroll work is almost invariably a closely interlacing design similar in feeling to that indicated in connection with the ivories of Mysore and Travancore. This is beautifully depicted in Mr. H. Tilly's *Glass Mosaics of Burma* (photograph No. 5) and in the embossed plaque (Plate No. 44-A, fig. 2, of this work).

Pagan work.

The writer is much indebted to Mr. E. Dawson, Sub-Divisional Officer of Myingyan, for having personally accompanied him to the rather inaccessible village of Pagan and there acted as his interpreter in studying this industry and in selecting the samples now shown in the Exhibition. The chief exhibits are a betel-box (Cat. No. 226) made by Maung Kywe of Pagan; a round box (Cat. No. 201) made by Ma Kyan Yi; a vase with dishes (Cat. No. 351) made by Maung Twa; and a table (Cat. No. 246) made by Maung Tha Shein of Pagan.

DIVISION 27. LACQUER-WARE OF BURMA.

Prome Gold Lacquer.

2. ***Prome Gold Lacquer.***—(*Plate No. 44-A, fig. 5.*)—After the article has been elaborately prepared in the way already described and left in its final varnishing as black or red, it is re-varnished and gold-leaf pressed on to the partially dried *thitsí* sizing. But should it be contemplated to elaborate a pattern in the gold lacquer, or any portion of it, a paint is prepared of finely powdered orpiment and gum. By means of a brush this is applied to the black or red surface, but the design must be completed before the sizing has entirely dried. The surface is then coated all over with gold or silver leaf and the article placed on one side to dry. It is next carefully washed with water when the elevated, arsenic-painted design is removed and the pattern thus revealed in black or red upon a gold or silver background.

Art Scheme.

The conception usually met with in Prome lacquer is a central panel in quasi-Chinese willow pattern, framed in scrolls of closely compacted floral ornamentations.

On arrival at Prome the writer was told that the industry had been entirely abandoned, since the Burmans had lost all interest in their own arts and taken in preference to imported goods. After a little search, however, some half a dozen shops were discovered where fairly good *hpungí* boxes, book-covers, plates and the like were made in this style of lacquering. The examples shown at the Exhibition were either purchased there and then or made to order. The best samples are a small box, gold lacquered outside and silver inside, made by Saya Pa, of Prome; also the book-board (fig. 5) and certain boxes and plates made by the same maker.

Useful Moulding Material.

3. ***Mandalay Moulded Lacquer.***—In Mandalay and elsewhere in Upper Burma one of the most interesting uses of *thitsí* may be studied. The oleo-resin is thickened with carefully prepared rice husk or cow-dung ashes, until it attains the consistence of putty. In this condition it is perhaps one of the most convenient and useful moulding materials known. In fact so admirable and suitable is it for all the higher forms of ornamentation by moulding, that one feels surprised that it should not have long years ago found its way to the Schools of Art in India, Europe and America.

Manipulation.

A stone or board previously dusted with fine ashes is used as the moulding table. The *thitsí* is then broken off in lumps of the required size and between the fingers is readily and easily moulded into the form of the bodies of animals, each leg, arm, finger, mouth or ear being separately made and stuck on in the desired attitude. By means of a few specially made wooden modelling tools, the details are sharpened up and when ready the figure is lifted off the table and transferred to the freshly sized portion of the object on which it is to be affixed permanently. It is then given a few finishing touches, before being varnished over with fresh *thitsí* and placed in the pit to dry. It sets so firm that it can with difficulty be broken and may be varnished, gilded, covered with minute coloured glass or even jewelled, provided these additions be applied before the material has set. In Plate No. 44-A (fig. 1) will be seen a *hpungí* box, the outer surfaces of which have been richly ornamented with moulded lacquer and the panellings of the medallions studded with coloured glass imbedded within the beadings of *thitsí*.

Modelling.

Lotus Thrones.

This art is largely practised in Mandalay, a whole street of artists being engaged in preparing the many-storied lotus thrones upon which the family idol is placed, as also *hpungí* coffins. These are richly ornate objects illuminated with coloured glasses and bass-relief grotesque figures, as also floral scrolls, pendants, etc., made from the moulding preparation of *thitsí*. The same material is employed in ornamenting the many-storied and many-trayed baskets in which Burmans store their treasures. The foundation of these is of course wicker-work lacquered and gilded, but round the outer surfaces and along the rims of the various trays there are rich borders of grotesque jewelled animals and floral scrolls of much delicacy in detail. In the preparation of these scrolls, blocks are, as a rule, used. The *thitsí* is rolled into a strip of the required thickness; it is then placed on the table and a mould made of soap-stone (flat or curved in any required shape) is pressed over it. The material is thus compressed into one large border piece—an inch or more in breadth—or into a whole series of parallel ribbons which, like the insertions in white embroidery, or the metallic braidings used in Europe for similar purposes, may

Mouldings.

DIVISION 27. LACQUER-WARE OF BURMA.

each be taken up and laid along the places where required. The work is thus rapid and the effect charming, though capable of infinite development on lines not attempted by the Burmans.

Panels.

Plate No. 44-A (fig. 2) shows an example of moulded *thitsí* in the form of a panel. This is usually made by a specially prepared layer of *thitsí* in which fine bone ash has been used in place of cow-dung ash. A thick layer of that material is placed over the plaque or other object and while it is still plastic, a soap-stone mould is pressed over it. If it be desired to illuminate the impression with coloured glasses or precious stones, the mould is removed before the pattern has been fully pressed out, the glasses or stones are affixed to their intended positions and the mould once more pressed over the impression. It is then allowed to set and may be gilded or otherwise coloured as desired. A plain black moulded panel, such as that shown on the illustration, very closely resembles richly carved black ebony and is even more durable since the *thitsí*, once it sets, is less liable to be broken off than the portions of a delicate wood-carving.

Imitation Ebony.

Manipur Lacquer.—In the Native State of Manipur which lies between Assam and Burma, lacquering, very similar to that described above in connection with Burma, is practised, the material being the same. It is mainly applied, however, to the ornamentation of sword scabbards, sword handles, leather belts, etc., which then look not that unlike inferior patent leather.

Awards for Division 27.—Lacquer-Work of Burma.

AWARDS.

Second Prize with silver medal to Maung Thaw of Mandalay for lacquered *hpungí* box.

Second Prize with silver medal to Messrs. Beato & Co. of Rangoon, for collection of lacquered work of Burma.

Third Prize with bronze medal to Saya Pa of Prome for a gilt lacquered tray.

Third Prize with bronze medal to Maung Tha Shein of Pagan for collection of lacquered work.

Commended for lacquered betel-boxes—Saya Nyain of Pagan.

Commended for lacquered ornamental table—Maung Tha Shein of Pagan.

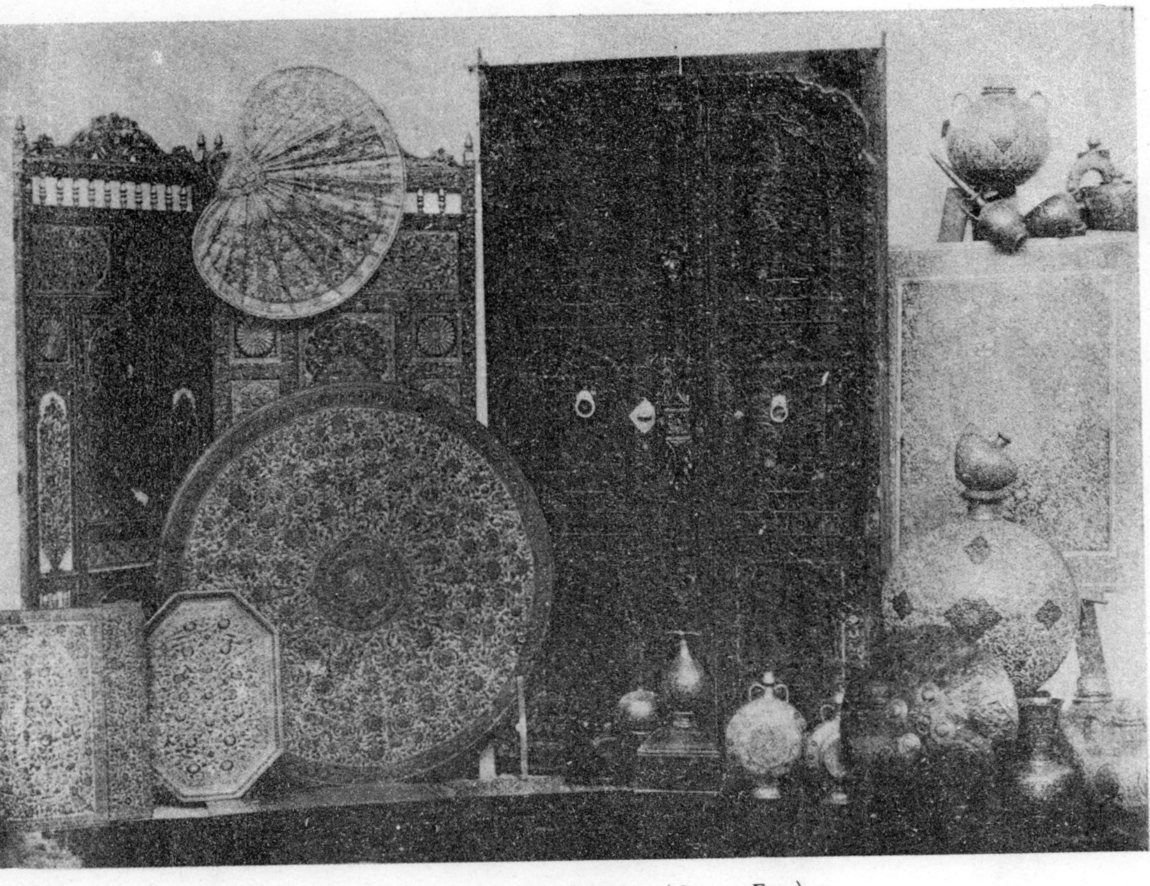

Plate No. 45 Varnished Wares. (Gesso, Etc.)

Commended for a lacquered teapoy—Ma Gyan of Mandalay. DIVISION 28. VARNISHED WARES.

Commended for a gold lacquered panel—Maung Pa of Prome.

Division 28.—Varnished (Gesso) Wares.

In most works on Indian Art the articles that it is desired to separate under this Division are often spoken of as lacquered and are thus treated as identical with the lac-wares of India and the lacquered-wares of Burma and Japan. But it may be said that in materials, methods of treatment, art designs and purposes for which made, they are perfectly distinct. In fact they are much nearer to the Painted wood and Papier Maché, dealt with under Divisions 17 and 18, than to Lac and Lacquer.

A writer in the *Indian Art Journal* has affirmed, and with much truth, that anything smeared with varnish is in India called Lacquer. Another writer, in the same *Journal*, observes that "the art product *par excellence* of Bikanir is a species of lacquer-work which may be applied to wood, stone or even glass and metal. It was, I imagine, first employed to the decoration of a large hall in the palace of the Maharaja." "The whole of the great hall called the *Rai Newas* is covered with ornament of this character." Varnish Smearing.

Methods and Materials.—Plate No. 45 shows an assortment of varnished wares from all parts of India and as stated on that Plate, perhaps the best collective name for the series would be *Gesso Wares*. In India they are sometimes spoken of as *muna-bathi*, when the design is thickly formed, and *lajawárdí*, when scarcely raised above the surface. The former is of course more expensive than the latter. In all the forms of this ware, however, certain peculiarities are persistent. The pattern is built up by some special preparation ; it is fixed by glue ; it is coloured and lastly varnished over the surface. The moulding material differs considerably in different parts of the country and according to the special purpose for which required. It is very often a paint prepared from finely powdered brick-dust and water ; or it is liquid plaster-of-paris ; or a powder made from certain shells (or simply chalk) mixed with some glutinous substance such as the pulp of the *bél* fruit ; or a paste made from the bean known Gesso Wares. Chief Characteristics.

DIVISION 28. VARNISHED WARES.

Process.

as the *dál*, mixed with a little fine lime; or it may be carefully prepared paper pulp. The moulding materials are laid on the glued surface by various methods and may be subsequently shaped or carved to the exact form required and still later coloured. They are usually applied as paint with a brush, at other times moulded with the fingers and in some few instances coloured dry starch is dusted through stencil paper on to a glued surface until the pattern is built up in that manner. In many of the special Indian manifestations of this art, the embossed surface (if one may for convenience speak of it as such), is covered completely over with gold leaf, a size or varnish having been given to cause the leaf to adhere. The elevated pattern may now be coloured thus leaving a gilded field, or the background may be picked out with colour leaving a floral design on gold above the coloured surface.

With these for general observations it may now be desirable to discuss the peculiarities of the better known centres of production.

Chief Centres and their Art Conceptions.

1. BIKANIR.—This Native State has for centuries been known to practice *gesso* ornamentation of a very superior kind. As just stated the *Rai Newas* Hall of the Palace is ornamented almost exclusively in this method or in a kindred art of *sgraffito* (see Plate No. 18—the rectangular panel) in which a layer of cement is carved (just before it sets) then painted and gilded. Most of the panels on the dado of the hall are done in this Indian *sgraffito*, but the upper ones, and the wood-work generally, are ornamented by *gesso* painting. In Plate No. 45 the large door and rectangular panel are from Bikanir. The former is one of the originals from the *Anup Mahal*, the latter is a reproduction carefully made from the numerous panels to be seen in the *Rai Newas* and other rooms of the older portions of the palace.

Old Work.

The doors appear to be much older than the wall decorations. The patterns on the panels of these doors, as also the scroll work of their frames, are strongly suggestive of the renaissance of Europe, a circumstance that may be accounted for by the intimate friendship (and in fact marriage relationship) that existed between the State and the Emperor Akbar. The designs appear to have been originally mainly gilded but both the varnish and the gold have faded and tarnished into a dull metallic brown which is exceedingly beautiful and a marvellous contrast to the vivid red, white, blue and gold of the more recent work.

Modern Work.

Some few years ago the suggestion was made to adopt the *gesso* work of Bikanir to some form or shape that might commend itself to European purchasers. For this purpose were accepted the characteristic and interesting oil bottles of Bikanir (*kopís*) that are made out of the inner layer of the camel skin. In consequence *gesso* painted and gilded *kopís* suddenly appeared in the shops of Indian Art dealers and rapidly became constant features of these stores. They are unquestionably fair samples of the ware, are moreover cheap and unbreakable. A paper in the *Indian Art Journal* (1892), by Colonel T. H. Hendley, C.I.E., gives an exhaustive series of coloured illustrations of these *kopís* and of certain painted tables in Bikanir, but makes no mention of the ancient doors and wall fittings of the Palace. To the right of Plate No. 45 as also Plate No. 43-B (fig. 4) of this work, will be seen a few *kopís* picked by chance from the very exhaustive assortment offered for sale at the Exhibition which were made at the Bikanir Central Jail.

2. IN SHAHPURA, in the Tonk State of Rajputana, there has for centuries apparently existed an industry in turning out a peculiar form of *gesso*-painted hide shields. It has been thought that these manifest a knowledge in the art of Japanese lacquering and it has been stated that a legend exists to the effect that the ancestor of the craft came from the East but was not a countryman of Hindustan. There is certainly one curious circumstance that lends countenance to this belief, namely, that the designs employed are, like many more of those seen in Rajputana, strongly Chinese or Japanese in character. In nearly every instance the undersides of these shields, specially along the margin, show clouds or even thunderbolts that closely resemble those painted on the walls of the old palace of Bikanir. See initial piece to page 170. But the designs are painted in *gesso* and the varnish used is copal, imported from Bombay for that purpose. The shield makers

Japanese Feeling.

DIVISION 28. VARNISHED WARES.

of Tonk doubtless from long experience have discovered that to impart a good polish and to prevent the design blistering off the hides, careful and elaborate treatment is necessary, but they do not by any means smooth, varnish and re-varnish their work a bit more frequently than is done by the Pagan lacquer workers, or in fact by many other lac and varnish workers all over India. They are accordingly no more entitled to the reputation of having acquired a knowledge of, or of practising, the art of Japan varnishing, than are the lac-turners of India.

3. HYDERABAD DECCAN.—Both in the town of Hyderabad itself and in Raichur, plates, trays and fans are painted and varnished in *gesso*. The background is usually in a rich enamelled green, the flowers large crimson patches with golden lines and gold stalks. It is customary for the ornamentations to radiate from a central point in wedge-shaped portions. The fans have usually peacocks and other animals dispersed within the foliage. The best samples at the Exhibition have been contributed by Subaya of Hyderabad, the plates (Cat. No. 240) costing about Rs. 10 and fans (Cat. No. 630) Rs. 12. The majority of panels furnished for the dado in Her Excellency Lady Curzon's *boudoir* at the Circuit House, Delhi, were made by Subaya. Two of these will be seen on the floor and to the extreme left in Plate No. 45.

Nossam and Hyderabad.

4. NOSSAM and NANDYAL, in the Karnul district of Madras, have for many years been famous for their *gesso* painted and varnished work. In the Madras Central Museum there is a beautiful circular table from Nossam which has been copied for this Exhibition and will be seen in Plate No. 45, the original being in the Loan Collection Gallery. This was made by Nandyal Chitar Subhanna (Cat. No. 5095), Rs. 54. The same artist made a fair number of the panels used in the dado of Her Excellency Lady Curzon's *boudoir* at the Circuit House, Delhi. The most convenient eye mark between the *gesso* work of Nossam and that of Hyderabad is the greater abundance of interspersed animals in the former. The paroquets are as a rule gracefully and boldly drawn and are placed in every conceivable attitude, but the peacocks, as is mostly the case all over India with that bird, have their tails screwed on the wrong way and the legs rigid and equine. In Sir George Birdwood's

Industrial Arts of India will be found (Plate 67) a most admirable example of this style of work, but instead of being on a green ground it is mostly on pure white.

DIVISION 29. WAX-CLOTH.

The Madras School of Arts has sent to the Exhibition many screens done in Nossam ware and portions of the Madras Room were specially designed in order to show the possible application of this art to modern household draping and furnishing.

Division 29.—Wax and Afridi Wax-cloth.

1. ***Beeswax.***—As already observed, Beeswax does not enter so very largely into the art crafts of India as might have been anticipated. In fact the chief if not the only use of that material is as a resist in certain forms of dyeing. These have been spoken of as hand-painted calicos. There may be said to be three chief centres in the production of these with characteristically different styles of work at each. (1) KALAHASTRI, in North Arcot district of Madras, where purely Hindu mythological subjects are produced on cotton cloth, which portray scenes from the *Ramayana* and *Mahabharata* in panoramic forms. (2) MASULIPATAM, where admirable chintzes appear to have been produced ever since the days of Arrian. As seen at the present day they are mostly coloured blue with indigo, and red with madder (*al*), and occasionally a little green or yellow—the designs being Persian and thus Muhammadan. For the most part the sheets and table cloths produced, represent the tree of life with birds resting on its boughs and animals reclining under its cool shade. In some of the samples, in the possession of the Indian Museum, Calcutta, and the Central Museum, Madras, the dyeing is so perfectly accomplished that at a little distance it is impossible to distinguish these goods from the finest embroidery. Beeswax is the material used as a resist in the production of all the finer Masulipatam and Coconada sheets—the goods that in ancient trade sometimes bore the names of these towns, at other times were called Rajamundris. (3) In BURMA—mostly in Rangoon—beeswax is printed over white, flowered silk, to prevent the dye that is subsequently given from colouring certain portions.

Resist in Dyeing.

Simulate Embroidery.

DIVISION 29. WAX-CLOTH.

White spaces on a pink ground may thus be produced and by ordinary block printing further elaborations of colour may be imparted within the white spaces.

Manipulation.

These are the main conceptions manifested, but there is an infinite gradation when all the minor centres are taken into consideration. A knowledge of the value of beeswax as an adjunct in calico-printing is, however, very nearly confined to South India and Burma. The place of beeswax is in Northern India mainly taken by the process of tie-dyeing that will be described under Class VII, Division 31. The melted wax is either printed by means of wooden blocks or is hand-painted by a brush of fine wires that may be very small and consist of only one or two wires or very large and formed something like a mop. This is the "Calmendar" (*kalmdár*, penbrush) mentioned by Tavernier when describing the *palampores* or bed-covers of Madras. The wax soaks completely through and thus may be used to protect both sides of the fabric from the dye subsequently given in the vat, or it may be used as a delimitating resist against the spread of dye imparted on one side only by a brush.

Chief Centres.

In the Exhibition a large series of hand-painted calicos have been displayed on the ceilings and as curtains and have come mainly from Kalahastri and Masulipatam, though Chingleput, Coconada, Salem, Madura, Mysore, etc., have also contributed. Further particulars will be found under Dyed Textiles, Class VII, below.

Tinsel Printing.

Throughout India beeswax is used, to a certain extent, as the adhesive substance in tinsel printing and as already observed it is also occasionally used in modelling and metallic casting.

2. ***Afridi Wax-cloth and Drying Oils.***—It is not contemplated to deal very elaborately with the art of smearing cloth in the fashion that has come to be known in India as wax-cloth. The writer has already published a fairly comprehensive report on the subject (see *The Agricultural Ledger, No. 12 of 1901*) and though the designs are often extremely curious, the interest in the subject mainly centres around its future industrial possibilities.

DIVISION 29. AFRIDI WAX-CLOTH.

Preparation of Roghan.

Operation.—Suffice it to say that the oil expressed from the *polli* seed (wild Safflower or *Carthamus Oxyacantha*) is boiled for 12 hours, then thrown into cold water when it assumes a new form and becomes the substance known in India as *roghan*. This is the material used by the Afridis in the manufacture of their wax-cloth. Yellow colour is obtained by mixing orpiment with the *roghan*; red with red-lead; white with white lead; silveriness by powdered mica; blue with indigo; green with orpiment and indigo; and gold and silver with either powdered leaf of these metals or imitation gold and silver leaf. To give consistence and body a little dry lime is added. The artizan takes in the palm of his left hand a lump of the coloured *roghan* about the size of a pigeon's egg. He very often, but not invariably, wears a leathern shield across the hand upon which the *roghan* is placed. In his right hand he holds a short iron style, about 6 inches long, which is pointed at one end. With the pointed end he works up the *roghan* and draws it out into fine threads. If it is too moist to draw out properly he works into it a small quantity of finely powdered lime. When he has succeeded to draw it out properly and regards the material as in a workable state, the end dangling from the small quantity on the style is applied to the cloth and the thread deftly wound this way and that, all the while being slightly drawn finer and finer. The main divisions of the pattern may have been previously marked or outlined with chalk on the fabric, but the details are worked up without anything to guide the operator, and, in the commoner designs, such as that of the Afridi dress cloth (*Mal-khosai* or *Panairakh*), it is never outlined in any way.

Pigments.

Manipulation.

Plastic Thread.

The rapidity and accuracy with which the pattern is worked up by threads of plastic *roghan* has to be seen to be appreciated and understood. The style is charged time after time from the store on the left hand and the little thickness or slightly rounded portion formed where each thread commences is most artistically utilised. The skilled artist can work from right to left with as much ease as from left to right, hence, just as in penmanship, the thick downward strokes and the fine upward hair lines, are each made to occur in their proper places.

DIVISION 29. AFRIDI WAX-CLOTH.

Adhesion of the Coloured Roghan.—No sooner has a line of the *roghan* been deposited on the cloth than the moistened tip of the finger is dabbled all along it. This has the effect of causing the *roghan* to sink into the texture of the cloth and to firmly adhere. In a very short time it dries or hardens and becomes quite permanent so that fabrics ornamented in this way may even be washed without materially disturbing the pattern. The combination of an oily substance with a metallic pigment and with lime, causes the material to dry most effectually, but much depends on the skill displayed in mixing and working up these ingredients. Sometimes also powdered mica (*abrac*) is dusted over the winding lines of *roghan* to give the pattern a silvery gloss, or gold leaf or imitation gold and silver powders may be similarly applied. In brushing or washing wax-cloth fabrics the

Fading of Colours.

imperfectly adherent particles of mica or gold may be removed but the bulk will remain, the coloured *roghan* itself can hardly be removed by ordinary treatment and is not even softened by the heat to which fabrics are usually subjected. The fading of the colours, that sometimes takes place, seems to be due to the use of inferior pigments such as white lead that consists mainly of barium sulphate, and more especially to the presence of sulphur in the colour materials employed.

Elaboration of the Design.—When solid patches of colour, such as the leaves or petals of flowers or the bodies of birds, have to be made, the style with its dangling thread is made to travel many times over the assigned space but always in the same

Solid Patches.

direction, not backwards and forwards; the perfectly parallel lines of *roghan* thus laid down are by the moistened finger compressed into the desired patches. Indeed so expert are the workers that all trace of the original parallel lines, of which such patches are built up, completely disappears. Where two or more colours have to be given, the operator usually applies all the patches and lines required of one colour before he proceeds to use the second or the third. The half finished table cloth or fire screen may in consequence often appear a most bewildering production from which it is difficult to discover the actual pattern in the operator's mind.

DIVISION 29. AFRIDI WAX-CLOTH.

The one point of special interest that has been brought out by the present Exhibition, so far as wax-cloth is concerned, is the fact that the writer was in error in thinking that the art was confined to Northern India and restricted to the particular oil employed by the Afridis. The personal and concentrated investigations conducted in connection with the Exhibition brought to light the fact that in two or three remote localities a precisely similar art prevails to that of Peshawar. In Baroda for example castor oil is boiled in the manner mentioned above and thrown into cold water in order to produce the *roghan* used in Pattan, a town in Baroda. The design and scheme of colours employed is also considerably different but the result is identical with that of Peshawar and Lahore. So again in Kach, linseed oil is similarly boiled and a *roghan* produced that is used as the basis of the wax-cloths of that State. Sample No. 1825 is a *mussala* (prayer cloth) made by Khatri Rangrej Rahman of Chowbari, Kach. This is a rich and elaborate design in green, scarlet, yellow and white, distinctly Muhammadan but with a strongly Hindu feeling in its ornamentation. The designs adopted in Kach by the local wax-cloth workers are unconnected with those of the Afridi country but like those of Baroda they vividly recall, in colour and technique, the characteristic forms of local embroidery. In fact, the only feature that is common to all the wax-cloths of India is that they are made by Muhammadans who are possibly descended from Pathans. It would thus seem fairly certain that not only have we neglected to make known the materials and principles of the Afridi wax-cloth but have failed to discover that all over India a knowledge exists in the treatment of oil and its utilization as a paint for textiles that may be of value to the art crafts of the world.

New Information.

Castor Oil.

Linseed Oil.

A Muhammadan Art.

It has commonly been affirmed that the Natives of India were unaware of the drying property of oil, in the manufacture of paint, until shown to them by Europeans. But there would appear little to justify a refusal to admit the indigenous character of the knowledge in the manufacture of *roghan*, the drying oil substance employed by the wax-cloth manufacturers. Moreover, it seems fairly certain that that knowledge has existed for many centuries

Native Painting.

DIVISION 29. AFRIDI WAX-CLOTH. and possibly may have been spontaneous in the various centres of wax-cloth manufacture.

Oil Paints. 3. ***Linseed Oil Paint.***—It is of course quite true, however, that in the majority of the paintings of India, such as the Sind painted toys and the *gesso* wares discussed above, water colours are used and fixed by lac or other resin varnish. In this connection it may be added that some years ago the writer had brought to him in London a sample of the well known Jaipur painted marble idols. He was asked if he recognised the article and replied unhesitatingly. He was next asked to examine it again more carefully. The observation was in consequence made that in almost every respect it was identical but that it smelt of English paint. This proved a useful hint since the idol had been cast in England, from imitation marble, and was a sample of goods that it was contemplated to pour into the dealers' shops of India and England as genuine Jaipur marbles. It is not known, however, how far this adventure succeeded but the fact of using a strongly smelling linseed oil paint was the only readily perceptible difference between the true and the false idol since all trace of the moulding had been effectually obliterated.

Jaipur Idols.

AWARDS FOR DIVISIONS 28 AND 29.—VARNISH WARES AND WAX-WORK.

AWARDS. Second Prize with silver medal to the Central Jail, Bikanir, for collection of *kopís.*

Second Prize with bronze medal to Khuda Buksh of Shahpura, Tonk, Rajputana, for a painted hide shield.

Second Prize with bronze medal to Khatri Rangrej Rahman of Kach for a wax prayer cloth (*mussala*) (No. 1825).

Third Prize with bronze medal to Usman Usta of Bikanir for panel of gilt *gesso.*

Third Prize with bronze medal to Calcutta School of Art, for painted *gesso* screen.

Third Prize with bronze medal for two table tops decorated with painted and varnished *gesso* to Nandyal Chitari Subhana of Kurnool, Madras Presidency.

Third Prize with bronze medal to Venganna of Kurnool, Madras Presidency, for a painted and varnished *gesso* tray.

Commended for two screens with *gesso* panels—School of Art, Madras.

Commended for *gesso* fan—Subaya of Hyderabad, Deccan.

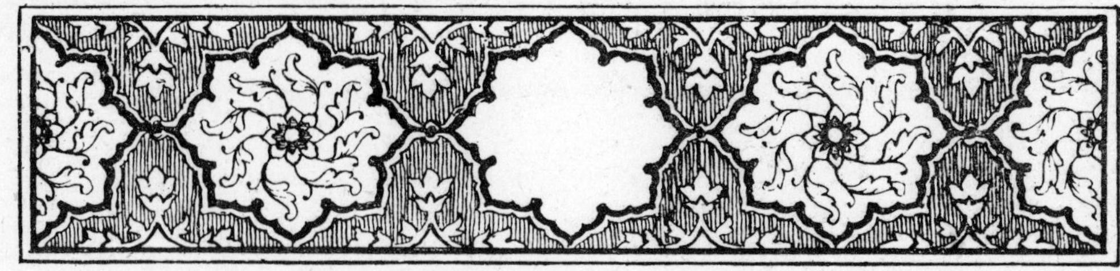

CLASS VII.—THE TEXTILES OF INDIA.

DIVISION 30. DYEING AND CALICO-PRINTING.

THIS of necessity is the largest and most important class of Indian Art Manufactures, and might be treated under various headings, such as the fibre used—Cotton, Wool, Silk, Gold, Mixed fabrics, etc., the method of treatment in the loom—Plain, Figured, Coloured, etc., as manifested by the piece-goods and broad-cloths, the muslins, velvets, gauzes, satinettes, brocades, carpets, rugs, etc., method of ornamentation subsequent to leaving the loom—Dyeing, Embroidery, Appliqué, etc., or the purpose served—a *Dútí*, *Sárí*, *Lúngí*, Shawl, Bed-cover, etc. The clothing of the people of India might almost be described as woven in the required shapes and sizes and but rarely cut into garments that fit the body. It is this circumstance, very possibly, that has given birth to the incongruous indifference, when European costumes are resorted to, for these being made to fit the body or even to serve the purpose for which they were originally designed. By far the larger portion of the people are dressed in cotton. Certain colours or methods of ornamentation are, as a rule, rigorously adhered to by the more important communities. Further, the designs usually met with have been elaborated after centuries of adaptation to the special purpose of each particular garment. It is perhaps needless to mention examples here, but as illustrative of the value of such considerations, it may be remarked that in Bombay the Marathas seldom wear printed cottons while the Gujaratis prefer them to all others. From these and such like considerations then, an impression may be obtained of the value of a study of the textiles as an object lesson in the Arts of India.

Fitting Garments.

It has been thought the course most likely to elucidate the more instructive features of this study, to refer the Indian Textiles to three classes as follows:—(1) Textiles Proper; (2) Embroidery and Lace; and (3) Carpets and Rugs.

DIVISION 30. DYEING AND CALICO-PRINTING.

The following are the groups that have been formed in the Textiles Proper as assorted within the Exhibition:—

(A). Artistic Treatment subsequent to the Loom.

Division 30. Dyeing and Calico-Printing.

Division 31. Tie-dyeing.

Division 32. Painting and Waxing.

Division 33. Tinsel-Printing.

(B). Artistic Treatment while on the Loom.

Division 34. Cotton—All kinds, such as plain, figured (*e.g.*, woven patterns).

Division 35. Silk—All kinds.

Division 36. Wool and Pashm—All kinds.

Division 37. Mixed Fabrics—such as Satinettes, Appliqués, etc.

The difficulty that besets every attempt at a scientific classification of artificial (that is to say manufactured) articles is exceedingly great and overlappings are unavoidable. For example, beeswax, lac and drying oils have already been indicated as materials used in the ornamentation of textiles. Such goods might, therefore, be either treated as illustrative of the use of certain materials or as methods of textile manipulation. So again it often happens that part of the ornamentation of a fabric may be done before and the remainder after being woven. With the Kashmir shawl it frequently becomes next to impossible to decide how far it should be regarded as loom-work, or as subsequent treatment with the needle. The *kinkhábs* and shawls of India are, moreover, sometimes spoken of as loom embroideries and are woven more as tapestries than as loom fabrics. The shuttle in these instances is a simple pencil of bamboo (or needle as it is called by the weavers) that is by the hand carried in and out of the exact number of threads of the warp that may be necessary in the production of the pattern. On this account it was deemed preferable (as suggested above) to raise embroidery to a distinct

Separation of Embroidery.

DIVISION 30. DYEING AND CALICO-PRINTING.

class, instead of placing that art as a division among the methods of subsequent treatment. Embroidery is in fact to the textiles what enamelling and damascening are to the metals. Dyeing, wax-painting and tinsel-printing have their counterparts in painting, tinning and lac-colouring, while appliqué, or patchwork, very closely corresponds to the encrusted metal wares. The student of Indian art will readily admit that these are more than fanciful comparisons, since it is found that a remarkable parallel exists between the corresponding art designs in the industries indicated, more especially in their relations to the ground material—a textile or a metal.

Division 30.—Dyeing and Calico-Printing.

Perhaps the most characteristic feature of an Indian village street might be said to be the bunting daily seen from one end to the other, which on closer inspection proves to be garments of every possible colour hung out by the dyers in order that the colours may be fixed or the textiles dried and bleached in the sun. It might almost be said of the crafts of India that none are so universally and frequently employed as that of the *rangrez* or dyer and the *chípígar* or calico-printer. With the exception of the sombre tints, prevalent in Bengal, the inhabitants of the rest of India (more especially the females) are gaily decked in brilliant colours. Almost every race or caste has its favourite

Special Costumes.

costume colour, or method of dressing. Moreover, festive seasons and ceremonials are marked by the use of distinctive colours in the costumes of the people. From these and such like reasons continuous employment is found for the dyer. And since the poor cannot possess more than a limited number of garments, the desire for tinctorial changes can alone be satisfied by the repeated bleaching and dyeing of the same fabric. To this circumstance may possibly be attributed the fact that the majority of the Indian

Fugitive Dyes.

dyes are fugitive, no effort having been put forth to discover the mordant by which they can be fixed. It is a common error to suppose all Indian dyes are permanent and all aniline dyes of necessity fleeting. To the desire for many changes in colour is doubtless largely attributable the modern popularity of aniline dyes. They are cheap, easy of application, fade readily and can

DIVISION 30. DYEING AND CALICO-PRINTING.

be repeated time after time without injury to the textile. But whether the advances of modern tinctorial science have benefited or injured India, it has to be admitted, as a fact, that perhaps considerably more than 50 per cent. of all the colour results attained at the present day are aniline or rather alizarine. And it has to be added that the better alizarine dyes are more beautiful and more permanent than a large percentage of the vegetable colours that are so much extolled by writers on Indian Art. Perhaps one of the most serious charges against these imported dyes is the ease with which old garments, carpets, etc., may be simulated, a circumstance that in itself refutes the charge of being more glaring than "the fine old vegetable dyes." In fact it is not the materials used by the dyers but the change in the taste of the people that is wrong. They have grown tired of pale, delicate colours and have turned to the opposite extreme for something new. When this craving for glaring colours—a depraved taste no doubt—has passed away, the Indian dyers with the pigments supplied them from the chemical works will no more need to revert to 70 or 80 per cent. of their old vegetable dyes, than the dyers of Europe find it necessary to revert to the woad of their forefathers. The majority of the Indian vegetable dyes are fleeting—that is to say, they gradually fade when exposed to light, especially the yellows and all shades that have yellow as an ingredient. The best colours are the blues and reds—indigo, *al* (*morinda*) and lac. But all Indian dyes are relatively expensive and troublesome and the danger lies in the fact that there are good and bad qualities of aniline. The dyer's art of India has recently suffered most seriously through the temptation given by the sale of the more inferior chemical dyes and the ignorance that prevails as to the exact process required to fix them. On the other hand the imported goods, pandering to the present desire for change, have degraded the taste for glaring colours and given the Indian dyer his models in vulgarity.

Change in Taste.

Indian Dyes Expensive.

The following classification may be accepted as denoting some of the more commendable methods and results attained in India :—

PLAIN DYEING.

Bengal.—The most highly esteemed dyers of this Province are those of Calcutta, Patna, Darbhanga, and Saran. The chief feature of the dyed fabrics of these towns might be said to be plain colours with narrow borders of a different shade imparted by crude methods of resist or discharge dyeing.

Assam.—Among some of the aboriginal hill tribes, dyeing is carried to a higher state of perfection than with the people of the plains, but usually each tribe possesses but one or at most two good dyes. The Nagas are famed for their bright *manjit* red, which in their hands gives a brilliant colour to the human hair employed in the ornamentation of spears. The blue used by most of the Assam aborigines is more nearly related to Chinese than to Indian indigo.

United Provinces.—There are few features of Indian life so striking as the sudden transition observable in the dresses of the people in passing from the Lower Bengal to the Upper Provinces, more especially the proficiency seen to be attained in calico-printing. The chief districts are Farukhabad, Kanauj, Lucknow, Bulandshahr, and Fatehpur.

Panjab.—There are many famed centres for dyeing, but perhaps the most characteristic feature of the province is the, skill attained in silk and wool dyeing in Amritsar, Ludhiana, and Kashmir—the brilliancy of the yellow, magenta, and purple floss silks used in the embroidery of the women's skirts and shawls (*phulkaris*). Calico-printing has also assumed certain very distinctive forms which will be described below.

Central Provinces.—In these provinces another revelation is given by the rich dark-red seen to be preferred by the people in the colouration of their garments. And this peculiarity extends right through the great central tableland to the confines of the Madras Presidency and north and west to Rajputana and Bombay. This took its birth very possibly in the locally produced *al* (*morinda*) dye, the *kharua* and *salu*.

Rajputana and Central India—are famed for the great skill of their cotton-dyers and calico-printers. The *pagris* worn by the Rajputs are as a rule pure white or delicately coloured. The skill attained at several centres such as Alwar and Kota is unsurpassed by the dyers of any other part of India. At the

Double-Dyeing.

former town a method of double-dyeing is practised. That is to say, a piece of muslin or net is coloured yellow on one surface and red on the other, or green on one side and red on the other. Any two shades may be so treated and the effect is perfectly kaleidoscopic, for not only does the flowing *sárí* show a different colour where a fold turns over, but the one colour is seen through the other in a perfectly bewildering fashion. Sir Thomas Wardle was one of the very first European writers to draw attention to this subject and his admirable example of an Alwar double-dyed muslin *sárí* has been quoted by many subsequent writers [see *Indian Art Journal*, Vol. I (1886)].

This art appears to be known to the dyers in some two or three towns of Rajputana and in Yeola near Nasik. In the last mentioned it is practised with the silks used in making *pitambar* waist cloths. It may have been the prototype of the shot muslins of Kota and of the shot silks of Amritsar and other towns of the Panjab and of the United Provinces. In Kota State most charming muslins are produced in which the warp may be a brilliant purple and the weft pale green, so that the textile shows the one and the other colour according to the angle at which viewed.

In the Exhibition will be seen a large assortment of double-dyed muslins made by Abdulla, Mahomed Bux, and Kamaluddin of Alwar.

The second great peculiarity of the dyeing of Rajputana and Central India may be said to be the perfection attained in the process of resist dyeing by tying up portions to which it is not desired to impart colour—Tie-dyeing or Bandana work (see Division 31).

Madras.—This Presidency in olden times had two features in the dyer's art for which it was famed, the use of the *chay* root (in place of the *al*)—for its splendid rich deep reds—and the employment of bees-wax as a resist in hand-painted, in place of block-printed, chintzes.

But it is perhaps needless to extend this introductory review of the peculiarities of the chief seats of the tinctorial art of India. The subject will be elaborated when discussing some of the more specially artistic manifestations. In passing, however, it may be

DIVISION 30. DYEING AND CALICO-PRINTING.

observed that Mr. Edwin Holder in the monograph on *Dyes and Dyeing in the Madras Presidency* gives useful particulars regarding the dyes used in South India, but makes no mention of the employment of wax as a resist nor of the superb results obtained by the dyers of Masulipatam, Chingelput, Salem, Coconada and Kalahastri in painted fabrics.

CALICO-PRINTING.

So very different are the styles of calico-printing met with in India that it becomes very nearly possible to arrange unerringly a promiscuous assortment of these goods to the actual towns where they were produced. This circumstance is very possibly largely due to the fact that they have been less keenly sought after by curio-hunters and in consequence (excepting in Madras) have been less seriously adapted to the demand for novelty. It may, therefore, be the most satisfactory course to deal with the calico prints province by province.

Bengal.—This art is met with in one town only, namely, Hajipur near Patna. The work consists of red and black stripes, circles and cones, printed all over a dull pink or yellow surface.

United Provinces.—In Lucknow, bed-covers (*lihaf* or *razai*) and shawls worn quilted (*fard*) are the chief articles turned out by the *chipigars*. They are made of fine quality of English cotton cloth and have usually a minute and complex pattern in a medley of colours, green, blue and red predominating on a white field. These goods are doubtless the origin of the "prints" worn by the domestic servant classes of Europe. Kanauj and Farukhabad used formerly to turn out chintzes on thick cloth (*gazi*, *garha*, *dhoti-jora*, etc.), but at present they use English cloth, and thus, with difficulty, can be distinguished from Lucknow prints except that the bed-covers (*palangposhes*) are mostly in larger and bolder designs. In the *fard* of both Lucknow and Kanauj, the field is usually covered by a minute flower closely compacted with a border pattern composed of two or three parallel scrolls. The Farukhabad calico-printers are, moreover, fond of the "Persian tree of life" pattern with a profusion of green leaves, the border being broad and with festoons of flowers encircling cones or demarcating conventional façades and balconies. The result may be described as heavy and overburdened.

DIVISION 30. DYEING AND CALICO-PRINTING.

Printing in Two Shades.

At JAHANGIRABAD (BULANDSHAHR) a very different style of calico-printing prevails, which, to some extent, has been recently imitated in Lucknow and Farukhabad. The ground is either yellow, flesh-coloured pale green, pale blue or more rarely white with a minute elaborate pattern in two harmonising colours. The yellow ground has the pattern in chocolate and pale green; the flesh-coloured ground with the pattern in pink and black; the grey with orange and black, and the white with pale blue and black The style is distinctly effective. The ceiling of the Main Transept of the Exhibition near the Refreshment Room will be seen to be draped in this style of calico-printing.

In JAFARGANJ near FATEHPUR still another highly peculiar school of calico-printing is met with. The ground is usually a dull neutral lemon yellow. This is traced all over by a large bold conception, usually the "Persian tree of life," large Persian cones, vases with sprays of flowers or bunches of carnation-like flowers. These are elaborated in blue and dark Indian red with the printed outlines of the patterns showing up in dark brown or black. The borders of the sheets are composed of medallions of flowers encircled by broad bands of red and blue with the interspaces filled in with fantastic Arabic inscriptions in white or black letters.

Use of the Brush.

A striking feature of this work is the circumstance that the large surfaces of the design are worked up with the brush over the top of the printed details. In this way shadows within the flowers or the ribs of the leaves show through the main brush colour. In fact the use of the brush in the production of this class of goods raises the craft to a higher platform than that of the ordinary calico-printer and one which in other parts of India is still further developed. The two bays on either side of the Main Transept will be seen to have ceiling cloths in the Jafarganj style, and those with large gracefully outlined and delicately coloured peacocks will be found specially worthy of study. A very large ceiling cloth similar to one that may be seen on the ceiling of the Lucknow Museum was received at the Exhibition too late to be

DIVISION 30. DYEING AND CALICO-PRINTING.

displayed to advantage, but it will richly repay examination as it is a splendid piece of work.

The boldness and freedom of Jafarganj work is a pleasing contrast to the severity and uniformity of the Lucknow, Kanauj and Jahangirabad work. Other districts in the United Provinces noted for their calico-prints are Agra, Multan, Mainpuri, Allahabad, Cawnpore, Bijnor, Mirzapur, Muzaffarnagar, Saharanpur, Meerut, Etwa, Jaunpur and Benares. None of these districts approach in artististic merit those already described. For example, Agra, as is but natural from its situation, shows a stronger leaning towards the style of calicos characteristic of Central India and Rajputana than to those of Oudh. The material is coarse, it is dyed in *al* and then printed in black or black and yellow patterns.

Mr. Saiyid Muhammad Hadi has written a useful monograph on *The Dyes and Dyeing of the United Provinces*. It will be found to contain information regarding every material used and all the methods of manipulation pursued. It should, therefore, be consulted by persons who desire to extend this study beyond the sketch here attempted,—namely the art conceptions of each school of calico-printing.

Central Provinces.—Calico-printing is not an important industry in these Provinces. The best results are obtained in Chanda, Nagpur, Bhandara, Narsingpur and Damoh. The colours used are mostly *al* red and indigo blue or the alizarine substitutes for these.

Panjab.—Following the course pursued with the United Provinces, the districts of the Panjab most noted for their calicos may now be briefly discussed and references made to the examples from each to be seen in the Exhibition. Kot Kamalia in Montgomery, Sultanpur in Kapurthala, Lahore and Kashmir are those most deserving of separate notice.

KOT KAMALIA.—The brush is largely used in the Panjab in aid of the block but apparently bees-wax is rarely, if ever, employed in any way as a resist in the Panjab brush-calicos. In Kot Kamalia the pattern, after being stamped all over, is elaborated by coloured patches or bands being brought up to the

DIVISION 30. DYEING AND CALICO-PRINTING.

required shade by hand painting the larger patches. *Pardas* are made in conjunction with *dewalgirs* (or dados) that very strikingly recall the old Persian *persiennes* [see *Indian Art Journal*, Volume I (1886)—article by Mr. J. L .Kipling]. These are in red, yellow and green with black outlines stamped on a white field. Very frequently, however, broad borders of white background and red cone patterns stamped at fixed distances apart have been brushed over in yellow, or large flowers printed in black have been brushed over with red; thus, in both instances, the details of the pattern show through a surface colour imparted last of all. The calico-printer of Kot Kamalia who obtained the highest reputation and printed all or nearly all the *dewalgiris* figured and described by Mr. Kipling (*viz.*, Yalla Yar) has died, and his descendants are by no means so successful as he was.

At SULTANPUR, in addition to work somewhat similar to that of Kot Kamalia, a distinctive and graceful style is met with unlike that of any other part of India. A fine quality of cloth is used and this is first dyed in salmon or ivory colour, then printed in terra-cotta red. The field is a most elaborate and closely compacted tracery in which the stems, leaves and flowers are, as it were, doubly outlined in a manner that forcibly recalls Sikh wood-carving, especially in the frequency of the composite flower that was possibly derived from the squamose flowering head of the plane tree. The borders are bold and in darker colours, with very often a balustrade-like division by means of inset pillars in Sikh style. In some respects this work seems as if accomplished by the colours being here and there discharged, but as opposed to this suggestion it may be added that none of the Panjab writers makes any reference to that process as being known and practised by the Panjab calico-printers. There is, however, in the Sultanpur work a soft harmony and a warm feeling that is most pleasing in the wall drapings of this part of the Panjab, that has only to be seen to be admired. One or two of the draperies and ceiling cloths both in the Main Gallery and in the Loan Collection Gallery are from Sultanpur.

Dyes Discharged.

LAHORE produces wall drapings and *abras* (quilts) on coarse cloth, the prevailing feature of which might be said to be

DIVISION 30. DYEING AND CALICO-PRINTING.

their shades of Indian red and faded blue and green. The dados and wall drapings are panelled and have figure borders running along the top. In the centre of each panel is very often a "Persian tree of life" with birds and other animals. Much of this work is brushed, such as the backgrounds of the panels. The borders frequently show wavy or zig-zag vertical lines in red, yellow, black and white alternations. The most noted calico-printer of Lahore may be said to be Jhandu who lives near the Wazir Khan mosque, and visitors to the Exhibition will have an opportunity (in the Artizans' Gallery) to witness that skilled artificer producing the wall drapings and curtains for which he has attained a very high reputation. He will also be seen engaged printing cotton velvets in squares suited for the manufacture of cushions.

AMRITSAR.—Some of the finer Panjab printed *sáris*, when on good quality cotton or muslin, approach very closely in colour effect to rich embroidered or brocaded fabrics. An excellent example of this will be found in the Amritsar *sári* shown by a coloured illustration in the *Indian Art Journal*, Vol. II, plate 5.

The calico-prints of GURDASPUR are very similar to those of Lahore with the exception that the field of the *abra* cloth or quilt is very often made up of a multitude of squares each containing one large conventional flower, but in so complex and dazzling a fashion as to become perfectly bewildering. Other districts noted for their calicos are Bahawalpur, Multan, Sialkot, Amritsar and Ferozpur, but the only one that need be detailed here is Kashmir. The best known calicos of KASHMIR are those of Sambar in Jammu and thus closely akin to the Sialkot work. They are of Persian design, but although often highly commended by Europeans are in reality inferior to many other Indian styles such as those of Kot Kamalia and Sultanpur, and are in no way comparable with those of Masulipatam. The Kashmir goods are mostly wall drapings, floor cloths and canopies. The ground colour is usually lemon yellow, the ornamentation of the field a medley of red and green with the borders made up of panels filled with geometric designs and zig-zag lines or with the cone-pattern severely and arbitrarily arranged.

Kashmir Calicos.

DIVISION 30. DYEING AND CALICO-PRINTING.

Several of the ceiling cloths displayed in the Exhibition will be found to come from Lahore, Gurdaspur, and Kashmir, so that the student has ample opportunity of examining these styles of work.

Rajputana and Central India.—The enumeration of the styles of calico-printing already made by no means exhausts India's resources in this form of the tinctorial art. Practically every Native State has something peculiar and distinctive of its own. Space cannot, however, be afforded to do more than refer to one or two well marked examples, each peculiar and charming, and which could not be omitted from even the most cursory sketch of the calico-printing of India.

AJMIR cloth is white or is dyed pale pink or a warm cream colour, then printed all over the surface in a delicate floral design boldly and sharply outlined in black, then elaborated with two or three shades of red from pink to almost red black. The fields of the shawls, bed-covers or ceiling cloths, are usually filled up with a fairly large floral elaboration of core-patterns, etc., but the borders are left pure white and have floral scrolls consisting of palmyra-like expanded fans or hibiscus-like flowers alternately dark and light red, while the end pieces (in *sárís* and *rumals*) are panelled by pillars and flowers in cusped arches. A large series of these beautiful and richly coloured fabrics will be seen in the Exhibition as ceiling cloths, wall drapings and table covers.

Jaipur Calicos.

The SANGANIR town of JAIPUR STATE must, however, be regarded as the very metropolis of the calico-printing craft of India so far as art conceptions and technique are concerned. Moreover, once upon a time Sanganir was a large and prosperous town where now there stands but a number of dilapidated hovels, occupied by a few poorly paid calico-printers. At the present day the fabric employed by them is English bleached cotton, but instead of being made into shawls, bed-covers, etc., the habit prevails of printing in strips or pieces and allowing the purchaser to make up in any way desired. The ground colour is usually white, blue or yellow, and the design may be described as realistic and graceful sprays of flowers or of the flame-cone built up of

DIVISION 30. DYEING AND CALICO-PRINTING.

flowers or of bunches of flowers or fruits resting within vases or plates. These are repeated all over the surface at fixed distances and usually in a diagonal fashion. There is no border or division of parts and the sprays are usually from 2 to 3 inches in size with the flowers conventional yet still recognisable. But the most surprising feature of all has to be now told, namely, that the fabrics are usually dyed on both sides and the patterns printed in such a way that they appear almost as vividly on the under as on the upper surface. Among the most frequent flowers may be mentioned the iris, the imperial pendant lily, the rose and the polyanthus with its gracefully nodding head of flower and revolute leaf margins, and many flowers and fruits of the plains of India such as the mango, brinjal, etc.,—modern designs very possibly. In the brinjal pattern, the fruit is deep purple brown and has a bright blue speck near the centre that gives the natural bloom while the characteristic leaves are softened and blended with a yellow background. In producing these charming effects of vivid floral designs, on pale harmonious backgrounds, the patterns are first printed all over every one of the colours required. Then the entire series of block patterns are covered over with a resist paste and the background painted in by the hand, a mop of cloth being used in place of a brush. The favourite backgrounds are pale blues, greens, lemon yellows, pure whites, or deep natural green-blacks. *Chadars* of the last mentioned colour are common, in which the floral ornamentation is confined to a narrow border and two end-pieces of red and yellow that consist of a series of erect floral patterns that might be described as depicting a well trained border of flowering shrubs.

Flowers of Temperate Regions.

Indian Flowers.

Obviously many of the Sanganir designs portray flowers that are not likely to have been seen by the calico-printers nor by the block engravers of Rajputana. In spite of this circumstance, however, there seems every reason to believe that the craft has been handed down for centuries and has come to us in all the purity of original inspiration. The nature, feeling and colour reciprocity, as also the technique in printing, are all perfect, while the absence of machine regularity gives a charm that places these goods above and beyond anything as yet accom-

DIVISION 30. DYEING AND CALICO-PRINTING.

plished in Europe. It has been observed that it is the quaintness and harmony in the Indian textiles that fascinates, but the skilful treatment of the Sanganir calico-printers is quite as wonderful as the goods are beautiful. Few, if any, of the modern schools of calico-printing in India (or in Europe for that matter) have approached the primitive workers of Sanganir and sad, therefore, is it to have to add that such perfection is rapidly being swamped by the popular wave for novelty and utility. The designs have been stolen and imitated and prints at a tithe of the old prices are being thrust on the markets that formerly afforded the means of existence for the Sanganir calico-printers. The student will find a rich display of Sanganir calicos, mostly derived from the Indian Museum, Calcutta, in the Loan Collection Gallery of the Exhibition. This will repay inspection as also the assortment offered for sale in the Main Gallery of which the piece No. 1117 obtained a second prize with bronze medal.

Designs Stolen.

JODHPUR.—In Jaipur itself an altogether different style of work is turned out which more closely resembles that of Agra and Jodhpur than Sanganir. It may, therefore, suffice to briefly describe the calicos of Jodhpur. These are printed as a rule on thick coarse cloth and like the Sanganir goods are in strips or pieces ready to be sewn together into the characteristic skirts worn by the females throughout the greater part of Rajputana. The prevailing ground colours are deep dark Indian red, or dark moss green or dull blue. The patterns are usually closely compacted in parallel bands an inch or so in breadth and arranged lengthwise along the fabric. Usually also they are purely conventional and almost geometric, but occasionally diagonal bands of flowers appear. When the ground is dark red or brown the patterns are bright red; when green the patterns are in lemon yellow and orange-red; or when blue the rosettes of flowers are in brilliant purple—an effect which when viewed near at hand, is startling and discordant, but when seen at a little distance becomes pleasing, more especially when the garments are worn and faded. The entire absence of white from these dress stuffs is one of their most remarkable features. The visitor will have an opportunity of studying a large series of these Jodhpur calicos,

Dark Stripes.

DIVISION 30. DYEING AND CALICO-PRINTING.

since they have been very extensively used for draping the walls in the Art Section and for covering the tables and shelves throughout the Main Gallery.

Rajputana Rumal.

UDAIPUR.—In Udaipur and elsewhere in Rajputana a quaint system of calico-printing on muslins prevails. This is usually done on the *rumals* that are tied tightly around the waist by men or worn loosely over the shoulders or round the head as *pagris.* The fabric is pure white or pale pink and the patterns consist of bunches of flowers, cone-patterns, etc., printed in two shades of dark red, the lighter shade fringing the darker, or occasionally green leaves and yellow flowers are shown. A large assortment of these very charming printed muslins will be found in the Exhibition, those coming from Jaipur, Udaipur, Ajmir, Jodhpur, Kota, etc., being specially worthy of examination.

Kota Calicos.

KUNARI in Kota State holds a high position among the skilled calico-printing centres of India. In addition to producing similar goods to those described in connection with Jaipur, Jodhpur and Ajmir, it also turns out a large quantity of goods of a commendable nature in which patterns are printed by a resist paste first, the fabric is then dyed for the background, washed, and the white patterns either left or subsequently coloured by block printing. In the Exhibition will be found an extensive series of this description such as the *pepáldah sárí,* blue-black ground with a scorpoid design in pale blue, and the *chamachálá sárí* a pattern, that can well be described as depicting cellular structure from the field of the microscope, drawn in pure white on a background of Indian red. In this, as in all the other similar examples of such goods, the ground colour is produced by brushing the surface with the dye.

In CENTRAL INDIA, UJJAIN may be mentioned as an important centre for calico-printing, but other towns are also noted such as Gwalior, Ratlam, Mundsaur and Indore.

Bombay Presidency has several noted centres for calico-printing but mainly in Gujarat, Ahmedabad, Bombay town, Surat, Broach and Baroda. In the Maratha country woven patterns are preferred to printed, but there are good calico-printers in Khandesh, Dharwar and Nasik. In Sind the art is carried to an

DIVISION 30. DYEING AND CALICO-PRINTING.

even higher platform than in Gujarat and the use of a resist paste is almost constant. The pattern is printed as required on the white ground and in Ahmedabad subsequently stamped over with a resist paste made of lime and gum; in Sind of fuller's earth and gum and in Surat of castor oil, bees-wax and *khakhan* oil (Salvadora). The fabric is then dyed the desired ground colour, which may be accomplished by brushing it over in one colour, or as separate panels in different colours with a flannel mop. In Sind, much as in Lahore, preference is given to faded colours and dull effects mostly in lemon yellow, green, brick-red or orange. If it be desired to produce a white pattern on a coloured ground, the resist paste only is imprinted and the textile then dyed when the resist paste, on being removed, shows the white pattern. Baroda and Kaira are perhaps the towns of greatest note and the prevailing colour used is blue-black or dark green, the design being mostly minute specks and the borders and end-pieces glaringly distinct, such as stripes in canary yellow, with green and red in alternating bands and similarly coloured rosettes or medallions in the middle of the field. A beautiful example of a Baroda *sárí* may be seen in the *Indian Art Journal*, Volume I (1886).

Baroda Calico.

Madras.—Of the Southern Presidency, Colonel George Bidie, M.D., C.I.E., some few years ago, wrote that "amongst Hindus everything connected with clothing is more or less regulated by the ancient and rigid laws of caste, so that the articles in this class also possess more or less of an ethnological interest. The brilliancy of the colours and their grouping in Indian textile fabrics are generally very different from European conceptions, but it will be found that some of their most characteristic designs are, so far as the choice and arrangement of colours are concerned, copies from nature, and therefore not unpleasant. The results, however, are often so remarkable that no European would venture to wear articles presenting such combinations, although on a dark-skinned people they do not seem at all out of place, and often have a most picturesque effect."

Madras Calico.

The people of South India certainly use more highly coloured and more boldly conceived designs in their calico-printed garments than is the case in any other part of India but

DIVISION 30. DYEING AND CALICO-PRINTING.

not more so than is in strict accord with Dravidian conceptions of art. Mr. Thurston very properly deprecates the degeneration that has recently taken place in Madras through the introduction of European prints in imitation of, or rather substitution for, the fine old designs of the country. He instances a sample, procured locally, in which rows of bicycles were depicted in alternation with trees on a piece of cloth intended for female attire. Such monstrosities are an insult to European knowledge and an outrage on Indian art. They have their parallel in the moral handkerchiefs, the sale of which some few years ago had to be prohibited because in addition to a scripture text they had printed on them a photographic reproduction of an Indian bank note, full size, as their central ornamental feature. It was soon discovered that these were put to a more successful fraudulent purpose than the contemplated conversion of India to Christianity. Some of the abominations here alluded to have been published as an object lesson, in contrast with Indian prints, in the *Indian Art Journal*, Volume VII, plates 92 to 93 (1897).

Imported Calicos.

Perhaps the most attractive feature of the South Indian calicos is, however, the very frequent use of bees-wax as a resist and their further discussion may, therefore, be reserved for Division 32 below.

AWARDS FOR DIVISION 30.—CALICO-PRINTING.

AWARDS.

Third Prize with bronze medal to Ganga Baksh Chimon Lall of Sanganir, Jaipur, for printed cotton curtains.

Third Prize with bronze medal to Jhandoo of Lahore for cotton prints.

Division 31.—Tie-Dyeing or Knot-Dyeing—Bandana Work.

Having gone into such details with the better known styles of calico-printing, it will hardly be necessary to do more than mention very briefly the various forms of resist-dyeing that have been assorted in the present position.

Manipulation.

BANDANA WORK.—The once famous Bandana handkerchiefs may be given as the best known example of tie-dyeing. The process is simple but so laborious that it could only have been invented or practised in a country where food was cheap and consequently human labour valued at an abnormally low figure. It

DIVISION 31. TIE-DYEING.

may be described briefly as follows:—The fabric is folded several times into half until reduced to a square or rectangular piece perhaps not more than one foot by a foot and-a-half in length and two or three folds in thickness. It is then damped and pressed over a block which consists of a piece of wood with a mass of nails or pins fastened all over it in elaboration of some design. It is then taken off the block and given to a girl (the *bandhani*) who purposely allows the thumb and forefinger nails to grow long with a view to their becoming an indispensable pair of pincers, by means of which minute particles of the cloth may be laid hold of readily. The raised up portions indicated by the block are seized and deftly tied by a string that may or may not have been coated with a resist paste. Great skill is needed not only to securely grasp all the layers of cloth at once but to so seize each portion that it may crinkle in a particular manner while being securely wound round and tied. Moreover the thread is not cut into separate pieces at each tied point. It is carried from the one to the other and is merely held in position by the turn upon itself that is given just before being carried to the next point. In consequence, when the operation of dyeing has been completed, the thread may be readily unwound and used again and again. The *bandhani* having finished her task, the fabric is given to the dyer who begins by immersing the folded up and compactly tied cloth in the lightest shade that it is intended to be given, say yellow. When finished, it is handed to the *bandhani*, who now impresses it upon a second pattern block, and proceeds to tie a still further series of raised up points. It is again dyed the next shade, say red, and if the pattern and scheme of colour desired be thus completed, the threads are unwound and the fabric opened out when it will be found to have a red field with a pattern in white and yellow points, repeated several times all over it. Instead of stopping with the red, a third series of points may be tied and the fabric dyed black when the pattern will appear in points of white, yellow and red on a black (or black-brown) field. Of this kind may be mentioned No. 4385 from Jodhpur which obtained a second prize with bronze medal as the best sample of tie-dyeing in the Exhibition.

Folding and Tying.

Stages in Dyeing.

DIVISION 31. TIE-DYEING.

Multi-Coloured Spots.

But should a still more elaborate design be contemplated, the dyeing and tying may be repeated indefinitely. For example, the first points tied may have been very large and the cloth so folded that when they are opened out they form perfectly circular white spots, squares or star-shaped patches, upon the first ground colour. These may now be dealt with separately and be tied and re-tied until the circles, the squares or the stars become variegated by concentric bands of colour, or a final special spot may be given in the centre of each by uncovering the tips so as to allow these portions of the tied up spaces to receive the desired tint; in fact such exposed portions may be specially coloured by means of a brush. But since the tying of points can never be absolutely complete, the very centre of each bears the tiniest speck of the final field colour.

Hand Work.

Instead of using a block to raise up the cloth at the desired points, the *bandhani* may simply proceed to tie up portions according to a pattern that she has practised until it has become a second nature. In this way she will work rapidly and outline a bird, a horseman or a flower, and pass over certain points in the design that require to be tied at subsequent stages, while carrying on a heated controversy with her neighbour or attending to her infant child. And she will return again and again to the further elaborations of one piece after another with a certainty of action that speaks intuition rather than training.

Zig-zag Designs.

But instead of circular, square or star-shaped spots, it may be desired to produce transverse bands or ziz-zag lines of one colour or another. For example, the *pagris* worn by the Marwaris are elaborately coloured in bands. This is accomplished by folding the cloth lengthwise into, say, four folds, then tying it at intervals by a series of patches of the desired breadth. If then dyed and subsequently opened out, it will be found to have a ground colour with zig-zag transverse bands of white. Having obtained this result, the ordinary point tying may next be resorted to with the result of producing a limitless series of effects.

CENTRES.—Cloth dyed by tying portions is generally known as *chunri*, and the art is practised throughout Central India and

Rajputana, as also Gujarat in Bombay. It is occasionally seen in Berar and Madras, but is extremely rare or quite unknown in the rest of India, although fairly largely practised at a few isolated localities, such as at Muttra. In Plate No. 48 have been shown two examples of tie-dyeing, namely figs. 6 and 7. The former is the characteristic system practised in Rajputana, more especially at Ajmir and Jodhpur, in which the final ground colour is black-brown, the pattern being in white, yellow and red spots. Fig. 7 on the other hand shows a piece of silk tie-dyed at Yeola, near Nasik. The custom prevails in that part of India of dyeing strips of silk with one half the breadth red with white spots, the other not dyed at all. Sir Thomas Wardle gives in the *Indian Art Journal*, Volume I (1886), three most beautiful coloured plates of tie-dyed work. Mr. Chobe Raghunath Das gives in the *Indian Art Journal*, Volume II, an interesting account of the Kota tie-dyeing industry, beautifully illustrated with coloured plates (Nos. 11, 12 and 13), the inspection of which will greatly help to elucidate the above brief description of this quaintly interesting craft. **DIVISION 31. TIE-DYEING.**

MASHRU WORK.—The term *mashru* means permitted, and has reference to the prohibition in Moslem ceremonial law to the use of pure silk by men, except in war or in the form of narrow borders. Mixed silk and cotton fabrics are, therefore, met with all over India, and many of them are exceedingly beautiful, as for example those with a wavy line or *khanjari*. In this style of work the warp is tie-dyed and the weft very possibly dyed but not tie-dyed. *Mashrus* both in pure silk or pure cotton or, still more abundantly, mixed silk and cotton have come to the Exhibition from practically every province. They constitute one of the most significant of Indian textiles though, until the appearance of Mr. A. Yusuf Ali's most admirable monograph on *The Silk Fabrics of the United Provinces*, they received but scant consideration. In connection with the organisation of the collections for the Delhi Exhibition, fairly careful inquiries were instituted into the subject of *mashrus*. From Chamba State has been received (No. 4417) a most remarkable example of tie-dyeing. It is a cotton fabric woven in alternate bands of cotton and gold thread, the cotton being tie-dyed so as to show

Mixed Fabrics.

Khanjari Patterns.

DIVISION 31. TIE-DYEING.

Manipulation.

large wavy formations in dark red within the cotton strips. In Benares the process of tying the warp was witnessed. It is done by men (*tanbandhas*) who earn from two to three annas, after labouring for ten hours daily, on the most monotonous of all occupations and one that must after a very few years exercise a very depressing influence on the operators. The warp is stretched and held tight. The men have given them small strips of birch bark from $\frac{1}{16}$th to 1 inch in breadth, according to the form of *mashru* desired. These strips they cleverly roll up and cause to encircle a certain number of threads of the warp. They then fix each band of bark by tying it with a string, and so expeditiously that the whole operation is completed before the observer has had time to see how it has been done. Time after time this is repeated, until the entire warp has been tied at intervals, equal to the breadth of the strips of bark affixed to it. It is then dyed and the strips of bark removed and when being arranged on the loom it is so adjusted as to cause the dyed portions to produce wavy lines (called the *khanjari*) across the breadth of the cloth. The price of *mashrus*, ornamented in this manner, depends upon the number of zig-zags within a given distance. Obviously it would be much easier and quicker to tie the warp with bands $\frac{1}{2}$ inch than $\frac{1}{8}$th of an inch in breadth. In plate No. 46, fig. 2, a fairly fine *khanjari mashru* will be seen and in fig. 4 one so fine that the zig-zags of the pattern are hardly visible to the naked eye.

Birch Bark.

Sangi.

SANGI.—Sometimes a wavy line is produced, not by tying but by a process of weaving, different coloured wefts being employed. Fabrics of this kind are known as *sangi*. They are cheaper, because easier produced, than the tie-dyed *mashrus*. The warp is of two colours and one of each kind being used together (hence *sang*—together), and by alternation they produce the wavy design. Azamgarh is famed for its *sangi* fabrics.

GULBADAN.—The name *gulbadan* is given to a textile that might be, not incorrectly, described as a cross between the *mashru* and the *sangi*, the warp being partially tie-dyed.

Double tie-dyeing.

Patola Silks.—One of the most beautiful and at the same time most interesting of all Indian textiles is that of the *petola*

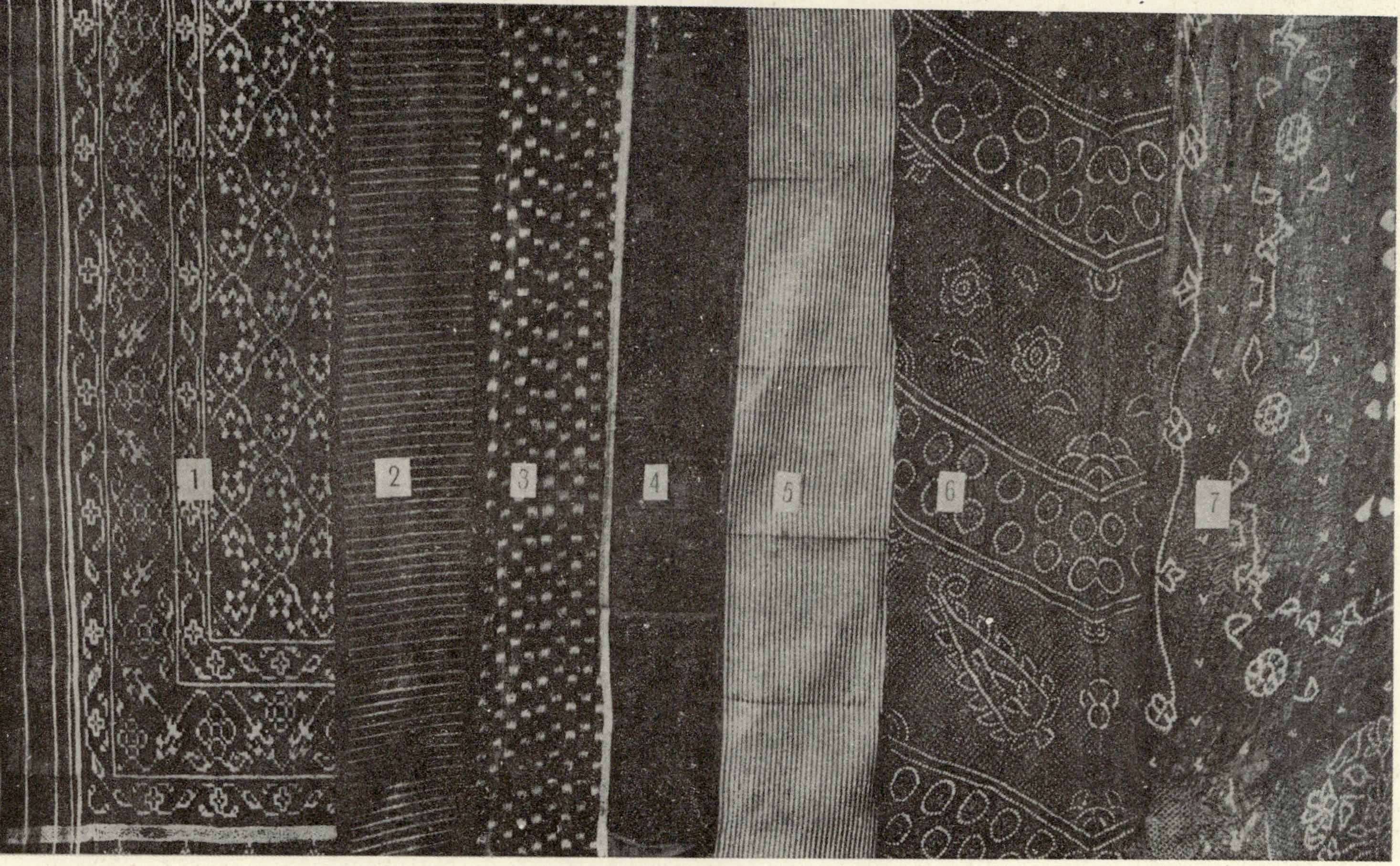

Plate No. 46 Tie-dyed-Fabrics

DIVISION 31. TIE-DYEING.

silk or wedding *sári* of the people of Gujarat. This lovely textile has curiously enough escaped the attention of most writers on Indian Art Manufactures. Mr. A. B. Gupte has fortunately, however, given the subject his attention and his description may be here reproduced:—"It is woven with warps and wefts which have been separately tied and dyed by the *Bandhana* or knot-dyeing process. The dyer takes a small bundle of the warp after it has been dyed in the lightest colour, and draws in pencil across it some lines at measured distances, according to the design to be produced. His wife then ties the silk, along the spaces marked, tightly round with cotton thread, through which the dye will not penetrate. The yarn is then dyed with the next darker colour found upon the warp, and the process repeated until the darkest colour is reached. The weft is then treated in the same way, being so tied and dyed that, in the loom, when it crosses the warp, each of its colours may exactly come in contact with the same colour in the warp. The little bundles of warp have next to be arranged in the loom by the weaver, who then takes the little bundles of weft one at a time, using each in its own place through the design."

Assorted Wefts.

Designs.—Plate No. 46, fig. 1, shows a portion of a *patola sári* but without being coloured it conveys little or no impression of the beauty of these warp and weft tie-dyed textiles. The light coloured portions are usually pure white, passing into yellow, the ground is maroon with the darkest patches in black-green. Some of the old examples occasionally picked up are very beautiful. A *sári* in the Loan Collection Gallery, sent by His Highness the Maharaja (Gaekwar) of Baroda will be seen to have a *patola* centre and rich gold borders and end-pieces. The colours are soft yet full and effective. But even the new *patolas* such as those shown in the Sale Gallery and made by Rama Chand Mul Chand of Pattan, Baroda, are fascinating. These were "Commended" by the Exhibition Judges and will be found worthy of careful study.

One of the most characteristic designs bears the name of the ancient town of Cambay (fig. 1), and there are many admittedly old designs and others comparatively new. As may be inferred,

DIVISION 31. TIE-DYEING.

they are most difficult to make and are accordingly very expensive. Once a design has been established it is repeated as long as it finds sale because of the labour in designing the colours of the warp and weft for a new pattern. In Europe doubtless the effect would be simulated by printing the pattern, but unless printed on both sides and dyed through and through the result would be but a poor substitute for the wonderful *patola* silks of Gujarat, which are woven with printed yarns, each thread of the weft being adjusted so as to bring its coloured portions into juxtaposition with the corresponding coloured portions of the warp.

Various Styles.

In the Cambay pattern a diaper is produced by a white line that forms meshes flattened laterally (*i.e.*, their greatest length vertical). Produced within these are three white flowers borne on dark-green stems in a maroon field, but the sprays lie as it were sideways to the length of the *sárí*. The border strips are not uniform, the end ones being broader and the pattern of these running vertically, whereas the side strips are narrow and the pattern drawn out lengthwise, much as in Penjdeh rugs.

Cambay.

Pattan-Baroda.

In the Pattan form there is no diaper, the pattern is laid sideways (*i.e.*, facing the sides not the ends of the *sárí*) and the border strips are carried within the field and portray a series of elephants, flowering shrubs, human figures and birds, repeated in that sequence and so placed that the feet are inwards or towards the centre of the *sárí*, not outwards as is customary with border patterns. The field colour in the Pattan *sárí* is dark blue-green with the patterns in red, white and yellow.

In Surat the background of the border is usually green while that of the field is dark red, see the *Indian Art Journal*, Volume I, No. 15 (1886),—a paper by Sir Thomas Wardle in which he gives a brief description and an admirably coloured illustration, which compared with Mr. Gupte's equally admirable coloured plate to be seen in the same volume conveys a comprehensive conception of these beautiful textiles.

But there is a point of some interest in these *patola* silks that may be added. From the design being produced by bunches of warp and weft, tie-dyed at fixed points, it is elaborated in squares and with step by step outline, like the embroidery on the meshes of net or gauze that was prevalent in mediæval times and which still lives with the peasantry of Europe. DIVISION 31. TIE-DYEING.

Mr. I. H. Burkill, Superintendent of the Industrial Section of the Indian Museum, Calcutta, has informed the writer that he had recently sent him a *patola* silk *sári* from Java with the request to have it identified. It would appear that these silks have for centuries found their way to Java and are there, just as in Gujarat, used as special bridal garments. Owing to being expensive and the difficulty in procuring them, they are handed down from mother to daughter and are never worn except on the wedding day. This very curious transportation of an artistic fabric and of its associations from one country to another is doubtless a consequence of the former close association of Java with the west coast of India. And it also goes to confirm the impression already conveyed of the antiquity of the art of *patola* dyeing and weaving. Java Trade.

As illustrative of the conservative character of many of the Indian Art Industries, it may be explained that while in Baroda, Mr. Lynn, the Baroda State Engineer, informed the writer that the dyers never teach their daughters certain parts of their trade in case they should marry husbands whom it might not be desirable to take into the craft.

AWARDS FOR DIVISION 31.—TIE-DYEING.

Third Prize with bronze medal to Chota Rungrej of Jodhpur for tie-dyed fabrics. AWARDS.

Commended for silk bandani work curtains—Mr. Shamji of Nowanagar State, Kathiawar.

Division 32.—Painting and Waxing in Calicos.

Accidental mention has been made above, under the heading of calico-printing, of methods of producing special effects, through the employment of a resist material along with the brush, in place of the block. The value of a resist is appreciated all over India by the calico-printers, but more with a view to giving background or field colours to certain large spaces, than as a direct method of ornamentation. With many of the high class calicos of South India, however, block printing might almost

DIVISION 32. PAINTING AND WAXING.

said to play a subordinate part and brush colouring, with wax as a resist, to become the chief method. The simplest and most beautiful results are those obtained on the red-coloured borders of the white *dhotis* that are worn by Native gentlemen in South India.

Early References.

The French traveller Bernier, who visited the Emperor Shah Jahan in 1663, gives a careful description of the splendour of his Court. In referring to the canopies and curtains of gold and embroidered silks in the Dewan-i-Am there occurs the following account of the draperies of the courtyard:—"It was red from without, and lined within with those *chittes*, or cloth painted by a pencil of Masulipatam, purposely wrought and contrived with such vivid colours and flowers, so naturally drawn, of a hundred several fashions and shapes, that one would have said it was a hanging *parterre*." Tavernier, a dealer in precious stones, who travelled in India early in the 17th Century and Dr. Fryer, who visited it during the close of that century, both allude to these cotton manufactures as "Calicuts"—a term derived from the place at which they were originally made. Tavernier says "chintzes or painted Calicuts, which they call *Calmendar*, that is to say done with a pencil—are made in the kingdom of Golconda and particularly about Masulipatam. These chintzes serve for coverlets for beds, for sofas, or table cloths, after the country fashion, pillow covers, handkerchiefs, but more especially for waistcoats, as well for the men and women in Persia."

Appliances.

The word "*Calmendar*" is *kalmdar* (pen-like) and is the instrument which to this day is universally used by the hand-painting dyers of South India. It is composed of a series of fine soft steel wires fastened brush-like at the extremity of a pencil. Bees-wax is heated in a dish and when melted to the required extent becomes the ink (if it may be so designated) that is used with the *kalmdar*. The border of the *sárí* or other textile is stretched across a softly padded table and the operator having previously indicated the main divisions of the pattern, proceeds to inscribe the details with hot wax. The fabric having been previously mordanted and in some cases dyed a pale pink colour seems to possess a special absorptive power over the hot wax; at all events it penetrates or is drawn through and through the textile. The rapidity and accuracy of the operation has to be seen to be appreciated. With apparent indifference the artist (for there is no other name that sufficiently meets his case) proceeds to draw with the steel pen (dipped every now and again into the liquid wax), the desired design. When completed the border of the fabric, with its pale yellow coloured wax design, is dipped into the dye solution and receives a second coating of red. When washed in hot water, so as to remove the bees-wax, the *sárí* is seen to have a pattern that looks like embroidery in two shades of red and equally formed on both sides of the fabric. This is briefly the chief method of procedure, and it may be repeated time after time, until a complex design in many colours has been elaborated. But in addition to using the pencil, large surfaces may be brush-coloured or even dyed in the vat, after all the portions where it is not desired to impart colour have been blocked out by wax. The bees-wax acts as a resist in preventing the action of the dye on the parts protected. When the colour has been imparted by brushing the surface, one side is invariably more brightly dyed and unless twice waxed and brushed on both sides, uniformity of colour when present indicates vat dyeing. So again the design is often simply outlined with wax, so as to prevent the spread of the colour beyond the limits of the colour form desired. The wax dyed fabrics, that are specially designed for export to the Straits, have the surface waxed and polished after the fashion characteristic of the goods of that country.

DIVISION 32. PAINTING AND WAXING.

Inscribed Pattern.

CHIEF CENTRES.—Colonel George Bidie, M.D., C.I.E., who devoted more attention to the study of this art than has apparently been done by any of his successors, brought together all, or very nearly all, the fine collections that are now to be found in our Museums. In one of his reports he wrote:— "In some cases the figures are printed on the cloth with wooden blocks, but all the finer *Palampores* are prepared by stencilling and hand-painting. The stencil plates are made of stout pieces of paper. On these the outlines of the pattern are first traced in ink

Stencilling Designs.

DIVISION 32. PAINTING AND WAXING.

and then perforated with minute holes in the most accurate manner with a fine needle. The stencil is then complete, and when in use, is placed on the cloth and covered with charcoal in very fine powder, which is rubbed so as to make it pass through the minute perforations and leave a tracing. The rest of the work is done entirely by hand, and thus considerable scope is given for the exhibition of individual taste in the selection and grouping of colours. The *Kalahastri palampores* contain mythological scenes, and are full of descriptions of these in the vernacular. Some of the more expensive Masulipatam-made *palampores* are virtually hand-painted pictures on cloth. The principal places of *palampore* manufacture are Eleimbedu in Chingleput District; Karnul, Kalahastri and Wallaja in North Arcot District; Anantpur and Tirupapiliym in South Arcot District; Jammalamadugu and Cuddapah in Cuddapah District; Kistna, Masulipatam and Godavari."

Art Conceptions.—The two dominant ideas that have regulated the separation of this art into widely different forms, may be said to be the uses to which they are put by the Hindus, as canopies over the idols, and by the Muhammadans, as praying carpets. In the former style, the design is mythological and portrays scenes in the *Ramayana* or *Mahabaratta.*

In the latter, the pattern is usually the conventional *mirhab* with the contained panel showing the "Persian tree of life," with birds resting on its boughs and animals reclining below its grateful shade, the earth being figuratively represented by a triangular mound of boulders below which a straight line is sometimes drawn to depict the rivers and seas with their countless forms of life.

Kalahastri Canopies.

Chief forms.—The most important centres for the production of Hindu canopies may be said to be Kalahastri in North Arcot, Salem, Madura, Palakolu and Masulipatam. In other towns *palampores* are made and used for domestic rather than sacred purposes, and these usually show sporting and rural scenes and are largely (especially within recent times) block printed, such as those from several villages in the Tanjore and Coconada Districts. The most important, in fact the only, centre at present where

DIVISION 32. PAINTING AND WAXING.

artistic *palampores* in the form of praying rugs, curtains, handkerchiefs, etc., are produced, may be said to be Masulipatam. In Dr. Bidie's time even more artistic results were attained at Eleimbedu in Chingleput and at Coconada than at Masulipatam, but from inquiries instituted by the writer in connection with the Exhibition this beautiful art has practically died out in these localities.

Chingleput and Coconada Sheets.

The samples, in the Indian Museum, Calcutta, of Chingleput and Coconada *palampores*, are exceptionally fine; far superior in fact to those found anywhere in the Madras Presidency at the present day. They consist very largely of designs worked in bees-wax with the pen-like brush (already described), not blocked out in large, mostly blue and dark red patches, as in the Masulipatams. Moreover, the patterns are in shades of red, brown and yellow on a white ground and with a very restricted use of blue. They are, in all the finer samples, formed on both surfaces, very possibly owing to double waxing having been resorted to and, therefore, double dyeing or vat dyeing. They are so perfect that at the distance of a few feet they can with difficulty be distinguished from the very finest Kashmir embroidered shawls. These most lovely calicos are for the most part done on the long narrow strips intended for use as *chadars* or shawls. The ends of the cloth have been opened out, twisted and tied up so as to form coloured fringes that in every detail simulate those of woollen shawls and are quite unlike the fringes shown on the cotton shawls of any other part of India. In the larger squares or *palanposhes* and *fards* or the canopies and floor cloths, the borders often consist of festoons of flowers, in the form of wreaths tied with ribbons and pendant tassels, that isolate certain portions or panels which are filled in with bunches of realistic flowers.

Coimbatore Curtains.

COIMBATORE is noted for its beautiful hand-painted curtains, sheets and handkerchiefs. These are done (or, to be more nearly correct, were done) on a white or grey mottled background. The prevailing pattern colour may be described as a light Indian red with a small admixture of green and dark red. The drawing is bold and liberal, consisting of scrolls with birds and animals freely intermixed. It proceeds primarily from two trees so compacted

DIVISION 32. PAINTING AND WAXING.

that it becomes difficult to trace the beginnings or endings of the design. The flowers are very large and numerous, so large in fact as to very nearly obliterate all other details. They are cleverly treated, the petals being outlined by pale coloured bands and shaded in with one or two tones of red. The border is wide, richly festooned with floral wreaths looped up and tied with ribbons in lover's knots, from which tassels of flowers are suspended in a manner that recalls Italian wall frescoing.

Masulipatam Praying Carpets.

In the Masulipatam wax-cloths, such as the praying-carpets, curtains, handkerchiefs, etc., the pattern nearly always assumes the form of a great central tree of life, accomplished in a rich deep red-brown with a profusion of blue. But while executed after the most approved Mughal model, they have a stronger taint of a former religious influence than is customary with goods made for and used by the Muhammadans. One of the most admirable features of this class of fabrics, for example, may be said to be the twin handkerchiefs, on each of which is depicted an immense moonstone-like circular design, that fills the entire square all but four triangular corner pieces. The medallion is composed of four zones and a central disc. As a rule, the zones are built up of the cone-pattern or flowing floral scrolls, the background being either white, blue, pink or dark red. The pink form is most characteristic of all Masulipatam work and is composed of a fern-like tracery on a white field that is elaborated by the *kalmdar* or is block printed with a light shade of the same red that appears all over the floral designs. But the charm of these handkerchiefs may be said to be the repose given by the claret-red (speckled with minute cone-patterns) used in the corner spaces. These great circular designs recall the moon-stones and discs of the Buddhist and Jain temples, and bear little resemblance to the Muhammadan art conceptions of any other part of India. But instead of circles, the handkerchiefs may have a square field in deep claret brown with a rich convoluted floral design outlined in yellow and with pale blue fittings. The borders of these squares are usually done in a double series of *jamewar*-like floral bands in white, red and blue that enclose elliptic spaces filled in by yellow florescence.

DIVISION 32. PAINTING AND WAXING.

Handkerchief Trade.

Throughout a great part of South India handkerchiefs were largely made and mainly for export. The traffic in these has recently, however, shrunk into small proportions and with hardly any prospect of a revival. They were usually glazed and with the pattern showing on both surfaces. These were in dark red with designs in blue, the outlines being picked out in white. The desired portions were coated with wax and the remainder dyed dark red, thus leaving certain patches in white. The wax was removed and the red parts next coated all over with wax and once more the specks to be kept white were also spotted in wax. The fabric was again dyed but this time in blue and the design thus completed. In all fabrics where large surfaces of waxing are necessary curious streaks of colour like a cobweb are seen over the surface. These appear to be due to the cracking of the wax-coating allowing the dye to penetrate, but this little defect is the certificate of the genuineness of the article.

Kalahastri.

Ceiling Cloths.—The mythological canopies and curtains used by the Hindus have perhaps been sufficiently indicated by the few brief references already made. One of the finest ever produced is the admirable example to be seen over the door in the Loan Collection Gallery. This has been contributed by the Raja of Kalahastri and is believed to be about 100 years old. The ground is white and the pattern almost entirely in soft but bright madder red, the spaces for the various scenes being richly canopied in foliage. In the Main Gallery a series of modern Kalahastris will be seen where they have been used as ceiling cloths. Those over the first half of the Main Transept are from Kalahastri itself. They are in large bold patterns, the human forms being in brilliant blue and bright yellow with the background in dark claret colour. To right and left of the Transept will be seen two or three other ceiling cloths, in mythological form. These have been received from Salem and may be said to be characterised by the paler colours used, more especially the lemon green, that takes the place of brilliant blue. The others from Madura are distinguishable by their deep dark red colourings, and lastly, the brightly coloured red and white cloths are

DIVISION 32. PAINTING AND WAXING.

from Pallakollo in Godavari. These were kindly procured by Mr. J. Cumming, I.C.S., Collector of Godavari. "In drawing and graphic composition of figures" wrote Mr. Havell "the Pallakollo canopies are almost unequalled."

But the contrast between all these modern mythological painted fabrics and the Loan Collection series, more especially the large canopy lent by the Raja of Kalahastri, will abundantly confirm the depravity of modern taste that is everywhere dominant in South Indian Art.

A lost Tanjore Art.

Loan Collection.—In the Palace of Tanjore, the writer discovered a form of wax-printing that seems to have been specially nurtured by the Rajas of that State. This was turned out at Karpur, a village in Tanjore District, but the art has for many years been discontinued. *Sárís* were specially woven of a good quality of cotton, in which a pattern previously conceived was worked out by threads of gold let into the weft, as in the manufacture of *jamdani* (flowered) muslins, but with this difference that the gold was made to form the background of the pattern, not the pattern itself. The next stage seems to have consisted in colouring the pattern. This was done by their elaborating a design in wax by means of the *kalmdar* or by the *kalmdar* and block printing combined. When waxed to the desired extent the fabric was dyed in rich clay red and subsequently certain portions were printed in darker shades of the same colour in order to give shadow effects. Where the waxing had been given, white or pink spaces were left on a rich soft red and these light coloured portions were still further ornamented by block printing. The gold wire was also toned down by the process of dyeing to which it was subjected, the result being a soft rich effect unequalled for artistic feeling by any of the printed or woven fabrics of the present day.

Mysore Examples.

Mysore.— From Bangalore has been received, through the co-operation of Mr. J. Cameron, Superintendent of the Museum of that town, a series of canopies dyed by the peculiar form of waxing practised in Mysore. The outlines of the human figures, of the plantains, palms and other details of the pattern are made in wax and the spaces within these are brush-coloured, the wax being used simply to prevent the colour from spreading beyond the desired spaces or the one from mingling with the other. **DIVISION 32. PAINTING AND WAXING.**

Burma.—In Rangoon, Toungoo, Mandalay, Tavoy and other towns of Burma, bees-wax is used as a resist in silk printing, or a preparation consisting of bees-wax, paraffin and turpentine is so used. The garment (usually white brocaded silk) is printed all over in some desired pattern (but in disregard to the design worked within the texture) by means of blocks coated with the hot wax. The fabric is then dyed a bright colour and when washed, to remove the wax, in hot water and fuller's earth, it shows a white pattern over a ground colour. A multitude of small special blocks are now employed and the white spaces are printed up in various colours as originally intended. A large assortment of printed Burmese silks will be found in the stall assigned to Messrs. Tara Chand Pursram of Bombay. **Burma Waxing.**

By way of concluding this brief account of the special wax-printed and hand-painted fabrics of India, it may be worth adding that it is curious this art should thus afford what may be accepted as an additional indication of a possible industrial and artistic relationship between certain communities of Southern India and the people of Burma.

AWARDS FOR DIVISION 32.—PAINTING AND WAXING.

Third Prize with bronze medal to Changalrayadu of Kalahastri for painted cloths. **AWARDS.**

Third Prize with bronze medal to Irshad Ali of Jaffergunj, Fathepur, for painted ceiling cloths.

Division 33.—Tinsel-Printing.

The line of separation that has to be accepted as dividing the style of textile ornamentation, discussed above under Division 29—"Wax-cloth," and that which becomes the special theme of the present Division, is extremely narrow indeed. The material used in wax-cloth ornamentation is an oleaginous substance (*roghan*) that is thickened with lime and coloured with pigments before being applied. In tinsel-printing an adhesive substance is printed over the texture and subsequently dusted with the colouring matter. But it often happens in the so-called wax-cloth work that the *roghan*, just before it sets, is dusted over with powdered talc or with **Definition.**

DIVISION 33. TINSEL-PRINTING.

gold and silver powder, with the object of giving a shimmer to the design or some portions of it. The dusting of an adhesive substance with colour is practically the definition of tinsel-printing, so that the separation is difficult to express in words, though the recognition of the two classes of coloured fabrics is exceedingly easy. They are characteristic of widely different purposes, peoples and places, so that there is a useful purpose served by their independent recognition.

Manipulation

In wax cloth the pattern is never printed by blocks; in tinsel-printing it is invariably so accomplished. In tinsel-printing glue, gum, lac or other adhesive substance is first printed over the fabric and gold leaf, silver leaf, tin-foil, mercury amalgam or other colour materials are pressed against the adhesive pattern. When gold effect is to be produced, the glue is previously coloured with the yellow aniline dye called *piori* and when silver is to be employed it is coloured with chalk. The fabric is printed with the glue, is dried in the shade, rolled up and bit by bit unrolled, moistened through a damp cloth being placed over it and, when sufficiently damp, gold or silver leaf is daubed all over the surface. The name *piori* is a curious adaptation in the aniline trade. Originally the pigment of that name was produced in India from cow's urine, and to falsify this origin the label on the packets of the imported *piori* shows a picture of a cow. The use of yellow or of white in the glue recalls the fact that in preparing certain forms of gold wire, yellow silk thread is used and white thread with silver.

Centres.—In various parts of India special manifestations of the art of tinsel-printing exist in which the effort may be said to be put forth to simulate the expensive embroideries of the neighbourhood. In many parts of the country, for example, a muslin printed and coloured with floral designs, has portions subsequently stamped with glue and these coated with gold or silver leaf. In the Panjab Room the curtains draping the balcony will be found to be double block and tinsel-printed in this fashion and the result very charming. This was made by Gulab of Lahore and obtained a reward by the Judging Committee.

Panjab.

DIVISION 33. TINSEL-PRINTING.

Jaipur. In Jaipur the art of tinsel-printing is carried to a state of high proficiency, many of the Sanganir calicos having first patterns printed with resist paste, then vat dyed, the resist removed and the floral designs on the pale blue or pale green ground printed with colour or tinsel. Ujjain and Mundsaur are also famed for their tinsel prints.

Nasik. In NASIK very curious and beautiful tinsel prints are produced. These appear to be accomplished by a coloured *roghan* stamped from moulds or blocks. The writer has not personally witnessed this process and the reports that have been published regarding it are contradictory and unsatisfactory. Dark coloured fabrics are stamped with a white or variously coloured adhesive substance. In consequence a diaper in green leaves usually encloses white, red or golden flowers. **Ahmedabad.** The tinsel prints of Ahmedabad are also more or less characteristic and beautiful and those of Madras closely resemble the Nasik prints. It is possible, that when the Nasik work is more carefully studied it may be found necessary to transfer the process to the heading of wax-cloth work, alongside of that of Morvi and Kach. It is retained in its present position chiefly because, according to all accounts, the material is printed by being pressed through a mould and not worked up by the hand as in the wax embroidery (if it may be so called) of Peshawar, Kach, Baroda, Chanda and other localities. In Chanda the wax material is made of boiled linseed oil thickened with a peculiar clay obtained locally and in some respects it seems to closely resemble the Nasik printing material.

Godavari Work. ***Loan Collection.***—There are many examples of tinsel printing in the Loan Collection Gallery most of them illustrative of the designs met with in the various provinces of India in which variously coloured textiles are spangled with gold or silver ornamentation. The most beautiful is a sheet contributed by the Madras Museum. This might, in fact, be shown as a splendid example of hand-painting with wax as a resist. It is said to have been made in Godavari. The field colour is a pale buff. The design, a double "Persian tree of life" completely interlaced but with the boughs open, gracefully branched, and richly clothed in long pale blue green leaves and bright pink flowers. Resting on

DIVISION 33. TINSEL-PRINTING.

the branches or walking under the shade are brilliantly coloured and crested pheasants. But the charm of this wonderful piece of work is the fact that the outlines of every twig, leaf, petal, or feather are cleverly rendered in gold. The border is broad and elegantly worked. It shows the, by no means unusual, festoonings of flowers, braced by ribbons and tassels and with bunches of realistic flowers placed above the saggings of the wreaths.

AWARDS FOR DIVISION 33.—TINSEL-PRINTING.

AWARDS.

Commended for a pair of curtains—Gulab of Lahore.

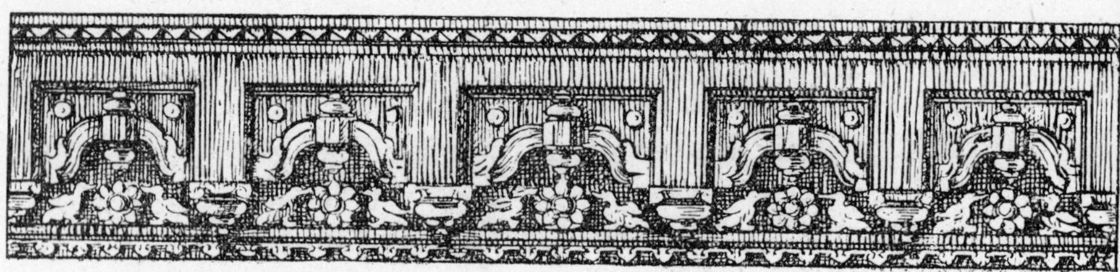

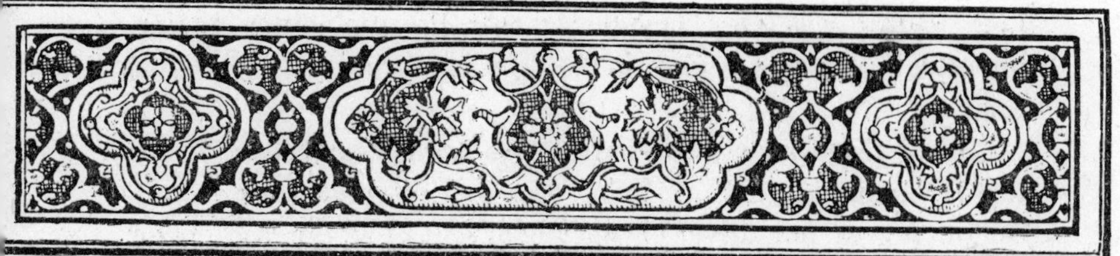

Division 34.—Cotton Manufactures.

MR. T. N. MUKERJI makes the following very forcible observation :—" Neither tradition nor history give any precise information about the time when cotton first appeared as an important article in the domestic economy of an Indian household. But as geology has preserved traces of early forms of life upon the earth, so has Indian society preserved in its different strata the manners and customs of pre-historic ages, side by side with the highest types of modern civilization. The trousers and coats made at the present day of the bark of *Sterculia urens* in the north, and of *Antiaris succedanea* in the south, show as much the kind of raiment worn by our forefathers as the charm written on the thin epidermis of the *Betula Bhojpatra* suggests the material on which they inscribed their sacred songs, after writing was invented. These, together with the leaf garments still worn by the Jowangs of the Orissa hills and the sheep-skin clothing of the North-west Frontier, were evidently the early forms of dress known in India."

DIVISION 34. COTTON.

Pre-historic Customs.

Historic Facts.—The manufacture of cotton was introduced into England in the 17th Century. But in 1641 " Manchester cottons," in imitation of " Indian cottons," were made of wool. So also the clamour against the Indian printed cottons was so great that in 1721 a statute was passed that prohibited the use of printed calicos and this was modified, in 1736,

Printed Cottons in England.

DIVISION 34. COTTON.

to permission provided the warp was entirely of linen. All this was changed with the discovery of Arkwright's machine and in 1769 Manchester had been placed in such a position of advantage that it was then recognised that the prohibition against imported goods was a violation of the first principles of political economy.

Steam Power.

Since these days a revolution has been accomplished in the textile industries not of India only but of the whole world. Steam power has driven hand labour out of all the markets for ordinary (that it is to say non-artistic) goods. Large factories for spinning and weaving have sprung into existence all over India and are year by year being multiplied. The outcry against them has been misguided and sentimental. To bolster up the effete methods and appliances of bygone times would of necessity involve the suppression of national progression and the exposure of India to an even fiercer foreign competition than at present. However much Indian art may be injured or individuals suffer, progression, in line with the manufacturing enterprise of civilization, must be allowed free course and the endeavour should be to aid rather than obstruct the progress of India's manufacturing enterprise. But with an exhibition designed to demonstrate Indian Art it became unavoidable to exclude all loom-power manufactures as also all hand-made goods that were not treated artistically. The observations that follow deal with actual exhibits and in consequence of necessity omit some of the most important groups of Indian cotton goods.

Chief Garments.—There may be said to be certain well recognised classes of cotton goods such as the *dhoti* (*dhotar*) or piece of plain cotton cloth generally having a coloured border and measuring about 5 yards in length and one and a quarter in width. This may be made locally or imported. It is worn by men. The *sári* (or garment corresponding to the *dhoti*) worn by women. This varies greatly in the material used and the designs of ornamentation employed, according to the wealth, position or caste of the owner. With the finer materials it is generally woven as a gauze and to the present day is largely hand-loom work. Speaking generally the chief difference between the *dhoti* and the *sárí* is the more closely woven nature and narrower coloured border of the *dhoti* or in the entire *sárí* being coloured, the pattern being either woven into it or calico-printed or embroidered. It is usually worn around the waist, the end being thrown over the head, in place of a shawl or *chadar*. With that economy in art that often mysteriously characterises native work, only the exposed portions are ornamented. The *sárí* is moreover as a rule delicately coloured, red, blue and green being the most generally used colours. One end of the *sárí* has usually a broad band of colour either woven in silk and gold or in the finer class *sárís* is attached. The *sárí* is one of the most graceful and picturesque of all garments and accordingly from an art point of view is perhaps the most interesting of all Indian fabrics. The *chadar* or shawl is a sheet usually about three yards long and one and a half wide. It is used by men and by certain classes of women only and is worn across the shoulders or in the case of females as a loose *sárí* (if it may be so described) or *dopatta* thrown over the head. The *pagrí* or *lúngi* (turban) is a long narrow strip of cloth worn by men around the head or as a band around the waist (*kamarband*). The *cholí* (*khana*) is the little bodice now very largely worn by females below the *sárí*. It is often of a rich material or is delicately embroidered. The *súsí* is the striped cloth used in making trousers and is sometimes a very beautiful material.

Economy in Art.

Lastly, if to this list be added two or three others such as the large shoulder sheet, often quilted, called the *fard* or *razái*, the similar sheet also often quilted and used as a bed cover the *liháf* or *palangposh*, the floor cloth or *jazim* or *farsh*, and the rug the *darí* or *satranjí*, the series of chief artistic textile articles of Native dress and household use may be regarded as complete.

These garments, etc., may be specially woven to size and shape or cut from the piece and sewn into the desired form. They may be dyed, embroidered, appliquéd or patched, the border being attached. Hence the cotton goods may be dealt with under several denominations of quality or methods of weaving.

DIVISION 34. COTTON: PANJAB.

But it would be beyond the scope of this catalogue to discuss more than the forms represented at the Exhibition and these for convenience may be grouped under two main sets, thus :—

(*a*) Long-cloths or Damasks.

(*b*) Muslins, Plain or Figured.

Long-cloths and Damasks.

These are mostly checked or striped and are perhaps best known collectively under the name of *ghatis*, sometimes called *andras*. They are fine quality cloths and may be either white or coloured but the patterns are usually woven, not printed. When checked (and of a thick material) they are, in Northern India, denominated *kheses*, and to the south *gabruns ;* and when striped are spoken of as *susis*. The loom for *khes* weaving is wider than is customary with other fabrics. The usual colours are dark red (for Hindus), dark blue (for Muhammadans), in both woven with white. But damask proper is ordinarily much finer in texture and is woven in white only or white bleached cotton alternating with unbleached or pale buff coloured cotton.

Many of the textiles here indicated closely resemble in texture the ginghams and checks of Europe. In the Exhibition a large assortment of *kheses* and similar fabrics have been received from all parts of India and will be found to reward careful inspection, since many are extremely beautiful. The following are those of perhaps greatest merit :—

Panjab.—From the DERAJAT and neighbouring country especially Dera Ismail Khan, Jhang, Multan, Shahpur, and through Kohat to Peshawar beautiful *kheses* are made. Other localities may be mentioned such as Muzaffargarh, Lahore, Sialkot, Firozpur, Karnal, Ludhiana and Patiala. The drills (*gabruns* or *gambrans*) of LUDHIANA closely resemble similar goods from Europe. The *lungis* of KOHAT and PESHAWAR (imitated in Ludhiana) are famous all over the East ; they are mostly in pale drab colour or dark blue with, in both cases, richly worked end-pieces in stripes of gold wire and coloured silk. In the *pagris* and *lungis* of SHAHPUR and MULTAN stripes in red, yellow and green are frequent. In GURDASPUR a special cloth is made known as *garbi loi*. It is exported all over India. The glazed *ghati* fabrics of JALLANDHAR (which imitate *gulbadans*) are well known, especially the diaper known by the poetic name of "the nightingale-eye" (*bulbul-chashm*).

DIVISION 34. COTTON: UNITED PROVINCES.

The textiles collectively designated *susis* are striped cotton goods, sometimes with a few silk threads in the warp. They are used for women's trousers (*pyjamas*) and are badly imitated by imported printed goods, though as made in the Panjab, machine-spun yarn is invariably employed.

United Provinces.—Mr. C. A. Silberrad has written a most learned and technical monograph on the *Cotton Fabrics of these Provinces* that the reader would do well to peruse. Space for only the briefest possible reference to the fabrics he describes can be here allowed and chiefly with the object of inviting attention to the selection on view at the Exhibition. The coarser broad cloth is known as *girant, garha* or *chandáha* and the finer goods as *tanzeb.* The best qualities of the latter are made at Benares, Bulandshahr, Fyzabad, Jaunpur, Mirzapur and Rai Barelli districts. When woven with a check pattern in colours they are called *chárkhánas,* when damasks they are *chauthais,* and one of the favourite designs is the *bulbul-chashm.* This consists of a double set of diagonal stripes forming small lozenge-spaces with usually a spot in the centre of each. So again the *gulbadans* (*pattidars* or *sangís*) have the pattern on one side. The warp is usually all of one colour, while the weft is of various colours; but the heddles are so arranged that it is on the pattern side of the warp for at least three-fourths of its length. The prevailing patterns are combinations of stripes and W-shaped markings. The *kánáwez* or double fabrics of ALIGARH are very beautiful and the *gabrúns* from AGRA (locally known as *nákhúnás*) have the warp white and the weft striped in various colours.

AGRA still enjoys a reputation for its checked and striped white cotton piece goods (*nákhúnás*), though competition with the imports have told seriously. The damasks of Rampur State have a considerable local market and are considered admirable of their kind. A fair assortment of the finer class *chauthais, gabrúns, gulbadans* and *nákhúnás* will be seen from Agra, Aligarh, Muzaffarnagar, Farukhabad, etc.

DIVISION 34. COTTON: CENTRAL PROVINCES.

Central Provinces.—The weaving of superior cotton cloth is a feature of Nagpur, Bhandara and Chanda Districts of these Provinces. The most famous are the cloths of the village of Umrer in NAGPUR and of Pauni in BHANDARA. The chief manufacture is *dhotis* (or *dhotar jodis*) the glory of which is the breadth and beauty of the borders. These are often woven in intricate patterns. It is on record that Pauni turbans have sold for as much as £20 apiece. In Nagpur has been erected one of the most successful cotton mills of India and these turn out, so far as intrinsic merit is concerned, goods not only equal to the best of the hand loom *dhotis* of old but equal, if not superior, to the finest imported articles. But unfortunately it has to be added that all trace of the highly artistic borders of former times may be said to have disappeared. Mr. Arthur Blennerhassett in his monograph on the *Cotton Fabrics* of these Provinces speaks of the *sáris* as "each kind having a different local name, according to its colour, design or border. Thus we hear of the *golabi rast* pink in colour; of the red *lal sendri*; of the blue *udi popri*; of the green *hirvi silari*. Some *sáris* are striped, others checked; some have coloured borders, some silver borders and some again golden ones. Among the most delicate of these fabrics are the *sáris* of BURHANPUR, with their variegated borders, interwoven with gold-plated thread *kalabathi*. Again, in SAMBALPUR, we have a *sári* called *phulia*. This is distinguished by a flowered border. Apparently peculiar to this district are the *sáris* known as *hansabali kapta* and *hansabali datapar*; the former is uniform in colour, and has a border of fanciful animals, such as fish, ducks, elephants; the latter *sári* is similar, only that the designs of the border occur also in stripes throughout the body of the cloth." These *hansabalis* are perhaps the most artistic fabrics of the Central Provinces.

In many of the older reports reference is made to the unbleached cotton gauzes interwoven with gold threads produced at Berhampur. Though still made, they are inferior nowadays since no one could give them the old name of "woven sunshine."

In BERAR, the AKOLA and ELLICHPUR Districts are well known all over India for their cotton goods, more especially their

DIVISION 34. COTTON: BENGAL.

checked and striped handkerchiefs. These are worn tied round the head or waist. Their beauty consists in the rich shades of *al* dye used in colouring the yarn.

Bengal.—The chief districts concerned in the cotton manufactures of Bengal are Burdwan, Birbhum, Bankura, Serampore, Nadia, Murshedabad, Jessore, Dinajpur, Rungpur, Bogra, Pabna, Dacca, Faridpur, Tipperah, Chittagong, Patna, Shahabad, Saran, Champaran, Monghyr, Bhagalpur, Cuttack, etc. Kassimbazar, Chittagong, Patna and Santipur have been famed for their cotton goods since the times of the East India Company's factories in these places, although the traffic is at present purely local. TIPPERAH has a fairly large trade in cotton weaving and DACCA, famous for its fine muslins, still holds a foremost position among the Bengal localities of cotton spinning and weaving. This will be presently dealt with under the separate section below devoted to "Muslins." The Brahman women of TIRHUT spin fine thread using very often *khaki* coloured cotton. From this, especially in Durbhanga district, is woven a cloth known as *kokti*. The Jahanabad (PATNA) muslins and broad cloths, so also those of RANGPUR and DINAJPUR, have fair reputations and are damask in quality and form.

An interesting monograph on the *Cotton Fabrics of Bengal* has been written by Mr. N. N. Banerjee, but it does not add materially to our knowledge of the artistic manufactures of the Province. He has failed to assort them under any practical system but described Plain muslins, Embroidered muslins, Figured muslins, other cloths of thick texture, cloths of thin texture, etc., and concludes with towels, *daris*, chikan work, etc.

Assam and Manipur.—A fairly large trade exists in the production of the shawls, *pagris*, etc., used by the various hill tribes. These are often highly ornate and brightly coloured but they can hardly be seriously viewed as indicative of a distinctive area of cotton manufacture. As in Burma so in Assam the art is a domestic one and acquires for the females of the household terms of approbation expressive of skill in warping, reeling, spinning and weaving. Mr. Samman's monograph of the *Cotton Fabrics of Assam* is so exhaustive that it would require many

DIVISION 34. COTTON: BOMBAY.

pages to even review the passages that refer to the particular class of goods produced and the art conceptions manifested by them.

Bombay.—Under the fostering care of the East India Company, Surat and Broach became important cotton manufacturing towns. In the diary record of 1777, some 30 different styles of cotton cloth are mentioned as produced in these towns, from the stoutest canvas to the finest muslin. A new era in the cotton trade of Western India opened, however, with the establishment of power loom mills in Bombay, Ahmedabad, Surat, etc., and since then the trade has largely changed its character. It has lost some of its former special local forms and entered into direct competition with English and German goods.

Mr. R. E. Enthoven has written a useful monograph on the *Cotton Fabrics of the Bombay Presidency* which should be consulted. Few, if any, of the hand looms produce artistic fabrics except in the form of *sárís* or turbans. The following notes may assist the visitor to inspect the goods shown at the Exhibition.

BELGAUM and DHARWAR are noted for their fine *sárís* which have bold silk borders and beautiful end-pieces. The red and dark blue *sárís* (*gulal-chikki*), the red and black *sárís* (*mungi chikki*), and the dark blue and white checked *sárís* (*bile khaddi*) are well known. The BIJAPUR *sárís* are viewed as of specially high quality. POONA is famed for its turbans and *lugadis*, *shalus*, *shelas* (scarfs), etc. The *shalu* is a *sárí* with gold brocaded border and end-piece. SHOLAPUR is an important centre in the cotton-weaving trade but it does not produce any very artistic goods. NASIK on the other hand is famous for its turbans, especially those produced in Yeola. *Lugadis* of cotton and silk mixed or cotton with silk borders are also largely made and carried all over the Presidency. In THANA *susis* are extensivly produced, that is to say the striped fabric used in the manufacture of trousers. It is hardly necessary to allude to the cotton manufactures of the town of BOMBAY as these are both well known and fall under the definition of ordinary commercial rather than artistic goods. The same might also be said of AHMEDABAD. The hand loom ***dhotars*** and *chalotas* have pretty silk borders and find a market all over the Presidency. SURAT turns out superior *lungis*, *sáris*, *susis*, etc., while BROACH gives attention to *razais* (bed quilt cloths).

KAIRA had formerly a large industry in cotton weaving, the goods being sent to Ratlam and other parts of Central India. Kaira, like many other towns, enjoys the reputation of having a water specially favourable to dyeing cotton goods.

Sind.—Coarse cloth (*dangari*) is manufactured in every village and *susis* at HALA. HYDERABAD is famed for its *agattis* or strings for supporting trousers; these are rainbow-coloured for men and of a gauze texture for women. It also turns out *khes* of exceptionally fine quality, the craft for this class of weaving being chiefly resident in Narapur, a town formerly well known for its fabrics. The Narapur *kheses* are exceptionaly well woven in red and green or red and yellow cotton and they are very cheap, each piece costing from R10 to R15. TATTA used to be renowned for silk goods and cotton chintzes, while KARACHI has some credit for its *lungis*, *kheses* and *susis*—the last mentioned being exceptionally well woven and the stripes carefully assorted.

Madras.—In the GODAVARI District certain villages around Coconada and Rajamundri have a high reputation for their cotton goods. The blue palampores (*palamposhes*) and fine shirting cloths of NELLORE were at one time largely exported from India to the West Indies but though they are still produced they are hardly if ever exported at the present day. The handkerchief trade was ruined through the emancipation of the slaves. Freedmen refused to buy the special articles of clothing that were the symbols of their former slavery. Recently the School of Arts, Madras, has tried to re-establish the trade in Nellore and Rajamundri handkerchiefs, by manufacturing these in the required shape, colour and perfume and sending out experimental consignments. But of all the ancient seats of cotton-weaving in South India Rajamundri is the only one that has to-day a fairly assured local position. The large assortment of beautiful fabrics shown to the writer on the occasion of his visit to that town, in connection with this Exhibition, showed that the weavers required only a helping hand to re-assert the old export trade, so far as may be possible. Similarly the *punjan* cloth of VIZAGAPATAM

DIVISION 34. COTTON: MADRAS.

was largely exported from Madras to Brazil, Europe and the West Indies. The only survival of this traffic is the export of blue cloth to French China from PONDICHERRY—a survival due to the French enactments regarding her colonies. It is believed, however, that the exact shade of blue in demand by the people of Siam and China cannot be produced very readily, except by the dyers of Pondicherry and the neighbouring British districts to the French Settlement of South India.

MASULIPATAM has for centuries enjoyed the reputation of producing exceptionally fine cotton chintzes. The trade in these has almost disappeared though if specially ordered these wax-dyed fabrics can be produced. MADURA has a fairly large trade in both cotton and silk goods, the special feature being the deep Indian madder red that used to be employed. This colour is now largely simulated by an imported alizarine dye that is much cheaper and the fabric when freshly dyed can with difficulty be distinguished from similar goods dyed with the old madder colour. A somewhat characteristic feature of the Madura cloths is a white silk thread woven through the red cotton so as to form a check about one inch in mesh. Madura painted calicos (chintzes) are much inferior to those of KALAHASTRI, in North Arcot, and still more so than the Masulipatam already briefly indicated.

Mr. E. Thurston has written a monograph on *The Cotton Fabric Industries of the Madras Presidency* that gives some useful particulars regarding the modern traffic. The chief themes expatiated on are the degraded taste (recently developed by the people, and largely through the influence of imported goods) and the position of the weavers, more especially in the carpet trade.

In ***Mysore*** special cotton weaving exists and good broad cloths (damasks) are turned out especially in BANGALORE. The chintzes of SHIMOGU and the printed cloths of BANGALORE are similar to those formerly produced at SERINGAPATAM.

In ***Burma*** weaving is a domestic industry carried on mainly by the women and in the more rural tracts rather than in the populous towns.

Muslins—Plain and Figured.

Mention is made in the *Mahabharata* of the presents brought to Yudhisthira as Paramount Lord; these included muslins from Ganjam, the Carnatic and Mysore. The most ancient statues commonly depict female figures draped in such fine materials that the form of the body is completely revealed, and only lines given to indicate drapery or the pattern of the border. Megasthenes speaking of the costumes of the people of India observed, that they wore flowered muslins. Marco Polo (*Book I, Chapter V.*) writes of the kingdom of Mosal in Asiatic Turkey: "All the cloths of gold and silver that are called Mosolins are made in this country; and those great merchants called Mosolins who carry for sale such quantities of spicery and pearls and cloths of silk and gold, are also from this kingdom." Commenting on this passage, the late Sir Henery Yule observes: "We see that mosolin or muslin had a very different meaning from what it has now."

DIVISION 34 COTTON: MUSLINS.

These and such like passages have been quoted time after time, by numerous writers, in order to justify the antiquity of the Indian art in weaving fine cotton goods. It may, therefore, suffice for the purpose of this work to at once deal with the chief centres of production and the goods displayed at the Exhibition.

Plain Muslins.—The muslins of Dacca have long been famous and received poetic names to denote their great beauty, such as the *mulmul khas*—the king's muslin, the *ábrawán*—running water (because if placed in a stream it could scarcely be seen), *baft hana*—woven air (because if thrown in the air it would float like a cloud), *shab-nam*—evening dew (a name given because if placed wet on the grass it could hardly be seen). The above and many such like names denote the great beauty and extreme delicacy of the Dacca muslins.

Poetic names.

The most exhaustive work on Dacca muslins and to this day the only satisfactory account of the industry concerned, is undoubtedly that written by Dr. James Taylor (*Descriptive and Historical Account of the Cotton Manufactures of Dacca*) and published by John Mortimer in 1851. Speaking of the fineness of the thread he remarks that "a skein which a Native weaver measured in my presence, in 1846, and which was afterwards

Early Account.

DIVISION 34. COTTON: MUSLINS. carefully weighed, proved to be in the proportion of upwards of 250 miles to the pound of cotton." Dr. Taylor then goes on to explain that the shortness of the Dacca cotton renders it unsuited to machine spinning but nevertheless the local muslin spinners were unable to use the American cotton which was given them for experiment and claim that the local fibre is superior for this purpose. The tendency of the fibres to expand with moisture is the criterion by which the Native spinner judges the quality of cotton. A common remark by the Dacca weavers, Dr. Taylor adds, is that the English yarn swells on bleaching, while Dacca spun thread shrinks and becomes stronger the more frequently it is subjected to that process.

Peculiarity of Dacca Cotton.

In Dacca muslins there are usually more threads in the warp than in the woof, the latter being to the former, in a piece weighing 20 tolas, in the proportion of 9 to 11. One end of the warp (as in mummy-cloths) is generally fringed, four or five threads being twisted together and knotted. The value of a piece of plain muslin is estimated by its length and the number of threads in its warp, compared with its weight. The greater the length and number of threads and the less the weight, the higher the price. It has been pointed out, however, that if a piece of muslin be cut in two and one half dressed and the other not, the value of the former would be pronounced as considerably less than the latter, hence it is difficult, if not impossible, to estimate the relative fineness of two samples without knowing the treatment to which they have been subjected. It is extremely difficult by the eye to recognise the difference between muslins valued at R150 and those at R600 the piece. A popular method of testing fineness was to ascertain if the piece of cloth could be passed through a lady's finger ring. In the time of Jahangir, muslins 15 yards long and 1 yard wide were manufactured that weighed only 900 grains and cost £40. Tavernier states that the ambassador of Shah Safy (A. D. 1628—1641), on his return from India, presented his master with a muslin turban 30 yards in length, so exquisitely fine that it could scarcely be felt by the touch. It has often been contended that even at the present day the hand loom muslins of Dacca were finer than any produced by machinery.

Valuation.

Extreme Fineness.

This is a mistake. The finest Dacca muslins do not exceed four hundreds, whereas several manufacturers in England can and do produce six hundreds. The demand for such goods is, however, exceedingly limited and steam power is never likely, therefore, to be employed in their production. The limited demand is the Indian hand labourer's chief safety with many of his artistic manufactures. **DIVISION 34. COTTON: MUSLINS.**

The finest of all the Dacca muslins used formerly to go under the name of *Mulmul Khas*—"the king's muslin"—(a name applied to all fine muslins nowadays whether Indian or foreign). This is made by the Dacca weavers in lengths of approximately 10 yards by 1 yard and it may contain from 1,000 to 1,800 threads in the warp. Such may occupy the weaver for at least five months and it can only be made during the rains when the moisture in the air enables the thread to be woven. It is said that as much as R50 per ounce may be paid for the yarn from which the finer muslins are woven. A price of R500 apiece would, therefore, not be exorbitant. At the Exhibition a fair assortment of fine muslins are shown by Sasi Mohan Basak of Nawabpur, Dacca, and also by Gokul Chandra Basak of Munshigunj, Dacca. The prices of these range from R150 to R600 for 10 yards (£4 per yard). **Humidity Essential.**

Figured Muslins.—The *Jamdani* or figured muslins have been spoken of as the *chef-d'œuvre* of the Indian weaver, and certainly they are the most artistic articles produced in Bengal. Dr. Forbes Watson in his most valuable work on the *Textile Manufactures and Costumes of the People of India* (p. 79) says that "from their complicated designs they have always constituted the most expensive productions of the Dacca looms. Those manufactured for the Emperor Aurangzeb are stated to have cost £31 whilst some manufactured in 1776 reached the extravagant price of £56 per piece. The manufacture of the finer *jamdanis* was long retained as a monopoly in the hands of the Government, the weavers, as stated by Raynal, being forbidden, under pecuniary and corporal penalties, to sell to any person a piece exceeding the value of 72 livres, or about three guineas. The Native or European merchants were obliged to **Figured Muslins.** **Prices.**

DIVISION 34. COTTON: JAMDANIS.

purchase these muslins through brokers specially appointed by Government." "In manufacturing figured (*jamdani*) fabrics," Taylor continues, "two weavers sit at the loom. They place the pattern, drawn upon paper, below the warp, and range along the track of the woof a number of cut threads equal to the flowers or parts of the design intended to be made; and then, with two small fine-pointed bamboo sticks, they draw each of these threads between as many threads of the warp as may be equal to the width of the figure which is to be formed. When all the threads have been brought between the warp they are drawn close by a stroke of the lay. The shuttle is then passed by one of the weavers through the shed, and the weft having been driven home, it is returned by the other weaver. The weavers resume their work with their pointed bamboo sticks, and repeat the operations with the lay and shuttle in the manner above described, observing each time to pass the flower threads between a greater or less number of the threads of the warp, in proportion to the size of the design to be formed."

Manipulation.

Patterns seen in Jamdanis.—The dominant feature of these art fabrics is unquestionably designs that are commonly accepted as Persian in origin. The fabric is usually grey cotton, ornamented with blue-black designs or occasionally with brightly coloured cottons and gold and silver wire. When made in the form of *sárís* the ends have large bold corner pieces, almost invariably developments of the cone (shawl) pattern. The field of these *sárís* has as a rule numerous small bunches or sprays of flowers, the most common being a circular design which suggests the jasamine (*chameli*). On one side is the tubular flower with its spreading petals and around and below are leaves that recall those of the sweet-smelling *sambak*. These and such like sprays may be scattered all over the surface or grouped in diagonal lines. The former condition is called *bútidar*, the latter *tercha* and when the floral ornamentations form a net-work that covers completely the field, the *jamdani* is spoken of as a *jalár*. At other times the poetic name of *panna hazara* or "thousand emeralds" is given when the sprays of flowers are connected together like the settings of a jewel; so also the

Persian Patterns.

Definition of Terms.

expression *phulwar* is used when a running floral pattern covers the entire field. When the flowers are large and life-like the *jamdani* is designated a *toradar*. DIVISION 34. COTTON : JAMDANIS.

The terms used to denote floral and other designs in *jamdanis* are identical with those employed in all other figured textiles. For example, *búti* is a single flower or figure not connected by a trellis or *jali*, or *búta* when the flowers are large. The various flowers depicted are denoted by further appellations, such as *chameli búti* (jasamine flowered), *gul daudi búti* (chrysanthemum flowered) and *genda búti* (or marigold flowered). When circular, the *búti* would be described as *chanda*, and *turanj* is the name for the so-called cone-pattern of the Kashmir shawls. A *pan-búti* would be heart-shaped like the betel leaf. *Fardi-búti* denotes minute spots or dots. *Tara-búti* is a star-shaped speck. *Jamewar-búti* generally denotes flowers of a large size arranged in rows. *Búti jhar-dar* denotes sprays of flowers.

Chief Jamdanis on View.

At the Exhibition a large assortment of all these forms of *jamdanis* and many others may be seen in the form of *sáris*, but the following are specially commended:—No. 182, a *Nilambari Jarao Shapa Terchi* with the diagonal floral pattern worked in wavy silver lines on a pure black texture. This was made by Gokal Chandra Basak of Rupganj, near Dacca. It has obtained a bronze medal and is valued at R500. No. 144, an *Asrafi Buter Chhit Jari* made by Sasi Mohan Basak of Dacca. No. 121, *Jarao Asrafi Buter Karchopi*, also made by Sasi Mohan Basak. It is much like the preceding, except that it is embroidered with flat massive gold wire heavily laid on the surface and bent backwards and forwards at the points of attachment. The central field flower has a cross in gold worked over it and the cone patterns are similarly overlaid with gold as if an afterthought. No. 171, *a Terch-Asrafi Miltheti*, made by Shaik Matabdi of Dacca and valued at R357. The field is covered with diagonal lines of black cotton flowers with, running across these, upright bands of gold rosettes and spots woven into and not embroidered ever the fabric. The corner pieces are so Names of Exhibitors.

DIVISION 34. COTTON: JAMDANIS.

large that they flow together and cover the end of the *sári.* They are boldly outlined in gold wire interwoven with the black and Indian-red cotton, the latter colour being toned down by the warp of dull grey cotton. This is a charming piece of work and is respresentative of an extensive series of highly artistic fabrics that have given Dacca an honourable position among the famed seats of the world's art productions. No. 189 is a silk *jamdani*, that is to say a grey cotton *sári* with the floral weft pattern in pale old gold silk. The blue cotton is also sparingly used and of a much paler and more artistic shade than is usually seen. This was made by Behari Lal Basak of Dacca. No. 185 is a *Jarao Jamdani Rumal* made by Radha Ballakh Basak of Dacca. This is a beautiful gauze texture in grey cotton with four bands of black scrolls having gold rosettes at close intervals. No. 143 is also a *rumal* or square sheet in *jamdani* made by Sasi Mohan Basak of Dacca. This is representative of a large series that may be seen at the Exhibition. These squares of flowered muslins, as they are sometimes called, have been used with a charming effect as table covers placed above some brilliantly coloured cloth to show up the rich design of the *jamdani*.

Squares or Rumals.

Embroidered Jamdanis.

Jamdanis may be elaborately embroidered with brightly coloured floss silks. This is mostly in bad taste; it rarely follows in any way the pattern of the *jamdani* and thus appears as an after-thought. They are, however, regularly produced, and are usually described as *Reshmi Karchopi Sárís.* The embroidery is done in blue, purple, green, scarlet and gold worked by satin-stitch into large rosettes, within glaring diapers of green that are at utter variance with the beautiful *jamdani* diapers below.

Nilambaris.

Occasionally and more especially with the cheaper *jamdanis*, brilliant colours are used. No. 11 is a white *sári* with the pattern in red, yellow and blue-black cotton, worked in a large and bold wavy design across the fabric. These coloured *jamdanis* are often woven on black cotton with massive designs in green, orange, ochre, yellow and white. No. 125 is an example of a *Nilambari Sári* of this kind. The corner pieces are in the usual cone-pattern, the outlines of the flowers, etc., being in yellow and red and the background dull green in massive patches above the black texture. This was made by Sasi Mohan Basak of Dacca and is priced at R40. From these and such like *jamdanis* the transition to the next group is only a matter of difference in price and the consequent loss of all expensive elaborations. **DIVISION 34. COTTON: JAMDANIS.**

It may be added in conclusion that a serious mistake has arisen through writers on Indian Arts transferring the *jamdanis* from woven to embroidered fabrics, the use of the expression "loom embroideries" having been thought sufficient distinction. But a consequence of this has been the entire destruction of the study of embroidery as a separate branch of Indian Art—a result highly undesirable. The reader should, therefore, consult the chapter on "Embroidery" for the *kasida* and *chikan* embroideries of Dacca—embroideries that by some writers have been dealt with conjointly with the *jamdanis.* **Loom Embroidery.**

Howrah and Santipur Coloured Muslins.—*Sáris* mainly in black or dark-blue muslin, or perhaps rather gauze, with brightly coloured (*jamdáni*) flowers are produced in Nadia, at the town of Santipur and elsewhere in Bengal, and are sold so extensively in Howrah as to become a feature of the cloth bazars of that town. The colours are often too brilliant to be artistic, but the assortment available both in scheme and design is so very extensive that a selection of a dozen highly artistic pieces becomes possible. They have been used by Europeans for bed-room curtains, especially those with white or grey ground colour and pink flowers. In the Exhibition a large assortment will be found and as they are extremely cheap and effective they are worthy of special attention. **Cheap Coloured Muslins.**

In Chittagong and elsewhere blue-black muslin *sáris* are largely made that show longitudinal (warp) stripes in Indian red, orange and green. This is usually called *Donga Kapur.* But striped muslins and other textiles of a much higher order are produced all over the country and are known as *Durias* or *Charkhanas.* No. 106 is a *Jarao Duria Dochesma* in which the stripes are black on one side and red on the other. No. 156

DIVISION 34. COTTON : JAMDANIS. is the very abundant *Azizullah* fabric woven of cotton and *muga* silk in alternate stripes.

Centres. In the ***United Provinces*** the town of Sikandrabad in the district of Bulandshahr; Mau in Azamgarh: Mahmudnagar in Lucknow; Jais in Rai Barelli; Tanda in Fyzabad; Mamudi in Hardoi; and Benares are famous for their plain, striped and flowered muslins.

Mr. Silberrad (Monograph *Cotton Fabrics*, p. 32) gives a most instructive description of the *jamdanis* of Tanda. The body of the muslin is a fine *tanzeb* (as already described) and the pattern is elaborated by a series of special weft threads from a series of spools left dangling from the web at their required positions. These are run through the desired number of warp threads two at a time, the heddles are then raised or depressed as the case may be and the shuttle weft sent across and back again. In this way the pattern is produced and in Indian muslin it is always brocaded on the surface of the fabric and in consequence more closely resembles needle-work, than is the case with power loom woven flowered muslins of Europe.

In the ***Panjab***, muslins used formerly to be largely produced at Delhi and to some extent are still made at Rhotak.

Rajputana has one or two localities that have a high reputation for muslins. Of these the foremost place has to be given

Kota. to KOTA. It would appear that the yarn at present used by both the Hindu and Muhammadan weavers of that State is, however, imported from Europe. A large assortment of these goods is shown at the Exhibition and have attracted considerable attention, though few only have been sold. They are exhibited by Bohrab Rajab Ali of Kota.

Chanderi. CHANDERI near GWALIOR and the town of Gwalior itself have similarly the reputation of turning out high class muslins; the Gwalior being mostly checked and figured. The border in Chanderis is usually silk and gold, the silk being double woven so that it shows two colours, one on each side. One of the best Chanderi muslins is No. 3123, a *saya* muslin, pale flesh-coloured, woven with gold wire. The border on one side is about 2½ inches broad and primarily referred to squares with a sort of tree-of-life pattern flowing by its branches from one square to the other. The end-piece is also elegantly woven with gold, the pattern being quaint. It proceeds from a small minute-like medallion and is thrown off obliquely to left in a long much branched and flowering arm, each spray being about 5 inches long and four of them cross the breadth of the fabric. **DIVISION 34. COTTON: JAMDANIS.**

INDORE and SARANGPUR produce unbleached muslins of considerable beauty.

Madras Presidency.—The town of ARNI in NORTH ARCOT is well known for its fine muslins, of which a fair series will be found in the Exhibition. The demand for these goods has in recent years declined very seriously. Colonel George Bidie wrote a long and interesting report on this industry which has been reprinted time after time since; the chief feature of which may be said to be that the cotton while being spun is kept damp by being stored in the green rind of the plantain stem and the yarn while being woven is also kept damp. It would appear that six hundred threads (*sindus*) are used in the weft of each piece of 16 yards long and 1½ yards wide, and are starched five times. It will thus be seen that the finest Arni muslins are about two or three times coarser than the best Dacca muslins.

Other muslins that have a high local fame are Adoni, Kampti, Madura and Tanjore and the satinettes of Ayyampet. The Venkatagiri muslin is mostly used for turbans; it is white with gold or coloured bands.

AWARDS FOR DIVISION 34.—COTTON.

First Prize with silver medal to Sasi Mohan Basak of Dacca for white muslins (plain). **AWARDS.**

First Prize with silver medal to Sheik Matabdi of Dacca for patterned muslin.

Second Prize with bronze medal to Gokal Chandra Basak of Dacca, for patterned muslins.

Commended for patterned muslins—Rada Ballabh Basak of Dacca.

Division 35.—Silk.

It would be wholly beyond the scope of a Catalogue, intended mainly to direct attention to the chief articles on view at the

DIVISION 35. SILK.

Indian Art Exhibition, to indulge in any lengthy discussion as to the origin of the sericulture of India. As in Hebrew so in Sanskrit, the greatest possible confusion exists as to the early names and synonyms that should be viewed as denoting silk. It is probably not far, therefore, from correct to affirm that all the undoubted references to mulberry silk, in early Hindu literature speak of it as an imported article and further that it is not until comparatively modern times that we have direct indications of a fairly extensive silk production in India. It is possible, however, that the *tasar* silk of Northern and Central India and the *eri* and *muga* silk of Assam may have been known and manufactured long anterior to the introduction of the mulberry-feeding insect.

Historic Facts.—Sir George Birdwood gives a most graphic and poetic sketch of the classic references to silk. Many other writers have followed in his footsteps and given *their* versions of the same story, each advocating some special aspect of interest or stating the arguments in favour of a particular view. The perusal of the literature of this subject leaves one or two facts in one's mind as significant and instructive. For example, so far as the classic literature of Europe is concerned, silk came originally from Serice (China) and carried with it its Corean name *sír* (in some form or other) into the languages of the countries to which the fibre or its textiles were conveyed.

Origin of the name.

The cultivation of silk in Europe was established by the Emperor Justinian about the year 550 A. D. He induced two monks to convey the eggs from China to Constantinople. From Greece it spread to Italy and later to France. The manufacture of silk in England, which dates from the time of Henry VI, received its greatest impetus through the Edict of Nantes in 1685, an edict that drove many of the best workmen of France to take refuge in England where they established the silk industry of Spitalfields.

Influence of the East India Company.

Though the East India Company need not be viewed as having introduced mulberry silk cultivation into India, it was through their strenuous efforts that it became an established industry in the plains, and that an export trade was organised both in raw and manufactured silks. Silk was doubtless largely imported by land routes from China, long anterior to its production having been attempted. But it is significant that no absolutely certain reference to silk occurs in the Vedas. In the *Mahabharata*, silk is mentioned among the presents brought by the Chiefs of India to their Paramount Lord. But there is nothing to prove that these offerings were not imported silks or even textiles derived from the *tasar* or other wild worms. It is thus by no means certain that such allusions prove the existence in India of an indigenous mulberry silk industry.

DIVISION 35. SILK.

It is, however, quite possible and indeed highly probable that several attempts may have been made to introduce the mulberry silk industry into India long anterior to the systematic endeavours of the East India Company. The writer, for example, found in 1882, during an exploration of Manipur, that not only were mulberry trees plentiful in that State, but that the true mulberry silk insect was also abundant in a semi-wild condition. There is little or nothing, however, to justify the supposition that this introduction within the geographical area of India, was brought about by the East India Company, more than that the forests of Manipur, which were found to contain a large percentage of tea trees, manifest the remains of a former tea industry, established by Europeans and long since forgotten. Manipur, from its very geographical position, may have had repeated interchanges with China, but the traffic between India and China was never, so far as is known, conducted through that State. Manipur might easily have had, unknown to the rest of India, a mulberry silk industry many centuries before India proper received that insect. But it is interesting to have to add that nowhere along the North-West Frontier (within the land routes of ancient communication with India) are there either mulberry trees or the mulberry-feeding silk-worm, except under the most careful cultivation.

Manipur Silk.

Lastly, the comparative silence of historians, as also of monograph writers, on the subject of the efforts to introduce or extend the cultivation of the silk-worm, during the various Muhammadan dynasties of India, is to say the least of it remarkable and goes a very long way towards the conviction that until the advent of the

Influence of the Mughals.

DIVISION 35. SILK.

East India Company mulberry silk growing was nowhere in India an important industry.

Wild Silks.

Forms of silk met with in India.—In addition to a fairly extensive series of races of mulberry-feeding worms, India has three well-known indigenous silk-worms, *viz.*, the *Tasar*, the *Muga* and the *Eri*. The first mentioned is widely distributed, being met with in all the lower hill tracts of the great table-land. It has, however, proved intractable or difficult of domestication. The cocoons are simply placed on the jungle trees on which the worm feeds and protected as far as possible from their enemies. The cocoons are reeled, but with considerable difficulty and great loss. *Tasar* textiles are usually of a dull or grayish straw colour, when not dyed, and are of a stiff texture. The second insect is confined to Assam and Eastern Bengal, and is more or less domesticated. It feeds on a species of laurel and yields a rich golden coloured silk that is fairly extensively employed in the art crafts of India. The last mentioned insect also exists in a state of semi-domestication. It is reared on the castor oil plant, but the fibre is devoid of the gloss and other properties, specially desired in silk by Europeans at least, so that a limited market exists and has always done so, for this particular fibre. It is reared chiefly in Eastern Bengal and Assam and to a certain extent in the United Provinces also. It is spoken of in the trade

"Herba."

as "Assam Silk," but was apparently the "herba" of the East India Company's returns and of the earlier reports and books of Indian travel. The writer was formerly of opinion that "herba" might have been the name of Rhea fibre. This he now thinks improbable. In 1679 the Madras Agent of the East India Company ordered 600 pieces of a textile which he explained "was called *arundee* made neither with cotton nor silk but of a kind of *herba* spun by a worm that feeds upon the leaves of the tree called *arundee*, which bears a round prickly berry of which oyle is made." There can be no doubt but that the "herba" there indicated was *eri* silk.

Forms of Wild Silk.

Under each of the wild species of silk there are several easily recognisable forms and these yield different qualities or kinds of silk, but except in the condition of the carded and spun silks that are employed fairly largely in the manufacture of velvets or plushes, it cannot be said that any one of the three (in spite of all the efforts that have been expended on them) have assumed or are likely to assume a position of importance in European commerce. From an art point of view the *muga* silk is the most interesting; since it is the silk employed in the *kasida* embroideries, shortly to be described, and moreover can be spun readily; while the *tasar* is difficult to spin and *eri* so exceedingly difficult that it is nearly always carded and spun. **DIVISION 35. SILK.**

Chief Manufactures.—It might be possible to classify the silks of India under two or three standards, for example, (*a*) the purpose for which woven—a *Sári, Dopatta, Rumal, Lungi,* etc; or (*b*) the nature of the textile—Plain or Figured Piece-goods, *e.g.*, Gauzes, Satins, Brocades or *Kinkhábs*, etc.; and (*c*) the localities of production. It may serve the purposes of this publication to dispose of all the ordinary goods, province by province, and to reserve the brocades or *Kinkhábs* for special treatment. It may also simplify the remarks that follow to commence with the United Provinces first, then to pass to the Panjab, Bengal, the Central Provinces, Rajputana and Central India, Bombay, Madras and last of all Burma. **Classification.**

Plain, Striped, Checked and Flowered Silks.

United Provinces.—The display of silk goods from Benares, Mirzapore, Azamgarh, Jalaun, Agra, Meerut, Allahabad, Budaun, etc., is so extensive and the information furnished along with these so varied and instructive, while, at the same time, the literature available regarding the silk industries of these Provinces is so voluminous, that it is next to impossible to compress into a few sentences anything like a satisfactory account of the interests involved or of the articles turned out. Mr. A. Yusuf Ali's most admirable monograph (largely drawn upon in the remarks that follow) runs to over 100 pages of closely printed matter and with its illustrations will be found highly interesting, but even that work is by no means exhaustive. **Centres.** **Literature Consulted.**

The silk fabrics of India may be studied according to two standards, *viz.*, the method of weaving or the patterns produced. In the present article the attempt will be made, as far as possible, to embrace both these features of interest, and the remarks that follow may be accepted as applicable fairly generally to the whole of India, not to the United Provinces only.

Comparison with Cotton.

Designs.—In connection with the account already given of the Flowered Muslins (*Jamdanis*), an effort will be found to have been made to define some of the more generally accepted names for the chief floral designs met with in that class of goods. The Flowered Silks will be described below under the heading of "Brocades," so that there remains to be discussed in the present position, the silk goods that might be described as holding a parallel position with the damask cottons.

In continuation, therefore, of the account of the various styles of cotton goods and of the patterns seen in these, it may serve a useful purpose if the terms more especially employed for the corresponding silk goods be here discussed. The simplest form is the stripe: when longitudinal or done in the warp the fabric is called *Doriya*; when across the width or in the weft, it is called *Salaidar*; when the lines are both in the warp and weft, the pattern becomes a check-*charkhana*; when the lines are diagonal, the fabric is spoken of as *Are-doriya*; when wavy or zig-zag, the fabric is *Khanjaredar*; when a series of small lozenge-shaped figures are formed by diagonal lines, the pattern is called *Ilayecha* and if the lozenges formed enclose a dot, often in gold wire, the pattern is called *Bulbul-chashm* (or nightingale's eye).

Stripes.

Checks.

Double lines with a running scroll or geometric pattern between, is called a *mothra*. This is used on the borders of *sáris*, etc., or as a division in some elaborate design. The term *bél* is the generic term for borders, but it is more specially applicable to running or floral scrolls. The term *aribel* is applied to borders of a wavy or zig-zag form.

Borders.

Flowered.

The word *bûti* denotes a flower, but when the flower is large it is denominated *bûta*. A running pattern of flowers or leaves, all over the textile, is designated *phulwar*. The term *jál* is given when lines, scrolls or other devices form meshes and enclose sprays of flowers (*bûta*). Lastly, when gold or silver is used as the field texture and the floral ornamentations are woven in coloured silks

DIVISION 35. SILK OF UNITED PROVINCES.

(such as in the *kinkhábs*) the design is spoken of as *minatashi* (or enamelled fabrics). It may be recollected that in the opening observations to this Class (page 238), the suggestion has been made of the possible comparison that may be made between the various forms of metallic and textile ornamentation, and it is pretty certain such comparison has existed in the minds of the Indian craftsmen and has thus doubtless influenced them in the elaboration of the designs that are now to be met with in both metals and textiles.

Comparisons.

Colours.—It is a common error to suppose that in Indian Art designs, pale or neutral colours must be and have always been used. This opinion doubtless arose from the preference shown for old rather than new carpets, brocades and shawls. That these and such like goods are better woven and more artistically designed than are modern examples, goes without saying, but the effect of time in toning down their colours appears always to be forgotten. Bright colours may in fact be described as a distinctive feature of most Indian arts, but unfortunately this very feature has been exaggerated by the modern facility in aniline dyes.

Aims of Decorative Art.

The essence of decorative art may be said to be conventionalism—the poetry of arts as it might be defined. It does not follow that in the scheme of colours adopted, the leaves in a floral design need be green any more than that the flowers and fruits must of necessity originate at their true positions botanically. To secure the effect and feeling not absolute adherence to every condition of nature is the aim of this branch of art. The flowers may, therefore, be brightly coloured and the leaves yellow or any other colour that may prove the complement to the stronger tints. Perhaps the most striking feature of Indian Art may be said to be this masterly treatment of colour in which the response and balance is invariably complete. Sir George Birdwood says "when the same form is used all over a fabric, the interchange of light and shade, and the effect of alternation, are at once obtained by working the ornament alternately in two tints of the same colour. Each object or division of an object is painted in its own proper colour, but without shades of the colour,

DIVISION 35. SILK OF UNITED PROVINCES.

or light and shade of any kind, so that the ornamentation looks perfectly flat and laid like a mosaic in its ground. It is in this way that the natural surface of any object decorated, is maintained in its integrity. This, added to the perfect harmony and distribution of the colouring, is the specific charm of Indian and Oriental decoration generally." In some of the gold and silk brocades presently to be discussed, in connection with Surat and Aurangabad, the toning down of bright colours is effected by the shading and outlining of the parts by complementary colours.

Balance in Colour.

There could perhaps be no more difficult subject of treatment than pure white marble. As seen in the Taj at Agra, however, the "Question" and "Answer" mosques in red sandstone, picked out in marble, give repose in colour as they balance in proportion the great tomb itself. "Beautiful as it is" says Fergusson "the Taj would lose half its charm if it stood alone. It is the combination of so many beauties and the perfect manner in which each is subordinated to the other, that makes up a whole which the world cannot match or which never fails to impress even those who are most indifferent to the effects produced by architectural objects in general." In the study of the coloured textiles of India, more especially the silk goods, harmony or balance in colours will be found cleverly accomplished. It is in fact with the scamped modern work only that this is neglected and such goods are in consequence glaringly vulgar. In the older textiles, where bright colours are employed, paler shades are invariably dispersed in such positions as to tone down or modulate the otherwise discordant note, with the result that it is not perceived colour effects have been produced, that would otherwise have risen from the surface and marred completely the design. With no other goods is this feature more strongly marked than in the flowered and coloured silks and the mixed silk and woollen or silk and cotton goods (the *himrus* and *jamawars*) presently to be described. In these, as a rule, minute patterns are assorted in severe lines, but monotony is saved and a charm accomplished mainly through the scheme of colours adopted.

Classification.

Chief Textiles.—The following may be given as the better known textiles procured in the United Provinces in which silk is exclusively or mainly used :— **DIVISION 35. SILK OF UNITED PROVINCES.**

1. *Brocades or kinkhábs (kamkhwabs).*—So far as these Provinces are concerned, *kinkhábs* are made at Benares only. They will be dealt with in a further paragraph.

2. *Pot Thán or Bafta.*—This is in reality a form of *kinkháb* in which the textile is more lightly woven and gold or silver wire more sparingly used. In fact the separation is one purely and simply in degree, between the *kinkhábs, baftas, amrus* and even the gold and silk gauzes or *abrawans.*

3. *Amru silks.*—May be described as a speciality of Benares, and are manufactured for persons whose purse will not allow them to procure *kinkháb* or *bafta* garments. In Europe they would be called brocades, but the line of separation between the *himrus* of the Deccan and the *amrus* of Benares is an extremely narrow one. The warp and weft in *himrus* are usually specially prepared cottons or they may be one or both in wool with the special flower wefts in silk mainly, but occasionally also in cotton. Many of the *amrus* produced in Benares have cotton or *tasar* silk warp and the special flower weft in a fine quality (mostly imported) of cotton yarn.

Mixed Fabrics. Fabrics of mixed textiles especially an admixture of silk are largely used by the Muhammadans in the manufacture of *pyjamas*, petticoats, etc. They may be in stripes of green, red, yellow, white and blue; or floral (jungle) patterns on various tints, such as *pistachio*-green, or *búti* patterns with the *chameli* or other flowers variously coloured on a dull background or in another shade of the same colour.

4. *Sangi.*—This class of goods may be spoken of as a speciality of Azamgarh, though produced also in Jalaun and Allahabad and to some extent in Benares as well. *Sangi* has already been incidentally alluded to in the chapter on Tie-dyeing. The wavy pattern (*khanjari*) worked across the *sangi* silks is a woven effect produced in order to imitate *mashru* or warp tie-dyed fabrics. **Two Threads.** The word *sangi* denotes the chief peculiarity of this series of textiles, namely the use, side by side, of warp threads treated together. In the *sangi* fabrics, the wavy line is carried on

DIVISION 35. SILK OF UNITED PROVINCES.

the surface until it might be said to simulate embroidery. They are either woven of pure silk or silk (often *tasar*) and cotton mixed, the warp being as a rule coarse and the weft fine. The most popular form is the *surkh zard*, or yellow *khanjari* on a red ground, and this is usually cotton and silk combined. A light red *sangi* has the yellow *khanjari* produced by a series of dotted lines as in the *gulbadan* textiles (presently to be described).

At times stripes or lines of *búti* work, in silk or gold wire, are woven across the *khanjari*. This is a speciality of Mubarakpur, near Azamgarh. So again *sangi nagshi* has a variegated series of *khanjari* stripes such as four small and two large in alternation.

Washing Silks.

5. *Gulbadan.*—This is a light texture fabric with a pattern much as in *sangi*, only that it is woven within the texture and not thrown on the surface. Sometimes also the warp threads are dyed in the manner described under the *mashrus* below.

Silks that answer to this name are produced all over Northern India and at one time were extremely popular and the manufacture gave employment to a large number of persons. The competition with European imported goods has however been very injurious to the indigenous craft. And moreover the cheaper and more attractive *sangi* textiles have also beaten the older and more expensive *gulbadan* work.

Tasar Weft.

When of pure silk, *gulbadans* are largely used by Hindus, or when mixed silk and cotton by Muhammadans. In the Aligarh *gulbadans*, the warp is of mulberry, and the weft of *tasar* silk. In the pure silk (*asli gulbadans*) of Karwi, the ground is red and the wavy lines white or green with white. The *susi* (or *char-khana*) checked and the *doriya* striped *gulbadans* are by some writers spoken of as distinct, but there seems no particular object in separating them—the difference is one in degree more than in technique, and with fabrics that may be of pure silk, of pure cotton or of cotton and silk mixed, this seems unnecessary. So again we have the *ilayecha* striped silks of Agra that differ from the *doriyas* of Azamgarh and Bulandshahr in quality only, the *ilayecha* being closer and better woven.

Tie-dyeing.

6. *Mashru.*—As explained in the chapter on tie-dyeing, the peculiarity of this kind of goods is that the warp has been tie-

dyed. The word *mashru* is taken to mean "permitted," and has reference to the observance (*fatwa*) that prohibits the use of pure silk for Muhammadans, except ladies or for men on special occasions.

Mashru work is expensive, but it is the most beautiful of all the forms of *khanjari*. It is largely produced at Benares, Azamgarh and Jalaun.

Satinettes.

7. *Ghatta or Satinette.*—This fabric is the speciality of several towns in Azamgarh district. Mr. Yusuf Ali derives the name "*ghatta*" from the Persian "*ghattidan*," to roll, and it would thus have reference to the chief process of producing the smooth glazed surface, characteristic of this class of goods, namely the passing of the cloth between hot rollers. They are of mixed cotton and silk but so calendered that the silk shows entirely on the upper surface. Of plain *ghattas*, pink is the favourite colour for women and yellow for men, or for wedding garments red with a yellow pattern, usually a *khanjari*. But they may be striped, checked or flowered.

The *ghatta* is in point of importance the silk fabric of these provinces that takes the place of the *gulbadans* of the Panjab. They are usually woven in pieces (*thans*) 9 yards long and 26 inches wide.

Gauzes.

8. *Abrawan* or Gauzes or Silk Muslins (*tanzeb*).—These are usually in plain colours, red or green, or they have patterns mostly small *bútis* or simply spots woven on them or specks produced by tie-dyeing. They are used by men for *kurtas*, and by women for *dupattas*, and are manufactured at Benares, Lucknow and Azamgarh.

CHIEF EXHIBITS ON VIEW.

Exhibits.

1. Muhamed Ibrahim of Mauza, Azamgarh, sends a beautiful series of silk muslins and gauzes as *dupattas*. These are admirably woven and will richly repay careful study.

2. Shaikh Karim Buksh, Satin Merchant, Azamgarh, contributes 12 samples of satin all brightly coloured but very well made.

3. Hafiz Shakrulla of Azamgarh sends a large collection of satinettes (in imitation *mashrus*,) also *ghattas*, *sangis*, etc. These are very excellent and some of them highly artistic.

DIVISION 35. SILK OF PANJAB.

They fully illustrate the foregoing observations on the kinds of silk produced in the United Provinces.

Panjab.—It will be found that so much detail has been indulged in, while discussing the silks of the United Provinces, that it becomes hardly necessary to do more than mention by name the silks of the other Provinces, except when special and

Centres.

peculiar goods are produced. The chief centres in the Panjab where both spinning and weaving silk are fairly important industries are :—Amritsar, Lahore, Patiala, Batala, Multan, Bhawalpur, Delhi, Jallandhar, Peshawar and Kohat. The names enumerated may be accepted as approximately denoting the relative values of these manufacturing centres. The bulk of the raw silk nowadays used, is imported from China *viâ* Bombay. Some few years ago it came from Bokhara *viâ* Peshawar. The quality of the silk goods has been lowered but the demand much increased, a far larger proportion of the people wearing silk than was customary a few years ago. The chief manufactures are as follows :—

Plain.

1. *Dariyais or Plain Silk goods.*—These are chiefly produced at Amritsar in pieces of 5 yards in length, and from 13 to 31 inches in breadth. They are in self colours but are often "shot" (*dhub-chan*).

Striped.

2. *Gulbadan.*—These are usually striped lengthwise. They are made to wash, and lustre is therefore not desired. They are usually pale green with scarlet stripes, dark green with scarlet, yellow with scarlet or crimson, purple with yellow, crimson with white or other such combinations. This kind of silk is much used by the wealthier Hindu and Sikh ladies for their closely fitting *pyjamas.*

Washing Silks for Europeans.

3. *Gardah or Gulbarra*—Is a term given to either *dariyai* or *gulbadan* silks when woven of fine counts. When made in white silk with stripes or checks in black, blue, or brown silk, it is called *dariyai charkhana*—a class of goods apparently designed to meet a European demand. BHAWALPUR is noted for a special fabric woven of silk and cotton threads together and subsequently glazed like English chintz.

4. *Khes and Shiya-khanis.*—The damask, already briefly indicated under cotton by the name of *khes,* may also be made

in silk and either plain, coloured, striped or in mixed checkers. These differ from the *dariyai* goods in the style of loom (many treddled) upon which fabricated and the method of weaving adopted. They have often a floss silk lustre and are massive and soft, with gold and silver wire very often freely intermixed. The best known examples of silk *khes* are the *shiya-khanis* of which His Highness the Nawab of Bhawalpur will be seen to have contributed a most beautiful and varied series.

DIVISION 35. SILK OF PANJAB.

Silk Damasks.

Both in Bhawalpur and Multan, the striped silks produced (*shiya-khanis*) recall to some extent the *jamewars* of Kashmir and the Deccan. The stripes show running scrolls or herring-bone patterns on the surface of the alternating bands of colour.

Striped Shiya-khanis.

5. *Kanawaz*—Is the name given to a thick fabric woven of yarns made by a large number of strands. It much resembles the thick stuffs imported from Bokhara and is satiny or velvety to the touch though not woven as an *atlas* or *satan* (the Indian form of the word satin).

6. *Kauni or Kinara.*—This is the name given to border strips. They are very largely woven separately and are sewn to the borders and ends of *sárís* and other garments. These are largely produced at Lahore, Jhelum and Kohat.

Borderings.

7. *Lungis or Pagris.*—Though more a special form of garment than a distinctive style of silk fabric, it may be worth noting that *lungi* weaving has become an important industry in certain towns of the Panjab, such as Peshawar, Kohat, Multan, Ludhiana, Shahpur and Bhawalpur. In the Artizans' Gallery, Gholam Hossein of Peshawar will be seen engaged at his craft as *lungi* weaver. An assortment of his beautiful goods is displayed around him and in the Main Gallery a large series from the towns above mentioned will be found, chiefly those made by Haji Malik Rahman of Peshawar, Kishan Das and Tulsi Ram of Bhawalpur, and Abdul Jabar of Kohat.

Lungis.

They are usually woven of finely spun and starched cotton yarn, mostly foreign, are of a steel grey colour and have borders and end-pieces in blue or red silk with a large percentage of gold wire. The finer class *lungis* may be entirely of silk, and in Kohat the borders are usually in stripes of many colours richly

Cotton or Silk.

DIVISION 35. SILK OF PANJAB.

Table Covers.

assorted. The Kohat *lungi* weavers, of whom Abdul Jabar may be mentioned, have recently taken to weaving curtains, table covers and overmantel drapings in *lungi* fashion; these are very beautiful articles for household draping. A large series of these are on view at the Exhibition. Dove-coloured and lustreless *lungis* (*palas*) with gold borders and ends are extensively made at Jallandhar.

Kashmir Embroideries.

8. *Kashmir.*—Lastly, one of the most promising features of the modern silk trade of the Panjab may be said to be the promise of a future greatness in the silk production of Kashmir. This is due to the enlightened action of His Highness the Maharajah and his advisers. It thus seems probable that in the near future this Native State may take an even higher position in silk production than it has as yet done. As represented at the Exhibition, Kashmir silks have attracted most attention in the form of the superb series of curtains and drapings embroidered with silk that have been lent by His Highness the Maharajah.

Historic Facts.

Bengal.—This province early became intimately associated with the endeavours of the East India Company to organise a mulberry silk supply for England intended to take the place of the silk procured through the Levant Company from Turkey. Kashimbazar—the Company's Indian Factory in Bengal—was thus temporarily raised to a position of considerable commercial importance, which it lost as rapidly with the subsequent decline in the Bengal traffic, due to the remarkable success of the Italian and French endeavours to rear the silk-worm. Tavernier wrote of Kashimbazar in the 17th Century that it furnished 20,000 bales annually, each weighing 100 livres. But the silk carried from Kashimbazar by both the Dutch and English merchants was of the coarse kind known as "country wound" and was suited for but few of the English goods even then produced. This circumstance led to strenuous efforts to improve both the quality of the silk and the nature of reeling, with the result that a large industry rapidly developed in what was known as ***korah*** silks.

At the present day the Bengal silk manufactures of most importance are the steam power factory at Ultadanga, near Calcutta (owned and worked by a Gujarati Muhammadan and run exclusively for the Burmese market). Of the purely Native interests, the following manufacturing centres for *korah* and other silks may be given :—Murshidabad, Bogra, Bankura, Midnapur, for mulberry silks; and Burdwan, Manbhum, Singbhum and Lohardugga, for *tasar* silks. Of artistic work only two need, however, be specialised :— **DIVISION 35. SILK OF BENGAL.** **Centres.**

1. MURSHIDABAD.—Mr. N. G. Mukerji gives an interesting review of the silk industry of this district in the *Indian Art Journal* (Vol. V., Pt. 38). He there writes "what is commonly, and everywhere, known as 'Berhampore Silk' is manufactured in four different centres. These are: Baluchar, Mirzapur, Khagra, and Islampur—all in the district of Murshidabad. Besides these four principal centres there are hundreds of villages throughout the district where pierced cocoons are employed for obtaining a coarse thread used in making *matkas*, of which the trade is very extensive." The *matka* textiles are in much demand by the Jains and other communities who object to taking life in order either to procure food or dress. The common sort of *matkas* are, however, made with silk waste and may be woven in stripes or checks. They are largely worn by the poorer classes who desire a silk *chadar*. They are also extensively exported to Assam. **Matkas.**

The name *korah* usually denotes plain, undyed silk piece goods. They are ordinarily made in lengths of 5 yards, but larger pieces up to 50 yards may be had. In width they are about 42 inches and may contain only 1,000 warp threads or as many as 2,400. The price is regulated by the number of threads in the warp. *Korah* silk handkerchiefs with striped borders are largely produced. Those known as *phulikat* are chiefly intended for the Rangoon market. **Korahs.**

But the *korah* silks may be striped as in the *rekhi* and *dhari* silks; or they may be checked (*chaukara*) as in the *matras* and *charkhanas*. It seems probable that most of the designs met with in Murshidabad and presumed to be purely indigenous, may be in reality survivals of art conceptions given to the district by the East India Company. Some few years ago the writer had the good fortune to be able to secure a most valuable treasure, now deposited in the Industrial Museum of Calcutta. This consists **Art Conceptions.** **Historic pattern book.**

DIVISION 35. SILK OF BENGAL.

of a pattern book kept by the officers of the Company as a record of the goods sent apparently from the Murshidabad district. There are in the book 906 cuttings of silk goods—all different patterns or descriptions. Against each has been recorded the report furnished either from home or communicated from Calcutta to the local officers. Some patterns are described as "Good," others "Bad," or it is observed that this and that "will not do," that the "olive of the ground colour is not approved," that "the pattern would do if the ground colour was clearer," that "the colours are bright and the patterns all approved," that others are "too dull" or again "not sufficiently lively," while still others are characterised as "middling." There are two records that furnish dates in the book as follows:—"The following patterns received from the Sub-Export Warehouse Keeper in his letter of the 28th April 1809," the other "3rd May 1805." The samples might be assorted under three groups in correspondence with the goods produced in India to-day, *viz.*,

Old designs.

1st—Murshidabad *Matras* and *Charkhanas*.

2nd—Azamgarh (*Ghattas*), Surat and Ahmedabad striped satinettes,

3rd—*Gulbadans* and *Sanglis* of the United Provinces and the Panjab.

In one or two instances the patterns are classified into "Soocs, Moosrsios, Moosrs, Alatcheigs, Alatchios and Alatches." What precise meaning could be attached to some of these terms the writer fails to perceive. They are doubtless mostly derived from the Turkish word that denotes a stripe. In Gujarat and Sind names are given to silks that recall some of these old East India trading terms, such as the *Atlash* and *Ailacho* silks of Sind. The *Soocs* seem to be striped *gulbadans* (or *dariyai charkhanas*); the *Moosrsios* are cotton satinettes; the *Moosrs* are silk satinettes; and the *Alatcheigs* have the flowers worked within the stripes (*mothra*) much as in the *jamewars* of Kashmir and the *himrus* of the Deccan. But without exception all the fabrics shown are striped along the length, not transverse to the warp, and there is no instance of a check amongst the lot. The stripes may be either narrow lines of colour alternating or such may form the boundary lines to strips usually with white as the ground colour upon which flowers in red or other shades are worked. This is the case in the series called *Alatcheig* the floral strips being made to alternate with a plain ground colour. Wavy lines are common but they are woven, that is, are never done by tie-dyeing, as in the *mashrus*, and they are confined within lines such as have been mentioned, or they cover the whole field, the *khanjari* being usually in pink on a white ground. **DIVISION 35. SILK OF BENGAL.**

If it be held that the pattern book shows the goods proposed to be exported from England to India, then it would appear that the present trade is a survival of an old industry, that the Company's imports simulated. In either case the intimate relationship of the East India Company with the Bengal silk traffic, and the magnitude of that traffic, is abundantly upheld by the circumstance that a pattern book, that most probably did not cover more than a period of 10 years, could contain a series of silks so extensive and diversified as that briefly indicated. It may be added that the pattern book was found in the house of a grandson or great-grandson of a clerk formerly in the employment of the Company's Agent at Berhampore. But the puzzle of puzzles is to grasp the reason of the one design being considered good and another bad. By most persons the "bad" would to-day be pronounced superior to the "good," so that without some knowledge of the purpose for which these minutely striped silks were exported, the standard on which they were judged cannot be discovered. **East India Company's Trade.** **Standard of Art Conceptions.**

Printed silks in the form of *nambali* handkerchiefs or *chadars* were formerly produced, but have been discontinued. They contained certain religious symbols or texts printed in brick-red over a yellow or golden coloured soft *korah* silk. **Printed Silks.**

Of the localities named above, the town of BALUCHAR has always enjoyed the reputation of producing the most artistic goods. On the opposite side of the river stands the town of Azamgunj which, like Baluchar, is largely occupied by wealthy Jains, many of whom are silk merchants. This circumstance doubtless accounts for the artistically woven fabrics and tie-dyed goods of Baluchar and Azamgunj, and for the intimate **Influence of Gujarat.**

DIVISION 35. SILK BROCADES OF BENGAL. relationship that exists between these towns in Bengal and the province of Gujarat. But it may be added that the famous silks of Baluchar are not produced in the town itself but in the numerous villages of that neighbourhood. Of these Bahadarpur holds the foremost position since it was the birth-place of Dubraj, the most famous of the Baluchar weavers.

Baluchar Brocades. Since Mr. N. G. Mukerji wrote his paper on Murshidabad silks, Dubraj, the master-weaver, has died. It is thus feared that the Baluchur *bútidars* (flowered *sárís*) of the future will scarcely equal those of the past. But at the Exhibition a large assortment will be found, contributed by Tinkari Saha, Durga Sankar Bhattacharji, and S. S. Bagchi, all of Baluchar, in Murshidabad. Many of these are very beautiful but cannot be compared with the *sárís* made by Dubraj, that may be seen in the Loan Collection Gallery and in the Industrial Section of the Indian Museum of Calcutta. What may be a surprise to most persons, however, is the fact that the Murshidabad *bútidars* were not considered **Made also at Ahmedabad.** by the Exhibition Judging Committee as equal to the corresponding goods sent by Parbhudas Patigara from Ahmedabad. It will thus be seen that the art of weaving this peculiar class of brocades or flowered shawls and scarves, is by no means confined to Murshidabad.

The ground colour of the characteristic Murshidabad *bútidar* is usually a deep purple (or dark red shot with blue), the pattern being elaborated by special weft threads of white, red, orange or green. Mr. Mukerji's coloured illustrations 9 *a* and *b*, also 10, are true to the style but by no means up to the quality of many in the Calcutta Museum. The loom used in producing these silks does not materially differ from that employed by the Dacca weavers of cotton *jamdánis* and the designs are for the most part similar, *viz.*, strongly Persian in feeling and conception. On this point Mr. Mukerji says:—"As a rule there are two *nakshas* for **Manipulation.** the borders, two for the *buts*, two for the *anchla* or ornamental end-pieces and one for the beginning and finishing up. The draw-boy manipulates a 'harness cord' for the *buts*, the weaver puts in a thread for the *buts*. At the next operation, *viz.*, the putting in of a weft thread for the ground, the draw-boy does nothing, then the draw-boy manipulates a 'harness cord' for the border while the weaver puts in a thread. At the next operation again the draw-boy does nothing, while the weaver passes the shuttle to put in another weft thread for the ground. At each operation, therefore, time is spent by the weaver not only in his own manipulation, but also in watching those of the boy. For rich designs as many as fourteen *nakshas* are sometimes employed. It is easy, therefore, to imagine how a piece of 5 yards long and 42 inches wide can take as long as six months for a weaver and his boy to weave."

DIVISION 35. SILK OF CENTRAL PROVINCES.

Double Coloured Silks.

2. BANKURA.—In this district a peculiar form of double weaving has for long been practised that is by no means devoid of artistic merit. Silk *sárís* are made in two colours, say green and yellow or red and yellow, the weft threads of the two surfaces being not kept absolutely distinct, so that the green surface looks as if shot in yellow and the yellow as if shot in green, so with all the other colours. The silk is also calendered so as to give it a soft satinette character. The chief drawbacks of this silk are its expense and defective weaving and dyeing—it is not uniform, so that a garment made of it has a patchy appearance.

Centres.

Central Provinces.—The most important branch of the silk craft, in these Provinces, is the production and utilization of *tasar* in Bilaspur, Raipur, Sambalpur and Chanda Districts. In the Sambalpur *tasar sárís*, the end-piece and borders are dyed yellow or crimson and occasionally blue.

Umrer Silks.

Mulberry silk is almost entirely imported from Bengal (except the minor supply which comes from Poona and is Chinese silk). It is fairly largely woven in Nagpur, Nimar and Bhandara Districts The major proportion is worked up into the well known borders for the cotton cloths [*dutis*, *lugras* (*sárís*) and *upernas* (scarves)]. As has already been incidentally mentioned, the Umrer *dutis* are famous all over a large portion of these Provinces, the dyers being specially successful in the tints they impart to the silk.

A fair amount of gold and silver wire is woven with the silk, in the borders and end-pieces of the better class goods of these Provinces. An extensive series will be seen in the Exhibition but except as examples of borders they hardly fall under the

DIVISION 35. SILK OF RAJPUTANA AND CENTRAL INDIA.

definition of Art Manufactures. In a further page, in connection with the subject of gold brocades, a brief notice will be discovered of Burhanpur silk *sárís* which may be accepted as completing the present brief reference to the silks of the Central Provinces.

Burhanpur.

Rajputana and Central India.—It is perhaps hardly necessary to devote a special chapter to the silks of these provinces. KOTA STATE and the town of CHANDERI in GWALIOR turn out a large amount of cotton *sárís* with silk or silk and gold borders. To some extent they also weave pure silk *sárís* richly adorned with gold borders and floral scrolls. Some of the Chanderi gauzes (*chadars*) have remarkably deep silk borders and these are double woven, brilliantly red on one side and deep blue on the other. A numerous assortment of Gwalior silk and cotton gauzes is on view. These are checked in gold and have broad end-pieces in gold with green, pink and purple flowers interwoven with the gold. These beautiful *sárís* have already been alluded to in the chapter devoted to "cotton muslins." In Kota the art of double dyeing is known and it is on record that silk *sárís* have been produced with crimson on one side and green on the other. The shot and rainbow coloured muslins and silk gauzes made by Bohra Raja Ali of Kota will be found fully represented by the series on view.

Centres.

Bombay and Sind.—Silk is manufactured in most towns of the Bombay Presidency, but with the exception of Bombay, Ahmedabad, Surat, Poona, Belgaum, Kolaba, Yeola and Thana, the goods turned out meet a purely local demand. If the *kinkháb* weaving be for the moment disregarded, as a speciality of Surat and Ahmedabad, it may be said that the silk goods produced by the towns of Gujarat are of a very ordinary character. This is somewhat significant, since (as observed in connection with Bengal and Madras) throughout a great part of India, even to the extreme south at Tinnevelly, the silk weavers claim to have come from Gujarat. They speak a language of their own that has been described as a dialect of Gujarati. The historic importance of Gujarat in the silk trade of India, is, therefore, an important factor to be considered, and, seeing that the mulberry silk-worm is not reared in that Province, the raw material must have always been imported

Association of Gujarat.

by sea and in the earlier days of the industry most probably to Surat by the Agents of the Dutch and British Trading Companies. **DIVISION 35. SILK OF BOMBAY.**

BOMBAY TOWN.—More recently and taking advantage of the cheap return freights from China, power loom mills have been established in Bombay that turn out a large amount of the spun silk goods that are sent to Burma. These mills also meet, to some extent, the special demands of the Bombay people and have doubtless largely undersold the hand-loom goods of the cheaper kind. In the Exhibition a set of the beautiful silk goods, turned out by the Sassoon and Alliance Silk Mill Co., Bombay, has been shown but not allowed to enter into competition with the Indian hand-loom manufactures, on the ground that the Exhibition was intended to exemplify Native Art Industries. According to the accepted definition of such, all power-loom goods produced by modern European appliances, whether worked by Natives or by Europeans and whether the patterns were of Indian or European origin, would be barred. **Sassoon Mills.**

The hand-loom weavers of Gujarat have for many years enjoyed a high reputation in the production of pure silk fabrics, plain, flowered and watered, and of mixed silk and cotton goods. Some few years ago, however, one of the largest silk merchants of England sent the writer samples of the particular kinds of goods that his firm were in the habit of importing from both France and Japan. He desired to have these circulated among the silk weavers of India in the hope of being able to open out an Indian market from which his firm might draw some portion of their annual supplies. The patterns were widely distributed and Indian corresponding goods procured. After the most careful inquiry it was found that the silks desired, as produced in India, were inferior in quality while being very much more expensive than the goods sent from Japan to England, to an annual value of over £1,000,000. The hope of Indian participation in the English market was thus reluctantly abandoned until such time as the Indian weavers have learned both to improve and cheapen their goods. **Gujarat Silks.** **Indian goods Inferior.**

These observations have been made here because much of the silk goods from the Bombay Presidency, on view at the Exhibition,

DIVISION 35. SILK OF BOMBAY.

such as the watered silks of Surat and the satinettes of Yeola, Poona and elsewhere, are very similar to the corresponding European goods and thus render comparison not only unavoidable but essential.

Poona Silks.

POONA.—For particulars regarding the Poona silk industry the reader should consult the *Gazetteer*. That article was written for 1885, and while true in all details it may be said that the industry has not since that date by any means prospered. For more recent particulars, Mr. S. N. Edwardes' monograph on the *Silk Fabrics of Bombay*, will be found most useful.

YEOLA.—The *pitámbars* (or *solas*) as also the *sáris* of Poona, Ahmedabad and Yeola, are known all over the Presidency. They are usually red, purple or yellow, or even green, blue or white, the Ahmedabad ones being very largely tie-dyed. One of the most ancient epithets for Vishnu is *Pitámbara* or the wearer of yellow garments. Mr. B. A. Gupte writes:—" The *paithanis* (female silk garbs), *pitámbars* (sacred cloths for males and females), *lugdis* (silk *sárís*), *phadkis* (female scarves) and *khans* (bodice pieces) from Yeola are in considerable demand among the higher classes of Natives, not only among the wealthy, who daily wear them, but also among those who appear in them only on festive occasions. The establishment of the industry at Yeola which now contains about 925 looms, dates from the beginning of the 18th Century when one Raghoji Naik, a relation of the present Patel, by the promise of a monopoly, induced a certain Shamdas Valji, a Gujarati bania, to bring silk weavers to settle at Yeola." This monopoly continued until abolished by a decision of the High Court on the 24th June 1864. (*See Bombay Gazetteer, Volume XVI., page 155.*) The silk used is imported from China, Bengal and Persia. The patterns are commonly taken from the *katári* dagger or the *bugdi* ear ornament, etc.

Yeola Silks.

Monopoly.

A narrow border is usually added to the *pitámbars* intended to be worn by men. Those used by females have broad borders and well formed end-pieces with often much gold wire. The field or centre of the *sári* may be ornate, the most frequent design being lines at right angles producing the checked (*chaukdi*) condition. The most beautiful *sáris* are those called *lugadis*.

DIVISION 35. SILK OF BOMBAY.

Thana Silks.

THANA silks were some few years ago better known to Europeans than were any of the other silks of the Presidency. The minute checked patterns and graceful geometric designs were produced by a process of double weaving. The goods were designed by Europeans and made mainly by Christians. When the fashion changed there was no further need for them, and moreover the few families that still produce these goods live on local sympathetic support more than on the merit of their goods. A full and instructive account of the Thana silk industry will be found in the District *Gazetteer*.

SURAT.—One of the most striking features of the Gujarat silk trade is the silk and cotton satinettes of Surat. These will be discussed in the chapter below devoted to "mixed fabrics," but in Surat a fairly large trade is also done in pure silk satinettes and in watered silks (both pure and mixed), very largely for the European and Hindu markets.

Chief qualities.

AHMEDABAD.—It would take many pages to give anything like a satisfactory account of the silk interests of this important and ancient capital of the silk and gold weaving crafts. The best known descriptions are the *magia* silks that are used in the preparation of *sáris*, the *khasi* silks and gold brocades (the *baftas* and *pot-tháns* of other parts of India). These are very expensive and often richly interwoven with gold. They will accordingly find a place along with the *kinkhábs* in the special chapter below devoted to that subject. But a large trade is also done in silk brocades without the use of gold—the *amrus* of other parts of India and in the silk and cotton mixed brocades—the *himrus*. At the Exhibition Parbhadas Rug Nath Petigara of Ahmedabad obtained a first prize with silver medal for brocaded silks, especially a *sári* which was pronounced equal to the finest old Baluchar *bútidars* of Murshidabad.

Silk brocades.

BARODA.—Under the chapter devoted to "Tie-dyeing" will be found a brief description of the *patola* silks of Baroda, Cambay and Surat, and the present brief abstract of the main artistic features of the silk industries of Bombay may, therefore, be concluded by the observation that the silk satins of KATHIAWAR, especially after being richly embroidered in their characteristic

DIVISION 35. SILK OF BOMBAY. fashion, are, for finish and delicacy of colour, hardly attained anywhere else in India. At the Exhibition it will be found that Lachman Das Bharanji of Amritsar has contributed a large assortment of Kathiawar embroidered silks and in Bhavnagar House an even finer series in the form of dresses, curtains, etc., may be seen.

JAMNAGAR, KACH.—In the Loan Collection two rather significant samples of *kinkhâbs,* sent from Sir Jamsetjee Jeejeebhoy School of Art, Bombay, are from Jamnagar. No. 1630 is described as a *dupeta* woven of orange red silk and gold, the latter being thrown almost completely on the upper side so as to form a diaper. On the reverse the diaper is in silk outlined in gold. The borders and end-pieces are attached. The former consists of two strips of silver in diaper pattern separated by narrow bands of red silk from a broad central band in gold diaper.

The end-pieces are woven with gold and silver; on the upper surface the *bútidars* are in silver on a gold field and on the under surface in gold on a silver field. The cones arranged in the centre of the terminal panel are floral, eight in number, but on the one extremity of the shawl the silver cones have the apex deflexed to the left, on the other to the right. This is a most significant peculiarity, but one that the writer is not aware to have observed in any other shawl. The deflection of the cone is usually to the left except when it appears as a corner piece or in other positions where symmetry dictates its inversion.

Sind.—Needle-work embroidered on silk and with silk thread is an important industry with the females of Sind. Silk weaving is chiefly carried on in the towns of TATTA and KARACHI. The quality of the goods recently produced has, however, been

Tatta Silks. much below that of former years. The silk fabrics best known are *garbi, gulbadan, atlas* and *ailacho.* The *garbis* and *ailachos* of Tatta were formerly in demand over a large part of Western and Northern India, but to-day they are almost unknown beyond the district.

From *Nasarpur* in Hyderabad a beautiful brocade (No. 562) has been received. This is in deep green with diaper check in crimson silk. The underside is glazed and the border is a cheap *kalábatun* shown on one edge only. The brocaded satinette *lungis* from Hyderabad (Sind) are very similar to those of Bhawalpur.

DIVISION 35. SILK OF SOUTH INDIA.

South India.—Silk manufacture at one time attained a high state of proficiency in Mysore, but recent efforts to extend the industry have not, it is believed, proved very successful. Madras Presidency can hardly be described as possessing any specific art conceptions of its own, connected with the silk industry. A few towns have a local reputation for their silk goods or mixed silk and cotton goods, as also for the extent to which they work up the local supplies of *tasar* silk; but there are no silk textiles that have more than a local repute. Moreover, all the silk manufacturing districts have felt the modern cheapening process and the facilities of foreign supply very greatly, so that the Madras silk industry must be regarded as declining rather than advancing. The raw silk worked up in the Presidency comes mainly from Bengal.

Modern Influences

BERHAMPUR.—The chief districts or towns noted for their silk manufactures are Berhampur (in Ganjam), where beautiful *sárís*, handkerchiefs, etc., usually in crimson (or lac) colour are produced. ANANTAPUR pure silk cloth is now hardly if ever produced, the looms being presently engaged in the production of mixed silk and cotton fabrics. Speaking of Dharmavaram in Bellary, Mr. Havell wrote some few years ago that "The most effective and characteristic cloth is one with a white ground of a wide check pattern, crimson borders and brocaded ends, sometimes with figures of flowers, birds, etc."

Checked Silks.

ARNI (North Arcot) is the seat of a well-known silk industry. *Sárís* (locally known as *Pattu Sarigai Pudavai*) are woven in checks outlined by gold threads and black, the meshes being in orange, dark brick-red, or green, orange and red. The borders are broad of a deep maroon with double rows of gold geometric scroll. In the Exhibition a representative series of these beautiful silks have been contributed by Y. N. Govindha Raju Chetee.

TRICHINOPOLY Town and several villages in the district as well, have fairly important silk interests, but chiefly in connection

DIVISION 35. SILK OF SOUTH INDIA.

Satinette.

with the manufacture of the mixed silk and cotton goods that have been described in connection with Northern India as satinettes (*himrus*). "Ariyalúr," Mr. Thurston (Monograph, *Silk Fabric Industry*, page 10) tells us, "is famous for the manufacture of female bodices, known as *thatturavikki*, worn by all classes." Mr. Havell gives particulars of the manufacture of the satin cloth of Ariyalúr. This he says is "distinct in style and of remarkable beauty in colour, as well as tasteful in the simple patterns woven, generally in stripes, across it. The *ravikkai* (Hindi—*choli*) worn by Native ladies is made of it. Only two men are engaged in this industry, which, as far as I know, has never been noticed before. A kind similar in style, but inferior in colour and execution, is produced in the town of Trichinopoly, embroidered with patterns in silver lace."

TANJORE has a very nearly silmilar industry to that of Trichinopoly, the bulk of the weavers being concerned in the production of the mixed silk and cotton fabrics, in demand by the Muhammadans, and which attains such perfection in Aurangabad.

Loan Collection.

While exploiting the palace of Tanjore, with the object of discovering articles of interest for this Exhibition, the writer found a large assortment of the most beautiful garments and textiles. A few of these have already been alluded to, in connection with resist dyeing (page 266), but it remains to be added here that perhaps the most superb brocaded silks met with anywhere in India, were those discovered in the Tanjore *toshakkhana*. In the Loan Collection Gallery a selection of these will be found—a series of perfectly bewildering beauty. Plate No. 80 gives but the faintest conception of these textiles. It shows the corner of a silk shawl or *sárí* in a crimson colour of such quality and depth that it seems as if the brocaded pattern in golden yellow green, white and blue silk was viewed through a transparent field. In every fold new tones are discovered and more vivid life portraitures detected. The writer received the information from the State officials that these silks had been made in Tanjore some few years ago. If this be correct we have here a second evidence of a far higher knowledge in the textile arts than could be inferred from the manufactures of the present day.

Brocaded Silks.

But in connection with the Loan Collection brocades and *kinkhábs* of Surat, it will be found that satin brocaded silks almost precisely similar to those of Tanjore were made in Surat from 75 to 150 years ago. **DIVISION 35. SILK OF SOUTH INDIA.**

Before passing away from the silk textiles of Tanjore, reference may be here made to the *kinkhábs*. A marvellous pair of trousers were discovered by the writer in the palace, the legs of which must be each at least 5 feet in diameter. These were made of a splendid gold brocade, the pattern of which, unlike the Persian designs of the *sârís* (just alluded to), will be seen to be *Chalukyan* or, as it might also be called, Dravidian style. The bird shown all over the surface looks more like a peacock than the classic goose of South India, but its tail is a canopy of flowers in silver wrought on a special background of gold, while from its beak dangles the usual spray of flowers. This splendid piece of gold brocade is said to have been made in the palace by the expert weavers that were formerly retained by the Rajas. It is shown in Plate No. 81, fig. 1. **Kinkháb.**

MADURA and DINDIGAL have both fairly flourishing silk and silk and cotton industries that are concerned in the production of goods closely resembling the *dariyais* and *gulbadans* of the United Provinces and the Panjab. These find an outlet in meeting the demand for washing silk dress stuffs in South India.

In COIMBATORE, silk weaving is a distinct industry, but what is of even greater interest the rearing of the mulberry silk-worm is on a fairly large scale. There is nothing very specially attractive or artistic in the goods turned out.

By way of concluding this very brief enumeration of the South Indian silk interests and silk goods produced, it may be worthwhile to add that the silk weavers of the greater part of the Madras Presidency claim to have come from Gujarat. They speak a dialect of Gujarati and employ names for their loom and all its parts and also for their yarns and textiles that are identical with those in use in Gujarat. The writer came across instances of this in Madura, Tinnevelly and Tuticorin, while organising the collections of silk textiles shown at the Exhibition.

This circumstance has a distinct bearing on the origin and

DIVISION 35. SILK OF SOUTH INDIA.

nature of the existing silk trade of at least the Southern and Western tracts of the Presidency. In fact it would point to the possibility of the methods of weaving and patterns found in the more Northern and Eastern parts of the Presidency, being more ancient than those associated with the Gujarati immigrants of the South, a conclusion that will be seen to coincide with similar observations in connection with the wood carving, silver, ivory and dyeing of the region in question.

Mysore.—A fair assortment of the silks of this State may be seen at the Exhibition. The observation would seem justified that the people of Mysore prefer dark red shot with blue giving the textile a purplish tint. In *sárís* this is usually bordered with the Persian cone-pattern along its inner edge. A good example of this may be mentioned as Nos. 3911 and 3912 made by Govinda Savajee of Bangalore. These are of a very high class, have broad gold borders worked in wavy lines and cost about Rs. 300 each.

B. Oosman Khan Salar Khan Sahib of Bangalore contributes a long and interesting series of Mysore silks. No. 54 is a green *sárí* checked in gold; No. 56 a violet *sárí* with gold wire checkered lines and gold *bútis*; No. 59 a red shot blue with brick-red border and gold diapers; No. 68 a rich magenta *sárí* in gauze texture with gold threads forming checks and narrow gold border.

Travancore and Cochin send a few series of their characteristic *sárís* both in silk and in cotton. These are woven as gauzes in unbleached (pale straw coloured) fibre with beautifully worked borders. In the form of *rumals* or *dopattas* they have usually boldly worked corner pieces inwrought with the weft so as to be softened in its colour by the silk carried above. This is peculiar to these States and recalls the old cotton textiles of Tanjore discussed above under the chapter of "Wax Resist dyeing."

Hyderabad (Deccan)—Has long been noted for its beautiful silks, more especially the brocades or flowered textiles of RAICHUR and AURANGABAD. In the Exhibition a fair assortment of these will be found but as the patterns employed are precisely those adopted in the fabrication of the mixed silk and cotton goods, known as *himrus*, the discussion of the flowered silks may be accepted as embraced by the account shortly to be given of the Mixed Fabrics. DIVISION 35. SILK OF DECCAN.

But before leaving this section, it may be desirable to invite attention to the chief brocaded silks shown. Those that have attracted most attention are the brocades contributed by the Industrial School of Aurangabad, of which mention may be made of No. 583, a rich electric blue, brocaded in a silk *jálí* around graceful gold *bútis*. Muhamed Habib shows a fine series of silk brocades and *Kamkhábs* (Nos. 541 to 547). Of these No. 546—a blue-black textile with a bold *jangla* design in gold, and No. 544—a satinette of delicate slate colour with a *jálí* in broad floral gold enclosing silver cones—are worthy of attention. Lastly, Muhamed Latif, also of Aurangabad, sends a set of brocades (Nos. 548 to 556); No. 553 is a drab satinette brocaded in silk *jálís* around gold *bútis*. The goods shown by this manufacturer have attracted much attention because of their soft colours and graceful patterns.

Burma.—Although a considerable quantity of silk is reared in Burma, a very large percentage of the yarn that is woven has always been imported both from China and the Straits. The objection to taking life held so strongly by the Buddhists, has necessarily retarded the progress of a silk rearing industry. In the older dynasties, the capture and removal to Burma of Manipuris was mainly occasioned through the necessity to secure silk workers. The descendants of these now form colonies in Prome, Ava and Amarapura. Mr. Hardiman has recently published a monograph on *Silk in Burma* but unfortunately devoted a small portion of his attention to the study of the artistic results. He tells us that the fabrics turned out fall under four groups:—(*1*) *bala*, (*2*) *acheik* or *lun*, (*3*) *gaik*, and (*4*) *sat*. The descriptions given of these do not suffice, without an intimate knowledge of Burmese, to convey any very clear conception of their respective peculiarities. The *bala* silks appear to be plain, striped or checkered and the other three forms to be striped but with various figures worked within the stripes. Mr. Hardiman's description may be here given:—" The word 'acheik' implies that the threads of the shuttles (as many as one hundred and twenty

DIVISION 35. SILK OF BURMA.

are used) hook into or across each of the other threads. The threads of the warp are of different colours, but the spools in the shuttles contribute to the flowered figures on the surface of the fabric. There are no raised figures, so that *acheik* cannot be properly called embroidery, embossment or tapestry, be the design what it may. Both sides are exactly the same; there is no right or no wrong side." It was, we are told, in King Mindon's reign that the threads were increased to 120 "the number employed before having been three only, in King Pagan's reign; and the term first used was not *acheik* but *waik* as the woof threads moved in zig-zag patterns only. The Burma or Manipur weavers who first introduced the *acheik* design lived at Amarapura near the Patodas-gyi pagoda." The wavy design shown on all these *acheik pasos* and *longyis* was hardly, as Mr. Hardiman suggests, derived from a foreign source, but is more likely intended to portray the wavy form of the balustrade alongside of the five processional paths around the circular pagoda at Mengun. Although this was only erected about 100 years ago, the Buddhist rails or processional walls, whether of stone or festoons of cloth looping over the shoulders of men, have in all stages of Buddhism been accepted as sacred emblems and become art conceptions both in architecture and decorative art. Be this explanation as it may, the silks of Burma may be accepted as either plain, striped, checked or brocaded—the last produced by the use of a large number of spools with special weft threads, or they are, as explained above under Division 32, wax printed fabrics. The favourite colours for the wavy patterned brocades are stripes of red, orange and green with white flowers worked transversely. In some the red predominates, making pink and red *pasos*, in others the yellows are the chief colours and in still a third the greens.

Influence of Mengun Pagoda.

In the Exhibition a large assortment of these goods are on view and will repay inspection, especially those in the stall held by Messrs. Tara Chand Pursram of Bombay, in the Jewellery Court. But when placed in competition with the silks of the whole of India, the Burmese goods were not considered by the Judging Committee as worthy of any special award.

Brocades, Kinkhabs and Cloths of Gold and Silver.

DIVISION 35. SILK, KINKHÁBS.

Brocades.

The term "brocade" is sometimes made to embrace all flowered or patterned silks in which the patterns are woven, not printed. A more restricted and accurate signification is often given, namely thick textiles so manipulated that the pattern is distinct from or supplementary to the weft and thrown on its surface. The root of the word "brocade" is identical with that in "broach" and means "to stab or transfix." It thus makes a direct reference to the small needle-like spools, that carry the pattern threads, being thrust between the warp (either by hand or machinery), in elaboration of the pattern. The process is in fact identical with that described in connection with flowered muslins. It is this act of passing special weft threads within the warp that has given origin to the superfluous and ambiguous expression of "Loom Embroidery."

Loom Embroideries.

Kinkhábs or gold brocades.

Indian brocades in pure silk are called *Amrus*; those with gold wire in addition to silk are *Kinkhábs*. These two terms might be accepted as naturally and conveniently separating the brocades, but unfortunately on the one extreme the transition is almost imperceptible from the so-called *Amrus* to the ordinary flowered silks, already fully discussed, and on the other from the *Kinkhábs* to the brocaded and other borderings, braidings and trimmings.

Cloth of Gold.

From time immemorial gold and silver wire have been drawn out to such a state of fineness that they may be woven into pure gold or silver cloth—"cloth of gold" literally—but more frequently the gold wire (*kalábatun*) is used as a special weft along with silk, or as special warp threads, in the fabrication of the silk brocades that in India bear the name of *kinkháb* (kincob) or more correctly *kamkháb*. For particulars regarding "Gold and Silver Wire Drawing," consult the Division below devoted to Gold Embroidery.

The poetic name—*Kamkháb*—literally means *kam*—little—and *khwáb*—dream. "Apart from its more cryptic meaning," writes Mr. A. Yusuf Ali, in allusion to Insha's punning lines, "the poet gives precedence to *Kamkhwáb* over the *Kákum* or *Sanjáb* fabrics, celebrated in Persian poetry; these were only seen by night, but the climax was reached when the *Kamkhwáb* came

DIVISION 35. SILK KINKHÁBS.

and was seen by the superior light of day, when there was no deception." Plate No. 47 shows an assortment of *Kinkhábs* and Plate No. 81 shows three more in detail.

Historic Facts.

Both "cloth of gold" and *Kinkháb* are mentioned in the *Vedas.* Megasthenes, speaking of the costumes of the princes of India, remarks that their robes were worked in pure gold. The rich stuffs of Babylon, brought from India, were in all probability gold brocades from Ahmedabad, Benares or Murshidabad. It would appear, however, that the *Kinkhábs* were originally woven of pure gold and that silk was added both to give a body to the textile and to afford a means of colour illumination.

Silk brocades.

Brocaded silks (*Amrus*) are made at Murshidabad, Benares, Bhawalpur, Multan, Ahmedabad, Surat, Yeola, Poona and Aurangabad. These have already been briefly indicated and will be still further dealt with in connection with "mixed fabrics." Although pure silk brocades are doubtless made, by far the most characteristic textiles of this kind are those with cotton or with wool, for both warp and weft, but with silk patterns brocaded over the surface. These are commonly designated *Himrus* (Plate No. 46-A) but, as already hinted, the isolation of the *Amrus* and *Himrus* is probably impossible and at the same time undesirable. So again a textile may be a silk brocade with simply a speck of *Kalábatan* (gold) thread to illuminate a particular feature of the pattern, just as a fabric of pure gold may be "enamelled," as the expression goes, by a speck of coloured silk. It thus becomes hopeless to arbitrarily restrict the names given to textiles, the more so since the same name or a derivative from it may, in the Provinces of India, have different meanings attributed to it. But if a liberal use of gold or silver wire be accepted as the condition that justifies the use of the name *Kinkháb,* then there may be said to be the following kinds of *Kinkhábs* :—

Classification of Kinkhabs.

1. Pure "Cloth of Gold" or Silver.

2. Brocades in which gold or silver thread cover the greater portion of the surface, and coloured silks are shown only here and there to outline or pick out the design. These are the *Kinkhábs* proper. Since they would be too heavy for garments they are mainly used for trappings, curtains, etc.

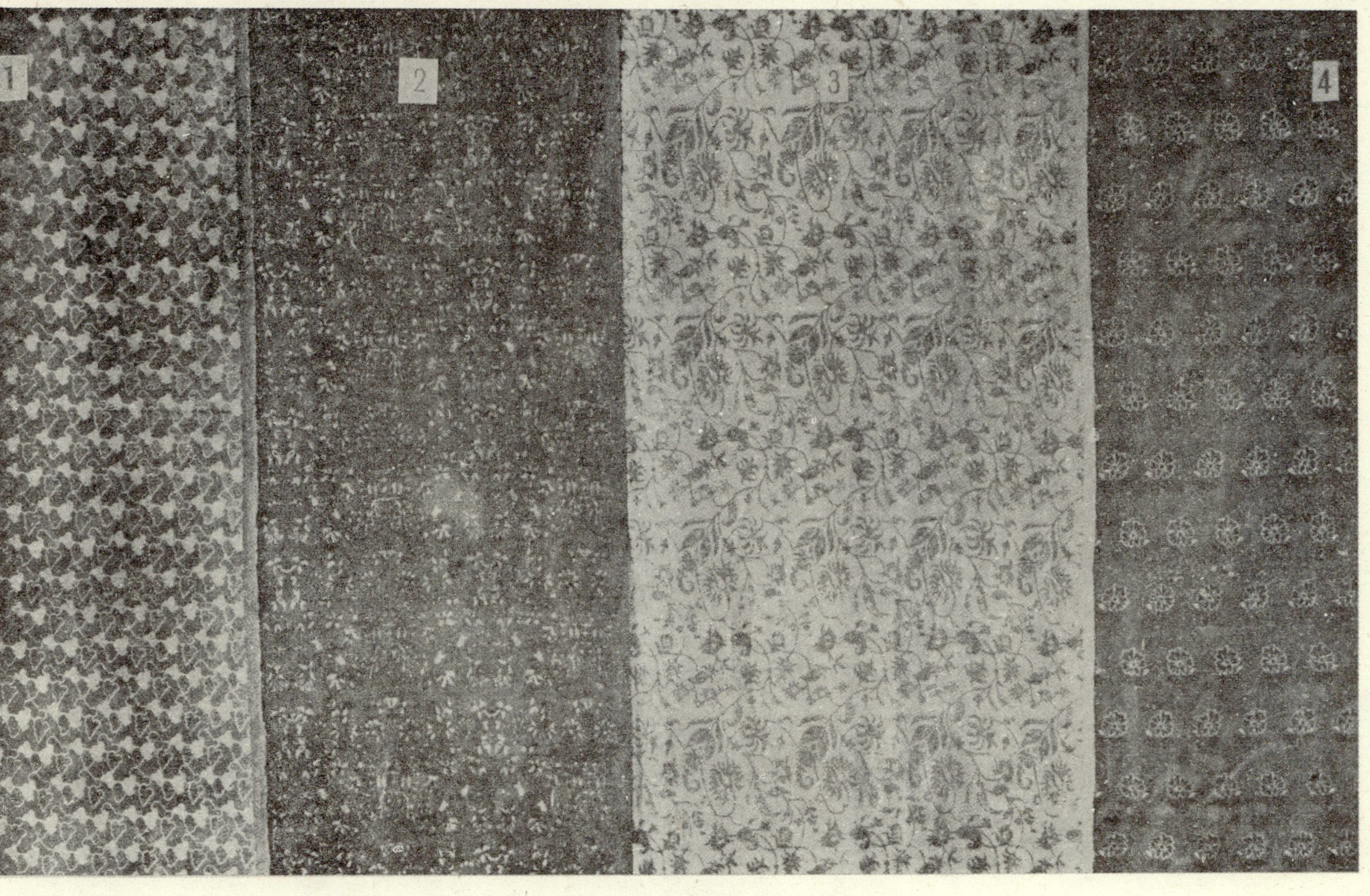

Plate No. 46-A Woven Patterns mixed Silk and Cotton (Himru.)

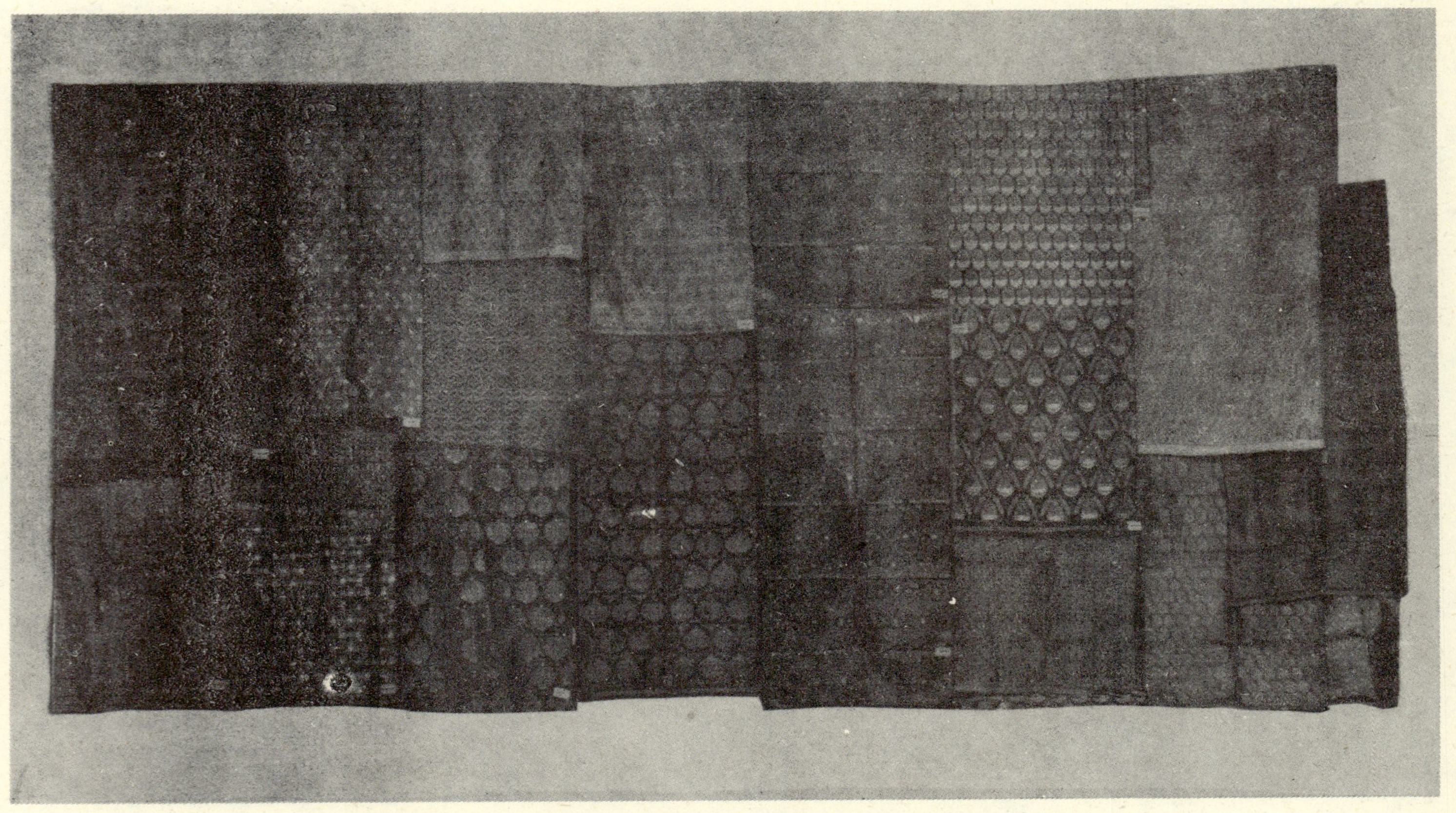

Plate No. 47 Kinkhobs (Gold Cloths of Benares, Ahmedabad, etc.)

3. Brocades in which the major portion of the texture is in closely woven silk and only certain portions of the pattern are in gold or silver thread. Fabrics of this kind are frequently called *Baftas* or *Pot-Tháns.* **DIVISION 35. SILK KINKHABS.**

4. Silk gauzes or muslins with certain portions of the designs in gold or silver thread or with gold borders and end-pieces sewn on to them. These are often called *Abrawans*, a name that denotes "flowing water," but in some parts of India the name "*Pot*" is given to this description of fabric.

It may assist the student to refer the *Kinkhábs* to provincial sections :—

Cloth of Gold. ***United Provinces***—AGRA.—In the Exhibition many good examples of "cloth of gold" may be seen. In the large glass case in which Messrs. Ganeshi Lall & Son of Agra show their rich embroideries, will be found superb dress stuffs woven of the purest gold or silver, but of such quality that the fabric is scarcely thicker or heavier than if made of pure silk. And what is perhaps more surprising still, these textiles may be even washed without either being torn or tarnished. In some of the finest qualities of "cloth of gold" the patterns are richly brocaded, in others embroidered with seed pearls and precious stones.

A large series of the more massive *Kinkhábs*, suitable for draperies, will be discovered among the goods procured from both Benares and Ahmedabad. A special bay has been set apart, in fact, for the *Kinkhábs*, but no attempt made to isolate them into the *Kinkhábs* proper, the *Baftas*, *Pots*, and the *Abrawans.*

Loan Collection. In the Loan Collection Gallery two sets of *Kinkhábs* are specially worthy of attention. These are as follows :—

A set contributed by His Highness the Maharaja of Benares, of which No. 1228 is a riding coat or *Angá Ghorecharlu.* This is a *Kinkháb* in *Jalidar* or elliptic meshes in gold, enclosing silver rosettes. No. 1229 is a *Kuba* or long coat made of *Kinkháb* woven in wavy lines (*Lahariadar*), of silk and gold. These two garments were used by the late Maharaja Udit Narayan Singh. They are bordered in gold embroidery and pearls.

No. 1226 is a *Balabar Anga* (or coat double-breasted and buttoning to the side). It is described as a *Kinkháb* of the *Gudre*

DIVISION 35. SILK KINKHABS.

pattern, that is to say piebald colour. The pattern is made up of right-angled triangles of gold separating strips of variously coloured silks into similarly shaped spaces. But there seems to be no sequence or recurrence in the strips of coloured silks which are in pale green, pink, brown, yellow, red, blue, black, etc., and repeated in any order. But the charm of this garment is in the *Kinkhâb* bordering or braid (*Kinara*). This is woven in gold with an elaborate and minute pattern in pale coloured silk. The stalks and foliage of the scroll are in dull metallic green. The flowers are composite, each floret outlined in gold. There is first one large flower in pale pink alternately inverted, and between two of these are ten similarly formed but smaller flowers in two or three shades of pale yellow, blue and brown. This coat was said to have been worn by the Maharaja Sir Ishwari Prasad Narain Singh Bahadur, G.C.S.I., and to have been manufactured in Benares.

The second set are the property of the Hon'ble Madho Lall, Rais of Benares—a gentleman who it will be seen acted as a member of the Judging Committee, and has for many years taken the keenest interest in the development of the art industries of India. No. 1223 is a coat (*Aba*). The material is a pale neutral yellow with a conventional design of the poppy worked all over it. The leaves are in silver, the flowers in gold and the stems in black silk. This wonderful design was reproduced especially for the Exhibition, and sold readily and several orders for further pieces of it were registered.

Poppy Pattern.

The following may be given as the names of the chief exhibitors and some of the more remarkable goods on view from Benares in the Sale Gallery :—

CHIEF EXHIBITS ON VIEW.

BENARES.—Perhaps the *Kinkbâb* that has attracted most attention, and deservedly so, may be said to be the one made by Bhagwan Das Gopi Nath of Benares. This is a restoration of a charming design found by the writer on an old garment in the possession of the Hon'ble Munshi Madho Lal of Benares, who kindly permitted it to be copied. The original has been figured as Plate No. 81, fig. 2. The ground or field colour is a rich

Poppy Pattern.

pale yellow silk and the pattern a conventional *Búta* which doubtless is intended to portray the poppy. This charming conception has already been discussed in connection with the design seen in "Encrusted Ware" (page 48).

Of other Benares *Kinkhábs* the following assorted under the names of the exhibitors are worthy of special study :—

1. Bhagwan Das Gopi Nath of Benares has a fine display, registered as Nos. 1501 to 1582. Many of these will be found to be white silks brocaded with white or coloured silks and having minute flowers of gold or silver at fixed intervals. Very often also the metallic threads form diagonal lines or diapers that enclose silk brocaded flowers.

2. Nur Mohammed Moulvi Khalilal Rahman and M. Rahmatulla Sardar of Mohalla Alipura, Benares, send a superb series of brocades. These are registered from Nos. 1272 to 1295. No. 1279 is a *kinkháb* on gamboge yellow silk with *búta pandars* in silver. No. 1282 is on emerald green with large flowers (*búta chasdars*) in gold outlined with red. No. 1277 is a grey brocaded silk in *jáli* form enclosing gold *bútis* with purple centres. No. 1281 is a black brocaded silk with *bútas* within the meshes of the brocade. No. 1284 is a *kinkháb* on dark brick-red with foliar *bútis* in the form of circular clumps of fronds. No. 1287 is a curtain (*purdah*) in cream silk with arborescent flowering *bútidars* in gold with purple centres (52 inches wide and 6 yards long). No. 1289 is a curtain (*purdah*) in pure white silk, with the *bútidars* of the last but in white silk with gold points. No. 1290 is also a curtain in pale green with *jangla* pattern with large gold foliage and silver flowers.

3. B. Balbhadra Das (Bhaddo Mal) of Benares has sent a collection of silk *sáris*, *chogas*, etc., registered as Nos. 1639 to 1650. Of these No. 1647 is a *sári* in white silk, brocaded with gold *jangla,* having silver, also pink and green silk flowers. No. 1649 is a black coat in silk, elaborately brocaded in gold floral *jális* enclosing cones. No. 1639 is a *sári* in dull yellow silk gauze with closely compacted *tercha* floral scrolls, the borders and end-pieces being in thick silver checkered damask, demarcated by narrow red lines which are broken up by gold spots—perhaps the

DIVISION 35. SILK KINKHABS: BENARES.

most beautiful *sárí* in the Exhibition. No. 1648 is a *choga*, purple silk completely brocaded in gold in *shikarka-kalaga* or scrolls of floral and animal forms surrounding large cones that have peacock and deer within. This is one of the most superb coats in the Exhibition and justly earns the award given it by the Judging Committee.

4. L. Dalu Mull Atma Ram of Benares sends a series of brocaded coats, vests, etc. These have been registered as Nos. 31 to 57. No. 55 is a jacket in gold *jáldárí* with opaque white flowers within the gold meshes. No. 57 is a coat with an elaborate *jangla* gold design all over the surface. All these articles of dress are in silk, muslins or gauzes.

5. Girdhar Das Hari Das of Benares sends an assortment of *amrus, pots* and *kinkhábs*. His goods have been registered under Nos. 1482 to 1574. No. 1565 is an *amru* or silk brocade on a field of sienna with dull green *bútas*, picked out in magenta. No. 1484 is a pale slate coloured silk, checked with silver and with gold rosettes within the silver meshes. No. 1572 is a flowered cotton muslin unbleached with diagonal floral scrolls in silver much like many of the *jamdánis* described in connection with the flowered muslins of Dacca.

6. Bulhadra Prosad Gobandhan Das of Benares sends a good series of *pots* or brocaded silks, registered as Nos. 1475 to 1481. Of these No. 1477 may be specially mentioned, a pale green brocaded silk, the silk pattern enclosing *chameli bútis*. No. 1478 is a *pot zard* or yellow silk brocaded in silver worked into diagonal checks athwart which a leaf is thrown. No. 1480 is a *kamarband tási* of six colours (green, pink, blue, red, yellow, purple) in bands ½ inch in breadth and with gold checks worked over their surfaces. These stripes run across the fabric and end in marginal gold *ghotas*.

7. Mohammad Husain Nakshband of Mohalla Alaipura, Benares, has furnished two *kinkhábs* in dull green with a delicate *jangla* pattern in gold (Nos. 1270 and 1271).

8. Moulvi Abdul Rahman Sardar of Mohalla Madanpura, Benares, has sent a good series of silk gauzes and brocades (*pots*), registered as Nos. 1251 to 1269. Of these the following may be

DIVISION 35. SILK KINKHABS: BENARES.

mentioned. No. 1259, a *rumal* in silk gauze of an ash-grey colour with gold *bútis* and borders. No. 1251, a *pot* in rosy pink with gold *terchi* bands and silver *bútis.* No. 1252, a silk *pot,* straw coloured with *terchi* bands or floral scrolls in gold with, between these, three rows of rosettes, two in silk and one in gold. No. 1254, a *pot* of olive green with diagonal spots alternately gold and silver.

9. Gopal Krishna Das of Gaighat, Benares, sends a large assortment, registered from Nos. 1383 to 1409. Many of these are *baftas* or pale coloured brocaded silks with *bútis* of gold or silver. Others, such as No. 1390, are pale coloured silks with cone-patterns composed of masses of brilliantly coloured small flowers. This maker has also contributed a series of simple silk brocades which he describes as "*khes.*"

Furrows of Gold.

10. L. Munna Lal Babu Lal of Benares shows a large assortment of all kinds of brocaded silks and *kinkhábs.* These have been recorded as Nos. 1410 to 1474. It would be a hopeless task to attempt to specialise the most attractive samples in this series. No. 1441 is a field of gold furrowed by very faint lines (red) and over the surface an elaborate design worked in silver and gold. This consists of large open cone-patterns filled with trees, animals, etc. No. 1417 is a pale green with silk brocaded designs and *jáli* lines in gold enclosing a gold cone. No. 1465 is a pale heliotrope silk with *jáldári* gold and enamelled specks.

11. Mullu Mul Girdhar Das of Benares has sent a long series of *kinkhábs* that closely resemble Ahmedabad work. These have been registered as Nos. 1307 to 1331. No. 1315 is perhaps the best example. This has the field obliquely furrowed in gold with a circular *búti* faintly outlined in red.

12. The weaving of *kinkhábs* may be studied in the Artizans' Gallery. Hara Prasad of Benares, who has contributed many good *kinkhábs* to the Main Gallery, has also set up looms and is ready and willing to show them and explain every detail to the visitor.

***Bombay*—** AHMEDABAD AND SURAT.—It does not seem likely to serve any good purpose to keep the gold textiles of Surat distinct from those of Ahmedabad. Both are exactly similar

DIVISION 35. SILK KINKHABS: AHMEDABAD.

in design and workmanship though, if anything Surat has recently shown more enterprise than Ahmedabad. A very extensive series of *kinkhábs* from these ancient seats of the craft is on view at the Exhibition. Following the system adopted above with Benares, an enumeration of the chief collections on view may be here given.

CHIEF EXHIBITS ON VIEW.

1. Perhaps the most instructive collection at the Exhibition may be said to be the series from Ahmedabad exhibited on behalf of the minor Jevabhai Chuni Lal Fatichand, and registered under Nos. 2451 to 2612. This was discovered by the writer in the Wazir District Court. It seems the owner, a *kinhkáb* dealer, died some 20 years ago and his estate has been under administration ever since. Moreover, it is understood many of these fabrics had been in stock for many years previously and are approximately 100 years old. Among the examples of the heavy gold work used for drapings, table covers, cushions, etc., there are many of great beauty such as small squares or table covers worked in the design figured by Sir George Birdwood (*Industrial Arts of India, Plate 68*), and many other equally charming fine old patterns. A feature of great beauty about this series is their pale rich tones. From the European stand-point these are infinitely superior to the modern glaring colours and wall paper designs of nine-tenths of the modern manufactures of Ahmedabad and Surat. One of exceptional merit is woven in gold and green but with such skill that in one position it looks as if entirely in gold, in another as if in silk. Many are in dark maroon coloured silk with flowers of various sizes and designs worked all over them—a very attractive one has large bunches of flowers resting within a vase-like construction that recalls many of the designs seen in the palaces of Delhi and Agra. The drawing-room of the Circuit House at Delhi was designed to show the possibility of adapting the art conceptions of Ahmedabad to modern house-furnishing. At the writer's suggestion the walls were panelled in carved teak wood, the frames being filled in with a set of dark red *kinkhábs* derived from Jevabhai Chuni Lal Fatichand's stock. It is hoped that the example of using these textiles, in

Pale Rich Tones.

House Furnishing.

place of tapestries, may be followed by others and thus lead to a new market for the *kinkháb* weavers of India.

DIVISION 35. SILK KINKHABS: SURAT.

2. Bhagwan Das Tribhwan Das of Chippopol, Ahmedabad, is one of the best known manufacturers of silk brocaded gauzes in India. He has furnished a large series to the Exhibition that have been registered under Nos. 934 to 978. This includes some superb *sárís* from Rs. 200 to Rs. 500 each, in all shades of colour and worked with gold, silver or coloured silks.

3. Hari Krishna Das Lala Bhai, merchant of Surat, sends an extensive assortment of silk and gold *sárís*. Many of these are in dark red with circular gold *bútis*. Most of these silk gauzes are admirably woven and in the richest and softest colours, tastefully picked out in gold or silver.

4. Parbhudas Rugnath Petigara of Ahmedabad has sent several *amru* silks and obtained a first prize with silver medal for them.

Black Kinkhabs.

5. Alybhoy Tajbhoy of Surat has sent a series of *kinkhábs* for which he secured a bronze medal. They have been registered under Nos. 2007 to 2022. No. 2013 is an elaborate gold design with silver points on blue-black silk. A feature of this manufacturer's goods appears to be his style of black silks with gold and silver brocadings. He has also contributed many very beautiful silk brocaded *sárís*.

6. Dayabhai Jagjivan Das Jarivala of Surat shows many very charming *kinkhábs* and brocaded silks. These have been registered under Nos. 2301 to 2325. No. 2315 is an amber coloured textile brocaded in dull yellow silk and forming a closely interlaced design through which sprays of flowers are thrown in silver wire that look like chains of pearls. Another sample is a *kinkháb* in black with a design in gold and silver, taken doubtless from the human hand. This was selected by Mr. C. L. Burns, Principal of the School of Art, Bombay, for the panelling of the Bombay Room and may be recognised in Plate No. 2.

7. Pranjivandas Dulabhram, 182 Haripura Bhavani Vad, Surat, has sent to the Exhibition a varied series of brocaded silks and gauzes. These are mostly in checks and stripes of gold with contained *bútis* in gold or silver. They have been registered

DIVISION 35. SILK KINKHABS: SURAT.

under Nos. 3415 to 3444, and will be found well worthy of the most careful study.

Loan Collection.

By way of comparison with the every-day goods, so to speak, it may be useful to once more direct the visitor's attention to the corresponding manufactures in the Loan Collection Gallery. Sha Udechand Ichhachand of Surat has contributed a fine old series of articles which, he says, were made in Surat from 75 to 150 years ago. Of these special attention may be given to a cotton *sárí*, dark blue with border in gold the scrolls being in metallic blue acutely bent and interlaced with a green scroll, the latter having pink and orange flowers. The end-piece is a plain gold panel surrounded by the bordering. The owner says this was made in Surat 100 years ago. Then to the silk *sárí* in rich purple red, brocaded with yellow silk borders and checkered design. It will be seen that the field of this garment has flowers (*bútis*) in alternate oblique rows brocaded in green edged with yellow, and blue edged with black. The end-piece is a panel of flowering trees in alternate green and blue. This lovely *sárí* is said to have been made at Surat 75 years ago. Attention may next be turned to the bright red *sárí* brocaded in yellow and green with the borderings or *béls* in blue. The Persian cones are much as in the example described from the palace of Tanjore and shown in Plate No. 80. The upper of these cones is in green silk, the lower in yellow—the two being separated by a border in white. The field of the *sárí* has blue *bútis* all over it. This is said to have been made in Surat 75 years ago.

Old Saris.

Eri silk.

A sample that may perhaps attract more attention than any of the others is, however, a *sárí* that would seem to be in spun *eri* silk. It is dyed a rich crimson and has yellow *bútis* laid sideways all over the field. This habit of placing the field *bútis* on their sides seems more or less peculiar to all the finer old *sárís* of Gujarat. The borders are in narrow black floral scrolls outlined with yellow. The end-piece is a panel of flowering trees with pale yellow green leaves. This exquisite piece of work is perhaps the finest example of Indian spun silk known. The peculiarity of the design being outlined in black and the flowers edged with a second shade of the substance colour are

DIVISION 35. SILK KINKHABS: SURAT.

conditions very constantly associated with the silk ornamentation of these gold *sáris*. It gives the softening harmony without which the bright colours would be unpardonable. In some of the Baroda examples, however, the black outlining has been carried perhaps a little too far.

Foliar cones.

The next article in Sha Udechand Ichhachand's collection, to which attention has to be directed, is a *sári* in bright crimson silk with gold scroll borders and end-piece in gold and inwrought many-coloured foliar cones, having the overturned tips assuming the condition of sprays. The bases of these cones show a few leaves tied in mimic fashion of vases. The petals of the flowers, just as in the last mentioned, are all bordered in the complement colour. The leaves are parti-coloured, the stalks and outlines of the leaves being in deep blue-black. This is one of the most marvellously beautiful brocades in the Exhibition and will richly repay the most careful study. It is also stated to have been made in Surat 75 years ago.

Satinette Brocade.

Lastly a sample of *amru* brocade. The field in this fabric is in deep metallic blue-green and it has a satinette texture. It is obliquely covered with *bútis* in jasamine form: the petals are red outlined in white and the leaves are simply yellow outlines. This is believed to have been made in Surat 100 years ago, and it is thus a most valuable model for the brocade silk weaver.

Flowers placed sideways.

Tarkas Harjivandas Jethasha Sitvala of Surat has also contributed to the Loan Collection Gallery a series of *kinkháb* squares, mostly in red with gold and silver floral and animal designs. One is a red striped *dusmal* in silk with blue borders, the stripes both in the border and field being in gold wire. This is said to be 100 years old. He has at the same time sent a *sári* in red silk with gold borders. This is embroidered all over in *bútis* that are laid sideways. They are black outlined with gold or yellow outlined with white silk and gold wire. This is also said to be 100 years old. Lastly, the same contributor has sent a *sári* said to be made of cotton, silk and gold, and to be 125 years old. The end-piece is the charm of this fabric. The flowering shrubs shown on it have a rosette of pale yellow-

DIVISION 35. SILK KINKHABS: BARODA.

green leaves and pale purple carnation-like flowers outlined in darker purple.

BARODA.—From the collection of gold brocades exhibited by His Highness the Maharaja of Baroda, the following may be specially commended:—No. 1055—A *Shallu* gold gauze *sári* in *asvali* pattern. This is very similar to the Aurangabad (Paithan) *sári* in the Sale Gallery (described below) only that the

Paroquet Pattern.

pattern is bolder though the severity of the black outlines somewhat mars the result. The border is a flowing, though sharply angular scroll, with the usual peacock in blue and green in place of the geometric design of paroquets in the Aurangabad sample. The scheme of colour is so similar in both that they might be said to have been made by the same person. No. 1057—A Benares Silk *Shallu* in magenta with a free all over pattern in gold with green spots and containing in the end-piece cones compacted of birds and flowers. No. 1058—Silk *Shallu* (*sulidar mundile*). The body is terra-cotta silk gauze striped with gold. The end-piece consists of gold check with a flowing scroll worked in the most delicate green, red and blue. No. 1061—Silk Paithani *Shallu*; red and blue with gold *motichur* border. It is a charming *sári*, double-woven with delicate purple blue on one side and crimson on the other. No. 1067—Silk *patola sári*, gold *asvali* pattern. This is built up of *patola* silk, centre and borders exactly as in the Aurangabad *sári* described below. The word *asvali* (possibly *asmani*) may mean blue and makes a reference to the prevalence of that colour in the design. The *patola* is in the usual deep brown red with green, bright red, white and yellow.

Hyderabad (Deccan).—Although Aurangabad and Raichur are more famed for their silk brocades (*amrus*) already described, and their mixed silk and cotton brocades (*himrus*), to be described below, than for their *kinkhábs*, still a fairly large manufacture of gold textiles exists. Aurangabad, or rather the neighbouring town of Pattan (Paithan), is in fact specially noted

Pattan Saris.

for a particular quality and pattern of gold and silk gauze. It would be next to impossible to convey anything like a conception of these marvellous textiles by a description alone. They

DIVISION 35. SILK KINKHABS: AURANGABAD.

are usually woven of dark or neutral orange-red silk and are checkered or striped with gold lines, the meshes or interspaces being filled up with various designs in gold, the most prevalent being the almost classic *Chalukyan* goose carrying an "olive branch" in its beak. The borders and end-pieces are woven separately and sewn on to the body cloth of the *sárí*, but instead of being in gauze they are formed of a compactly woven and firm silk brocade, with a large admixture of gold. The most striking peculiarity of these brocades and end-pieces is the persistence of exceptionally bright and showy colours, namely, moss green, canary yellow, pale metallic blue and bright pink. These are worked into flowing angular scrolls on a field of pure translucent gold and are framed by narrow bands composed of graphically depicted green paroquets or peacocks, placed usually head and tail in the vertical bands and in the transverse ones with each alternate bird looking over its shoulder at its neighbour. The end-piece, framed with such a border, is a veritable "field of gold" upon which large Persian cone-patterns are seen to spring from vases and to be supported right and left by a pair of peacocks.

Pattan Asvali Pattern.

The graceful *ensemble* of the sprays of brilliantly coloured flowers that are employed to form the Persian cone-pattern—the beds of flowers in this garden of paradise—strikes the key upon which the scheme of colour and ornamentation of these marvellous shawls is formed. But the harmony is perfectly wonderful: the cones are alternately outlined in red and blue: certain flowers within them are red outlined in white, or white outlined in red, or blue outlined in white, or white outlined in blue, but they are all different and yet natural and artistic. So again the gorgeous peacocks with their green blue plumage, give the justification for the green paroquets and bright blue flowers of the border patterns.

Sir George Birdwood (*Journal of Indian Art, Part 37—1892—Plate 77*) has figured and described a beautiful example of these Pattan gold *sárís* and if the reader has not the opportunity to inspect the numerous examples shown in the Exhibition, he would do well to consult the publication named. The specimen

DIVISION 35. SILK KINKHABS: AURANGABAD.

described by Sir George Birdwood is in the possession of His Majesty the King and was taken from India, during the historic visit, as Prince of Wales, to this country in 1876.

Pattan gold Saris.

There are several very beautiful examples of these Pattan *sárís* to be seen in the Exhibition. In the Loan Collection Gallery, as already detailed, His Highness the Maharaja (Gaekwar) of Baroda shows several, all more or less historic in interest, since known to have been worn by certain Maharanis during their wedding ceremonials. In the Sale Gallery one of the finest ever exhibited will be found. This was discovered by Mr. Percy Brown while exploiting the resources of Aurangabad for the Exhibition. The owner originally possessed two, but having fallen into adverse circumstances and failing to sell these art treasures had one of them burned to recover the gold of which it was woven. The other was secured for the Exhibition and has been sold to the Industrial Museum of Calcutta. The history given of this *sárí* by the exhibitor, is curious and interesting. "The famous *sárí*" he writes "was prepared for the Maharaja Bhosla of Nagpur in 1853 at the cost of Rs. 2,200, but as his kingdom was annexed, it did not reach the Royal family. It was, therefore, left with Baba Shetha of Paithan, under whose direction the work was produced. As the Shetha became bankrupt, it was offered for sale at Aurangabad." Plate No. 82 is intended to represent this Aurangabad (Pattan) *sárí*, but without colour the mere outline of the design is meaningless.

Industrial School of Aurangabad.

The Industrial School of Aurangabad has contributed a set of gold *kinkhábs* manufactured there. Abdul Aziz of Aurangabad sends some very creditable *kinkhábs* such as No. 484—a dark green ground with gold over which a *jálí* of green *bûtis* and silver wire, picked out with blue and pink, has been thrown.

Panjab.—There is no authentic information as to the present existence of a *kinkháb* Industry at Delhi or anywhere in the Panjab. Doubtless during the times of the Mughal Emperors, however, there were State *kinkháb* weavers. At all events some of the finest *kinkhábs* in the Exhibition are those that date from about the time of Akbar and for a couple of centuries subsequently. The Rajas of Kashmir and Chamba had in those

DIVISION 35. SILK KINKHABS: PANJAB.

days many friendly dealings with the Emperors and rendered on more occasions than one services that doubtless were rewarded by many acts of personal distinction and decoration. Some of the most beautiful gold enamels and also gold *kinkhábs* in the Exhibition are those that seem in every likelihood to have been procured from, if not made at Delhi, about the period named. For example there are in the Exhibition two *kamarbands* that for artistic skill and workmanship are unsurpassed by any of the larger and more showy examples. Of these No. 4419 is a splendid work of art woven of pale green silk as the body material but almost completely covered by the purest gold and silver. The pattern of the central portion of the *kamarband* is a diaper of green silk looped together in elliptic spaces of about one inch in length, within which a trefoil leaf is worked in silver outlined with dark green on a gold surface. The border or *bél* is an open graceful silk scroll in pale green, outlined and veined with a darker shade, and with flowers in pure white silver, pendant within its arching lines. The end panel is a plain field of the purest gold with, worked over the surface, six lilies growing from separate stems as if on the ground. The leaves with their parallel veins are so vivid and life-like that one involuntarily feels them to ascertain if they are not painted instead of being woven. The flowers, of which five scapes are seen to arise from each plant, are woven in silver outlined and veined in green silk, every detail being faithfully portrayed, so that the species of lily might almost be determined. This wonderful piece of weaving could neither have been designed nor woven by an inhabitant of the plains of India, where such plants are quite unknown. The trefoil leaf of the *jálí* is also very remarkable but might easily be the wild oxalis or the common parochetus of the Himalaya. According to the information furnished by His Highness the Maharaja of Chamba, this *kamarband* was owned by Raja Balibhadar in A. D. 1590.

Loan Collection.

The other, No. 4420, is a *kamarband* woven of exceedingly finely spun cotton (perhaps in 150 counts) and natural *khaki* colour very possibly. The borders and ends are in gold *kinkháb* woven with a body of pale green silk. The margins of the *bél* are zig-zags

Very fine Cotton.

DIVISION 35. SILK KINKHABS: TANJORE.

of gold and green outlined with black and over the gold is worked a *búti* in purple, outlined in a deeper shade, the leaves being green outlined in black. The end-piece is simply a broader form of the same design as in the border. This beautiful *kamarband* is believed to have also belonged to Raja Balibhadar in A. D. 1590.

Bengal.—MURSHIDABAD—Is often spoken of as turning out *kinkhábs*, but at the present day at all events little or no gold and silver wire is used and the goods produced are, therefore, the *Amrus* or silk brocades described above.

Central Provinces.—Abdulla Miyan of Burhanpur in Nimar District has sent several large and beautiful gold *sárís* that much resemble the Aurangabad work detailed above. In the Burhanpur examples the field or body of the *sári* is usually pale blue spotted with red and the gold borders are woven as lines of elephants but the end-pieces are much as described— a field of pure gold over which brilliantly coloured floral cones supported by peacocks have been thrown.

Madras.—TRICHINOPOLY AND TANJORE.—Reference has already been made to the splendid *kinkhábs* to be seen in the Loan Collection Gallery, procured from the Tanjore palace. Plate No. 81, fig. 1, shows a *kinkháb* covered with the classic goose but, in the same glass case where that textile is displayed, will be seen several *sárís* of the Aurangabad type that doubtless may have all been made in Pattan. These are fine old examples of which it would be most instructive to obtain historic particulars.

Gulbadan.

But in both Trichinopoly and Tanjore the so-called "*gulbadans*," regularly manufactured, often contain so much gold wire as to entitle them to a position among the *kinkhábs* rather than the brocaded silks. The name *gulbadan* given to these textiles by the manufacturers has here, it will be observed, a totally different signification to what it receives in Northern India. The best series on view at the Exhibition are those made by Kanatchi V. Ramaswami Baghavatar of Trichinopoly. His No. 377-4 is a pale green *hari gulbadan*, striped lengthwise with orange and yellow with gold *bútis* between the lines. No. 377-9 has a black field with buds of white and gold. This is described as a *muksi kallidar gulbadan.* Lastly No. 378-1 is a *sárí* in maroon coloured silk woven in satinette and having circular gold spots. The backs of most of these quasi-*kinkhábs* are glazed as in the silks of Sind, Multan and Bhawalpur.

This very cursory account of the *kinkháb* industries of India may be concluded by a few observations that in the writer's opinion largely account for the undoubted degeneration witnessed during the past 20 years or so in the *kinkhábs* of India.

European Feeling.

Vested Interests.—Before passing away from the *kinkhábs*, it seems necessary that the strongly European feeling of many of the modern examples should be explained. As has been indicated in more positions than one in this work, the unavoidable influence of European domination and civilization is being felt in every direction and is operating often very injuriously on the arts and crafts of the country. Popular favour has turned to goods and designs presumed to be those approved of and used by Europeans, with the result that the older manufactures have been either starved to death or distorted into new forms, in supposed accord with the modern fashion In Benares, the writer was enabled, through the enthusiastic co-operation of the Collector, Mr. Radice, to visit all the leading *kinkháb* weavers at their factories and to discuss with them the origin of the designs in use. It then transpired that there are usually three persons concerned with the *kinkháb* trade—the designer who is invariably a Muhammadan; the weaver who may be either a Hindu or a Muhammadan; and the vendor or trader who is almost invariably a Hindu. Some of the difficulties in improving the trade proceed from the confliction of the vested interests of these three persons. For example, the weaver starches or sizes his goods before sending them out and by mutual agreement between all three classes a *kinkháb*, once it is sized, cannot be taken back again into stock. This habit is said to have originated through the traders sending goods on inspection that were retained until seriously injured, then returned. By all three persons agreeing that goods once sized shall not be taken back by either the weaver or the trader, the habit of sending out on inspection these expensive goods was effectually checked, but the result may be said to be an

Sizing of Kinkhabs.

DIVISION 35. SILK KINKHABS.

injury to the industry since if it be so desired to purchase goods not sized this becomes impossible.

The design is drawn on thin sheets of mica and when approved by the trader is set on a miniature frame by the designer and given to the weaver. By tying his warp threads on to the yellow silk tags on the model frame and drawing them through the comb, the loom is set and the work may be then carried out by a person almost quite unfamiliar with the design.

Sketches on Mica.

Decadence of Taste.—While examining a large series of old designs one of the chief *kinhkáb* manufacturers expressed amusement at the interest shown in worthless old mica sketches, long out of fashion. He explained that he possessed a book of great value from which all his most successful designs had, for some years past, been taken. On being desired to show this treasured pattern book, he produced a sample-book of English wall papers. It was learned that the weaver in question had, some years ago, been sent to London in connection with an Exhibition. While walking down a street he saw, in the window of a shop, a display of wall papers and thinking some of these would be of use to him in India, passed within the shop and had presented to him the pattern book he had found of such infinite value ever since. This at once explained the monstrous degeneration perceived in the Benares *kinkhábs*, and it is deplorable to think of fabrics woven at a cost of perhaps £10 sterling a yard being produced on the model of a wall paper sold very possibly at 4 pence the piece. But such unfortunately is the case and not in Benares only but throughout India the fine old art designs that have been attained after centuries of evolution are being abandoned and models utterly unsuited and far inferior artistically are being substituted. The writer can confidently affirm that he found in at least 50 per cent. of the important silversmiths' workshops of India, the illustrated trade catalogues of European firms and stores being employed as the pattern books upon which their silver plate was being modelled. One might multiply indefinitely examples of the wall paper and price catalogue kind, for few if any of the art industries of India are free from the taint of "European fashion." Mr. N. G. Mukerji in his paper on Murshidabad

English Wall papers.

Silks deals forcibly with the decline of Native taste and puts the popular notion tersely in the following sentence :—"The growing demand in India is for stuffs that *look* silky and catch the eye by their finish and the 'European elegance' of pattern." It is this "European elegance" that is ruining the art conceptions of India by depriving them of their originality, sentiment and poetry, and in no class of manufactures is this more apparent and deplorable than in the textiles.

DIVISION 35. SILK KINKHABS.

AWARDS FOR DIVISION 35.—SILKS.

AWARDS.

First Prize with gold medal to Bhagwan Das Gopi Nath of Benares for *kinkhábs.*

First Prize with silver medal to Parbhudas Rugnath Petigara of Ahmedabad for brocaded silk *sárí.*

First Prize with silver medal to Nur Mohammad Maulvi Khalilul Rahman and M. Rahmatalla Sardar of Benares for *kinkháb.*

First Prize with silver medal to L. Mathura Das of Benares for *kinkháb choga.*

First Prize with silver medal to Baba Shetha of Pattan, Aurangabad, for brocaded gauze *sárí.*

Second Prize with bronze medal to R. Balbhadra Das (Bhaddo Mal) of Benares for *kinkháb choga.*

Second Prize with bronze medal to Budhu Bhusan Biswas, Baluchar, Murshidabad, for brocaded silk exhibited by Tinkari Saha of Baluchar.

Third Prize with bronze medal to Kutooh Shaikh of Baluchar, Murshidabad, for brocaded silk exhibited by Durga Sanka Bhattacharji of Baluchar.

Third Prize with bronze medal to the Industrial School, Aurangabad, for *kinkháb.*

Third Prize with bronze medal to L. Dalu Mal, Atma Ram of Benares, for *kinkháb choga.*

Third Prize with bronze medal to Alibhoy Lagbhoy of Surat, for gold *kinkháb.*

Commended for gold *kinkháb sárí*—B. Oosman Khan Salar Khan Sahib of Bangalore City.

Commended for a *patola*—Ramachand Mulchand of Baroda.

DIVISION 36. WOOL AND PASHM.

Commended for *kinkháb lungi*—Hayat Mahommed of Bahawalpur.

Commended for *kinkháb*—Girdan Das Hari Das of Benares.

Division 36.—Wool and Pashm.

Unsuitability of Wool.

Wool takes a very subordinate position among the art crafts of India. This proceeds doubtless from two circumstances, *viz.*, its unsuitability as a material of clothing to the climatic conditions of the greater part of this country and its very perishable nature when subjected to the conditions that prevail in India. There is also a further circumstance of some value, though a consequence very possibly of the preceding, namely, the relatively inferior quality of the wool afforded by the sheep of India.

Fleece of a Goat.

In Kashmir, a large and highly artistic industry has, for centuries, had a world-wide fame, but the material used is the under fleece of a goat and, therefore, a kind of hair rather than wool: this is known as *pashm.* The goat from which it is obtained inhabits the Alpine tracts of the North-West Himalaya more especially the Northern slopes into Western Thibet.

It is in the Panjab, therefore, that woollen goods attain importance and no apology need be given for the foremost position being assigned, in the remarks that follow, to that province and its frontier State of Kashmir.

Literature.

PANJAB.—Dr. Forbes Watson's great work on *The Textile Manufactures and Costumes of the People of India* devotes many pages to the subject of wool. It also republishes the Jury Reports of the Exhibition of 1851, where the Kashmir *Pashminas* and Shawls were for the first time displayed to Europe in a sufficiently exhaustive manner to convey a fair conception of their merit and beauty. Mr. B. H. Baden Powell's *Hand-book of the Manufactures and Arts of the Panjab* was, in reality, the Official Report of the Panjab Exhibition. It affords much useful information, regarding the woollen manufactures of Northern India, 30 years ago. It also republishes *in extenso* Mr. Moorcroft's still earlier and most admirable and detailed account of the Kashmir shawl manufactures (*Travels*, Volume II, Chapter III) an article that has been drawn upon by every subsequent writer. Sir George Birdwood's *Industrial Arts of India*, while it does

DIVISION 36. WOOL AND PASHM.

not devote a special chapter to the woollen manufactures and shawls, gives many useful particulars, more especially in the chapters devoted to embroidery and carpets. Mr. Kipling, in connection with the report on the Calcutta International Exhibition and in numerous subsequent papers, has afforded useful details regarding these manufactures. In 1885 Mr. D. C. Johnstone wrote a monograph of *The Woollen Manufactures of the Panjab*, and shortly thereafter Mr. T. N. Mukerji wrote his *Art Manufactures of India*, in which a special chapter is devoted to woollen fabrics, but only the most incidental allusion made to Kashmir shawls.

Collections at the Exhibition.

It will thus be seen that from these and such like works, a fairly extensive range of information is available, but had nothing been written, a description of a tithe of the collections on view at the present Exhibition, might run to a volume of several hundred pages. His Highness the Maharaja of Kashmir has, for example, contributed a series of shawls and curtains, both loom and embroidery work, of so extensive and varied a character that it may, with perfect safety, be affirmed, on no other occasion has such a display been made. It was found that after stocking all the available show cases with shawls and curtains there was an overflow sufficient to drape a large portion of the walls of the Loan Collection Gallery, the walls of the entire transept of the Exhibition and also of the dining room at the Circuit House at Delhi. But even this superb series by no means indicates the whole of the treasures on view. From one end of India to the other Kashmir shawls have been received on loan from the nobility of India, many being of historic value and such as to afford useful data in any effort to fix the dates when at least some of the most beautiful designs may have first appeared in India. This huge mass of material does little more than indicate one-half the collections on view, since in the Sale Gallery may be seen quite as extensive and varied a series as in the Loan Collection Gallery. These have been contributed by the private manufacturers of Kashmir, Lahore, Amritsar, Ludhiana, etc., as well as from traders all over the country.

Draperies of the Exhibition.

It may thus be said that over 500 shawls and *chaddars*, of the kind usually designated Kashmir, are on view and that in

DIVISION 36. WOOL AND PASHM.

price they range from Rs. 50 to Rs. 10,000 each—the total value of the collection being well over £40,000.

The writer thus feels that to do justice to this subject, would necessitate a careful and minute study of the technique of the woollen shawls and kindred textiles and a laborious study of all the designs met with before he could be in a position to analyse the results obtained by the beautiful series on view.

Since neither the necessary time nor the space can be devoted to this most attractive study, the reader must be prepared for the remarks that follow dealing with but the salient points of the subject. It may, however, be useful to follow the example adopted under both Cotton and Silk, namely, to reserve the more artistic goods—Shawls and Brocades—for separate treatment.

Wool and Pashm.—The woollen manufactures of India generally may be said to consist of woven or felted blankets and piece-goods, of a very coarse nature usually, and only occasionally ornamental.

Sources Of Wool.

In the Panjab, the finest plains wool is that of Hissar, but Ferozepur, Lahore, Jhang, Shahpur, Peshawar, Dera Ismail Khan, Amritsar, Multan, Rawal Pindi and Jhelum each and all produce wool in fair quantity and quality. A large proportion of the wool worked up in the province, more especially that used in adulteration or as a substitute for *pashm*, comes from Australia. Bikanir also supplies a good quality of wool that is now being largely drawn off by Karachi to foreign markets. *Pashm* usually comes through Srinagar, Kullu and Bashahr to the Panjab and is consigned to Amritsar, Lahore and Ludhiana. Foreign *pashm* comes from Bokhara, *viâ* Kabul and Kirman to Bombay and Amritsar and is known as *kirmani*, but an even still more inferior wool known as *wahat shahi pashm* comes from Persia.

Foreign Wool.

A fair proportion of the woollen goods produced on hand looms in India, is woven of English yarn.

Woollen Mills.

There are several woollen power-loom mills in India, the best known being those at Dhariwal, Cawnpore, Bombay and Bangalore; but so far these are mainly concerned with the production of goods in competition with imported textiles rather than with Indian hand-loom goods.

Namdas or Felts.—These are made out of unspun wool. They are used as bed and floor rugs, for horse cloths and such like purposes. Certain wools are better suited for felting than others, but the felting property may be artificially produced by the use of soap or of a mixture of chalk and gum. When the latter is used, the felting is inferior and will not stand either a shower of rain or the simplest washing. Patterns are occasionally worked within the felts by so arranging the felting material as to leave spaces for the coloured wools to be inserted in their required positions, or the result is more expeditiously attained by the pattern being made from coloured felts, clipped up and the portions assorted as desired, then subsequently imbedded in the general felting material. Bhera, Kohat, Bannu, Hazara and Dera Ghazi Khan have a considerable traffic with the rest of the province in the supply of their coloured felts. Kohat and Bannu make very large felts sufficient to serve as floor carpets, but the designs are crude and in aniline dyes exclusively. Kashmir has, within the past 20 years, done a large trade in the supply of white or variously coloured felt rugs that are more or less richly embroidered by wool in chain stitch. These will be discussed below in the chapter devoted to the form of Embroidery.

DIVISION 36. WOOL AND PASHM.

Floor Carpets.

Piece Goods.—From the artistic stand-point, the manufacture of blankets and country cloths (*alwáns* and *lois*) from ordinary wool may be disregarded, so that it may be accepted that the chief woollen fabrics of artistic merit are those made of *pashm* or *shâll* wool (hence called *pashmina*). These are in the form of *chaddars, rumals, doshalas*, etc., long-cloth or serge of plain colours (*pashmina alwán*); *jamawars* or patterned *alwáns*, usually striped, and *bhabla, garbi*, or *patti* cloth and *chaddars*, etc. (the modern Rampur *chaddar*), which has woollen warp and cotton weft. This is softer, finer in texture and equally warm with the pure *pashmina* and has recently gained much in popular favour. But unfortunately, to the discovery of the advantages of this combination has to be attributed the success of the foreign power-loom manufacture of Rampur *chaddars*, now so largely imported and sold as Indian workmanship. *Nakti pashmina* (imitation *pashmina*) is a name given to the Rampur *chaddars* made of Rampur or foreign wools so treated as to closely resemble *pashmina*. *Pattu* is a term given to a fabric woven of wool or

Pashmina.

Rampur Chaddars.

DIVISION 36. WOOL AND PASHM.

goat hair treated so as to resemble *pashm* or a mixture of *pashm* and cotton. *Alwán* is either *ek tara* or *do tara* according as a single or double thread is used in weaving. *Malida* is the name given to *pashmina alwán* that has been shrunk (felted), softened by soaking in soap-nut (*rita*) treaded on by men with bare feet and pulled out by wedges hammered within the roll while exposed to the sun.

Centres of Manufacture.

The chief seats of the artistic woollen manufactures are Kashmir, Ludhiana, Simla, Kangra, Amritsar and Gujrat. Sirsa, Hissar and Rohtak are noted for their good blankets. It is perhaps needless, however, to specialise the manufactures of these towns since they will have to be dealt with in the chapter devoted to Shawls and again under the class devoted to Embroidery.

A fairly extensive assortment of fine quality *pashmina* serges will be seen in the Exhibition either as piece-goods or done up in dress lengths, with a fringe worked on the two ends so as to cause them to appear like very long and narrow shawls. They are mostly white, grey or blue in colour and of all qualities from the coarser heavy fabric suitable for gentlemen's wear, to the finest serges for ladies' dresses. A large assortment will also be found with the front panel, yoke, collar and cuffs, embroidered in silk by a sort of French knot stitch. The best series are exhibited by Davi Sahai Chamba Mall of Amritsar.

UNITED PROVINCES.—These Provinces are by no means self-supporting in the matter of wool. A fair quantity is produced in Agra and Mirzapur, but by far the best wool comes from the hill districts of Garhwal, Almora and Naini Tal. But the supplies drawn from the Panjab, Rajputana, Sind and foreign countries, meet the major portion of the demands of these provinces.

Piece-Goods.—The manufacture of coarse cloth and inferior blankets may be said to be the chief goods produced, if the manufactures of the Cawnpore Woollen Mills be disregarded.

Namdas.—Felting is to some extent practised at Bahraich. Patterns are usually obtained by making thin felts of the desired colours and cutting these up in the shapes of the contemplated designs. They are then assorted on the felting surface and fresh coloured or white felting wool distributed over the surface. The coloured design is thus, as it were, imbedded within the felt.

BENGAL.—Except in the province of Behar, the rearing of wool and the production of woollen goods may be said to be practically unknown in Bengal.

BOMBAY.—Wool-weaving in the form of blankets and sacking is more or less practised in every district, and felting to an even greater extent. The best wool used is reported to be that of Rajputana, Marwar, Kathiawar and the Deccan. The prevailing colours are white for Sind and Gujrat and black for Deccan and Khandesh wools. Sind and Baluchistan wool has become an article of importance in Karachi, but all the fair qualities come from beyond the province, being mostly Rajputana, more especially Bikanir wool.

Descriptions of Wool.

Felts or Namdas—Are made in almost every district. They are used as saddle cloths and mattresses (*burnus*). A felt cape is also largely used in Gujrat called a *ghumti* or *mochla*. This is thrown over the head as a sort of waterproof covering worn during the rains. As in all other parts of India, felts are produced by compressing a thin layer of damp wool spread out for that purpose on a mat. The mat with its layer of wool is rolled up and unrolled, the while being pressed, until after two or three hours the fibre completely unites through its own natural tendency to curl.

SIND AND BALUCHISTAN.—The *namdas* or felts of both Sind and Baluchistan are often of excellent quality and tastefully coloured or richly embroidered. The *namda* saddle cloths of the Baluchis are highly artistic but mainly because of their being embroidered.

CENTRAL PROVINCES.—The rearing of sheep is a fairly important undertaking in Jabalpur, Nagpur, Chanda, Wardha and Raipur. Hoshangabad and Saugor have some reputation for their blankets and *namdas*.

RAJPUTANA AND CENTRAL INDIA.—Blankets of fair quality are made at Jaipur, Bikanir and Jodhpur—those of Todgarh in Ajmir being considered the best. Bikanir is famed all over India

DIVISION 36. WOOL AND PASHM.

for its serges and at many parts of Rajputana the *Jat* or *Vaishnava* women spin and weave a textile used in the preparation of warm under-skirts and *sárís.* The chief places noted for these are Alai, Khajwana and Indana.

The *namdas* or felts of Jodhpur and Jaipur are exceptionally fine. They are pure white and are often ornamented by a sort of appliqué method by which successive layers of dog-tooth cut fringes and flowers of white or of red or orange coloured felts are attached to the *namda.*

MADRAS AND MYSORE.—The black wool of Mysore, Bellary and Kurnool and the white wool of Coimbatore are the two qualities best known. The sheep of Madras proper, namely, from Ganjam to Tinnevelly, yield hair rather than wool. The only manufactures are carpets and blankets. Of the former, there are five centres of production—Bangalore, Ellore in Godavari, Masulipatam in Kistna, Walajanagar in North Arcot and Ayyampet in Tanjore. The woollen mills of Bangalore turn out serges and other textiles; here and there all over the Presidency ordinary country blankets are made.

Shawls and Chaddars.

Disregarding for the moment the popular classification of these textiles, according to size, shape and purpose, in other words into plaids, shawls, handkerchiefs, table-covers, curtains, scarves, etc., it may be said that there are two main forms or methods of production, *viz.*, the *Tili* or *Kanikar* and the *Amlikar.*

Loom *versus* Needle.

The former have the patterns elaborated on the loom, the latter by means of the needle. The one is woven, the other embroidered. This exceedingly simple and useful separation unfortunately is no sooner stated than it has to be withdrawn, for, excepting with the very most expensive loom shawls, the needle is invariably used to furnish certain portions of the design in all loom shawls. In fact Kashmir shawls are more frequently produced as the combination of *kanikar* and *amlikar* methods than of either the one or the other by itself.

Patchwork.

Another useful hint for classification may be had from the circumstance that many shawls (it would be safer to say the majority of the Kashmir shawls) are made by a sort of patchwork.

That is to say where the patterns are to be loom woven (*tili* work), they are formed in ribbons or strips that may be twelve to eighteen inches in breadth or not more than half to two inches broad. These flowered ribbons are woven on exceedingly curious little looms, of so primitive a character, in fact, that it is difficult to believe the results seen could have been obtained by such means. The ribbons are then cut to the desired lengths, are sewn together in fulfilment of the scheme of pattern and are attached to a plain central piece or field. The border strips are often woven of silk with a *pashmina* extra weft: the object of such borderings being to give them the strength and weight desired. The field or body of the shawl, etc., is woven of the purest and finest *pashm*.

DIVISION 38. WOOL AND PASHM.

Ribbons.

A patchwork shawl of the kind indicated might be described as the most characteristic of all the many forms and conditions produced in Kashmir. But instead of being *tili* work, it may be *amlikar*. For this purpose pieces of *pashmina* of the required quality and colour are produced. These are cut up into various patches and shapes and all are sewn together in elaboration of the scheme contemplated. They are then completely embroidered over the surface, the result being the production of an *amli* shawl that sometimes so closely resembles *tili* work that it may be a matter of the greatest uncertainty to distinguish the one from the other. Patchwork loom shawls are usually formed of pieces of one breadth throughout their length, and are in fact strips or ribbons sewn together. Patchwork embroidery shawls are composed of irregularly formed patches, the separate pieces elaborating the main colour effects desired. This difference is a useful one in determining doubtful instances but even this may be utterly overthrown, since it is customary to find, what might not inaptly be described as restoration shawls, that is to say, shawls built up of two or more old shawls, the border pieces having been cut off in strips and sewn on to new textures. In such instances perfectly straight strips of *amli* work may be found.

Embroidered Patchwork.

Restoration Shawls.

It will thus be seen that it would be arbitrary, however desirable from a systematic point of view, to separate Kashmir shawls into loom-woven and needle-embroidered, though it would be

DIVISION 36. WOOL AND PASHM.

Needlework Cheaper.

equally misleading to ignore the existence of these two styles, since needlework (contrary to the popular acceptation of hand-work) is very much cheaper than loom. In fact the degree of needlework detected on a loom shawl may be accepted as the extent of the weaver's admission of defective workmanship. It is thus of the very greatest importance to be able to distinguish the two styles. But for the frequency of their combination in one and the same textile, the writer would in fact have preferred to deal with the *amli* work under Class VIII. But by *amli* work should be understood that particular form of embroidery designed exclusively to imitate *tili* work. All other forms of embroidery, met with in Kashmir, and even the shawl stitch when applied to other purposes (such as the modern tea-table cloth) than shawls, will be dealt with under Class VIII, and not in the present article. It will thus in fact become necessary, under Class VIII, to revert to these shawls in order to make clear the additional forms of embroidery met with in Kashmir.

Other Embroideries.

Centres.

Centres of production.—For many years the production of these shawls was confined to Kashmir. When Ranjit Singh commenced to extend his rule all over the Panjab, shawl weaving was almost confined to the Muhammadans resident in Kashmir, but through the encouragement then given them, many of the weavers came and settled in Amritsar. The great famine that visited Kashmir in 1833 A.D. drove, however, many of the weavers into the Panjab and weaving colonies were in consequence established at Amritsar, Ludhiana, Nurpur, Gurdaspur, Sialkot, Lahore, etc. Fearing the opposition of these new centres of production, the Kashmir authorities prohibited the export of the wool, but supplies came to the Indian weavers through Simla and Kullu, also Peshawar and Kirman. This disadvantage led, however, to an inferior article being produced in the Panjab centres, or at all events gave these a name for inferiority which they still bear. France was for many years the chief foreign market for these shawls. French agents accordingly came every year or even resided permanently in the towns of production and hence gradually exercised a considerable influence over the industry. The Franco-Prussian war was a severe blow, however, to the

Reputation.

Markets.

traffic, and the check thereby given has never been remedied. In fact the fashion has changed in Europe and America, so that these shawls are now mainly curiosities or are used as draperies.

During its prosperity the vast profits of the Kashmir shawl trade led to their production by power-loom, more especially at Paisley. Some 30 to 40 years ago it was an admitted necessity in Scotland that a bride should receive a Paisley imitation Kashmir shawl. Although these shawls had the severity of all power-loom fabrics they reproduced every detail of the Kashmir originals and the resulting cheapening process greatly helped to destroy the European demand for both the Kashmir original and the Paisley imitation, and reacted injuriously also on the Indian market. The shawl weavers of India look entirely to India as their market and it was perhaps an unfortunate circumstance that they ever established a continental market for their goods.

In India expensive Kashmir shawls have for centuries been much sought after by the princes and nobles. The possession of one or more of priceless value was an admitted mark of nobility, and accordingly such shawls were treasured and handed down from generation to generation. Some of the finest Kashmir shawls are, therefore, those belonging to the older families of India. The Loan Collection will accordingly be seen to possess a series of the greatest beauty and some of them very old and historic in interest.

Manipulation or Fabrication.—It would serve no useful purpose were the writer to attempt a description in a few sentences of all the stages of manufactures and the methods and contrivances adopted in the Kashmir shawl trade. It is essential that persons who desire a comprehensive conception should consult some of the numerous technical works that exist. One of the most interesting may be said to be that written by Moorcroft—a distinguished traveller and botanist—who visited Kashmir some sixty years ago. It may suffice the purpose of the present publication to abstract a few passages from his most admirable paper on Kashmir shawls:—"When the warp is fixed in the loom, the *nakash*, or pattern drawer, and the *tarah-guru* and *talim-guru*, or persons who determine the proportion of yarn of different

DIVISION 36. WOOL AND PASHM.

colours to be employed, are again consulted. The first brings the drawing of the pattern, in black and white. The *tarah-guru*, having well considered it, points out the disposition of the colours, beginning at the foot of the pattern and calling out the colour, the number of threads to which it is to extend, that by which it is to be followed, and so on in succession, until the whole pattern has been described. From his dictation, the *talim-guru* writes down the pattern in a kind of character or shorthand, and delivers a copy of the document to the weavers."

Tojis or Special Needle-like Shuttles.

"The workmen prepare the *tojis*, or needles, by arming each with coloured yarn of the weight of about four grains; these needles, without eyes, are made of light smooth wood, and have both their sharp ends slightly charred to prevent their becoming rough or jagged through working. Under the superintendence of *tarah-guru*, the weavers knot the yarn of the *toji* to the warp. The face or right side of the cloth is placed next to the ground, the work being carried on at the back or reverse, on which hang the needles in rows, and differing in number from four hundred to fifteen hundred, according to the lightness or heaviness of the embroidery. As soon as the *Ustad* is satisfied that the work of one line or woof is completed, the comb is brought down upon it with a vigour and repetition apparently very disproportionate to the delicacy of the materials."

Twilled cloth.

"The cloth of shawls, generally, is of two kinds, one plain, or of two threads, one twilled, or of four. The former was, in past times, wrought to a great degree of fineness, but it has been of late less in demand. The various twilled cloths are usually from 5 to 12 *girahs* or nails wide. Shawls are twilled and are commonly about 24 nails broad and differ in their extent of field. Two persons are employed in weaving a cloth of this breadth. One throws the shuttle from the edge as far as he can across the warp, which is usually about half way. It is there seized by the second weaver, who throws it onwards to the opposite edge, and then returns it to his companion, who, in his turn, introducing his finger into the warp, forwards the shuttle to the edge whence it started, and then recommences the operation. The cloth thus made is frequently irregular, the threads of some parts of the woof being driven up tightly, and in others left open, from which results a succession of bands, sufficiently distinguishable whilst without colour, but still more obvious when dyed. The open texture is in a degree remediable by the introduction of fresh threads; but there is no sufficient cure for that which has been much compacted. One might be led to suspect that there existed some radical defectiveness in the principle of this mode of weaving not readily mastered, were not pieces of cloth found occasionally of an almost perfect regularity of texture. But the greatest irregularity is discoverable in those shawls which have the deepest and heaviest borders and a further examination compels me to retract an observation somewhere made, of the artist being so much engrossed by attention to the work of the pattern as to neglect the structure of the field. The edge of the warp in the loom is filled with the heavy thread of the *phiri*, or seconds yarn charged also with colour, so that in a few lines the front of the worked part advances beyond that of the plain part of field, and an endeavour to equalize this betrays the weaver into a work which proves fruitless, and, in general, the heavier the embroidery on the border, and of course, the higher the price of the shawl, the less regular is the structure of the cloth."

Reparation of defects.

"Such indeed in some instances is the degradation of the cloth in the field, as to induce some foreign merchants to cause it to be removed, and another piece to be engrafted within the edge of the border. But in this case there is no other remedy than in a judicious selection of a sheet of the same breadth and fineness; for, although two breadths of the narrow cloth might fit the vacant spaces, yet these must be joined by the *refugar* in the middle; and although this can be so done that the band differs not in thickness from the rest of the cloth, yet the joint is discernible when held between the eye and the light, from the threads in the joined breadth being not continuous in the same line, whereas any irregularity of this nature is drowned in the edge of the border. The best practice to ensure a good field seems to consist in weaving the border, in every case, separately and inserting the field by the *refugar*."

Substitution of Fresh Field.

The quality of the shawl cloth is estimated by the number of

DIVISION 36. WOOL AND PASHM.

strokes of the *tuftin* or comb that are given to the inch. Thus some are spoken of as 100s, 200s, 300s, 500s, and the very finest up to 1500s, in the *girah* ($\frac{1}{16}$th of a yard).

Division of Labour.

The writer discussed the necessity of having one man to design the pattern, another to allot the colours to be used, a third to draw up a written description, and a fourth to weave the shawl. One of the Kashmir shawl weavers overhearing the conversation observed that he saw nothing extraordinary in that and sagely added that one man composes music, a second makes it his profession to print the music, a third to sell copies of it and a fourth to perform the same. Later on the weaver in question, when asked to sign his name, in proof of certain payments, drew a flower at the bottom of each page of manuscript and so accurately that it could be at once identified from spurious imitations. He could not write, but designing patterns was to him a second nature and a particular *búti* became his signature.

Signature of Weaver.

Chief Forms or Shapes of Shawls.—There may be said to be two chief forms of shawls and one of *pashmina* cloth in which brocading or embroidery are resorted to for ornamentation. The shawls will be dealt with in the remarks below and the cloth reserved for a special section. The English word "shawl" came from the Hindi *shâll* and thus carries with it a token of the early association of England with the Kashmir shawl trade. There are two chief forms of shawls:—

1st: Do-shalla or Twin-shawl—(*Plate No. 50*—four examples in centre of plate).—These are long narrow shawls always sold in pairs. The pattern varies according to the central field or *matan* and the border *palu*. When the *matan* is plain, the shawl is *khali-matan*. If four colours are sewn together it is *char-baghan*. If there be a central medallion of flowers, etc., in the *matan*, the shawl is spoken of as *chand* (moon), and if it has corner flowers these are *kunj*. When an end panel is distinctly developed, that is to say is broader than the side borders, the shawl is spoken of as *shahpasand* or *palledar* (King's pattern), and if the end-pieces are only equal to the borders it is *chardaur* or *dordar*. When the pattern is woven or embroidered so that it is the same on both sides, the shawl is a *dorakha*.

Terms.

Colours.

The prevailing colours are white (*safed*), black (*mushki*), crimson (*gulanar*), scarlet (*kermizi*), purple (*uda*), blue (*ferozi*), green (*zingari*) and yellow (*zard*).

2nd: Kasaba or Chaddar-Rumal—(*Plate No. 50* top corners and *Plate No. 51* middle line).—These are more or less square shawls. They have assumed their present forms and qualities very largely in consequence of European demand. The *adahkat* (*posi*) or half shawl is also a European suggestion. It is so embroidered or woven that when folded across the middle, the pattern will show on both exposed surfaces. If there be thus revealed three strips of ornamental work, it is *tehri bel*, and if only two, *dohri bel*. The Rampur *chaddar* is a fine quality shawl, woven for the most part with woollen warp and a specially prepared silk sometimes even cotton weft. The wool used is of course the finest and purest *pashm* or the whole fabric may be *pashmina*. They are usually twilled or may have a damask pattern worked in the plain colour. They are also very frequently embroidered in the shawl stitch fashion with narrow borders and inside corner pieces or by pale coloured or white silk by the knotted braid form of embroidery already mentioned and to be more fully discussed in the special chapter on Embroidery. Plate No. 50 (bottom right corner) shows a *chaddar* with embroidered border.

Rampur Chaddar.

Patterns.—The series of long shawls (*do-shallas*) and square shawls (*rumals*) at the Exhibition from Kashmir, Amritsar, Ludhiana, and in the Loan Collection Gallery from all parts of India, is so extensive and varied that it would be hopeless to attempt a description of even some of the more remarkable examples. One conception runs through them all, namely the Persian "cone" or "flame" pattern, what in India is often spoken of as the "Kashmir shawl pattern," and by the Kashmiris is known as *butha* (*buta*). The deflexed tip of the "flame" is usually turned toward the left, rarely the right, as in the Plate No. 2 of Mr. Kipling's paper on the *Industries of the Panjab*, given in Vol. IV of the *Indian Art Journal*.

Centres of Manufacture.

Kashmir.—The following are the chief exhibitors of *Do-shallas* and *Rumals*:—His Highness the Maharaja of Kashmir

Kashmir.

DIVISION 36. WOOL AND PASHM.

has sent to the Sale and Loan Galleries 200 shawls. As already observed, in more places than one, it would be hopeless to attempt a description of these since they represent practically every design that has ever been conceived in this line of textiles. The *Rumals* are exceptionally fine, especially those with bold patterns in black and brown. One of the shawls belonging to the Srinagar Museum is valued at Rs. 22,000 and many in the Exhibition will be seen at Rs. 3,000 to Rs. 10,000.

M. Abdul Aziz of Fateh Kadal, Srinagar, has sent a fine series—many of them remarkably good, especially a *do-rakha* or double woven shawl with patterns the same on both sides, and an *amlikar rumal* of the *charbaghan* (the four garden) style with green alongside of red and yellow in the same position to blue.

Woven Map of Srinagar.

Picture shawl.—Major Stuart H. Godfrey has sent to the Exhibition a shawl that has excited the greatest possible interest. As a piece of colour it is very admirable but in point of design it is devoid of artistic interest. The remarkable feature about this shawl, however, is the fact that it is a panoramic map of Srinagar and depicts the city with its palaces, people, mountains, lakes, rivers and even avenues of trees with the names embroidered beneath each. Major Godfrey says of this wonderful fabric:—"This specimen of the Kashmir hand-worked shawl was purchased at one of the sales of the surplus shawls of Kashmir, held by the Accountant-General, Jammu and Kashmir State. An account and photogravure of this shawl was published in the *Magazine of Art* in August 1901. The design is a plan to scale of the city of Srinagar as it stood in the time of Maharaja Sir Ranbir Singh, G.C.S.I., by whose orders the shawl was made. The shawl was, it is said, designed for presentation to H. M. the King Emperor, then Prince of Wales, had the Royal visit to Jammu extended to Srinagar. The chief places in and around the city can easily be identified from the shawl." Sir George Birdwood (*Indian Industrial Arts, p. 367*) alludes to the fact that His Majesty actually did receive during his tour in India a shawl worked with a map of the city of Srinagar.

Chamba.

CHAMBA.—This State has sent to the Exhibition a black

pashmina chaddar (No. 4421), believed to have been procured in the time of Raja Umed Singh, A. D. 1750. It is entirely loom-work, the end-pieces showing a series of floral cones rising from flat basins. The flowers are large, the majority purple, outlined with fainter shades. Other flowers are blue outlined in purple, and still others grey outlined in white. They are all composite in type, the scaly heads forcibly bring to mind the *Centaurea*. **DIVISION 36. WOOL AND PASHM.**

AMRITSAR.—There are several very excellent collections of shawls such as those sent by Khan Muhamed Shah and Saifud-din. This firm were at one time merchant princes when the shawl trade was in its glory. They have for some years practically ceased to trade in shawls and those shown are mostly very old samples that have been handed down from one owner to another as models of perfection. No. 1308 is a *chinikar asli* shawl—white field with blue-black *palledar* designs, chiefly consisting of the cone pattern with alternating floral scrolls. This is represented in Plate No. 83, fig. 4. No. 1309 is a white shawl with flowers in rich pink and blue—the cone being boldly and gracefully drawn. No. 1311 is a *rumal* woven on one side only but very elaborate and beautiful. No. 1313 is a *sarrakh palledar* (*shahpasand*) shawl in deep dark red. The border shows cusped arches in blue, red and green, enclosing fantastic developments of the cone. **Amritsar.**

Davi Sahai Chamba Mall of Amritsar shows a superb series of shawls, *rumals* and *chaddars*, which it would take many pages to describe. One of these, a *dokakha* shawl, is shown on Plate No. 83, figs. 2 and 3. The former represents the under side with the cones turned to the right and the latter a portion of the upper surface with the cones in the normal position. This is so admirably woven that the pattern is completely developed without recourse having to be made to the embroiderer.

Rajputana.—BIKANIR.—His Highness the Maharaja of Bikanir has contributed to the Loan Collection Gallery many very charming fine old shawls—all loom-woven and of the most delicate colourings. These are mostly one to two hundred years old. No. 2134 is a white Kashmir shawl with border richly woven in cone pattern, the cones being made up of wreaths of flowers **Bikanir.**

DIVISION 36. WOOL AND PASHM.

springing from a miniature vase (Plate No. 83, fig. 1). The overturned top of the cone is a spray of minute flowers. No. 2137 is a similar shawl in rich deep red with large cones. No. 2139 is a *dulai* or shawl in stripes of blue, red and grey, with intervening bands of white and with open scrolls within the bands—a *jamawar* shawl. Lastly, No. 2138 is a dark green-blue shawl with floral cones. This is one of the most beautiful in the series.

United Provinces.—LUCKNOW.—Nawab Hyder Mirza sends two very delightful *do-shallas* to the Exhibition. No. 39 is in white *pashmina* with loom-woven borders. The general scheme of colours may be said to be red and blue with a multiplicity of cones, the corner pieces being middle work, large cones, fringed with excrescences of small cones of various sizes and shapes. Both the border pattern and the field between the great cones of the end panel, appear to be built up of fan-like expanded flowers that closely resemble the pink. This shawl will be seen in Plate

Sikh Design.

No. 50-A. The particular design indicated is said to have originated with the Sikh dignitaries and is thus probably about 200 years old.

No. 40 is a superb *do-shalla* with a red centre and very deep borders and end-pieces. These are composed of an infinity of much elongated cones hooking into each other in every direction and gemmating into still more elongated cones that unite overhead and form a sort of mimic mirab arches. This design defies description, though the general tone may be said to be a soft blending of pale red and delicate blue. But here and there and everywhere the most unexpected surprises in colour occur, such as the long tapering beak of the cone having a prominently black outline, the lower half of the same cone being in red outline; or the upper half of another may be outlined in an ivory white that rises from the surface in a manner that demarcates the design in a most remarkable fashion. The border is a graceful scroll of poppies with the flowers shown in side view, in full face view, and also in bud; the crumplings of the petals being indicated by a mottling of the blue and red colourings.

BENARES.—Mr. B. Moti Chand, Rais of Benares, has sent to the Exhibition (Loan Collection Gallery) some splendid Kashmi shawls. One of these (No. 1653) is a *do-shalla* said to be very old. It is woven of white *pashmina* and has broad strips of loom woven borders and end-pieces. The lines of attachment of these are cleverly covered by needlework embroideries of an inch or so in breadth, leading on to the white *pashmina* cloth. The charm of this particular shawl is the peach bloom effect produced. The ground colour is dull Indian red, the patterns are worked in sapphire blue, bordered with black, and the twigs and leaves are outlined in pale orange. This is the general scheme but it is elaborated by a blending and balancing of the colours that is most fascinating. For example the outlines of the cones are blue in one, yellow in another, red in a third and white in a fourth, but there are double lines around the cones and these blend from one tone to the other along their length. Thus the cones with a blue outer border have an inner edging of yellow that passes into orange and red along its length. Those with yellow have an inner fringe of blue similarly shaded, and those with white have red. The large cones are also double, one within the other. From the inner cone a fringe or dangle of trellis sapphire extends to the outer cone and this is rendered in the deepest blue.

DIVISION 36. WOOL AND PASHM.

Blending of Colours.

The general tone is therefore blue on red. The end-pieces are composed of eight strips sewn together. It is not stated how old this shawl may be, but it would seem to be several centuries.

Embroidery or Amli work (*Plate No. 51*).

When a pattern is to be embroidered, it is drawn on a piece of paper, outlined by needle pricks and transferred to the textile by finely powdered charcoal being rubbed through the puncturings of the stencil on to the cloth.

Both shawls and *jamawars*, as already stated, may have their coloured patterns worked exclusively by the needle. This has in fact been so often alluded to that it may perhaps be viewed as superfluous to specially assign a paragraph to this subject. The stitch employed is invariably a form of parallel darning, the thread being made to nip up the loops of the warp but only occasionally allowed to penetrate the texture. This is so cleverly accomplished that it is often almost impossible to distinguish such embroidery from loom work. In fact the Kashmiri weaves so

Darning Stitch.

DIVISION 36. WOOL AND PASHM.

Imperfect Weaving.

badly that one portion may have the wefts firmly compacted, another be loose and open. These evidences of careless weaving the Kashmiri has no hesitation in accepting as a perfectly true indication of the character of his work, but he smilingly explains that these and such like defects can be entirely removed by the embroiderer. With this object in view threads are carried within the texture until the imperfections are completely obliterated.

Finishing Touches.

But in addition to repairing defects, the embroiderer is very largely employed in giving finishing touches to woven patterned shawls. The outlines of the design are sharped up by wool or silk threads run round the most minute details in each and every shade of colour that may be required. The stitch employed for this work is a sort of obliquely overlapping short darn. Then again while border pieces may be so neatly joined to the body of the shawl that the union can with difficulty be either seen or felt, still this feat is further improved by the embroiderer carrying the design of coloured ornamentation of the border for an inch or so on to the fabric of the shawl and thus across the line of union. By this means the union is not only still further disguised but strengthened. So in the same way corner pieces (*kunj*) are often needlework, while the borders are woven. (Plate No. 50 A.)

Union Embroidered Over.

In the Exhibition may be seen an extensive series of *amlikar* shawl work. Most have the embroidery in *pashm* and are intended purely and simply to imitate the *kanikar* work. Others are in silk and in both darn and chain stitch. These are very possibly an evolution from the handkerchiefs that were and are still made in Kashmir, Chamba and Kullu, and are probably more ancient in design than the Muhammadan conquest of Kashmir. Fringing the top of Plate No. 51 will be seen a series of embroidered handkerchiefs. It is somewhat significant that these very frequently show a strong tendency to animal ornamentation if not to mythological scenes – thus pointing to a possible Hindu origin. In the needlework shawls done in the plains of India, this peculiarity seems to have been greatly developed, so much so in fact that a shawl or *rumal* with animal portraiture, might almost at once be pronounced as not having been made in Kashmir.

Embroidered Handkerchiefs.

DIVISION 36. WOOL AND PASHM.

Murshidabad Gold Medal Shawl.

One of the most superb *amlikar do-shallas* in the Exhibition is No. 20 – a *shahpasand* shawl exhibited by Trailakhya Dass of Murshidabad and Dacca. It is presumed to be very considerably over 100 years old and to have been made in Amritsar. It is priced at Rs. 6,900 and has been sold to His Highness the Nizam of Hyderabad. The border represents a conventional scene of the King on an expedition accompanied by his nobles and army. A somewhat remarkable feature and one not uncommon with shawls of probable Hindu origin (or made in the plains of India), is the fact that the cones are inverted or have the wind blown tips of the flames deflected to right not to left as is customary with Kashmir shawls proper. In the Pattan gold *sárís* (already fully discussed) it is customary for the cone to be inverted (see Plate No. 82). Further it may be added there are seven such cones, not eight as in most of the *shahpasand* style. Plate No. 84 shows this wonderful shawl which in point of excellence of needlework at least is unsurpassed by any other sample in the Exhibition.

Jamawars or Brocaded Woollen Piece goods.

Woollen Brocades.

Jamawars are pieces of a fixed length, such as that required for the manufacture of a *choga* or coat, or suitable for a lady's dress. They are in reality brocaded woollen goods which may be entirely in wool (*pashm*) or partly cotton, and have the floral designs or brocaded portions either in *pashm* or silk. They may be loom-wooven throughout or ordinary *alwán pashmina* (piece goods) middle embroidered. In the latter case the pattern runs lengthwise but so completely covers the breadth that like wall-papers the patterns unite when sewn together. The ends are fringed so that in some respects they resemble the Scotch plaid. In the *jamawars* of Kashmir, the ends are woven straight on from the textile, but in those of Amritsar and Ludhiana they are sewn on. This is a useful hint by which the goods of these various places may, as a rule, be recognised.

Designs.

There is an infinity of designs met with in the *jamawars* and these are referable largely to two groups, the *rega-butis* or small flowered, and the *kirkha-butis* or large flowered. Plate No. 50 (to the extreme left) shows two *kirkha-butis*. A third series are the *jaldars* or patterns that assume more or less the

DIVISION 36. WOOL AND PASHM.

Striped French Muslins.

reticulation of a net. Some of the earliest designs are, however, stripes and in consequence it is sometimes affirmed that *jamawars* are woollen textiles with striped designs —the textiles which the French are said to have taken to imitating in their striped muslins. But it would seem much more likely that many of the designs presently seen in the *jamawars* of Kashmir at least, were originally made from designs given by the French agents who came to purchase the shawls. At all events the Kashmiris refer many patterns, especially of borderings and dress trimmings, to a Mr. Prinsep who took charge of the Kashmir shawl industry on behalf of the then Maharaja. He doubtless exercised a pronounced influence on at least the goods that are admittedly European in intention, such as the *rumals* and dress-piece *jamawars.* In Europe, *jamawar* dress pieces are "Turkish shawls," a curiously interesting suggestion of the association of striped textiles with Turkey.

Punjab Jamawars.

But the Kashmiris who had left the "Happy Valley" during the great famine, and settled in Amritsar, Ludhiana, Gujrat and Sialkot, etc., soon found lucrative markets in some of the great Muhammadan centres (Lucknow, Hyderabad, etc.) for their *jamawars.* A mixed textile of silk and cotton (*himru*)—presently to be described—was in extensive demand by the Muhammadans of India for the manufacture of their coats and other garments. The designs used by the *himru* weavers of Hyderabad (Deccan) were accordingly carried to the Panjab and there imitated in wool or wool and silk, with the result that a new inspiration was given for the *jamawar* weavers and there came into existence the long series of profusely floral designs that are sometimes called *jangla* or *phuldár* and *guldar.* Of these many are clearly copies from European wall papers or Brussels carpets, in which flowers are depicted life-like with every detail of perspective and shadow—incongruous details that cause the patterns to rise from the surface instead of remaining below as in all truly Indian flat surface decorations.

Jalalpur Jamawars.

In JALALPUR near Gujrat there sprang into existence a peculiar style that survives to this day. This consists of broad stripes, alternating with narrow ones, the prevailing colours being shades

DIVISION 36. WOOL AND PASHM.

of red, more rarely blue, with white or yellow backgrounds for the chief floral scrolls. These are woven of wool but of very ordinary quality, so that the texture is heavy, coarse and open. The patterns employed are also formed by a sort of zig-zag outline, due doubtless to a slightly different method of weaving from that of the *jamawars* of Kashmir. There are, for example, no brocaded or additional weft patterns. Striped *jamawars* of this style were at one time fairly popular as curtains and drapings generally but they have gone out of fashion and are hardly manufactured at the present day.

Collections on view.

In the Exhibition a long series of *jamawars* may be inspected, both from Kashmir itself and from the various towns in the Panjab where the manufacture of this class of goods has assumed relatively greater importance than in Kashmir. The following are some of the principal collections on view :—

LUDHIANA.—Ashan Shah & Co. No. 930—a modern *gular* or flowering design with the ground black, the flowers large, closely aggregated and in every conceivable colour, with elaborately shaded and brilliantly coloured green leaves. Price Rs. 450. No. 931—Similar but with pink field and flowers and leaves very bright.

No. 933—A *Jamawar-jaldar* with orange ground and a completely reticulating tree bearing here and there small red and green cones. No. 934—Pale blue field with graceful bunches of flowers, two inches in size, dispersed in regular lines across the breadth. No. 935—Grey field with purple and orange flowers. No. 936—Brown field with large pink and white carnation-like flowers surrounded by sprays of small purple flowers. No. 937—*jamawar-jaldar* pale brown with soft sprays of pink, blue and green flowers. No. 938—A *choga* or coat, described as a *sozankar purnatan*, is made from a richly needle-embroidered *jamawar*. No. 918—*Jamawars* of Jalalpur only with narrow strips bearing delicate scrolls along their surfaces as in the Amritsar *jamawar* figures in Mr. Kipling's paper on the *Industries of the Panjab*, Volume IV, Plate No. 4 of the *Indian Art Journal*.

These have been detailed because they are representative of

DIVISION 36. WOOL AND PASHM. all the modern Punjab *jamawars* and not because of the possession of any very special merit over other collections.

AMRITSAR.—Khan Mahomed Shah and Saifuddin send a few exceptionally charming *jamawars* of which attention may be directed to:—No. 1314—*Safed jamawar*, a bold example in large cone patterns, arranged almost in transverse lines and with a liberal intermixture of green leaves and red and blue flowers. No. 1316 is spoken of as a *basanti* and is very similar to the preceding except that the field is yellow. No. 1318—A *choga* of cloth (*mushki*, black) richly brocaded in red. No. 1319—A black (*mushki*) piece with delightful purple red and blue *jals* with green within the meshes. This is perhaps the most beautiful sample in the Exhibition, and when compared with modern work shows how seriously the art conceptions of these fabrics have declined.

AURANGABAD.—It is interesting to conclude this brief reference to the *jamawars* or brocaded woollen goods of India by a reference to the fact that the *himru* weavers of the Deccan appear to have realized the desirability of their participating in this trade instead of calmly allowing their fine old designs to be reproduced by the Kashmiris. Muhamed Latif of Aurangabad has contributed two woollen *himrus*, woven apparently of European woollen yarn. They are in the most brilliant colours possible but the designs are excellent.

Division 37.—Mixed Fabrics.

So much has already been written on the subject of textiles made of Silk and Cotton, Cotton and Wool, Wool and Silk and such like combinations, that there now but remains the task of linking these up in their true position as Mixed Fabrics. The prohibition in Muhammadan ceremonials against men wearing pure silk, very possibly, was the great incentive to the invention of methods by which the artistic effects of silk might be secured without violation of that injunction. Some of the most beautiful textiles of India are of this nature, such as the *ghattas*, *mashrus*, and *himrus*. But it seems fairly established that the East India Company had much to do with the introduction of many of the patterns as also the extension of the production of certain goods of this kind. The *alatches* of Agra and *alatchios* of Surat do

Incentive to Mixed Textiles.

not differ from the *alatchios* of Berhampur and both are, or rather were, very largely mixed silk and cotton goods. The intimate relationship that existed between the Company's traffic with Indian silks and that with Turkish, may at once suggest the origin of both these Indian names from the Turkish *Alcha* or *Aláchá*, striped.

DIVISION 37. MIXED FABRICS.

The chief mixed textiles of India are of course the *ghattas* (satinettes), the *mashrus*, the *sangis*, the *pattus* or flannels, and the *himrus*. A further group, but one that is perhaps better placed under Embroidery, may be said to be the Appliqués. The *himrus* of all the Indian mixed fabrics are the most important, from the stand-point of artistic treatment. After having furnished a very brief provincial review of the mixed textiles, the present chapter may, therefore, be mainly devoted to the discussion of the *Himrus* or Brocaded Cotton and Silk goods.

BENGAL.—Cotton and *tasar* silk are often woven together in this province, especially in Bankura and Manbhum, the fabric being known as a *garbhasuti*. But that name, as also *asmani*, is given to mixed mulberry silk and cotton. The *baftas* of Bhagalpur are soft and glossy. They are made of silk and cotton and much resemble the *shuja khanis* or *susis* of Bhawalpur and Multan. The name *bafta* in other parts of India is synonymous with *pot*, and means a brocaded silk. *Azizulla* and *ajiji* are names given in Bengal to a textile largely produced in Dacca that consists of alternate strips of cotton and *muga* silk.

So much has been written above regarding the silk and silk and cotton textiles of Murshidabad and the neighbourhood, that it is hardly necessary to add in this place that the *seraja* (=Shiraz very possibly) cloth of Maldah is an almost identical mixed textile with much of that already described.

Satinettes.

UNITED PROVINCES.—The *mashrus* (permitted textiles) and the *ghattas* (satinettes) already fully discussed are perhaps the best known examples of mixed silk and cotton in these provinces. In fact these are with the *himrus* of the Deccan the chief mixed textiles of India. The reader will find full particulars regarding the *mashrus* in the chapter on Dyeing, supplemented with the

DIVISION 37. MIXED FABRICS. facts recorded under Silk. With regard to the satinettes, it was felt undesirable to sepa -ate these from the *atlas* or satins proper, and they have accordingly been disposed of under Silk. The *susis* or *charkhanas* (checks) and the *doriyas* (or stripes) are also very largely mixed with cotton, but hardly call for separate treatment in this place. These textiles are often glazed on the reverse side by a preparation made of quince seed. *Sangi*, although a term that denotes a particular method of twin warp weaving, is sometimes given to a fabric of cotton and mulberry silk, just as *gultar* denotes mixed cotton and *tasar* silk.

PANJAB.—The *gulbadans* and *khes* already discussed under Silk, are often made up with a cotton warp. They are thus mixed textiles and are known as *garbhis*. The *susi* or *sufis* (from *musufa*=pure) made at Multan and Kohat are similarly fabrics with a cotton woof and silk warp. *Lakar* are woollen goods with silk borders or silk lines. The same may be said of the *lungis* (largely used as *kamarbands* or as *chaddars*) and these have long silk ends.

CENTRAL PROVINCES.—The *mushrus* of Minar have a silk warp (often *tasar*) and a cotton woof. The Bhandara and Sambalpur *sáris* are mostly cotton with silk borders and ends. In Seoni, *tasar* is never woven by itself but invariably mixed with cotton.

BOMBAY AND SIND.—An extensive series of mixed fabrics are produced in these provinces which, leaving out of consideration the series of cotton *sáris* with silk or gold and silk borders, may be stated as follows :—The *garbha-sutis* or textiles with a cotton warp and silk weft are produced at BELGAUM

Garbha-sutis. (especially Gokak), at POONA and at NASIK, where they may be had in an extensive artistic series, such as the squares or checks (*chaukati*) and the *anjiri* with red warp and green woof. Of AHMEDABAD it is said that the two best known kinds of *garbha-suti* are *mashru* and *magia*. In both the woof is entirely cotton. In SURAT a large trade is done in *mashrus* or satinettes which are produced in two qualities called *ilaichas*

Elaichos. or *elaichos*. There is also a fair trade in reply to a European demand in watered silks both as pure silks or much more abundantly in the form of silk and cotton mixed. Sir Thomas Wardle (*Journal of Indian Art*, Vol. I, Pt. 15, plate 6) gives four samples of Surat satinettes with yellow silk geometric designs that are very characteristic of the goods usually designated *elaicho*. They are certainly not *kinkhábs* though mainly used like the most of the *kinkhábs* in the manufacture of men's coats and waist-coats. **DIVISION 37. MIXED FABRICS.**

In SIND the textiles known as *garbi* and *ailacho* are often made of mixed silk and cotton.

MADRAS.—A very large proportion of the silk textiles of South India have in reality to be described as mixed silk and cotton, such as the satinettes of Ayyampet in Tanjore, of Arcot and Malajahnagar in North Arcot, and of Ariyalur in Trichinopoly. The traffic in these is very large owing to the great centres of Muhammadan population such as Hyderabad where they are used in the manufacture of trousers and waist-coats. This subject will be reverted to in the account of—

The Himrus of Cotton and Silk Brocades.

The word *Himru* literally means a textile intended for use in the cold season. It is woven of cotton but peculiarly spun so as to form a thick soft fabric that feels as if made of wool. It is also brocaded in silk, the major portion of which is somewhat clumsily carried behind from one point to the other in the design and thus forms loose masses that constitute an extra and very warm layer. In consequence of these accumulations of more or less loose silk, the *himrus* have as a rule to be lined and thus when made up into coats for men or bodices and trousers for women, become literally warm clothing for the cold season. The *himrus* are thus usually very distinct from the satinettes,—the *mashrus*, *ghattas*, *garbha-sutis* and *elaichos* (already fully disposed of)—in that the silk is not thrown on the surface as an upper layer, but only appears here and there in elaboration of the pattern. **Himrus.** **Definition.**

AURANGABAD is the chief centre in the *himru* trade of India, though TRICHINOPOLY has a fair share in the traffic and was at one time more important than at present. To a limited extent similar goods are made of pure silk and these are turned out not only at AURANGABAD but at SURAT, AHMEDABAD, BENARES and

DIVISION 37. MIXED FABRICS.

elsewhere and are generally designated *amrus* or brocaded silks. The *Jamawars,* already described, are very largely woollen *himrus.* It is sometimes a matter of uncertainty how far it is possible to separate the flowered satinettes from the *himrus.* The Nawabs of Surat have for several generations used fabric for their coats that has been described as *Nawab's-himru.* It would appear to be a satinette worked in purple but much resembling many of the *himrus* of Aurangabad.

Examples on View.

Plate No. 46-A shows a series of four characteristic Aurangabad *hímrus.* Fig. 1 is a rich geometric design in two shades of blue, the pattern being outlined in white. This resembles the long series of Surat satinettes, that may be seen in the Exhibition, in which the designs are elaborated on a geometric basis. Fig. 2 is a beautiful purple fabric with an intricate pattern in red, blue and green. Fig. 3 is perhaps the most prevalent design seen in the *himrus.* The field is usually pale slate coloured and the pattern an open floral scroll with miniature cones mixed up with the flowers and foliage. The design is mostly worked in two shades of pale purple and moss green. In the Exhibition there may be seen perhaps 50 different phases of this pattern that vary in size and method of linking up the details and in their schemes of colour which range from pure black to brown and purple (such as fig. 2), also green, blue, maroon and scarlet to grey, slate, khaki, orange, yellow or white; the floral effects being in strict accord with the ground colour. Fig. 4 is representative of the extensive series of *himrus* that might be denominated *butidars.* That is to say they have a flower or spray of flowers repeated in transverse lines. The ground colours may, as in figs. 2 and 3, be almost any shade though black and dark blue or dark maroon seem the favourites for *butidars.* In the example shown, the flower (*búti*) is in richly toned purple, bordered with white and with a tiny blue-green leaf that shows in the print as a white speck. A fourth very distinct series of *himrus* closely resembles the striped *jamawars.* That is to say, they are composed of two or more stripes with variously coloured border lines between the stripes and with floral scrolls or geometric designs worked along the surface of the stripes.

Range of colours.

Jamawar Pattern.

DIVISION 37. MIXED FABRICS.

The following notes on the Aurangabad *himrus* may be of assistance to persons who desire to study these very charming textiles :—

The Industrial School, Aurangabad, sends a large series (Nos. 556—588), but amongst them are many pieces in pure silk. Muhamed Habib, merchant of Aurangabad, furnishes a long series of *kamkhábs* and brocades (registered as Nos. 541-7), also *himrus* (registered as Nos. 486 to 511). Of the latter one is especially charming, *viz.*, a soft buff with faded blue *jali* in green with pink flowers. Another is a white texture, "Spot pattern" in blue flowers with pink and green specks. Fazal Hussain of Aurangabad has supplied a good assortment of *himrus*—(Nos. 529 to 540). Of these No. 533 is a thick, warm material in blue-black with rows of jasamine flowers in white, picked out in red and with green leaves. No. 529—a satinette in rich red with white lines edged with green. Abdul Aziz of Aurangabad contributes an assortment of *himrus* (Nos. 512 to 528). Of these mention may be specially made of No. 512, a *himru* of Indian red field with *jali* in green and *bútis* in pink and yellow. No. 517, an orange yellow field with *bútis* in green, purple and pink. Ameruddin of Aurangabad sends a set of *himrus* (Nos. 476—483). Of these No. 478 is very bright—a red brocaded with purple and white spots. No. 480 is a *himru* described as a *babari jal*—a complex design in purple edged with white worked on a dark green background. Muhamed Latif of Aurangabad sends a set of *jamawars*, *himrus* and brocades (Nos. 548—556), already alluded to under both Silk and Wool.

In point of texture and durability few Indian fabrics appear so directly suited to European purposes as the *himrus*. Like the *kinkhábs* they might be extensively used for wall drapings, curtains and upholstery purposes. Some of the finer qualities might also be largely employed for ladies' dresses and others for the manufacture of gentlemen's ties and fancy waist-coats or even dressing gowns. The *himrus* may be washed, the only difficulty being with the mass of loose silk on the under surface. The visitor to the Exhibition will, at all costs, admit that the magnificent display of *himrus* from Aurangabad, Surat and

DIVISION MIXED FABRICS. 37. Trichinopoly, indicate a class of goods that has been much neglected by the pioneers of possible outlets for Indian manufactures in Europe and America.

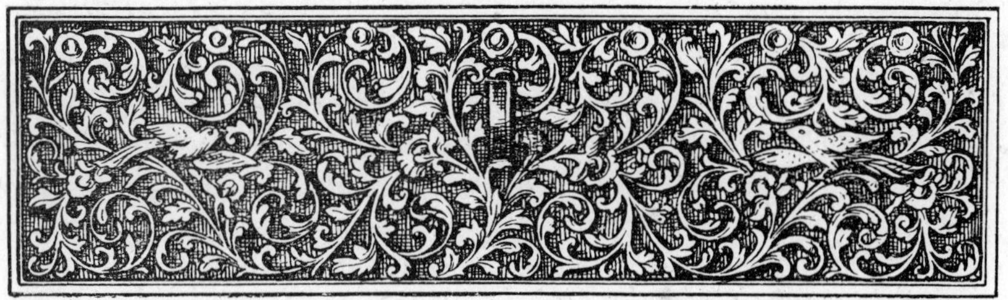

CLASS VIII.—EMBROIDERY, BRAIDING AND LACE.

THIS exceedingly important class of Indian artistic work has been specially designed to include all forms of needlework, but to exclude textile ornamentations accomplished on the loom, such as are seen in the manufacture of *kinkhabs*, brocades, *jamdanis*, tapestries, carpets, etc. It has already been urged that the expression "loom embroideries," given by many writers to certain kinds of ornamental textile work, has not only tended to prevent a proper comprehension of the special features of these, but has greatly obscured the study of embroidery proper. The bobbins used by the Indian craftsmen, in some of their more delicate forms of brocading, are, it is true, so minute that they fully deserve the name of eyeless needles. But they are thrust within the actual warp while the fabric is being woven and do not, therefore, differ in principle or in the result attained from the elaborately and intricately designed surface shuttles of the power-loom brocade weaver. It seemed to the writer accordingly desirable that an Indian Art Exhibition, such as the present, might rigorously enforce, and with advantage, the acceptance of Embroidery as an art accomplished subsequent to any and every stage in weaving, however large or small the loom might be. In other words, when the threads are thrust within the warp and secured in parallel lines by the weft, such should be defined as an act of weaving, not of embroidery. It is of no consequence whether these threads be broached by a shuttle or by a needle. In this view Embroidery is freed from the restraint involved by weaving a pattern and is seen to possess individualities and

Definition.

characteristics of the greatest beauty and interest that are largely lost sight of when merged, as is customary, with certain corresponding forms of loom work. In fact it may be said the weaver but tries to imitate laboriously and artificially the results attained with facility by the embroiderer, though in some cases (notably that of the Kashmir shawls), loom work is both more difficult and more expensive than embroidered While that is so, there is distinctly more individuality and less restraint in the embroidered designs than in the woven patterns (as seen in Kashmir shawls), and this is abundantly true of all textiles when the corresponding results of the shuttle are contrasted with those of the needle.

A cursory inspection of the Indian embroideries shown in the Exhibition, will reveal one or two aspects of collective interest that may be here indicated before the respective styles of work are taken up and studied critically. Embroidery will be noted to attain its highest development in Northern or North-West India. It is more frequently found among the inhabitants of the hills than of the plains. It is a pastoral art in its inception. As a rule highly coloured embroideries are found in temperate tracts and white embroideries in tropical countries.

The present Exhibition being confined to Indian Art, articles of Ethnological interest had to be excluded. But from a historic point of view it would be of advantage to extend the study of a difficult subject, like that of needlework, so as to embrace the results attained by the aboriginal tribes as well as that by the skilled artificers of the civilized communities. Throughout the mountainous tracts of India embroidery, in some form, is nearly always met with. The stitches employed and the art conceptions displayed by these aboriginal tribes are of the greatest possible value, in conveying a conception of the knowledge possessed by the people of India, prior to the Muhammadan conquests and domination. A study of the embroideries characteristic of the hill tribes of Assam and Upper Burma would very possibly afford materials for the production of an epitome of the needlework not of India only but of the world. And some of the examples met with in these tracts are of a very advanced order and exceedingly beautiful, such as the line-darn stitch embroideries of the Kamptis and Singphos. These recall forcibly the work of the Brahuis of Baluchistan. The graceful scrolls worked by the women of Manipur on their garments, in satin-stitch, are indicative of art conceptions possibly of the greatest historic value, since clearly uncontaminated by Saracenic feeling. The embroideries of the Garo and Khasia hills are similarly very beautiful and will richly repay critical study and comparison with the best results in the more advanced provinces of India.

The following may be given as the chief groups of textile ornamentations that fall within the present class:—

Division 38.—Darn, Satin, Stem, and Feather Stitches; embroideries mostly with coloured floss (filoselle) or *muga* silk and usually on cotton or woollen fabrics.

Division 39.—Tent, Cross, Knotted, and Herring-bone Stitches, also Button-holing.

Division 40.—Chain Stitch with silk or wool and on silk or woollen textiles.

Division 41.—*Chikan*-work and Drawn Stitch Embroideries, mostly in white thread and done on cotton or linen cloth-washing embroideries.

Division 42.—Net-work usually in satin or chain stitch and either on black or on white net with affixed spangles or beetles' wings.

Division 43.—Lace—this may be referred to Cushion, Point, Torchon and other such groups and may be either knitted by bobbins or worked by a crochet hook or needle or it may be produced on net or other textiles; the materials are cotton, linen, or silk thread, or gold and silver wire. The separation from Division 41 often becomes extremely difficult and the use of gold and silver wire in lace manufacture similarly renders it sometimes difficult to separate the laces proper from gold embroidery and braiding

Division 44.—Laid, Crewel, Appliqué and Quilted Embroideries in silk, cotton or linen, such as that on *pashmina* cloth and *chaddars*. Many of the forms of work assigned to this position differ from the next Division almost entirely in the material used.

Division 45.—Gold and Silver Wire Embroidery done on a frame (*karchob*) and consists chiefly of two forms, *viz.*, *zardozi* (on velvet or satin) and *kamdani* (on muslin). These are mainly accomplished as "couching" or "laid" embroideries, attachment being made by an additional thread from behind brought up on purpose at repeated intervals.

Division 46.—Braidings and Trimmings, that is to say, embroidery on narrow strips of net, velvet or other material done in various stitches mostly "laid" or "couching" and with silk or gold wire and tinsel spangles (*gota* and *kinara*). This is in reality a special form of *zardozi* work, but by many writers *kinkháb* borderings are also placed along with *zardozi* braidings and trimmings with the result of once more linking together needle and loom work. There would, however, be less harm in so doing than with the larger textiles since the makers of all forms of braids, trimmings, borderings, etc., are usually constituted a perfectly distinct craft, from the weavers or the embroiderers. Moreover, once the separation of loom from needlework bas been recognised, there might be no great necessity for their isolation in every minor industry where either the one or the other art or both combined may be practised.

Indian Method of Sewing.

Stitches Employed.—There is a peculiarity of all Indian needlework that may in passing be mentioned in this place since it doubtless has something to say to the styles of work produced, namely, the fact that the needle is pulled away from, not drawn toward, the operator. In other words, the action of sewing adopted in India is just the opposite to that pursued in Europe. The persistence with which the inhabitants of Eastern countries work in this so-called "opposite direction" seems due to the lesser development of the extensor muscles of the body and not a perversity in character. To the same circumstance is due the crouching gait of the people, of the plains of India more especially—the leg being swung, not pulled forward, and in consequence is never fully extended. Of the same nature is the overhead habit of swimming and the jerking of the playing marble by the forefinger of the right hand from between the forefinger and thumb of the left, instead of being propelled by the forcible extension o

Opposite Direction.

the thumb. Hence to the same cause also, whatever that may be, must be attributed all the agricultural and industrial operations where strength and skill are put forth in pulling or drawing, not in pushing or propelling.

By each and every race of people in India the needle is therefore inserted within the fabric and the thread drawn away from the operator. The persistence, however, with which certain races practise one stitch of needlework in preference to others, gives an importance to this study that seems to have been neglected very largely, alike by writers on Indian Art and Ethnology. For example, the intimate and constant association of some of the higher forms of the art with the Muhammadan faith is certainly significant and must be accepted as accounting for many of the better known designs met with in India. Prior to the conquests of the Muhammadans there can be no doubt the needle was not in much demand since the garments of the Hindus were mostly worn in the condition in which woven. Still, the extremely local character and intimate association with distinct races and aboriginal tribes, of many of the Indian forms of embroidery, point to their being indigenous. Moreover, the stitch used very materially influences the nature of the designs adopted. For example, curves would be next to impossible with darn or satin stitches, but very easily attained by chain stitch. And this is precisely the character of the embroideries met with in districts where the one or the other form of needlework prevails. So again since the loom very largely simulates embroidery, the influence of the needle on the methods and appliances of weaving must have been much greater than is at present recognised. Similarly the preference for embroidered garments has largely dictated the class of fabrics to be woven. For example it is customary for darn stitch to be employed on coarse cotton and chain stitch to be used on silk or woollen fabrics. The former covers the textile, the latter ornaments certain isolated portions of it. The one corrects the inferiority of the garment, the other adds to its luxurious merits. But there is a limit to surface ornamentation, and, speaking generally, that is reached when propriety and necessity have been passed, hence darn stitch often appears like chain stitch as a sumptuary

Ethnological Bearings.

Influence of Stitch on Art.

On Industries.

DIVISION 38. DARN, SATIN, Etc., STITCH. ornamentation. From these and such like considerations, therefore, it may be accepted that the actions and reactions of embroidery on the artistic feelings and industrial attainments of the people of India is likely to have been considerable and far-reaching.

Principle of Classification. In the Exhibition an extensive series of embroideries may be studied, and it will be found that to these have been devoted a very much larger portion of the Exhibition than has been assigned to any other class, except perhaps the Textiles. In dealing with the embroideries it becomes therefore essential to discuss them Division by Division. But it may be desirable to here explain that when two or more stitches are employed on the same fabric, the position assigned has been determined by the nature of the stitch most abundant or that which constitutes the chief feature of interest in the style.

Division 38.—Darn, Satin, Stem, and Feather Stitches in Indian Embroideries.

In all the forms of Embroidery placed in this Division the ornamenting threads are carried in more or less parallel lines or bundles of lines across the surface of the fabric. In the *darn* stitch, for example—the one perhaps most frequently met with in India—the needle runs along nipping up small portions of the textile at intervals. In the *satin* stitch, the needle catches a hold of the sides or outlines of the structures to be ornamented and returns backwards and forwards until the required covering has been effected. Occasionally it goes round and round so that the work is double, that is to say it is the same on both sides. So also it is not infrequent for *satin* stitch to be padded or cushioned by patchwork or by thick threads first sewn over the portions that are to be subsequently elaborately embroidered. By *stem* stitch, outlinings are very often done, the return loop or stitch carried below, being much shorter than the forward upper one. The effect produced may be said to be continuous lines. In *feather* stitch the lines of sewing are worked diagonally in a graduated series of V shapes, each fitting within the other. This stitch thus takes its name from the plume of a feather. It is occasionally used in filling up large flat surfaces that have to be coloured.

One of the most prevalent stitches in the white embroideries described below under Division 41—*Chikan* work, is in reality a form of minute satin stitch. This is seen to be gradually developed when the embroidery of one district is compared with another until it becomes ordinary satin stitch. The only ground for the isolation of the *chikan* work from the satin and other stitches then becomes the practical one of the widely different purpose served. **DIVISION 38. DARN, SATIN, Etc., STITCH.**

The variations within and between all these stitches of parallel embroidery are numerous and call for critical study by those who have the opportunity of so doing. In the present article it may suffice to denote a few of the better known examples :—

Panjab Darn Stitch.—(*Plate No. 48, fig. 8.*)—One of the most admirable papers written on any branch of Indian Art is the brief account given by Mrs. Flora Anne Steel on the "*Phulkari work in the Panjab.*" Her closing and graphic sentence comes on the reader with a feeling of deep disappointment, since, had Mrs. Steel extended her essay to all forms of Indian embroidery, she would have rendered an incalculable service to India that a lady only can do. To few Indian ladies have there been given, in so remarkable a manner as to Mrs. Steel, the gifts of accurate observation and fluent narration. In all fairness therefore to the numerous writers on Indian Embroidery it may be said that with the single exception of Mrs. Steel's paper on *Phulkaris*, nothing has been written that is of the least merit from the stand-point of India's advantage. Mrs. Steel has depicted the persons who engage in *Phulkari* embroidery, the process and stitch that should be accepted as alone deserving of that name, the best old examples of that work, and the modern degraded forms commonly met with nowadays. **Phulkari Work.**

She has also in the most unmistakable manner indicated the influences that have combined to bring about the ruin of the art. No apology need, therefore, be made for drawing upon Mrs. Steel's most interesting paper further than to regret the unavoidable necessity of having to give but a few passages from it. "The word *Phulkari* means a 'flowering work', and might therefore be applied to any embroidery. It has, however, in a **Uses of Phulkaris.**

DIVISION 38. DARN, SATIN, Etc., STITCH.

great measure, been restricted to one particular kind, which is only employed as a decoration for the *chaddars* or head veils of women, and in one or two districts to the petticoat also. By the natives themselves the work is divided into three branches: 1st, the true *Phulkari*, where the pattern is diapered at intervals over the cloth; 2nd, *bagh* or garden, where the whole surface is ornamented by a connected pattern; 3rd, *chobes*, where the edges alone are ornamented and the centre left plain. The distinctive feature of the original *Phulkari* work, uncontaminated by exotic amendments, is the stitch, which is purely and simply a darning stitch, done entirely from the back. It is a curiously distinctive work, following the track of certain peoples and tribes with unvarying certainty, modifying itself to new conditions, and so becoming of positive ethnological value."

"It seems indubitable that wherever the stalwart Jat tribes of the south-eastern plains came from, with them came the original *phulkari* workers; for the art, almost unchanged, lingers still in its best form among the peasants of Rohtak, Hissar, Gurgaon, Delhi, and to some extent in Karnal. Rohtak may be said to be its home, and here, says the Census Returns, the Hindu Jat, untouched by Muhammadanism or Sikhism, thrives thickest."

In the old samples Mrs. Steel explains the green and white threads when present were usually in cotton, not silk. "This points probably to an older time still, when silk was unknown, or too rare for common use; this is the more probable, because we find some tribes in Hissar using wool. Another peculiarity is that the fabric itself is employed geometrically as an inner decoration; so that the medallions and diamonds, etc., are not merely patterns of silk worked on, but a combination in yellow and madder-brown. This is distinctive of the original work, and is only possible where absolute accuracy of thread-counting is observed. It is only to be found nowadays amongst the true Hindu Jats, even the infinitely more refined workers in Hazara and Jhelum being unable to work the small stitches and big spaces required in this mixed decoration."

Thread Counting.

Association with the Jats.

Referring to the *bagh* work of Hazara and the neighbouring districts, Mrs. Steel writes: "It is worthy of remark that Mr."

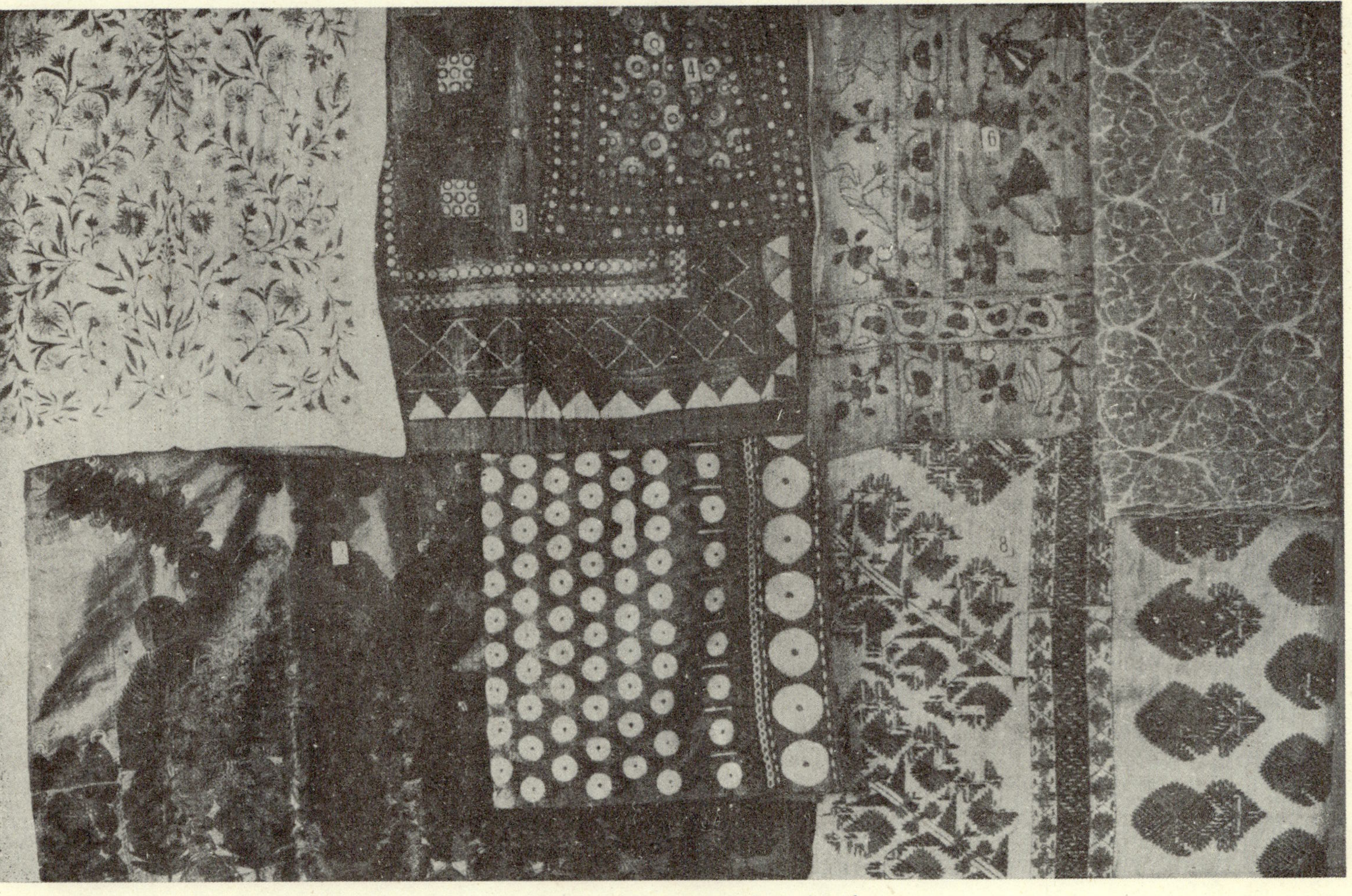

Plate No. 48 Satin and Darn Stitch Embroideries

DIVISION 38. DARN, SATIN, Etc., STITCH.

(now Sir Denzil) "Ibbetson in his 'Panjab Ethnology' remarks that the very tract where we find this *bagh* work at its best was originally peopled by Hindu Jats, who were afterwards conquered by Muhammadan tribes. Curiously enough, the modification in style is just what might be expected under such circumstances. The fabric becomes finer, the labour in consequence infinitely greater; while the embroidery ceases to be a decorative adjunct, and becomes the cloth itself. At the same time, the distinctive stitch, the distinctive merits, which had caught the stranger's eye, remain. It is free-work in servitude; and while in Rohtak at the present day the Jat woman works for herself, in Hazara and the neighbouring districts the fine work is all done to rich orders, and most big houses keep dependents constantly embroidering." The Hazara work is of course done with the usual care "yet even here the first 'rift within the lute' may be detected, which, I have no doubt, led to the present degradation of the *phulkari* art. I allude to the preliminary sketching out of the ground work by threads, to avoid the almost inevitable mistakes which were sure to arise in counting such fine threads. One miss, prolonged over a whole diagonal, throws out the whole pattern, so the women, by 'plane-tabling' the ground into squares, provided for the rectification of small errors. It is beautiful work, but quite unsuited, with its surface of floss silk, to life in the fields."

Plane-tabling Designs.

The two forms of work discussed by Mrs. Steel, *viz.*, the true *phulkari* and the *bagh* form, instantly become apparent when the plates given by her are examined. In the absence of these it may be said that in the former the ornamentations are remotely dispersed, and moreover large portions of the field colour are shown within the *bútis* or flowers in order to outline the details. In the latter the whole field surface is covered with silk, the outlining being done by methodical and parallel lines of the field texture (perhaps not more than $\frac{1}{16}$th of an inch in diameter). But the modern degenerations are not confined to the "plane-tabling" of the pattern by means of superfluous and discordant lines of green thread. The normal *phulkari* stitch is about $\frac{1}{4}$ of an inch in length, the needle making three or four at each insertion and nipping up the portions of the field at the exact positions

Method of Outlining.

DIVISION 38. DARN, SATIN, Etc., STITCH.

required. Seen on the upper surface, the fabric is thus closely compacted with bands of silk that are separated by very neat parallel furrows of the field cloth. In the cheap modern work no attempt is made to secure parallel bands of silk and the stitch is prolonged for half to as much as 2 inches. The colours have all been changed and in place of the rich golden yellow on an Indian-red field, picked out with white or occasionally with specks of green or a dark indigo blue field with purple embroidery, the field in modern goods is a black, blue or scarlet, mostly woollen textiles and the embroidery is in green, red and purple, offensive, staringly ugly, aniline cheap dyes. Such are the "atrocities that are now teaching the beauties of Indian art to many an admiring circle in England."

Modern Atrocities.

Mrs. Steel's condemnation of the modern traffic in *phulkaris* is more than deserved. The writer may add that while in Ludhiana, in connection with the present Exhibition, he was shown a consignment of several bales of *phulkaris* that were ready for despatch to America. The dealer showed the pattern that had been furnished to him by a European trader and smilingly observed that it paid him to make such stuff, but he could not see what the people in America thought beautiful or found useful in these monstrosities in black, green and red. The design was not Indian at all and the stitches of embroidery were fully an inch in length. Mrs. Steel makes no mention of the *shishadar phulkaris, viz.,* the forms in which a striking effect is produced by the insertion of circular pieces of looking-glass within the design. These are held in position by being button-hole stitched all round. This has a quaint, barbaric effect. The glass used is made at Karnal. It is blown into globes, silvered inside and then broken into the required shapes and sizes necessary for the *shishadar phulkari* or the glass mosaic plaster work seen in the palaces of the nobles. The habit of using mirror glass in embroidery is very wide-spread in Northern and Western India and is met with from Peshawar to Lahore, Amritsar, Hissar, Sind, and Kathiawar. In the last mentioned country it occurs in the bodices worn by the ladies and in the *natis* or head dresses of the children (see Plate No. 48 fig. 4).

Shishadar Phulkaris.

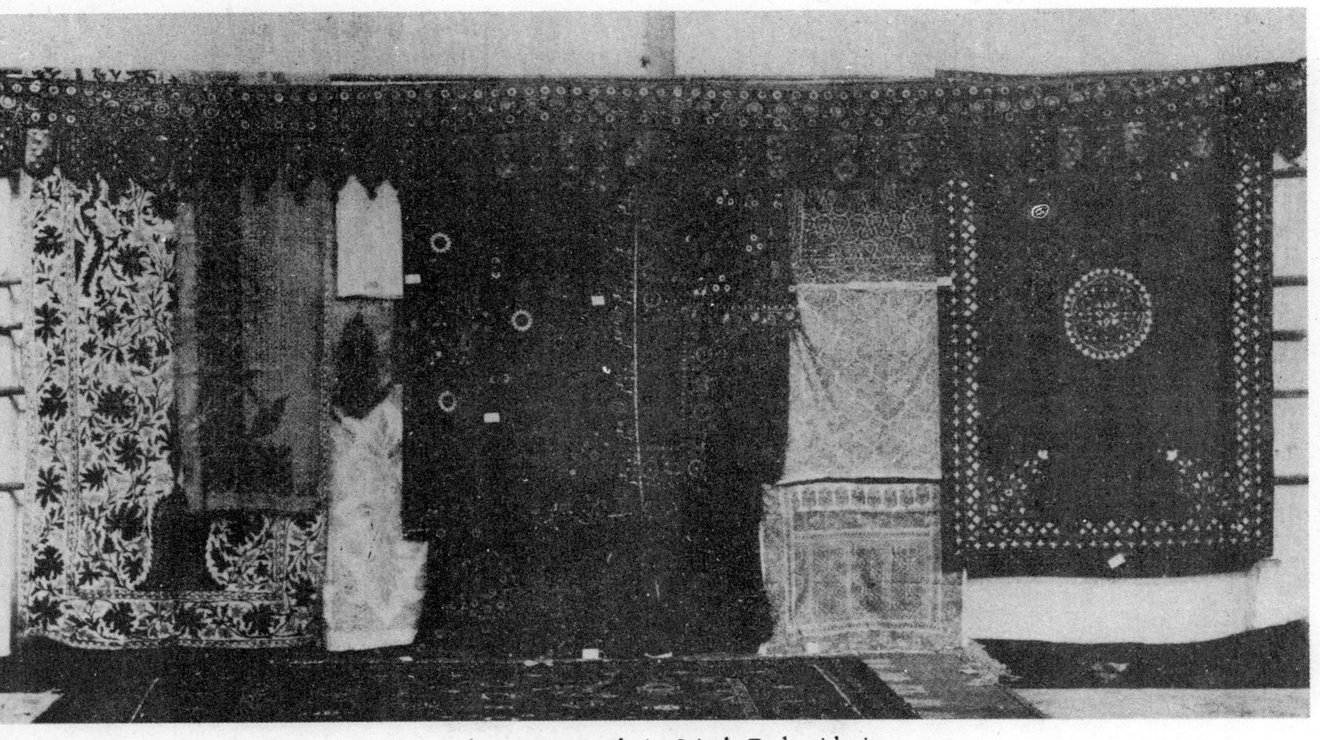

Plate No. 49 Chain Stitch Embroideries

DIVISION 38. DARN, SATIN, Etc., STITCH.

Phulkari Stitch lost.

The present brief observations on the Panjab *phulkari* embroideries may be fittingly concluded with one or two sentences abstracted once more from Mrs. Steel's paper: "On turkey red the *phulkari* stitch is lost, and so long stitches, eye service, and illegitimate patterns creep in." "A growing demand for pure style at fair prices is the only remedy, and that lies in the hands of the buyers." "But so surely as Jubilee *baghs* sell and buyers say no one will see the work when it is draped at the top of a door with a Japanese fan and a peacock feather, so surely will the *phulkari* art be forgotten. Already the native women look at some of my most cherished treasures critically and remark: 'Those must be very old; we don't work like that nowadays.'"

In the Exhibition an extensive series of Panjab *phulkaris* will be seen, *viz.*, from Rohtak, Hissar, Sialkot, Amritsar, Lahore, and Rawalpindi. The series from Hazara (Plate No. 48, fig. 8) will be found specially worthy of study; they are mostly on white cotton with purple and green silk and have a large admixture of an entirely different stitch (shortly to be described). The bulk of the Panjab embroideries may thus be accepted as made by Hindu and Sikh women and to have been so made, very possibly for centuries. Along the frontier from Peshawar to Quetta, a very different style of work is, however, met with, that must be accepted as peculiar to the Muhammadans if it does not denote an even remoter aboriginal origin. Since the major portion of this work is done, like that of Hazara, in a stitch that is perhaps best described as a form of herring-boning, it will be dealt with under Division 39, and it is only here alluded to in order to enforce recognition of the widely different character of at least a large number of the so-called *phulkaris* of Hazara, Peshawar, Kohat, Bannu, the Western Panjab, Sind, and Baluchistan—(Plate No. 48, figs. 2 and 5)—a tract of country that differs very greatly from the Southern and Eastern Panjab—the home of the *phulkari* proper.

Frontier Embroideries.

Kashmir Shawl Embroidery.—(*Plate No. 51.*)—In this Native State, a form of darn stitch has attained great proficiency. The needle is run along the surface of the finest textiles, catching the tiniest loops of the warp without penetrating through the

DIVISION 38. DARN, SATIN, Etc., STITCH.

thickness. So completely and minutely is this done that the embroidery covers every detail of the surface until it is often a matter of the greatest uncertainty to distinguish loom from needlework. This subject has already been discussed in the chapter devoted to Shawls and *Chaddars*, more especially the observations regarding *amlikar* shawls. It is, therefore, not necessary to repeat particulars already given regarding the embroidered shawls that may be seen at the Exhibition. In all the finer and more artistic work the thread used is invariably made of *pashm* and is not only run within the shawl texture but is blended so completely with it that it is difficult to insert a pin between the stitches of embroidery and the field texture.

Cheap Embroidery.

In addition to darn stitch, two or three other forms of needlework are met with in Kashmir shawls, table cloths and curtains. The outlines of the patterns in woven shawls are sharpened up by stem-stitching, with *pashm* thread. In all the cheaper embroidered *chaddars*, such as those produced very extensively in Ludhiana and other towns of the Panjab, the embroidery is done with coarse *pashm* or even imported woollen yarn, in stem and feather stitches. In the finer forms the embroidery is in darn stitch and so minute that the individual stitches can, with difficulty, be recognised by the naked eye.

Kashmir Curtains.

His Highness the Maharaja of Kashmir and Jammu has most obligingly lent the superb series of drapings that are to be seen in the great transept of the Exhibition and in the Loan Collection Gallery. These are curtains (25 feet by 10 feet) of strong, white cotton cloth richly embroidered with silk, mostly in two or three shades of red and purple. One of these curtains is shown to the left of Plate No. 51 and has a pair of peacocks worked on it, in which the effect of the plumage has been fully conveyed. The curtain alongside and to the right of the same plate is in *pashmina* of a rich maroon colour and elaborately embroidered in silk. The stitch employed in these wonderful and fine old examples of embroidery is mostly stem and feather, but a fair admixture of chain stitch is also occasionally seen.

Table covers.—In *rumals* (*handkerchiefs*), especially those intended as table covers, the material used in embroidery is very

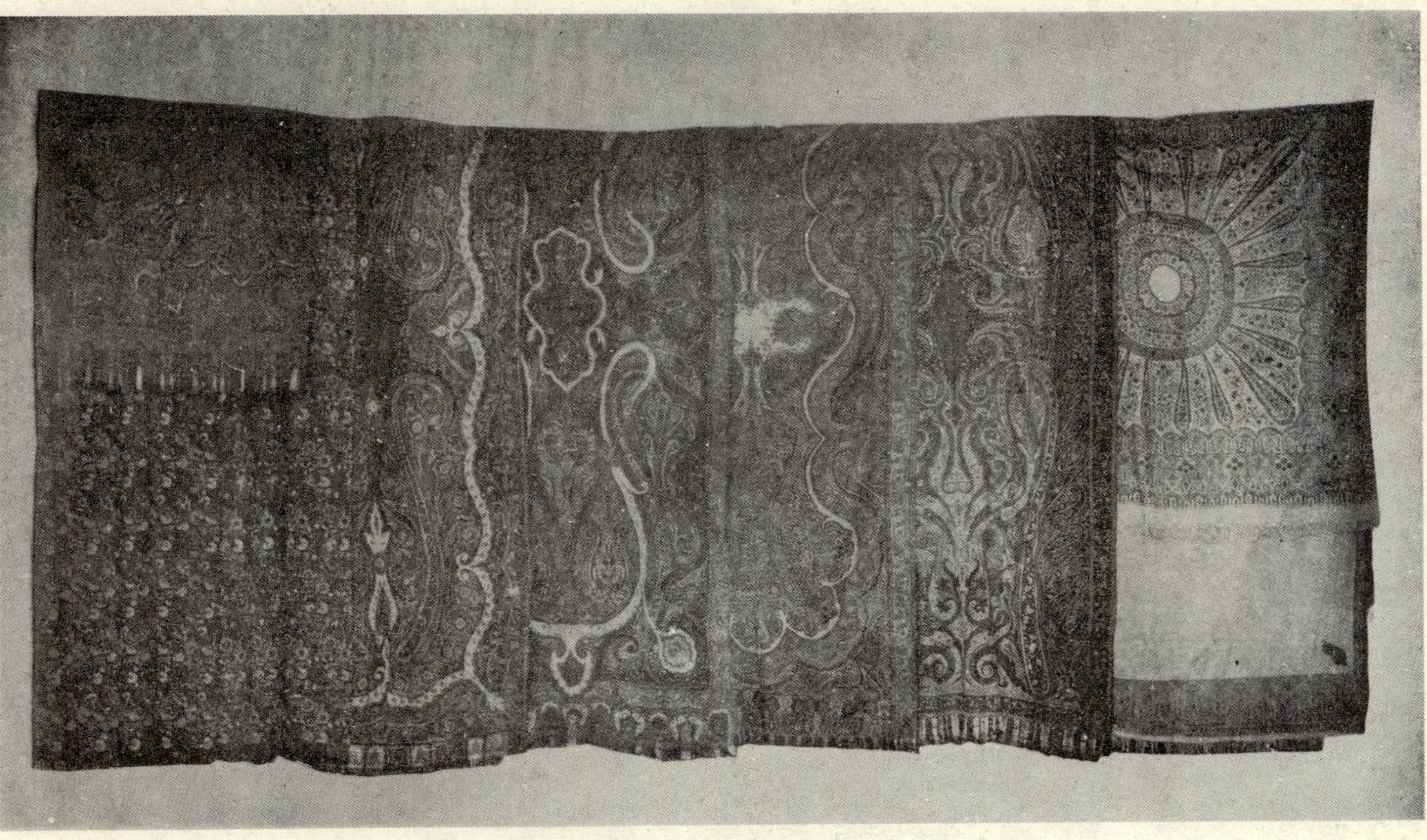

Plate No. 50 Kashmir Shawls

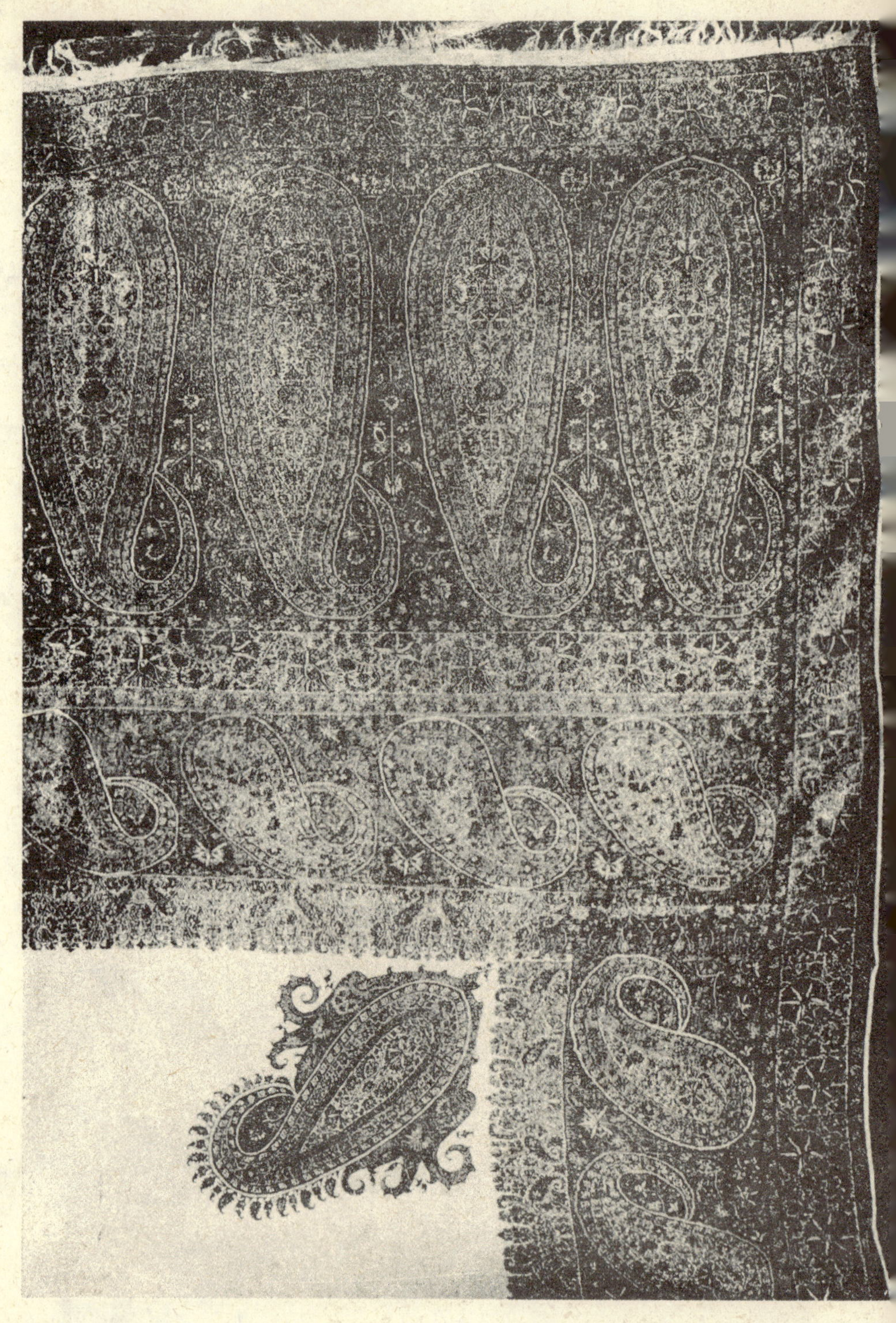

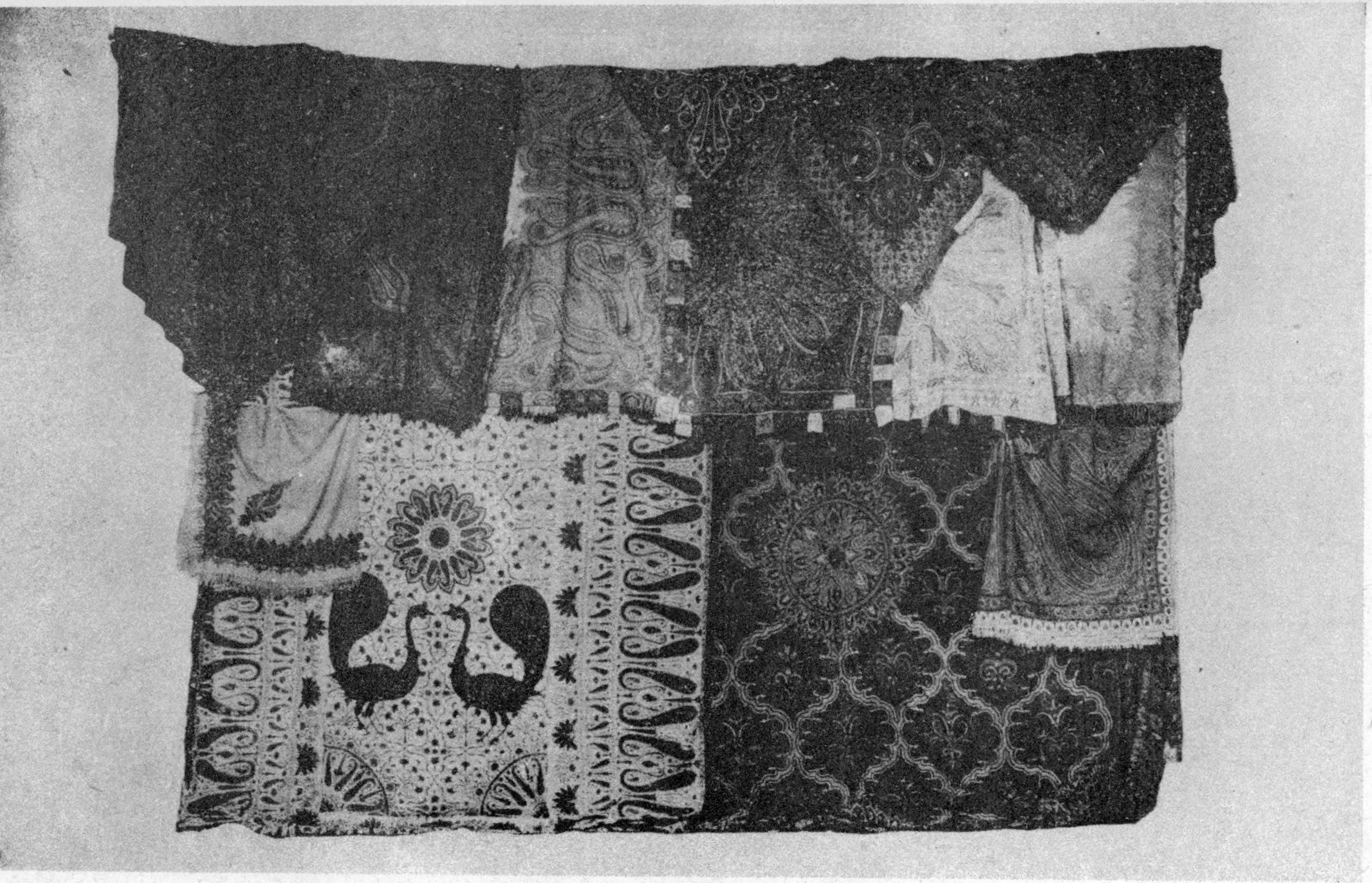

Plate No. 51 Kashmir Embroideries

largely, if not entirely, silk and the stitches are mostly chain and satin. The examples shown along the top of Plate No. 51 are embroidered *rumals*, those that constitute the topmost row of all are done in chain and other stitches worked with silk thread. When it is desired to produce the same effect on both sides, the Kashmiris rarely employ double satin stitch but prefer to embroider first one side and then the other. In fact the quality of Kashmir embroidery may be judged of by the smallness of the extent and the uniformity and neatness in which it is carried to the under side; hence it becomes simply a matter of time and money to secure double embroidery.

DIVISION 38. DARN, SATIN, Etc., STITCH.

Double Embroidery.

Within the past few years, a large and rapidly expanding new industry has been created in Kashmir, namely, the production of small tea-table cloths, table centres and such like articles on white cotton or linen in darn stitch embroidery neatly and elaborately worked, with the brightest of European coloured washing silks. Plate No. 48, fig. 1, shows a table cloth in this style of work. Such cloths are remarkably cheap and attractive though usually a good deal over coloured and much too elaborate in design to be regarded as art productions. The sample shown is one with less work than is customarily given. It is possible, however, that this new branch of embroidery may gradually settle into more artistic forms and become of the greatest value to the shawl embroiderers of Kashmir, many of whom have been feeling keenly the gradual decline in popularity of their traditional craft. In the Exhibition will be seen a large assortment of these modern embroideries.

Washing Embroideries.

CHAMBA AND KANGRA.—As in Kashmir so in the mountainous countries of Chamba, Kangra, and Kullu, the shepherdesses as also the ladies of the palaces have from time immemorial wiled away their leisure hours in embroidering cotton handkerchiefs. This is done by a form of double satin stitch so that there is no right and wrong side. Plate No. 48, fig. 6, shows a Chamba handkerchief in its most characteristic form, namely, with brilliantly coloured flowers and animals depicted in rhythmic form around sporting or mythological human groups. They are quaint, of the sampler type and historically of interest but not of a very high artistic order.

Embroidered Handkerchiefs.

DIVISION 38. DARN, SATIN, Etc., STITCH.

United Provinces.—DELHI, AGRA, AND BENARES.—These towns have been famous for many centuries for their rich embroideries, both in gold and silver wire as also in silk thread. The former may be reserved for treatment under Division 45—Gold and Silver Embroideries, even although they may and often are satin stitch in form of needlework. The latter—the silk embroideries—of Delhi and Agra more specially, are perhaps better known in Europe than are any of the other styles of Indian work. They originated very possibly with the grandees of the Moghal Court and for many years were met with exclusively on heavy textiles, such as velvet and satin, having a lining of coarse cotton to carry the weight of the massive work placed on the surface. This style of work was used mainly for men's coats, caps, collars, and other such purposes. Within recent years an important development has taken place through the demand for silk embroidery in forms suited to European requirements. Superb curtains, screen cloths, table centres, etc., in silk, satin, or velvet and richly embroidered with coloured silks and a restricted admixture of gold and silver thread, are now produced both at Delhi and Agra. The designs are mostly padded or cushioned, and the embroidery, which is satin stitch in form, is accomplished very largely by the use of two needles, one acting from below and employed to bind the upper thread or braid in the required position. It is entirely frame-work and is done on the top not the under surface as is the case with *phulkari* embroidery. Plate No. 54, fig. 3, shows a superb piano cover worked mostly in coloured silks and in designs derived from the Taj at Agra. This was made by Ganeshi Lal of Agra, and has been purchased by His Highness the Nizam of Hyderabad.

Silk Embroideries.

Embroidered Gowns.

Her Excellency Lady Curzon has given a great impetus to another modern aspect of the Delhi and Agra work by placing extensive orders with the chief embroiderers for robes and gowns. In consequence there has come into existence a purified and refined style of embroidery that bids fair to considerable expansion in the future. In the Exhibition there will be seen a large assortment of ladies' gowns and dress pieces embroidered both in coloured silk and in gold or silver, but in which no trace exists of the overburdening that characterised the work of this kind produced some few years ago. The better known silk embroiderers are Messrs. Manick Chand and Messrs. Kishen Chand, of Delhi; Ganeshi Lal, of Agra.

DIVISION 38. DARN, SATIN, Etc., STITCH.

Sind and Baluchistan and Kathiawar.—Darn and satin stitches are extensively used by the people of Sind, Baluchistan, and Kathiawar, though in forms and conditions that make them as widely remote from most of the embroideries already discussed as from each other.

Picture Embroidery.

In the Exhibition will be seen a piece of embroidery exhibited by Mr. C. K. Khilnani, of Karachi, and made by his expert embroiderer Faiz Mahomed. This represents the fisherman's daughter walking along the sea-shore with a basket of herrings under her arm. The subject is English, the silk used in the embroidery very possibly European. The picture could hardly, therefore, have had assigned a place in an Exhibition of Indian Art, but from the fact that the stitch of needle employed is distinctly Indian, namely, the Kashmir darn stitch; the picture has therefore been shown though it is the one discordant note in the entire series of embroideries. The attempt at reproducing a painting by the needle instead of the brush recalls the time when in Europe embroidery was given a place among the high arts instead of being assigned to its true position as a decorative art. The skill of the embroiderer manifested by this picture is simply marvellous. There is perhaps no example of modern embroidery in the Exhibition that can be compared with it for technique. The subject alone has been the cause of its exclusion from a foremost position in the list of awards.

Brahui Embroideries.

In Baluchistan, there are several widely different forms of embroidery, each characteristic apparently of distinctive races of people. To Mr. R. Hughes Buller, the Census Officer of Baluchistan, the writer is indebted not only for the splendid series of embroideries shown both in the Loan Collection and Sale Galleries of the Exhibition, but for much useful information regarding the country and its people from which these have come. Among the Brahuis both darn and satin stitches are practised, the latter being often double and mainly utilized on

DIVISION 38. DARN, SATIN, Etc., STITCH.

linen or cotton handkerchiefs and table cloths; the former is the chief stitch used on the beautiful work shown on their dresses. It would seem, however, that the Bugli women, while they also employ the stitch peculiar to the Brahui ladies, to a much greater extent, resort to the form of herring-bone stitch already incidentally mentioned in connection with Hazara and the Afghan Frontier. This will be reserved for discussion under Division 39.

Plate No. 87 shows a Brahui lady's dress made of rich maroon coloured satin, elegantly embroidered in thick floss silk. This was obligingly lent by Mrs. Yate, of the Residency, Quetta, and is one of the most beautiful in the extensive series on view. The stitch would appear to be a form of satin, worked very possibly over pins or cords so as to bring it up into folds or ridges. The design is primarily geometric but certain of the colours cross from one ridge to another and thus cause the notched or toothed outline that is more or less peculiar to this style of work. There is a great front pocket that assumes the condition of a panel to the frock. This has two oblique openings for the hands on either side of the central attachment of a flap. Over the breasts are panels that resemble the linen fronts of a European shirt, while from the shoulder and running along the top of the sleeves are two bands of embroidery that end in broad cuff pieces.

These are the special constructive features of the Brahui dress and they are completely covered with the line form of satin stitch embroidery except the shoulder bands which are invariably done in wool or coarse silk, and in stem and feather stitches not in satin stitch. The silk used in the front panels is mostly dark red, orange, green, white and black, the pattern being outlined in black and picked out by a bold conception in white embroidery. This striking use of black and white, amid elaborations in Indian red or purple may be taken as the dominant feature in the scheme of colour of the Brahui embroideries. The isolation of the pattern by narrow bands of the field material recalls, of course, the Jat embroideries (*phulkaris*) of the Eastern Panjab, but there the comparison begins and ends. It would be exceedingly curious were a study of the races cognate with the Brahuis, such as the Khonds and Gonds of the central table-land of India, to reveal the existence of work similar to that of the Brahuis which otherwise stands by itself as one of the most strikingly peculiar and beautiful forms of needlework met with in India.

DIVISION 38. DARN, SATIN, Etc., STITCH.

Double Satin Stitch.

In the Loan Collection a beautiful example of colour silk double satin stitch embroidery from Quetta will be seen (No. 2907). This may be called a tea-table cloth of white cotton which in design is first referred to squares by lines of black silk worked in cross-stitch. Within each of the meshes thus formed as also around the crossing points of the meshes medallions have been worked in a sort of Maltese cross fashion. These are produced in such a complexity of colour that the effect is perplexingly difficult to describe but very beautiful. One is in dark metallic green with purple specks, the next purple with green, a third blue with dull orange, and so on. It is a double satin stitch so that it is the same on both sides.

Kathiawar Choklas.

In Kathiawar two widely remote forms of embroidery are met with: one satin in much elongated stitches, with very crudely formed boundary lines of the field texture; the other chain stitch. The former may be seen in Plate No. 48, figs. 3 and 4, and the latter will be discussed under Division 40. Occasionally both forms are combined as in the *nati* shown (fig. 3). It may be said that the satin stitch of Kathiawar is the needlework of the peasant as the chain stitch is that of the upper classes. It is customary when a girl gets married for her wedding dresses to be tied up in one or two embroidered handkerchiefs. These are called *choklas;* after marriage they are usually affixed to the walls of the bed-room as ornaments. They are made of coarse blue cotton cloth, so completely covered by a greatly drawn out satin stitch of purple floss silk that hardly a trace of the original material is visible. Occasionally also (as in the sample in Plate No. 48, fig. 3) they are ornamented with a border of patchwork in red or white cotton. The *nati* (fig. 4) is the child's head-dress upon which the Kathiawar females expend so much patient labour. It consists of a little cap that ends in a square fold intended to hang down the back. It is usually

DIVISION 38. DARN, SATIN, Etc., STITCH. richly embroidered with both satin and chain stitches and has very frequently small pieces of glass let into central features of the pattern. The *Torans* are quaint strips of cloth with tags suspended from the bottom. These are intended to be placed over the doors of the inner room of the peasant's house. They are made of several differently coloured bits of cloth, subsequently richly embroidered. With the poor they are of cotton in satin stitch, with the rich of silk and mostly in chain stitch. In the Exhibition will be seen an extensive series of these, two being specially made and 10 yards long. In the Bhavnagar Room will be seen a large collection of *choklas*, *natis*, and *torans* affixed to the wall or hung across the clothes rack in the manner customary in a Kathiawar house.

Bombay.—The Bombay School of Art sends two very effective pieces of this work, one a square in old gold coloured satinette embroidered with bold lines of floral scrolls running along its length. The stems are in dark purple, the leaves green and the flowers in three shades of light purple. The broad border appears as if made in imitation of a carpet. The second piece is described as a window blind made in Delhi. It is on pale straw coloured satin embroidered in gold loops into a squamiform surface, each has a quaint flower in pale slate and brown colours worked within it.

Kasida Embroideries.

Bengal.—DACCA.—In Eastern Bengal and thus far away from the tract of country discussed above, in connection with darn and satin stitch embroideries, occurs another surprisingly interesting centre of these styles of needlework. The Abbé de Guyon writing of the *zardozi* work of Dacca in 1774 said: "From Dacca come the best and finest embroideries in gold, silver and silk, and those embroidered neck-cloths and fine muslins which are seen in France." Dr. James Taylor in his *Cotton Manufactures of Dacca* (1851) gave a detailed account of these embroideries that has been drawn upon by most subsequent writers without anything material having been added to the record of the craft. Taylor was of opinion that it was introduced in the 9th Century from Bussora—a conjecture strengthened by the fact that the chief exports go to Bussora and Jedda.

Embroidery.

DIVISION 38. DARN, SATIN, Etc., STITCH.

The cloth (usually common cotton) is stretched on a frame after the pattern has been stamped over the surface. The needlework is done in *muga* silk of an old gold colour, is accomplished by Muhammadans and mainly by the females as a pastime or to secure a small additional sum to the family earnings. Plate No. 48, fig. 7, shows a good example of this style of work. It is known as *kasida* embroidery. Formerly *kasida* embroideries were entirely in darn stitch but recently chain stitch has been introduced. A large assortment of *pagris*, *handkerchiefs*, loin-cloths and purdahs, embroidered with *muga* silk will be seen in the Sale Gallery of the Exhibition. These are exhibited by Rokman, Krista Hari, and Sasi Mohan Basak, all of Dacca. Some will be seen to be diapered in dark Indian red silk as well as the cloth of gold *muga* work. For bed-room curtains they are extremely good and very cheap, considering the amount of work that is expended on them, but from not being done on both sides they have to be lined.

The reader should compare this brief notice of *kasida* embroideries with the particulars recorded above regarding the *jamdani* muslins.

Azamganj Satin Stitch Embroideries.—(*Plate No. 85.*)—In the Loan Collection a small series of embroidered *kamarbands* (waist belts) will be found. These are perhaps the most beautiful examples of this style of work in the entire Exhibition. The plate given shows six of these, but unfortunately it fails to convey any sort of impression of their great beauty. Without the aid of a lens it is almost impossible to detect the individual threads of silk and the colours are so chaste that they look like the most delicate paintings. Work of this kind is not done at the present day and is so far superior to any of the artistic productions of Bengal, that but for the presence of a colony of art weavers and of wealthy Gujarati merchants in the town it would have been almost safe to have concluded that these *kamarbands* were not made in Azamganj. There is nothing the least like them produced anywhere else in India so that little would be gained by excluding them from recognition as Bengal embroideries.

DIVISION 39. TENT, CROSS, Etc., STITCH.

Burma.—In the Industrial Section of the Indian Museum, Calcutta, there has been preserved an embroidered sheet of woollen cloth. This was originally shown at the Calcutta International Exhibition of 1883-84. It is richly embroidered by Satin Stitch in a charming series of faded blues and purple. In the centre is depicted a mythological scene with Chinese-like contorted clouds. The border is a graceful and most artistic scroll. For many years the manufacture of these beautiful embroideries in silver spangles and painted pictures proceeded at Mandalay and Prome. In the Loan Collection Gallery may be seen the specimen here specially alluded to, as well as several other very beautiful examples of satin stitch of a kind little, if at all, inferior to the work of Japan.

AWARDS FOR DIVISION 38.—DARN AND SATIN STITCH, ETC., EMBROIDERIES.

AWARDS.

First prize with gold medal to Trailokya Nath Das, of Dacca and Murshidabad, for a pair of Kashmir shawls.

Second prize with bronze medal to Davee Sahai Chamba Mall, Amritsar, for collection of *phulkaris*.

Commended for embroidered tea cloths—Lassoo, of Srinagar.

Commended for *muga* silk *kasida*—Ramjan Bibi, of Dacca.

Division 39.—Tent, Cross, Knotted, Herring-bone, and Button-hole Stitches.

The forms of embroidery that it is intended to place in this position are not very important in the sense of being characteristic of particular forms of commercial embroideries, though they are exceedingly interesting from a historic point of view. Nearly all the aboriginal stitches in Indian embroidery would fall into this position, and among these a curious combination of herring-boning and button-holing is especially prevalent, that looks far more difficult than most of the stitches of the civilized races.

Definition of Stitches.

It may be here useful to denote what the writer accepts as the chief features of each of these stitches. By *tent* stitch is meant a series of parallel lines of thread, of the same length, carried across any particular part of a fabric, more especially to strengthen a union of two pieces or to form the dividing line in a pattern. When these are crossed at right angles by a second series of

DIVISION 39. TENT, CROSS, Etc., STITCH.

similar lines it becomes the simplest conception of *cross* stitch. One of the most beautiful developments of the cross stitch is that known as the Persian, but this is very little practised in India. *Knotted* stitch is produced by the thread being wound round the needle and fixed by the needle being returned through the centre of the knot. *Herring-bone* stitch might almost be described as an open and extended form of cross-stitch in which the crossing is made near the point of emergence. Lastly, *button-hole* stitch is a sort of half chain with loops passing round the edge of the fabric. The following may be given as some of the better known examples:—

Cross Stitch.—HISSAR—SIRSA.—These methods of embroidery are all well known and numerous variations exist between each until it becomes next to impossible to separate the one from the other. Mr. J. Lockwood Kipling says of Hissar:—"The embroidered woollen *ohrnas* or *chaddars* of the district are worthy of mention, for though nothing could be more homely than the material, or more simple than the design, they are thoroughly good and characteristic in effect. Two breadths of narrow woollen cloth are joined with curious open work, and covered with archaic ornaments in wool and cotton thread of different colours, needle-wrought in a sampler stitch. The cloth is a fine red, though somewhat harsh and coarse in texture, and though all the designs are in straight lines, human figures and creatures are sometimes oddly indicated. The price of these *chaddars* was originally about Rs. 4, but since a sort of demand has arisen among amateurs interested in Indian fabrics, the rate has been doubled. It is scarcely likely that this woollen *phulkari* or 'flower work' will grow, like the silk and cotton one, from a domestic manufacture for local use into a regular production for export trade. Similar *chaddars* are made and worn in the Sirsa district."

From Hissar and Sirsa the use of cross stitch extends through Bikanir and Jodhpur along the entire length of the mountainous tracts that form the back-bone of Rajputana and deflected south it reaches the hilly parts of Central India and the Central Provinces. The cross stitch is essentially aboriginal though as a special

DIVISION 39. TENT, CROSS, Etc., STITCH.

feature to produce certain effects it is resorted to occasionally by the embroiderers in every branch of needlework. A good illustration of cross stitch from Bikanir is given in the *Indian Art Journal*, Vol. IV, Plate 21, Part 33, page 5.

Knotted Embroidery.

Knotted.—IN BHAWALPUR, MULTAN, MONTGOMERY, JHANG, and DERA GHAZI KHAN a form of embroidery occurs not infrequently that might be described as a knotted form of crewel. The thread passes through and through repeating the same pattern on both sides, but a twist or knot is given by alternately looping one over the other in a short darn stitch. This style of work is generally done on thin muslin, the samples at the Exhibition from Bhawalpur being in strips of red and black running lengthwise. Collectors of Indian Art textiles sometimes pick up (as great treasures) old samples of Chinese knot embroidery. Some few years ago Chinese embroidery was very popular with the Parsee ladies and large quantities were then imported. These are the fine old Indian examples of Chinese knot embroidery, and of course they are not Indian in any sense of the word. But in the finer forms of Lucknow *chikan* work there is seen a distinct example of knotting in Indian embroidery. This is known as the *phanda* stitch (see below).

Knotted Marginal Rim.

Herring-bone Stitch.—FRONTIER EMBROIDERIES.—As has been incidentally mentioned in several places, the most striking feature of the aboriginal embroideries of India is a closely compacted form of herring-boning. The thread turns on itself and crosses to the opposite side, interlacing with the previous loop. If the distance covered be considerable, the needle is purposely passed within the strands of two or three of the previous loops, much as in darning a hole. So again by using the half chain stitch of button-holing, before crossing from side to side, a knotted line is formed around the surface that is being interlaced. This in various forms occurs in the embroideries of Hazara, Peshawar, Kohat, Bannu, Dera Ghazi Khan, and Quetta.

Skirts and Bodices.

In PESHAWAR ladies wear silk skirts called *langahs*. Messrs. Mull Chand and Son send to the Exhibition an extensive series of these, of which No. 4357 (Plate No. 48, fig. 5) may be specially mentioned. They also contribute an excellent set of embroidered bodices—*kurtas*— No. 4359 being especially good. There are some 20 different patterns amongst these, the skirts are made of silk and are about 6 yards long and 28 inches wide, are of every possible shade from deep maroon to canary yellow and embroidered all over in large showy flowers, the leaves and stalks of which are in chain stitch and mostly in yellow or green and the flowers are large medallions of white, crimson or purple, picked out with green. The medallions are formed by white silk worked like the spokes of a wheel from the axle to the rim but interlaced in a composite form of herring-bone stitch. The bottom of the skirt has a strip of three or four inches of stout cotton lining, doubtless to cause the skirt to hang but also to give support to the great medallions of white silk that form the bottom fringe.

DIVISION 39. TENT, CROSS, Etc., STITCH.

In a few of the skirts the medallion style is absent, and *bûtis*, cones or sprays of flowers are worked every two inches or so. In one example of maroon silk, the pattern is outlined in a lax form of chain stitch in white or yellow, the interiors of the leaves being filled in with green and of the petals with dark blue.

Double Herring-boning.

In PESHAWAR also it is possible to purchase examples of a most remarkable development of this style of work. From PANJDEH coats are received that are made in coarse cotton richly embroidered in silk by a stitch that might not inaptly be described as a sort of double herring-bone. The leaf or other surface, to be covered by silk, has its outline formed by the button-hole chain while the herring-boning threads are run across in so compacted an interlacement that they can with difficulty be separated. The prevailing colours are dark maroon, purple, scarlet, dark metallic green, cobalt blue and lemon yellow. Along the skirt of the coat the design consists of numerous erect stems (about 2 feet in height) formed of diamond-shaped bands of alternating colours that give origin to four to five whorls of ascending compound leaves. The stems bear terminal as also axillary floral rosettes in a manner strongly suggestive of the Imperial lily. On the back of the coat near the collar the design brings to mind the Arabic tree of life in the form of masses of date palms with pendant clusters of fruits. The sleeves are purely ornamental and are

DIVISION 39. TENT, CROSS, Etc., STITCH. accordingly permanently sewed up by the surface embroidery being made to go through both layers.

From DERA GHAZI KHAN, DERA ISMAIL KHAN, BANNU, and QUETTA a further manifestation of this same style of double herring-boning is met with in the embroideries seen on leather belts. In the Loan Collection Gallery No. 2909 is a sword belt embroidered in what is there called *kundi* work. This is perhaps the most wonderful and elaborate needlework met with anywhere in India. The green leather on the sword side of the belt is covered by a mass of circular buttons or medallions of embroidery, done in yellow silk. These are worked from a central point in closely compacted herring-bone stitch, the margin being secured by a ring of imitation chain stitch worked simultaneously with the return of the threads to the centre. These buttons of embroidery are not more than ¼th of an inch in diameter and are assorted in lines separated by bands of chain-stitch work. On other parts of the belt the medallions are much larger, are of yellow, green, purple, white or blue silk, and an inch and a half in diameter. They have often central discs elaborately embroidered in chain stitch.

Embroidered belts.

Similar belts have been exhibited by Nawab Sir Imam Buksh Khan Mazari, of Dera Ghazi Khan, and a large assortment will be found in the Sale Gallery made by Esa of Dera Ghazi Khan.

Baluchistan.—Under the chapter devoted to darn and satin stitches, mention has been made of certain forms of embroidery met with in Baluchistan, but it is necessary to say something of the double herring-bone stitch that is abundantly used by certain classes of people in that country. The following notes taken from the collections on view may exemplify the points of greatest interest. QUETTA.—No. 2902.—A cotton dress with long front pocket, embroidered in purple magenta silk. The threads are carried from opposite sides diagonally over a band and are made to loop around each other in the middle. This stitch is used to cover long strips which start from a sort of cross on the shoulders and stretch down over the breasts like imitation straps. No. 2903 illustrates another form of Baloch embroidery done by the Bugli women. Bands of yellow and green cotton are sewn on to the cotton garment in a sort of patchwork, they are then embroidered over the surface, the stitch being usually that above described, but often with two threads simultaneously looping around each other midway. It is customary when appliqué is resorted to, for the embroidery to consist mainly of large circular buttons or medallions in yellow, red and purple. So also No. 2904 shows a silk dress in opaque yellow, embroidered in orange, green, brown, and dull brick-red. The stitch used is mainly herring-boning, the threads looping through each other. But in this instance large patches are literally woven by the needle in the manner in which a stocking may be repaired. Lines appear to be run across in one direction and the return threads are subsequently worked through these in regular meshes until the whole surface is covered. No. 2912 is a Baloch female shirt (dress) with the breast ornamented in immense medallions 2 inches in diameter, made up of zones of herring-boning stitch separated by rings of chain stitch.

DIVISION 39. TENT, CROSS, Etc., STITCH.

Applique Embroidery.

Lastly in SIND, the so-called herring-bone stitch is frequently resorted to by the embroiderers. Dark purple silk from Bokhara is ordinarily the ground material used in the manufacture of *chaddars*. These are curiously embroidered in a quaint design that may be spoken of as consisting of masses of circular patches or medallions compacted together in a most striking manner. Plate No. 48, fig. 2, shows a portion of one of these silk shawls. They are embroidered for the most part with deep orange-coloured floss silk, the stitch employed being there called *dandh-take*, but it is simply the cleverly compacted form of the herring-bone work already fully discussed. In Sind as in Peshawar, it is not so firmly compacted as in some of the other manifestations. The outlines and stalks of the pattern are done in chain stitch, but occasionally also there are introduced spiral formations in chain stitch worked in white and yellow silk alternating with dark green. This style of embroidery is said to be done by the Hindu ladies of Bhiria near Hyderabad in Sind, and a *chaddar* so embroidered used formerly to be very much more frequently worn than at the present day.

Aggregations of Medallions.

DIVISION 40. CHAIN STITCH.

Good samples are exhibited by Mr. C. K. Khilnani, of Karachi who has sent to the Exhibition many marvellously beautiful works of art. In the Indian Museum, Calcutta, there are several samples of these *dandh-take* shawls, but on the finest muslin and embroidered both in orange and crimson silk. They are exceedingly beautiful embroideries which collectors of such textiles would do well to secure good examples of, since the art seems to be rapidly declining in local favour and may in the near future be entirely lost.

Embroidered Muslins.

AWARDS FOR DIVISION 39.—TENT, CROSS, ETC., STITCHES IN EMBROIDERY.

Third prize with bronze medal for Brahui female dress embroidered.—M. Ibrahim of Quetta.

Division 40.—Chain Stitch.

This form of embroidery has been incidentally alluded to as employed in conjunction with several of the forms of needlework already discussed. It has further been observed that it lends itself more readily to floral and other ornamentations, where curved lines are essential, than is the case with most of the stitches already discussed. In consequence it is the form of embroidery most frequently used on silks and other expensive materials where surface covering is not desired. It consists of a series of looped stitches thrown around the needle and inserted one after the other within the immediately preceding stitch, thus giving the effect of a chain. Its most satisfactory use is to describe an outline rather than to cover surfaces, but all the same in Bokhara, Peshawar, Kashmir, Gujarat, Kathiawar, Kach, and Sind, it is extensively and successfully employed to cover surfaces of any size desired. In fact chain stitch is one of the most characteristic and prevalent of Indian forms of embroidery. Sir George Birdwood appears to be alluding to this form of embroidery when, speaking of the work of Kach and Kathiawar, he says :—" It is of the same style as the well-known embroidery of Resht on the Caspian. Either the Armenian merchants introduced the style into Cutch or from Cutch into Persia."

Definition.

Following the course pursued with other forms of needlework, the manifestations met with may be taken up in sequence commencing with the Panjab and passing West and East to South. **DIVISION 40. CHAIN STITCH.**

Panjab.—BOKHARA SOZNIS.—The form of chain stitch embroidery that is perhaps best known is the Bokhara *sozni* or bedcover. This is usually in coarse cotton cloth elaborately covered with great medallions in purple and red. As a rule they are overloaded with ornamentation and, strictly speaking, are, therefore, not very artistic. Since made beyond the frontier of India, they may be accepted as disposed of by these few observations, the additional information only being added that the chief exhibitor of Bokhara *soznis* is Haji Mian Gulam Saudani. **Soznis.**

PESHAWAR SOZNIS.—These are much less known though very much more artistic than the Bokhara. Instead of manifesting great meaningless patches of colour, the Peshawar *soznis* are most intricately and elaborately conceived and the design runs through every part and is consistently maintained. The scheme of colour, instead of purple and crimson, might be described as blue and green with a fair admixture of dull Indian red. Plate No. 49, fig. 2, shows a portion of one of the three or four exceptionally fine old Peshawar *soznis* that are on view at the Exhibition. It is not necessary to attempt a description of these since the design can be studied from the plate. It may suffice, therefore, to add that these *soznis* are exhibited by Haji Safdar Ali, of Peshawar, and have secured a first prize with silver medal in recognition of their high artistic merit.

AMRITSAR.—Lachman Das Bharany, of Amritsar, shows a fair assortment of chain stitch embroideries most probably made in Kathiawar or Kach.

KASHMIR.—It has already been observed that in the embroidery of woollen *rumals* and table covers, when silk is used, the stitch employed, especially to form outlines, is very frequently chain. But to the public generally the chain stitch of Kashmir is more prominently associated with embroidered felts (*namdas*) and woollen curtains, than with shawls. Within the past few years a large trade has arisen in these goods to such an extent, in fact, as to have induced some of the carpet manufacturers to open special branches to deal with this important new trade. **Namdas.**

DIVISION 40. CHAIN STITCH.

The felts, mats, or woven curtains are usually in natural coloured wool or in pale shades of grey, green, blue, or red. They are then embroidered in a bold floral design mostly after the Persian praying rug pattern with one or two border scrolls. The embroidery is done in coloured *pashm*, and the value of the rugs or curtains depends principally upon the quality of the material and size of the chain stitch. On cheap materials the stitch is purposely made large; with fine materials greater care is displayed in the embroidery. A floor rug, say five feet long, may be priced at from Rs. 4 to Rs. 40, according to the quality of the felt and the nature of the embroidery.

In the Exhibition a large display of these chain stitch embroidered felts (*namdas*) and curtains may be seen, the chief exhibitors being :—Samad Shah & Sons and Mahomed Joo, of Srinagar, Kashmir.

GUJRAT.—A most useful paper on the subject of the chain stitch embroideries of this province will be found in the second volume of the *Journal of Indian Art* from the pen of Mr. B. A. Gupte. The coloured illustrations there given, if consulted by the reader, would greatly help to elucidate the meaning of the brief observations that can alone be offered in this work. The women of both Kach and Kathiawar almost invariably wear embroidered garments, so that it is not difficult to understand the high proficiency in the art that has been there attained. Commercial embroidery is produced by men chiefly in the towns. In Kach and Kathiawar the embroiderers are mostly Hindus, in fact the women, as a rule, do all their own work. In Surat the embroiderers are nearly all Muhammadans. In Surat, Baroda, Ahmedabad and other towns of Gujrat, chain stitch is largely practised, for the most part on English woollen broad cloth. The silk used in the needlework is brilliantly coloured, rather too much so for artistic results. The work in fact is marred by the bright green leaves and showy flowers that are universally present. But there is a feature of Gujrat, Kathiawar and still more so Kach embroideries of this description that must be here recorded, namely, that the colouring of surfaces is done in zones of various tints thus, as it were, indicating the shadows, veins, etc. Although this is not usually carried to the extent of destroying the first principle of flat decoration, in the more pretentious examples, shading is distinctly used to an injurious extent.

DIVISION 40. CHAIN STITCH.

In the Sale Gallery of the Exhibition, a large assortment of these embroideries will be seen, and in the Loan Collection Gallery many of great beauty and historic interest will be found. Of the Loan Collection, the following may be specially mentioned as deserving of study :—

SURAT.—Lady's dress, in dull *khaki* yellow, embroidered by chain stitch in maroon and dark blue, around circular pieces of mirror—the silk and the glass forming flowering sprigs. It is described as a silk *ghaghara* or gown, made 125 years ago. It is exhibited by Sha Udechand Ichhachand.

KATHIAWAR.—Allusion has already been made on more than one occasion to the circumstance that Kathiawar is one of the great centres of chain stitch embroidery. The visitor, who will take the trouble to visit the Bhavnagar House, will discover there a display of embroidered skirts, bodices, handkerchiefs, curtains, that will doubtless call forth the greatest admiration. The ground materials are neutral coloured satins, mostly shades of purple, blue, green and yellow, all richly embroidered. Around the bottom of the skirts are thrown narrow embroidered borders, while the surfaces of the skirts themselves will be seen to be elegantly embroidered with sprays of flowers (*bútis*), the colours used displaying none of the vulgarity for glaring colours just described in connection with the modern Surat and Ahmedabad work. A superb collection of old skirts will also be seen in the Sale Gallery, many of which were picked up by the writer while on tour, as also by his assistant, Mr. Percy Brown. The late famine in Gujrat and Kathiawar, it is feared, may have to be accepted as the pathetic cause for many of these beautiful embroidered fabrics being offered for sale.

KACH.—It is probable that the most artistic centre for chain stitch embroidery in India is Bhuj—the capital of the promontory of Kach. Mr. Brown, who specially visited Bhuj in connection with this Exhibition, was enabled, through the liberal co-operation rendered by His Highness the Rao of Kach, to secure from

DIVISION 40. CHAIN STITCH.

that State a very excellent collection of both modern and ancient chain stitch embroideries. Plate No. 49, fig. 1, shows an old *shamiana* of rich maroon silk embroidered in four large clusters of flowers with birds nestling within them, also a central medallion showing the resplendent sun. The border might be described as consisting of a scroll in sun flowers, each alternate flower being one half obstructed by a large moth. This very admirable piece of needlework is so old that it can scarcely be handled, but it is unquestionably one of the most artistic samples in the Exhibition.

Ramji Proshottam Mochi, of Bhuj, exhibits an attractive series of Bhuj embroidered skirts (*kurtis*), (similar to the figure in the *Indian Art Journal*, Vol. II, plate 15).

Turning now to the Loan Collection Gallery, two or three samples of Bhuj work are, perhaps, the most wonderful examples of Indian chain stitch ever exhibited :—

Bhuj Embroidered Petticoat.

The petticoat (No. 1123) in white satin elaborately embroidered in chain stitch figured in Plate No. 86, will be found well worthy of careful study. The pattern was first traced with pencil, then embroidered. The design, like that in Bhuj silver, is unrestrained. It flows from one part to the other without regard to design or proportion, and in consequence it breathes of life. It is a veritable glimpse at nature as it may be seen in the jungles of India—a profusion of flower and foliage closely intermixed. The leaves are in vivid green, the lighter shades in moss green to lemon yellow and the darker tints passing almost into blue. The flowers are as numerous, varied, and brilliant as in the most luxuriant forest glades in the tropics, but they are all

Tropical Life.

in secondary or tertiary shades of orange, purple, red, and blue. The border is done on black satin, the stalks of the floral scrolls being in orange, the leaves green, the flowers white, outlined in pink. This is one of the most showy garments in the Exhibition—a master-piece of skill made by the best artist in Kach at a cost of Rs. 600. The illustration here given conveys a fair conception of its elaboration, but falls far short of the reality, which is as complex in colour as in design—a perfect paradox—that just misses being at once the most beautiful and most offensive work of art in the Exhibition. This is, however, the peculiarity of all the chain stitch embroideries of Kathiawar and Kach. Their vivid colours, often on a black background, do not, as a rule, appeal to the art conceptions of Europeans. **DIVISION 40. CHAIN STITCH.**

Embroidered Bodice.

The specimen No. 1124 is a bodice in the same design as the petticoat just described, but much more minute and intricate. The field is a deep pink orange, nearly every particle of which is covered by green foliage with yellow sheaths and veins. The flowers are bunches of roses, convolvuluses and sprays of jesamine, hopelessly jumbled together into masses of colour that are certainly very charming in general effect but completely lost as an artistic conception. It is like no other work to be seen anywhere in the Exhibition, except perhaps the enamels of Bhuj itself. The shoulder pieces are on black satin and even more detailed than the other parts; a rose, for example, not one inch in diameter is seen to have 20 petals, each coloured with 3 or 4 shades of red, but the chain stitch, in which it is worked, is so minute that the individual stitches cannot be seen by the naked eye. This is without exception the most wonderful piece of embroidery in the Exhibition. It was made by Mauji China, of Bhuj.

Other Bhuj Examples.

Less conspicuous, but nevertheless beautiful and interesting, are the following:—No. 1138—a petticoat richly embroidered. It is in dull metallic green embroidered in purple, yellow, white, and blue chain stitch. The pattern consists of an alternate flowering tree with birds on it and a peacock with expanded tail. The border is a floral scroll outlined in two shades of purple with yellow and white fillings to the leaves and petals and blue outlinings to certain flowers. The most marked peculiarity of this sample is the prominent use of two or three shades assorted in bands, giving the effect of light and shade but not to an injurious extent. No. 1137 is also a petticoat, but in yellow satin. Its best feature is the border scroll in a greatly expanded fan-like design, alternately blue and purple with green leaves No. 1131 is a yellow petticoat in rich satin elaborately embroidered by chain stitch in alternate floral and peacock design.

SIND.—Like Kathiawar and Kach, Sind has many embroiderers, who use very largely the chain stitch. The chief centres

DIVISION 41. CHIKAN WORK.

Embroidered Leather. are Shikarpur, Rohri, Karachi, and Hyderabad. The *soznis* of Shikarpur are well known but have nothing very distinctive. In Hyderabad, Sind, a large trade is done in embroidered camel saddle cloths. These are made of *sambar* leather with the borders and cordons worked up in designs of appliqué in green leather embroidered over the surface with chain stitch of silk, gold and silver wire. A sample of these camel cloths will be seen on Plate No. 43—B., fig. 1.

AWARDS FOR DIVISION 40.—CHAIN STITCH.

AWARDS. First prize with silver medal to Haji Safdar Ali, Peshawar, for *sozni.*

Second prize with bronze medal to Summad Shah, of Srinagar, Kashmir, for embroidered shawls.

Commended for *kasida*—Gokul Chandra Basak, of Dacca.

Commended for silk embroidered border—Mochi Rugha Fakira, of Bhuj, Kach.

Commended for embroidered felt saddle cloth—Mirza Sher Ali, of Quetta.

Commended for embroidered garments—Nur Mahomed Khamusa, of Bhuj, Kach.

Division 41.—Chikan work and Drawn Stitch or White Embroidery on Cotton, Silk, etc. Washing Embroideries.

This may be briefly described as a form of embroidery done on some white washing material such as calico, muslin, linen or silk. There are various methods and stitches, shortly to be described, that are more or less characteristic, but the most frequent is the ordinary satin stitch combined with a form of button-holing.

The great centres of this form of embroidery are Calcutta, Dacca, Lucknow, Peshawar, Madras, Bhopal, and Quetta. In Madras, silk is the material most generally employed and the form of needlework there practised is almost exclusively satin-stitch, though the so-called drawn work and one or two of the special stitches that characterise the *chikan* work of Northern India are to some extent adopted. Accordingly, Madras silk embroideries are not usually classed as forms of *chikan* work but are placed along with the satin-stitch embroideries generally.

White silk Chikan.

So again the exceedingly beautiful but imperfectly known white embroidery of Baluchistan has never before been assigned its true place, namely, along with the *chikan* work of Eastern Bengal and Lucknow. It differs, however, very materially from all the others and stands out by itself as constituting a class of work that calls for separate recognition. It is double satin-stitch but the patterns are very quaint and aboriginal. So again the Bhopal white work is a form of silk embroidery in satin-stitch a quilting embroidery in which very frequently a padding of some coloured material is employed which shows faintly through the sewing thus producing a most graceful and highly artistic effect. A similar form of padded or quilted embroidery is met with in Quetta.

DIVISION 41. CHIKAN WORK.

The needlework of this Division may be usefully referred to three great sections, *1st: Chikan work proper; 2nd: White satin stitch; 3rd: Kamdani or gold embroidery on white cloth.*

1st: Chikan work proper.—It may help to elucidate the classification that the writer has adopted, if the *chikan* work proper be first dealt with. For this purpose it seems desirable to give the position of importance to that of Lucknow, though in historic sequence it is probable that the craft originated in Eastern Bengal and was only carried to Lucknow during the period of luxury and extravagance that characterised the latter term of the Court of Oudh. The Kings of Oudh attracted to their capital many of the famous craftsmen of India, hence Lucknow, to this day, has a larger range of artistic workers than are to be found in almost any other town of India. Lucknow *chikan* work is perhaps the most remarkable of these crafts as it is the most artistic and most delicate form of what may be called the purely indigenous needlework of India. The following is a brief enumeration of the chief stitches used by the Lucknow embroiderers:—

Description of the Stitches Employed.

(*a*) *Taipchi.*—This is usually done by women and is the simplest and cheapest form of work. It consists of a sort of darn stitch in which the thread is drawn through the fabric in more or less parallel and straight lines. The design is simply outlined and is ordinarily done on muslin.

DIVISION 41. CHIKAN WORK.

(*b*) *Khatao* (*or Khatawa*).—This is a form of appliqué produced on calico or linen, never on muslin. Minute pieces of the same material as the fabric are sewn to the surface, in elaboration of the foliar and floral designs, but these are so minute that it requires very careful observation to detect that the design is mainly in appliqué, not embroidery. The details are then filled in by *taipchi* or some of the other stitches to be shortly described. *Khatao* is one of the two forms of what are collectively designated the flat embroidery of Lucknow, in contradistinction to the forms of embossed or knotted *chikan* work.

Opaque Embroidery.

(*c*) *Bukhia*.—This is the true flat *chikan* work of which *khatao* is but the cheap imitation. It might be described as inverted satin-stitch. In other words the thread is mainly thrown below and is employed in effecting opaque spaces and lines on fine muslin. The needle nips the material on the upper surface by minute stitches thus outlining the petals, leaves, etc., while the thread is carried below and accumulates in compact masses, until the fine muslin on the embroidered portions is no longer transparent. It is this effect that the skilful worker desires to produce and which has received the name of *bukhia*.

Knotted.

(*d*) *Murri* (*rice-shaped*).—This form is practised on muslin only. The thread may be described as forming numerous knots or warts of a pyriform shape. These are in reality produced by a sort of minute satin-stitch but the embroidered patches rarely exceed one-eighth or even one-sixteenth of an inch in size, and thus look like French knots.

(*e*) *Phanda* (*millet form*).—This is simply a small and less elongated condition of *murri* stitch. The knots are very minute and practically spherical, that is to say, not drawn out (or pear-shaped) as in *murri*. The presence of *phanda* is the surest indication of the high class of the work. The knots are very frequently not more than one thirty-second part of an inch in size and in that case are aggregated together to form the filling of leaves or petals. This is one of the most graceful developments of Lucknow embroidery and the one that may be described as most characteristic of this great centre of needlework.

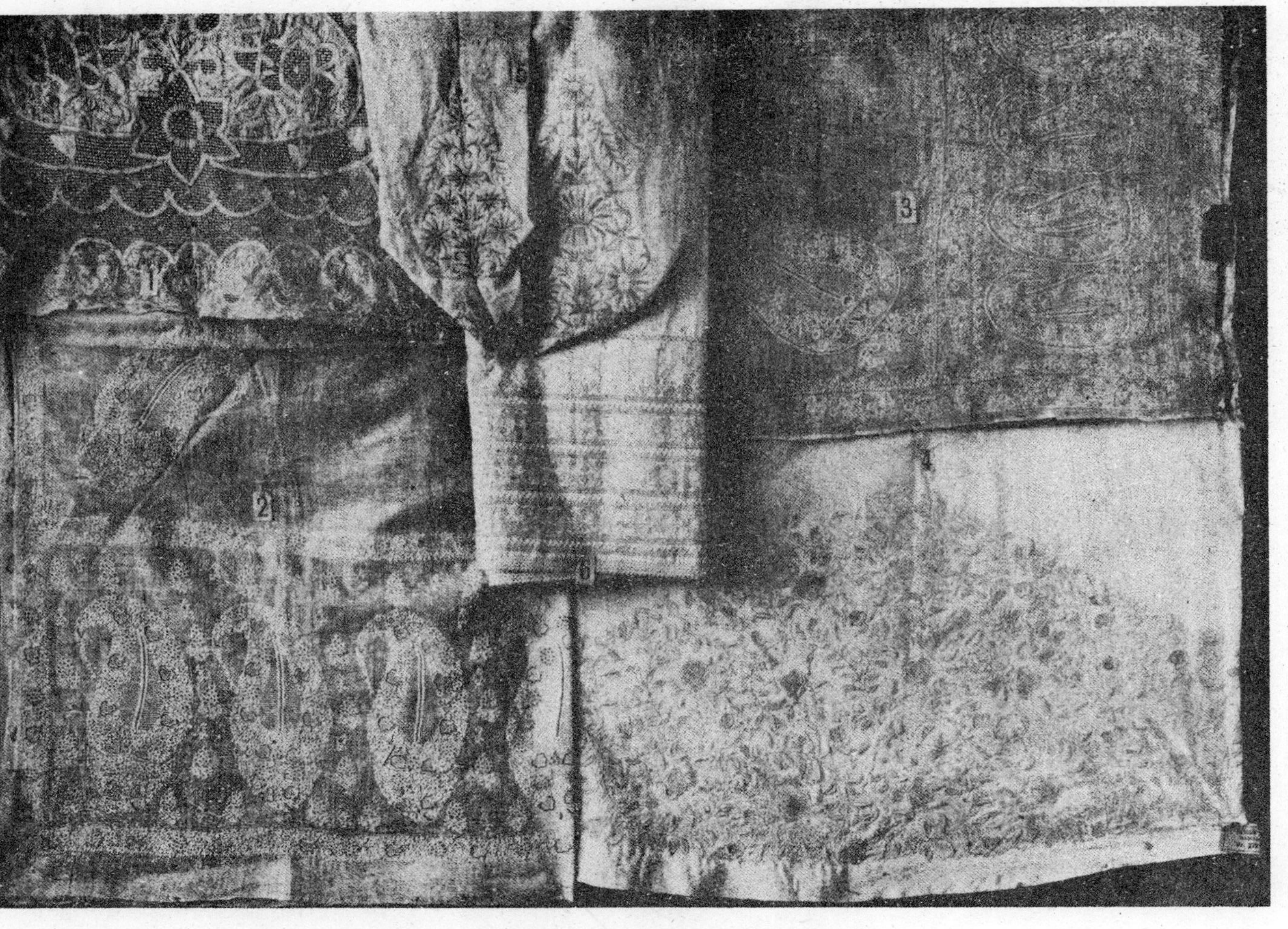

Plate No. 52 Chikan and Drawn Work Embroidery

DIVISION 41. CHIKAN WORK

Drawn-stitch or Box-work.

(*f*) *Jali* (*fishing net*).—This when met with in *chikan* work is commonly spoken of as drawn stitch, but as a matter of fact the Lucknow embroiderers regard the drawing out of a thread (*tar*) as a slovenly imitation of true *jali* embroidery. In true *jali* the strands of the warp and weft are pushed on one side by the needle and held in that position by a sort of extremely minute button-holing. There are various forms of *jali* in Lucknow *chikan*. The chief are the following:—*Madrasi-jali*—this consists of a series of minute squares usually about $\frac{1}{16}$th inch in diameter Of these one is opened, the other left closed and the third broken into four still more minute openings. *Calcutta-jali* (as produced in Lucknow) consists of a series of openings one-half the size of the *Madrasi* but assorted in parallel bands with alternating bands not perforated. In neither of these forms are any threads drawn out. Lastly, the *siddhaur* (simple) *jali* (usually produced by the women) is drawn *jali* and is the form seen in all cheap work. The openings are irregularly shaped, approximately squares, but usually not bound by button-holing in any form. In Calcutta *chikan* work this is called box-work, especially in the larger or coarser condition as practised with calico and linen tea-table covers.

Tasar Silk.

A feature of Lucknow *chikan* must be here mentioned, namely, that yellow or tasar silk is largely used in the filling of petals or leaves. *Phanda* work is, as a rule, done in tasar. This peculiarity instantly distinguishes the *chikan* work of Lucknow from that of the rest of India.

Chief examples on View and Names of Important Exhibitors.

Kedar Nath Ram Nath & Co., of Lucknow, have secured a gold medal for a splendid series of examples of this work. Of these the following may be specially mentioned:—Of *taipchi* a dress piece or *sári* (No. 4931), price Rs. 50; a coat (No. 4919), Rs. 10; a *kurta* (No. 4920), Rs. 10. Of *murri* work native caps (Nos. 2543 and 2544), price Rs. 65; lady's dress front, cuffs, and collar (No. 4918), Rs. 38; insertions (No. 4913), Rs. 24. Of *phanda* work a large assortment of which the following may be specially alluded to: native cap (No. 2558); a d'oyley (No. 2547), Rs. 25;

DIVISION 41. CHIKAN WORK.

a *choga* (No. 4925), Rs. 195; an *abba* (or small *choga*) (No. 4924), Rs. 225; a lady's handkerchief (No. 2573), Rs. 250—the finest piece of this kind of embroidery in the Exhibition—it manifests almost every stitch known to the *chikan* worker; another handkerchief (No. 2574) shows *phanda*, *murri*, *bukhia* and the three forms of *jali* work, Rs. 300; a dress piece (No. 4930), Rs. 200. Of *bukhia* work a handkerchief (No. 2581), Rs. 200; a native cap (No. 2563), Rs. 6; a lady's dress with front panel, cuffs, collar (No. 4936), Rs. 20; a cap (No. 2590), Rs. 25; Plate No. 52, fig. 2, shows a sample of Kedar Nath Ram Nath's work.

Sham Sundar Ghazi Ram, of Lucknow, were given a silver medal for their collection. They showed many samples of great beauty of which the following may be specially mentioned:—a *sárí* (No. 2128), Rs. 437; insertions (No. 2122), Rs. 22; a handkerchief (No. 1358), Rs. 31. Plate No. 52, fig. 3, shows a sample.

A bronze medal was awarded to Alla Buksh Faiz Buksh, of Lucknow, for a fine series of samples of which the *dupatta* (No. 2533) may be specially mentioned.

Ganga Prasad and Ganesh Prasad, of Lucknow, have very many excellent samples of *chikan* work, a panel for a lady's dress being specially worth attention.

Ashiq Ali, of the Chauk, Lucknow, shows admirable *chikan*, the *sárí* in *phanda* work (No. 2195) being specially good.

When compared with Lucknow *chikan* work that of Calcutta and Dacca has to take a distinctly second position. At the same time for certain purposes the Calcutta work has its own merits. It is for example better suited for tea-table cloths where repeated washing is necessary. S. C. Pyne & Co., of the New Market, Calcutta, are the only exhibitors and their show is by no means so good as it might have been.

It is satisfactory that the Judging Committee have been led to recognise the purely indigenous form of embroidered lace (if the expression be permissible) by the award of a gold medal to this division.

2nd: Satin Stich on white-washing material more or less combined with chikan work proper.—It is next to impossible to draw hard-and-fast lines between the various forms of needlework.

Certain stitches are sufficiently abundant to give useful lines of isolation, but every now and again more than one stitch is met with on the same fabric and modifications occur in the stitch until the one type of work blends into the other. As already explained one of the most prevalent stitches, in *chikan* work, is in reality a minute form of satin stitch. This is developed until in certain localities it becomes ordinary satin stitch. The only ground of association with *chikan* work then becomes the circumstance that it is done on a washing material and mostly with white thread.

DIVISION 41. CHIKAN WORK.

There were two or three great centres for this class of work, namely, Madras, Bhopal, and Quetta with Kashmir and Peshawar as also some of the frontier towns of the Panjab that manifest special forms of white embroidery, that have to be found positions somewhere and are perhaps best associated with the *chikan* work.

PESHAWAR.—Some years ago Mr. Lockwood Kipling wrote of this town:—"Colourless embroidery or *chikan-doz* is wrought here as delicately as in Kashmir, and, as in chased copper, there is considerable affinity between the work of Srinagar and Peshawar. The *burka* or Muhammadan ladies' out-door mantle, garments of all sorts, and the *sozni* or quilt are the objects to which this work is applied. The effect is scarcely, perhaps, commensurate with the labour and delicacy of the work. Some of the patterns wrought on fine muslins are nothing short of exquisite in line and quantity, but a close examination is necessary for a just appreciation of their beauty. There is no 'cutting out holes and sewing them up again' as in English, Bengal, and Madras *chikan* work. Sometimes tiny pieces of muslin cut out in the shape of leaves are applied either on the surface or between two surfaces and outlined with fine stitches. It is only by holding the work against the light that these delicate patterns can be fairly made out. Excepting the *sozni* or quilt, none of this work is made for European use. In Peshawar, as in Lucknow, much of this embroidery is done by women and children, whereas in Kashmir the industry is confined to men."

In the Exhibition Messrs. Mull Chand & Sons will be seen to have furnished an assortment of *burkas* and other white embroideries.

DIVISION 41. CHIKAN WORK.

QUETTA.—A large display of Baluch white embroideries are on view, and Mr. R. Hughes Buller has also deposited in the Loan Collection Gallery many of great beauty from his own private collection. Plate No. 52, fig. 6, shows a Brahui embroidered skirt. There are several very distinct styles. It is said to be mostly made by *Kandahari* women living in Quetta. The goods turned out are *chaddars* of English bleached cotton with broad embroidered borders in white silk. The stitch most prevalent is a form of double satin done in silk. The pattern is accordingly the same on both sides. The design might almost be viewed as a continuous elaboration of the tree of life with intermixed stars and squares assorted as borders. On the margin it is also customary to show a narrow strip of torchon lace, but in a design and method of production that seems quite original. The best form of this lace might be described as resembling a double row of wheels linked together.

The samples most worthy of inspection are the *chaddars* Nos. 2635, Rs. 75; the *pugri* or *langota*, No. 2632, Rs. 37.

Another form is similar to the appliqué embroidery of Bhopal and will be described below under Division 44.

A table cloth in the Loan Collection Gallery may be here briefly indicated. It is No. 2607 and is called a *shabaka*. This is a most peculiar and characteristic form of white embroidery. Threads are drawn out right and left to demark the limits of the pattern to be worked. Some of those withdrawn lines are worked up, making what the Calcutta *chikan*-workers call a line of box-work border, while others are not. The main pattern is formed which consists of a series of triangles joined end on end, and worked in conjunction with the lines drawn out. The sewing is made to go through and through in a form of double satin stitch, so that it is the same on both sides. It is done with white silk and the pattern is usually worked into squares by double lines of ordinary stitching. In the corners of the cloth are also worked large cone-patterns.

MADRAS.—Embroidery of a peculiar kind has attained a high proficiency in Madras. This consists for the most part of washing white silk superbly embroidered in silk. The chief firm for this class of goods is Daday Khan, Mount Road, Madras. In the Exhibition will be seen a large assortment of the work turned out by him mostly in the form of ladies' dresses, the panels, cuffs, etc., being all beautifully embroidered. It is not to be wondered at that this splendid display has secured a first prize with silver medal. A specimen has been shown, on Plate No. 52, fig. 4.

DIVISION 41. CHIKAN WORK.

In addition to dress pieces, Daday Khan also shows an assortment of cuffs, collars, handkerchiefs, and afternoon tea-table cloths. The last mentioned are elegantly embroidered in what is called washing gold. They form a class of goods quite distinct from the extensive series of other tea-table cloths from many towns that each claim admiration ; those of Madras have a dignity and purity of design all their own that is quite charming.

BHOPAL.—(Plate No. 52, fig. 5.)—Sends an assortment of white embroideries well worthy of special recognition. The most interesting work it seems, however, preferable should be treated (as already stated) under Division 44. The Victoria Girls' School of Bhopal contributes drawn embroideries of excellent workmanship but in European designs and methods.

3rd: Kamdani or Gold and Silver Embroidery on white cotton cloth and muslin.—The term *kamdani* usually denotes light embroideries in which gold and silver wires are used—the opposite condition in fact to *zardozi*, the heavy embroideries that fall under Division 45. But there is a class of goods that neither seems to find a place under *chikan* work, as ordinarily accepted, nor under *kamdani* as just defined. These are the piece-goods that might be spoken of as hand-embroidered *jamdanis*. *Chikan* work, though doubtless it includes piece-goods, usually has the more restricted meaning of special embroideries, such as prepared *chogas*, special panels for dresses, cuffs, collars, caps, handkerchiefs, etc. *Chikan* work in fact takes the place in India that lace holds in Europe. Piece-goods sold by the yard and with a particular pattern embroidered in cotton, silk or gold and silver wire at fixed intervals all over do not by most persons fall either under the definition of *chikan* work or of *kamdani*, no more than embroidered net sold by the yard would be treated as lace (see remarks below under Division 42).

DIVISION 41. CHIKAN WORK.

By whatever name the embroidered piece-goods are known, there will be seen in the Exhibition a display of unequalled beauty in the form mainly of ladies' dress pieces in fine muslin and hand-embroidered with numerous designs either in cotton, silk or gold and silver. These come chiefly from Lucknow and are exhibited by most of the firms that show ordinary *chikan* work. If made of fair quality of muslin, the 9¾ yards suitable for a dress will cost about Rs. 10, and from that price up to Rs. 250 every grade in quality of muslin and richness in embroidery may be seen. In many of average quality, say Rs. 15 to Rs. 30 for a dress length, a charming effect is produced by the sparing use of *muga* or *tasar* silk threads within the embroidery. Many of the samples with gold and silver wire are wonderfully artistic and by no means so heavy as might be anticipated from the amount of metallic wire which they contain.

There has been a fair demand for these needle-embroidered muslins, but by no means to the extent that their great beauty seemed to give expectations of. It is thus to be hoped that the greatest observations may tend to direct attention to these very beautiful goods.

AWARDS FOR DIVISION 41.—CHIKAN WORK.

AWARDS.

First prize with gold medal to Kedar Nath, Ram Nath of Lucknow, for collection of *chikan* work.

First prize with silver medal to Daday Khan of Madras for a superb series of silk dress pieces embroidered in silk.

Second prize with silver medal to Sham Sunder and Ghasi Ram, of Lucknow, for a cotton *sári*.

Third prize with bronze medal to Alla Buksh Faiz Baksh, of Lucknow, for collection of *chikan* work.

Commended for collection of *chikan* embroidery—Mr. S. C. Pyne of Calcutta.

Commended for dress-pieces—Ganga Pershad and Ganesh Pershad of Lucknow.

Division 42.—Net-Work—Net Embroidery.

Division 43.—Lace and Knitting.

There perhaps would be no material advantage gained by the rigorous separation of the embroidery of net, as met with in

India, from the manufacture of lace as understood in Europe. It is commonly affirmed that lace is of modern introduction into India and is purely a Western art, which even in Europe only dates from about the 15th Century. That opinion may be correct and it certanly is so when attention is concentrated on the three chief forms of lace, *viz.*, point, cushion, and crochet laces. These might be defined as textiles made by sewing, twisting, and knotting thread; the first by means of a needle and one thread, the second by numerous threads worked from bobbins, and the third by one thread and a crochet hook. In other words laces are not woven on a loom or machine by which two threads (or two sets of threads) at right angles are simultaneously bound together by a mechanical contrivance. Neither are they needlework embroideries on woven textiles. But while that definition would be accepted by most persons, certain forms of embroidered net, such as the Limerick tambours, are regularly viewed as lace; so also are numerous manifestations of embroidered appliqué and of embroidered braiding work, such as the Carrick-ma Cross laces. These do not differ in principle from some of the forms of *chikan* work already discussed, which are purely Indian and have been practised for many centuries. It will thus be seen that a restriction of lace to fabrics produced from threads that are sewn, twisted, or knotted together by the hand is not absolutely upheld though it is a useful one to enforce.

DIVISIONS 42 AND 43. NET-WORK. LACE.

Definition.

In India there would appear to have existed a large traffic, for many years past, in embroidered net sold by the piece. This class of goods can hardly be said to differ from the *chikan* and *kamdani* work already fully discussed. In fact the chief difference lies in the circumstance that the one is embroidered on cotton cloth and the other on net. So in the same way the isolation of embroidered nets, when sold as piece-goods, from the Limerick laces, or specially prepared articles of dress, is an exact parallel with the separation advocated above of *chikan* work proper from *kamdani* embroideries.

Net Work.—HYDERABAD.—In various centres all over India, net is regularly utilised in needlework embroidery. In Hyderabad, for example, a fairly prosperous industry would appear to have

DIVISIONS 42 AND 43. NET-WORK. LACE.

existed for many years in which net is embroidered in chain stitch. For this purpose the cloth is stretched on a light frame. The thread is held in the left hand below and drawn up above by the hook, the loop of the chain formed and the hook once more returned through another mesh to catch the thread.

In the Exhibition will be seen an extensive series of these Hyderabad embroidered nets both in the form of piece-goods and special garments. No. 245 is a piece of black net with white silk worked into a floral design at fixed intervals all over the surface. This exactly resembles the *jamdani* textiles of Bengal except that it is on net and the pattern is embroidered, not woven. No. 246 is in *tercha* design, that is to say, the *bel-dari* runs obliquely across. No. 247 is a maroon coloured net with white silk flowers (*bútis*)—all these and many others were made by Muhamed Burhan, of Hyderabad.

Kamdani embroidered nets are also regularly produced ; that is to say, nets in which gold and silver wire are more or less employed as also coloured silks or even wools. No. 242 is an embroidered net with *jalis* or meshes, formed by gold wire and spangles with, at the crossings, stars of dark green, alternating with brick red, embroidered in wool. In the centres of the meshes are placed trifoil *bútis* in gold wire. This was made by Muhamed Burhan and costs R219 for 8 yards. In another sample a minute chain runs obliquely across (*tercha*) with intervening *bútis* worked in gold wire and spangles attached by orange-coloured thread from below.

MADRAS.—Similar embroidered nets with silk or gold or silk are extensively produced at Madras by various makers such as Daday Khan, of Mount Road, and by Muzaffar Hussain, of Triplicane, Madras. These may be either on white or black net and very often have beetles' wings fixed within rings of gold wire.

As a curiosity it may be said in passing, that the use of beetles' wings in textile ornamentation, would appear to be fairly ancient. In the Loan Collection Gallery a *sina-band* or breast covering (No. 4415) of crimson velvet richly embroidered with gold, will be seen to have a liberal admixture of beetles' wings.

This was presented by the Maharaja Ranjit Singh to Wazir Nathu, of Chamba.

DIVISIONS 42 AND 43. NET-WORK. LACE.

DELHI.—The embroidery of net seems to be a fairly established industry in Delhi, not merely for the production of narrow strips and special pieces such as those dealt with below under Lace, but for piece-goods embroidered in imitation of the Lucknow *chikan* and the Dacca *jamdani* textiles.

Lace.—There would appear no reason to doubt but that the manufacture of lace, as accepted above, was introduced into India by the missionaries. It has attained to considerable proficiency in Southern India more especially, and for years past has left the precincts of the Convent and School and assumed the condition of a village industry. According to some writers there may have been several independent introductions in different localities. The village industry as seen for example in Quilon and its neighbourhood has been attributed to the Portuguese and Dutch. Be that as it may, scores of women and children may be seen any day at Eravipuram, for example, actively engaged making cushion lace. In fact lace-making has become as much an industry of the people of Quilon and of many other parts of South India, as carpet weaving may be said to be in Mirzapore or Agra. The number of bobbins used depends on the age and experience of the operator.

In South Travancore there seems no doubt the art was introduced by Mrs. Mault in 1818, and from Nagercoil it was carried to Idaiyangudi in Tinnevelly, to Madura and to other centres. In many of the Convents in South India such as those of Madras town, there are large and prosperous lace schools that have furnished many of the splendid examples of Limerick laces on view at the Exhibition.

In Hyderabad, Mrs. Pratt, wife of a missionary, unpicked some pieces of lace to discover for herself the method by which they were made, and shortly thereafter organised a large school for lace-weaving in connection with her husband's mission.

In Mirzapore in the United Provinces there is another missionary school teaching lace and in Delhi still another. From these and other such institutions have been received the varied and

DIVISIONS 42 AND 43. NET-WORK. LACE.

rich display of lace on view at the Exhibition, a selection from which has been shown on Plate No. 53. These are as follows:—

Fig. 1.—Real Limerick point lace made at the Presentation Convent College, Vepery, Madras.

Fig. 2.—Pillow lace from the London School, Mirzapore.

Fig. 3.—Point lace from the London Mission School, Nagercoil, South Travancore.

Fig. 4.—Necktie from the Idaiyangudi Lace School, Tinnevelly.

Fig. 5.—A bertha made of real Limerick lace worked by Sister M. Berchmans of the Presentation Convent, Maclean Street, Madras. This sample obtained the first prize.

Fig. 6.—Lace from the Nagercoil School.

Fig. 7.—Pillow lace handkerchief from Idaiyangudi Lace School.

Fig. 8.—Embroidered net fron the Baptist Zenana Mission, Delhi.

Before passing away from the subject of lace, the writer would desire attention to the lace borderings shown on the Quetta embroidered shawls, coats, etc. This is clearly lace, not embroidery, and is a form most probably of torchon lace. There is nothing to show that this has been derived from missionary schools. It is reported to be peculiar to Kandahar and is probably the first record of Asiatic lace.

Knitting.—Closely allied to lace manufacture is the art of knitting. It may be observed that knitting seems to have been unknown in India prior to the efforts of the missionaries. It is called *jorab-bunna* and is taught in most female schools. Stockings and such like articles, knitted both by imported and Indian worsted, may be purchased at most of the towns of Northern India and a regular trade has been recently organised in the manufacture at Bombay, Lahore and elsewhere of socks, banians, etc., by machinery.

Izarband Knitting.—This curious industry may be said to date from the Muhammadan conquest of India, since prior to that the Hindus wore *sáris* and *dutis*. not garments cut, shaped and sewn together so as to fit the body. In the absence of

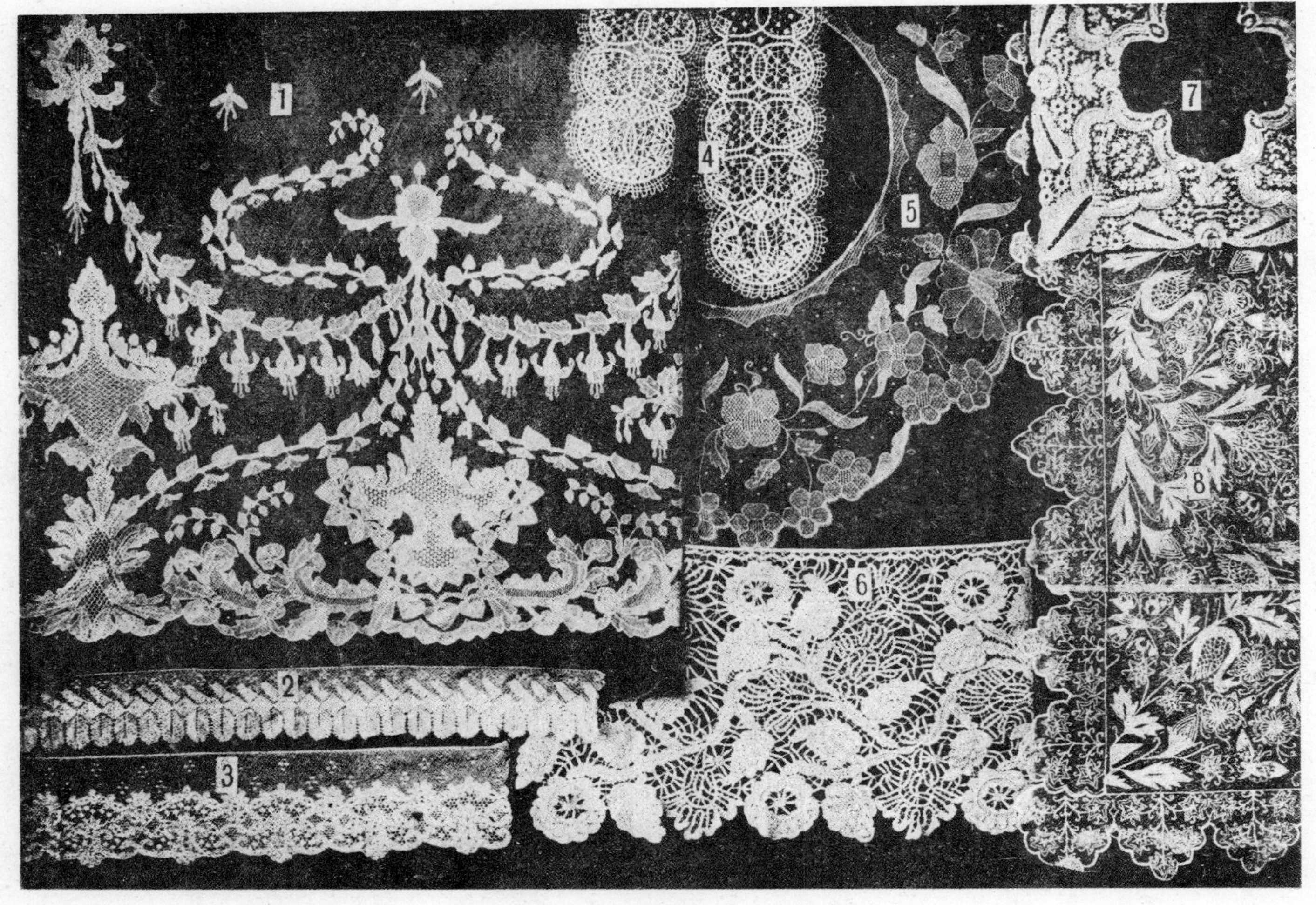

Plate No. 53 Network and Lace

trousers, there would be no occasion for waistbands or girdles such as those used for tying up the *pyjamas* and made by the Patwas (Hindus) and Ilaquebands (Muhammadans). These are not woven on a loom but are knitted by bobbins (*naras*) from a frame. Usually the *izarband* is simply a fine net of uniformly coloured silk, but at times it is richly ornamented, the silk being variegated and with beautiful tassels in gold or silver wire attached. In consequence of this craft has come into existence the manufacture of tassels to be used on cushions, bed-ties and many such articles, some of which are simply plaited not knitted as in the *izarband.* In the Panjab the places most noted for *izarbands* are Amritsar, Batala, Delhi, and Lahore, but throughout India most large towns have their noted *Patwas* or *Ilaquebands.*

Naichas or flexible *hukka* tubes are often highly ornate articles and the outer coverings of these are plaited of silk and gold or silver wire by a process that seems inexplicable without the deft fingers and lissom body of the *Patwas* apprentice.

In the Exhibition the large assortment of *Izarbands* and *Naichas* will be found exceedingly interesting, and their presence denotes the existence in India of some knowledge of the art of knitting and plaiting threads together in the formation of textiles. In the Loan Collection Gallery the *naichas* exhibited by His Highness the Nawab Bahadur of Murshidabad will be found specially worthy of study.

Division 44.– Laid, Crewel, Appliqué and Quilted Embroideries.

It has been thought desirable to emphasise the existence in India of widely different styles of needlework. There might be no great advantage gained by their isolation one from the other were it not possible that, when separately recognised, they may be more highly appreciated. The goods placed into the present position can with difficulty be isolated from those that fall into the next Division.

Laid, or as it is sometimes called couched, embroidery includes all forms in which the ornamenting material is laid on the surface of the textile and held in position by small stitches, usually

DIVISION 44. LAID, CREWEL, Etc., EMBROIDERIES.

brought from the back by a special needle for the purpose. Various forms are produced by the distance apart and position of these attachments. "Basket couching" denotes a form where the binding threads are so regulated as to simulate basket work: "brick stitch" when in rows with the attachments alternating: and "diaper couching" when in diagonal lines. But in "laid embroidery" it is also very often the case that the ornamental material is upheld by some padding placed beneath for that purpose—hence the term "couching."

The forms of laid or couching in India are so numerous that a special work might be devoted to their narration. The writer can, therefore, attempt to indicate but a few of the better known and more artistic examples. These are:—

Braiding Embroideries. – There is a form of braiding which in India is called *Dori*-work commonly seen on *pashmina* fabrics. It appears to have been first started in its present form, in Kashmir, about 50 years ago and possibly at the suggestion of the French traders. Originally, and to this day, it is a stitch still worked with gold braid (*dori*) on certain shawls or portions of shawls. As seen on *pashmina* dress-pieces, on *chogas*, *chaddars*, etc., it consists of a flat silk braid, white or pale coloured, about the thickness of ordinary knitting worsted. A long piece of the braid is thrown loosely around the neck and hangs to the left side. The end is taken in the left hand and laid upon the fabric. It is then fastened by the needle being driven beneath it, thus casting a loop of thin thread over the braid which is next turned at right angles and a second stitch passed underneath. When this has been done, the embroiderer gives his sewing thread one or two turns around the braid, close to the surface of the cloth, and then once more lays the braid down and thrusts the needle beneath it. The twist of the thread given around the braid as also the turning and returning of the braid itself, with each two stitches, causes it to assume the beautiful knotted appearance that is so much admired in this style of work. The designs most generally met with are elaborations of the cone, in endless conditions and sizes. Occasionally on reversible shawls it is worked on both sides, and within the past few years tippets or capes have appeared that are lined with skin inside and elaborately *dori*-embroidered on the outside. DIVISION 44. LAID, CREWEL, Etc., EMBROIDERIES.

It is somewhat curious that, although this stitch in braiding seems to be purely indigenous, the writer is not aware of its having been previously described. Dr. Forbes Watson (*Textile Manufactures,* etc., published in 1866) gives in Plate IX a most excellent illustration but simply calls it "ornamental braiding." Baden-Powell in his *Manufactures and Arts* simply observes that, "it is best done in Kashmir, whence some very magnificent specimens are occasionally seen; but it is also done with considerable success both in Amritsar and Ludhiana. This is in fact a kind of braiding done with silk thread and a peculiar stitch."

In the Exhibition will be seen an extensive series of embroidered *pashminas* and *chaddars,* many of them exceedingly beautiful. The most noteworthy examples are those shown by Davee Sahai Chamba Mall, of Amritsar; by Ashan Shah, of Ludhiana; and by Samad Shah and Sons and Mahomed Joo, of Kashmir.

Appliqué Embroideries.—In place of braids, pieces of variously coloured cloths are often laid on the surface of other textiles and embroidered along the margins and over the surfaces by way of giving attachment. Here and there all over India and Burma the habit prevails of obtaining certain effects by clipping up one textile and applying portions of it to the surface of another. Patchwork becomes in Kashmir a high art as has been fully detailed in connection with the shawls of that State. In Hyderabad, Sind, camel saddle cloths are ornamented by one colour of leather being sewn on the top of another and subsequently needle embroidered by chain stitch. The Brahui women of Quetta resort to appliqué as an additional method of ornamentation with their herring-bone stitch embroidery. The *chikan* workers of Lucknow use patches of the same material sewn on to their white embroideries to produce dense or opaque effects. In several kinds of lace, appliqué and braiding are well-recognised methods of obtaining certain results. Patchwork.

In Burma appliqué assumes a specific form and gives origin to the embroidered wall drapings known as *kalagas.* These are made both of cotton and woollen cloths. The field material is

DIVISION 44. LAID, CREWEL, Etc., EMBROIDERIES.

usually black or red. They portray in the central panel some mythological scene, the faces and hands of the human figures being usually pieces of white cotton cloth painted in the desired manner, while the foliage, trees, and flowers are all pieces of cloth of the necessary colours and forms. "The result in Burma is a gorgeously coloured screen, which is used to decorate the house on festive occasions or to partition off a portion of it for a guest. The *kalaga* also forms a gay roof-covering for the bullock cart when the family travels to one of the large pagoda feasts." *Kalagas* are largely made at a suburb of Rangoon, known as Kemmendine.

In the Exhibition it will be seen that Messrs. Beato & Co., of Rangoon and Mandalay, have supplied a large assortment of *kalagas,* as also two that are very old and much more artistic, because simpler than the every-day articles. Messrs. Tara Chand Pursram, of Bombay and Rangoon, also show a large collection of *kalagas* and other spangle embroideries of Burma.

Quilted Embroideries.—Throughout India preference is shown for cotton rather than woollen goods. To obtain the required warmth necessary for the cold season many methods of softening and rendering the fabric massive have been invented such as that discussed in connection with the *himru* textiles. An even more general practice, however, consists in packing soft, loose cotton wool between two layers of cotton cloth and quilting

Quilts.

the two together. With the common classes of people the quilts are simply dyed or printed. In fact the production of sheets for this purpose has been one of the greatest incentives to artistic progress in the dyer's craft. With the upper classes, quilting more often assumes the form of embroidery and elaborate designs are worked, the padded or raised up portions acting the part of couching to subsequent embroidery.

Quilted *soznis* are extensively produced in Maldah, Rajshahye, Nadia, and Puri. If the *kasidas* of Dacca and the *chikan* work of Calcutta be excluded, these embroidered quilts might be spoken of as the only examples of artistic needlework met with in Bengal. In addition to being largely embroidered, Broach in the Bombay Presidency has the reputation of having

DIVISION 44. LAID, CREWEL, Etc. EMBROIDERIES.

invented woven quilts, the various squares in the double textile being hand-loaded with cotton before being closed by the loom.

When applied to garments quilting comes to assume ornamentation that has the additional advantages of warmth and strength much as in the smock-frock of the English farm labourer.

BHOPAL.—In this State quilting is carried to a high state of proficiency. A *choga* is made of very fine white Chinese silk and lined with a good quality of white cotton. On the lining is sewn, by appliqué, patches of red and blue-coloured cotton in elaboration of the desired pattern. Such ornamentations are shown along the margin, around the sleeves and cuffs, the neck or collar, and down the back as a great panel and also along the shoulders. When the appliqué is complete, the silk is laid over and securely sewn on to its lining by every detail of the outlining of the appliqué being stitched. The result may be said to be that the red and blue appliqué shows through the silk in a subdued and charming fashion.

It is understood that Her Highness the Begum of Bhopal takes a special interest in this form of embroidery, and in consequence the art has been carried to great perfection, every shade of colour being used and designs of the most complex character developed. It is accordingly satisfactory to note that the Judging Committee of the Exhibition have awarded a silver medal to Abdul Aziz Khan for his display of this class of embroidery now on view.

QUETTA.—It would seem that with many of the tribes in Baluchistan, the habit prevails of thickening the cotton garments worn by them by quilting certain portions and colouring them in the manner fully described above in connection with Bhopal. Mirza Sher Ali, of Quetta, obtained a bronze medal for a *choga* embroidered in this manner.

AWARDS FOR DIVISION 44.—LAID EMBROIDERIES.

AWARDS

Second prize with silver medal to Abdul Aziz Khan, of Bhopal, for an embroidered *choga*.

Third prize with bronze medal to Mirza Sher Ali of Quetta for embroidered *choga*.

Division 45.—Gold and Silver Wire Embroidery.

DIVISION 45. GOLD AND SILVER EMBROIDERY.

It seems probable that to the majority of persons the expression "Indian Embroidery" would suggest almost exclusively the form of gold and silver work that forms the special theme of this chapter. From being universally done on a frame it is called *karchob* work and as already observed there are two forms—the heavy and massive (*zardozi*) and the light and graceful (*kamdani*). The former is worked on velvet or satin with usually a heavy cotton lining to give support to the gold work, while the latter is on muslin or fine silk. They are mainly accomplished as "couching" and "laid" embroideries, that is to say, certain portions of the design are cushioned so as to raise the embroidery above the general level, while in still other instances gold braidings or specially formed gold wires are laid in the required fashion and attachment given by yellow silk brought by a needle from below. As a rule gold wire thread can neither be woven on a revolving spool nor sewn by a needle, unless specially prepared and very expensive. Accordingly gold wire embroidery is almost of necessity "laid."

Chief Forms.

Laid Embroidery.

Before proceeding further with the subject of gold embroidery, it seems almost indispensable for a proper understanding of the chief features of the art, that a digression should be made in so far as to convey some sort of conception of the art of wire drawing.

Gold and Silver Wire Drawing.

The Plate No. 53-A which Munshi Sher Mahomed has obligingly furnished, gives a faithful conception of one phase in the wire drawing industry of India. Like a great many other crafts gold wire drawing, at least in its present form, would appear to have been first practised by the Muhammadans. It does not, however, follow that the Hindus did not possess a cruder and more laborious process of their own long anterior to the conquests of the Pathans and Moghals. In fact the references to gold textiles, in the most ancient writings of India, almost of necessity, involve such knowledge. Moreover, there are many oddities, both in wire drawing and gold weaving, that suggest their being survivals of former and cruder methods and styles than are at present practised.

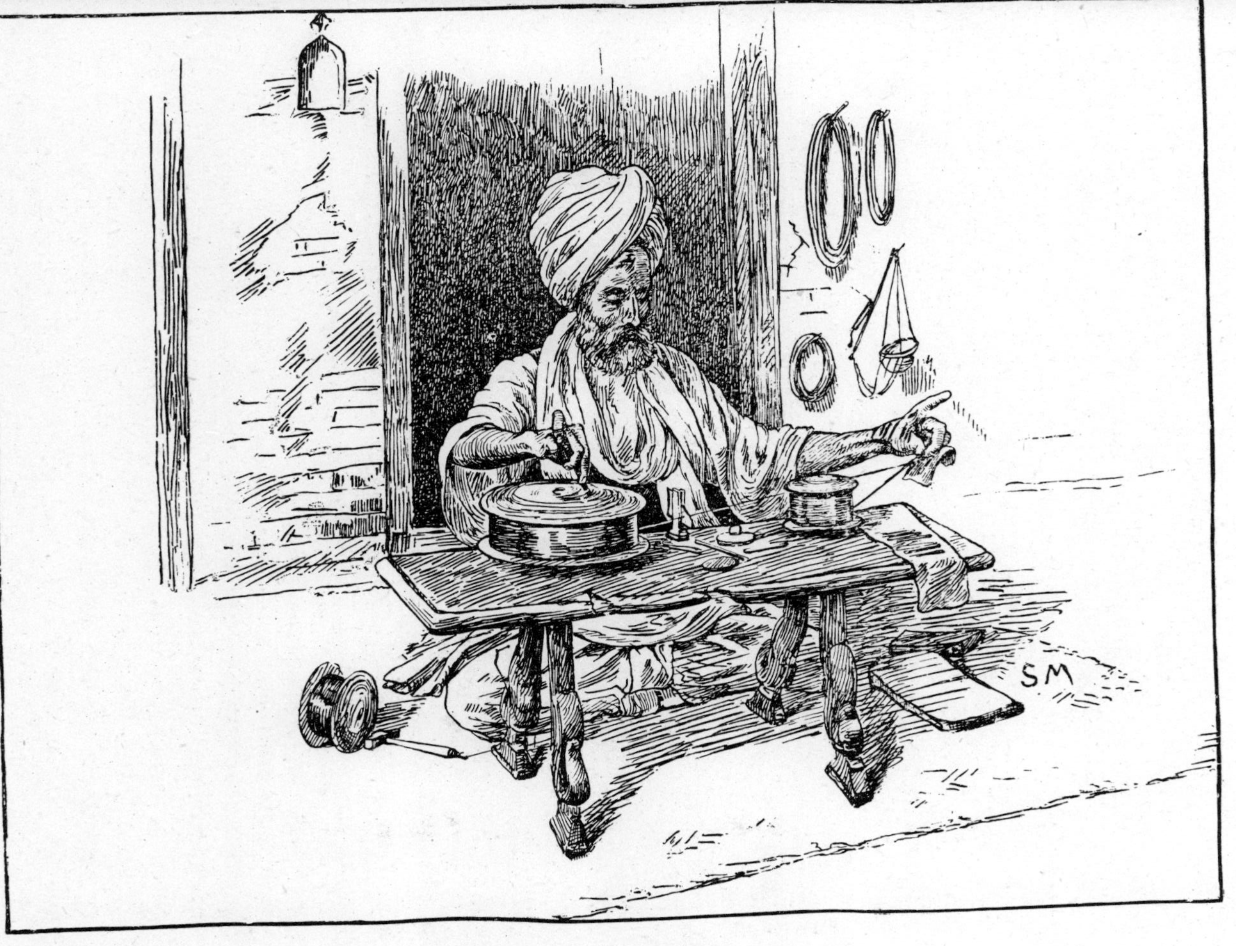

Plate No. 53–A Gold-wire Drawing

DIVISION 45. GOLD AND SILVER EMBROIDERY.

Perhaps one of the earliest complete accounts of wire drawing may be said to be that written by the distinguished novelist Colonel Meadows Taylor, but he has been followed by so many others that there may be little advantage in giving here an abstract account. It is impossible, however, to attempt more than to indicate the main features of the craft and exclusively those that have a bearing on art manifestations.

Manipulation. A bar of silver, say a foot long and half to three quarters of an inch in thickness, near the middle, and slightly tapering at both ends, is first gilded. This is accomplished by once or twice wrapping gold leaf around it and placing it in the furnace till the gold fuses and unites with the silver. Thus prepared the bar is drawn out and for this purpose it is inserted by one of its ends within a round opening in a massive sheet of strong iron, fixed in an upright position. The protruding portion is seized by a powerful clamp and forcibly pulled through the opening. It is returned by the other end, to a smaller and again to a still smaller opening, time after time, until the gold-coated silver bar is drawn out and gradually assumes the thickness of a hair and is many miles in length. But such is the ductility of the gold that, however fine it may be desired to produce the silver wire, it will be found uniformly and completely coated with gold. This is the finest and most important stage.

The wire is now cleverly flattened by being hammered as it passes across an anvil. The skill in this stage consists in so adjusting the motion of the wire (or rather series of wires) across the anvil that each stroke of the hammer will flatten them uniformly. The next stage consists in winding the flattened wire around a silk thread. This is done in order to make the wire both appear larger and thicker than it is, and to impart to it at the same time the flexible or fibrous quality, as well as the strength, necessary to allow of its being woven.

Silver Wire. Silver wire is produced by exactly the same process except that the bar is not gilded. Pure gold wire would be useless and by gold wire is, therefore, meant silver wire coated with pure gold in the manner described. **Imitation Gold.** But imitation gold and imitation silver wire are so extremely prevalent that precisely similar

Russian Gold. articles may be found, the one costing many times the value of the other, when the difference lies exclusively in the quality or nature of the wire used. The major portion of the imitation gold wire used in India is imported and comes mainly from Russia.

It would also appear that an inferior form of gold wire is produced by partially gilding the fine wire as it passes through one of the last of the iron plates. But an even more serious mode of depreciation lies in the fact that silver may be alloyed with a fair amount of copper before losing its ductility, and the gold or silver wire thus produced is much cheaper but unfortunately tarnishes readily. The gold effect is also temporarily heightened by the use of yellow silk and turmeric, worked into the silk during the winding stage. The pure wire is known as *sona-kalabatun* and the inferior as *rasi-kalabatun*. So again the gold wire may be so sparingly wound round the silk as to show interspaces. This is always a sure sign of inferior work. But instead of being drawn out to the fineness indicated, the gold may be left as a fairly thick wire. This is known as *badla*, and is largely used in embroidery and in the manufacture of plaited and woven trimmings.

Tarnishing Wire.

By way of concluding these jottings regarding gold and silver wire drawing, it may be said that it has been estimated Delhi alone produces over 300,000 miles of these wires per annum.

Lahore, Delhi, Agra, Benares, Murshidabad, Ahmedabad, Ahmednagar, and Burhanpur are the places most noted for the manufacture of gold, silver, and tinsel wires. But all large towns, especially those that were formerly the seats of Muhammadan governments, have as a rule gold and silver wire drawers. The gold, silver, and tinsel spangles, that are used so largely with gold and silver embroideries, are called *sitaras* or *taras*. The forms of drawing, flattening, spinning, plaiting, etc., of gold and silver wire are innumerable. To a large extent they originate the various recognisable qualities met with and give the distinctive styles to the weaving and embroidery, that are characteristic of most of the towns of India.

Having now conveyed some conception of the art of wire-drawing, it may be desirable to revert to the study of—

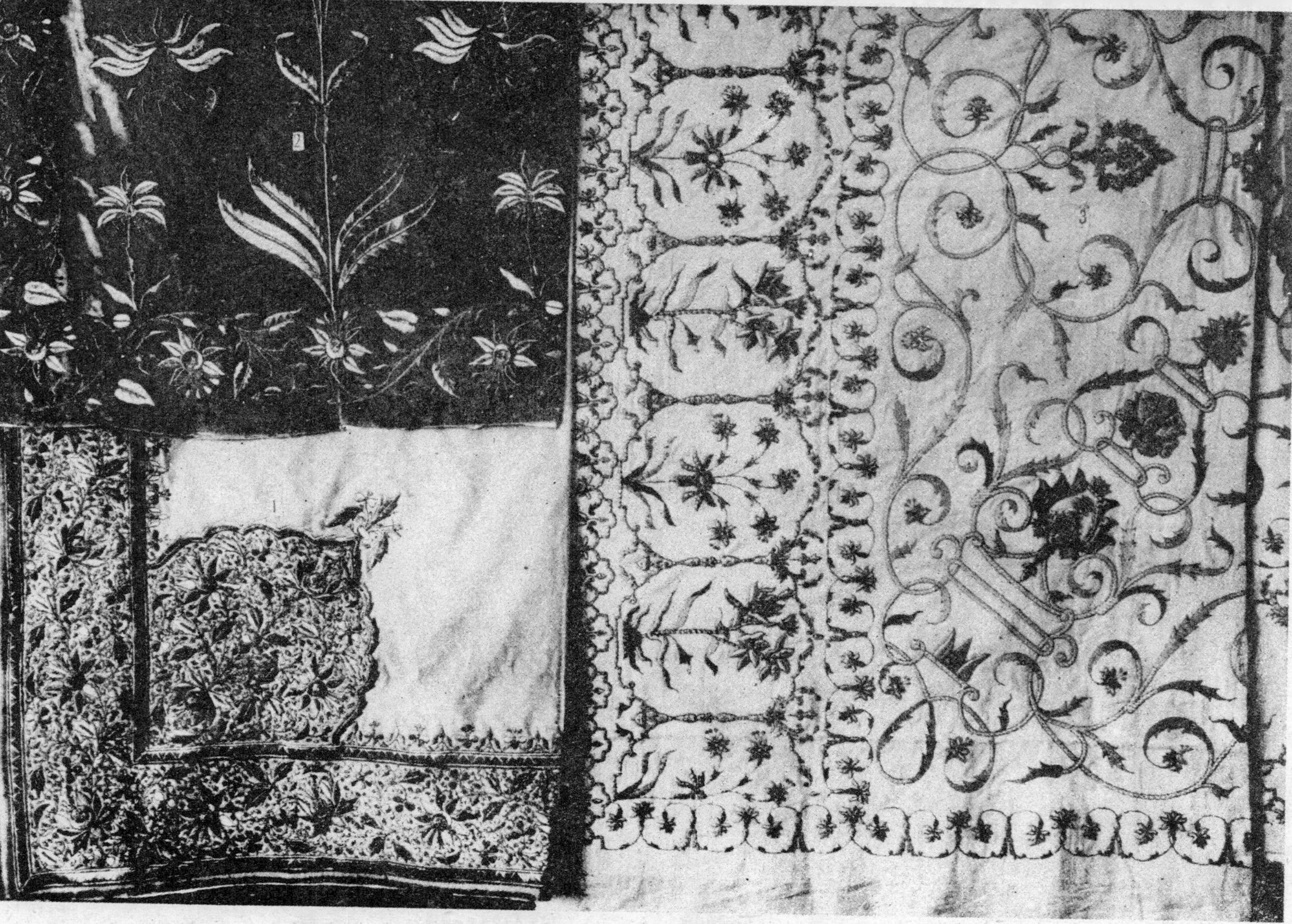

Plate No. 54 Gold and Silver Embroidery

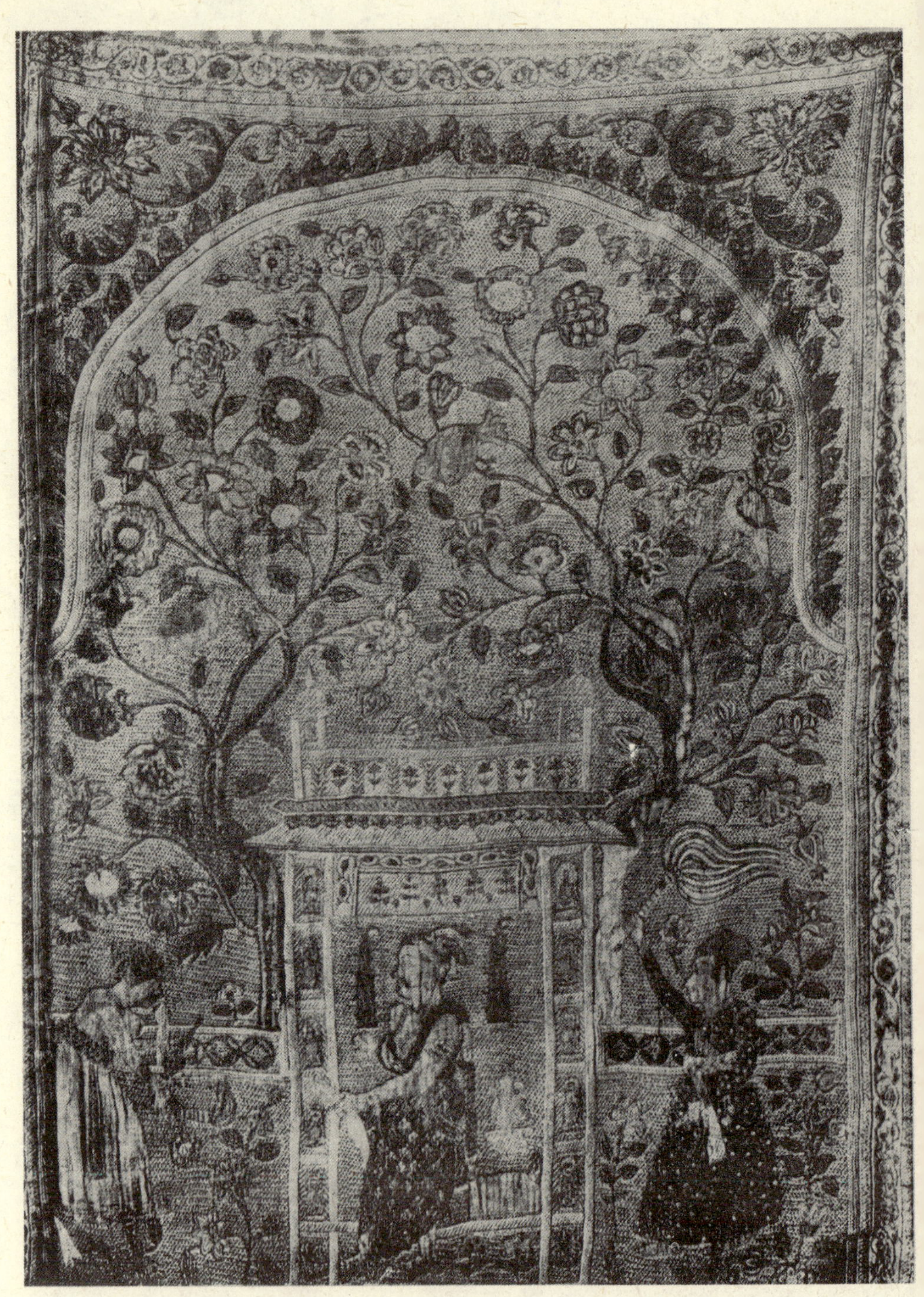

Plate No. 54-A Portion of Old Maharatta Kanat in Possession of His Highness the Nawab of Murshedabad

Gold and Silver Embroidery.

DIVISION 45. GOLD AND SILVER EMBROIDERY.

Wire produced by some such process as that briefly indicated above, is now specially spun, plaited, spirally twisted or otherwise prepared, in the form required for each particular style of work. The cloth having been printed or stencilled with the contemplated design, is stretched on the frame and certain portions are cushioned by having sewn over them coarse woollen thread, or by having pieces of card-board affixed as may be desired. This is the *bharat-kam* (literally "work filled in") or couched embroidery so extensively resorted to in the preparation of saddle cloths, *masnads*, coats, caps, etc.

Mr. Percy Brown gives in Plate No. 55 an illustration of the Agra *karchob* (frame) embroiderer engaged at his work with, on the wall behind, a sample of his embroidery. Plate No. 54 shows three samples, out of a long series, that have obtained awards at the Exhibition. These are as follows:—

Fig. 1.—An embroidered piano cover made by Manik Chand, of Delhi. It is on pale buff-coloured silk velvet and is worked in the purest quality of gold.

Fig. 2.—An embroidered curtain in dark buff-coloured silk velvet, worked in the purest and most massive gold. The design is a graceful one drawn mainly from the lily. It was made by Kishan Chand, of Delhi.

Fig. 3.—A large white silk curtain embroidered in gold and pale coloured silks, from designs taken from the Taj. It was made by Ganeshi Lal & Son, of Agra and Simla.

In passing it may be added that these superb pieces of work have all been purchased by His Highness the Nizam of Hyderabad. They have been specially singled out from the bewilderingly beautiful display, not because of their having received awards but in consequence of their being indicative of a modern tendency to depart from the massive style, characteristic of this work. Sir George Birdwood (*Industrial Arts of India*, page 368) says:—"The gorgeous gold embroidered velvets (*makhmal*) of Lucknow, and of Gulbargah, Aurangabad, and Hyderabad in the Deccan, used for canopies of costly state umbrellas of dignity, elephants' cloths, horses' cloths, and State housings and caparisons

DIVISION 45. GOLD AND SILVER EMBROIDERY.

generally, are largely represented in the Indian Museum. In form they have remained unchanged from the earliest periods of Indian history, but their sumptuous gold scroll ornamentation is in design distinctly of Italian Sixteenth Century origin. The Portuguese were in the habit of sending satin to India to be embroidered by natives in European designs."

Massive Embroidery.

The massively heavy embroidery of elephant trappings and *masnads* (the gold carpet placed in front of the throne) still exists, and a large assortment will be seen among the goods shown by not only the three exhibitors above named, but by Gopi Nath Lachmi Narain, of Lucknow; by Bhagwan Dass Gopi Nath, of Benares; by Girdhandas Paramand, of Hyderabad; by Baboo Gopal Krishna Das, of Benares; and many others. Mr. Baden Powell gives in his *Manufactures and Arts* a plate (page 96) that is fully illustrative of much of the old style of gold embroidery—a display of gold which crowds out by its massiveness all trace of design. But the diversities and local characteristics of *bharat-kam* are as numerous as are the seats of the craft. There is hardly an important locality of production that does not show something in its gold embroidery that is as distinct as are its ruined tombs, mosques, and palaces—something that marks the individuality of its rulers and of the dynasty of which, perhaps, it was the capital. The schools of embroidery might in fact be studied as archaic records. In a work, however, that professes to indicate the most interesting features of the collection presently on view, space obviously cannot be afforded for the details that might be set forth on this theme. The reader who may first examine the dignity of style shown in the Delhi and Agra work, next the ostentatious grandeur of Lucknow, and lastly the barbaric simplicity of Burhanpur gold embroidery, will get a fair impression of the value of the study. But it is in the details of wire drawing, in the form of wire used, in the nature of the stitch employed and the degree of combination with precious stones and silk that the most fruitful directions of classification are given.

Individual Characteristics.

It is much to be regretted that it is impossible to find space to critically discuss the extensive series of *zardozi* work at the Exhibition. These have come from every province, but more

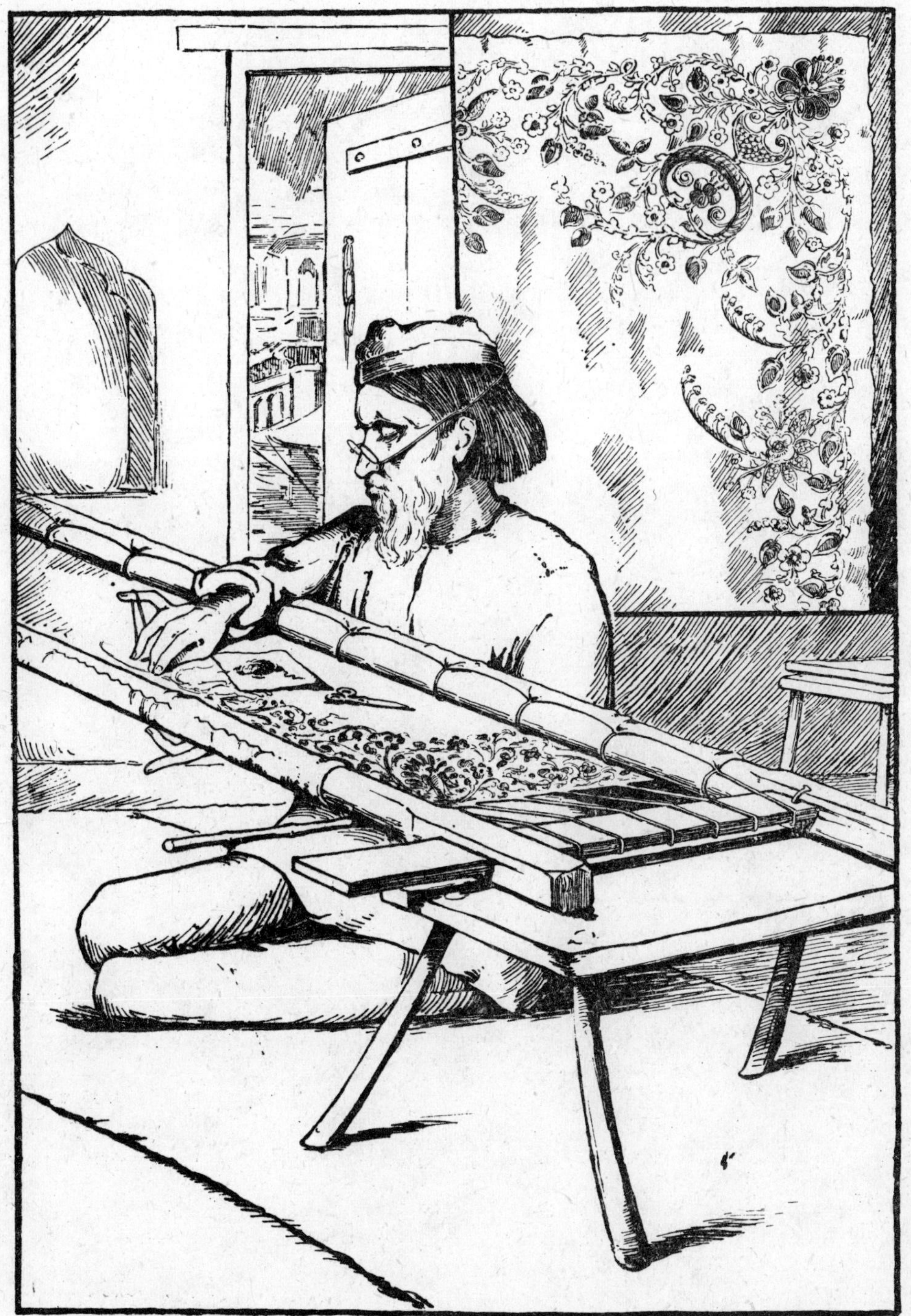

Plate No. 55 Embroiderer, Agra

DIVISION 45. GOLD AND SILVER EMBROIDERY.

especially from Agra, Aurangabad, Benares, Bombay, Delhi, Hyderabad, Lahore, Lucknow, Surat, etc.

Loan Collection.—As already mentioned, there are two sections in the gold and silver embroideries—the *zardozi* and the *kamdani*—that correspond very closely to the *kinkhabs* and the *gauzes* in the woven textiles In the Loan Collection Gallery there are many charming examples of both of these that are well worthy of special study.

His Highness the Nawab of Murshidabad exhibits a *kanat* or wall of a tent that is composed of many richly embroidered panels separated by uprights or supporting poles placed within the material. No. 999, one of the panels, is shown on Plate No. 54-A. This was obtained as a loot from the Maharattas by Nawab Ali Verdi Khan in 1744 A. D.

It is a fine old screen, each panel of which represents a garden scene within a *mirab* arch. It is worked in delicately coloured silks by satin stitch, the background being formed by gold sewn by a needle apparently around cords of yellow silk. The designs had apparently been first freely drawn with a brush on the canvas that forms the body material. Though somewhat stiff, the pose of the figures is excellent, the drawing careful and the ornamentation good and the style of needlework, especially that of the field of gold, one that is hardly, if ever, practised at the present day.

The *masnad* with pillows shown by Sir Desai Raja Bahadur of Savantvadi is not only very beautiful but it illustrates the peculiar style of gold embroidery in that State which in many respects will be seen to differ materially from the gold work of the rest of Bombay Presidency.

Division 46.—Braidings and Trimmings.

It may perhaps be regarded as superfluous to have provided a special division for the goods thrown into this position, since, on the one hand, they are simply specially woven ribbons brocaded with silk or with silk and gold; and, on the other, are narrow strips of cloth embroidered with silk or silk and gold. In other words they differ from the goods already discussed only in the sense of being narrow bands that are used as special trimmings.

DIVISION 46. BRAIDINGS AND TRIMMINGS.

Instead of weaving the whole fabric in gold or mixed gold and silk, the very general habit prevails of weaving the borders or end-pieces of *sáris* and other garments in silk or in silk and gold mixed, the body of the garment being in some commoner material such as cotton. These *kinkhab* borderings are often but most erroneously spoken of as "gold laces." True laces knitted or worked by the needle of cotton, linen, silk, or gold and silver wires are produced in many parts of the country and these and these alone, as already repeatedly urged, should of course be called Lace. The expression "Braidings" or "Borderings" would be much more accurate and equally expressive, the more so since special looms and other appliances are largely used all over India in the manufacture of the borders and ends made separately and subsequently sewn on to fabrics. The craft engaged in weaving these borderings and trimmings is more or less distinct from that of weaving generally.

The chief trimmings produced are :—*Gota*—a narrow bordering with the *badla* form of gold wire as the warp and silk as the weft. *Lais*—(from the English Lace)—a narrow fabric with silk as the weft and the warp containing both *badla* and *kalabatun* gold wire. These, by the looms used, might be described as knitted more than woven into an open texture.

But in addition to woven borderings, there are numerous embroidered forms that, as already said, are simply narrow strips of *zardozi* or *karchob*; these are often elaborated with spiral cords of gold and variously shaped gold spangles attached by the needle and thread brought from below for that purpose. Braiding may thus be regarded as accomplished either by sewing together various spirally prepared trimmings or wires or by weaving these with silk into borders or *kors* and *kinaras*. The patterns in *kors* are often very beautiful, but so numerous that a volume might be written before anything like a comprehensive conception could be conveyed of them.

The series of braidings and trimmings shown in the Exhibition will be found most attractive and interesting, especially those from Surat, Ahmedabad, Aurangabad, and Hyderabad. Many of the last mentioned are braids woven in the finest and purest gold thread, the pattern being embossed by means of a stamp, or are repoussed by a punch. This curious effect seems fairly lasting for the trimmings may be worn for years before the embossing is completely destroyed.

DIVISION 46. BRAIDINGS AND TRIMMINGS.

If space could be afforded, much of great interest might be written on the numerous forms of both woven and embroidered trimmings that have no corresponding piece-goods. For example, in the Wazir country trimmings for the bottom of the sleeves and trousers are specially made and brought for sale into Bannu. These are regularly spoken of as embroideries, but as a matter of fact they are woven, though in a style that resembles very much more the knitting of a stocking than the weaving of a textile. Thick cords of purple silk warps appear to be plaited in pairs, the series of such pairs being bound together by the passage of the woof. To elaborate a pattern, the warp threads are cut off as desired, and differently coloured ones tied on in their places and used to the extent desired. To effect results that could only be attained by the woof needle, embroidery is resorted to.

It is thus possible that in the Wazir country is to be seen one of the most primitive of all looms and one that might be described as producing a fabric that may, not inaptly, be described as a cross between woven and knitted. It is probable that one of the most fascinating industrial studies that could be engaged in would be the investigation of the methods and appliances used by the *gota*, *kor*, and *kinara* weavers and embroiderers of India.

The collections of most interest on view are those sent from Gwalior—mostly *kinkhab kors* in blue, red, and green with gold patterns worked in the silk.

Of the braids of Surat both woven and embroidered in gold and silver with green and white silk that are sent by Pranjivandas Dalabram, the most beautiful is No. 3442—a (*kor*) braid woven of gold and silk as a gauze. Similar work is also exhibited by Chunan Lal Har Kishan Das & Co., of Surat.

From Aurangabad *kors* or *kinkhab* borders have come in abundance, and many of them superlatively beautiful. No. 951 is a *ganga-jamni* (gold and silver) braid spoken of as *anar-dani* because of the minute grain-like meshes formed within the gold.

DIVISION 46. BRAIDINGS AND TRIMMINGS.

No. 963 is designated a *feet* and is a gauze-like braid with red silk weft and gold warp. No. 982 is a *pallu sunheri* woven of gold warp and orange silk weft, then repoussed by hand punching. So also No. 981 is a *pallu* braid in *ganga-jamni* form very neatly repoussed.

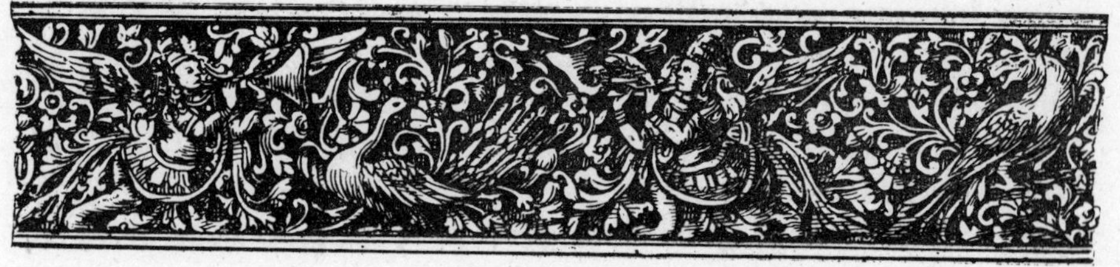

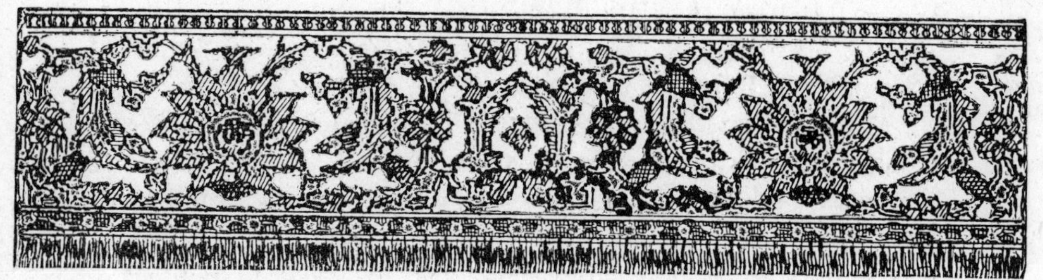

CLASS IX.—CARPETS, RUGS, MATS, BASKETS, Etc.

WHILE this class is by no means so important as almost any of those that have gone before, it is none the less interesting. All writers seem to agree in thinking that pile carpet-weaving, like a great many more of the arts of India, came from Persia. With that opinion there would seem no great occasion to demur, though it is quite probable that India possessed a carpet-weaving industry of its own (possibly not in pile carpets) long anterior to the advent of any Persian influence. There are methods and designs met with here and there, in the Indian carpet trade, that are very possibly indigenous and which have greatly tended to bring about the peculiarities that allow of Indian carpets being at once recognised from those of other countries. DIVISION 47. CARPETS.

Mr. John Kimberly Mumford, in his most admirable work "*Oriental Rugs*," has fallen into the popular notion of assuming that from Akbar's time there had been originated and developed the large trade in Indian carpets, of which Mr. Vincent Robertson affirms, "The spread of this manufacture extended over the whole of India and as late as the middle of this century was practised, very much in its integrity, from Kashmir to as far south as Tanjore" To this Mr. Mumford adds his quota of assumptions:—"It is almost inexplicable," he says, "that a system so strongly grounded, so literally and figuratively inwoven with the family and civil life of the people, could, in so brief a time, have been destroyed; but such seems to have been the case. The apparent first cause was the desire of the Indian Government to furnish

DIVISION 47. CARPETS.

occupation for its prisoners in jails throughout the Empire, and incidentally to neutralize the expense of maintaining the corrective system. Brought thus into competition with prison labour, the caste weaver was undersold, and had no resource save to cheapen his product and increase its volume."

Although the present is hardly the proper place nor time to indulge in a controversy of opinions and theories, the writer feels, that in view of the fairly large interests involved, as manifested by the display of carpets on the walls of this Exhibition, it is incumbent to remove misapprehensions that may be calculated to injure the Indian craft of carpet-weaving. It is probable that were statistics called for, it would be found there are more looms in the factories of the Amritsar carpet weavers than in all the Government Jails of India put together. This is a statement quite capable of verification, and it is an important one in view of the ruin these Jails are commonly assumed to have brought on private enterprise. It is always very easy and, moreover, an acceptable argument in Europe and America, to extol the value of the caste and communal systems, in fostering and developing art, and to attribute defects in goods produced to the disappearance of these saving influences. Now in the case of carpets, the art is admittedly one that was introduced by the Muhammadans and which attained its greatest perfection under the guidance of the Muhammadan rulers. Caste could, therefore, have little to say to it in the past, any more than it has at present. Moreover, there is absolutely no proof of carpet-weaving at any period having been either so large or so widespread as at the present day. That the Emperors of Delhi and Agra encouraged the art and kept their State weavers as they doubtless had their State artificers in each and every craft, is probably correct. That the weavers could and did produce, under these circumstances, marvellously beautiful carpets goes without saying. Moreover, it is fairly certain that at many important centres of administration all over the Empire there were State factories, though the *Ain-i-akbari* has little to say about them. That carpet-weaving had become an established industry of the people, owned and supported by them, such as Mr. Vincent Robinson would appear to believe, is quite another matter.

There is little or nothing to show that the princes and nobles of India used woollen pile carpets in the past more extensively than they do at the present. With invaders and conquerors who had personally known and experienced in cool climates the advantages of such carpets, the desire for them would naturally be greater than with the people of a tropical country who seek rather coolness than warmth. The Indian sumptuary desires are more naturally met by gold *masnads* than by expensive carpets, so that there is little to support the belief that after the death of Akbar's grandson, the carpet-weaving of India was anything like as large or important as it is at the present day. This much in fact seems fairly certain, namely, that the present traffic is almost exclusively the outcome of the interest aroused by the London Exhibition of 1851. The few carpets, that were sent from India to that great show, caused the dealers of Europe to direct attention to this country as an unexploited area of supply. It would scarcely have been defensible even had the evil consequences of to-day been anticipated, for the Government to have put æsthetic limitations on India's participation in this or any other branch of foreign trade. But in all fairness to the persons who have interested themselves in the modern traffic, it must be upheld, in the clearest possible manner, that the mistakes that have been made are entirely a consequence of the European and American dictation of supply. Oriental carpets are of necessity expensive and the traffic in them must be restricted. The idea seems to have at once occurred that if a cheaper article could be produced by India than comes from Turkey and Persia, a large and profitable trade might be organised. Patterns were accordingly sent to India, the quality prescribed, and the price fixed at an almost impossible figure. The result could hardly have been otherwise than a steady deterioration in quality and artistic merit.

The writer has personally visited all the better known carpet factories of India, and from one corner of the country to the other has heard the same story :—" This is the class of carpet we are compelled to manufacture. We would much rather turn out a better article but we are in the hands of this person and that who takes all our carpets." In practically every such instance the actual letters with their accompanying designs have been brought out in support of the statement that the fault lies with the dealers, not the manufacturers. It is not a case of supply and demand but rather one in which the terms of that axiom have to be reversed.

Prior to the advent of the home trader with his patterns and his prices, there did not exist an Indian carpet supply. Nor were there in India persons with capital and enterprise prepared to originate the conditions of an advantageous supply market. The blame must be exclusively laid to the door of the purchaser, but while that is so a wholesome reform might now, as it seems, be inculcated by a prohibition being laid on all State production, whether in Jails or Schools of Art, of carpets below a certain quality or in patterns other than those prescribed for each institution. By some such means it seems possible that an improved standard might be attained. But that India does not desire the present low grade traffic, can be abundantly demonstrated. Few, if any, cheap carpets are to be seen in the houses of the Europeans resident in India. Hardly any Indian carpets, good or bad, are to be seen in the palaces of the Natives. But where Indian carpets are used, they are almost invariably of a good quality and in rich oriental design. The cheap carpets are exclusively made for export. Moreover, the demand in India for expensive carpets and rugs from Turkey, Persia, Herat, Panjdeh, Seistan, and Baluchistan, shows that there is in India itself a considerable market, and one of great future possibilities, for higher grade carpets than are made in this country at the present day.

Division 47.—Pile Carpets.

With these very brief introductory remarks, the course adopted with other classes of goods may be followed in this, namely to discuss the collections on view, province by province.

Panjab.—There may be said to be four or five fairly important centres of carpet-weaving in this province including Kashmir. These in their order of importance may be said to be Amritsar,

Kashmir, Lahore, Multan, Hushiarpur Batala, and Bahawalpur, also Kohat and Bannu. But to that enumeration has to be added Peshawar— the great emporium of the transfrontier traffic in carpets from Afghanistan, Turkistan, and even Persia.

The transfrontier supply is exceedingly important and appears to have been so for many years if not for centuries. In fact it might almost be affirmed that the spasmodic supplies of the so-called "Lahore carpets" mentioned in some of the returns of the East India Company, had reference to transfrontier and not to Indian woven carpets.

LAHORE.—In the early records of the Panjab, such as Honigberger's *Thirty-five Years in the East*—a work that deals specially with Lahore prior to its date of publication (1852), there is no mention of an indigenous carpet-weaving industry. Mr. Baden Powell (*Manufactures and Arts of the Panjab*—1872) makes mention of a few carpets from the Lahore and other jails of the province, but says practically nothing regarding an Indigenous industry. Mr. Lockwood Kipling (in reply apparently to Mr. Vincent Robinson's paper in the *Society of Arts*—March 1886) wrote:—"It has been said that the Panjab Jails have injured the indigenous industry of carpet-weaving. It would be more like the truth to assert that they have created such as exists. It was not until the Exhibition of 1862, that the Panjab was known beyond its border for the production of carpets and then only by the productions of the Lahore Jail executed for a London firm."

The carpets in the Lahore Museum that are most treasured are those picked up at Peshawar. These have been the models most generally followed by the modern weavers and they are for the most part Herat carpets with the minute and intricate design of the *henna*-flower. In Indian trade carpets of this class are often spoken of as *lahori*, but the exact same pattern in a Kaleidoscopic arrangement and re-arrangement of colours was found by the writer to be the chief design turned out by the carpet-weavers of Ellore in the Madras Presidency. The comparative importance of Lahore as a centre of carpet-weaving may, however, be judged of by the fact that no exhibits except the Loan Collection from the Lahore Museum will be seen in the Exhibition.

DIVISION 47. CARPETS.

AMRITSAR.—This is perhaps the most important carpet-weaving centre in India. There are numerous factories ranging from that of Messrs. Davee Sahai Chamba Mall with over 300 looms down to several with only 8 or 10 looms. This large and prosperous industry appears to be quite modern. No carpets were apparently sent from Amritsar to the Lahore Exhibition of 1868. In the *Gazetteer* it is stated that the industry is mainly in the hands of wealthy Hindus, who, under European supervision, employ Muhammadan weavers all working on the contract system and entertaining their own staff of workers. The Native States and Central Asia are ransacked for old and choice patterns, while the utmost care is taken in the selection of the warp, the wool, and the vegetable dyes. *Pashmina* wool is used for the finest descriptions of carpets and the work is all done by hand. In the *Indian Textile Journal* (July 1900), will be found a long and detailed account of this industry, the conclusion being arrived at that the industry may be considered a well paying one and worthy of the favourable consideration of capitalists. Mumford estimates that there are 5,000 men and boys in the carpet industry of this town. "The out-put of the Amritsar looms," he writes, "therefore, is perhaps the best by which to judge the present day carpet production of India. That part of it which is handled by American firms is probably the best which these factories have to show, better no doubt by reason of the fact that the agents dealing directly with India can and do dictate concerning designs, colours, and all the points of construction." This is a most unfortunate admission for a writer of Mr. Mumford's stamp, to whom purity of design and colour is the first and only criterion on which a rug or carpet can be or rather should be judged. But it is a statement true, not of Amritsar only, but of all the carpet centres of India, and accounts far more for the present degraded state of the trade than may be laid to the charge of "Thugi Jail Labour." At the present Exhibition the famous firm of Messrs. Davee Sahai Chamba Mall have a large display of carpets; some of these are perhaps the finest made and most expensive shown in the Exhibition, having been woven of the purest *pashm* wool. But it is an open secret that many of this wonderful

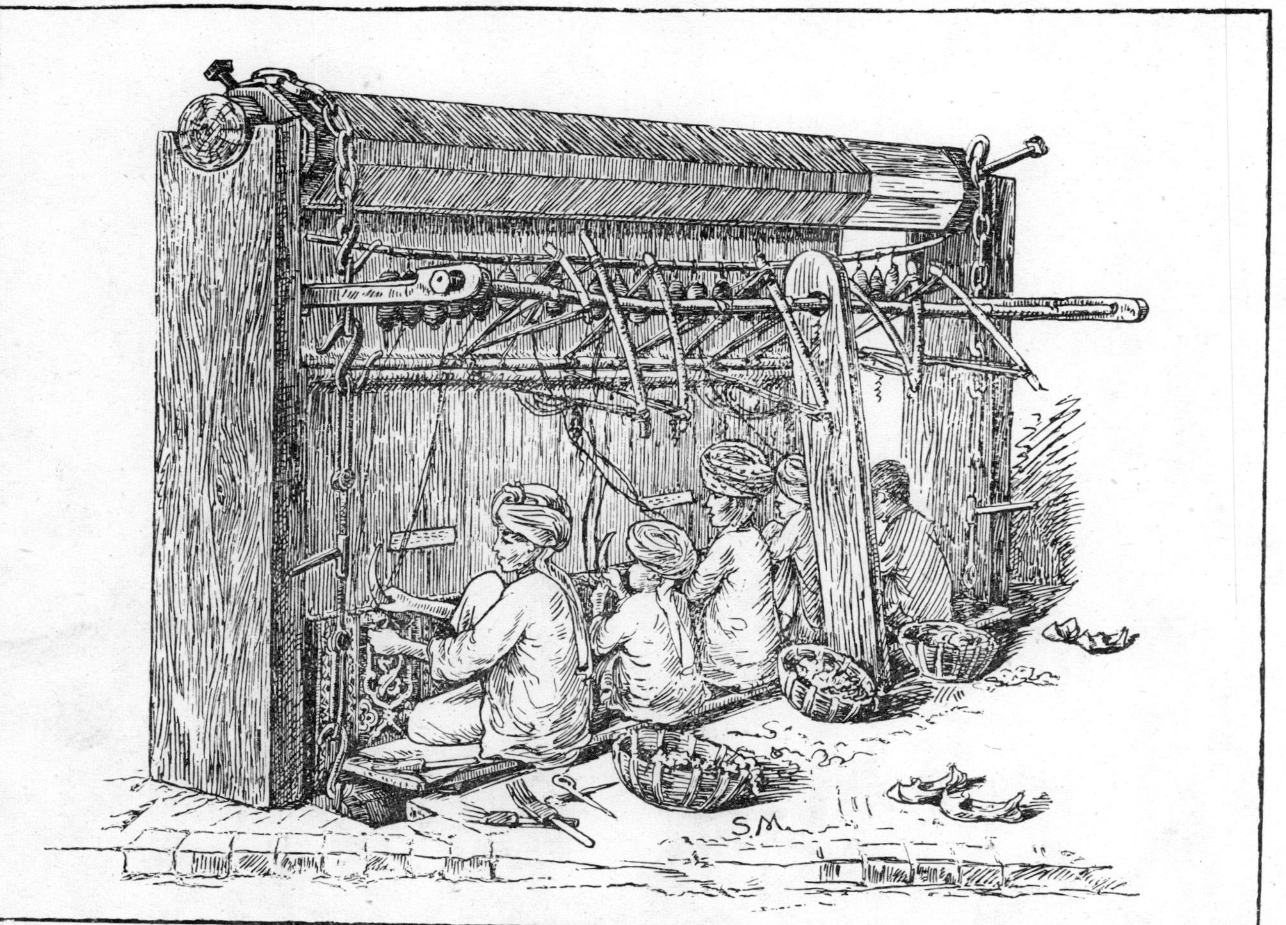

Plate No. 55-A Carpet Weaving

series have been condemned because of their having been woven in dull faded colours, in imitation most probably of old carpets. At almost every carpet centre the writer was told that American buyers demanded faded colours, hence doubtless have come into existence most of the very un-Indian carpets to be seen all over India, such as those in greys and faded greens, in place of the bright almost liquid colours of the old masters.

DIVISION 47 CARPETS.

KASHMIR.—Three exhibitors have sent numerous carpets to the Exhibition. These are the Kashmir Manufacturing Company, Baines Brothers, and Mitchell & Co. The first mentioned has secured a gold medal and the second a silver medal for their carpets. The firm of Mitchell & Co. sent only a few rugs, but these were very charming, perhaps the best woven and most artistically coloured of any Indian rugs in the Exhibition. Both the Kashmir Manufacturing Company and Baines Brothers sent copies of the famous Ardebil Mosque carpet, the original of which is in the Victoria and Albert Museum of South Kensington. This, like perhaps one half of the carpets shown at the Exhibition, has been copied from the famous book on Oriental Carpets, published by the Imperial and Royal Austrian Commercial Museum, a work that has exercised a far greater influence on the carpet trade than could have been foreseen by its authors. From one end of India to the other, the plates of that work, either in original or as specially copied by Indian draftsmen, are to be seen in the factories of even the humblest workers. While it has thus tended greatly to raise the tone of carpet-weaving in India, it has also had the injurious influence of destroying what little distinctions formerly existed between the chief centres of production.

Old Carpets from Kashmir.

Loan Collection.—Perhaps the most interesting series of carpets in the Exhibition are those which the writer discovered in Bijapur and which he was fortunate enough to procure on loan through the generous co-operation of Mr. W. W. Drew, Collector of the District. Plate No. 57 shows two of these wonderful carpets, from which it will be seen that they may be accepted as the prototypes of many of the carpets now commonly spoken of as Indian. Along with these carpets has been received the following most interesting note from which it will be learned that they

DIVISION 47. CARPETS. are believed to have been made in Kashmir about 250 years ago. It will thus be seen that long prior to the creation of the present carpet manufacturing industry, Kashmir would appear to have turned out carpets of great beauty:—"Ten old carpets are sent for the Exhibition, nine of which are old woollen pile carpets lent by the Custodians of the Asar Mahal, and the remaining one—a cotton *jainamaz* carpet—lent by the custodians of the Jamai Mosque."

"The woollen carpets have been preserved in the Asar Mahal, an old palace which has acquired sanctity in the eyes of the Muhammadans on account of its containing the relics (Arabia Asar-relics) of the Prophet in the shape of two hairs of his beard. These relics were brought to Bijapur in the time of Ibrahim Adilshah II (1580—1626) and during his reign and those of his successors appear to have been widely known throughout the Mussalman world, as is evidenced by the rich offerings made by the foreign Muhammadan potentates to the Asar. It is, however, not known whether these carpets were presents. They were probably ordered out by King Mahamad Adilshah. An old

Carpets, 250 years old. manuscript *Haft-Kursi-e Padshahan,* gives the date of their arrival from Kashmir in the year A.H. 1067 equivalent to 1657 of the Christian Era, which is the last year of Mahamad Adilshah's reign. This date is probably authentic as after Mahamad, the decline of the Bijapur kingdom had commenced and it is not likely that costly foreign materials could have been ordered out after his reign. It is, therefore, almost certain that the carpets are about 250 years old and probably made at Kashmir. The carpets are supposed to be used only once during the year, when they are spread in the upper halls of the Asar Mahal on the birthday of the Prophet, the 12th of Rabi I. They have, however, been much damaged in bygone days by the apathy and to a certain extent helplessness of the custodians. A few of them were sent out about twelve or fifteen years ago to Yeroda Jail to be repaired and lined with canvas with a view to better preservation."

Cotton Dari. "Not much is known about the cotton *jainamaz,* a carpet from the Jamai Mosque. A local tradition is that it is one of the few

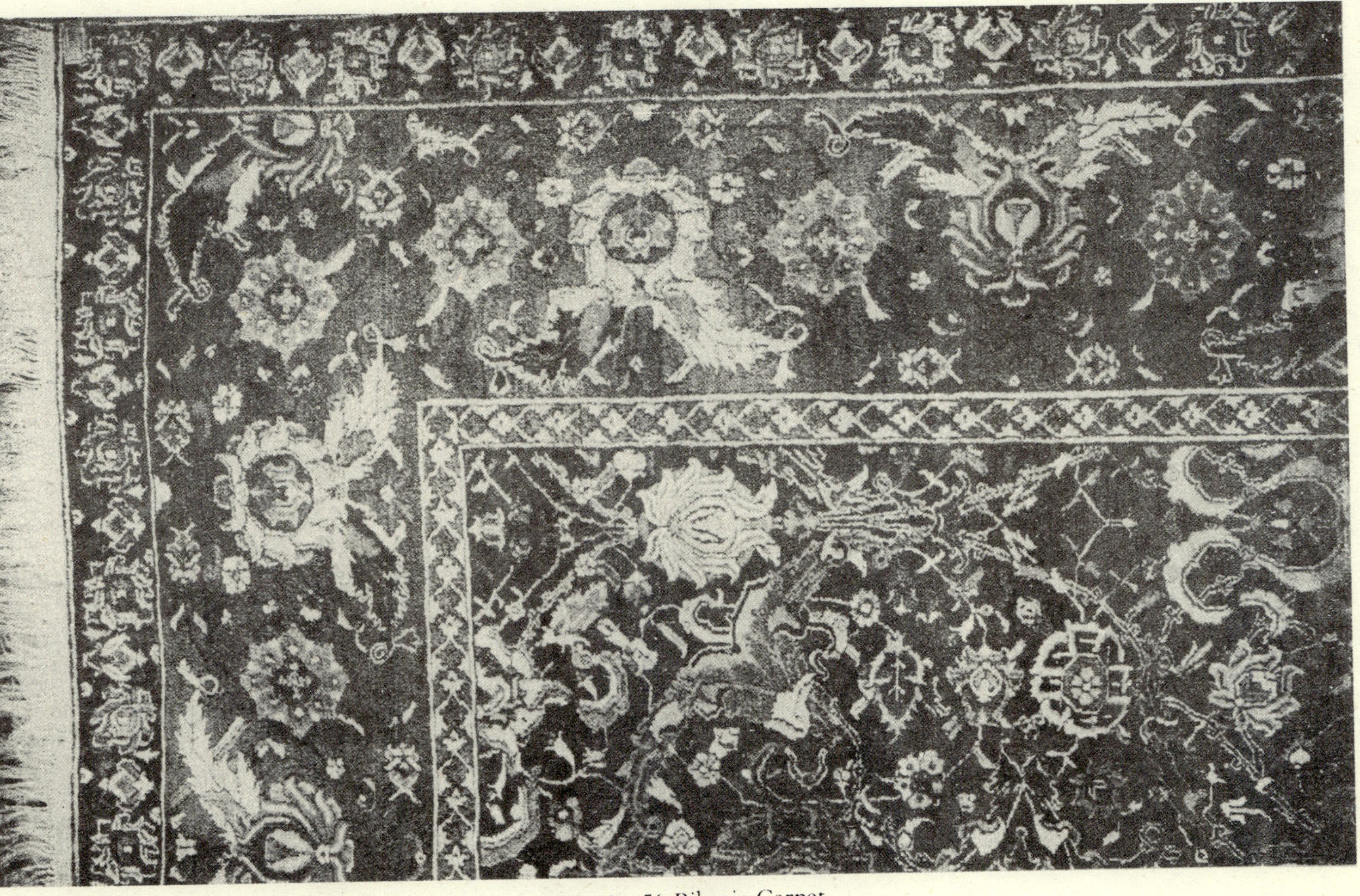

Plate No. 56 Bikanir Carpet

carpets left in the mosque by the Emperor Auranzeb after the conquest of Bijapur in 1626, he preferring the bare floor to carpets for prayers. The carpet would thus appear to be about 200 years old and is probably of local origin as carpet-weaving was and is still one of the industries of Bijapur and the pattern goes to confirm this opinion."

MULTAN.—This is one of the localities of India that enjoys the reputation of having had an indigenous carpet industry of its own long anterior to the introduction of carpet-weaving from Persia. In the *Gazetteer*, however, it is suggested that "it seems likely that rugs and carpets brought over from Turkistan, in the course of its large and long established Pawindah trade, may have served as the original inspiration. The patterns have a decidedly Tartar air. They are excessively bold and yet not clear in detail. The usual size of the stitch, together with a peculiar brightness in the white, and their rather violet, red, and yellow, give them a somewhat aggressive and quite distinctive quality of colour." They are usually disproportionately long for their width, a peculiarity noticeable in all carpets that come from countries like Persia and Turkistan, where the apartments are long and narrow.

BAHAWALPUR—Produces carpets that in no material way differ from those just described for Multan. The pile is long, loose, and boldly coloured. Recently His Highness the Nawab has directed attention to the utilization of the immense supplies that are running to waste in his country of the wild silk-cotton from *Calotropis gigantea*. In the Loan Collection Gallery two rugs from this new material may be seen and, it is believed, will at first sight be mistaken for silk.

HOSHIARPUR and BATALA—May be taken as modern offshoots from the carpet-weaving of Amritsar. There is nothing of a descriptive character regarding their carpets and rugs.

PESHAWAR has been alluded to above as the emporium of the Afghan, Turkoman, and Persian carpets that find their way into India. A very large and choice collection of these has been received from Haji Mian Safdar Ali and is now on view mainly in the great transept of the Exhibition.

DIVISION 47. CARPETS.

Many of these belong to what is known in India as Panjdeh rugs, but which should rather be described as Turkoman or Tekke (commonly called Bokhara) rugs. They are mostly rich bright maroon in colour and have great medallions (called in India elephant foot-prints) over the surface. In Peshawar and also at Quetta the traders speak of these medallions as foot-prints of the camel as seen on the sands, the white portions being the high lights.

In addition to Bokhara rugs, large numbers of Herat carpets find their way into India and are readily purchased even at the high prices demanded which may be said to rule about twice the price of rugs of the same size and quality made in India. They pay a high export duty before being allowed to leave Afghanistan, but in spite of all disadvantages, those shown have sold more readily than any of the numerous high class Indian carpets on view at the Exhibition. In fact the results of this Exhibition, so far as they have gone, may be said to be a pronounced indication in favour of the transfrontier rugs of Peshawar and Quetta.

KOHAT and BANNU.—In these towns and one or two other places along the North-West Frontier a peculiar form of rug is made that is called a *nakhai*. This is constructed by pulling out the weft threads in loops for an inch or so protruding between each pair of the warp strands. These loops are not cut, but when the rug is finished they become twisted. The designs are usually in purple, crimson with black-yellow, and occasionally green worked in crude geometric patterns. They are not exactly art textiles, but cannot be said to be devoid of artistic feeling and they represent a characteristic style of work that it will be unwise to omit entirely. There will be seen to be a large assortment on view.

RAJPUTANA and CENTRAL INDIA.—There are many centres where carpet-weaving has flourished for many years. Those that are best represented at the Exhibition and which, therefore, deserve special consideration are Jaipur, Bikanir, and Ajmir.

JAIPUR.—Some half a dozen carpets and rugs have been shown on the walls of the Exhibition as representative of the produce of the jail looms of this State. These are beautifully

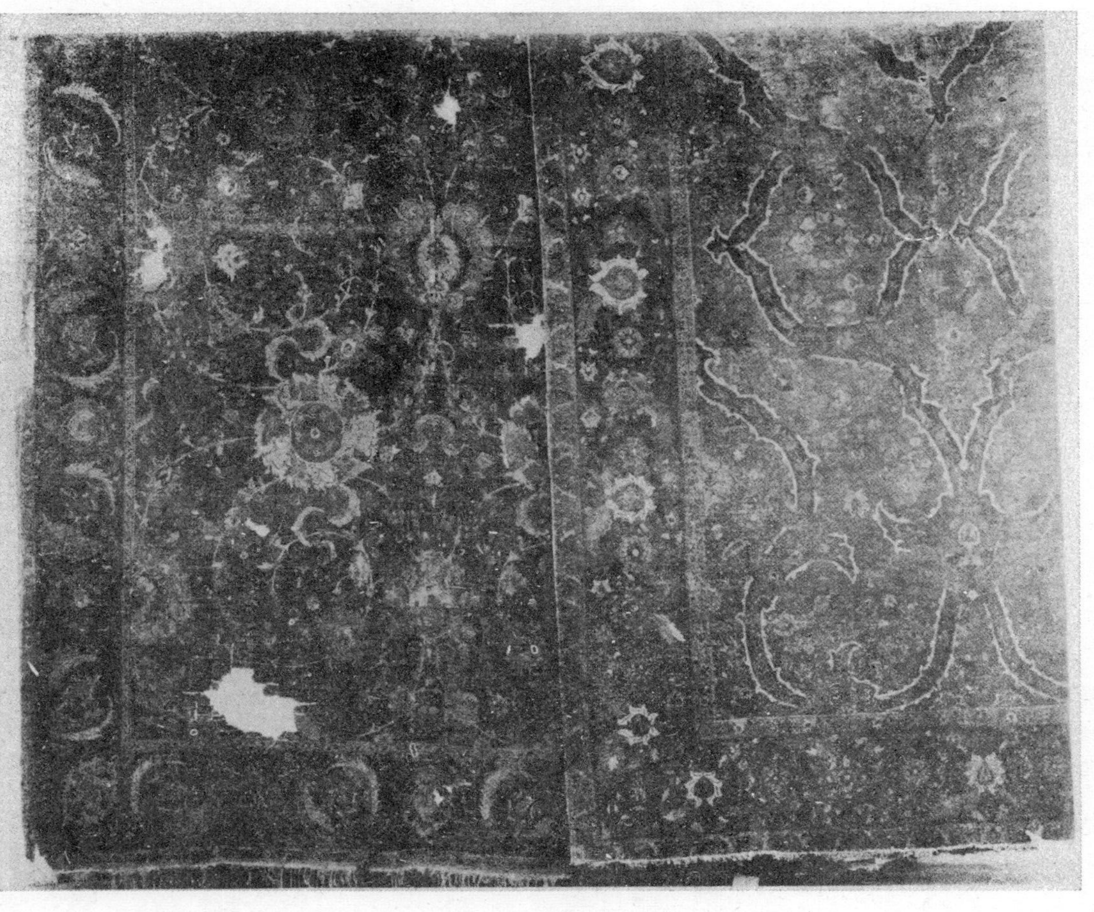

Plate No. 57 Old Pile Carpets of Bijapur

finished, of excellent wool and splendid colours. One of the most historic carpets in India is in the possession of His Highness the Maharaja of this State, and it has been utilized time and again in the carpets that are produced. Mr. Mumford says of Jaipur that "the carpets woven copy the designs found chiefly in the rugs of eastern and middle Persia. They nearly always present the cypress tree and also many animal forms, laid upon a ground of dark red, blue, or ivory white. The borders have a swaying vine pattern, with the customary floral adjuncts."

BIKANIR—Has through the enlightened action of His Highness the Maharaja attained a higher position of merit than has been reached by any of the modern centres of production The Vienna patterns have been closely followed, the dyes carefully supervised and the wool used of a very superior quality. In fact Bikanir produces the best wool in India, and it is thus pre-eminently suited to become a great carpet-weaving centre. Plate No. 56 shows one of the best Bikanir designs.

AJMIR—Turns out many excellent carpets and one of the most beautiful rugs in the Exhibition being from there, but copied both by Jaipur and Bikanir. This is a dark brown or deep maroon with the imperial lilv portrayed most vividly in rich grey and pale yellow.

Sind and Baluchistan.—The carpets manufactured in Sind closely resemble those of Multan. Sir George Birdwood describes them as "the cheapest, coarsest, and least durable of all that are made in India. Formerly they were fine in design and colouring, but of late years they have greatly deteriorated." Speaking of Baluchistan, Sir George Birdwood continues:—"The carpets and rugs are made of goats' hair which give them their singularly beautiful lustre, finer even than that of the Indian silk carpets and more subdued in tone, although the dyes used in Baluchistan are richer. The patterns are usually the fantastic geometrical character found in Turkoman rugs from which the patterns of the early 'Brussels carpets' were derived. They are laid on either a deep indigo or deep madder red ground and traced out in orange brown and ivory white, intermixed with red when the ground is blue and with white when the ground is red.

DIVISION 47. CARPETS.

The ends terminate in a web-like prolongation of the warp and woof beyond the pile, and when striped in colours or worked in a small diaper, form a most picturesque fringe."

This is an excellent description of 99 per cent. of all the rugs and carpets that arrive by camel caravans at Quetta and a large proportion of those that reach India through Peshawar as well. Mr. Mumford is possibly correct, however, in transferring them from the position of being Indian carpets and placing them under Turkoman. They are rarely made even in Baluchistan, but come from Afghanistan and mainly from Seistan. But it is curious to note that Mr. Mumford speaks of their decline in quite as severe terms as he deprecates the decline of Indian. "The modern Baluchistans have fallen, he says, about as far from the high standard established by the old ones as any rugs which find their way out of the East to-day." Plate No. 58-A shows one of the finest of the series of Seistan rugs to be seen at the Exhibition. The print fails utterly to convey even a trace of the charm of this wonderful rug which has been purchased by Mr. Phipps and thus will most probably be carried to the United States of America.

Perhaps the best examples of the transfrontier rugs and carpets that find their way into Quetta are the few sent by Major Ramsay and Major Showers that will be found in the Loan Collection Gallery.

United Provinces.—Three or four centres are well known for their carpets and have been noted for many years. These are Agra, Mirzapore, Jhansi, Jabalpur, and Allahabad.

AGRA.—The Agra Central Jail has been awarded a gold medal for its collection of carpets. It seems unnecessary to specially instance from the examples on view, but the verdict of a body of experts, such as those who formed the Judging Committee, seems a remarkable refutation of the sweeping condemnation that has been made of all Indian jail-made carpets. It was somewhat unfortunate that Messrs. Otto Weylandt & Co. should have sent their best carpets to the Loan Collection. They were in consequence excluded (just as the fine old Bijapur carpets were) from competition with the large assortment of other Indian carpets shown in the Sale Gallery.

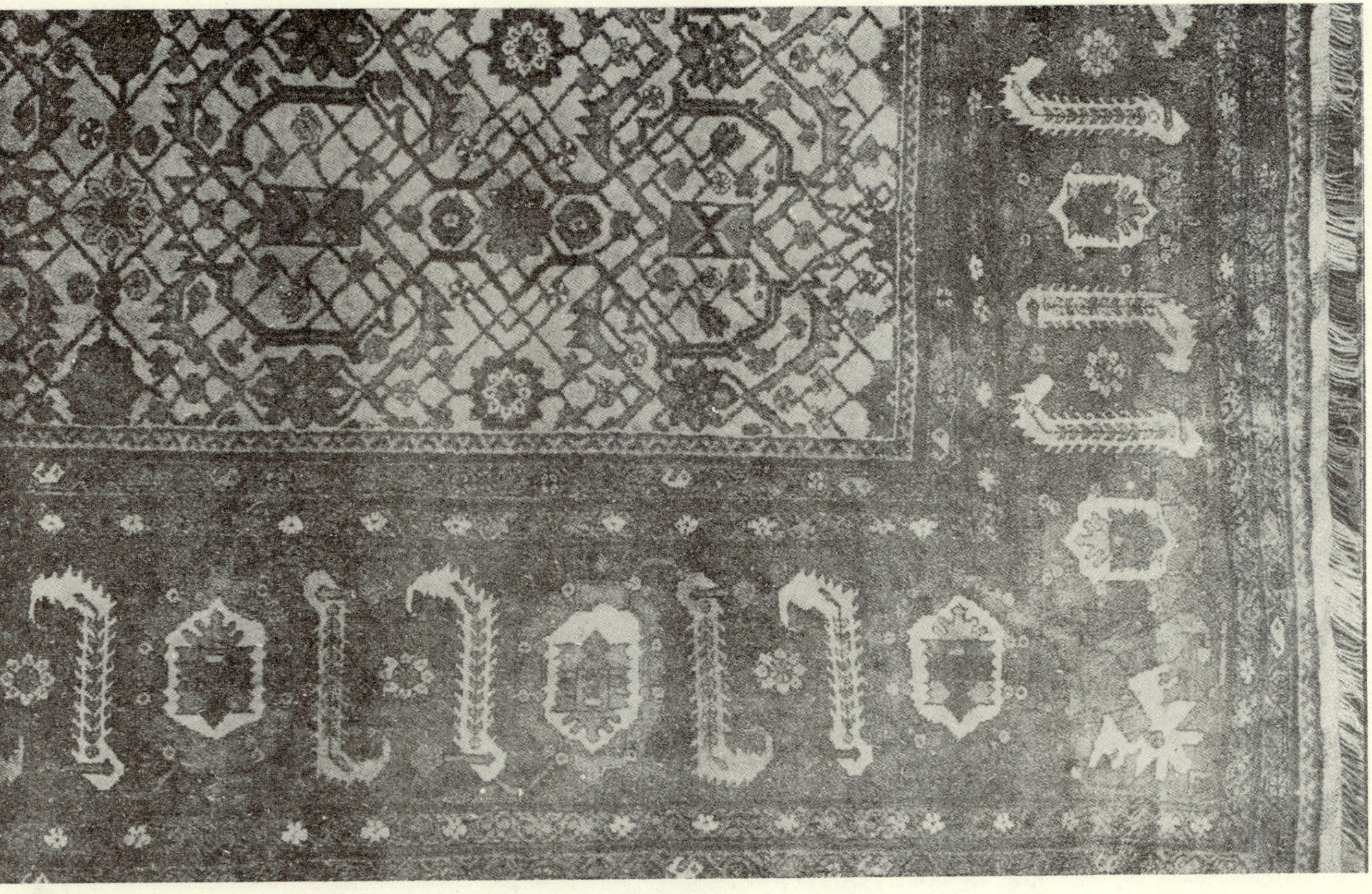

Plate No. 58 Warangal Carpet in Silk

There is no mention of the manufacture of carpets in Agra during the time the *Ain-i-akbari* was written, nor any record down till the closing years of the East India Company. Mr. Mumford says:—"In point of size and thickness the Agra carpets of to-day are fit successors to those of the olden time. They were of enormous weight and solidity. The designs are similar to those common in the time of the Mughal ascendancy, the cone forms playing an important part." So far as the writer can discover there is little of any special character to distinguish the carpets of Agra from those of Amritsar or any other centre where high class carpets are produced.

DIVISION 47. CARPETS.

ALLAHABAD, JABALPUR, and JHANSI—Are often spoken of as producing carpets, but none from either of these centres have been received at the present Exhibition, and it is believed their production must be very limited, Jhansi holding perhaps a higher position than either of the other places.

MIRZAPORE.—Mr. A. W. Pim who wrote the monograph on *Woollen Fabrics in the United Provinces* offers some trenchant remarks regarding the carpet industry of this town:—"The output is large, and has increased during the present few years; but the industry does not appear to be in a flourishing condition, nor to rest on a healthy basis. The manufacturers are in general men of no capital, who work by means of advances given to them by local contractors, receiving Rs. 4 per square yard of carpet supplied." "The patterns, which are usually stiff and conventional, are divided into three classes according to the character of the border known as *hashiya barik*, *bari hashiya* and *sozan*. The best patterns are derived from Persian sources, but of late years European firms have supplied models to be copied at Mirzapore."

Carpets have been received at the Exhibition from the following firms:—A. Tellery, E. Hill & Co., and Shaikh Abdool Karim. The assortment is fairly representative of the best work turned out at this centre which may perhaps, and not incorrectly, be classed as the head-quarters of the cheap commercial carpets of India. Mr. Mumford, an expert on carpets whose views of the various Indian styles have already been placed on liberal quotation, observes regarding Mirzapore:—"There is probably no city in India whose carpet industry has known a more extraordinary series of ups and downs than has that of Mirzapore." "It was only a little while after the introduction of the Mirzapore carpets into England, that English firms began to lower the quality of them. Efforts to restore it scored desultory success, and as late as 1867 the fabrics maintained a fairly good reputation. The jail system coupled with precipitate trading, finally finished them." "The present development is doing something to redeem the industry, but merely to the end of securing a satisfactory workshop, and probably not with any view to again producing the fabrics as they were before the great era of decadence began."

Bengal.—The lower provinces of India can hardly be said to possess a carpet-weaving industry. There is no wool worth speaking of in Bengal and the only carpets that need be mentioned are those from Gaya. While poor in quality, these possess an individuality that recalls the Ramchandra carpets of Ellore. They are possibly of Hindu origin though the weavers are Sunni Muhammadans. A good supply of these will be found in the Exhibition mostly made by Shobrati and Hussain Bux of Obra.

Madras.—The carpets exported from Masulipatam and Cocanada were those that first attracted attention in Europe as being specially Indian These were doubtless a century or so ago made practically at the same centres as at the present day. Mr. E. Thurston in his monograph of *Woollen Fabric Industry* of the Presidency, gives the seats of present day carpet-weaving as follows:—Ellore in the Godavari district, Masulipatam in the Kistna district, Walajanagar in North Arcot district, and Ayyampet in the Tanjore district.

ELLORE.—The weavers are Muhammadans, too poor to purchase the materials required or to subsist while a carpet is being woven. The business is there done by advances. Mr. Havell holds that while "there may be a falling-off in treatment of colour and in the execution of the details of patterns, compared with the finesse in the working of Indian carpets made twenty or thirty years ago, but the blame of this can hardly be attributed to the weavers themselves, and the mischief is not so serious but that a judicial encouragement of the weavers would soon remedy it.

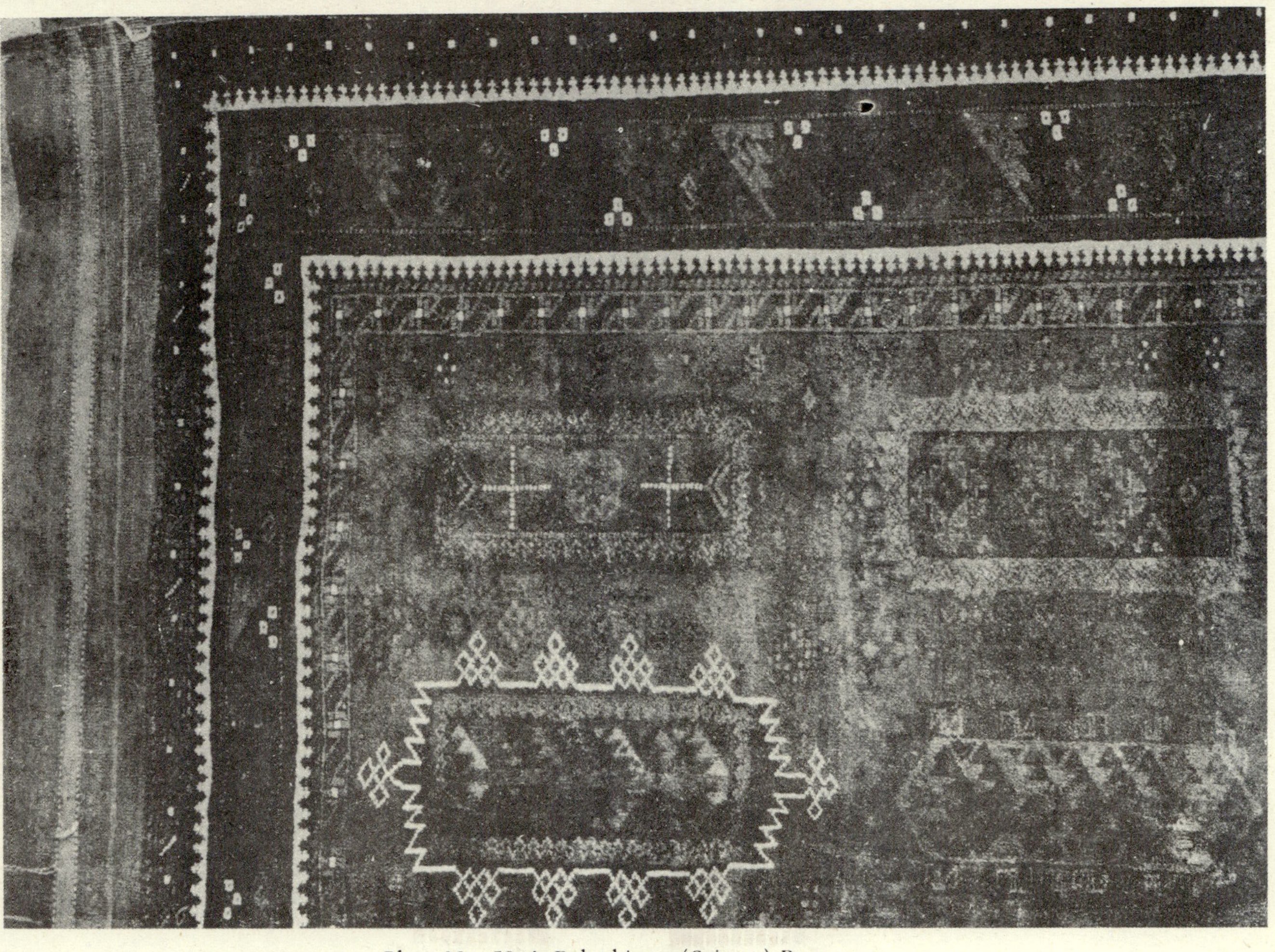

Plate No. 58-A Baluchistan (Seistan) Rug

DIVISION 47. CARPETS.

The best patterns in use are not inferior to those of old South Indian carpets, which are held up to the disparagement of modern productions. The outcry against the deterioration of Indian carpets, as far as South Indian carpets are concerned, is, in my opinion, not called for. Aniline dyes are very rarely used, as they are at Warangal and other places in Hyderabad, and I have seen carpets from the native looms at the three seats of the industry—Ellore, Masulipatam, and Ayyampet, which are in no respect inferior to old specimens in the hands of connoisseurs in London or in native houses and palaces. I cannot but think that jail manufactures, which are generally altogether inferior in colour and design, are passed off as coming from the caste weavers' looms. The good work, to which I refer, is not at all easy to obtain, and the unbusiness-like habits of ordinary native workmen doubtless react against their trade."

During the inspection of the Ellore factories made by the writer in connection with this Exhibition, it was found that one carpet was being reproduced in half a dozen different schemes of colour. With much trouble the manufacturers were persuaded to send to Delhi a few of their older designs. These will be found in the Exhibition. The following report on these carpets sent by the writer to Mr. J. A. Cumming, the Collector of the District, may be here published :—" Three classes of carpets were shown to me :—

(*a*) Carpets of foreign design, mostly Persian, in which almost universally the colours were poor, weak, defective in every direction, so that the carpets in this class were, in my opinion, about the most inferior produced in India.

(*b*) Carpets collectively designated as the design known as Ram Chandra. These, as a rule, are good, the colours being in direct adaptation to the pattern and well blended, but the quality very low, the wool being mostly hair and the number of threads to the inch usually not more than 5 to 8. The field of these carpets is commonly some shade of orange or flesh-colour with a thin diaper of trellice and rosettes thrown across. The border is usually in shades of deep red with blue. The effect is not at all unpleasing and, if better made (not less than 10 to 12 threads to the inch), would sell readily at Delhi.

DIVISION 47. CARPETS.

(*c*) By far the most interesting article shown to me by Mr. Banerjee was an old rug, which I regard as the original style of Rajamundry and Ellore. It might be described as a reproduction, in pile carpet, of the exceedingly fine grass mats that formed so striking a feature of the exports from the Northern Districts of Madras a century and more ago. The field was dull white with corner pieces and a central medallion. It was very finely and compactly woven by a process that the weavers described as the 'velvet' method. I could not discover the special feature that led to this compactness as I had only a few minutes of daylight at the factories. But I may add that it is more compact than could be supposed from the number of threads to the inch, so that I assume there is some peculiar stitch or knot employed in its fabrication. The effect is to simulate most closely the fine texture of the old grass mats."

MASULIPATAM.—Sir George Birdwood says that "the Masulipatam carpets were formerly the finest produced in India. The English importers insisted on supplying the weavers with the cheapest materials and we now find that these carpets are invariably backed with English twine. The spell of the tradition thus broken, one innovation after another was introduced into the manufacture." Mr. Mumford observes of this town that:—"It was here that the first British settlement was established in 1620. Even then the city, though small, was renowned for its fabrics. From fine, closely woven, beautifully designed rugs, they have, under the sweat-shop system, taken on the cheaper character of much of the Indian output. These rugs were at one time widely sold in the United States, but have lost caste since the large importation of other and better fabrics began." No examples of Masulipatam carpets have been received at the Exhibition.

MADRAS.—The School of Arts has, at the writer's suggestion, reproduced two old carpets from the collection in the Madras Museum. These are Ram Chandra carpets and may have been originally made at Ellore or Masulipatam. They are now on view as also two or three more from the same institution. The prevailing feature of all these is the rich deep brown-red. The carpet hung across the transept in front of the main door as a great curtain was made in the Madras School of Arts and in point of design and colouring is superior to any of the carpets sent by the private manufacturers of Ellore.

MALABAR.—Sir George Birdwood alludes to the carpets made in this district as being the only pile carpets of pure Hindu design and free from either European or Saracenic influence. The writer failed to secure examples of these for this Exhibition.

HYDERABAD.—The Warangal carpets shown at the Exhibition of 1851 may be said to have been both a surprise and a revelation to many. "The peculiarity of these rugs," says Sir George Birdwood, "of which several remain in the Indian Museum, was the exceedingly fine count of the stitches, about 12,000 to the square inch. They are also perfectly harmonious in colouring, and the only examples in which silk was ever used in carpets with a perfect satisfactory effect. The brilliancy of the colours was kept in subjection by their judicious distribution and the extreme closeness of the weaving, which is always necessary when the texture is of silk."

Of these wonderful rugs two have been sent out from the Victoria and Albert Museum and are now on view at the Exhibition: these are probably part of the original consignment alluded to above by Sir George Birdwood. In the Exhibition will also be seen three superb examples of Warangals exhibited by His Highness the Maharaja of Tipperah. One of these has been reproduced in Plate No. 58. This charming silk textile, like most of the Warangals, has the peculiar property of changing colour according to the position at which viewed. The ground is a dull grey white which in certain positions turns almost black.

Dr. Forbes Watson (*Textiles and Manufactures*) gives a short account of the Warangal carpets and rugs and furnishes several very excellent illustrations. Plate No. X is a coloured representation of a carpet almost identical in scheme of colours and design with some half a dozen that may be seen in the Sale Gallery. These have been sent by His Highness the Nizam. The prevailing colour effect may be said to be scarlet and white with the floral scroll of the field blue black or white and designs of the border red picked out with white on a blue background

DIVISION 47. CARPETS.

which is only shown by the narrowest outlinings to the red patterns. Within the corners and cutting off a portion of the field are usually placed squares in the colourings of the border. A feature of these Hyderabad designs may be added, namely, that the floral scrolls have the stems of the veins angularly bent in the fashion seen and described above in the Aurangabad gold brocaded *sárís*.

AURANGABAD.—The technical school of this town has sent one or two small rugs that are admirably made and in excellent designs and colours. It is to be hoped this may obtain the encouragement it deserves.

MYSORE.—The jail in Bangalore has for many years been noted for the good quality of carpets turned out especially during the term of its administration by Colonel P. H. Benson, I.M.S. In the Exhibition will be seen some excellent carpets from this Jail. While in Bangalore, Colonel Benson drew the writer's attention to a fragment of a very old carpet which had the local reputation of being one of the old Hindu designs of Mysore State. At the writer's suggestion, Mr. B. K. Venkatavaradaiyengar, the President of the Mysore-Delhi Exhibition, had this carpet reproduced, and as shown on the walls above the Bellary and Mysore carved wooden doors, there is a strong suggestion obtained of their possible close affinity in art conception. The writer has ventured to reproduce in Plate No. 58-B, this old Hindu or possibly Chalukyan carpet. The green-canopied design over medallions that would appear conventionalization of the double-headed goose of Mysore dispersed over a white field, are distinctly effective and quite unlike any other style of carpet met with in India.

Bombay.—Along the western coast of India it has often been maintained that Persian traders early established themselves and brought their skilled artificers to manufacture the goods for which they found a ready sale at the courts of the Emperors, Kings, and Nobles of India. In this way it is presumed carpet-weaving was established. Certain it is that one of the earliest seats of this craft so far as the reports of travellers uphold was the ancient city of Cambay. The Dutch naturalist and explorer, John

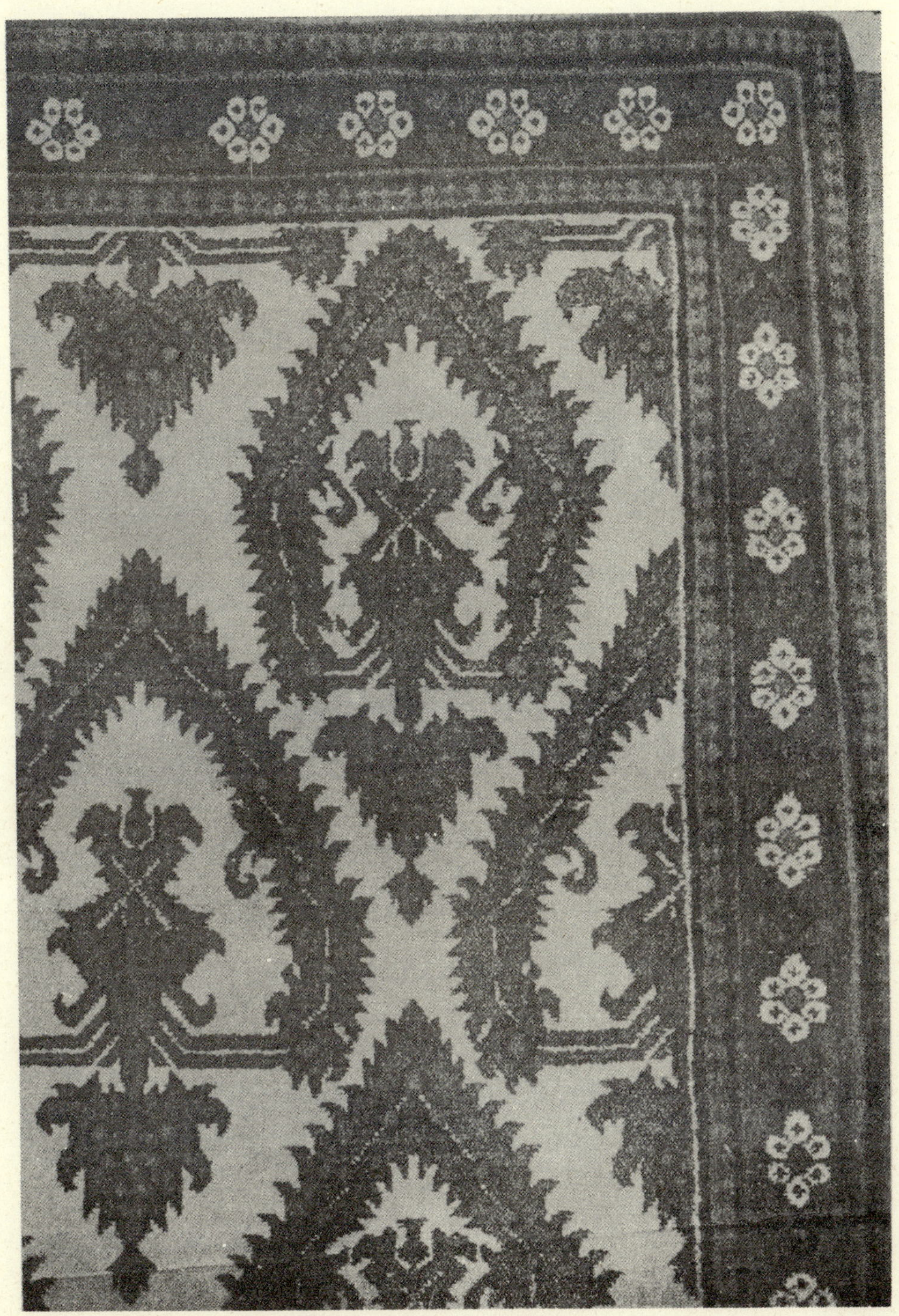

Plate No. 58-B Old Hindu or Chalukyan Carpet

Hayghen Von Linschoten, who came to India in 1596, speaks of Cambay thus:—"They make likewise many carpets called Alcatiffs, but they are neither so fine nor so good as those that are brought out by Persia and another sort of coarse carpet that are called Banguays which are much like the striped Coverlets that are made in Scotland serving to lay upon chests and cubbords."

DIVISION 47. CARPETS.

BOMBAY.—The School of Art in Bombay has sent one or two remarkably beautiful carpets which have obtained a bronze medal.

AHMEDABAD—Is not represented at the Exhibition, but for some years a fairly extensive business has been conducted by two private firms, the carpets being confined chiefly to America.

POONA.—The Yeroda Jail has long had the reputation of turning out excellent carpets. The writer was agreeably surprised, on inspecting the jail, by the richness and purity of the designs possessed by this prison. On making inquiries, he discovered that some 30 years previously these had been obtained from some old carpets in the possession of the Jamai Musjid of Bijapur. It was this circumstance that ultimately led to the Bijapur carpets being secured on loan (see above in connection with the remarks regarding Kashmir). It would thus appear that the Poona Jail has been the means of distributing some admirable carpets all over Western India, that could not otherwise have been secured. And what is more, it is largely due to the circumstance of the Bijapur carpets having been lined when they were sent to Yeroda to be copied, that they are in the state of preservation they are now in. Instead of the Yeroda Jail having exercised a debasing influence on the carpet manufactures of Western India, it has absolutely conservated what might otherwise have been lost.

Among the admirable rugs shown by this jail is a charming reproduction of a fine old *Kirmani*, a fragment of which has been in the possession of the jail for many years. The Superintendent of Prisons, Poona, had this reproduced for the Exhibition in silk with about 40 stitches to the inch. It is a rich lemon yellow field with marvellously worked floral design. It has not only been sold but orders booked for several replicas. Another rug

DIVISION 47. CARPETS

that has attracted considerable attention is one woven of natural-coloured wool.

BARODA.—*The Pearl Carpet* (*Plate No. 59*).—Perhaps if any one article could be singled out as more freely discussed at the Exhibition than any other, it would be the Pearl carpet of Baroda. This would appear to be the article described in the following from Sir George Birdwood's *Industrial Arts of India* as a *chaddar*:—"The most wonderful piece of embroidery ever known was the *chaddar* or veil made by order of Kunde Rao, the late Gaekwar of Baroda, for the tomb of Mahommed at Medina. It was composed entirely of inwrought pearls and precious stones, disposed in an arabesque pattern, and is said to have cost a crore (ten millions) of rupees. Although the richest stones were worked into it, the effect was almost harmonious. When spread out in the sun it seemed suffused with a general iridescent pearly bloom, as grateful to the eyes as were the exquisite forms of its arabesques."

The circular portion shown in the Plate was probably originally intended as the veil or canopy, and the rectangular carpet shown on the walls of the Loan Collection Gallery close by is one of the four such pieces that are said to have formed the carpet. According to the official report that accompanied these most curious and interesting exhibits, it affirms that the entire series is believed to have cost Rs. 60,00,000. His Highness the Gaekwar is permitting these wonderful exhibits to be taken to Delhi. The field is in seed pearls, the arabesque designs in blue and red being worked out in English glass beads with medallions and rosettes of diamonds, rubies, emeralds, freely dispersed. To place on the four corners of the carpet were constructed four large weights in solid gold thickly set in diamonds. One of these weights will be seen hard by the carpet. Needless to add, this superb gift never went to Mecca.

AWARDS FOR DIVISION 47.—PILE CARPETS.

AWARDS.

First Prize with gold medal to the Kashmir Manufacturing Company, Srinagar, for woollen carpets.

First Prize with gold medal to the Agra Central Jail for collection of carpets.

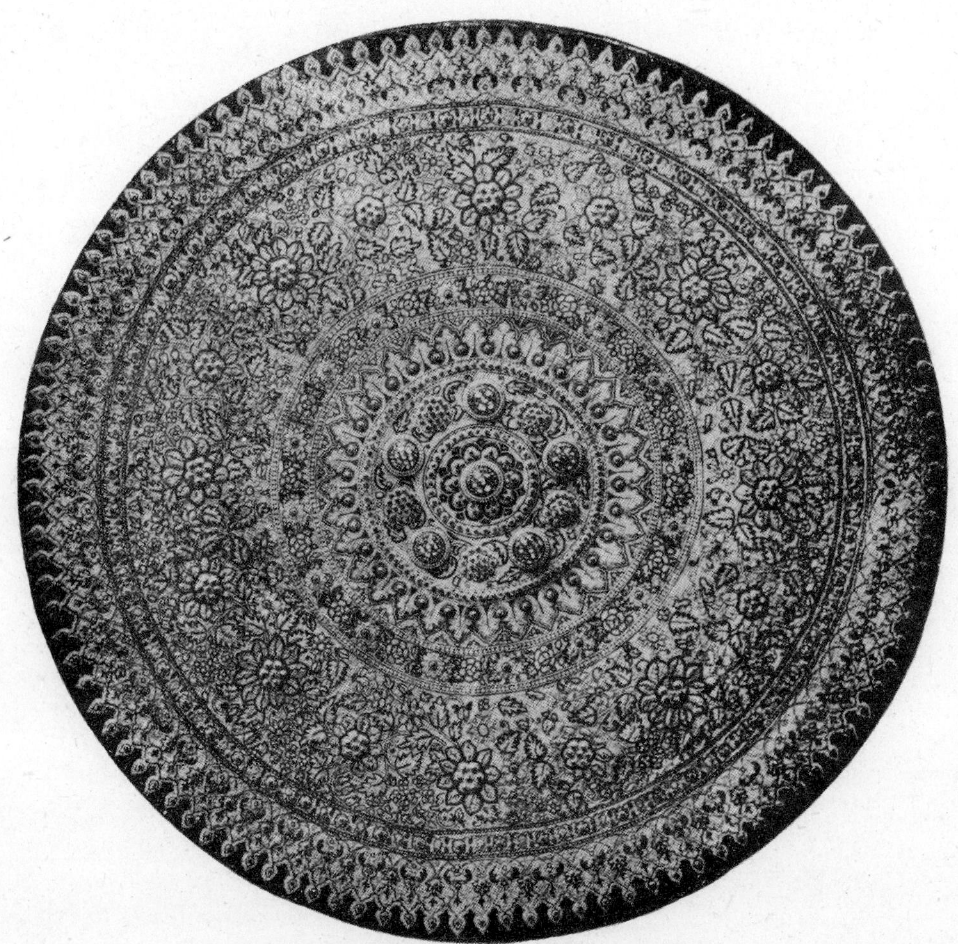

Plate No. 59 Pearl Carpet of Baroda

DIVISION 48. COTTON CARPETS.

Second Prize with silver medal to Haji Mian Safdar Ali, of Peshawar, for pair of Panjdeh rugs.

Second Prize with silver medal to Messrs. Baines Bros. & Co., Srinagar, for collection of Kashmir carpets.

Third Prize with bronze medal to Yeroda Jail, Poona, for rug No. 705.

Third Prize with bronze medal to Bombay School of Art, for carpet No. 1665.

Third Prize with bronze medal to A. Tellery, Mirzapore, for collection of carpets.

Commended for woollen carpet No. 1398, Messrs. Davee Sahai Chamba Mall, Amritsar.

Division 48.—Cotton and Woollen Carpets in other than Pile Stitch.

So much has been said regarding the pile carpets, the *kalins, kalichas,* or *galichas* of India, in the foregoing notes regarding the exhibits on view, that it is hardly necessary to describe the *daris* and *shatranjis.* These are plain not pile carpets and just as the *galichas,* which are usually in wool, may occasionally be made of cotton, so the *daris,* which are ordinarily of cotton, may sometimes be found made of wool. It would seem probable that the carpets of India prior to the Muhammadan conquests belonged almost exclusively to this description. *Dari* means a rug and *shatranji* a carpet. They are usually transversely striped but only occasionally do they show floral or geometric designs within the strips, such as in the *khas* fabrics of India and the *khilims* of Persia and Turkistan.

Cotton.—It would take many pages to convey anything like a fairly satisfactory account of the numerous and varied assortment of cotton *daris* and *shatranjis* on view. They are universally used by the poorer classes as praying carpets (*jainamaz*) of the Muhammadans, and have in consequence often much more art displayed in their manufacture than might be anticipated. Some of the more noteworthy are those from Rangpur in Bengal (blue and white), Agra, Aligarh, Bareilly, and Bulandshahr of the United Provinces; Jaipur and Bikanir in Rajputana; Bahawalpur, Multan, Gujrat, Sialkot, Peshawar of the Panjab: Dharwar,

DIVISION 48. COTTON CARPETS.

Belgaum, Ahmednagar, Raladgi, and Cambay in Bombay; Vadavedi and Adoni in Madras.

Plate No. 60 gives a representative series drawn from both the Sale and Loan Collection Galleries, but without showing the colour values, it fails to convey any very satisfactory impression of their beauty. To the left is a portion of the superb old *shatranji* of which the official report has already been given in connection with the Bijapur carpets. It will be seen that the local tradition goes to show that this *shatranji* was presented by the Emperor Auranzeb after the conquest of Bijapur in 1626. It is a rich Indian red field with, hanging in the middle, a lamp symbolical of the faith. This carpet would appear to have been woven more like a tapestry than an ordinary *dari*, and the patterns seem as if separately made and interwoven in their places on the loom.

Over the top of Plate No. 60 will be seen two of the ordinary forms of *daris*—one the classic striped form obtained from Jaipur, the other the floral and animal style made at Bikanir.

To the extreme right is a fine old *shatranji* lent by Sirdar Gurdat Singh, of Lahore. This is about 100 years old and is in the style of cotton carpets produced at Multan and Bahawalpur some few years ago.

In the middle of the plate is a *shatranji* from Yeroda Jail, Poona, that has been much admired. It is in deep chocolate brown field with a pattern in blue and white. This recalls in design some of the finer examples of Seistan rugs. It is one out of a large series of splendid *daris* and *shatranjis* that the writer found in the Yeroda Jail. These wonderful cotton carpets are doubtless well known to the residents in Western India, but until shown on the walls of this Exhibition were quite unknown to the bulk of the persons who interest themselves in Indian Art Manufactures. They give a lesson that might well be learned by the manufacturers of cotton carpets throughout India, namely, that if they would abandon the blue and white forms of *daris* and *shatranjis* and produce richer and more varied designs such as those of the Poona *daris*, a larger market might be found in India for *shatranjis* than has as yet been attained. There can be little

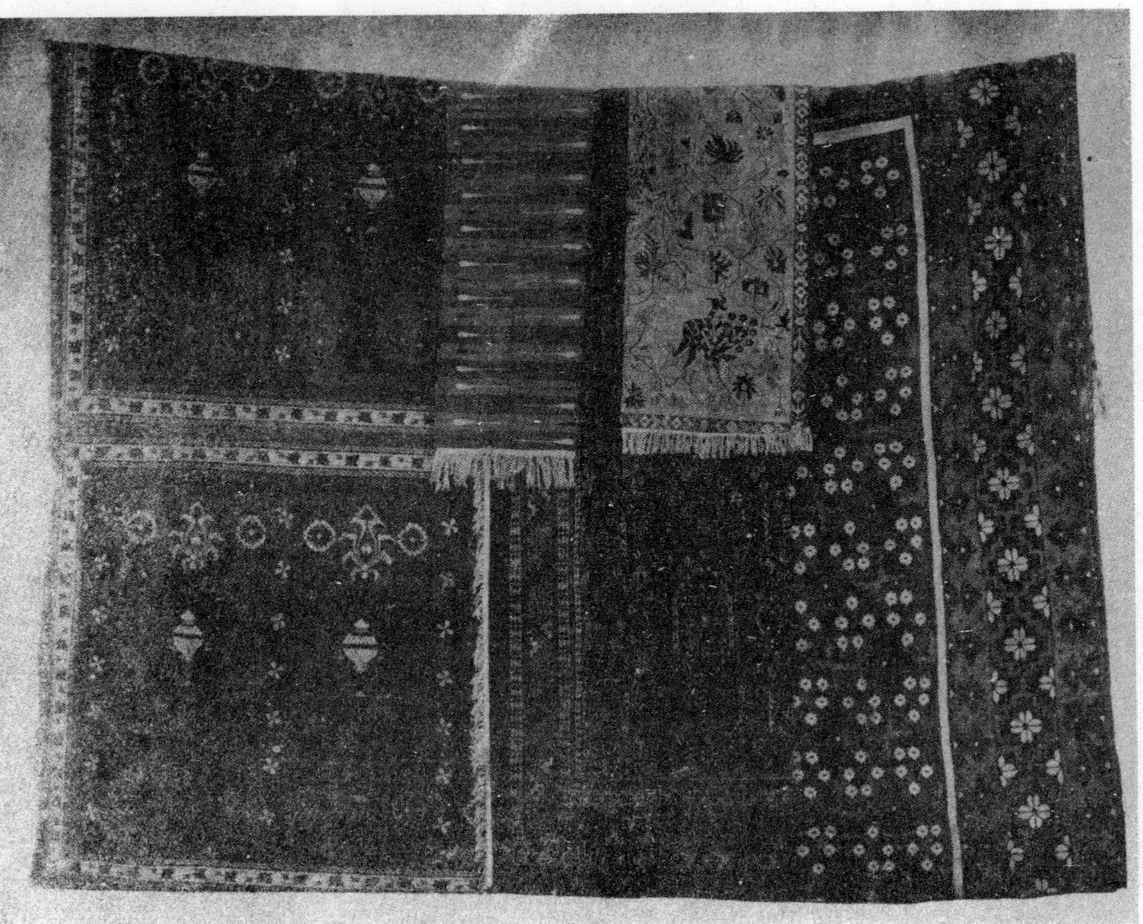

Plate No. 60 Cotton Carpets (Daris.)

doubt that a cotton carpet, if neatly and substantially woven, would be more acceptable to the inhabitants of tropical countries than a woollen one. Cotton plain carpets would be preferable to cotton pile carpets which have hitherto alone been tried to any extent. **DIVISION 48. COTTON CARPETS.**

Woollen Daris and Shatranjis—Though not met with very abundantly in India are still made and are much admired. The Bhutias of Darjeeling and the people of Nepal and Eastern Tibet weave strips of striped woollen thick cloth which, when sewn together into sheets, closely resemble the Kurdish *khilims.* These are largely used as rugs and are very beautiful. The people of Darjeeling also weave thick *chaddars* of white and blue that are very beautiful and find a distinct place among the art treasures of the people resident in the eastern side of India but are hardly seen elsewhere.

In BIKANIR, rugs are regularly woven in wool but in the same form as the cotton *daris.* The pattern used recalls the barbaric cross stitch embroideries of Hissar and Sirsa. An admirable example of this style of work will be seen on the walls of the Exhibition.

In QUETTA, rugs and camel saddle cloths are largely woven in wool and richly ornamented with shells. They are in stripes with patterns worked within them, and to all intents and purposes should be classed as a form of the fabrics known as *khilims.*

AWARDS FOR DIVISION 48.—COTTON CARPETS.

Second Prize with silver medal to Yeroda Central Jail, Poona, for a cotton *dari*—No. 204. **AWARDS.**

Division 49.—Mats and Baskets.

Although India has a most varied assortment of the articles that should find a place in this Division, comparatively few are of artistic merit. In the Exhibition the selection of grass mats from Ganjam and Tinnevelly will be found worthy of special study, especially the latter which are remarkably fine.

From Eastern Bengal come the famous *sitalpati* mats which have a great reputation for being exceedingly cool when slept upon. They are made from the bark of a reed that grows in marshy places and are often exceedingly beautifully made and

DIVISION 49. MATS AND BASKETS. artistically woven. A large assortment may be seen in the Loan Collection Gallery.

One of the greatest curiosities in the way of mats may be said to be the fact that ivory is cut up into strips of such fine texture that it is literally woven. Many ivory mats may be seen, some in the Sale Gallery and others in the Loan Collection Gallery. Of the latter the more interesting are those exhibited by His Highness the Maharaja of Tipperah, by Nawab Salimullah, of Dacca, and by the Maharani of Bharatpur.

AWARDS.

AWARDS FOR DIVISION 49.—MATS.

Third Prize with bronze medal for grass mats made in Tinnevelly.

Commended for grass mats No. 4611—Cochin State.

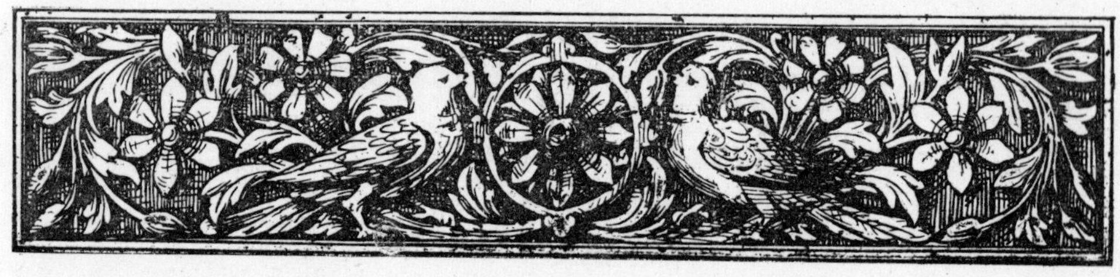

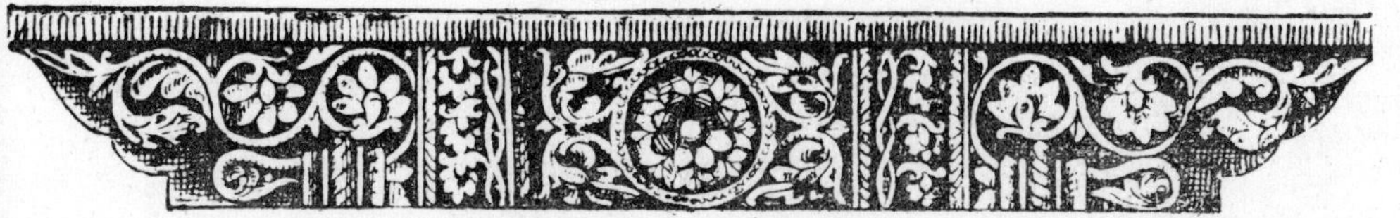

CLASS X.—FINE ARTS.

BY MR. PERCY BROWN, ASSISTANT DIRECTOR,
DELHI ART EXHIBITION.

IT is generally accepted that the higher flights of art, such as picture painting and sculpture, usually spoken of as the Fine Arts, are little known and still less practised by the natives of India. In a sense this is true as an examination of their art work has revealed very little that may legitimately come under this head, but in the examples that do occur some of the productions are of such a high order that they well deserve mention. Conveniently to describe these it has been found desirable to resolve this class into two Divisions :—(*a*) Articles "in the round" such as those executed in marble, metal, wood, terra-cotta, and plaster of Paris, and (*b*) Work done "on the flat" as pictures (oil and water colour), book illustrations, etc.

(*a*) DIVISION 50. STATUARY, Etc.

(a) Division 50.—Statuary, etc.

Under this head may be included the numerous statuettes of mythological subjects and figures carved in marble or cast in metal which are produced in so many parts of India and Burma. To the student of religion, many of them—noticeably those turned out by the stone carvers of Jaipur—are no doubt interesting, but to the artist the major portions are crude and child-like in the extreme and can hardly be placed among the Fine Arts. Tied down to reproduce each particular figure in a certain attitude, the sculptor is restricted by the rules of his religion to a limited number of poses, so that action except of a stiff and unnatural character is rarely found. Some of the carved marble representations of animals are, however, of a much more life-like appearance, the "Nandi" or sacred bull being occasionally a fairly faithful copy from nature; a small specimen from Gaya shown in the Exhibition being specially worthy of mention. The same remarks apply to metal work, the subjects being generally of a similar character to those in the material previously dealt with, and although

(*a*) DIVISION 50. STATUARY, Etc.

one cannothelp but admire the beauty of workmanship and delicate finish of some of the mythological groups from Madura, neither the design nor composition are particularly commendable. A noteworthy exception, however, to the above is found in some of the productions of the brass workers of Jaipur. These take the form of miniature copies of scenes from country life, charmingly natural representations of bullocks and country carts being their particular "forte." The action, modelling, and feeling of movement are admirably portrayed and it seems strange that artists who can execute such wonderfully life-like miniatures, do not attempt something larger and more ambitious which, if carried out with the same amount of feeling and quality, would mark them at once as sculptors of no mean order.

There is little doubt, however, that the very highest form of fine art in India is to be met with in the terra-cotta statuettes made in Lucknow. They are about the size and in a sense similar to the well-known Tanagra figures, but hardly attain that breadth of treatment and feeling of freedom that is the charm of these classic productions. This is probably due to a difference in process as, where the Greek modeller worked with his material in a soft plastic state, the Lucknow sculptor usually tools and carves his, while his clay is what is known as "green," that is, the stage between the wet and the dry. The former method tends to a soft, free, and voluptuous style, as witness the beautiful rounded forms and flowing draperies of the one, while the latter inclines more to a hard, detailed effect and is thus admirably suited to the realistic subjects usually depicted by the Lucknow craftsman. Although he has shown in the Exhibition that he can, when he so desires, represent domestic scenes in the most delightful manner, the Lucknow modeller is never so happy as when portraying, in its most repugnant form, poverty, disease, and old age. Some of his figures although barely six inches high have been weeks in preparation and the artist appears to have taken a pleasure in lingering over his repulsive beggars and dying, famine-stricken wretches, so as to ensure the representation of every detail. As examples of the realistic school of sculpture, they take a very high position.

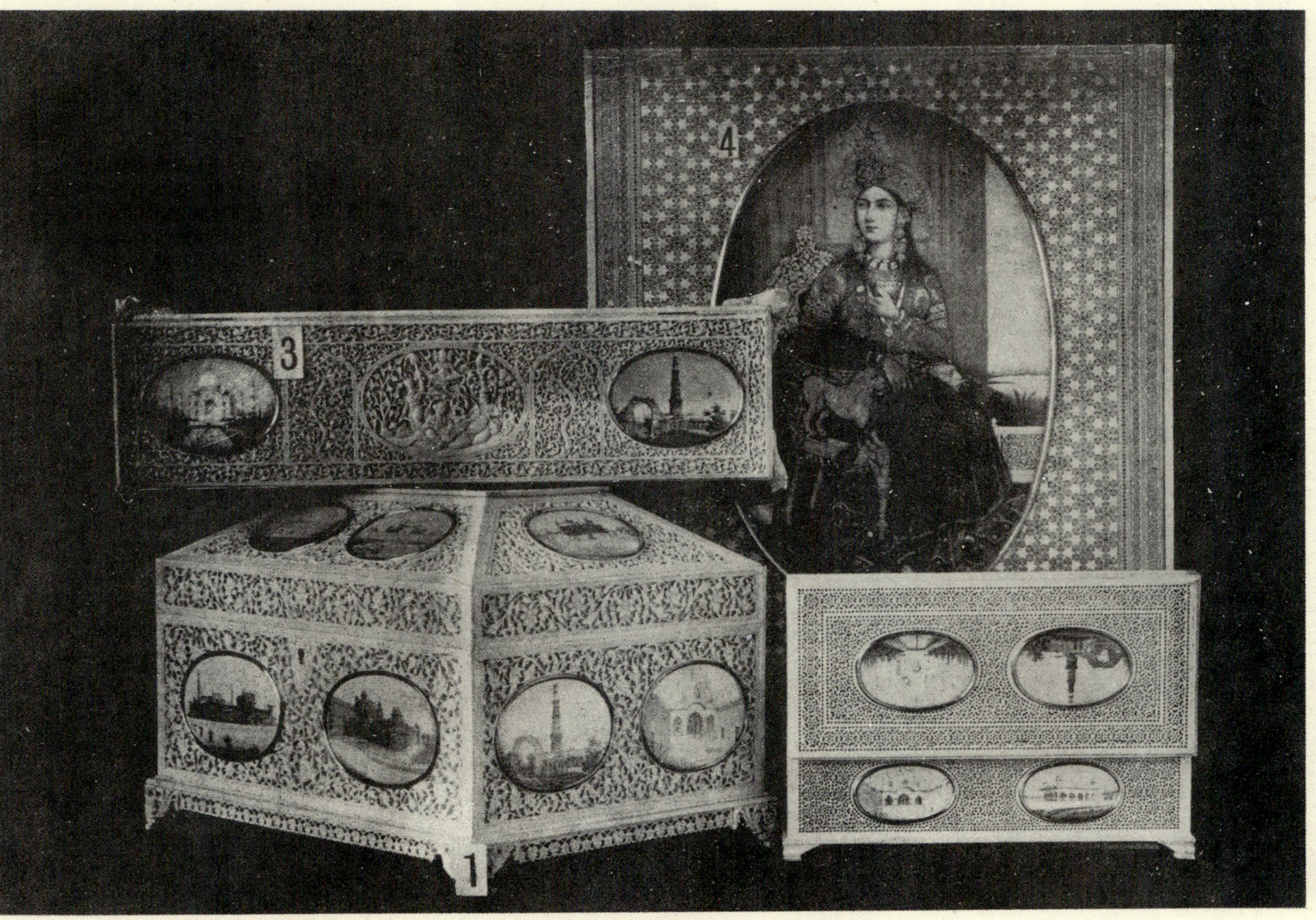

Plate No. 61 Miniature Painting on Ivory

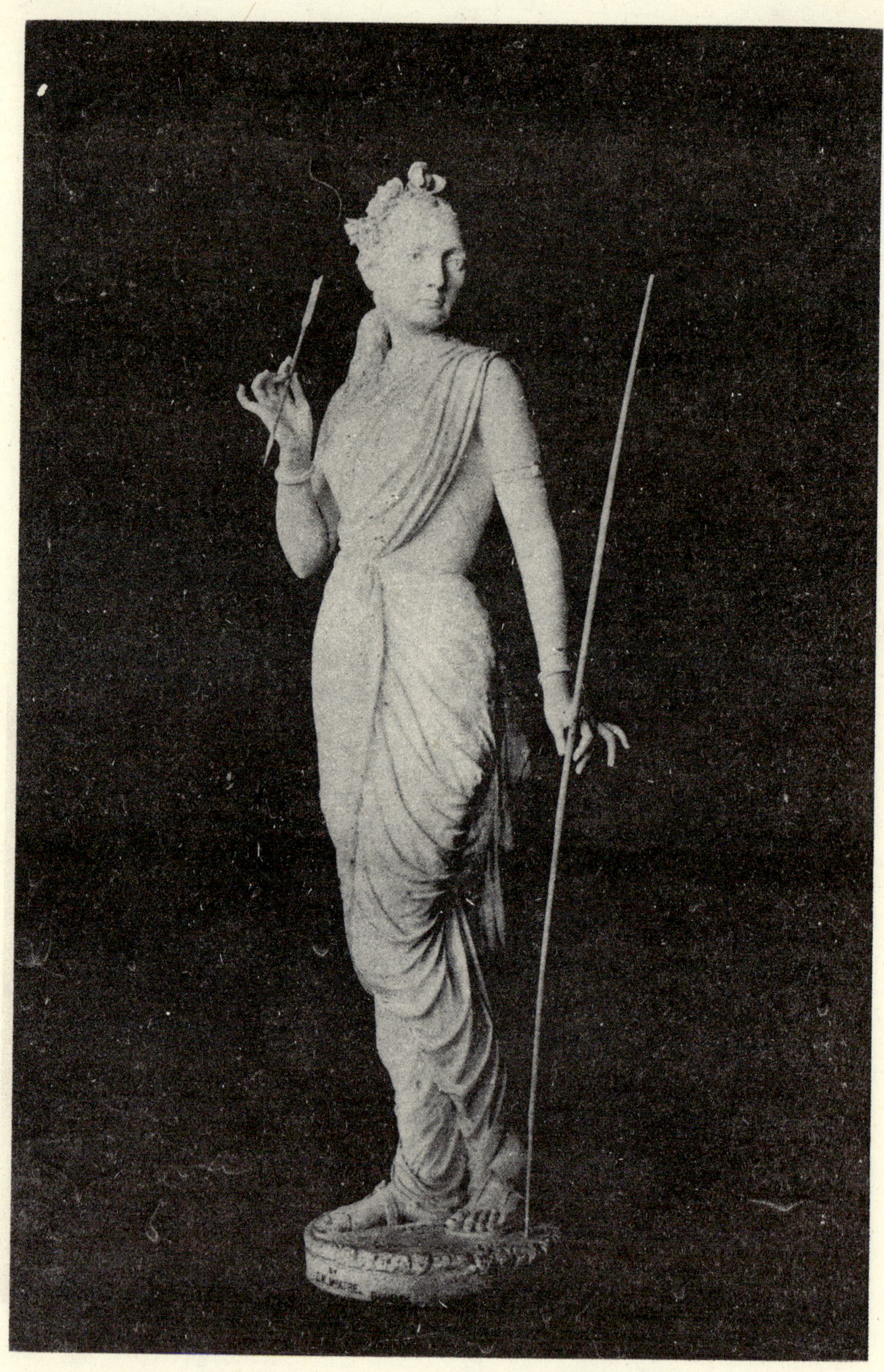

Plate No. 62 Statue Parvatti (as Shabaree) in Plaster of Paris

(a) DIVISION 50. STATUARY, Etc.

WOOD.—Although used to a large extent in decoration, the Indian sculptor has not produced much statuary in this material. Two striking examples face one on entering the Exhibition building, representing two "Caryatid" figures, but these are reproductions to half scale, made under the supervision of the Madura Technical School, of large architectural supports in stone from the great temple of that place. They serve to illustrate the character and style of the work of the sculptors of that period.

The Burman, however, has used teak wood with very favourable results in his attempts at statuary and some of his productions in this material are remarkably good. The groups he occasionally fixes on to his carved and perforated screens and archways (alas! often to the detriment of the general effect of the design) are extremely sculpturesque and frequently his gong stands are statues in themselves. Here and there on some of the monasteries and temples one finds friezes of panels to a fairly large scale, pictures in wood, panoramas illustrating mythological scenes which show how versatile the Burman is when working in his favourite material. His single figures, however, usually mythological although sometimes natural, but touched with that delightful feeling of conventionalism which makes his work so charming, are remarkably well sculptured and may be considered well worth a place among the Arts.

A different class of work from that previously described are the plaster models contributed by the past and present students of the Schools of Art, which form a not unimportant display and call attention to the large amount of study of this kind that is now being carried on at these institutions. Modelling in this form is a comparatively recent introduction, and it is at present perhaps too early to judge whether it will ever become really understood by the art student of India. As this art is entirely Western in its character it should, it is considered, be regarded from the same point of view as European Statuary and be described accordingly. If, however, the observer chooses to look at these works from the standpoint of Indian indigenous art, they are so immeasurably superior to any of the ordinary bazar productions that a comparison

(a) DIVISION 50. STATUARY, Etc.

is almost impossible, a striking exception being the Lucknow terra-cotta, which has been dealt with previously.

The subjects treated are all complete figures or busts taken directly from life and are either bronzed or painted, a practice which removes the harsh effect of the white plaster and at the same time tends to hide some of the more superficial faults. A study of the numerous examples in the Exhibition reveals, in some of them, a certain amount of aptitude on the part of the modeller in seizing a likeness which is encouraging, but the greater portion of these productions are in other particulars somewhat ordinary. The principal faults are a lack of feeling, which it is feared will take some time to overcome, and an ignorance of the construction of the figure or face which only a long and constant study of life and antique can remedy. This latter is probably the root of the whole matter, for although the training given is of the best, the length of time devoted by the average art student to conscientious study is generally somewhat limited. He is generally too eager to become a professional artist to spend long over the ordinary School of Art routine.

CHIEF FINE ART EXHIBITS ON VIEW.

Of the religious subjects carved in marble, Jaipur exhibits a large assortment, some of which are good of their kind, but the exaggerated poses of many and the custom of touching them here and there with gold and vermillion detracts somewhat from the good qualities these occasionally possess. A very rustic conception of a cow and calf in a charmingly natural style is worthy of mention, but its resemblance to a similar composition in plaster of Paris to be seen occasionally in Europe, places it not altogether above suspicion. Specimens of the same art, but of a more dignified character and with the details better drawn and more delicately modelled, are some of the white marble statues of Buddha from Rangoon.

Of the models in metal of a mythological character some good specimens from Madura and Tirupati were exhibited. Manufactures of this class are usually executed in what is known as the "ceri perdú" process, a method equivalent to the better known one of " waste moulding " in plaster. Briefly, the figure

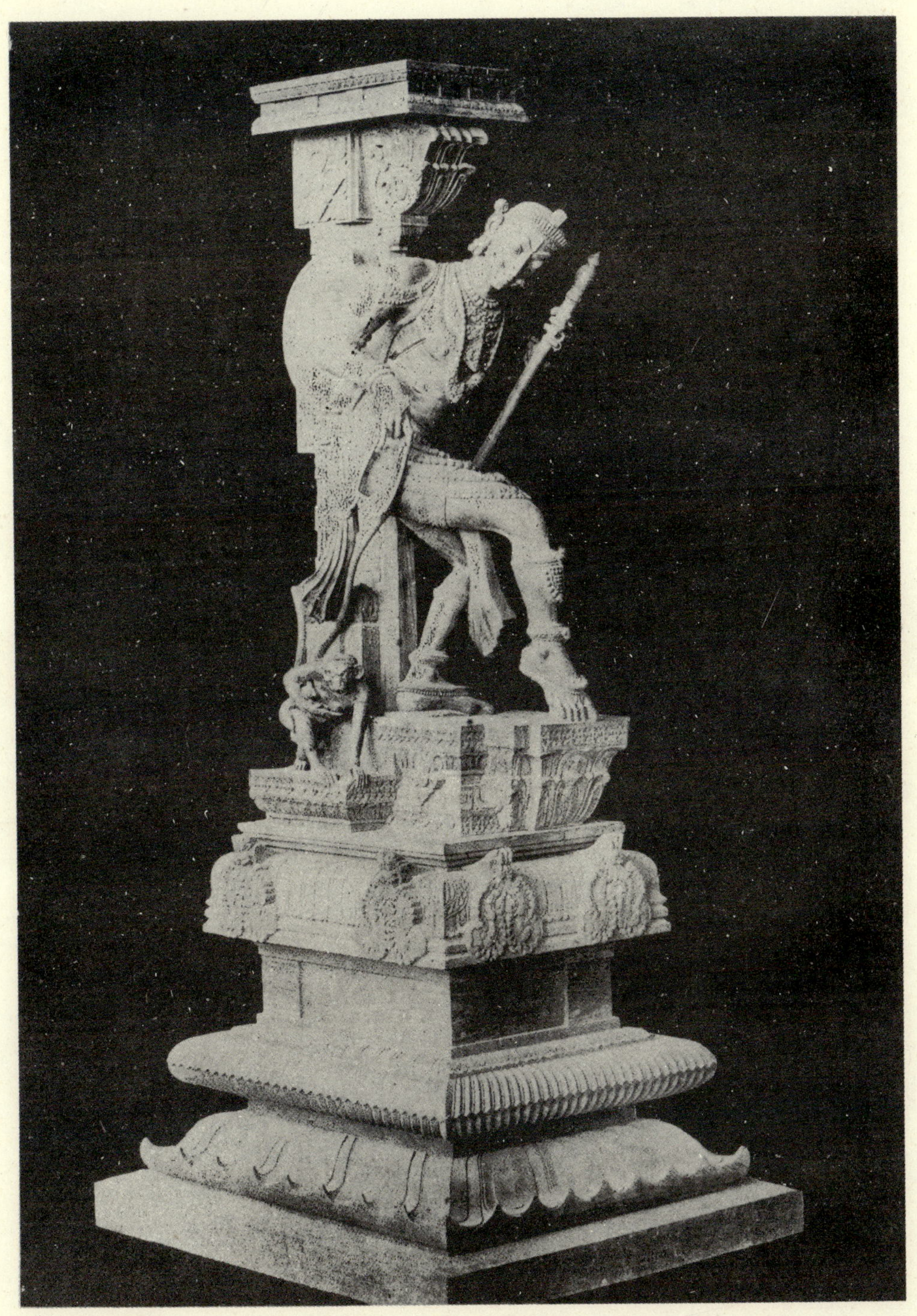

Plate No. 63 Copy in Wood of Stone Pillar in Madura Temple

(a) DIVISION 50. STATUARY, Etc.

is first modelled in wax and over this a layer of clay or similar material is worked. The wax is then melted out and the clay thus forms a mould or "matrix" of the original wax figure into which the liquid metal is poured, which, when set, takes the exact shape of the wax model. After a certain amount of chasing and polishing the article is finished. This process, varying somewhat in the details, is the one by which most of the cast metal figures are prepared.

Clay modelling is represented by the terra-cottas of Lucknow, the series exhibited being entirely the work of one man, Bhagwant Singh, the modelling master of the Lucknow Technical School, a modeller by caste and an artist by instinct. His principal compositions are "a Banya's wife with her child," "Famine," "Beggars," "a Cripple," and several groups of figures working at ordinary bazar trades and occupations. His Banya's wife is an extremely pretty conception and distinctly different in every way from the groups of blind beggars. The versatility of this artist's subjects renders a study of his work never tiring. Without looking at his hollow, sightless eye-sockets, the action of the blind beggar at once suggests the infirmity under which he is labouring. That the modeller goes direct to nature for his studies goes without saying, and this, combined with a most retentive memory for every characteristic detail of the human form or fold of drapery, has resulted in a very instructive and realistic series of examples of Fine Art.

A varied collection of plaster figures, the work of the Schools of Art, was to be found distributed about the Exhibition. Of these perhaps none has been so much criticised as the work of Mr. G. K. Mhatre of Bombay. This artist received his early training at the Sir Jamsetjee Jejeebhoy's School of Art and is now working as a professional sculptor in a studio in Bombay on the most approved European lines. His exhibits were two in number, both statues about 5 feet high representing "Parvatee as Shebaree" and a female figure entitled "To the Temple." The latter, which is perhaps the more natural of the two, has come into prominence before, being exhibited in the Sculpture Court at the Paris Exhibition of 1900. It depicts a very graceful

(a) DIVISION 50. STATUARY, Etc.

native girl clothed in soft, clinging draperies, incense in hand, going to her devotions. *Parvatee* is a somewhat similar conception but smacks rather more of Paris than the East in some of its details. In both, however, the drapery and general modelling is carefully considered and Mr. Mhatre is to be congratulated on having produced these very conscientious studies. Of the less ambitious works reproduced in a similar material, M. Rajahram Shejwalker of the Lahore School of Art sends a delicate little piece of work entitled " a Mahratta woman " and Mr. Markote of Bombay a spirited likeness in imitation bronze of a Fakir. The Madras School of Arts contributes a number of painted plaster figures, a realistic series of subjects executed in a remarkably realistic manner.

AWARDS FOR DIVISION 50.—STATUARY, ETC.

AWARDS.

First Prize with gold medal to Mr. G. K. Mhatre of Bombay, for modelled figure of a girl.

First Prize with gold medal to Bhagwant Singh of the Lucknow Technical School, for figures modelled in clay.

Commended —Modelled statuette of a Mahratti girl—Rajahram Hari Shejwalker, Lahore School of Art.

(b) Division 51.—Painting.

This may be said to be broadly divided into three distinct styles. The Buddhist, exemplified by the frescoes on the walls of the caves of Ajunta, the Muhammadan style as shown by the book illustrations and portrait pictures of the Moghul artists and still carried on to this day, and the modern style of oil and water colour painting as practised in the Schools of Art. The first mentioned is more decorative than pictorial so that it can hardly be classed among the Fine Arts, and is therefore omitted from a description of what is intended to be an account of painting in the pictorial sense only. The earliest true pictures therefore, of which we have any records are the productions of the old Moghul painters who from all accounts carried on this work with unusual difficulty owing to the well-known Muhammadan objection to the delineation of natural forms. It is interesting to find that probably the earliest encouragement they received was from the broad minded Akbar who in a characteristic speech

(b) DIVISION 51. PAINTING.

is alleged to have said :— " There are many that hate painting, but such men I dislike. It appears to me as if a painter had quite peculiar means of recognizing God : for in sketching anything that has life, and in devising its limbs one after the other, he must come to feel that he cannot bestow individuality upon his work, and is forced to think of God, the only giver of life, and will thus increase his knowledge."

Authorities appear to be of one opinion with regard to this style of painting, namely, that it was originally introduced from Persia. There, from an early date, book-illustrating was a greatly advanced art and no doubt some of the beautifully illuminated manuscripts of the Persian Artists soon found their way into India. The similarity between the painted illustrations from Ispahan and the work of the Moghul portrait painters shows that they were both of the same school, but the strong Chinese feeling which here and there is so noticeable seems clearly to indicate that many were in no little way influenced by the production of Mongol Artists. An analysis of a number of these paintings, both ancient and modern (for the works of the present day differ in the main very little from those of years ago), reveals a mixture of faults and good qualities that is somewhat bewildering. To the casual observer the want of atmosphere, the total disregard of all the rules of perspective, and the general stiffness of the composition condemn them absolutely, but a closer study brings to light the artist's capabilities for portraiture which, combined with a sense of harmony of colour and a grasp of decorative effect, renders these pictures peculiarly interesting. The process of painting by which these works are executed is known as " body colour," that is water colour mixed with white, which gives them a solidity or " body." The paper used is an ordinary and often comparatively thin country-made article. From the picture painting described above grew the art of miniature painting which is carried to a considerable degree of excellence in Delhi. These miniature paintings are usually executed on ivory by means of the " body colour " mentioned above and generally depict historical scenes, architecture, or portraits. The colours now used are nearly all obtained

Miniature Painting.

(b) DIVISION 51. PAINTING.

from Europe except the gold and white, which are made locally. Owing to the extreme fineness of the technique, the brushes require to be very small and delicate and are manufactured from the fur of the tails of young squirrels.

Although this art is usually regarded as a comparatively modern one, there is no record of the date of its introduction into Delhi. It is surmised by some that it was first imitated from the miniatures which, with our grandfathers, took the place of the photography of to-day. The writer had an opportunity of studying the original drawings from which miniatures are copied belonging to one of the hereditary painters of Delhi. The subjects were varied and included portraits, conventional patterns, durbar and religious scenes. They were mostly executed on old scraps of country-made paper and many showed signs of having been traced from still older drawings, the local colouring being roughly washed on afterwards, this making a kind of "working drawing" from which the more elaborate miniature paintings are, in the hands of a trained painter, comparatively easily evolved. The method of tracing is peculiar and shows how many of these drawings have been handed down from generation to generation. A piece of thin transparent paper being placed over the original picture, the whole design is carefully and closely pricked through with a sharp point or needle until the top paper bears a copy of the original drawing traced out in minute holes. This is then placed over the ivory or paper on which it is proposed to transfer the picture, and powdered charcoal dusted over it, which penetrates the pricked holes and traces the drawing through, really a process of stencilling. Some of the drawings shown were evidently copied from illustrations in old European books, but the bulk of them appeared to have been obtained from very early and no doubt in some cases contemporary drawings of the personages or events usually depicted by these artists.

Modern Oil and Water Colour Painting.

The art described above is an indigenous fine art of India, but an exotic form has of late years become so prominent and is assuming such proportions that it needs more than passing mention. This is the oil and water colour painting now produced in no small quantity by the students and teachers of the Govern-

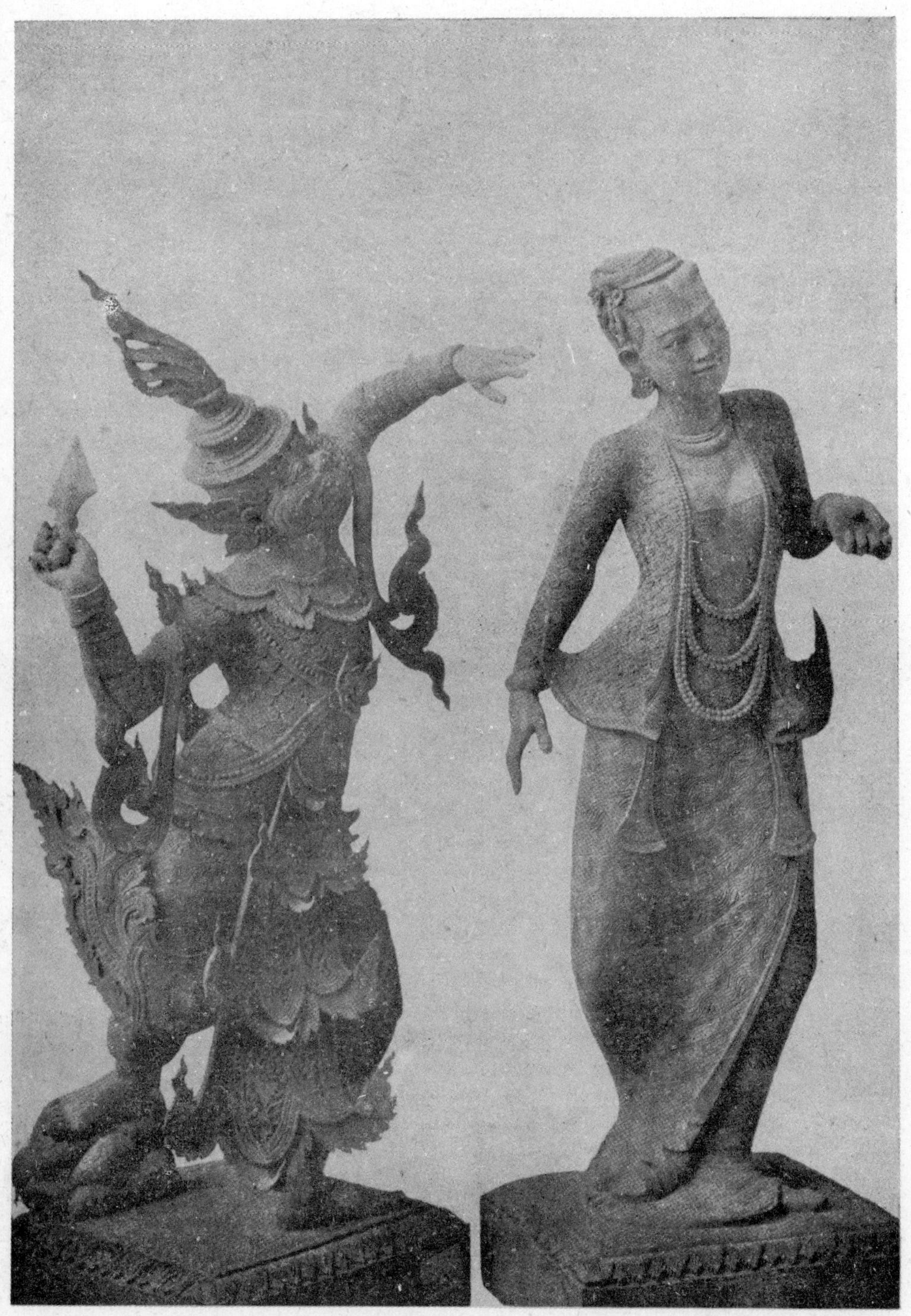

Plate No. 64 Burmese Sculptures in Wood

(b) DIVISION 51. PAINTIN .

ment Schools of Art. Until its introduction from Europe there was no oil painting of any kind practised throughout the country, but the number of pictures executed in the medium shown in the Exhibition reveals the fact that oil picture painting as a branch of study as well as a means of livelihood is being taken up very seriously by a rapidly increasing class. Some of the work displayed in the Entrance Hall of the Exhibition was remarkably good, in the life studies the modelling and feeling of living flesh being well reproduced, and one or two landscapes showed an atmosphere and a consideration for composition which is worthy of remark. Much, however, of the work shown was of a very ordinary character, the drawing being decidedly defective and the technique and colouring in most cases crude.

CHIEF EXHIBITS ON VIEW.

Of paintings in the Muhammadan style a large series was exhibited, mainly in the Entrance Hall. A fine collection of mythological scenes with beautifully designed and illuminated ornaments were kindly lent by the Maharaja of Alwar.

They represented scenes from early Hindu History and as schemes of colour, although the general composition and drawing might be criticised, they were remarkably good. Forming part of the same loan but somewhat different in style and character of subject from those previously mentioned, was a set of water colour paintings, portraying the entry of Lord Lake and Akbar the Second into Delhi. The costumes, arms and armour, trappings, and the features of the personages taking part in the great procession are most carefully delineated. One cannot help but feel that these partake however more of the character of a decorative frieze than a series of pictures, but looked at from whatever standpoint their good qualities are noticeable. The drawing, colouring, and general feeling of pomp and splendour are wonderfully expressed. Another very fine series of pictures of this school of painting was contributed by Rai Bahadur Janki Nath Pandit of Delhi. This consisted of 72 illustrations from the *Ramayana.* The donor gave the following particulars regarding these. "Rama Churitur :— These pictures formed part of a Sanscrit Ramayana which was written in golden letters in Kashmir during Jehangir's time and

(b) DIVISION 51. PAINTING.

this about 300 years ago. The text for some reason was destroyed and the pictures taken out and preserved. It is known that the book remained in the King's Library for centuries but fell into the hands of a soldier during the Mutiny of 1857, when shortly thereafter it was purchased by me. The beauty of these paintings is remarkable and their faithful portraiture of Indian life of considerable historic value."

One of the glass cases in the Main Gallery contained a very fine collection of illustrated books contributed by a number of Native Princes, Nobles, and gentry from different parts of the country. A series lent by the Maharaja of Alwar is specially worthy of mention. One of these was a very historic manuscript copy of the "Gulistán of Sheikh Maslih-ud-din Sadi of Shiraz." The illustrations are beautiful examples of illuminating and were the work of Ghulam Ali Khan and Buldeo, painters of Alwar. A selection from the library of the Nawab Bahadur of Murshidabad was also well worth careful study. For beauty of colouring, decorative effect and general suitability to the purpose for which they were executed, the paintings in these books could hardly be excelled.

Three pictures which provoked some considerable criticism and discussion were two oil paintings and one water colour by Abanindra Nath Tagore. In imitation of the Muhammadan School of painting, they exhibited a knowledge of drawing and a grasp of the harmonious arrangement of colours that at once attracted attention. The best of the three was no doubt the one entitled "The last days of Shah Jehan" and represented two figures in a marble columned "Imambárá," the one with a very natural turn of the head gazing across the water at the "Taj Mahal." The foreshortening of the head of the figure was one of the most striking parts of the picture. The delicate colouring and soft effect of the whole composition was most pleasing. "The capture of Bahadur Shah" was hardly so good as the picture previously described. The usual conception of the scene is rather more dramatic than the one here shown which represents a very quiet scheme of colour with three or four figures, the proportion of some of these being open to criticism. A noticeable part of the effect however is the admirable harmony displayed in the colour of

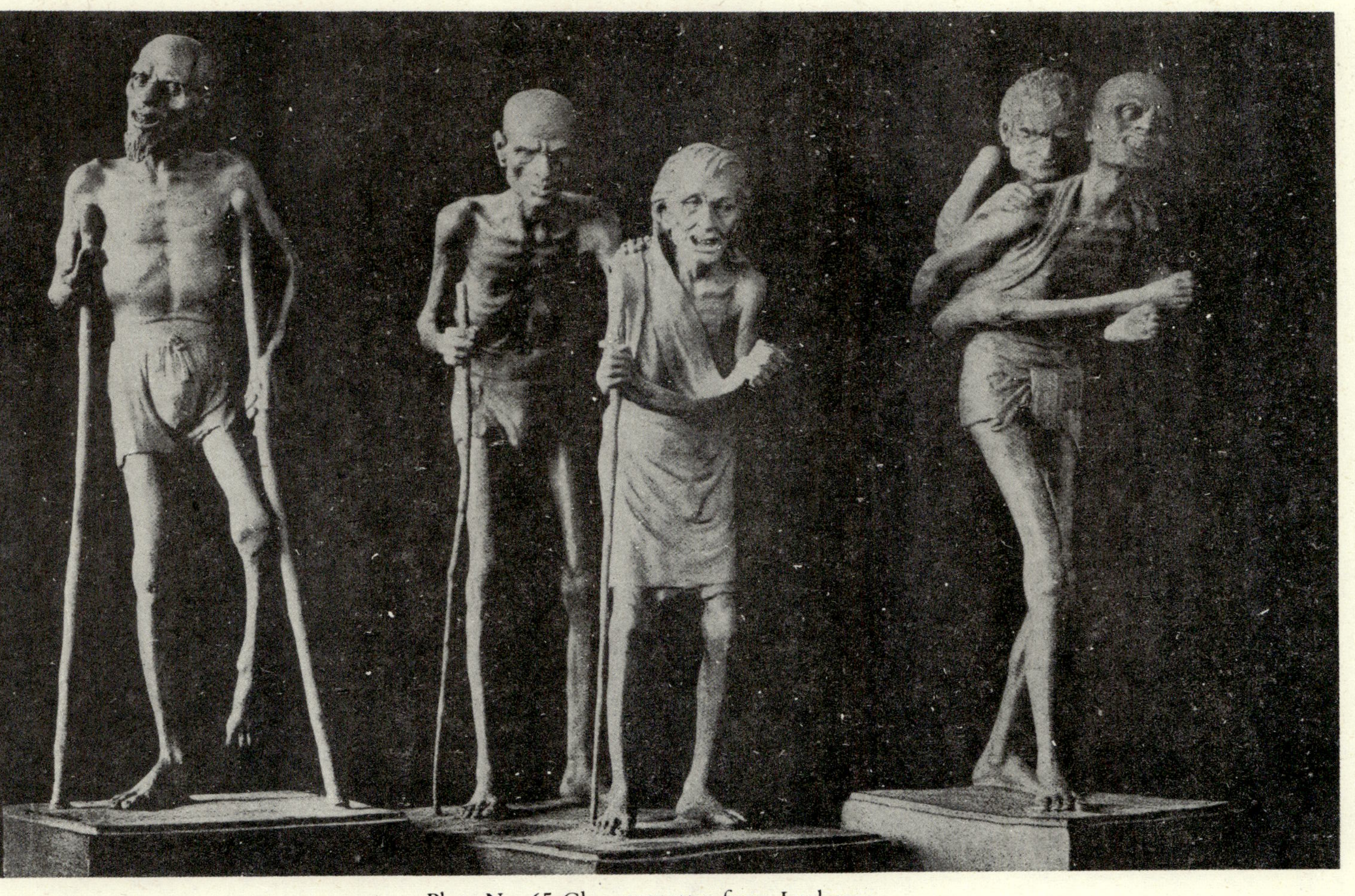

Plate No. 65 Clay statuettes from Lucknow

the old king's costume with the blue and gold dress of his guard. The remaining picture is executed in "body colour" touched with gold and silver. It depicts the "Construction of the Taj." The quality of the drawing is somewhat mixed, in some places being decidedly wrong, but the most striking part of the effort is the exceptionally good modelling of the features which appear to have been copied from early likenesses, they are in fact early Muhammadan paintings but infused with a feeling of life that was rarely attained by those artists. The whole effect of this particular composition is most rich and decorative.

(b) DIVISION 51. PAINTING.

MINIATURE PAINTINGS.—An interesting collection of miniature paintings on ivory was exhibited by Fakir Chand and Raghu Nath Das of Delhi. A quantity of this work chiefly representing architectural scenes was displayed by this exhibitor on his beautiful caskets in the Division devoted to Ivory. This is a favourite method in Delhi of enriching articles executed in this material and when carefully arranged these small painted panels, usually oval in shape, add to the interest of the design. Muhammad Husain Khan, also of Delhi, exhibited a very complete collection of miniatures both on ivory and paper. His subjects were most varied and included portraits and architectural scenes. Chief among these was No. 4157, a frame containing pictures of the Kings of Delhi; a collection of historic interiors from Agra, Delhi, and Amritsar, No. 4178; and a very fine portrait of Nur Jehan Begum, No. 4161.

Of the School of Art style of painting in oils, two portraits of Panjabis by M. Sher Muhammad of the Lahore School of Art deserve special mention. They show a knowledge of technique and a familiarity with the intricate modelling of the human face that places them considerably above the ordinary work of this kind.

AWARDS FOR DIVISION 51.—PAINTING, ETC.

AWARDS.

Second Prize with silver medal to Abanindra Nath Tagore of Calcutta for picture entitled "Last hours of Shah Jahan."

Second Prize with silver medal to Muhammad Husain Khan of Delhi, for a set of miniature paintings.

Second Prize with silver medal to Qazi Abdul Salam of Alwar for decorative book-binding.

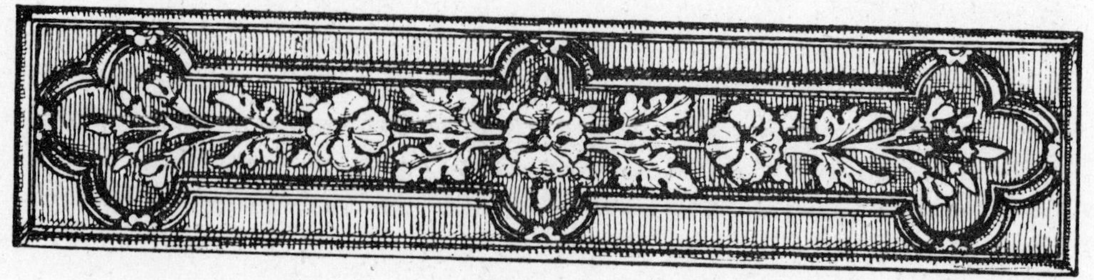

II.—LOAN COLLECTION GALLERY.

CHASED STEEL.

THE large gallery that will be found on the left of the transept has been designed for the Loan Collection. The rich and varied display assorted within its glass cases or hung on the walls, has been procured from the palaces of the princes and nobles and from the various provincial Museums of India, with, in addition, a large contribution from the Victoria and Albert Museum of South Kensington, London.

Ten Classes.

CLASSIFICATION.—It will be found that the exhibits have been grouped into the ten classes formed in connection with the Main Gallery, except that Class X has been carried to the great transept and shown in conjunction with the Fine Arts of the Sale Collection. The assortment of the classes and of the divisions under these, has been in strict accord with that detailed on pages 2 and 3 above. It has not, however, been found desirable, nor indeed necessary, to establish each and every one of the 50 divisions. The goods under most of the classes are less numerous in the Loan than in the Sale Gallery and are capable of artistic grouping, and to some extent also, of assortment in sets that correspond with the names of the owners. Thus for example in Class I, Metal Wares, it will be seen that while the chief divisions, such as "Gold and Silver Plate," "Enamels," etc., have had separate glass cases assigned to them, many of the larger assemblages such as the Arms have been grouped according to the names of the exhibitors, in place of into every possible division such as for "Iron, Lead and Tin goods;" for "Tinned,

Fifty Divisions.

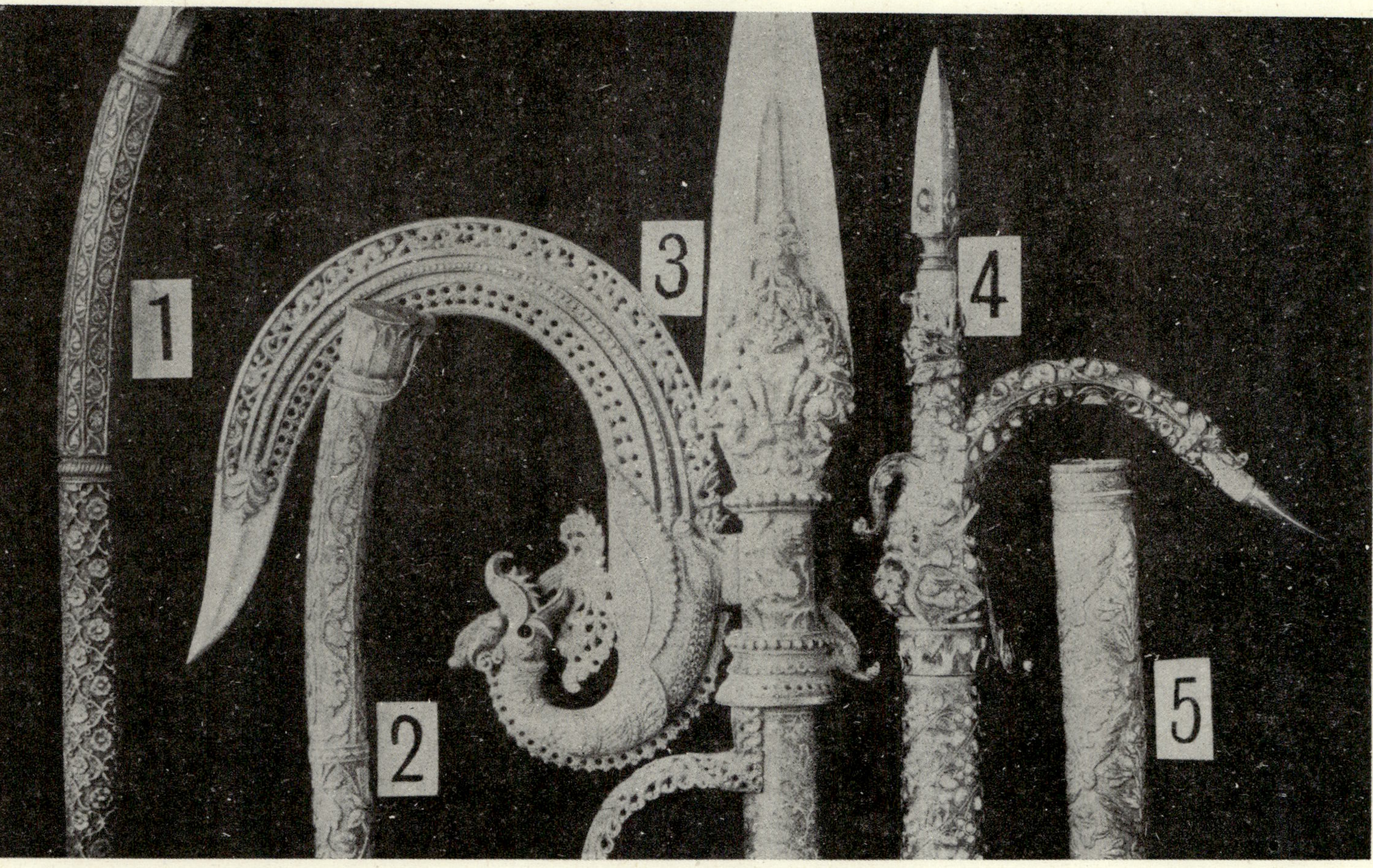

Plate No. 66 Carved Steel

Painted and Lacquered wares;" etc. Moreover the character of the goods for each division having been already fully discussed, it in many cases remains only to indicate by the names of the exhibitors the chief examples of each division. It is believed the visitor may find the course adopted the most instructive for Loan Collections and the least burdensome. Acting on this belief, opportunity has been taken by the writer, in connection with the Main Gallery, to refer, division by division, to the goods in the present gallery that should be studied by those specially interested in any particular description of art ware and to refer to the pages of the Main Gallery section where descriptions and other such particulars may be found.

Main Features.

COURSE TO BE FOLLOWED.—In the remarks below, therefore, the acccount of this gallery will keep two main ideas in view as follows:—(A) To exemplify the chief features of the Loan Collection; (B) To record the names of the chief exhibitors. In pursuance of these two purposes the writer will endeavour to link up all that has gone before by referring to the passage where the goods of the Loan Collection have already been discussed. In fact the remarks that follow will only supplement what has been said where it is felt that additional particulars may be of value to the visitor. Lastly, in order to preserve relationship to the owners, the course will, as a rule, be followed to discuss in the position of greatest interest all the collections sent by each person.

CHIEF FEATURES OF THE LOAN COLLECTION.

Class I.—Metal Wares.

The Loan Collection Metal Wares may be said to be specially rich in Division 1, Iron and Steel Arms: Division 3, Enamelled Wares: Division 4, Gold and Silver Plate: Division 5, Damascened and Encrusted Wares, and Division 6, Old Copper and Brass, especially the collections of idols, lamps, etc.

Chiselled Steel.

CHISELLED STEEL, TANJORE.—Among the arms special attention must be directed to the examples of carved or chiselled steel. These have already been referred to (page 14 and Plate No. 4). There are several sets in the Exhibition that specially deserve study, but those from the Madras Museum stand out as perhaps the finest of all. It is recorded that the swords, gauntlets,

ENAMELS.

elephant goads (*ancus*), daggers (*khanjars*), maces (*gargaz*) of this fine series were procured from the Tanjore palace. Plate No. 4 shows a selection of these, but Plate No. 66 gives one of the goads in greater detail. The steel will be seen to be richly chiselled while the handle is elegantly damascened in silver.

BIKANIR.—His Highness the Maharaja of Bikanir contributes the second series of chiselled arms. This consists of several iron sticks (*gedias*) and spear heads. Plate No. 66, figs. 1, 2, and 5, shows three of these. The State armourer informed the writer that the one shown as fig. 2 (No. 2146 of the invoice) was an iron *gedia* made at Gujarat; it is in carved steel diaper pattern with drooping fuchsia-like flowers. This is reported to have been made about 300 years ago and to have been procured in the time of His Highness Anup Singh as loot from the fort of Aduni in Gujarat. Nos. 2147 and 2150 are spear heads damascened in silver and gold, the borders being cut steel. These were also obtained from the fort of Aduni in Gujarat.

Three Hundred years old.

JODHPUR.—In a further paragraph the arms from Jodhpur will be discussed in connection with damascening. Their chief interest lies in the beautiful examples of that art, which they manifest, but at the same time it may be mentioned in this place that many of them have also the barrels and steel fittings of the matchlocks admirably engraved and chiselled. Plate No. 72 shows three of these matchlocks; figs. 1 and 2—more especially the latter—manifest excellent chiselled steel.

Matchlock Fittings Chiselled.

Enamelled Ware.—The chapter on this subject (pages 21-30) alludes to several of the Loan Collection samples. It may be useful to amplify the information there furnished by the following special notes from the chief exhibits in the present gallery.

LONDON.—The Victoria and Albert Museum of South Kensington, has furnished one or two articles to which special attention may be invited in this place, such as the fine examples of Lucknow and Rampur enamels and the elephant goad, the handle of which is both richly jewelled and beautifully enamelled in Jaipur style (see Plate No. 66, fig. 4, and Plate No. 68-A, fig. 3).

JAIPUR STYLE.—Plate No. 67 shows three samples of enamelling. Fig. 1 is a sword from the United Provinces (No. 2655) in

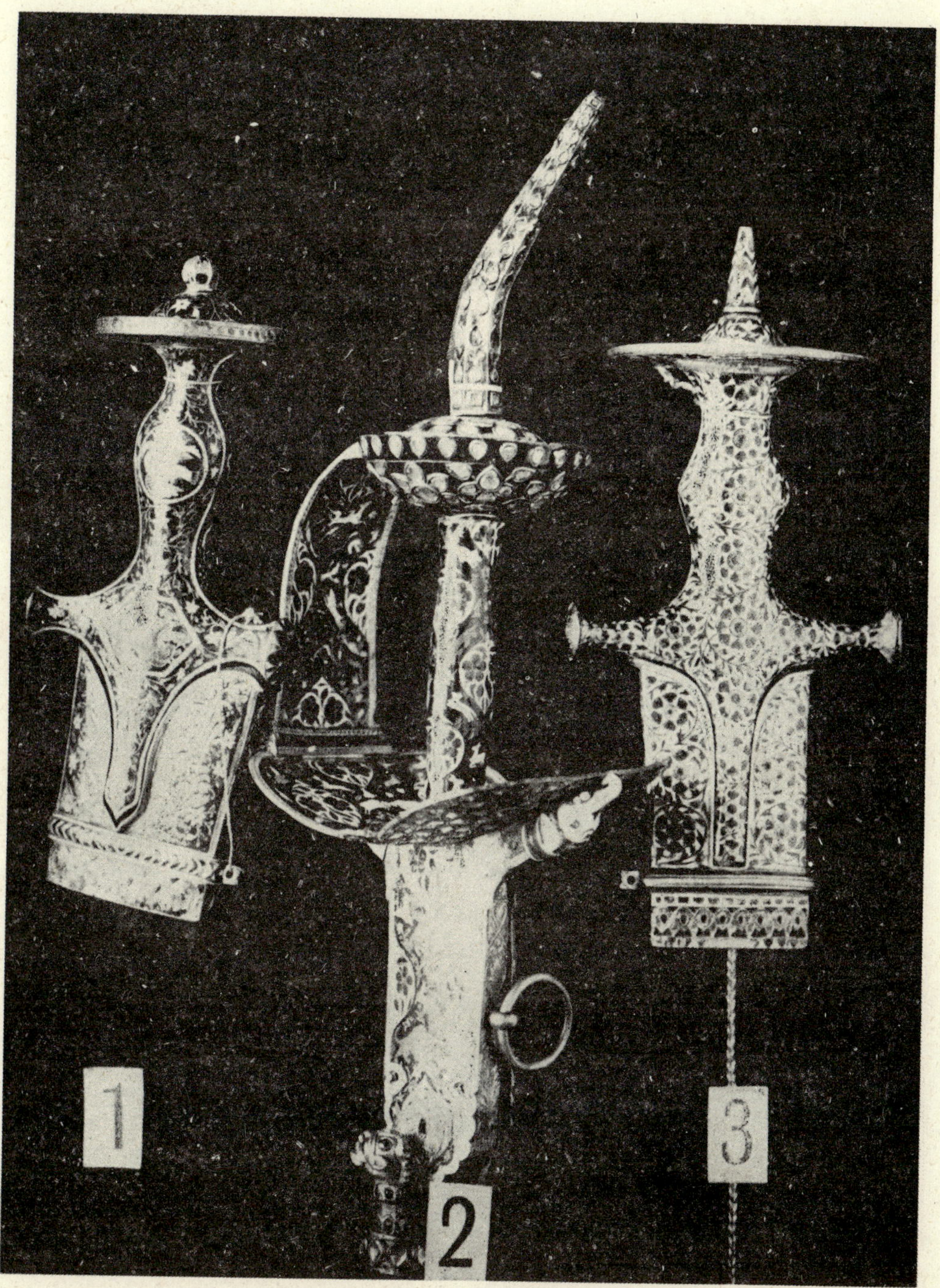

Plate No. 67 Sword Hilts in Jaipur Enamel

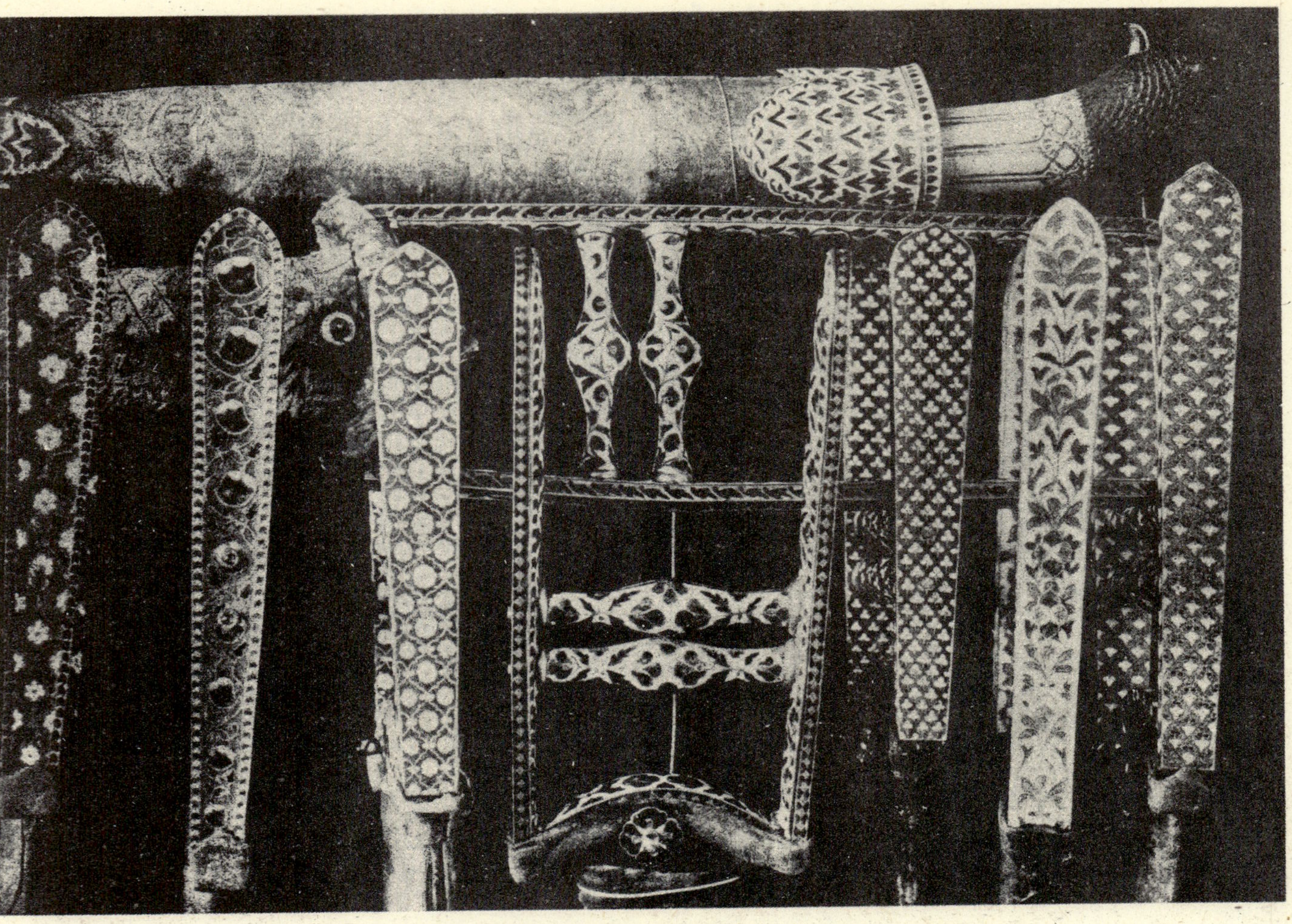

Plate No. 68 Enamelled Daggers Exhibited by His Highness the Maharajah of Chamba, Jaipur Style very possibly

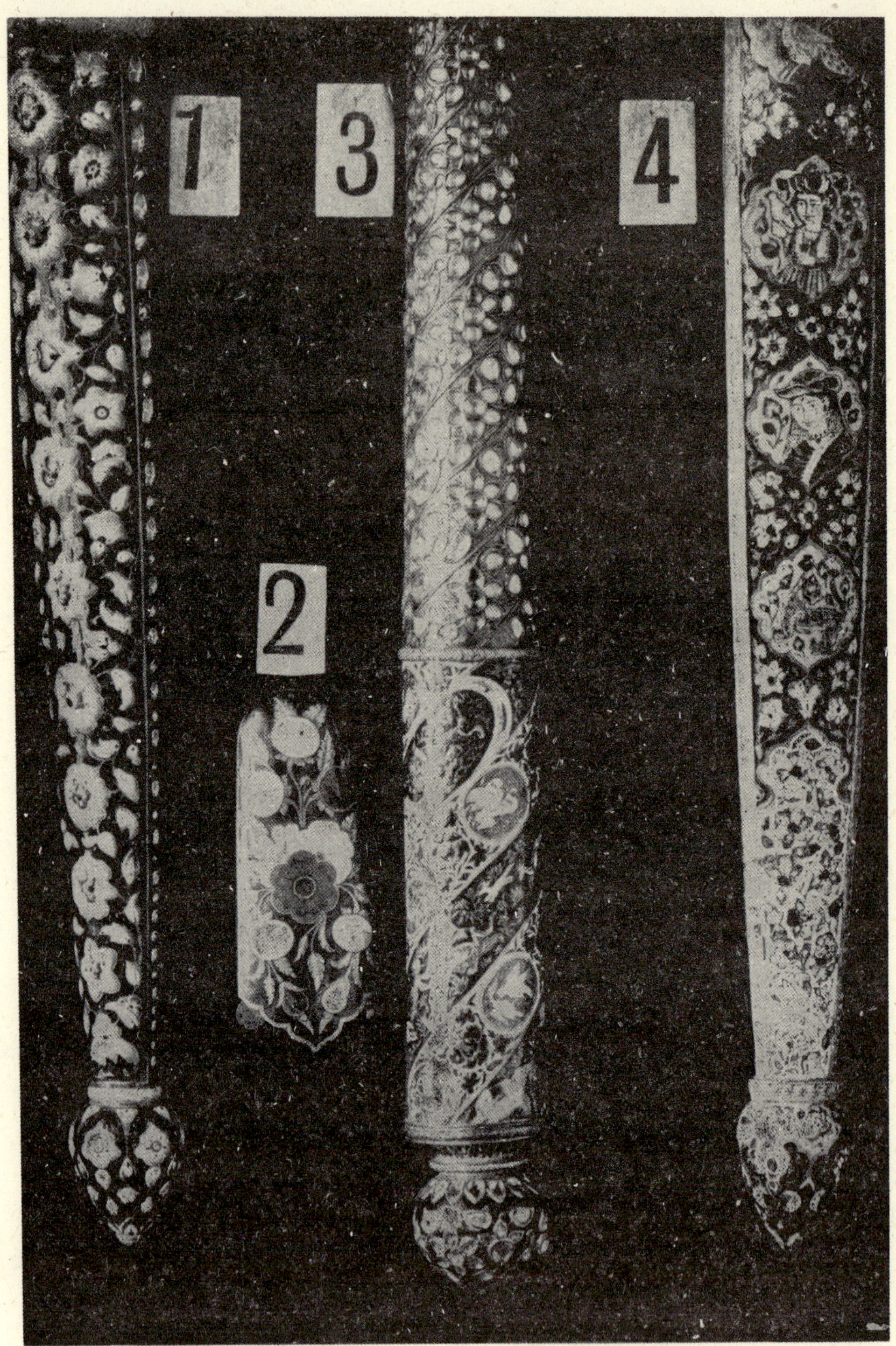

Plate No. 68-A Bhawalpur, Jhalawar, and Kach Enamels

which the enamelled field is of a transparent red with floral scrolls worked over it in white and with green leaves and birds mostly also in white. Fig. 2 is a sword exhibited by His Highness the Maharaja of Cooch Behar. The field is green with medallions dispersed all over. These have special fields in white with, worked over them, scrolls in deep transparent red. The main field shows animals in yellow, white, and blue colours. Fig. 3 is a *talwar* exhibited by His Highness the Maharao of Udaipur. The field is greenish white, flowered in deep red with blue centres and green floral scrolls.

Chamba Enamels.

CHAMBA.—His Highness the Raja of Chamba sends a superb series of gold enamels. These are shown in Plate No. 68. They are in Jaipur style. Commencing from the right they are as follows:—(1) Enamel in ruby red ground with white flowers, green leaves outlined in gold. (2) Sapphire field with ruby and white flowers and gold diaper. (3) Ruby red field, white flowers, and gold diaper. (4) Field white, flowers ruby red, leaves green, outlined in gold. (5) Field green, trifoil pattern white, outlined in gold. (6) Field white, flowers sapphire, leaves green outlined in gold. (7) Field dark blue, flowers white, leaves minute green, outlined with gold. (8) White field, red flowers, and green leaves. (9) Field white, iris flowers blue, leaves green.

BAHAWALPUR.—Plate No. 68a shows a series of enamels that have been already more or less alluded to, but of which it appears desirable to record a few additional facts. Fig. 1 is a dagger scabbard (see p. 23) exhibited by His Highness the Nawab of Bahawalpur. The sheath is completely enamelled, field dark green, flowers blue with white and red centres, handle in fossil ivory (see page 173).

KACH.—Fig. 2 is a sword tip (*kholi*) (p. 24); field green, leaves gold engraved, flowers in blue, yellow, and pink. The prevalence of blue caused the failure of the photographic reproduction. This is exhibited by His Highness the Maharao of Kach and was made by Mulji Naranji.

A pair of finger rings, made by artists of old times; the field is of green, with the flowers pink and yellow. These are exhibited by Sardar Rana Shree Jalam Sanghji.

ENAMELS.

The Bhuj workers seem to have attained a higher proficiency in the art of enamelling than has been acquired in any other part of India, not even excepting Jaipur. Their glaze is uniform throughout, is firm and enduring, and they seem to be able to graduate their colours so as to give the shadings of petals. But their colours are devoid of the depth and transparency of Jaipur enamels. The Bombay School of Art has for some years been pioneering improvements in the art of enamelling. The collections contributed will be found in the Main Gallery and it will be seen, page 30, that a medal for its display has been awarded to the School.

JAIPUR.—Fig. 3 is the handle of a jewelled and enamelled *ancus* from the South Kensington collection. The enamelling would appear to be in Jaipur style.

Sporting Scenes.

JHALAWAR.—Fig. 4 shows a dagger from this State having a crystal haft and richly enamelled scabbard. The field is green but carries medallions, the colours of which are pale blue supporting figures and animals mostly in red. In one medallion a hare is being caressed, in a second it is caught by a hawk, and in a third the hawk has returned to the hawker.

Crown for the Deity.

JODHPUR.—His Highness the Maharaja has sent some very interesting enamels of which the following are specially deserving of study:—No. 3506, a helmet of the deity Nathji Maharaja. It is about 80 years old. Is enamelled in green and white zig-zag (*lahria*) lines and has 222 diamonds with one large emerald. It weighs 64 tolas and is an article of worship with the people in the State. Dagger (No. 3508) with the handle in green enamel on silver. A pair of gold bangles (No. 3512) with alligator heads enamelled in green and red and studded with diamonds, rubies, etc.

Historic Sword.

LUCKNOW.—In this collection there are many good bits of enamelling in the Lucknow style, but none so interesting nor so good as the sword exhibited by His Highness the Maharaja of Benares. This was presented by the King of Oudh to Maharaja Balawant Singh in 1768 A.D. The hilt is in silver and the enamelling in the characteristic intricate pattern, with large surfaces of silver exposed. The pattern is in a graceful scroll with conspicuous blue flowers and green leaves having orange coloured

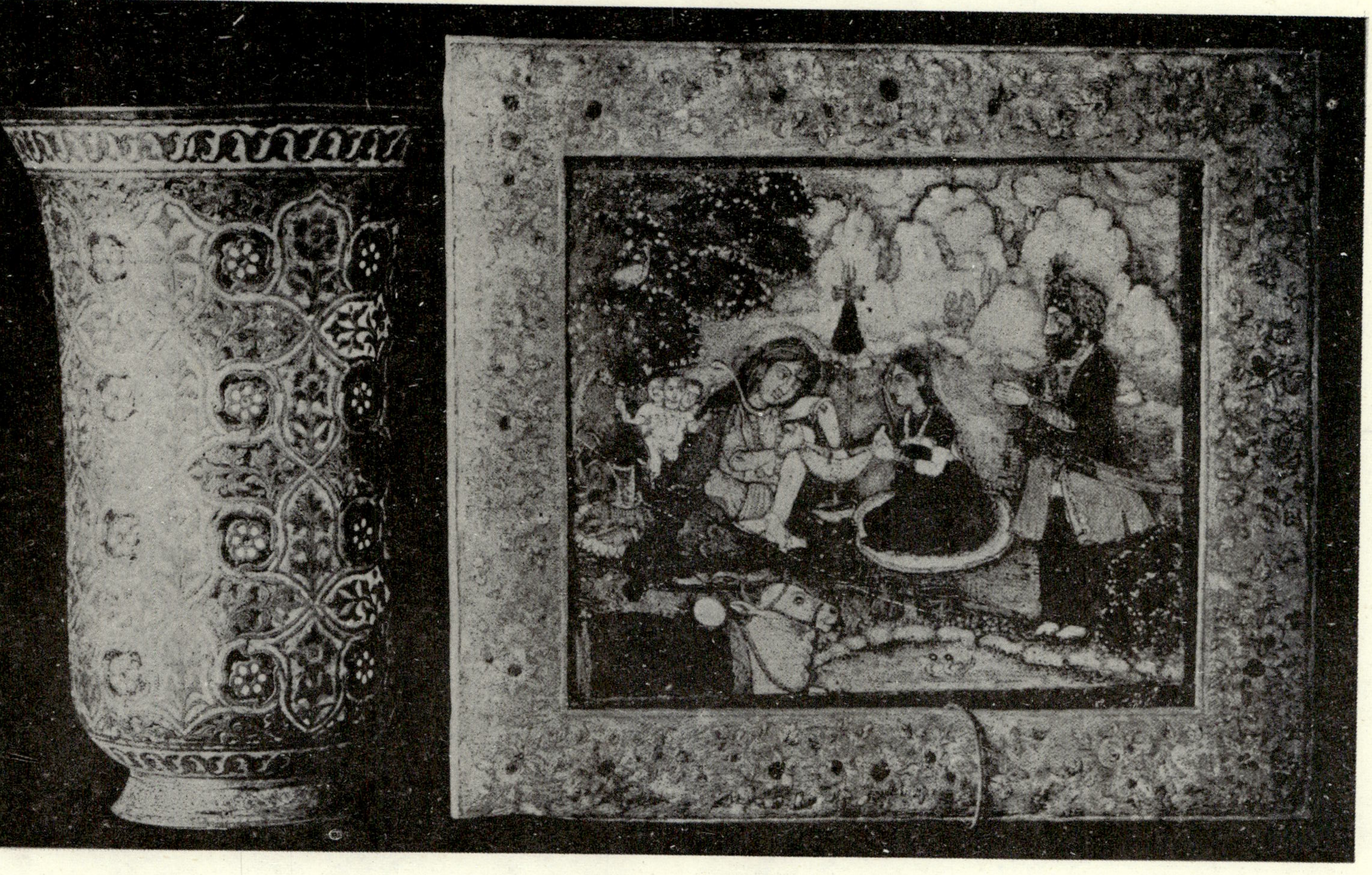

Plate No. 69 Kashmir Enamels

also pale turquoise blue shadings—a style that recalls the oval box seen on Plate No. 6. On the other the modern form of birds, with the arbitrary circular tail of the peacock, as in Plate No. 6,—Rampur *hukka,* are seen on the scabbard. It is thus fairly certain that the scabbard enamellings are much more recent than those on the hilt of the sword itself. **ENAMELS.**

The Nawab Hyder Mirza of Lucknow exhibits an enamelled *attar-dan.* His Highness the Maharaja of Bikanir shows a large silver *hukka* (No. 2115) richly enamelled in Lucknow style, valued at Rs. 700. It comprises oval medallions with floral ornamentations and peacocks, pheasants, etc.

PANJAB.—In the Panjab Room will be seen a few examples of the old enamelling of this province. These were done on chased copper, the lower portions being charged with dark blue enamel. Good specimens are lent by the Lahore Museum. His Highness the Raja-i-Rajgan of Kapurthala also sends one and Sardar Sarup Singh of Lahore another.

KASHMIR. (Plate No. 69).—The Sri Pratap Singh Museum contributes an enamelled plate, in style quite unlike anything done at the present day in Kashmir; it resembles very closely Persian work. It portrays Shiva and Parvati with the Raja in the attitude of devotion. In the same plate has been shown an exceptionally fine specimen of the usual style of Kashmir enamelling. The Raja, General Sir Amar Singh, K.C.S.I., has lent to the Exhibition a superb *aftaba* and *tasht* from his unique collection of the artwares of the State that will be seen as the great central feature of the metal trophy.

Gold and Silver Plate.—The collections received from the Princes of India, under this division, are so extensive and diversified that space can alone be provided to acknowledge the names of the owners and in passing to mention here and there some of the examples that amplify the particulars already afforded. But a collection of very special interest may be said to be the silver plate contributed by the Victoria and Albert Museum of South Kensington.

PANJAB.—Dewan Bhagwan Das of Lahore has sent a fine old Kashmir silver vase. His Highness the Nawab of Bahawalpur

GOLD AND SILVER PLATE.

has contributed perhaps one of the most interesting of all the collections of silver and gold plate in the Exhibition. His Highness the Raja-i-Rajgan of Kapurthala shows a gold plate of great beauty. Raja General Sir Amar Singh of Jammu shows some remarkably fine examples of old Kashmir and Thibetan silver, especially a coffee pot and a smoking pipe.

RAJPUTANA AND CENTRAL INDIA.—His Highness the Maharaja of Bikanir exhibits many articles in silver, such as a portable throne made by Kesho Thathera: a silver *hindola* or idol cradle made in Jodhpur, also a silver swing shown at the entrance into the Loan Gallery: this was made by Chhoga Thathera. A collection of gold and silver articles such as a claret jug, in form of a duck, a silver rose water sprinkler in "China style," a pair of silver ducks made by Rattu and Kesa Thathera of Bikanir. His Highness the Maharao of Udaipur has sent to the Exhibition *hukkas* of silver and gold.

His Highness the Maharaja of Jodhpur has sent (No. 752) a *golab-dani* of silver the bottom portion of which is done in neillo work the remainder gilded. In form it is also very quaint, being composed of two trumpet shaped portions supporting a pair of tigers. No. 754—a complete set of elephant jewellery in silver, the head covering being made up of a mass of embossed flowers The bangles are 3 feet long and composed of seven plates with connecting links.

CENTRAL PROVINCES.—Though curious and interesting historically, the silver and gold plate and ornaments from these provinces are not very extensive nor imposing. The following may be specially mentioned:—a silver engraved *hukka* exhibited by Babu Tantya Naidu of Saugor, a silver belt sent by Maktum Hussain, Jamadar of Chanda, a collection of silver and gold ornaments sent by K. Anand Rao Sharma, Tahsildar of Chanda, a pair of gold ornaments lent by Padisal Luxmiah Shahookar of Chanda and, lastly, a pair of gold ornaments sent by Tota Baliah Shahookar of Chanda.

UNITED PROVINCES.—There is a large assortment of old silver from these provinces of which the following may be mentioned:—a silver *hukka* exhibited by Raja Rameshur Bux Singh of Sheogarh:

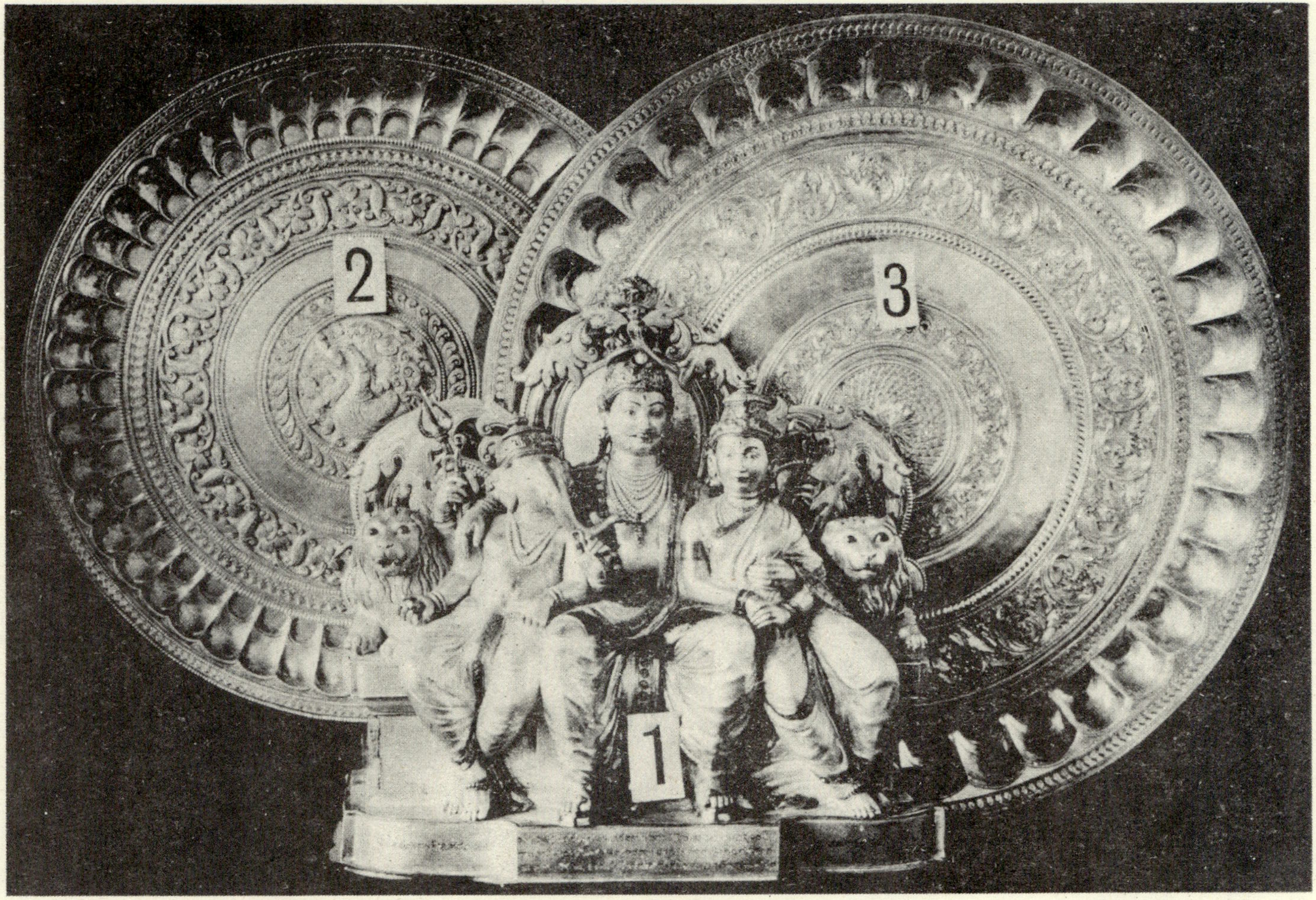

Plate No. 70 Bijapur Silver

GOLD AND SILVER PLATE.

a similar *hukka* by Maharaja Jug Mohan Singh, C. I. E., of Rai Bareilly: a silver *aftaba* exhibited by Rana Sheo Raj Singh of Khajur Guon, Rai Bareilly: a silver vase, shown by the Nawab Hyder Mirza of Lucknow. A large series of silver and silver and gilt ware contributed by the Hon'ble Munshi Madho Lal of Benares: a similar collection by His Highness the Maharaja of Benares: a collection of silver articles exhibited by Pandit Gauri Shanker Misra of Benares: a silver swing for the idol sent by Joshi Parmanand and Keshoji of Benares: a collection of silver lent by B. Moti Chand of Benares.

Nepal Silver.

BENGAL.--His Highness the Maharaja of Tipperah has sent to Delhi a selection of silver plate and a silver *hukka*. The most interesting examples of silver from this province very possibly may be said to be the example of *mandila* filigri work (see p. 38) contributed by His Highness the Nawab Salimullah of Dacca. For Exhibition (administration) purposes Nepal has been placed in the Bengal circle, and it has, therefore, to be remarked in this place that the four silver vases sent by His Excellency the Prime Minister of that State are most interesting and curious. But for the shape, which looks as if elaborated from an English flower pot, they would have occupied a high position as they are clearly the expression, by the goldsmith, of art conceptions that appear in the agglutinated and accumulative wood work by that State as in most of its arts. One of these silver vases has been shown in Plate No. 71. The Industrial Section of the Indian Museum, Calcutta, has placed on view a selection, from its treasures in gold and silver plate. These are very useful types by which to compare the work in the Sale Gallery. But they are not very old samples since they were procured in connection with the Calcutta International Exhibition of 1884.

BOMBAY.—The collection of silver that has attracted perhaps the most attention is the small series which the writer was able to procure in Belgaum (Plate No. 70). These are exhibited by Rao Bahadur R. C. Artal, Deputy Collector of Belgaum. It consists of a silver image representing Shiva seated on a throne with his wife "Parvati" on his left and their son "Ganapati" on the right. The grace and dignity of the female figure is quite

GOLD AND SILVER PLATE.

charming while the attitudes of all the others are considerably above the usual standard of Indian silver statuettes. The two richly engraved silver plates sent by Mr. Artal are very admirable examples of an almost lost style but one of which traces appear and reappear all over the central table land of India between Mysore on the west and Ganjam on the east. The *basawanna* or sacred bull in the action of rising (not shown in the plate) is very natural and is cleverly formed. The roll of the hind quarters with the elevation of the shoulder and the flesh-like texture of the surface of the animal, is truly wonderful. This is perhaps one of the best pieces of hammered silver in the Exhibition. It, as also the idol of Shiva, were made by Huwapabin Shirgappa Kanchgar of Bail Hongal of Belgaum, Bombay. The Bombay School of Art exhibits a small but excellent series of silver repoussé such as a hanging basket, a *toda*, or buckle, etc. The silver sporting shield, though hardly in Indian style, is an excellent piece of beaten silver.

KACH.—From this State have come many most curious and interesting samples of silver. The Rana Sardar Shree Jalam, Sanghji, has contributed a sugar basin made by Sutar Harji Rattansi of Bhuj and a tea pot by the same maker that seem to combine some quaint old English ideas with the work of Bhuj. From the Bhuj Museum have come some *Jambhaia* handles that are very well worth inspection.

BARODA.—His Highness the Maharaja Gaekwar has sent many very interesting samples of silver to the Exhibition, but the majority show such a striking resemblance to the work of Tanjore and Madura as to suggest the probability of their being in reality South Indian work. The silver *hindola* or idol swing is one of the most pretentious examples of silver in the Exhibition, but cannot be said to possess artistic merit above the most ordinary type. The gold *kalas* or corner pieces of the pearl carpet have already been described. They each weigh 514 tolas of gold and are closely studded with large diamonds. They were made under the orders of His Highness the late Maharaja Khanderao Gaekwar for presentation to the tomb at Mecca. But as the Hindu court and subjects greatly disapproved

GOLD AND SILVER PLATE.

of the Gaekwar's proposed trip to Mecca the idea was abandoned. The other articles shown by His Highness the Gaekwar of Baroda may be reviewed as follows:—No. 1024, a silver filigri model of a State elephant with gold gilt *howdah* (contributed by the Baroda Museum). No. 1046, a silver *kasandi* (*garrah*) upper portion painted in water colours and coated with lac, design quaint but not elegant. No. 1027, a silver kamal—*seat* of Mahadev—the *nandi* below the lotus flower supporting Shiva. No. 1028, a silver *sinhasan* (throne of Mahadev) partly gilt, with *nandi* resting on lotus in front of the five-headed cobra and within a canopy—doubtless procured from South India. No. 1036, a silver perforated *pan-dan*. This is punched by a minute square punch into a mass of openings arranged in a diaper fashion until it resembles filigri at a distance, but is much superior, the silver surface appearing like a woven texture—in a sort of *patola* pattern. No. 1042, a silver *gela* (*musak*-shaped water bottle) in silver. Seems done in Poona repoussé. No. 1043 is a silver *surahi* richly chased in a pattern similar to that on the common *surahis*. No. 1049 is a silver *lota* furrowed and with floral medallions at fixed interspaces—very similar to the engraved *lotas* of Trichinopoly.

Imitation Filigri.

MADRAS.—Perhaps the best known gold ornaments of South India are those produced at Vizianagram. One of the pieces placed on the knop of the back hair is shown on Plate No. 71. It is interesting to compare the design there shown with the ornamentation elaborated on the back of the turtle on Plate No. 77. Both belong to the same period and school of decorative art (see p. 182) and need not be further discussed. The following are the contributors of Vizianagram jewellery:—K. Ramayyammpur Dachipatti Chetti Garu, Mr. W. H. Gillman, D. Ramgan Garu, all of Vizianagram.

Court Jewels.

The Receiver of the Palace at Tanjore shows a few out of the superb collection of court jewellery in his charge. At the writer's suggestion he sent only those in gold, not expensive jewelled ornaments. The samples of gold plates and other head ornaments hardly if at all differ from those of Vizianagram. It is not clear whether these were not actually made at

GOLD AND SILVER PLATE. Vizianagram and may not therefore be in any way characteristic of Tanjore.

The Trevandrum Museum exhibits two or three very fine pieces of the peculiar style of damascening met with in Travancore State (see page 46 and Plate No. 11-A, figs. 13 and 14).

MYSORE.—His Highness the Maharaja of Mysore contributes an excellent sample of embossed or repoussé silver in the form of a large tympanum depicting the patron saint of the State. It is in a carved wooden frame with the armorial bearings ("the double-headed eagle") of Mysore on the top, and represents the goddess *Chamundy* of the Mysore Royal House, slaying the demon *Mahishasura*: the figure on the left is that of *Saraswati*, the goddess of learning attended by her maid and that on her right, *Lakshmi*, the goddess of wealth attended by her maid.

From the palace has also been procured a splendid silver plate in Poona style which depicts in zones the various scenes from the Ramyana. The Bangalore Museum shows some excellent silver statuettes (page 32).

BURMA.—In the Loan Collection Gallery will be seen the finest examples of silver plate in the Exhibition. Some of these are old samples, others were specially made for the present Exhibition but have already been secured for the Rangoon Museum. Plate No. 9-A shows three exceptionally fine samples—that in the centre having obtained from the Judges of this Exhibition the gold medal for being the finest piece of silver plate shown at the Exhibition in any style. It was made by Maung Yin Maung of Rangoon. The illustration most unfortunately fails to convey anything like a faithful impression of the characteristic features of this wonderful piece of work.

Damascened and Encrusted Wares (*See pages 42-51*).—The series of these wares on view in the Loan Collection very far excels anything to be seen in the Sale Gallery—a circumstance that abundantly confirms the opinion already advanced that the art of ornamenting one metal by the adhesion of portions of other metals, in artistic assortment, originated with the necessity for arms and armours. The decadence of the craft was doomed with the modern impersonal character of warfare and with the

Decadence of Damascening.

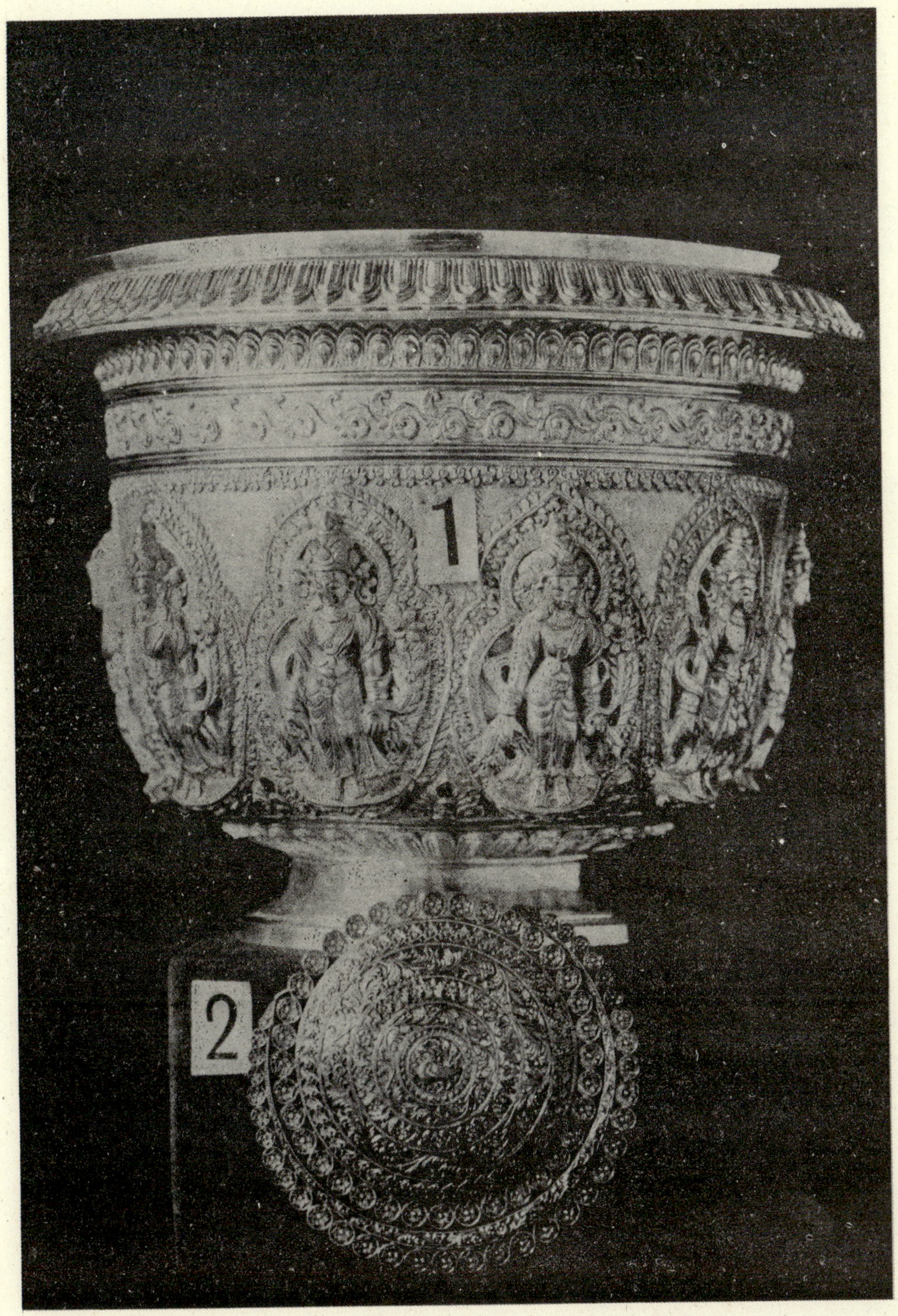

Plate No. 71 (No. 1) Nepal Silver, (No. 2) Vizianagram Gold

DAMASCENED AND ENCRUSTED WARES.

discovery of methods and materials of destruction accomplished at great distances. The final blow was given to the craft by the reign of peace and commerce, consequent upon the British supremacy. The more worthy samples on view may be studied in a provincial sequence, as has been done with the silver and gold plate, but space cannot be afforded to do much more than to mention the names of the contributors. The Victoria and Albert Museum of South Kensington, London, shows a splendid set of damascened and encrusted wares. These might perhaps be first inspected before giving attention to the collections derived from the armouries and museums of India.

PANJAB.—Nawab Mohamad Ali Quzlbash of Lahore sends a fine old matchlock damascened in gold. His Highness the Raja-i-Rajgan of Kapurthala sends a fair series of arms, swords, etc. Raja Kirti Singh of Shekhupura contributes a large assortment of admirable weapons, such as a dagger with a beautiful jade handle, set with jewels, many daggers damascened with gold, two sets of armour richly damascened in gold, and lastly beautiful gold damascened gauntlets.

RAJPUTANA AND CENTRAL INDIA.—The Raja Sahib of Ratlam has sent a coat of arms made of steel, with floral gold damascening, in a style which, it is believed, originated in Rampore State. A *talwar kona*—so called from its peculiar shape, is supposed to have been made in Persia and the enamelled work on the sheath to have been done at Jaipur State. The Maharao Raja of Bundi shows guns and swords richly damascened in gold.

His Highness the Maharawat of Deolia, Pertabgarh, has furnished a useful series of arms. A sword inlaid with gold is specially interesting. It was damascened at Pertabgarh on Rampur steel; a *kattar* gold damascened; a matchlock with the butt inlaid with ivory and damascened with gold said to have been made at Makran and used by the late Maharawat Dalput Singh.

Many very fine collections have been contributed by His Highness the Maharaja of Alwar. Of these a sword made by Mohomed Ibrahim and damascened by Thakursi Parsad is very interesting. Many similar swords may be seen which manifest

DAMASCENED AND ENCRUSTED WARES.

Pearls within the blade.

the greatest skill, for example one with pearls made to run within a longitudinal groove. A mace damascened in gold will repay careful study. It was prepared about a century ago for Maharao Raja Bakhtawar Singhji by Sheik Gul Ahmad. Other samples may be mentioned such as a gauntlet gold damascened : a hatchet of Cabul make—the handle and the blade plated with gold embossed with flowers. This is made of *kheri* iron and is supposed to have been done by Cabul artists. Lastly, armour plate richly damascened in gold purchased by Maharaja Binai Singhji.

His Highness the Maharao of Udaipur has sent a splendid collection of old historic weapons, many of them beautifully damascened. These include shields, arrows, swords, gauntlets, helmets, etc.

Matchlocks.

JODHPUR.—His Highness the Maharaja has kindly permitted his armoury to be freely drawn upon, the result being a superb series of matchlocks and other weapons of great artistic and historic interest. Of these 15 are of special merit, many having the barrels and fittings elaborated with *Zar Nashan koft* work. In this a small opening is first cut in the field and a piece of gold or silver encrusted. This is subsequently hammered and chased into the desired floral pattern in the manner described in connection with Sialkot, page 48. Plate No. 72, fig. 3, shows one out of many examples of this most beautiful work. Of other weapons the following may be mentioned:—No. 3507 is a dagger (*peshkabz*) of *kassoti* stone, jewelled with rubies and gold bands. This is the stone used by jewellers to estimate the amount of gold in jewellery. No. 3509 is another dagger, the handle of Makrana marble, inlaid with gold and studded with rubies and emeralds. No. 3510 is a dagger with rock crystal (*bittor*) handle engraved and studded with rubies. No. 3516 is a dagger with the handle made of *singhism* stone studded with rubies and emeralds, the latter carved. No. 3517 is a dagger with handle of inferior rock crystal called *bittor*. This is richly studded with gold recesses within which rubies and emeralds are imbedded. The guard covering the attachment is enamelled in dark green. No. 3515 is a sword (*khanda*), the handle of which is in silver with deep transparent massive green enamel, set with trifoil-like pattern of three rubies

Jewelled Daggers.

Fine old Sword.

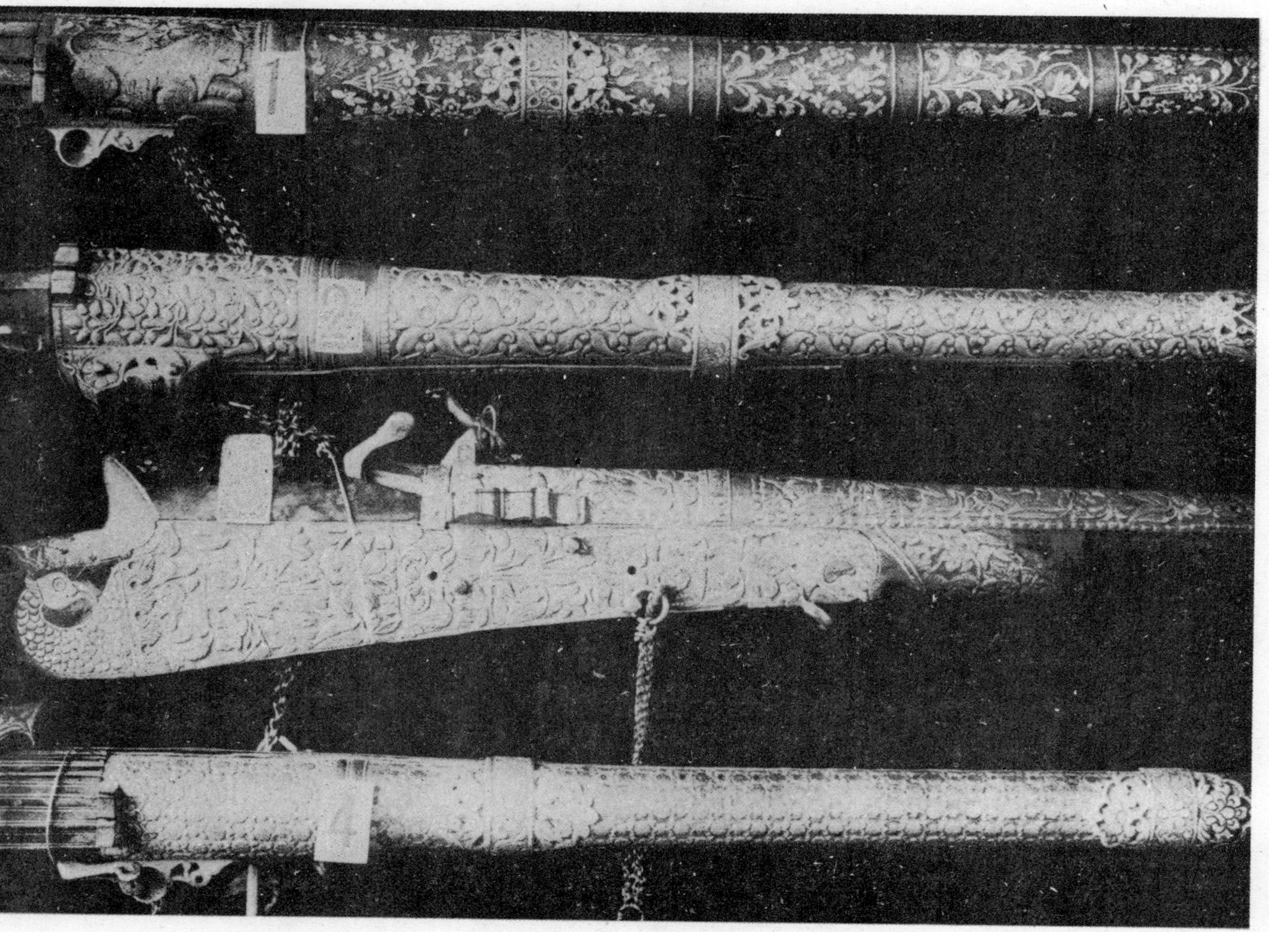

Plate No. 72 Chiselled and Damascened Matchlocks

DAMASCENED AND ENCRUSTED WARES.

and one diamond. There are 91 diamonds and 296 rubies. This was made in the time of Maharaja Abhai Singh, 150 years ago.

His Highness the Nawab of Tonk has similarly contributed a most interesting set of arms and armour such as matchlocks with gold damascening, chain armour, battle axe, daggers, shields, and gauntlets—all damascened in gold.

His Highness the Maharaja of Indragarh has sent to the Loan Collection a set of arms and armours. These embrace swords with *laharia* work, gold damascened shields, swords, spears, etc., many with old ivory and fish-tooth handles. So also the Thakur Lal Singh of Peepaldah of Kota has sent spears, daggers, etc., all gold damascened.

HYDERABAD.—A collection of old *bidri*-ware is shown by His Excellency Maharaja Kishen Parshar Bahadur, Prime Minister of Hyderabad.

BENGAL.—The Industrial Museum of Calcutta has sent some extremely interesting examples of Gujarat and Sialkot *koft*-work procured by that institution some 20 years ago. These show how the unpopularity of the goods has resulted in a serious depreciation in the merit of the articles turned out. The Calcutta Museum also furnishes many excellent examples of Tanjore encrusted ware which, like many other loan collections, manifest the cheapening process as having practically ruined the art.

UNITED PROVINCES.—Raja Rameshur Bux Singh of Sheogarh, Rai Bareilly, exhibits a collection of old arms made of iron, ornamented with deer horn (*bichwa*) and gold damascening, also knives of *foulad* with handles of *yashab*.

Maharaja Jug Mohun Singh of Rai Bareilly sends a sword, one side *foulad* and the other of iron: a spear with attached pistol made of iron and bamboo. Nawab Hyder Mirza of Lucknow has sent to this collection a small curious sword inlaid with silver. It is called *neemch* and has *ganga-jamni* work on the handle. B. Moti Chand of Benares shows a sword richly jewelled, the gold being engraved in sporting and hunting scenes in a quasi-European style.

His Highness the Nawab of Rampur sends a shield damascened in silver with deer's horn fittings. Nawab Ahmad Ali Khan

DAMASCENED AND ENCRUSTED WARES.

contributes a sword with *foulad* handle said to have been used by Nadir Shah and has his name damascened on the blade. He also sends a dagger with *sonahra* work.

Shah Wahid Alum, Deputy Collector of Benares, sends a splendid collection of arms consisting of spears, daggers, swords, etc. Most of these are historically interesting, many going back to the old Kings of Oudh. The owner says: "Burhan-ul-mulk and Safdar Jang, ancestors of the Kings of Oudh, were natives of Iran and were fond of arms of native manufacture. During the reign of Wajid Ali Shah, the last King of Oudh, arms were neglected and these daggers with some others fell into the hands of a Tahsildar of Oudh. A relation of this gentleman subsequently came to Jaunpur with these arms and married and died leaving a widow behind him who locked up all her late husband's property, including these daggers, till the passing of the Arms Act when they were confiscated and sold by public auction. The present owner being Tashildar of Jaunpur at the time purchased them."

Very old Oudh Weapons.

BENGAL.—Colonel His Highness the Maharaja of Cooch Behar, already alluded to as having sent a superb sword richly emamelled, also exhibits a shield beautifully inlaid and jewelled. Rai Mani Lal Nahar Bahadur of Azimganj shows an interesting collection of old *bidri* work. His Highness the Nawab of Murshidabad—one of the most liberal of the contributors to the Exhibition, also sends a small but beautiful collection of both gold and silver *bidri*. Syed Asad Reza of Purnea contributes a collection of old *bidri* illustrative of the style of work in that part of Bengal.

Bidri.

Nepal.

His Excellency the Prime Minister of Nepal shows a good series of *khukries*, some very ornate, others intended more to show the shape and quality of the knives made in Nepal.

BOMBAY.—Sardar Rana Shree Jalam Sanghji of Kach sends many daggers and other arms richly inlaid with gold (*vara* work) and often beautifully engraved.

Tanjore ware.

MADRAS.—Tanjore encrusted ware will be found represented by some fine old samples such as in the collection secured from the palace of Mysore and one or two good bits from Mr. J. Andrew, Collector of Tanjore.

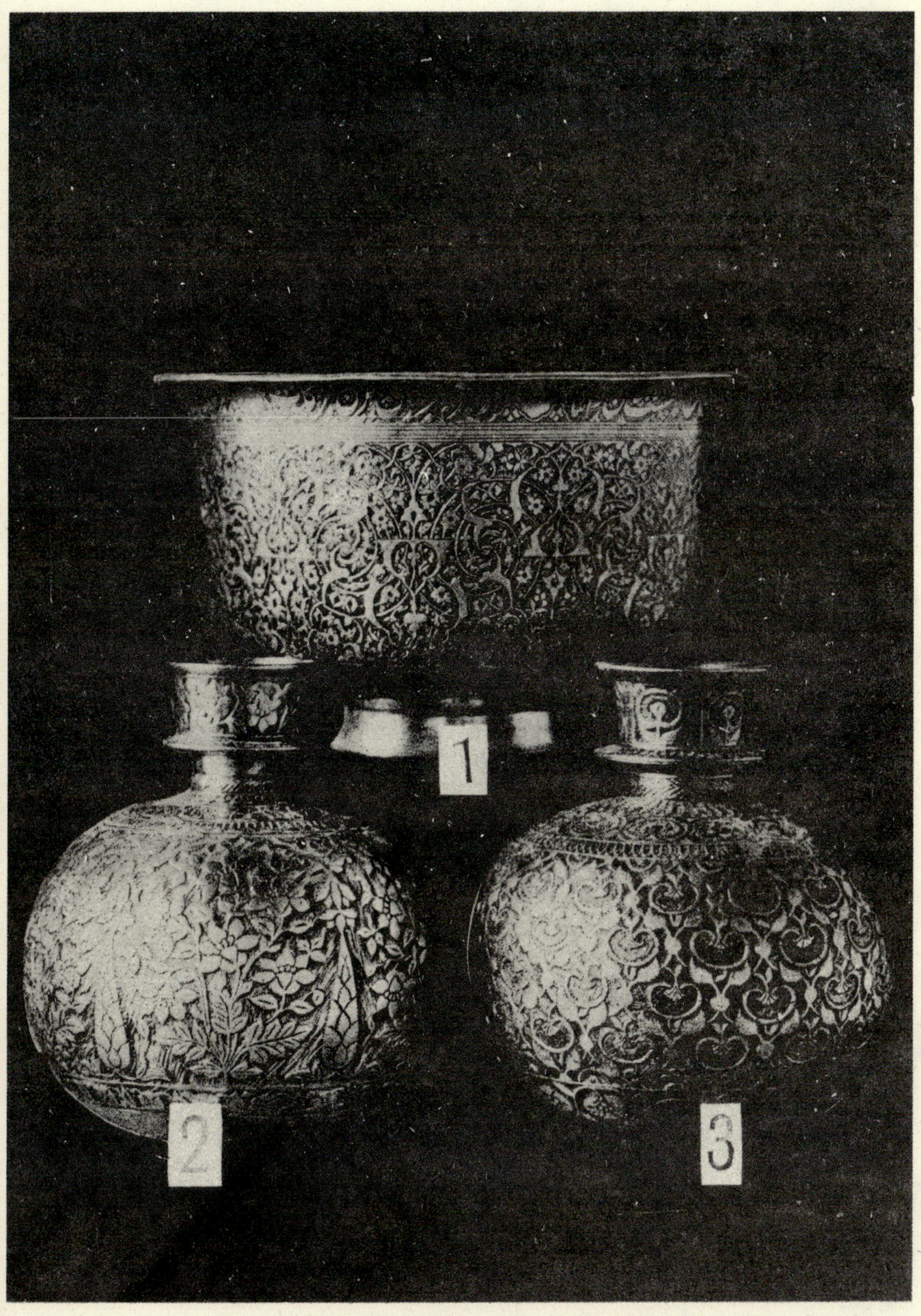

Plate No. 73 Copper and Brass Bowls from Victoria and Albert Museum, South Kensington

DAMASCENED AND ENCRUSTED WARES.

Copper and Brass.—The Victoria and Albert Museum of South Kensington has sent many very choice old bits of Indian brass and copper. The authorities of that Museum have fixed the probable dates of these samples and for comparative study they are accordingly of the highest interest and merit. Plate No. 73 shows a selection out of many of the copper and brass work. Fig. 1 is a bowl (*katora*) copper chased and backed with lac. It is worked in the arabesque style met with in Peshawar and Kashmir (see pages 16-17), but in the sample here shown the scroll is interlaced with spiral lines not commonly met with in modern examples. According to the label on this charming example, it dates from the 17th Century. Fig. 2 is a *hukka* bowl in brass chased and backed with lac. The flowering design, within foliated arcades, is very unlike anything produced at the present day in India. It is said to be from Nurpur in Kangra—a locality that has no reputation in India for its brass and copper wares and is most unlikely to have ever developed a form of *hukka* bowl seeing that the population are practically non-smokers. According to the label this beautiful piece of brass work dates from the 18th Century. Fig. 3 is another *hukka* bowl in brass chased in a conventional trellis. It is also said to have come from Kangra and to be 18th Century work. In the writer's opinion both this and the preceding are more likely to be Persian than Indian work. The present example has been chased, not punched in the Indian fashion.

Reputed Kangra work.

PANJAB.—The Lahore Museum sends a very complete series of Kashmir brass and copper, that dates back for some years and marks in a striking manner the recent deterioration that has taken place. Sardar Sarup Singh of Lahore exhibits an old brass candlestick. Dewan Bhagwan Das, Magistrate of Lahore, sends a copper dish and scent bottle in *filigri*.

BENGAL.—The Raja of Mourbhanj sends a collection of brass. The Industrial Museum, Calcutta, sends an extensive series of brass and copper wares.

BOMBAY.—The School of Art exhibits a large series of the hammered brass and copper work of its pupils.

MADRAS.—The School of Arts has made a great display of

DAMASCENED AND ENCRUSTED WARES. the extremely high relief work done in copper by its pupils. The Madras Room has in consequence many panels in this style of work that are marvels in technique, the idols standing from the surface in ¾ relief. The Madras Museum makes by far the best display of old bronze and copper and brass ware. Many of the samples shown have already been both figured and described in the *Indian Art Journal* so that it is only necessary to refer to them very briefly in this position. On the stair-case leading to the Loan Collection Gallery will be seen, right and left, most of the copper and brass treasures from the Madras Museum, such as the marriage lamp with 22 *chirags* suspended by chains from the various arms of the candelabra. This will be seen on Plate No. 12. On the landing and opposite to the lamp has been placed a spirited figure of Shiva (*Nadesa*) dancing within a loop of flame. Throughout the gallery may be discovered many more examples of the Madras Museum superb collection of old metallic idols and animals.

High Relief work.

Old Bronze Idols.

Bangalore Museum contributes several very carefully made idols with canopies in the same style as described on page 59 (Plate No. 13). These all manifest the Chalukyan demon spouting forth life—what the writer has called a *yali*.

Class II.—Stone and Glass Wares including Inlaid Stone.

There is very little to be added regarding these goods to what has already been detailed in pages 63 to 79, but the samples shown are so far superior to those of the Main Gallery that they will naturally attract special study. Of these the place of honour has of necessity to be given to the delightful series of jade, crystal and other such articles, as also to the historic tablets in marble-inlaying that have been sent to India by the Victoria and Albert Museum of South Kensington, London. One of the tablets has already been briefly alluded to (page 76 and shown on Plate No. 17-A), namely that showing Orpheus charming the animals. The other is in the form of a circular table with pieces of *pietra daura* let into it, that came from the fort at Delhi.

Historic Inlaid Marbles.

Of the jade, agate, and crystal ware from South Kensington, the following may be specially mentioned :—Plate No. 74, fig. 1

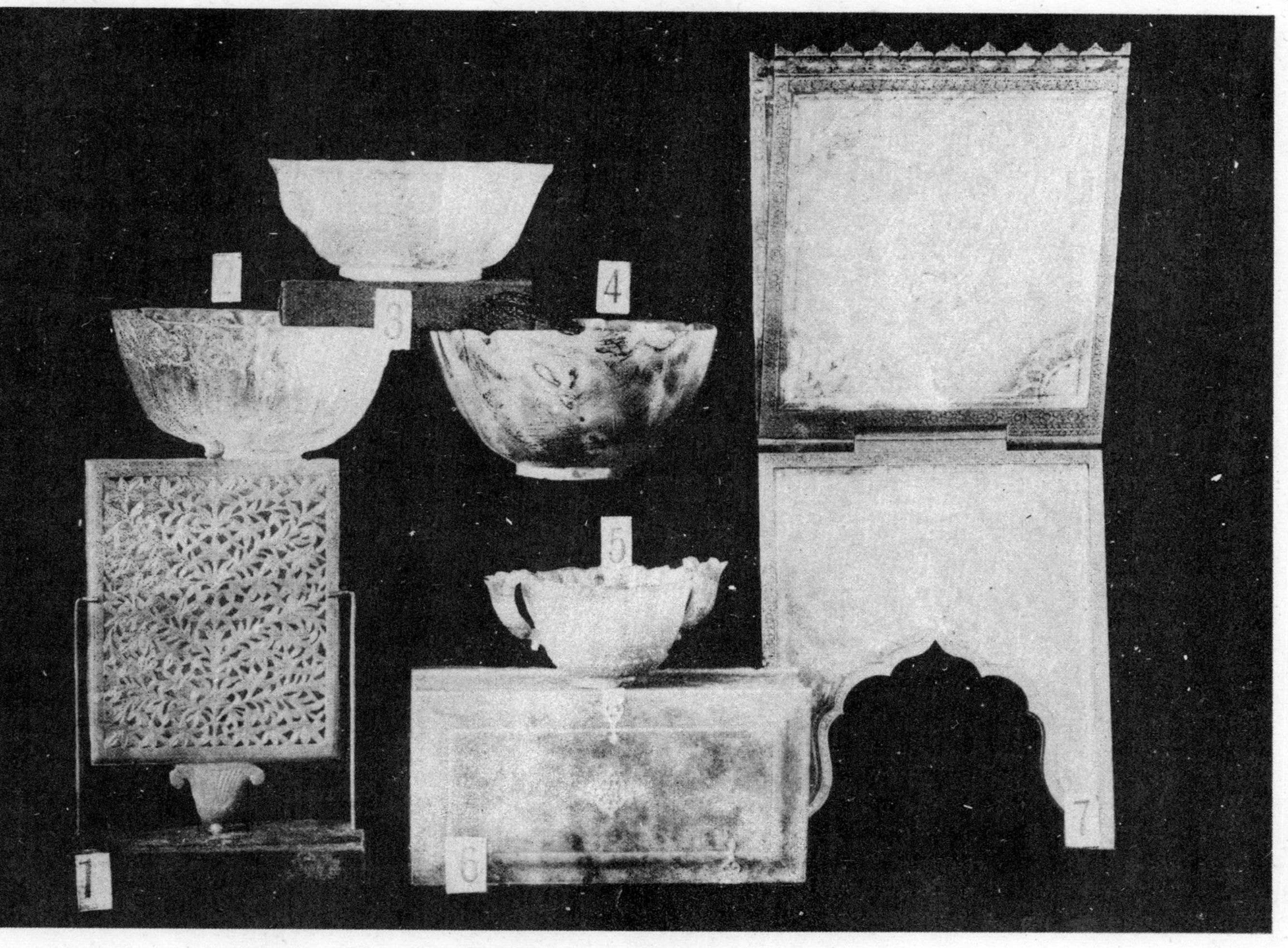

Plate No. 74 Jade Agate and Rock Crystal

JADE WORK.

Jade and Agate, etc.

shows a green jade rectangular carved and perforated plate in Indian style. Fig. 2 is a bowl in rock crystal, deeply fluted and carved outside: the stalks within the grooves support pendant lilies. This is supposed to have come from Agra and to have been made early in the 17th Century. Fig. 3 is another rock crystal bowl engraved with floral designs and having recurved handles. This is supposed to have come from Cambay. Fig. 5 is another agate bowl fluted and having handles in the form of the cornucopiæ. It is believed to be Indian.

In addition to these samples South Kensington Museum has also sent several very admirable examples of jewelled jade.

PANJAB.—His Highness the Maharaja of Kashmir and Jammu has sent from the Sri Pratap Singh Museum a splendid sample of jade that has been shown on Plate No. 75, fig. 2, and has already been alluded to (page 73). Major Stuart Godfrey has sent from Leh many interesting examples of engraved stones used as moulds. On Plate No. 74, figs. 6 and 7, will be seen examples of Bhera jade-stone work.

RAJPUTANA AND CENTRAL INDIA.—UDAIPUR.—His Highness the Maharaja of Udaipur contributes two charming jewelled jade *hukka* bowls. These are shown on Plate No. 75, figs. 7 and 8. The former has the pattern elaborated in carved emeralds and the latter in rubies. Many of the swords and daggers already discussed, as obtained from the various States of Rajputana and Central India, have jade or crystal handles often richly jewelled. In Plate No. 75 a few of the more characteristic ones have been shown. The dagger, fig. 1, will be found described on page 73.

UNITED PROVINCES.—Mir Fida Hussain, Rais of Nagram, Lucknow, sends a rosary of stone. Pundit Gauri Shanker Misra of Benares, a series of stone animals, *e.g.*, an elephant, a cow, etc., also spoons of *aqiq* stone.

BENGAL.—Mr. C. W. McMinn, of Tipperah, has sent a remarkably fine set of inlaid table tops in the best style of Agra work. These have already been briefly alluded to (page 78) and shown on Plate No. 17-A.

JADE WORK.

STONE WORK.

BOMBAY.—The Chote Sahib Molvi Sahib of Cambay has contributed a most interesting collection of carved agates, cornelians, illustrative of all classes of work and every stage in manufacture. (*Conf.* with page 73.)

MYSORE.—His Highness the Maharaja of Mysore has sent on loan a selection of the carved stone work as also of the inlaying in marble illustrative of the work being done for the new palace of Mysore. These have already been referred to on pages 69 and 78.

MADRAS.—Tanjore palace has contributed a few very admirable black stone idols and figures, similar to those produced at Madura.

Class III.—Ceramic Wares, Glass Mosaics.

In the Loan Collection Gallery there are no specimens of this class of such importance as to necessitate detailed descriptions. The Nagpur Museum shows a small set of the pottery formerly produced at Burhanpur. Babu Mall, Engineer, Raushanpura, Delhi, exhibits a few statues in clay.

The Victoria and Albert Museum has supplied some interesting examples of glass mosaics from Siam that probably may be regarded as the prototype from which may have been derived the Burmese glass work.

Class IV.—Wood-work.

In accordance with the divisions established on pages 100-1 for the class here indicated, the following remarks may be offered regarding the articles shown in the Loan Collection Gallery:—

Architectural Wood-carving.

PANJAB.—The entire fittings of the Panjab Room are intended to demonstrate the various styles of the province. The Panjab Museum has, however, contributed on loan many of the special features of these fittings, such as the carved *chaukat* with its *mehrab* arch from Bhera and several *bokharchas* from Amritsar. The Kashmir Manufacturing Company show a four-fold walnut screen in the modern style of Kashmir wood-work, described above on page 109. Mr. B. N. Bosworth Smith exhibits a carved doorway in the Bhera style already fully discussed.

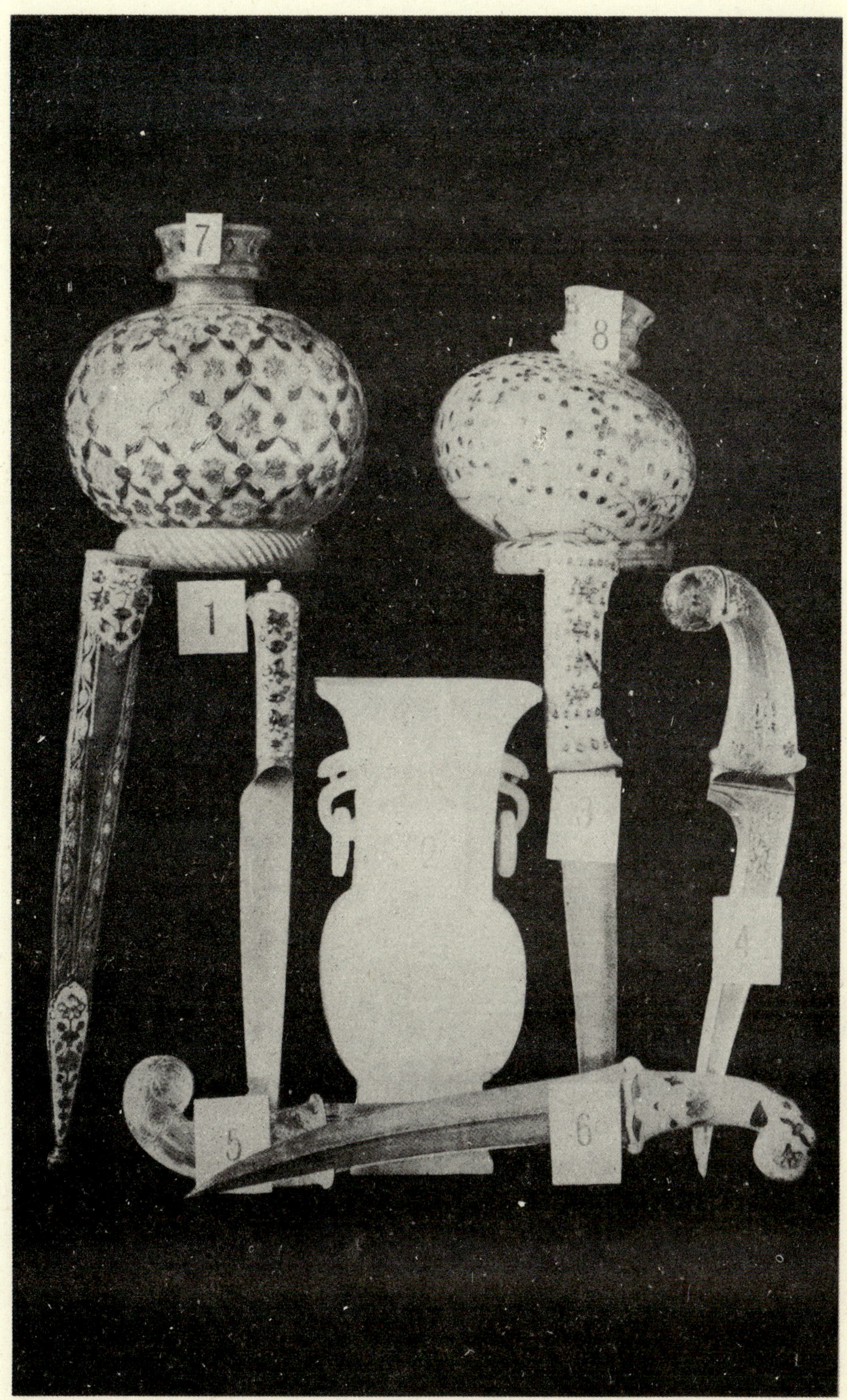

Plate No. 75 Jewelled Jade and Rock Crystal

ARCHITECTURAL WOOD-WORK.

UNITED PROVINCES.—A carved wooden screen made by Nek Ram, carpenter of Farukhabad. This has already been discussed (page 111) and shown in Plate No. 23.

RAJPUTANA AND CENTRAL INDIA.—The fine old carved doors from Chittor fully described and figured above (page 117) on Plate No. 26, are, according to one report, believed to have been made of sandal-wood.

BOMBAY—AHMEDABAD.—In the text of the Main Gallery (pages 122—6) full particulars will be found of the style of wood-work characteristic of that part of India. In the Loan Collection Gallery will be seen a screen made by Somnath Bhudar Das of Ahmedabad. This is one of the best of work, but owing to its being shown in this gallery has not been judged along with the samples specially submitted for competition. It is shown on Plate No. 27 to the right.

MYSORE.—His Highness the Maharaja of Mysore has generously allowed many of the carved doors and door-frames of his new palace at Mysore to be shown at Delhi. Of these several will be seen to be richly carved in animal and floral panels and scrolls. A carved wooden vase with graceful floral wreaths manifest the high proficiency that is outlined by the carvers of that State.

COCHIN.—The Dewan of Cochin has sent to Delhi a carved and inlaid chair that is worthy of study as illustrative of certain features that are perhaps local in origin.

Inlaying and Appliqué in Wood-work.

The Victoria and Albert Museum has sent some interesting examples of ivory and mother-of-pearl inlaying. These have been already briefly alluded to (page 208, Plate No. 43-D). It will be seen that in the older examples of this art a larger use of lac was customary than at the present day.

RAJPUTANA AND CENTRAL INDIA.—From Bikanir have been received two sandal-wood doors richly inlaid and overlaid with ivory. These have already been discussed (page 180), but it may be added that they belong to the balcony of Guj Mandir (elephant palace) and were made by Delhi workmen at the time of Surat Singh, 80 years ago. Being in sandal-wood they recall the still older Chittor doors that are also supposed to be made of sandal-

INLAYING. wood. From Bikanir has been received a work-box delicately and elaborately inlaid with ivory and mother-of-pearl, the latter being in a fairly well marked bed of lac. This is reported to have been made at Alwar.

KOTA STATE—Is chiefly known for its inlaying or veneering with mother-of-pearl (to be discussed in a further paragraph), but the act of inlaying with ivory is also well known. In the Loan Collection Gallery there will be seen a box inlaid with ivory said to have been made by Munna, a carpenter of the State.

MYSORE.—His Highness the Maharaja of Mysore has kindly permitted some of the beautiful examples of inlaid work presently being prepared for the new palace to be sent on loan to Delhi. Some of these have been shown on Plate No. 32, and it will be seen that the collection forms an imposing feature of the Loan Collection Gallery.

Sandal Wood-work.

MYSORE.—The Bangalore Museum sends a book slide in rich sharp deep carving, a form not very usual with the carvers of the State. His Highness the Maharaja of Mysore has contributed a superb series of carved sandal-wood, most of the pieces of which have already been alluded to, discussed, and figured (pages 150—2, Plates Nos. 36-A, 38, and 39).

MADRAS.—The Madras Museum sends two carved plaques of Mysore work.

Painted Wood-work and Papier Maché.

CALCUTTA and LAHORE Museums have amplified to some extent the collections of papier maché already discussed (pages 163—8) and a few good samples have also been procured both from KASHMIR and BIKANIR, but these do not seem to call for any special reference in this place. Perhaps the chief articles in the Loan Collection Gallery that need be mentioned here are the realistically painted wooden groups of gods from Mysore.

TANJORE palace has sent a model of the famous temple of that place elaborately painted in the style customary in that country. The model in question has, in the writer's opinion, been utterly ruined by being painted. It was an old model that he

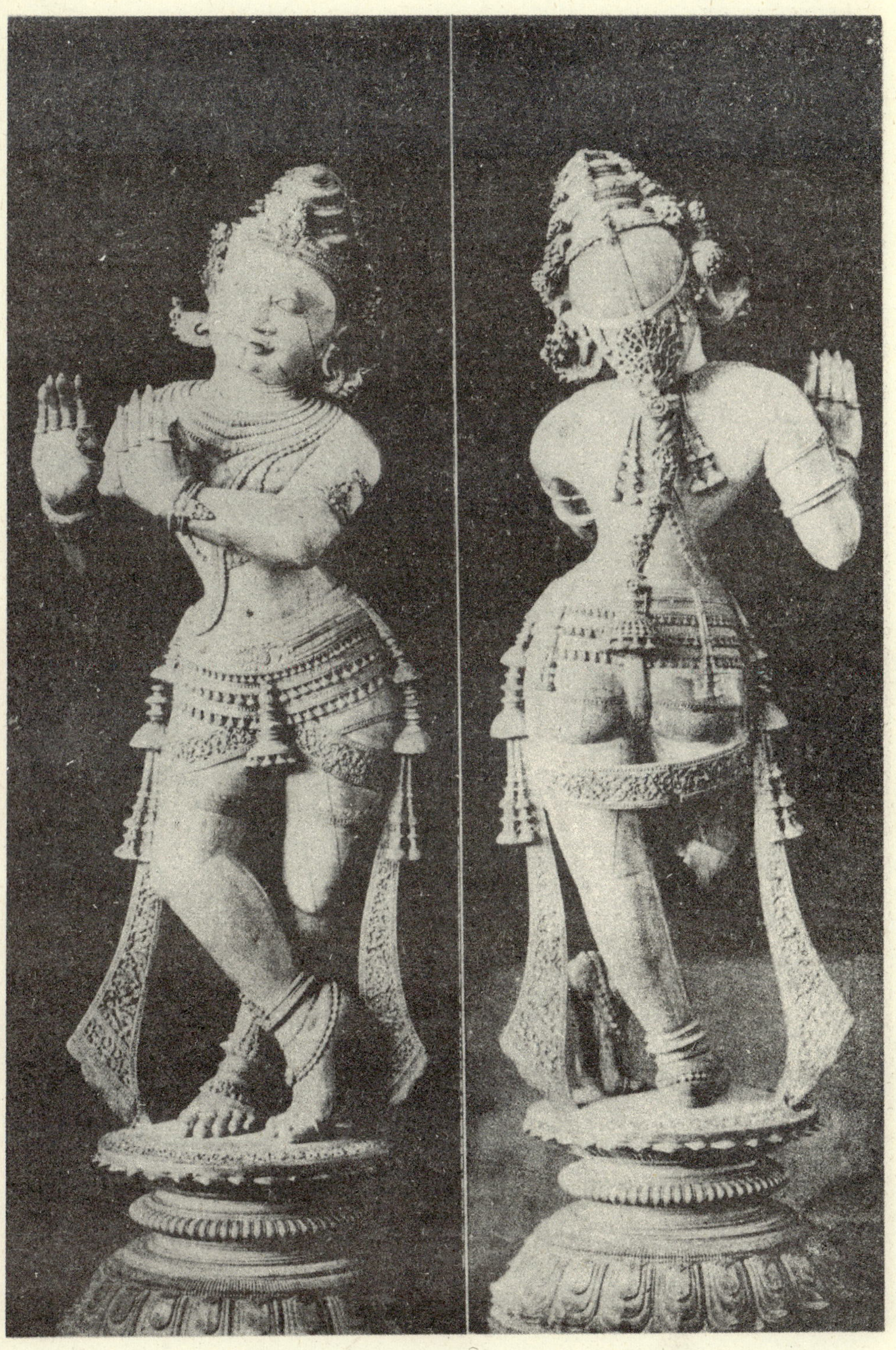

Plate No. 76 Krishna—Old Ivory from Orissa

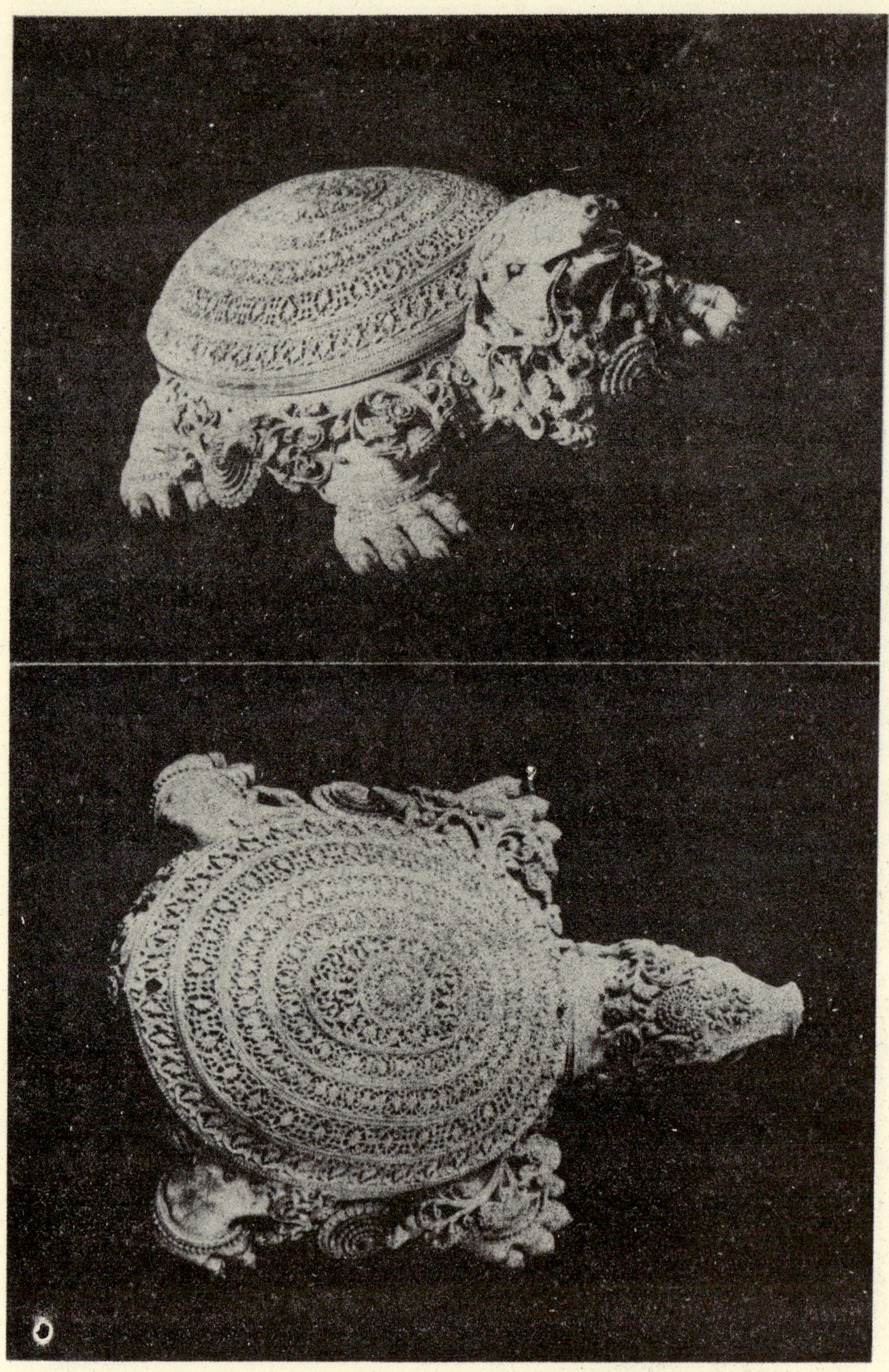

Plate No. 77 Mythological Tortoise—Old Ivory from Orissa

found in the palace and asked to have sent to Delhi, but it never occurred to him to warn the authorities not to paint the model in the modern most inartistic style of temple ornamentation. **PAINTED WOOD.**

From BIKANIR has been received a *hindola* of wood painted and gilded. It is supported on elephants, the piers or uprights are made up of numerous small flowers with in front of each a human figure. Over the cradle are three peacocks with outspread tails made of mirror glass.

Class V.—Ivory, Horn, Leather, Shells, etc.

The articles that fall into this class have been already so fully discussed (pages 170—208) that it will only be necessary to allude in the briefest possible terms to the chief exhibits in the Loan Collection Gallery. Of these perhaps the first position should be assigned to the collections from the Victoria and Albert Museum of South Kensington. A selection of these has been given in Plate No. 79 and the samples there shown have been discussed on pages 185-7.

PANJAB.—*Lahore.*—A set of bed legs in ivory have been sent by Bhai Gurdit Singh, Rais of Lahore.

RAJPUTANA AND CENTRAL INDIA.—On page 180 reference will be seen to a collection of charming thumb guards sent to the Loan Collection by His Highness the Maharao of Udaipur. From the same palace has been received a pair of carved ivory *kalamdans* in a delicate and graceful style of work, the pens, scissors, and other requirements being all made of ivory. *Bharatpur State* **Ivory Mats.** shows in this collection an ivory mat of some interest and beauty. His Highness the Maharaja Holkar of *Indore* has furnished a *punkah*, a *chauri*, and a *kalamdan* of ivory and sandal-wood.

UNITED PROVINCES.—His Highness the Maharaja of Benares has sent a series of ivory models. Pundit Gauri Shanker Misra of Benares shows a *kalamdan*, an album of pictures of the kings and princes of India, and other such articles in ivory.

BENGAL.—His Highness the Maharaja of Cooch Behar contributes an ivory mat to this gallery; and similar mats have been sent by the Nawab Salimulla of Dacca, as also His Highness the Maharaja of Tipperah. His Highness the Nawab Bahadur of Murshidabad contributes a pair of ivory teapoys and a large

IVORY, HORN, Etc. collection of ivory models. His Highness the Maharaja of Tipperah furnishes an ivory chair and a splendid pair of tusks. By far the most interesting examples of ivory from this province are, however, three small pieces from the Chief of the Nayagarh State. Old Ivories. These have been fully described and illustrated (pages 182-3, Plates Nos. 76 and 77) and need not be further detailed.

BOMBAY.—The School of Art has contributed four pieces of ivory carving. His Highness the Nawab of Junagadh State has sent ivory combs.

MADRAS.—His Highness the Maharaja of Travancore has contributed many interesting examples of ivory fully discussed above (pages 185-9, Plates Nos. 41, 42, and 43).

MYSORE.—His Highness the Maharaja of Mysore has sent so many excellent pieces of ivory that many pages might have to be devoted to their discussion. These have already been briefly indicated (pages 189-90, Plates Nos. 40, 42, 43, and 78).

Turning now to *Horn, Antlers, Porcupine quills* (pages 193-9), in the Loan Collection will be seen a few exhibits of interest not exemplified in the Main Gallery. Of these mention may be made of a bow made of buffalo horn sent by His Highness the Maharaja of Alwar; powder-flasks of horn engraved or inlaid sent from many parts of India such as Jodhpur, Kota, Bulrampur, and Baroda; and tiger claw ornaments such as the belt sent by Mrs. Leslie Porter of Lucknow.

Leather and Skins.

These have been treated so very fully in connection with the Main Gallery (pages 199-205, Plate No. 43-B) that it is only necessary to enumerate the names of the chief exhibitors in the Loan Collection Gallery.

PANJAB.—His Highness the Nawab of Bahawalpur sends rhinoceros hide shields with enamelled bosses. Sirdar Mohamed Behram Khan of Mazari, Dera Ghazi Khan, two Baluchi leather shields inlaid with brass.

RAJPUTANA AND CENTRAL INDIA.—His Highness the Maharawat of Pertabgarh and His Highness the Maharao of Mewar (Udaipur) show rhinoceros hide shields richly ornamented with jewelled bosses.

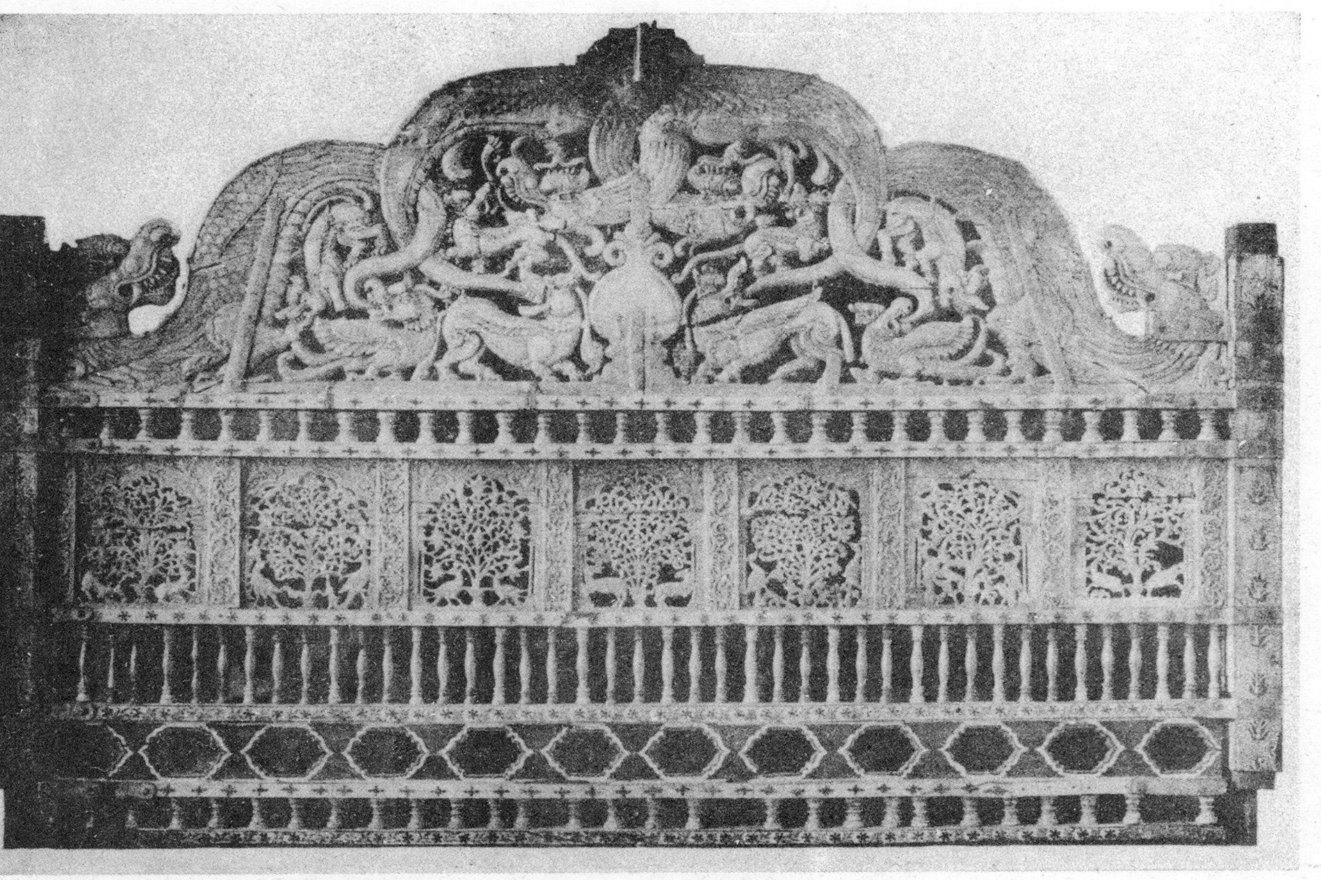

Plate No. 78 Ivory Screen from Mysore

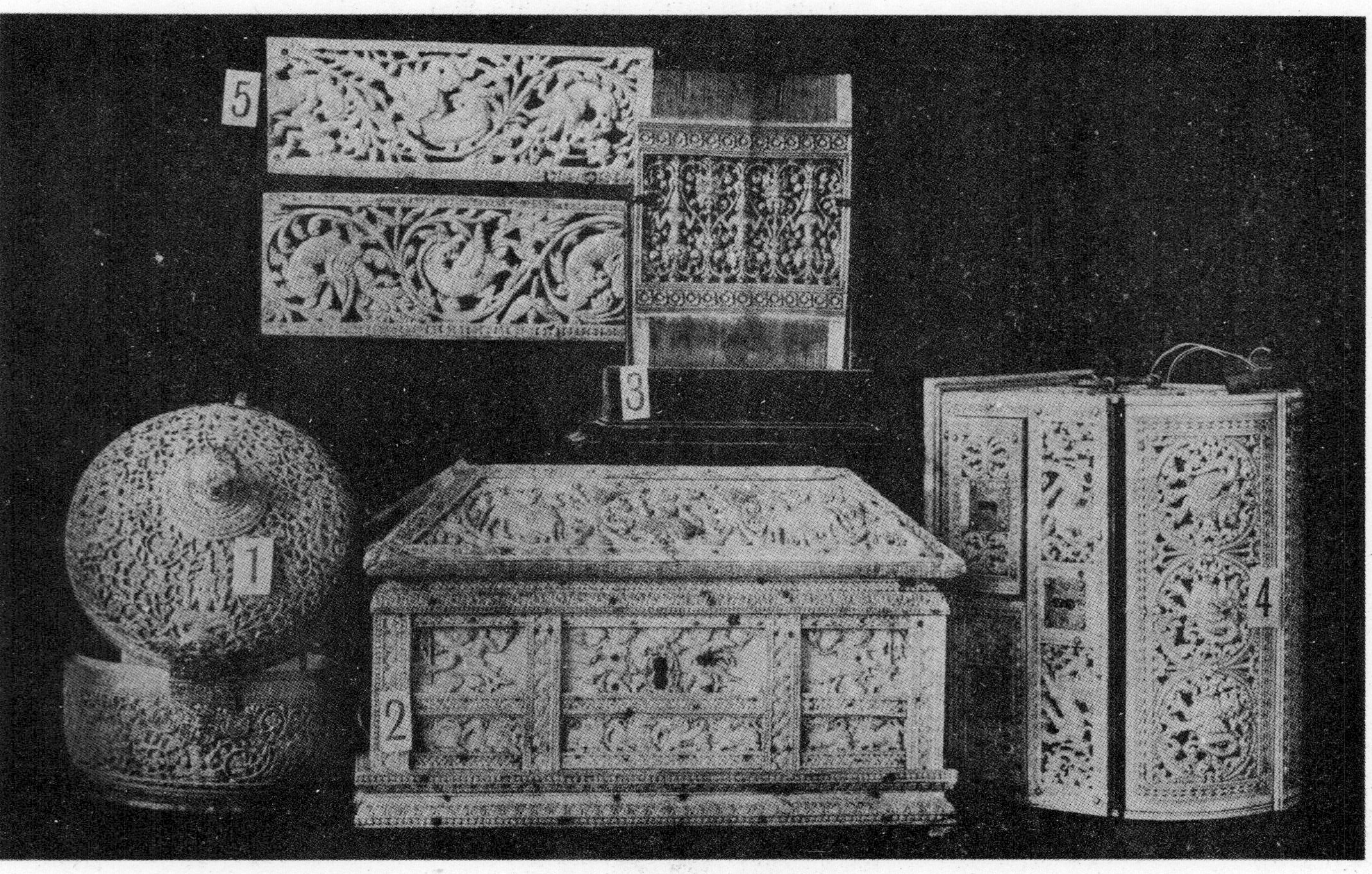

Plate No. 79 Old Ivories from the Victoria & Albert Museum, South Kensington

BOMBAY.—His Highness the Maharao of Kach and His Highness the Maharaja Gaekwar of Baroda as also the State Museum of Baroda have contributed carved rhinoceros shields. TEXTILES

Shell and Mother-of-Pearl.

The Victoria and Albert Museum has sent several examples illustrative of the use of mother-of-pearl. The best have already been alluded to (page 208, Plate No. 43-D) and need not be further discussed.

His Highness the Maharao Raja of Bundi, His Highness the Nawab of Tonk and Raj Bijaya Singh of Kumari, Kota, send examples of mother-of-pearl work.

Class VI.—Lac, Lacquer and Varnished Wares.

The examples in the Loan Collection Gallery that fall into this class are neither so extensive nor so materially different from those fully discussed in connection with the Main Gallery (pages 209-35) as to call for special treatment in this place. The Industrial Section of the Indian Museum contributed an example of gold enamel from Prome and the Madras Museum a fine old example of a circular table of Nossam *gesso* work (Plate No. 45). His Highness the Maharaja of Bikanir shows some superb examples of *gesso* work in the form of doors, State chairs, etc. These have been fully discussed above (pages 225-7) and shown in Plate No. 45. They are reported to have been made over 100 years ago. The pattern seems to break out entirely by itself as if inlaid or made of a different material from the common background. **Gesso Work.**

Class VII.—Textiles.

DYEING, CALICO-PRINTING, TINSEL PRINTING, ETC.

The Lahore Museum as also the Calcutta and Madras Museums have contributed sets of most of the styles of dyeing and printing discussed in connection with the Main Gallery (pages 236-52). Most of the Native States have also sent contributions of this nature, but they are not of sufficient interest to justify a repetition of much that has already been so fully discussed. His Highness the Raja of Chamba exhibits a very curious example of *Mashru* or Tie-dyed cloth (*conf.* with page 255). This consists of a cotton fabric woven in elaborate bands of cotton and gold threads

TEXTILES. in alternate bundles, the cotton being dyed so as to show large wavy formations in dark red within the cotton strips.

Wax-printing has been dealt with in fair detail, in the account of the exhibits in the Main Gallery, but it is desirable to record here one or two special contributions that are to be seen in the Loan Gallery. The Raja of Kalahasti sends a fine old Darbar ceiling cloth that was made 80 years ago. It cost originally Rs. 800. In the Palace of Tanjore a very curious and interesting form

WAX-DYEING. of wax-dyeing was discovered by the writer. This has been already discussed (page 266), but the samples on view in this gallery will repay inspection.

His Highness the Maharaja Gaekwar of Baroda has sent some fine old silks, amongst which one will be found to be classed as a *patola* (page 256).

It may help to elucidate the chief features of the Textiles shown in the Loan Collection, to enumerate, province by province, the chief exhibits on view.

Silk Textiles.

PANJAB.—His Highness the Raja of Chamba has sent some of the most superb gold *kinkhabs* to be seen in the Exhibition. These will be found fully described above, in the chapter devoted to such fabrics, but it is necessary in this place to specially draw attention to them. Dewan Bhagwan Das of Lahore exhibits silk *lungis*. His Highness the Raja-i-Rajgan of Kapurthala shows several silk *lungis* that illustrate the work of his State.

UNITED PROVINCES.—His Highness the Maharaja of Benares shows several *kinkhabs* of historic interest illustrating the old designs of Benares. The Hon'ble Munshi Madho Lal exhibits two *kinkhab* garments of great beauty.

BOMBAY.—His Highness the Maharao of Kach exhibits a collection of silk, the Raja of Mourbhanj shows a set of silk garments; His Highness the Maharaja Gaekwar of Baroda contributes an extensive series of great beauty and historic value. Tarkas Harjvandas Jethasa Sitwala of Surat sends a collection of *kinkhabs*. Of these the following may be mentioned:—A red striped *dusmal* in silk with blue border, the stripes both in the border and field being in gold wire. This is said to be 100 years old.

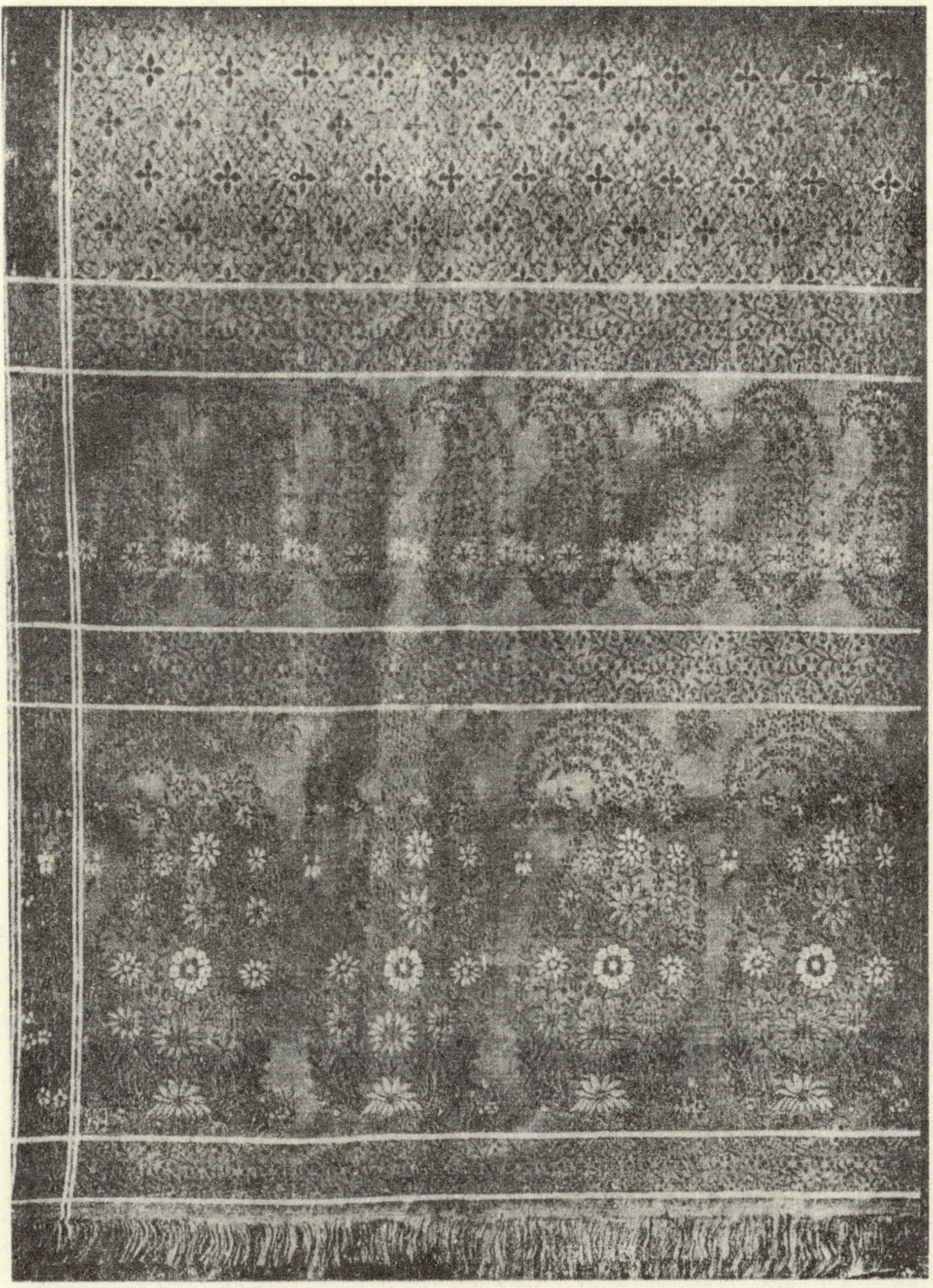

Plate No. 80 Brocaded Silk Sari from Tanjore Palace

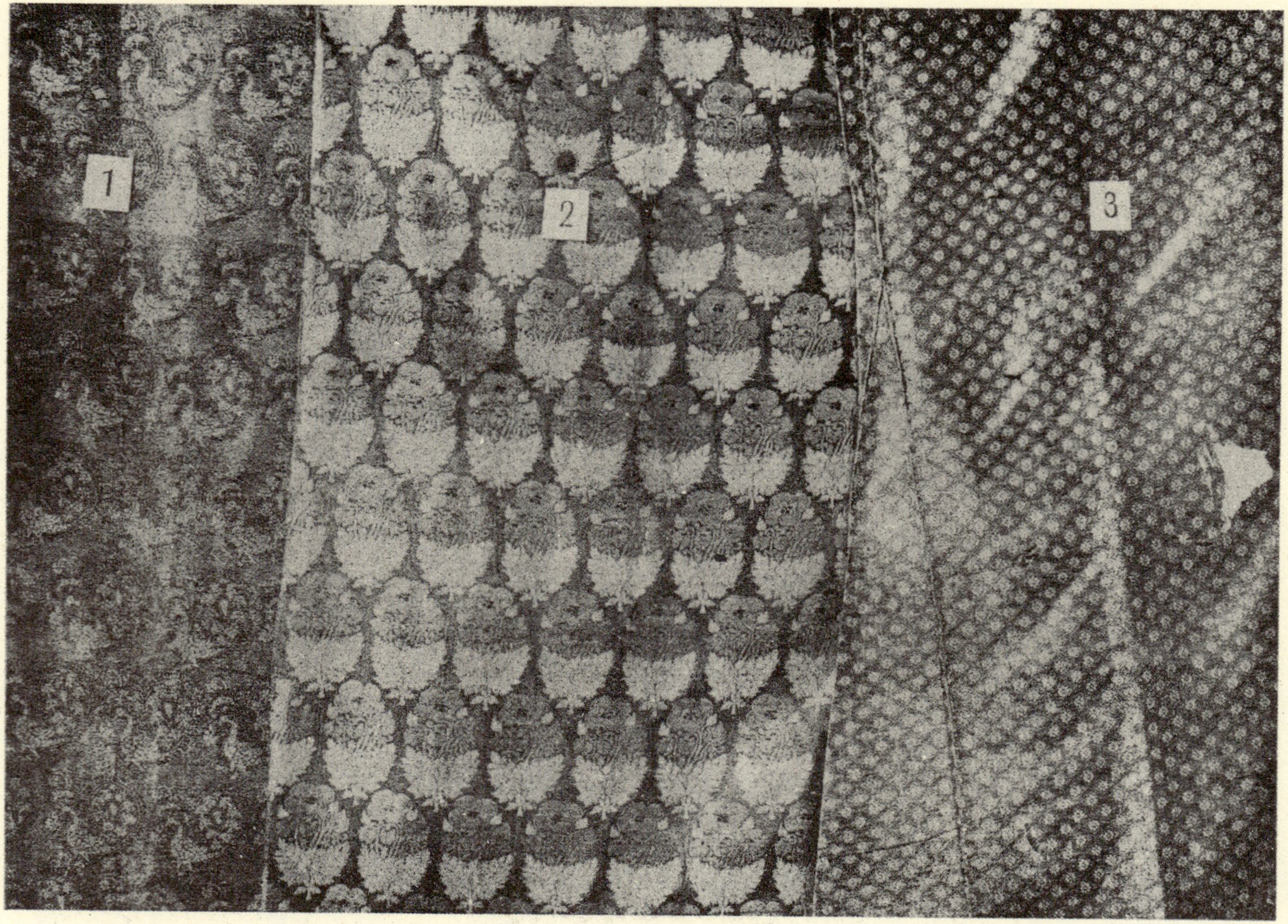

1

2

3

Plate No. 81 Old Kinkhabs from Tanjore and Benares

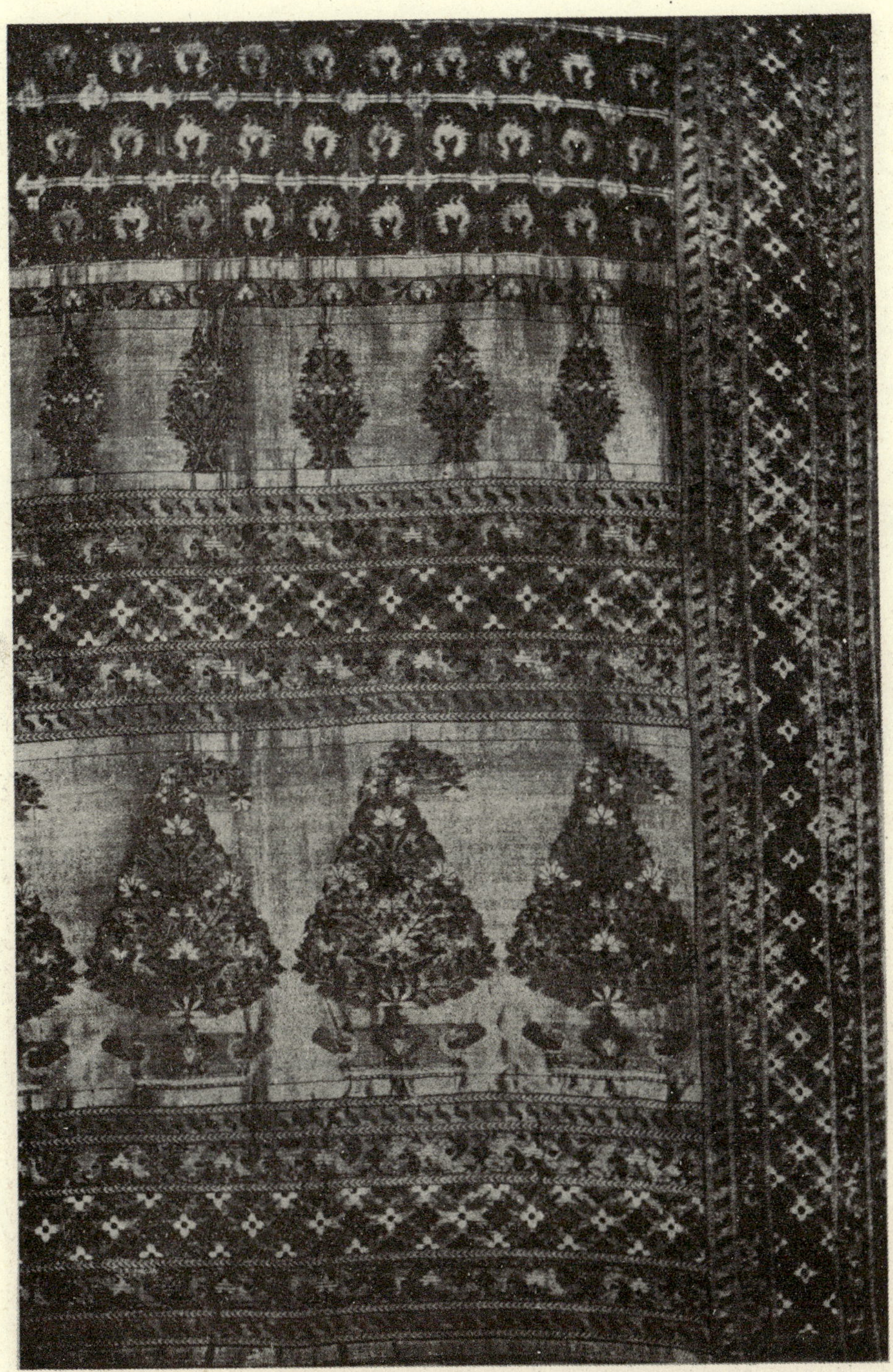

Plate No. 82 Aurangabad (Pattan) Silk and Gold Sari

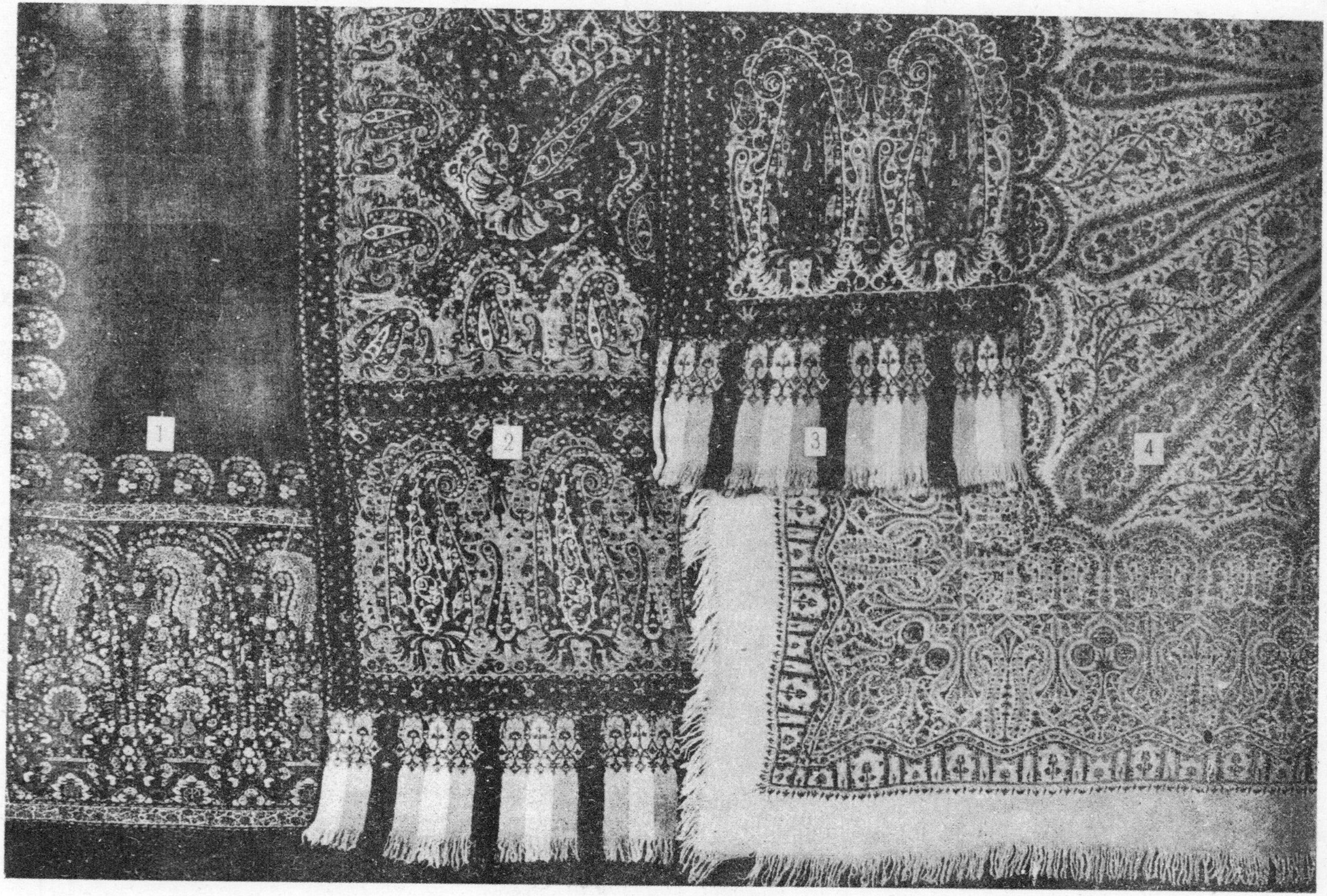

Plate No. 83 Kashmir Loom Shawls

EMBROIDERIES.

A *sárí* in red silk and gold borders, but embroidered all over in *bútis* laid sideways; these are black outlined with gold, yellow outlined with white, silk and gold wire. This is also said to be 100 years old. A *sárí* said to be made of cotton, silk, and gold and to be 125 years old. The end-piece is the charm of this fabric. The flowering shrubs have a rosette of pale yellow, green leaves with pale purple carnation-like flowers, outlined in darker purple. Sha Oodechand Itchhachand Vakharvala of Surat has contributed a full series of silk brocades, most being over 100 years old.

Wool and Pashm.

The following acknowledgment of the exhibitors in the Loan Collection of woven and embroidered shawls, *chaddars* and *pashmina* may be useful as a future record :—His Highness the Maharaja of Kashmir, Bhai Manohar Lall of Lahore, His Highness the Raja of Chamba, Major Stuart Godfrey, His Highness the Maharaja of Bikanir, Nawab Hyder Mirza of Lucknow, B. Moti Chand of Benares, Sha Oodechand Itchhachand Vakharvala of Surat, and Joshi Parmanand and Keshoji of Benares.

Class VIII.—Embroideries.

This group of artistic textiles has been dealt with in so exhaustive a manner, in connection with the Main Gallery, that it is only necessary as a record to enumerate the names of the chief exhibitors in the Loan Gallery :—Nawab Mohammad Ali Qazlbash of Lahore, Nawab Sir Imam Buksh Khan Mazari of Dera Ghazi Khan, Bhai Gurdit Singh of Lahore, His Highness the Raja-i-Rajgan of Kapurthala, His Highness the Raja of Chamba, Mian Sahib Serai of Hajipur, Dera Ghazi Khan, His Highness the Maharaja of Kashmir, the Chief of the Magassis, Baluchistan, His Highness the Maharaja of Bikanir, the Hon'ble Munshi Madho Lal of Benares, His Highness the Maharaja of Benares, B. Moti Chand of Benares, B. Rama Das Pursotam Das of Benares, B. Indar Narain Singh of Benares, Rai Mani Lal Nahar Bahadur of Azimganj, His Highness the Nawab Bahadur of Murshidabad, His Highness the Maharaja of Tipperah, Surat Chandra Raja of Kachu Khali, Triliocham Dewan of Baradow, Raiong Murung of Ranikheong, Hakim Ratan Chand of Fort Sandeman, Nawab Sir Shahbaz Khan, Chief of the Bagtis, Mrs. Yate, Residency,

EMBROIDERIES.

Quetta, Mrs. R. Hughes Buller of Quetta, Wadera Qaiser Khan, Chief of the Magassis, Kalat, Sardar Rana Shree Jalam Sanghji of Kach, His Highness the Maharaja Gaekwar of Baroda, Sha Oodechand Itchhachand Vakharvala of Surat, Seth Nagindas Javerchand Javeri of Surat, Sitvala Keshavbhai Kalamobhai of Surat, Pranjivandas Dulabhram of Surat, the Receiver of the Palace Estate, Tanjore, the Sir Desai Raja Bahadur of Savantvadi, Mylapore Convent, Nagercoil Lace School, Dr. K. M. Appiah of Mysore, the Bombay School of Art, and Industrial Section, Indian Museum, Calcutta.

Class IX.—Carpets, Mats, Etc.

The Victoria and Albert Museum of South Kensington exhibits two Warangal carpets; Nawab Mahomed Ali Qazlbash of Lahore sends two old woollen carpets in Multan style; Messrs. Baines Bros. of Kashmir exhibit a *pashmina* rug reproduced from Mumford's Oriental Rugs and made to order for the Hon'ble J. P. Hewett, Chief Commissioner of the Central Provinces; Nawab Sir Imam Buksh Khan Mazari of Dera Ghazi Khan sends a Baluchi carpet; Bhai Gurdet Singh of Lahore, an old cotton *dari* made in Multan; Dewan Bhagwan Das of Lahore exhibits a woollen carpet; His Highness the Nawab of Bahawalpur sends two carpets made of "*ak*" fibre; Mian Sahib Serai of Hajipur, Dera Ghazi Khan, sends a collection of Baluchi rugs and carpets; Messrs. Otto Weylandt & Co. of Agra exhibit two woollen carpets; His Highness the Maharaja of Tipperah contributes silk carpets; the Custodians of the Asar-i-Sharif and Jame-Mosque at Bijapur exhibit nine old carpets and a *dari*; Major J. Ramsay of Quetta sends a *Panjdeh* carpet and rug; Major Showers of Kalat exhibits a carpet; Sirdar Sir Nauraz Khan of Kharan, Baluchistan, contributes a carpet, and Wadera Qaisar Khan, Chief of the Magassis, Kalat, also sends a carpet.

Class X.—Fine Arts.

Following the example adopted in the other classes it may serve a useful purpose if an enumeration be here followed of the chief contributors to the Loan Collection under this class:—

PANJAB.—Rai Mohan Lal of Lahore sends a copy of the

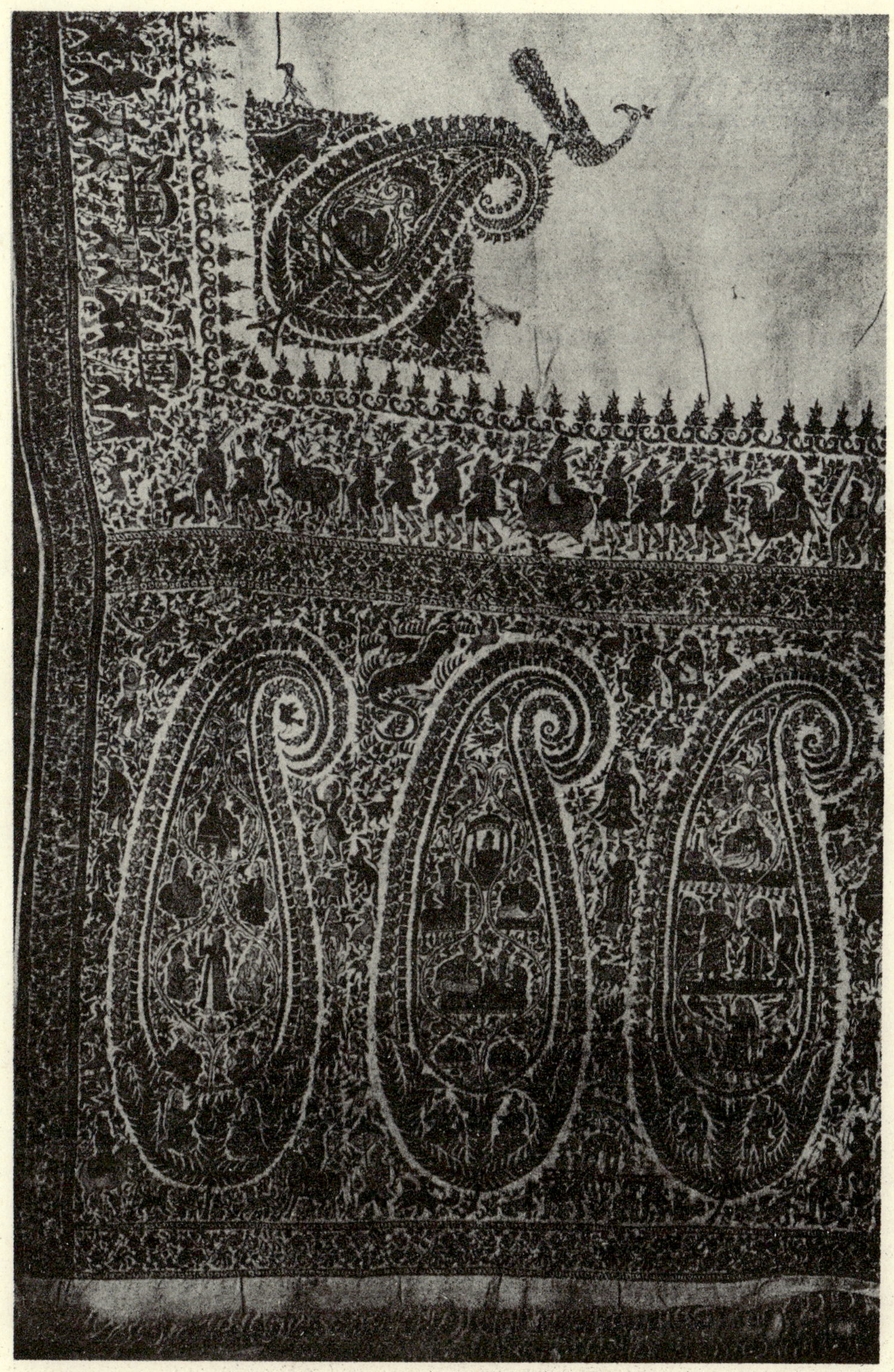

Plate No. 84 Needle-work Kashmir Shawl, very Old, made in the Punjab

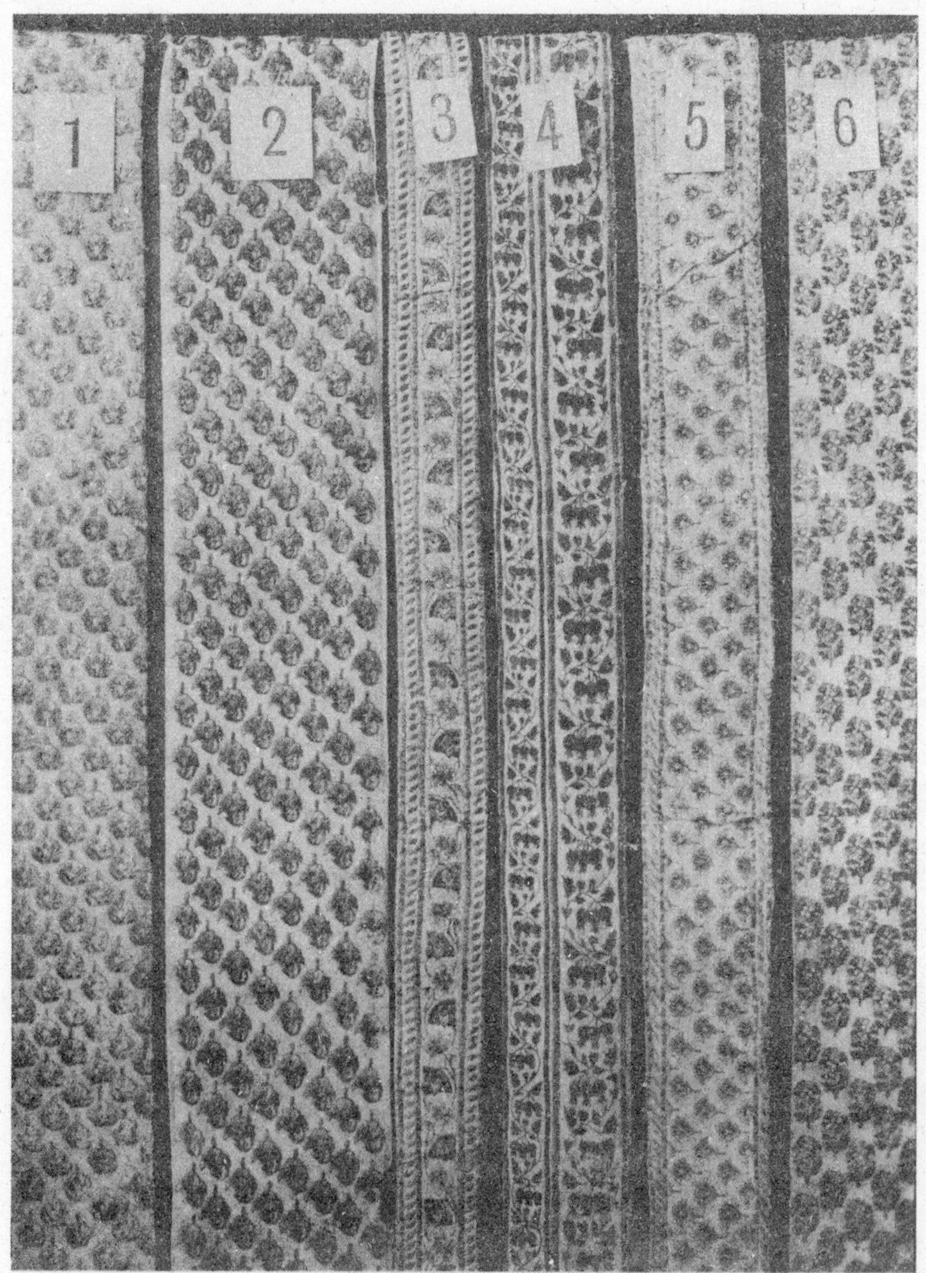

Plate No. 85. Satin Stitch Embroideries from Azamganj in Bengal

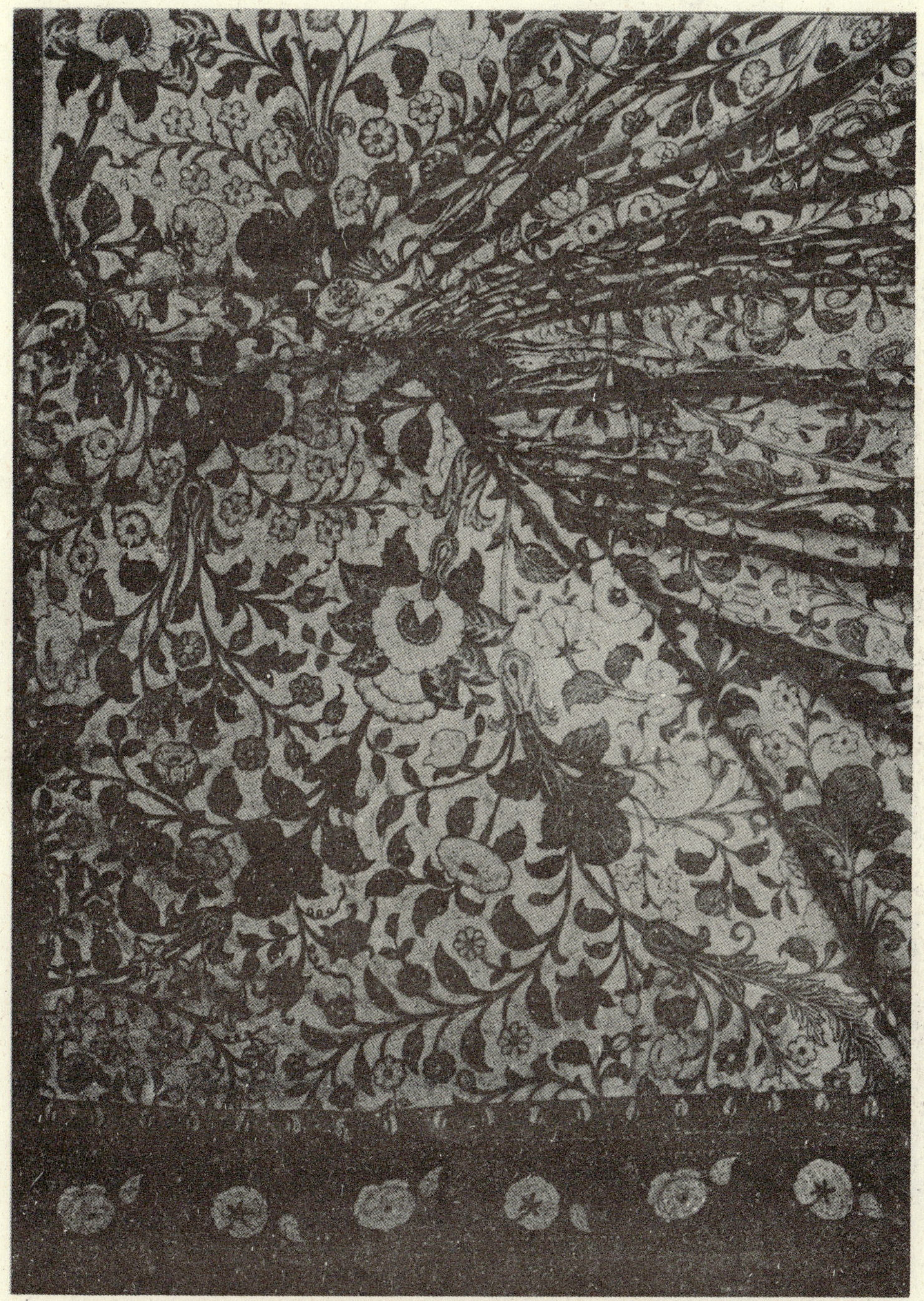

Plate No. 86 Chain Stitch Embroidery from Kach

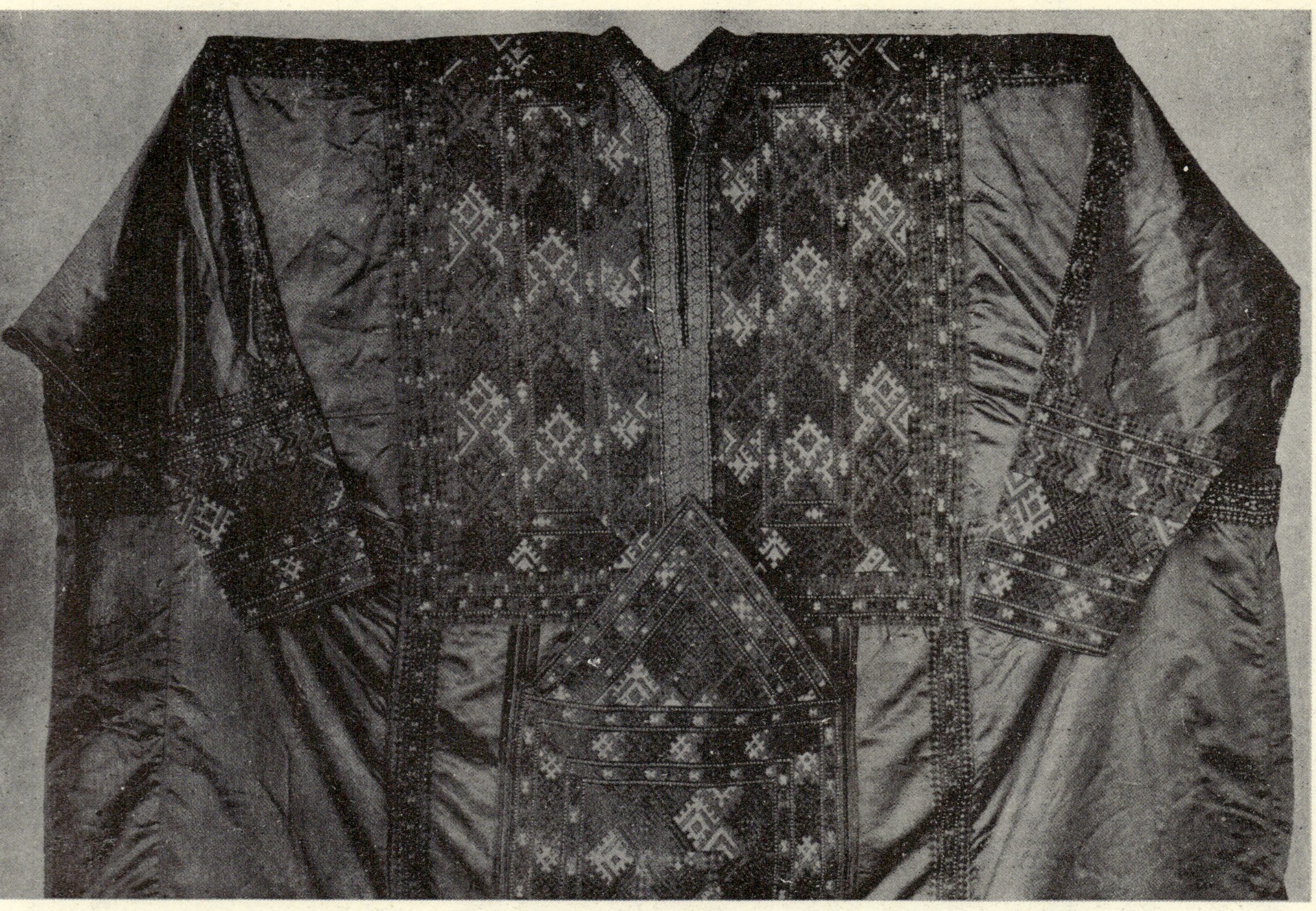

Plate No. 87 Brahaui (Double) Satin Stitch in Ladies' Dress

"Mahabharatha." Fakir Sayed Qamaruddin Khan Bahadur of Lahore sends a picture of the Emperor Akbar and a copy of the "Shahnama." M. Sohan Lal of Lahore contributes a collection of Hindu mythological pictures. The Lahore Museum shows a selection of old Sikh Darbar pictures. Bhai Gurdit Singh of Lahore contributes two pictures. Nawab Ghulam Mahbub Subhani of Lahore shows a copy of the "Pand Namah" and an illuminated copy of the "Dewan Hafiz." Bhai Hardial Singh of Lahore exhibits four old pictures. Lala Ram Sarn Das of Lahore contributes two illuminated books. Bhai Monohar Lal of Lahore shows ten old pictures representing the ten *gurus* of the Sikhs. Dewan Bhagwan Das of Lahore sends ten pictures. Raja Kirti Singh of Shekhupura exhibits 250 old pictures drawn by the Kangra painters. **FINE ARTS.**

RAJPUTANA AND CENTRAL INDIA.—His Highness the Maharaja of Alwar has furnished a splendid series of fine old pictures and a still more valuable collection of illuminated books. Of the former special attention may be given to the three panoramic views of the State entry of Akbar II. Of the latter the *Gulistan* may be mentioned. This is valued at Rs. 1,75,000 and was written by Agha Mirza of Delhi, a single page taking one fortnight and the whole book 12 years. The borders of the pages were designed and painted by Natha Shah and Kari Abdur Rahman of Delhi, and the illustrations were painted by Ghulam Ali Khan and Buldeo, artists of Alwar. Each border required from two to four days to paint. One of the pictures represents apparently a scene in Burma or the far East with the officers of the East India Company on board barges along with soldiers and flying a peculiarly striped form of the Union Jack.

His Highness the Maharaja of Marwar (Jodhpur) sends a collection of pictures. The Bharatpur State contributes five pictures representing elephants and horsemen.

UNITED PROVINCES.—His Highness the Maharaja of Bulrampur of Gonda (Oudh) contributes a collection of illuminated books. Raja Rameshur Bux Singh of Sheogarh, Bareilly, sends a series of old pictures. Pandit Gauri Shanker Misra of Benares exhibits a collection of pictures. Kanwar Narindro Bahadur of

FINE ARTS. Sandela sends also a collection of pictures. Nawab Gulam Hussain Khan of Lucknow shows a good series of old pictures.

BENGAL.—His Highness the Nawab Bahadur of Murshidabad contributes illuminated books. Abanindra Nath Tagore of Calcutta sends through the Principal of the School of Art, Calcutta, three pictures that were so much appreciated as to receive a silver medal.

MADRAS.—Goondal Pandit Laxshmunchar of Mysore contributes an old picture. His Highness the Maharaja of Mysore sends a large series of mythological pictures. The School of Arts, Madras, contributes several paintings done by its pupils.

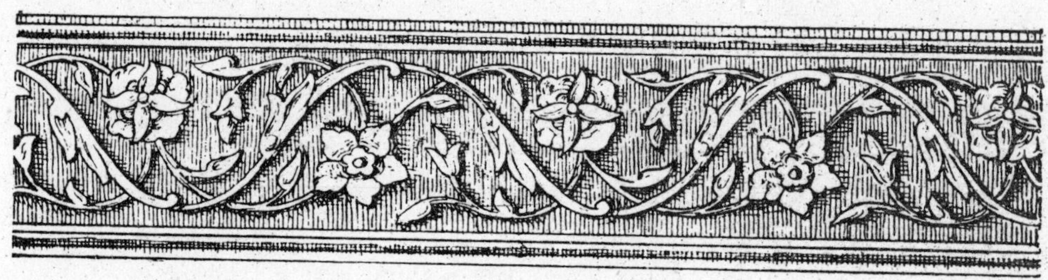

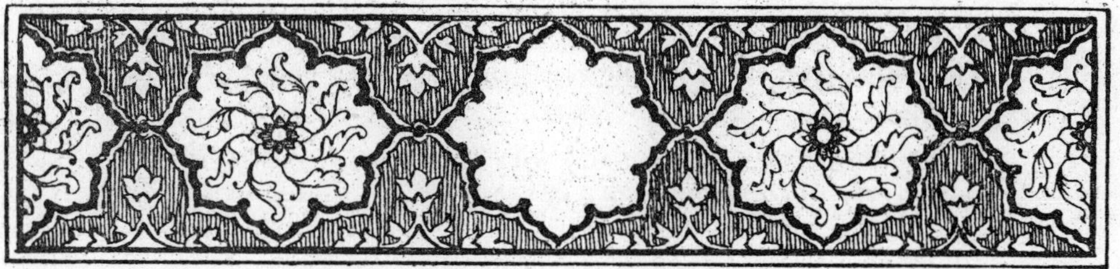

III.—JEWELLERY COURT.

IT was considered desirable that the Exhibition authorities should not undertake to organise a collection of precious stones and jewellery. The alternative course was deemed the preferable one, namely, for a special building to be set apart, in which a selected number of the better known jewellers of India might be permitted to open stalls and to sell their goods as they desired. Accordingly the Jewellery Gallery was prepared and the space sold to the jewellers who were thereby free to make their own arrangements. The sales made by them were in consequence not subjected to the payment of any further Exhibition charges. At first it was intended to restrict the gallery to the display of jewellery, pure and simple, but ultimately the concession was made of allowing the occupants of space in the Jewellery Court to display and sell their own gold and silver plate, subject to the class of goods shown being in strict accord with the definitions of an Indian Art Exhibition. The Jewellery Court was thus treated as more or less distinct from the general Exhibition. There were therefore no medals or awards made for the goods shown in that gallery. In some cases the jewellers displayed the values put by them on their more important goods: in others they were not valued, but it has been calculated, and perhaps not far from correctly, that the contents of the Jewellery Gallery were close on £1,000,000 in value.

Allotment of Ground Space.

No Awards.

Total Value.

The following were the occupants of space in the Jewellery Court—commencing on the right hand side and passing down the gallery to the end and back by the opposite side:—

1. MOTILAL DAYABHAI & CO., 280, KALBADEVI ROAD, BOMBAY.—This firm besides having both wholesale and retail

branches are also manufacturing jewellers and diamond merchants. The principal articles exhibited by them in the Jewellery Court were:—

A pair of anklets (*paijams*) with diamonds, rubies, emeralds, and pearls valued at R1,00,000. Diamond bangles valued from R10,000 to R20,000. Necklaces set with diamonds, rubies, and pearls at from R10,000 to R30,000. A pair of gold cups and saucers set with diamonds, R20,000. A silver salver with an allegorical history of the Ramayana. Burmese bowls of unique design in silver. An emerald tea service of Kashmir pattern. A pair of silver centre pieces of unique pattern.

2. P. ORR AND SONS, MADRAS.—This firm of jewellers and gold and silver-smiths claim to be the pioneer manufacturing firm of India. Their factory at Madras, in which they employ upwards of 600 artizans, is reputed to be the largest and best appointed establishment of the kind in India. They turn out not only jewellery, gold and silver ware, but also scientific instruments. A speciality is made of the hand chased "swami" silver ware. Their examples of this work, shown at their stall in the Exhibition, formed one of the most interesting features of their display. It is not possible to give a full description of the valuable and beautiful collection of goods exhibited by this firm, but special mention may be made of the following:—

A diamond brooch containing a blue diamond of a very rare shade set between two white stones, with a diamond drop of a beautiful pink tint. All old Indian stones of the first water. A diamond head ornament, in the centre of which is set a large diamond weighing nearly 134 carats—a magnificent stone but slightly yellow in colour. A pink pearl remarkable for its perfect shape and colour and a fine emerald and diamond necklace with pearl cluster drops.

3. TARACHAND PURSRAM RAMSWAMI, 63, MEADOW STREET, BOMBAY.—This firm have an extensive display of both old and new jewellery and all forms of Indian artwares that will be found well worthy of study. The firm have branches in Calcutta and Rangoon and conduct an extensive business as dealers in art curios as well as being jewellers, diamond merchants, and silver-smiths.

4. MESSRS. T. R. TAWKER AND SONS OF MOUNT ROAD, MADRAS.—This firm having secured the whole of the western extremity of the gallery have a superb display. They are manufacturing jewellers and silver-smiths who pay special attention to the subject of Indian jewellery. Their collection of exhibits, which includes some jewels of great intrinsic value, claims additional merit by the fact that several pieces are of historic interest. Of these a large emerald, weighing upwards of 18 carats—a stone said to have been set in the signet ring of the Mughal Emperor Shah Alum. This gem which is of the rich emerald hue so much sought after, is a perfect specimen, and bears the name of the Delhi monarch and the date inscribed in Persian on its face. Another stone, a carved emerald contained in a necklace, is reputed to have originally found a place as one of the State jewels of the "Tiger of Mysore," Tippu Sultan. Several very fine ruby necklaces are shown, one being composed of stones of exceptional size and colour that took the firm many years to bring together. A necklace of 42 grand emeralds has also taken much patience to collect, some of the gems having been obtained from the old family jewels belonging to the Tanjore Raj. Such are a few of the fine jewels exhibited by this firm and it may be added that their display has been valued at R60,00,000.

5. RAI BUDDREE DAS BAHADUR AND SONS OF 152, HARRISON ROAD, CALCUTTA.—This firm exhibits necklaces, *sirpatches*, brooches, bangles, rings, etc., of pearls, rubies, emeralds, diamonds, etc. The following are some of their most prized specimens:—

The large ruby—*chatterputty maneck*. This is believed to be very ancient and to have been owned in turns by Hindu and Muhammadan Kings. It is in size about 2 inches long and 1½ inches broad and is set in a *sirpatch* with pure Indian diamonds. The pearl necklace—the pearls in this are large, round, and well matched, the collection having taken 30 years to bring together. Three-row pearl necklace—this consists of many exceptionally fine pearls. The pearl drop necklace—these are well matched drop pearls. Green diamond—a rare and large stone called *Banasputty*. It is said to be very old and is described as of first water and surrounded by other small white diamonds. Diamond drop tiara—this consists of numerous old white diamond drops in the shape of grapes. The firm has also some very large, rare, ancient, loose stones such as diamonds, sapphires, emeralds, catseyes of unusual size and weight, collected from private sources for years past.

6. GANESHI LAL AND SON OF AGRA AND SIMLA.—This firm have an extensive display of all classes of jewellery as also antique jade and crystal. The following may be accepted as denoting some of their more remarkable exhibits:—

A necklace of old emeralds, diamonds, and pearls, valued at R1,25,000. Necklace of old rubies, diamonds, and pearls, R6,000. Pendant of old emeralds weighing about 40 carats and diamonds converting it into a *kalgi*, R55,000. A pair of bracelets set with old rubies and diamonds, R40,000. A single diamond scarf pin—the diamond weighing 51 carats, R1,10,000. A very old and fine white jade cup with carved handle, R15,000. Very old gold enamelled *hukka* complete, R13,000.

7. SRI RAM JANKI DAS OF DELHI.—This firm have a good display of jewellery. A special feature of this work is their traffic in jade stone. They have a curious and interesting assortment of this work both ancient and modern and either simply engraved or jewelled. The following are some of their more interesting exhibits:—

A necklace of stone valued at R4,000. A necklace of pearls set with diamonds and sapphires, R1,100. An Indian *jhumar* (jewel for the head) set on one side with diamonds and on the other with rubies and pearls, R1,500. A seven row necklace, R2,000. A jewelled drop necklace set with pearls, sapphires, and diamonds, R2,500. A seven diamond ring, R1,600. A jade plate with a tea cup set with diamonds, emeralds, rubies, and pearls, R6,000. A handsome aigrette fully jewelled, R7,000. An oval jade plate set with diamonds, pearls, turquoises, rubies, and emeralds, R4,000.

8. SUGUNCHAND SOBHAGCHAND, JEWELLER AND DEALER IN ALL KINDS OF PRECIOUS STONE, JAIPUR.—The special feature of this firm is their extensive transactions in gold enamelling. They have practically in fact absorbed the Jaipur enamelling craft

and have all the best workmen in their employ. The principal articles exhibited by this firm are as follows:—

A cup set with large diamonds, emeralds, pearls, and rubies, R6,00,000. A gold belt set with large diamonds, R3,00,000. A diamond necklace, R3,00,000. A pair of bracelets set with large diamonds and rubies, R75,000. A pearl necklace, R1,25,000. A two row pearl necklace, R1,50,000. A two row emerald necklace, R75,000. A gold enamelled tea set, R10,000. A gold enamelled picture frame, R5,000. An enamelled bottle case, R3,000. A green diamond ring, R20,000. A large pearl aigrette, R25,000. Large pearls valued at R55,000. A large assortment of lockets, bangles, rings, etc., in gold enamel.

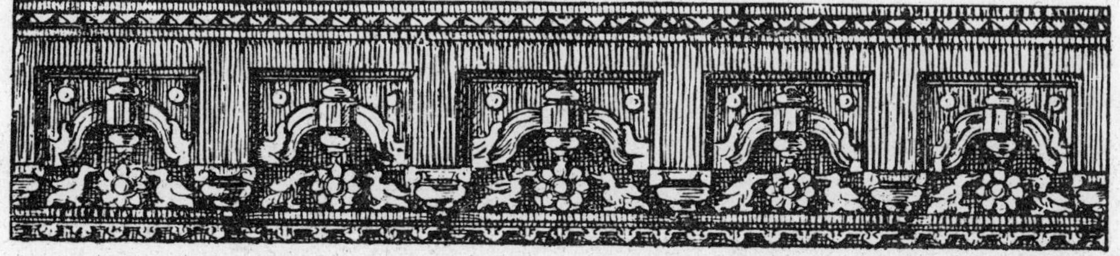

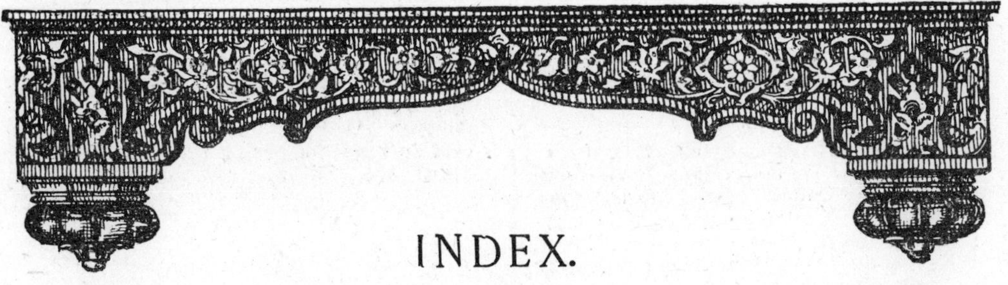

INDEX.

THIS Index has been referred to two sections, *viz.*, names of places and a general enumeration of the articles described, including the vernacular names given to these.

It is thus hoped that this treatment may serve the double purpose of an index while becoming at the same time an Abstract Gazetteer to the centres of Artware production in India. By consulting the passages indexed, under the names of towns, the visitor to India may not only ascertain the articles of greatest interest, to be looked for in each of these, but he may discover the names and addresses of the better known manufacturers as well. To assist the reader vernacular names have been rendered in italics and the names of the Classes and Divisions of manufactures in small capitals.

A

An Abstract Gazetteer to the Centres of Art Production in India.

The quotations of pages, given below, it will be observed, have been rendered in the sequence of the classification adopted. In the text the system has been pursued of mentioning, by name only, all the places that produce very similar manufactures. In the present enumeration a few additional names have been recorded and reference made to the passage or passages where the corresponding goods are described. In a good few instances names of places, like names of persons (especially when met with in quotations or descriptive labels and advertisements), are spelt in two or more ways. This index is intended to give the more generally accepted rendering and thus in some few instances to correct the text.

B

C

D

E

F

G

H

L

M

N

O

P

Q

R

S

T

U

V

W

Y

B

General Index and Glossary.

A

B

D

E

F

G

H

J

K

M

N

O

P

S

T

U

V

W

Y

Z

No. 1945 R. & A.—11-12-1903.—5,000.—J. E. F.